CPA Exam Study Manual

Auditing & Attestation

2007/2008

Kaplan CPA Review

This publication is designed to provide accurate and authoritative information in regard to the subject matter covered. It is sold with the understanding that the publisher is not engaged in rendering legal, accounting, or other professional service. If legal advice or other expert assistance is required, the services of a competent professional should be sought.

President: Andrew Temte
Vice President: Dave Wiley
CPA Content Manager: Teresa Coile Anderson

© 2007 by Kaplan CPA Review, a division of Kaplan Professional Companies

Published by Kaplan CPA Review

   1905 Palace Street
   La Crosse, WI 54603
   (608) 779-5599
   www.kaplanCPAreview.com

All rights reserved. The text of this publication, or any part thereof, may not be reproduced in any manner whatsoever without permission in writing from the publisher.

Printed in the United States of America

Contents

Introduction 4
Frequently Asked Questions 5
How to Study Auditing: A Guide for Taking the CPA Exam 9
Ch. 1 Overview of Auditing 10
Ch. 2 Sarbanes-Oxley Act of 2002 46
Ch. 3 Audit Opinions 56
Ch. 4 Compilations and Reviews 96
Ch. 5 Audit Risk 116
Ch. 6 Evidence Gathering 138
Ch. 7 Internal Control 185
Ch. 8 Accounts Receivable and Revenues 255
Ch. 9 Statistical Sampling 264
Ch. 10 Inventory and Accounts Payable 290
Ch. 11 Auditing and Technology 303
Ch. 12 Flowcharting 326
Ch. 13 Cash Receipts and Cash Balances 330
Ch. 14 Special Reports and Other Reports 337
Ch. 15 Long-Term Liabilities and Contingencies 381
Ch. 16 Payroll 389
Ch. 17 Land, Buildings, and Equipment 398
Ch. 18 Investments 408
Ch. 19 Other Issues in Auditing 415
Cram Essentials 454
Essay Writing on the CPA Exam 521
Exam Strategies 550
Index 586

INTRODUCTION

Thank you for choosing Kaplan CPA Review to guide your preparation for the CPA exam. You are about to embark on a journey that is unparalleled in your academic and professional training until now. Success on the CPA exam requires your total commitment of focus, discipline, time, and energy. We are here to guide you to those all-important words: "I passed!"

Kaplan, the leader in standardized test preparation for nearly 70 years, is dedicated to helping you pass the CPA exam the first time. Inside this book, you will find study notes and outlines as well as comprehensive questions and answers for the Auditing & Attestation section of the CPA exam. Other volumes published by Kaplan CPA Review cover the remaining three sections of the exam. We realize you have a very busy life, and we have structured this volume to include only the topics you need to know for the exam. We do not include a lot of extra material that is unlikely to be tested. You do not have time for that!

We realize that everyone's needs are different when it comes to preparing for an important exam. Some people require only a brief refresher of well-known concepts; others look for a more in-depth review. Our Kaplan CPA Review Learning System is designed to provide you with the level of preparation *you* need. In addition to this Kaplan CPA Review Study Manual, the following companion products in our Learning System include study tools that are geared to all learning styles and that provide the flexibility today's busy professionals require:

- Kaplan Activity Planners to provide day-by-day guidance.
- Lesson and Problems Videos (available online or on optional CDs) providing more than 100 hours of instruction across all four sections.
- Online CPA QBank containing 3,000 T/F and 2,200 M/C questions, Testlets, and Simulations.
- Audio CDs presented as a series of Q&As providing more than 22 hours of strategic retention exercises.
- 2,100 Flashcards for hours of critical topic review.
- E-mail an Instructor and E-mail Lessons provide additional assistance.

We appreciate the opportunity to guide your study for the CPA exam. We wish you the best of success. Check our Web site at *www.kaplanCPAreview.com* for free resources to help you get ready for the exam, and practice with sample exam-like questions. Call us today at 800-CPA-2DAY (800-272-2329) or e-mail us at *cpainfo@kaplan.com* to take the first step towards passing the exam and getting on with the beginning of the rest of your life.

We're Kaplan. We build futures one success story at a time. Let yours be our next one.

FREQUENTLY ASKED QUESTIONS
ABOUT THE AUDITING & ATTESTATION SECTION OF THE CPA EXAM

Q: When should I start the application process to take the CPA exam?

A: First, you need to be certain that you have all education and other requirements fulfilled for the state where you want to have your scores reported. Go to www.cpa-exam.org and click on "Apply Now" and then follow the links to find your state. Be positive that you have (or will have) the hours and the courses that are required. Laws vary considerably by state and tend to change over time. Do not take the requirements for granted; check on the rules of your state. Second, keep in mind that the approval process can take up to six or seven weeks. You probably need to send in your application at least two months prior to when you want to sit for one or more parts of the exam.

Q: Can I begin the application process prior to completing all requirements so that I can sit for the exam as soon as I am qualified?

A: Check your state requirements. However, most states specify that the requirements have to be completed prior to beginning the application process.

Q: What is an NTS?

A: The NTS is your "notice to schedule," which indicates that your application has been approved. At that point, you can contact Prometric at *www.prometric.com/CPA* to find a test center and schedule an exam. Prometric is the company that administers the CPA exam. Make sure that you carefully read the NTS; it contains a lot of helpful information.

Q: Do I have to take the CPA exam in a particular state?

A: No, as long as you are properly approved and scheduled, you can take the CPA exam in any Prometric Center regardless of its location. For example, you can take the exam as an Iowa candidate but sit in a testing center in Hawaii.

Q: How long do I have to pass all four parts of the CPA exam?

A: That depends entirely on the law of the state where you are having your scores reported. Be certain to check by reading the rules of your state when you go to *www.cpa-exam.org*. The time can vary considerably by state.

©2007 Kaplan CPA Review

Q: When is the CPA exam offered?

A: The CPA exam is given in four windows during the year: January–February, April–May, July–August, and October–November. Each section of the exam can be taken once in each window. Thus, you could potentially sit for Auditing and Attestation (as well as all other sections) a maximum of four times in any calendar year.

Q: Should I take all four parts of the CPA exam in one window?

A: That depends almost entirely on your ability to prepare for the exam. Most experts feel that a total of 250–400 hours is needed to prepare properly for all four sections of the exam. Many individuals take one or two parts per window unless they have a sufficient amount of time available to prepare for more. It is not unusual, though, for a candidate to take one part at the beginning of a window and a second part toward the end of that same window.

Q: Which part of the CPA exam should I take first?

A: There are a lot of different theories about which part should be taken first. One theory holds that you should take the part that you feel most positive about at the beginning so that you increase the chances of getting off to a good start. Other theories, though, do exist.

Q: Is the CPA exam only given by computer?

A: Correct. Starting back in 2004, the CPA exam was switched from a paper and pencil exam to a computerized exam. A multitude of changes in the exam took place at that time.

Q: What does the Auditing and Attestation exam look like?

A: Auditing and Attestation opens with 24 multiple-choice questions. When those 24 are submitted by the candidate as being complete, a second testlet of 24 more questions are given and then a final 24 appear. For Auditing and Attestation, there are a total of 72 multiple-choice questions that make up the first portion of the exam.

Q: Should I guess if I do not know an answer?

A: The grade is computed based on the questions that you get correct. Therefore, you should answer all questions even if you must guess.

Q: After I answer a question can I go back and change my answer?

A: Each of the three testlets in Auditing and Attestation has 24 multiple-choice questions. Until you finish a testlet, you can always change your answers. Once a testlet has been submitted, you cannot go back and change those answers.

Q: Are all of those multiple-choice questions in Auditing and Attestation actually graded?

A: Of the 72 multiple-choice questions, 60 are graded while the other 12 are being tested for future use and do not affect the candidate's grade. However, you cannot tell which ones are graded. Unfortunately, it is possible to spend a long time attempting to answer a question that is not even graded.

Q: Do all of those multiple-choice questions have the same value?

A: No, each question is individually weighted through a complicated mathematical process. In simple terms, answering a complex question correctly is worth more than answering an easy question correctly.

Q: After finishing the 90 multiple-choice questions, what happens next in Auditing and Attestation?

A: In all parts of the CPA exam other than Business Environment and Concepts (BEC), there are also two simulation questions. Each is like a small case study. A piece of information is provided and then a wide variety of questions are asked that can include matching, fill-in-the-blank, spreadsheet work, et cetera. In addition, the simulation contains a written communications question where the candidate has to compose a memo, audit documentation, a letter, or the like. Finally, there is a research question. In that question, the candidate is given access to a database of official pronouncements and must enter search terms to find a passage that answers a query that has been given. This research is very much like an Internet search.

Q: So, Auditing and Attestation is made up of 72 multiple-choice questions and two simulations. How is a grade determined?

A: Three grades are determined: one for multiple-choice, one for the written communications question, and one for the remainder of the simulation. Those grades are then weighted by factors of 70, 10, and 20 to arrive at a final grade. For example, a grade is determined for the multiple-choice questions and then that grade is multiplied by 70% to arrive at that portion of a candidate's total grade.

Q: What is a passing score?

A: A candidate must make a score of 75 to pass. However, because of the complex weighting system, that does not equate to getting 75% of the questions correct.

Q: I understand what multiple-choice questions look like. How can I see an example of a simulation?

A: Go to *www.cpa-exam.org* and click on "Tutorial and Sample Exams." Kaplan CPA Education's Complete Learning Systems also provide candidates with a variety of practice simulations.

Q: How long are the exams?

A: Regulation is 3 hours, Auditing and Attestation is 4.5 hours, Financial Accounting & Reporting is 4 hours, and BEC is 2.5 hours.

Q: How much of that time should be used for the two simulations?

A: The AICPA recommends 45 minutes for each simulation in Financial Accounting and Reporting and also in Auditing and Attestation but only 35 minutes for each simulation in Regulation. That is probably a good allocation of time. Therefore, in Regulation, the candidate should spend about 110 minutes on the 90 multiple-choice questions and 90 minutes on the two simulations. Do note that this means that you would need to average answering each multiple-choice question in Regulation in less than 75 seconds. You can certainly make that pace but you have to stay focused to do so.

Q: How difficult are the questions on the CPA exam?

A: Not surprisingly, the complexity of the questions tends to vary significantly. However, almost anyone who has been around the CPA exam will assert that the breadth of the questions is more challenging than the depth. In other words, most questions are not extremely difficult but the exam tends to cover every possible topic. You have to move your thinking from one topic to another very quickly. The first question might be on itemized deduction while the second is on dividend income and the third on the taxation of partnerships. Few questions are necessarily difficult but that constant movement of topics from one to another poses a challenge.

Q: What is the pass rate on Auditing and Attestation?

A: The pass rate on each of the four parts is roughly in the 40% to 44% range. It is a difficult exam but it is certainly not impossible. People who put in enough hours tend to pass.

Q: Where can I get more information on Kaplan CPA Review?

A: Go to *www.kaplanCPAreview.com* or send an e-mail to *CPAinfo@kaplan.com*.

HOW TO STUDY AUDITING: A GUIDE FOR TAKING THE CPA EXAM

STUDY MANUAL – AUDITING & ATTESTATION

FIVE STEP SOLUTION APPROACH TO SUCCESS

An overall approach for the CPA exam: All candidates should complete the tutorial and example questions on the AICPA's website to obtain experience with the computer-based testing.

Step 1: Carefully read the entire question before looking at the answers.

- Do not jump to the conclusion that you know the answer before you have read the entire question. Such action could actually result in you misreading the question and answering incorrectly.

Step 2: Determine the concept being addressed in each question.

- This will allow you to narrow your focus on one key topic area and will make the question much easier to answer.

Step 3: Identify the pertinent information in the question.

- Be careful, there are many times when all of the information provided in the question is not relevant to the present situation. You must determine what information to use and what information should be ignored.

Step 4: Anticipate the answer *before* looking at the answer choices.

- If you have already formulated an answer before reading the answer choices, it will be much easier to recognize the correct answer.

Step 5: Read all of the answers and select the best alternative.

- This is especially important, since sometimes your final choice answer may be 'all of the above,' 'none of the above' or combinations such as 'a and c only.'

Note: All multiple choice questions are graded based upon the number correct, weighted by a difficulty rating. There is no penalty for guessing, thus, you should answer *all* the multiple choice questions. In most cases, there are at least two obvious incorrect choices- eliminate these first, then review once again the concept being addressed and make your best 'educated guess' between the two remaining choices.

Overview of Auditing

Study Manual – Auditing & Attestation
Chapter 1

Study Tip: Almost every person has some habit or fondness that eats up a lot of their time. For some, it is television, while for others it is card playing, going to the movies, or the like. When you first begin to study for the CPA exam, determine what activity you use to waste time. Do not avoid this activity completely, but work to reduce that time to a specific but reasonable amount each week. This will help you take control over your time and find the time needed to properly prepare.

INTRODUCTION

There are three forms of CPA attestation engagements—examinations, reviews, and the performance of agreed-upon procedures.

1. An *examination*, referred to as an "audit" when it involves financial statements, normally results in a *positive opinion*, the highest form of assurance provided. When performing an examination, CPAs select from all available evidence a combination of evidence that limits to a low level of risk the chance of material misstatement.

2. A *review* is substantially less in scope than an audit and normally provides *limited assurance* ("We are not aware of any material modifications that should be made"), rather than a positive opinion with respect to whether the information follows the appropriate criteria.

3. An *agreed-upon procedure* is the third form of attestation engagement, in which a CPA and a specified party that wishes to use the information may mutually decide on specific procedures the CPA will perform. Agreed-upon procedure engagements result in a report that describes the procedures performed and related findings.

PURPOSE OF AUDITING

- To systematically obtain sufficient, competent evidence regarding an entity's assertions (historic financial information).
- To evaluate the evidence in order to determine the correspondence between those assertions and established criteria (generally accepted accounting principles, or GAAP).
- To communicate the results to interested users, such as shareholders, potential shareholders, creditors, analysts (underwriters and credit rating bureaus), and

financial information monitors (regulatory agencies and stock exchanges) in the form of a report. The report is intended to add credibility to the financial information being distributed.

ROLES OF MANAGEMENT, BOARD OF DIRECTORS, AND AUDIT COMMITTEE

- Management: While the auditor is responsible for forming and expressing an opinion on the financial statements, *the responsibility for the preparation of the financial statements and for their content rests with the management of the entity*. (Don't forget this.)
- Board of directors: The board of directors is elected by the shareholders to guide and oversee management.
- Audit committee: An audit committee is a special committee made up of members of the board of directors who are *neither* officers *nor* employees of the company. It is responsible for the appointment and compensation of the external auditors, and the external auditors report to the audit committee rather than to management. The audit committee works with the external auditors to reinforce independence from management. Audit committees are often responsible for various activities of the company's internal audit staff and other control matters.

CONSIDERATIONS IN PLANNING AN AUDIT

A. Prior to accepting an engagement for the financial statement audits, the auditor should perform certain procedures to make certain that acceptance is appropriate under the circumstances. Part of the process involves developing an understanding of the client's business and industry.

B. Also, the auditor should have established policies and procedures to meet the quality control objective relative to the acceptance of a client. The objective is to avoid association with a client whose management lacks integrity.

C. Information that may be gathered and procedures that may be followed include:

- Obtaining and reviewing financial information of the proposed client.
- Inquiring of third parties, such as bankers, legal counsel, and others, regarding the prospective client and its management.
- In the case of a first-time audit, communicating with the predecessor auditor, as required by auditing standards.
- Considering special circumstances that may cause the firm to regard the engagement as having special risks.
- Evaluating the CPA firm's independence and ability to service the client's needs.
- Determining that acceptance will not violate regulatory requirements or the Code of Professional Conduct.

In producing financial statements, the management of the reporting company makes an overall assertion that the financial statements follow generally accepted accounting principles in the United States. In making this overall assertion, management makes five specific assertions about the various account groups and the financial statements taken as a whole:

1. *Valuation or allocation*: Each transaction and each account balance have been included in the financial statements at appropriate amounts.

2. *Existence or occurrence*: All reported assets, liabilities, and equities actually exist, and all transactions did occur. The auditor wants to be sure that the accounts are *not overstated*.

3. *Presentation and disclosure:* All accounts are properly classified and described, and all relevant information is disclosed.

4. *Completeness:* All transactions and accounts have been included within the financial statements, and nothing has been omitted. The auditor wants to be sure that the accounts are *not understated*.

5. *Rights and obligations*: All assets are the rights of the reporting entity, and all liabilities are the obligations of the reporting entity.

An auditor attempts to corroborate the above assertions in order to provide reasonable assurance that no material misstatements exist in any of the assertions. (Be sure to know these very well for the CPA exam.)

MATERIALITY

Definition: *Materiality* is anything of a size or type that would influence the judgment of a reasonable person relying on the information.

Materiality pervades almost all audit practice decisions. A preliminary judgment of the size component of materiality is set at the beginning of an audit, but is continuously reassessed as new information is gathered. Therefore, materiality is a significant consideration that requires well developed, professional judgment.

MISSTATEMENTS

Definition: *Misstatements* are anything that is stated incorrectly. There are three types of misstatements that are of direct concern to an independent auditor:

1. *Error*—an unintentional mistake in the financial statements, such as a mathematical or clerical mistake.

2. *Fraud*—an intentional act that results in a material misstatement in financial statements.

3. *Illegal act*—violations of laws or governmental regulations, including acts committed by management and the entity's employees acting on behalf of the entity.

ASSURANCE

- An independent auditor cannot offer an unconditional guarantee (absolute assurance) that the financial statements are presented fairly in accordance with GAAP. Absolute assurance would require that *audit risk* be reduced to zero. (Audit risk will be discussed more later.)
- This is impossible because an audit opinion is based upon *sampling* of data (rather than examining all data), *judgmental assessment,* and *estimates* (all of which are subjective).
- Therefore, an independent auditor seeks to collect competent and sufficient evidence that is persuasive rather than conclusive, thereby providing reasonable assurance that financial statements are presented fairly according to GAAP.
- Reasonable assurance is provided when risk of a material misstatement is reduced to an acceptably low level. The auditor uses his or her *professional judgment* to determine when the *risk level* has been reduced to a level low enough to allow for the issuance of *reasonable assurance.*

ILLEGAL ACTS

A. **Direct Illegal Acts.** A direct illegal act is a violation of laws or governmental regulations that directly applies to the financial statements. For example, a liability for income taxes that has not been properly reflected in the financial statements in order to comply with the Internal Revenue Code would be a direct illegal act.

- An auditor's responsibility for detecting illegal acts relating to the violation of laws and governmental regulations having a direct and material effect on the financial statements is the same as the responsibility relating to the detection of errors and fraud.
- The auditor must provide reasonable assurance that such acts did not occur.

B. **Indirect Illegal Acts.** An indirect illegal act is a violation of laws or governmental regulations that indirectly applies to the financial statements. For example, violations of laws and regulations of the Occupational Safety and Health Administration or the Food and Drug Administration may have an indirect effect on the financial statements:

- They are generally small, frequently relate to the operations of the entity rather than to the financial statement assertions, and are often hidden.
- In many circumstances, an independent auditor has no basis for determining whether this type of law or regulation has been violated.
- The auditor has no responsibility to search for indirect illegal acts; however, if an auditor becomes aware of evidence that indicates the possibility of an indirect illegal act, the auditor must understand the nature and circumstance of the act and obtain sufficient evidence to evaluate the effects of the act on the financial statements.

Professional Standards and Audit Responsibilities

Introduction

In the United States, the audit work of a CPA is guided by U.S. Generally Accepted Auditing Standards (GAAS). Historically, these standards have been produced by the Auditing Standards Board of the AICPA. Because of accounting scandals such as Enron and WorldCom, the U.S. Congress created the Public Company Accounting Oversight Board to set standards for the independent audits of *publicly traded* companies. The AICPA still sets standards for the independent audits of privately held companies.

The Professional Standards most directly related to the Auditing and Attestation section of the CPA exam are:

- Statements on Auditing Standards
- Public Company Accounting Oversight Board Pronouncements
- Statements on Standards for Attestation Engagements
- Statements on Standards for Accounting and Review Services
- Statements on Quality Control Standards

There are ten generally accepted auditing standards, referred to as GAAS. *All* of the auditor's work must follow GAAS, which are currently established by the Statements on Auditing Standards (SAS) produced by the Auditing Standards Board of the AICPA. The ten general statements are divided into three categories consisting of general standards, standards of fieldwork, and standards of reporting. Therefore, these standards apply to audits of both publicly held and privately held companies.

Generally Accepted Auditing Standards

The following mnemonic should assist you in remembering the ten standards: TIPPICANOE. Each of the summary phrases of the mnemonic is italicized in the discussion below.

T—Training and proficiency

I—Independence

P—Professional care

P—Planning and supervision

I—Internal control

C—Competent evidence

A—Accounting principles

N—No new principles (consistency)

O—Omitted disclosures

E—Express an opinion

A. General Standards.

- *Training and proficiency.* The audit is to be performed by a person or persons having adequate technical training and proficiency as an auditor.
- *Independence.* In all matters relating to the assignment, independence in mental attitude is to be maintained by the auditor or auditors.
- *Professional care.* Due professional care is to be exercised in the performance of the audit and the preparation of the report.

B. Standards of Fieldwork.

- *Planning and supervision.* The work is to be adequately planned, and assistants, if any, are to be properly supervised.
- *Internal control.* A sufficient understanding of internal control is to be obtained to plan the audit and to determine the nature, timing, and extent of tests to be performed.
- *Competent evidence.* Sufficient competent audit evidence is to be obtained through inspection, observation, inquiries, and confirmations to afford a reasonable basis for an opinion regarding the financial statements under examination.

C. Standards of Reporting.

- *Accounting principles.* The report shall state whether the financial statements are presented in accordance with Generally Accepted Accounting Principles (GAAP).
- *No new principles (consistency).* The report shall identify those circumstances in which such principles have not been consistently observed in the current period in relation to the preceding period.
- *Omitted disclosures.* Informative disclosures in the financial statements are to be regarded as reasonably adequate unless otherwise stated in the report.
- *Express an opinion.* The report shall either contain an expression of opinion regarding the financial statements, taken as a whole, or an assertion to the effect that an opinion cannot be expressed. When an overall opinion cannot be expressed, the reasons therefore should be stated. In all cases where an auditor's name is associated with financial statements, the report should contain a clear-cut indication of the character of the auditor's work, if any, and the degree of responsibility he or she is taking.

  General standards relate to the overall method of performing the audit. Fieldwork standards relate to the specific work carried out by the auditor. Reporting standards relate to the form and content of the auditor's report that accompanies the financial statements. A detailed discussion of the ten basic standards follows.

A. General Standards.

1. *Training and proficiency.* An auditor must be knowledgeable about accounting and auditing, the client's industry, and the specific company, and they must have the

experience to make appropriate evaluations. Technical training is generally achieved by formal education and demonstrated by passing the CPA exam, with the proficiency resulting from practical experience. Training and proficiency are maintained by continuing professional education.

2. *Independence.* Independence is important because it allows auditors to make unbiased evaluations of the assertions made by management. Also, the public has more faith in the work of an auditor if the auditor is independent. For this reason, an auditor must be independent both in fact and in appearance.

   a. For every audit engagement, an auditing firm must identify all of the "covered members":

   - A covered member of an audit engagement is every person on the engagement team, and anyone who can influence the engagement or the members of the engagement team.
   - The firm itself, as a separate legal entity, is also a covered member.
   - A covered member can have no direct financial interest (such as ownership of stock or bonds) or relationship with an audit client.
   - The independence rules extend to a covered member's immediate family (defined as a spouse or spousal equivalent and any dependent).
   - The only exception is that the immediate family member can work for the client as long as the person is not in a position to influence the client's financial statements. This would normally exclude members of management.

   b. Further, the independence rules extend to a covered member's *close relatives* (defined as parents, siblings, and children who are not dependents).

   - Close relatives cannot have a material financial interest in the audit client and cannot hold a key employment position with the client where there is a significant relationship to the accounting or financial reporting function. (A close relative could not, for example, be the controller of the client.)
   - Any partner of the firm or professional employee who is not a covered employee for a particular engagement can hold equity shares in the client but not more than 5% of the outstanding stock.
   - An auditor may not render an opinion on statements of the current year until all fees from the prior year's audit have been paid.

3. *Professional care.* This standard requires that auditors observe each of the fieldwork and reporting standards.

   a. Although not infallible, an auditor is responsible for exercising reasonable care to ensure that the audit is carried out as well as the *average auditor* would have done.

   b. The auditor should exercise professional skepticism throughout the audit process, which involves a questioning mind and a critical assessment of audit evidence.

c. While the auditor should not assume that management is dishonest, neither should the auditor assume unquestioned honesty.

B. Standards of Fieldwork.

1. *Planning and supervision.* An audit of financial statements is a complex process and cannot be carried out efficiently without an appropriate amount of planning.

    a. Adequate planning is demonstrated by the creation of an *audit program*, which is required for every audit engagement.

    b. Supervision is the process of directing the efforts of assistants in conjunction with the audit objectives, and determining whether the objectives are achieved.

    c. All audit work should be reviewed by an auditor with adequate technical training.

2. *Internal control.* Internal control is comprised of all policies and procedures to ensure that the systems within a company operate effectively as intended.

    a. The purpose in an independent audit of gaining an understanding of internal controls is to provide assurance that the financial information being generated by the company does not contain material misstatements. In understanding an entity's internal control, an auditor must consider five components:

        - Control environment—Is internal control a priority of the owners and the management of the entity?
        - Risk assessment—Are the entity's accounting and control systems able to anticipate problems and adapt to them before they occur?
        - Control activities—Does the entity have general control policies and procedures in place throughout?
        - Information and communication—Are the accounting systems capable of delivering the proper information to the correct party in a timely fashion?
        - Monitoring—Does the entity work to make sure that internal control evolves with changes over time?

    b. After coming to an understanding of the five components of internal control, a preliminary assessment of *control risk* is made.

        - If the assessment is that control appears to be poor, the auditor sets control risk at the maximum level and must perform a maximum amount of substantive testing or use substantive testing that generates audit evidence of a particularly high level.
        - If, however, the assessment appears to be good, the auditor considers whether or not testing the internal controls would save audit time and cost.

- If no reduction in audit time is expected, then control risk is still set at the maximum level and a maximum amount of substantive testing is performed.

3. *Competent audit evidence.* Evidence gathering is referred to as substantive testing.

   a. It is testing that confirms an account's ending balance and verifies the transactions that affected its ending balance.

   b. An auditor can use a wide array of testing techniques including inspection, inquiry, observation, recalculation, and confirmation.

   c. The actual amount and quality of evidence to be gathered depends upon the professional judgment of the auditor.

C. Standards of Reporting.

1. Implicit reporting requirements.

   a. *No new principles (consistency).* The report shall identify those circumstances in which GAAP has not been consistently observed in the current period in relation to the preceding period. The objective is to provide assurance that the comparability of an entity's financial statements is not materially affected by inconsistent application of GAAP from period to period. Assurance of consistency is implied.

   b. *Omitted disclosures.* Disclosure can be assumed to be adequate unless the report states otherwise. This is another implicit requirement.

2. Explicit reporting requirements.

   a. *Accounting principles.* The auditor's report must explicitly state whether the financial statements are presented in accordance with GAAP. Because GAAP is not static, it is difficult to determine what the "pool" of generally accepted accounting principles is at any given point in time. For this reason, a GAAP Hierarchy has been established with five levels of authority with the higher levels having the highest priority. For businesses, the top level of the GAAP Hierarchy consists of FASB Statements and Interpretations, APB Opinions, and AICPA Accounting Research Bulletins.

3. *Express an opinion.* The report must contain an opinion on the financial statements taken as a whole or a clear indication that an opinion cannot be expressed.

   a. When an opinion cannot be rendered, the reasons should be stated.

   b. If the auditor's name will still be associated with the financial statements, the report should contain a clear-cut indication of the character of the auditor's examination and the degree of responsibility the auditor is taking.

c. This is an explicit requirement.

SOURCES OF GENERALLY ACCEPTED ACCOUNTING PRINCIPLES

As mentioned earlier, there is an established GAAP Hierarchy with five levels of authority. For businesses, those five levels are:

Authoritative GAAP

1. FASB Statements and Interpretations, APB Opinions, and AICPA Accounting Research Bulletins.

2. FASB Technical Bulletins, AICPA Industry Audit and Accounting Guides, and the AICPA Statements of Position.

3. AICPA Accounting Standards Executive Committee (AcSEC) Practice Bulletins and FASB Emerging Issues Task Force consensus positions.

4. Implementation guides published by the FASB staff, AICPA Accounting Interpretations, and practices that are widely recognized and prevalent generally or in industry.

Other Non-authoritative Accounting Literature

5. Other accounting literature such as FASB Concepts Statements, textbooks, articles, and speeches.

   - For governmental entities, the Government Accounting Standards Board (GASB) establishes standards rather than the FASB.
   - Audits of government organizations, programs, activities, and functions, and of government assistance received by contractors, nonprofit organizations, and other nongovernment organizations must adhere to Generally Accepted Government Auditing Standards (GAGAS).
   - The Comptroller General establishes these standards and they are often referred to as "The Yellow Book."

ACCEPTING THE ENGAGEMENT AND ENGAGEMENT LETTERS

INTRODUCTION

There are several steps that will be taken by an auditor before accepting an audit engagement. The first step is client contact that may occur in various ways. The reporting company may contact the auditor about a possible audit, or the auditor may contact the reporting company.

Depending upon the size of the reporting company, an audit committee may be the auditor's point of contact. If an audit committee does exist, it is generally made up of members of the board of directors who are neither officers nor employees of the company.

An audit committee is responsible for the appointment, firing, and compensation of the external auditors. The external auditors report to the audit committee, rather than to management. Audit committees are often responsible for various activities of the company's internal audit staff and other control matters.

ACTIVITIES OF AUDITOR PRIOR TO ACCEPTING CLIENT

A. It is important that an auditor establishes policies for deciding whether to accept (or continue serving) a client in order to minimize the likelihood of being associated with an organization whose management lacks integrity.

   1. As soon as discussions start, the auditor should request a tour of the reporting company's facilities and begin to gather information about the reporting company.

   2. The initial information gathered will help the auditor decide whether or not to accept the engagement.

   3. It will also assist the auditor in evaluating the assertions made by management.

   4. It is possible that the reporting entity may be having the same discussions with several auditing firms at the same time.

B. The initial information gathered by the auditor will include the following:

   1. The industry of the reporting entity.

   2. The form and ownership of the reporting entity.

   3. The financing arrangements.

   4. Why the reporting entity requires an audit.

   5. Whether or not there have been any previous auditors.

   6. If there were previous auditors, who they were and why they are being changed.

   7. The history of the company.

   8. The company's future plans.

   9. What types of systems and records are in place.

   10. The knowledge and competence of accounting and financial personnel.

   11. Copies of past financial statements, interim financial statements, and tax returns.

   12. Whether or not all transactions are posted.

13. Whether or not the ledgers and subsidiary ledgers are in balance.

14. Whether or not reconciliations are up to date.

C. *Audit conference.* The reporting company should interview each of the auditing firm(s) and then extend an offer to the firm considered best suited for the work. Prior to accepting the engagement, an audit conference should be held between the client (audit committee if applicable) and the auditor, the purpose of which is to establish an understanding as to the nature of the engagement and the responsibilities of the parties. At this conference:

1. The client should be informed of the problems associated with an initial audit as opposed to the normal problems of a subsequent audit.

2. The client should be informed of the nature of an audit examination of financial statements, and a determination should be made as to whether an audit will be of benefit to the client.

3. The client should inform the auditor of any communications between the audit committee and the predecessor auditors.

4. The auditor and client should establish what responsibilities the auditor will and will not be assuming.

5. The auditor should make clear the responsibility being assumed in connection with the detection of errors and fraud.

6. The audit timing, the proposed outcome, and the audit fees should be discussed.

PREDECESSOR AND SUCCESSOR AUDITOR

A. Predecessor Auditors.

Definition: A predecessor auditor is an auditor who has reported on the most recent audited financial statements or was engaged to perform but did not complete an audit of any subsequent financial statements and has resigned, declined to stand for reappointment, or been notified that his/her services have been or may be terminated.

1. If it is the first year the auditor is examining the client's financial statements and the financial statements have been examined by other auditors in previous years, the auditor is required to communicate with the predecessor auditor.

2. The responsibility for initiating communication with the predecessor auditor rests with the successor auditor.

B. Successor Auditors.

Definition: A successor auditor is an auditor who is considering accepting an engagement to audit financial statements or an auditor who has accepted such an engagement.

1. Because the information being sought by the successor auditor is confidential, the client must grant permission for the contact to be made.

2. If the client will not grant this permission, the auditor would normally withdraw from consideration as the successor auditor.

3. However, the auditor may continue if the reason for the denial is viewed as legitimate.

4. The successor auditor should make the following inquiries of the predecessor auditor prior to accepting the engagement:

    a. Facts that might bear on the integrity of management.

    b. Disagreements between the auditor and management concerning accounting principles, auditing procedures, or other significant matters.

    c. The existence of illegal acts or fraud.

    d. The existence of communications between the auditor and the audit committee. This is a particularly important question because anything the independent auditor encounters that would have a significant impact on the financial statements must be communicated to the audit committee.

    e. The predecessor's understanding about the reason for the change in auditors.

    f. Any other information that may be of assistance in determining whether to accept the engagement.

5. If there are any circumstances (e.g., litigation, disciplinary proceedings) that prevent the predecessor auditors from giving a complete response, the predecessor auditor should indicate that the response is limited.

ACCEPTING THE AUDIT

A. After the audit conference and communication with the predecessor auditor, the auditor must determine if the engagement should be accepted. Among the factors to be considered are the following:

1. Whether the auditor has adequate knowledge of the client and the industry to perform in accordance with the needs of the client.

2. Whether the client will benefit from an audit examination of the financial statements.

3. Whether the auditor is appointed early enough to adequately plan the audit to obtain sufficient competent audit evidence for the formulation of an opinion on the financial statements.

4. Whether it is in the auditor's best professional interests to accept the engagement.

B. There are no authoritative guidelines on how to decide whether to accept an engagement; however, the auditor should consider the following questions:

1. Are there known accounting or auditing problems?

2. Are the records in good condition so that an audit is actually possible?

3. Is the auditor completely independent of the reporting company?

4. Does the management demonstrate adequate integrity?

5. Does the auditor have sufficient knowledge of the industry so that proper evaluations can be made? (An auditor does not have to possess sufficient knowledge about the industry when the engagement is accepted, but it is necessary by the time the audit work begins.)

ENGAGEMENT LETTER

A. If the engagement is accepted, the auditor should establish an understanding with the client regarding the services to be performed.

1. Although this understanding may be obtained orally or in writing, it must be documented in the audit documents and is generally obtained through the use of an engagement letter.

2. The engagement letter is sent to the client, who indicates approval by returning a signed copy to the auditor.

3. The understanding *must include* four elements:

    a. The objectives of the audit (the expression of an opinion on the financial statements).

    b. The responsibilities of management:

    - Management is responsible for establishing and maintaining effective internal control over financial reporting.
    - Management is responsible for identifying and ensuring that the client complies with all applicable laws and regulations.
    - Management is responsible for preparing the financial statements, all financial records, and related information, and making them available to the auditor.

- Management must provide the auditor with a representation letter at the end of fieldwork.
- Management must adjust financial statements to correct material misstatements.
- Management is responsible for affirming in the representation letter that the effect of uncorrected misstatements aggregated by the auditor is immaterial.

  c. The responsibilities of the auditor:

- The auditor will conduct the audit in accordance with U.S. GAAS.
- The auditor will ensure that the audit committee is aware of any reportable conditions that came to the auditor's attention.

  d. The limitations of the audit:

- An audit gives reasonable, rather than absolute assurance.
- Material misstatements may remain undetected.
- If the auditor is unable to form or has not formed an opinion, the auditor may decline to express an opinion or decline to issue a report.

B. Additionally, an engagement letter *may also include* the following:

1. Timing and the estimated completion date.

2. Arrangements with respect to client assistance.

3. Involvement of specialists or internal auditors.

4. Arrangements regarding communication with the predecessor auditor.

5. The basis on which fees are computed and billed.

6. Additional services to be provided related to regulatory requirements.

7. Other additional services.

8. Any limitation or other arrangement regarding the liability of the auditor or the client.

9. Conditions under which access to the auditor's audit documents may be granted to others.

10. A statement of the mechanism by which notification will be made of any changes in the original arrangements necessitated by unknown or unforeseen factors.

C. An engagement letter is used primarily to prevent misunderstandings between the client and the auditor as to the nature of the engagement and the responsibilities being assumed by the auditor. The engagement letter also serves as a useful reference in preparing for current and future engagements.

D. Sample Audit Engagement Letter.

Farris & Company AUDITORS
26000 Taylor Lane
Clarksville, OH 45113

July 1, 2006

Mr. James Ridge
Chairperson of the Audit Committee
Ridge's Valley View Farms
10000 Lebanon Road
Clarksville, OH 45113

Dear Mr. Ridge:

In accordance with the agreement reached in our audit conference on June 1, 2006, we are to perform an audit of the balance sheet of Ridge's Valley View Farms as of December 31, 2006, and of the related statements of income, retained earnings, and cash flows for the year then ended in accordance with generally accepted auditing standards. Those standards require that we plan and perform the audit to obtain reasonable, rather than absolute, assurance about whether the financial statements are free of material misstatement, whether caused by error or by fraud. Accordingly, a material misstatement may remain undetected. Also, our audit is not designed to detect error or fraud that is immaterial to the financial statements. If for any reason we are unable to complete the audit or we are unable to form an opinion on the financial statements, we may decline to express an opinion or decline to issue a report as a result of the engagement.

While an audit includes obtaining an understanding of the company's existing internal control sufficient to plan the audit and to determine the nature, timing, and extent of audit procedures to be performed, it is not designed to provide assurance on the internal control or to identify reportable conditions. However, we are responsible for ensuring that the audit committee is aware of any reportable conditions which come to our attention. Our findings regarding your internal control, including information about material weaknesses, will be reported to you in a separate letter at the close of the audit.

You and your management are responsible for the financial statements, establishing and maintaining effective internal control over financial reporting, identifying and ensuring that the company complies with the laws and regulations applicable to its activities, making all financial records and related information available to us, and providing us with a letter that confirms certain representations made during the audit.

In addition to the performance of an audit, we will prepare the federal and state income tax returns for the year ended December 31, 2006.

Whenever possible, we will use your company's personnel. We will provide your staff with a package of schedule formats required by our staff for the audit. We understand that your staff will prepare all of the schedules in this package. This effort should substantially reduce our time requirements and initiate a more efficient audit.

Based upon our discussion with your personnel and after a preliminary review of your accounting records, we estimate the cost of this audit engagement and the preparation of the aforementioned tax returns to be approximately $100,000. The charges for our services will be at our regular hourly rates plus out-of-pocket expenses. This estimated cost could be affected by unusual circumstances we cannot foresee at this time. However, if we should encounter such problems, we will contact you as soon as possible to discuss such circumstances. An interim billing of $30,000 will be delivered on or close to November 30, 2006, with a final billing upon delivery of the audit report and tax returns (on or about March 15, 2007).

We appreciate this opportunity to be of service to you. Please do not hesitate to contact us if you have questions about the engagement or desire other professional services.

If these arrangements are in accordance with your understanding, please sign and return the enclosed copy of this letter to us.

Very truly yours,

Dylan Farris, CPA

Accepted by:_____

Title:_____ Date:_____

OVERALL AUDIT PLANNING REQUIREMENTS

AUDIT STRATEGY

A. Subsequent to client acceptance of the proposal, an overall *audit strategy* must be developed.

   1. The auditor should *plan the audit* to obtain *reasonable* and not absolute *assurance* that material misstatements are detected.

   2. Absolute assurance is not attainable because of the *nature of audit evidence* (not every transaction is tested, and human errors can occur in the testing) and the *characteristics of fraud* (it is usually hidden).

B. During planning, the auditor will:

1. Consider management's assertions.

2. Make a preliminary assessment of materiality.

3. Assess audit risk.

4. Specifically assess the risk of material misstatement of the financial statements due to fraud.

C. The first standard of fieldwork states that the work is to be adequately planned, and assistants, if any, are to be properly supervised.

1. In order to make certain there is adequate time to plan and execute the examination of financial statements, early appointment of the auditor by the client is desirable.

2. However, appointment of an auditor near or after the year-end date does not preclude the auditor from accepting the engagement.

D. Management's assertions.

1. An independent auditor provides reasonable assurance that the five assertions made by management are free from material misstatements.

2. In planning and performing an audit, the auditor considers these assertions for the various financial statement accounts, and plans audit tests which will reduce the risk to an acceptably low level that a material misstatement exists.

3. When all of these assertions have been met for an account, the account is in conformity with generally accepted accounting principles.

MATERIALITY

A. Preliminary assessment of materiality.

1. As previously stated, materiality is anything of a size or type that would influence the judgment of a reasonable person relying on the information.

2. An auditor must consider materiality in planning the audit and designing audit procedures.

   a. At the beginning of the audit, the auditor should set a preliminary standard for the *quantitative* aspect of materiality and all misstatements of this amount or more will be viewed as material.

   b. The quantitative standard is usually set based upon past annual and interim financial statements using the size of net income, net assets, and the like. This assessment should be reviewed throughout the audit as more information is obtained.

3. *Other misstatements* will be judged based on their cause.

AUDIT PLANNING PROCEDURES

A. While planning and supervising the audit, the auditor should keep in mind that the overall goal of the audit is to *gather sufficient, competent evidence so that the risk of material misstatement is reduced to an acceptably low level.*

B. If the auditor's goal is achieved, the auditor has provided reasonable assurance that the financial statements present fairly, in all material respects, the financial position of the client and the results of its operations and its cash flows in conformity with accounting principles generally accepted in the United States.

C. In planning the audit engagement, the auditor will:

1. Consider obtaining additional information from the predecessor auditor.

2. Perform analytical procedures.

3. Evaluate internal controls.

4. Develop a written audit program.

5. Consider supervision needs.

6. Consider the timing of audit procedures.

D. The auditor may want to summarize the overall audit plan into a planning memorandum.

UNDERSTANDING THE CLIENT AND CLIENT'S INDUSTRY

A. The nature, timing, and extent of planning will vary with the size and complexity of the audit client, experience with the client, and knowledge of the client's business.

B. To develop an overall audit strategy, the auditor will want to gain an understanding of the client's operations, business, and industry and may consider the following:

1. Client considerations:

    a. The business and industry.

    b. Accounting policies and procedures.

    c. The methods used by the entity to process significant accounting information, including the use of computers and computer service centers.

    d. Financial statement items likely to require adjustment.

- e. Conditions that may require extension or modification of audit procedures (e.g., risk of misstatement, related party transactions).

2. Audit considerations:

   a. Anticipated reliance on internal control.

   b. Preliminary judgments about materiality levels.

   c. The nature of reports expected to result from the examination.

C. In addition, the auditor may consider performing the following review and inquiry procedures during planning:

1. Review correspondence files, prior year's audit documents, permanent files, financial statements, and auditor's reports.

2. Review current year's interim financial statements.

3. Discuss matters that may affect the audit with firm personnel responsible for nonaudit services to the client.

4. Request assistance from specialists and consultants.

5. Establish the timing of the audit work.

6. Consider staffing requirements.

7. Inquire about current business developments affecting the entity.

8. Discuss the type, scope, and timing of the examination with management, directors, and the audit committee.

9. Consider the effects of new accounting and auditing pronouncements.

10. Coordinate the assistance of client personnel in data preparation including internal auditors.

D. The auditor should obtain a level of knowledge of the client's business that will enable effective planning and performance of the audit in accordance with generally accepted auditing standards. This knowledge helps the auditor:

1. Identify areas that may need special consideration.

2. Assess conditions under which accounting data are produced, processed, reviewed, and accumulated.

3. Evaluate accounting estimates for reasonableness (e.g., valuation of inventories, depreciation, allowance for doubtful accounts, percentage of completion of long-term contracts).

4. Evaluate the reasonableness of management representations.

5. Make judgments about the appropriateness of the accounting principles applied and the adequacy of disclosures.

COMMUNICATE WITH PREDECESSOR AUDITORS

A. Subsequent to acceptance, the successor auditor may wish to make additional inquiries of the predecessor auditor.

B. Although a second communication is not required, the information obtained can be extremely valuable in planning the audit. Additional communications with the predecessor auditor may include the following:

1. Reviewing the predecessor's audit documents primarily for opening balances and consistency of application of accounting principles.

2. Making inquiries regarding matters affecting the conduct of the examination, such as audit areas requiring an inordinate amount of time or audit problems arising due to the condition of the accounting system and records.

ANALYTICAL PROCEDURES

A. The auditor is required to perform analytical procedures in planning the audit, as well as in an overall review near completion of the audit.

B. During the planning stage, the objective of analytical procedures is to assist in planning the nature, timing, and extent of audit procedures that will be used to obtain evidence for specific accounts.

C. Analytical procedures consist of evaluations of financial information made by a study of plausible relationships among financial and nonfinancial data.

D. Perhaps the most familiar example of analytical procedures used in auditing is the calculation of ratios. However, analytical procedures range from simple comparisons of information through the use of complex models such as regression and time series analysis.

E. The typical approach consists of:

1. Developing an expectation for the account balance.

2. Determining the amount of difference from the expectation that can be accepted without investigation.

3. Comparing the company's account balance (or ratio) with the expected account balance.

4. Investigating significant differences from the expected account balance.

F. When developing an expectation, the auditor must attempt to identify plausible relationships. These expectations may be derived from:

1. The information itself in prior periods.

2. Anticipated results such as budgets and forecasts.

3. Relationships among elements of financial information within the period.

4. Industry information.

5. Relevant nonfinancial information.

G. Relationships differ in their predictability:

1. Relationships in a dynamic or unstable environment are less predictable than those in a stable environment.

2. Relationships involving balance sheet accounts are less predictable than income statement accounts. (Balance sheet accounts represent balances at one arbitrary point in time.)

3. Relationships involving management discretion are sometimes less predictable (e.g., decisions to incur maintenance expense rather than replace an asset).

H. Principal limitations concerning analytical procedures include the following:

1. Inadequate guidelines for evaluation (e.g., should the ratio be the same as last year?).

2. The inability of the auditor to determine whether a change is due to a misstatement or is the result of random change in the account.

3. Cost-based accounting records that hinder comparisons between firms of different ages and/or asset compositions.

4. Accounting differences that hinder comparisons between companies (e.g., the use of LIFO versus the use of FIFO).

5. Analytical procedures that present only "circumstantial" evidence in that a significant difference will lead to additional audit procedures as opposed to direct detection of a misstatement.

CONSIDERATION OF INTERNAL CONTROL

A. An auditor must obtain a sufficient understanding of internal control to plan the audit.

B. This understanding should include knowledge about the design of controls and whether the client has placed them in operation.

C. This understanding must be sufficient to allow the auditor to:

1. Identify types of potential misstatements.

2. Consider factors affecting the risk of misstatements.

3. Design substantive tests.

D. In addition, as noted above, the auditor must identify a planned assessed level for control risk for each of the five management assertions in each account.

AUDIT PROGRAM

A. Planning the engagement involves the consideration of the nature, extent, and timing of work to be performed.

B. The auditor should prepare a set of written programs.

C. These programs aid in instructing assistants in work to be done by setting forth the evidence-gathering procedures that the auditor prescribes in order to accomplish the objectives of the examination.

SUPERVISION REQUIREMENTS

A. The auditing firm should give consideration to the need for adequate supervision.

B. At each staff level, a clear indication is necessary as to:

1. The types of decisions that may be made by that level of staff.

2. The party or parties to be addressed for other decisions or resolution of questions.

3. The responsibilities for review of work performed at other levels.

C. Supervision involves directing the efforts of assistants who are involved in accomplishing the objectives of the examination and determining whether those objectives were accomplished. It includes:

1. Instructing assistants.

2. Keeping informed of significant problems encountered during the audit.

3. Reviewing the work performed by assistants.

4. Dealing with differences of opinion among audit personnel.

D. Assistants should be informed of their responsibilities and the objectives of the procedures they are to perform.

E. Assistants should also be directed to bring to the attention of the auditor who has final responsibility for the engagement any accounting or auditing problems so he/she can assess the significance of the problems with respect to the audit.

F. The work of each assistant should be reviewed to determine whether it was adequately performed and to evaluate whether the results are consistent with the conclusions to be presented in the audit report.

G. The auditor with final responsibility and the assistants should be aware of the procedures to be followed when differences of opinion among firm personnel cannot be resolved.

   1. Persons who do not agree with the final conclusion should be able to document their disagreement and, if necessary, disassociate themselves from the resolution of the matter.

   2. In this situation, the final resolution of the matter should also be documented.

TIMING OF AUDIT PROCEDURES

A. Tests of controls and substantive tests can be conducted at various times.

   1. The timing of tests of controls is very flexible; they are often performed at an interim period, and subsequently updated through year end.

   2. An auditor also has a certain amount of flexibility in planning the timing of substantive tests.

B. Before applying procedures at an interim date, an auditor should consider the incremental audit risk involved, as well as whether performance of such interim procedures is likely to be cost effective.

C. The auditor who intends to apply audit tests at an interim date should consider whether the accounting system will provide information on remaining period transactions that is sufficient to investigate significant unusual transactions, other causes of significant fluctuation, expected fluctuations that did not occur, and changes in the composition of the account balances.

OTHER AUDITOR RESPONSIBILITIES

A. The auditor is not required to possess sufficient knowledge of the client's industry at the time of acceptance of the audit.

B. However, if, as a result of planning an engagement, the CPA determines that he/she does not possess the industry expertise or the professional competence necessary for the engagement, the CPA may take steps to obtain the knowledge necessary to complete the engagement in a competent manner or, if this is not practical, he/she should refuse (or withdraw from) the engagement.

C. If withdrawing, the auditor may, if appropriate, expect compensation for the services performed.

NEW STATEMENT ON AUDIT STANDARDS #114: THE AUDITOR'S COMMUNICATION WITH THOSE CHARGED WITH GOVERNANCE

CPAs must communicate certain matters related to an audit to those who are "charged with governance of the client." This includes the board of directors and the audit committee. The matters to be communicated are significant and relevant for overseeing the financial reporting process. The purpose of the communication is to (a) provide an overview of the scope and timing of the audit; (b) obtain relevant information; and (c) provide timely observations that may arise from the audit that could be relevant to overseeing the financial reporting process.

A. Sound governance principles require that:

1. Auditors have access to audit committee as necessary.

2. The Chair of the audit committee and, when relevant, other members, meet with the auditor periodically.

3. Audit committee meets with the auditor without management present at least annually. Many matters will be discussed with management prior to a discussion with those charged with governance. It would not, however, be appropriate to communicate to management questions about management's competence or integrity.

B. Matters to be communicated to those charged with governance are:

1. Auditor responsibilities under GAAS.

2. Overview of planned scope and timing of audit.

3. Significant findings from the audit.

C. The communication process.

1. Significant findings should be communicated in writing to those charged with governance when the auditor believes oral communication would not be adequate.

2. Other communications may be oral or in writing.

3. The auditor should communicate on a sufficiently timely basis to enable those charged with governance to take appropriate action.

D. Adequacy of the communication process.

If the auditor believes it was inadequate and cannot be resolved, the auditor may: (1) modify opinion on basis of a scope limitation; (2) obtain legal advice; (3) communicate with third parties (e.g., a regulator); or (4) withdraw from the engagement.

E. Documentation

If communications are oral, retain notes concerning the communication. If the communication is in writing, retain a copy.

QUESTIONS: OVERVIEW OF AUDITING

1. Which of the following criteria is unique to the auditor's attest function?
   A. Familiarity with the particular industry of which the client is a part.
   B. Independence.
   C. Due professional care.
   D. General competence.

2. When an auditor becomes aware of a possible client illegal act, the auditor should obtain an understanding of the nature of the act to:
   A. evaluate the effect on the financial statements.
   B. determine the reliability of management's representations.
   C. increase the assessed level of control risk.
   D. recommend remedial actions to the audit committee.

3. Which of the following professional services would be considered an attest engagement?
   A. An engagement to report on compliance with statutory requirements.
   B. The compilation of financial statements from a client's accounting records.
   C. An income tax engagement to prepare federal and state tax returns.
   D. A management consulting engagement to provide I.T. advice to a client.

4. After fieldwork audit procedures are completed, a partner of the CPA firm who has not been involved in the audit performs a second, or wrap-up, audit document review. This second review usually focuses on:
   A. fraud involving the client's management and its employees.
   B. the materiality of the adjusting entries proposed by the audit staff.
   C. the fair presentation of the financial statements in conformity with GAAP.
   D. the communication of internal control weaknesses to the client's audit committee.

5. The auditor's report may be addressed to the company whose financial statements are being examined or to that company's:
   A. chief financial officer.
   B. president.
   C. chief operating officer.
   D. board of directors.

6. The fourth standard of reporting requires the auditor's report to contain either an expression of opinion regarding the financial statements taken as a whole or an assertion to the effect that an opinion cannot be expressed. The objective of the fourth standard is to prevent:
   A. an auditor from reporting on one basic financial statement and not the others.
   B. restrictions on the scope of the audit, whether imposed by the client or by the inability to obtain evidence.
   C. misinterpretations regarding the degree of responsibility the auditor is assuming.
   D. an auditor from expressing different opinions on each of the basic financial statements.

7. In an audit of financial statements in accordance with generally accepted auditing standards, an auditor is required to:
   A. determine whether control procedures are suitably designed to prevent or detect material misstatements.
   B. search for significant deficiencies in the operation of internal control.
   C. document the auditor's understanding of the entity's internal control.
   D. search for significant deficiencies in the operation of internal control.

8. To exercise due professional care, an auditor should:
   A. design the audit to detect all instances of illegal acts.
   B. critically review the judgment exercised by those assisting in the audit.
   C. attain the proper balance of professional experience and formal education.
   D. examine all available corroborating evidence supporting management's assertions.

9. The third general standard states that due care is to be exercised in the performance of an audit. This standard is ordinarily interpreted to require:
   A. limited review of the indications of employee fraud and illegal acts.
   B. thorough review of the existing safeguards over access to assets and records.
   C. objective review of the adequacy of the technical training and proficiency of firm personnel.
   D. critical review of the judgment exercised at every level of supervision.

10. What is the general character of the three generally accepted auditing standards classified as general standards?
    A. Criteria for competence, independence, and professional care of individuals performing the audit.
    B. Criteria for the content of the auditor's report on financial statements and related footnote disclosures.
    C. The requirements for the planning of the audit and supervision of assistants, if any.
    D. Criteria for the content of the financial statements and related footnote disclosures.

11. The audit work performed by each assistant should be reviewed to determine whether it was adequately performed, and to evaluate whether the:
    A. audit procedures performed are approved in the professional standards.
    B. auditor's system of quality control has been maintained at a high level.
    C. audit has been performed by persons having adequate technical training and proficiency as auditors.
    D. results are consistent with the conclusions to be presented in the auditor's report.

12. A CPA is *most likely* to refer to one or more of the three general auditing standards in determining:
    A. whether the CPA should undertake an audit engagement.
    B. requirements for the review of internal control.
    C. the scope of the CPA's auditing procedures.
    D. the nature of the CPA's report qualification.

13. What is the meaning of the generally accepted auditing standard that requires the auditor be independent?
    A. The auditor's sole obligation is to third parties.
    B. The auditor must be without bias with respect to the client under audit.
    C. The auditor may have a direct ownership interest in the client's business if it is not material.
    D. The auditor must adopt a critical attitude during the audit.

14. The primary purpose of establishing quality control policies and procedures for deciding whether to accept a new client is to:
    A. minimize the likelihood of association with clients whose management lacks integrity.
    B. anticipate before performing any fieldwork whether an unqualified opinion can be expressed.
    C. enable the CPA firm to attest to the reliability of the client.
    D. satisfy the CPA firm's duty to the public concerning the acceptance of new clients.

15. Which of the following factors would *most likely* cause an auditor not to accept a new audit engagement?
    A. An inadequate understanding of the entity's internal control.
    B. An inability to perform preliminary analytical procedures before assessing control risk.
    C. Concluding that the entity's management probably lacks integrity.
    D. The close proximity to the end of the entity's fiscal year.

16. The objective of tests of details of transactions performed as substantive tests is to:
    A. comply with generally accepted auditing standards.
    B. evaluate whether management's policies and procedures operated effectively.
    C. detect material misstatements in the financial statements.
    D. attain assurance about the reliability of the accounting system.

17. Which of the following standards requires a critical review of the work done and the judgment exercised by those assisting in an audit at every level of supervision?
    A. Due care.
    B. Proficiency.
    C. Audit risk.
    D. Inspection.

18. During the initial planning phase of an audit, a CPA would *most likely*:
    A. discuss the timing of the audit procedures with the client's management.
    B. evaluate the reasonableness of the client's accounting estimates.
    C. identify specific internal control activities that are likely to prevent fraud.
    D. inquire of the client's attorney as to whether any unrecorded claims are probable of assertion.

19. Which of the following statements is **FALSE** about materiality?
    A. Materiality judgments are made in light of surrounding circumstances and necessarily involve both quantitative and qualitative judgments.
    B. An auditor considers materiality for planning purposes in terms of the largest aggregate level of misstatements that could be material to any one of the financial statements.
    C. An auditor's consideration of materiality is influenced by the auditor's perception of the needs of a reasonable person who will rely on the financial statements.
    D. The concept of materiality recognizes that some matters are important for fair presentation of financial statements in conformity with GAAP, while other matters are not important.

20. For all audits of financial statements made in accordance with generally accepted auditing standards, the use of analytical procedures is required to some extent:

	In the planning stages	As a substantive test	In the review stage
A.	No	Yes	Yes
B.	Yes	No	No
C.	No	Yes	No
D.	Yes	No	Yes

21. The element of the audit planning process *most likely* to be agreed upon with the client before implementation of the audit strategy is the determination of the:
    A. evidence to be gathered to provide a sufficient basis for the auditor's opinion.
    B. schedules and analyses to be prepared by the client's staff.
    C. pending legal matters to be included in the inquiry of the client's attorney.
    D. methods of statistical sampling to be used in confirming accounts receivable.

22. The in-charge auditor would *most likely* have a supervisory responsibility to explain to the staff assistants:
    A. why certain documents are being transferred from the current file to the permanent file.
    B. what benefits may be attained by the assistants' adherence to established time budgets.
    C. how the results of various auditing procedures performed by the assistants should be evaluated.
    D. that immaterial fraud are not to be reported to the client's audit committee.

23. Which of the following would an auditor *most likely* use in determining the auditor's preliminary judgment about materiality?
    A. The entity's annualized interim financial statements.
    B. The results of the internal control questionnaire.
    C. The anticipated sample size of the planned substantive tests.
    D. The contents of the management representation letter.

24. In planning an audit, an auditor would *most likely* obtain an understanding of a continuing client's business by:
    A. performing tests of details of transactions and balances.
    B. reviewing prior-year audit documents and the permanent file for the client.
    C. reevaluating the client's internal control environment.
    D. reading specialized industry journals.

25. An auditor obtains knowledge about a new client's business and its industry to:
    A. develop an attitude of professional skepticism concerning management's financial statement assertions.
    B. make constructive suggestions concerning improvements to the client's internal control.
    C. evaluate whether the aggregation of known misstatements causes the financial statements taken as a whole to be materially misstated.
    D. understand the events and transactions that may have an effect on the client's financial statements.

26. The senior auditor responsible for coordinating the field work usually schedules a pre-audit conference with the audit team primarily to:
    A. provide an opportunity to document staff disagreements regarding technical issues.
    B. give guidance to the staff regarding both technical and personnel aspects of the audit.
    C. discuss staff suggestions concerning the establishment and maintenance of time budgets.
    D. establish the need for using the work of specialists and internal auditors.

27. The element of the audit planning process *most likely* to be agreed upon with the client before implementation of the audit strategy is the determination of the:
    A. timing of inventory observation procedures to be performed.
    B. procedures to be undertaken to discover litigation, claims, and assessments.
    C. evidence to be gathered to provide a sufficient basis for the auditor's opinion.
    D. pending legal matters to be included in the inquiry of the client's attorney.

28. Which of the following procedures would an auditor *most likely* include in the initial planning of a financial statement audit?
    A. Determining the extent of involvement of the client's internal auditors.
    B. Considering whether the client's accounting estimates are reasonable in the circumstances.
    C. Obtaining a written representation letter from the client's management.
    D. Examining documents to detect illegal acts having a material effect on the financial statements.

29. Which of the following is required documentation in an audit in accordance with generally accepted auditing standards?
    A. A flowchart or narrative of the accounting system describing the recording and classification of transactions for financial reporting.
    B. An internal control questionnaire identifying policies and procedures that ensure specific objectives will be achieved.
    C. An audit program setting forth in detail the procedures necessary to accomplish the engagement's objectives.
    D. A planning memorandum establishing the timing of the audit procedures and coordinating the assistance of entity personnel.

Answers: Overview of Auditing

1. **B** Without independence, the auditor cannot objectively issue an opinion.

2. **A** Illegal acts have financial statement implications in that the client may be faced with fines or penalties as a result of the illegal acts. Such contingencies should be recognized in the financial statements. Thus, the auditor must obtain an understanding of the illegal acts in order to consider their potential financial statement effect.

3. **A** An attestation engagement is an engagement that provides either positive or negative assurance concerning financial information. An engagement to report on compliance with a statutory requirement provides negative assurance that is an attestation engagement.

4. **C** QC 10-1.19 states that the purpose of a financial statement audit is to express an opinion regarding the statements and if they are "presented fairly, in all material respects, in conformity with generally accepted accounting principles." All the other choices are items that would be considered by the reviewing partner, but the emphasis is on whether the financial statements support the opinion paragraph of the audit report.

5. **D** The independent auditor's report should be addressed to the client, the board of directors, or the stockholders, depending on the circumstances.

6. **C** The objective of the fourth standard of reporting is to prevent misinterpretation of the degree of responsibility the auditor is assuming when his or her name is associated with financial statements.

7. **C** The auditor is required to document the auditor's understanding of the entity's internal control. The form and extent of documentation may be influenced by the size and complexity of the entity, but in all audits this understanding must be documented.

8. **B** The third general standard is: Due professional care is to be exercised in the performance of the audit and the preparation of the report. Exercise of due care requires critical review at every level of supervision of the work done and the judgment exercised by those assisting in the audit.

9. **D** The third general standard requires the independent auditor to perform his or her work with due care. Exercise of due care requires critical review at every level of supervision of the work done and the judgment exercised by those assisting in the audit.

10. **A** The general standards concern the auditor as an individual and describe his audit competence, need for independence, and they require due professional care.

11. **D** The first standard of fieldwork requires supervision of assistants, if any. Supervision involves directing the efforts of assistants who are involved in accomplishing the objectives of the audit and determining whether those objectives were accomplished. An element of supervision is reviewing the work performed by each assistant to determine whether it was adequately performed and to evaluate whether the results are consistent with the conclusions to be presented in the auditor's report.

12. **A** General standards refer to the training and proficiency of the auditor.

13. **B** Since the auditor is working in an "attest" function, he or she can have no interest in the client operations or else his or her objective judgment would be biased.

14. **A** QC 90 states that policies and procedures should be established for deciding whether to accept or continue a client in order to minimize the likelihood of association with a client whose management lacks integrity. Suggesting that there should be procedures for this purpose does not imply that a firm vouches for the integrity or reliability of a client, nor does it imply that a firm has a duty to anyone but itself with respect to the acceptance, rejection, or retention of clients.

15. **C** CPA firms should have quality control systems that include policies and procedures for deciding whether to accept or continue a client in order to minimize the likelihood of association with a client whose management lacks integrity. Accordingly, if a new client's management probably lacks integrity, an auditor would likely not accept the new audit engagement.

16. **C** Substantive tests are defined as tests of details and analytical procedures performed to detect material misstatements in the account balance, transaction class, and disclosure components of financial statements.

17. **D** QC 90 states that policies and procedures should be established for deciding whether to accept or continue a client in order to minimize the likelihood of association with a client whose management lacks integrity. Suggesting that there should be procedures for this purpose does not imply that a firm vouches for the integrity or reliability of a client, nor does it imply that a firm has a duty to anyone but itself with respect to the acceptance, rejection, or retention of clients.

18. **A** The planning phase of the audit involves making preliminary judgments about materiality, audit risk, and timing of procedures. The other answers are procedures that would be completed during the evidence gathering phase, rather than the planning phase.

19. **B** AU 312 states that, in planning the audit, the auditor should use judgment as to the appropriately low level of audit risk and the preliminary judgment about materiality levels in a manner that can be expected to provide, within the inherent limitations of the auditing process, sufficient audit evidence to obtain reasonable assurance about whether the financial statements are free of material misstatement. Materiality levels include an overall level for each statement; however, because the statements are interrelated, and for reasons of efficiency, the auditor ordinarily considers materiality for planning purposes in terms of the smallest aggregate level of misstatements that could be considered material to any one of the financial statements. For example, if misstatements aggregating approximately $100,000 would have a material effect on income, but such misstatements would have to aggregate approximately to $200,000 to materially affect financial position, it would not be appropriate to design auditing procedures that would be expected to detect misstatements of approximately $200,000. The lower amount is normally used. Materiality is "the magnitude of an omission or misstatement of accounting information that, in the light of surrounding circumstances, makes it probable that the judgment of a reasonable person relying on the information would have been changed or influenced by the omission."

20. **D** Analytical procedures are required by GAAS in the planning and review stages of an audit. Analytical procedures are substantive audit tests, but as a substantive test, they are used to plan the audit and in the final review.

21. **B** The other answers involve judgment by the auditor only and as such, the decision process only involves the auditor. Schedules and analyses to be prepared by the client's staff, however, would necessarily have to involve the client, since the client will be preparing the schedules.

22. **C** Supervision involves directing the efforts of assistants who are involved in accomplishing the objectives of the audit and determining whether those objectives were accomplished. The in-charge auditor, as part of his supervisory responsibility, should review the work of each assistant to determine whether it was adequately performed and to evaluate whether the results are consistent with the conclusions to be presented in the auditor's report. This review and evaluative process should be explained to staff assistants by the in-charge auditor.

23. **A** In planning the audit, the auditor should consider his preliminary judgment about materiality levels. In some situations, this is done before the financial statements under audit have been prepared. In such a situation, the auditor's preliminary judgment about materiality might be based on the entity's annualized interim statements or financial statements of one or more prior annual periods. The other answers are incorrect because the auditor's preliminary judgment about materiality levels is considered in planning the audit, before sample sizes and substantive test are planned, and before internal control questionnaires and management representation letters are prepared.

24. **B** AU 311 states that knowledge of an entity's business is ordinarily obtained through experience with the entity or its industry and inquiry of personnel of the entity. audit documents from prior years may contain useful information about the nature of the business, organizational structure, operating characteristics, and transactions that may require special consideration. Other sources may be audit guides, industry publications, financial statements of other entities in the industry, textbooks, periodicals, and individuals knowledgeable about the industry.

25. **D** An auditor obtains knowledge about a new client's business and its industry as part of audit planning. The auditor should obtain a level of knowledge of the entity's business that will enable him/her to plan and perform the audit in accordance with generally accepted auditing standards. That level of knowledge should enable him/her to obtain an understanding of the events, transactions, and practices that may have a significant effect on the financial statements. Knowledge of a client's business and industry can help an auditor provide constructive suggestions.

26. **B** AU 311 states that a pre-engagement audit conference is a meeting between the senior auditor and the other members of the audit team to discuss the time and review the general plan of the audit. Specific personnel are assigned to specific areas at that time, and each member of the team is evaluated to determine if each member is independent of the client. A list of related parties is distributed to enable staff members to recognize related party transactions when they encounter them.

27. **A** The client is responsible for counting inventory, and the auditor is responsible for observing the client's count. Since the timing of the observation depends on the timing of the count, there must be agreement between the auditor and client regarding the inventory observation procedures before the auditor finalizes an audit strategy for inventory. The other answers are evidence-gathering issues that are decided by the auditor without specific regard to timing and other client concerns. Independently of the client, the auditor determines the extent of evidence needed in the audit, the nature of procedures to follow in the audit, and the scope of issues to be addressed in a legal letter.

28. **A** AU 311 states that the procedures that an auditor may consider in planning the audit usually involve a review of his records relating to the entity and discussion with other firm personnel and personnel of the entity. An example of those procedures is to determine the extent of involvement, if any, of consultants, specialists, and internal auditors.

29. **C** In planning the audit, the auditor should consider the nature, extent and timing of work to be done and should prepare a written audit program. This program, or set of programs, should present in reasonable detail the audit procedures considered necessary to accomplish the objectives of the audit.

SARBANES-OXLEY ACT OF 2002

STUDY MANUAL – AUDITING & ATTESTATION
CHAPTER 2

Study Tip: Decide how many days you will be able to use to prepare for each section of the CPA exam. Divide that number of days into three equal periods of time. During the first third, focus 100% of your time on learning new material. In the second third, allocate 60–70% of your time to new subjects with the remainder for reviewing previously covered topics. For the final days, 30–40% of the coverage should be new areas with the rest for review. When taking the exam, all topics need to be kept fresh in your memory until you walk in to take and *pass* the CPA exam.

SARBANES-OXLEY AND THE PCAOB

A. Background.

PCAOB was created under the Sarbanes-Oxley Act (SOX) to register, inspect, and discipline accounting firms that audit public companies. It also has the full authority and responsibility to develop standards for the audits of publicly held companies.

The duties of PCAOB are set forth in Title I, Sections 101–109 of SOX.

B. Title I.

1. Section 101.

   a. Establishes PCAOB as an independent, nonprofit body to oversee the auditors of public companies in order to protect the interest of investors and further the public interest in the preparation of informative, accurate, and independent audit reports for public companies.

   b. Consists of five members appointed by the SEC, no more than two of whom can be CPAs.

2. Section 102.

   a. Requires accounting firms that audit public companies to register with PCAOB.

   b. Makes it unlawful for any person who is not registered to prepare or issue an audit report of a public company.

c. Requires disclosure regarding any criminal, civil, or disciplinary actions pending against a registered CPA firm in connection with an audit report.

3. Section 103.

   a. Requires PCAOB to establish or adopt standards (e.g., auditing, ethics, quality control, independence) related to the preparation of audit reports.

   b. In April 2003, PCAOB voted to establish its own professional auditing standards rather than delegate standard setting to the Auditing Standards Board (ASB) of the AICPA.

   c. Standards set to date include:

      - Temporarily adopted existing ASB auditing standards under the title *Interim Professional Auditing Standards*.
      - Issued *Auditing Standard No. 1*, "References in Auditors' Reports to the Standards of the PCAOB." This standard requires registered public accounting firms to state in an audit report that the audit was conducted in accordance with the standards of the PCAOB rather than in accordance with GAAS. This creates two sets of auditing standards—one set for public companies and one for nonpublic companies.
      - Issued *Auditing Standard No. 2*, "An Audit of Internal Control Over Financial Reporting Performed in Conjunction With an Audit of Financial Statements." This standard requires the auditor to:
         * Evaluate management's assessment of internal control over financial reporting.
         * Make his or her own assessment as to the effectiveness of internal control over financial reporting.

         This standard requires that an integrated audit be performed over the financial statements and the effectiveness of internal controls over financial reporting. The auditor must express two opinions in all reports on internal control over financial reporting—an opinion on management's assessment process and an opinion on the effectiveness of internal control.

      - Issued *Auditing Standard No. 3*, "Audit Documentation." This standard requires audit documentation to be able to stand on its own with no need for oral and written explanations.
         * Audit documentation must contain sufficient information to enable an experienced auditor, having no previous connection to the engagement, to understand the work that was performed, who performed it, when it was completed, who reviewed the work, and the date it was reviewed.
         * There is a presumption that the audit documentation establishes the fact that the audit work was performed. If there is no audit documentation, then there is a presumption that the work was not performed.

- The auditor must document significant findings or issues.
- Audit documentation must be completed within 45 days after the auditor's report is issued. If documentation is changed after the 45-day period, then the changes must be dated and include who made the changes and the reason for the changes. The original documentation must not be discarded. Audit documentation must be retained for seven years.
  - Issued *Auditing Standard No. 4,* "Reporting on whether a previously reported material weakness continues to exist." This standard establishes requirements and provides guidelines that apply when an auditor is engaged to report on whether a previously reported material weakness in internal control over financial reporting continues to exist as of a date specified by management.
    - The standards of the PCAOB do not require an auditor to undertake an engagement to report on whether a previously reported material weakness continues to exist.
    - An engagement to report on whether a previously reported material weakness continues to exist is a voluntary engagement and is not required by the PCAOB.

4. Section 104.

   a. Requires PCAOB to conduct inspections of public accounting firms to assess compliance with SOX, PCAOB, SEC rules, and professional standards related to audits of public companies. These inspections include the review of audit and review engagements of the firm as well as the evaluation of the firm's system of quality control.

   b. There are two types of inspections:

      - Regular—annual inspections for registered firms that audit more than 100 public companies and triennial inspections for registered firms that audit less than 100 public companies.
      - Special—can be authorized by PCAOB or requested by the SEC at any time.

5. Section 105.

   a. Requires PCOAB to establish procedures for the investigation and discipline of registered public accounting firms and their accountants.

   b. Disciplinary actions can include:

      - Temporary suspension or permanent revocation of registration of firms or individual auditors.
      - Civil penalties ranging from $2,000,000 to $15,000,000 for registered firms and $100,000 to $750,000 for individuals.
      - Additional training or continuing professional education.
      - Censure.

- Other appropriate sanctions.

6. Section 106.

    a. Establishes that non-U.S. public accounting firms that prepare audit reports with respect to any U.S. public company are subject to PCAOB's rules.

7. Section 107

    a. Requires all PCAOB rules to be approved by the SEC.

8. Section 108.

    a. As an amendment to the Securities Act of 1933, authorizes the SEC to recognize as "generally accepted" for purposes of the securities laws, any accounting principles established by a standard setting body that meets certain criteria. In April 2003, the SEC recognized the Financial Accounting Standards Board (FASB) as the accounting standard setter.

9. Section 109.

    a. Provides that funds to cover PCAOB's annual budget be collected from registered accounting firms and public companies. Amounts due from public companies are referred to as "accounting support fees" and are based on the average monthly U.S. equity market capitalization of publicly traded companies.

QUESTIONS: SARBANES-OXLEY ACT OF 2002

1. As a result of the Sarbanes-Oxley Act, the Public Company Accounting Oversight Board (PCAOB) has been created. Which of the following is not true?
   A. The PCAOB is a government agency.
   B. The PCAOB comes under the oversight and enforcement authority of the SEC.
   C. The PCAOB will be funded by fees charged to all publicly traded companies.
   D. All public accounting firms that participate in the preparation of an audit report for a company that issues securities must register with the PCAOB.

2. In registering with the Public Company Accounting Oversight Board (PCAOB), a CPA firm must provide significant information. Which of the following is not a required disclosure?
   A. A list of all audit clients.
   B. Information about any criminal actions pending against the firm.
   C. The annual fees from each client that is an issuer of securities, divided between audit and non-audit services.
   D. A list of all accountants participating in the audit of each client that is an issuer of securities.

3. Any CPA firm that is registered with the Public Company Accounting Oversight Board (PCAOB) is subject to periodic inspections. Which of the following statements is true?
   A. These firms must undergo inspection by the PCAOB as well as peer review by an outside CPA firm.
   B. All firms will be inspected annually by the PCAOB.
   C. All firms will be inspected every three years by the PCAOB.
   D. Larger firms will be inspected annually whereas all other firms will only be inspected every three years.

4. According to the standards of the Public Company Accounting Oversight Board (PCAOB), the management of a company that issues securities must accept responsibility for the effectiveness of the company's internal control over its financial reporting. Which of the following is not also a responsibility of the management?
   A. Must provide a written plan each year for updating the internal control over the financial reporting.
   B. Must evaluate the actual effectiveness of internal control over the financial reporting.
   C. Must support the evaluation of internal control over the financial reporting with sufficient documented evidence.
   D. Must prepare a written assessment of internal control over the financial reporting.

5. According to the standards of the Public Company Accounting Oversight Board (PCAOB), the auditor of a company that issues securities must audit the company's internal control as well as its financial statements.

   Which of the following statements is true about the reporting process?
   A. The two reports must be combined.
   B. The two reports must be separate.
   C. The report on internal control must be issued at least 45 days before the report on the financial statements.
   D. The two reports can be combined or can be separate.

6. A CPA firm is issuing separate reports based on audits of an issuing company's internal control over financial reporting and its financial statements. Which of the following statements is true according to the standards of the Public Company Accounting Oversight Board (PCAOB)?
   A. The report on internal control has to be dated as of the balance sheet date.
   B. The report on internal control has to be dated at least 21 days prior to the date of the report on the financial statements.
   C. Both reports have the same date: normally, the last day of audit field work.
   D. The reports might have the same date but they will often have different dates.

7. According to the standards of the Public Company Accounting Oversight Board (PCAOB), the independent auditor must audit the internal control over the financial reporting of any company that issues securities. Assume that the company provides a written assessment that internal control is effective. Assume also that the auditor uncovers a material weakness in internal control that cannot be rectified before the end of the audit work. What action should be taken by the auditor?
   A. The auditor should resign from the engagement.
   B. The auditor should provide a disclaimer.
   C. The auditor should modify the report being given.
   D. The auditor should issue an adverse opinion on the effectiveness of internal control.

8. According to the standards of the Public Company Accounting Oversight Board (PCAOB), the auditor of a company that issues securities must audit the company's internal control as well as its financial statements. What is the recommended timing of these two audits?
   A. The internal control audit should be performed first followed by the audit of the company's financial statements.
   B. The financial statement audit should be performed first followed by the audit of the company's internal control.
   C. The internal control audit should be performed first unless there is an adequate reason for doing the financial statement audit first.
   D. The two audits should be integrated.

9. According to the standards of the Public Company Accounting Oversight Board (PCAOB), what is the general definition of a control deficiency?
   A. An internal control system that simply is not operating as intended.
   B. An internal control system that is not being monitored properly.
   C. A situation where the design or operation of an internal control does not allow employees, in the normal course of performing their assigned functions, to prevent or detect misstatements on a timely basis.
   D. A situation where an inherent limitation has been noted but no corrective action has been taken by the company or its officials.

10. An independent auditor is performing an audit of a company's internal control in connection with its financial reporting under the standards of the Public Company Accounting Oversight Board (PCAOB). A control deficiency has been uncovered. What are the two possible types of control deficiencies?
    A. Current and noncurrent.
    B. Design and operations.
    C. Computer and manual.
    D. General and application.

11. According to the standards of the Public Company Accounting Oversight Board (PCAOB), what is the definition of a material weakness in internal control?
    A. A flaw in the design or operation of internal control that has allowed a material misstatement to be included in a set of financial statements.
    B. A significant deficiency (or a combination of significant deficiencies) in internal control that results in more than a remote likelihood that a material misstatement in the annual or interim financial statements will not be prevented or detected.
    C. The discovery of a problem in either the design of internal control or its operations that is so serious that the likelihood of problem is viewed as greater than reasonably possible.
    D. The uncovering of any aspect of internal control that requires modification before the company's internal control can provide reasonable assurance that no material misstatements exist in the published financial statements.

12. According to the standards of the Public Company Accounting Oversight Board (PCAOB), an independent auditor who issues an opinion on financial statements for a company that issues securities should include a scope (or second) paragraph. What is the problem with the following example of that scope paragraph?

    We conducted our audits in accordance with the standards of the Public Company Accounting Oversight Board (United States). Those standards require that we plan and perform the audit to obtain assurance about whether the financial statements are free of material misstatement. An audit includes examining, on a test basis, evidence supporting the amounts and disclosures in the financial statements. An audit also includes assessing the accounting principles used and significant estimates made by management, as well as evaluating the overall financial statement presentation. We believe that our audits provide a reasonable basis for our opinion.

    A. The statement about the Public Company Accounting Oversight Board is stated incorrectly.
    B. The statement about assurance is stated incorrectly.
    C. The statement about misstatements is stated incorrectly.
    D. The statement about estimations is stated incorrectly.

13. For how long does the Sarbanes-Oxley Act require registered CPA firms to maintain audit documentation generated to support an audit report?
    A. Three years.
    B. Five years.
    C. Seven years.
    D. Ten years.

ANSWERS: SARBANES-OXLEY ACT OF 2002

1. **A**   The Sarbanes-Oxley Act was set up so that the PCAOB would not be a government agency but would be self-funded from charges to the companies being regulated. All firms must register with the PCAOB if they plan to work in any way with a company that issues securities. To enable a proper degree of government control, the PCAOB is under the oversight and the enforcement authority of the SEC.

2. **A**   The CPA firm only needs to provide a list of the audit clients who issue securities. If a company does not issue securities, it is not viewed as a public company and does not come under the jurisdiction of the PCAOB.

3. **D**   For firms working with companies that issue securities to the public, the inspection process by the PCAOB takes the place of peer review which, based on the number of accounting scandals that have occurred, was not working as intended. Firms that audit more than 100 companies that issue securities are inspected by the PCAOB annually. The rest of the CPA firms registered with the PCAOB will be inspected every three years.

4. **A**   The PCAOB requires management to accept responsibility for internal control, and then evaluate it each year, documenting the results. Based on that evaluation, the management must prepare a written assessment of the internal control.

5. **D**   The PCAOB leaves the decision about reporting to the parties involved. The CPA can issue one report to cover both audits or can issue separate reports. When the reports are separate, both reports must be included in the annual report of the company.

6. **C**   The date that is included indicates the last day of audit responsibility for the CPA. Consequently, the last day of field work is used for all audit work whether it is on the financial statements or the internal control.

7. **D**   The auditor is carrying out an audit and has discovered a material weakness. An adverse opinion should be rendered to properly alert the parties interested in the financial statements of the issuing company.

8. **D**   The PCAOB has stated that to reduce time and cost the two audits should be integrated as much as possible rather than looking at them as two entirely separate engagements.

9. **C**   The definition of a control deficiency established by the PCAOB is not particularly different than that which was previously being used. There is always a problem with internal control when misstatements will not be prevented or detected in a timely manner. Answers a and b are examples rather than serving as a definition.

10. **B**   When a control deficiency is discovered, it can relate to the way by which the system with its policies and procedures was designed. Perhaps the design did not accomplish what it was supposed to accomplish. There can also be a deficiency in the operation of one or more controls. The system can be designed perfectly but the people may be performing their tasks in a deficient manner.

11. **B**   This definition comes from paragraph number 10 of PCAOB Standard 2. It focuses on the existence of a significant deficiency in internal control so that material misstatements are neither prevented nor detected.

12. **B** The audit report required in Standard 1 by the PCAOB is basically the same as the traditional standard audit report issued prior to the creation of the PCAOB except that the standards of the PCAOB are mentioned rather than U.S. generally accepted auditing standards. In the example given, the one mistake that is made is that "assurance" is mentioned without clarifying that the auditor only seeks "reasonable assurance."

13. **C** The Sarbanes-Oxley Act wanted to ensure that CPA firms would not destroy audit documentation too quickly and, therefore, mandated this period of time for saving all audit documents and other evidence gathered.

AUDIT OPINIONS

STUDY MANUAL – AUDITING & ATTESTATION
CHAPTER 3

Study Tip: People get tired of studying, especially when studying seems to get into a rut. As long as you are preparing efficiently, do not make any changes. However, if putting in the hours of study has become a real trial, try changing your location. For example, if you normally study in your den, begin working at the kitchen table for a few days. Creating any typ of change can be refreshing, and it can keep the preparation process from becoming drudgery.

TYPES OF AUDIT OPINIONS

The audit report is the end product of all the work that is performed in an audit examination. There are five basic types of reports that may be issued by the auditor at the completion of an audit examination.

1. *A standard report with an unqualified opinion.* This report will be issued following a normal examination without any unresolved difficulties or special situations.

2. *A standard report with explanatory language.* The explanatory language is added to the standard report when one of the following circumstances arises:

   - An opinion based in part on the report of another auditor.
   - Unusual circumstances requiring a departure from generally accepted accounting principles (GAAP).
   - Substantial doubt about the entity's ability to continue as a going concern.
   - Inconsistency in application of GAAP.
   - Certain circumstances affecting comparative statements.
   - Selected quarterly financial data required by the SEC has been omitted or has not been reviewed.
   - Supplementary information required by the FASB or GASB has been omitted or has not been determined to be in conformity with appropriate guidelines.
   - Other information in the document containing the financial statements is materially inconsistent with the statements.
   - The auditor wishes to emphasize a matter.
   - Comparative financial statements in which prior period statements were examined by a predecessor auditor or have a different opinion in the current report than in the previous report.

3. *A qualified opinion.* This is required in certain circumstances involving:

- Departures from GAAP in the financial statements (unless the auditor has determined that an adverse opinion is appropriate).
- Restrictions on the scope of the audit (unless the auditor has determined that a disclaimer of opinion is appropriate).

4. *An adverse opinion.* This is required when departures from GAAP are so material and pervasive that the financial statements taken as a whole are not presented fairly.

5. *A disclaimer of opinion.* This is issued when the auditor has not performed an audit sufficient in scope to form an opinion on the financial statements. A disclaimer is also necessary when the auditor is not independent with respect to the client.

An auditor must never issue a "piecemeal opinion" (expressing on certain items within financial statements when the auditor has disclaimed an opinion or has expressed an adverse opinion on the financial statements taken as a whole). The prohibition on piecemeal opinions does not prevent the auditor from expressing an opinion on certain financial statements and disclaiming on others.

STANDARD REPORT

Assuming that no special problems arise, the auditor will issue a standard report. The form of the auditor's standard report on financial statements of a nonpublic company covering a single year is as follows:

Independent Auditor's Report

To: Board of Directors and Stockholders
XYZ Company

We have audited the accompanying balance sheet of XYZ Company as of December 31, 2005, and the related statements of income, retained earnings, and cash flows for the year then ended. These financial statements are the responsibility of XYZ Company's management. Our responsibility is to express an opinion on these financial statements based on our audit.

We conducted our audit in accordance with U.S. generally accepted auditing standards (GAAS). These standards require that we plan and perform the audit to obtain reasonable assurance about whether the financial statements are free of material misstatement. An audit includes examining, on a test basis, evidence supporting the amounts and disclosures in the financial statements. An audit also includes assessing the accounting principles used and significant estimates made by management, as well as evaluating the overall financial statement presentation. We believe that our audit provides a reasonable basis for our opinion.

In our opinion, the financial statements referred to above present fairly, in all material respects, the financial position of XYZ Company as of December 31, 2005, and the results of its operations and its cash flows for the year then ended in conformity with U.S. GAAP.

Burton and Company
March 1, 2006

The first paragraph of the standard report is referred to as the introductory paragraph, the second as the scope paragraph, and the third as the opinion paragraph.

- The introductory paragraph indicates that an audit has been performed, names the company, identifies the financial statements by name and year, specifies that the statements are the responsibility of the company's management, and states the auditor's responsibility (to express an opinion on the statements based on the audit).
- The scope paragraph specifies that the audit was conducted according to U.S. GAAS; indicates that the audit was planned and performed to obtain reasonable assurance that the statements are free from material misstatements; explains that evidence supporting amounts and disclosures has been examined on a test basis; indicates that an assessment was made regarding accounting principles, significant estimations, and statement presentation; and states the belief that the audit provides a reasonable basis for the opinion.
- The opinion paragraph begins with the phrase, "In our opinion," to show that this is not a guarantee, but an expert judgment. It also indicates that the statements present fairly in all material respects the financial position, results of operations, and cash flows. Finally, it indicates that the financial statements conform to U.S. GAAP.

In addition to the three paragraphs of the report itself, notice four other items included on the auditor's report: the title, the addressee, the auditor's signature, and the date of the report. Key details relating to these items include:

- The title of the report is "Independent Auditor's Report." This title was chosen to establish a clear separation in the mind of the reader of the financial report between the client and auditor. The word *independent* must be in the title.
- The addressee of the report may be the company itself, the board of directors (or trustees), the shareholders, or a third party who engaged the auditor to perform the examination. The report should never be addressed to the management of the company, or to any officers of the company.
- The signature will simply be the manual or printed signature of the auditor.
- The date of the report establishes the ethical and legal responsibility of the auditor. This date should be the date on which audit fieldwork was completed. Under normal circumstances, this concludes the auditor's responsibility for any type of evidence gathering. If the auditor dates the report later than the completion of fieldwork, then the auditor will be responsible up to the date used on the report. If the auditor dates the report earlier, then the auditor will still be responsible for information that could have been obtained up to the date of completion of fieldwork.

A special problem can arise in dating the report when the auditor receives information about the client subsequent to the completion of fieldwork, but prior to the issuance of the report. If, for example, the auditor were to complete the fieldwork on March 1, then hear on the radio on March 5 of a major fire at the firm's warehouse, the auditor will become responsible for the new information. The auditor should return to the client, let us say on March 7, to obtain relevant information about the fire, and then consider the need for a footnote disclosure of this subsequent event.

The financial report will thus contain a footnote that refers to an event occurring on March 5, creating a dilemma for the auditor. If the report is dated March 1, the completion of fieldwork, a reader of the financial reports will be concerned by the reference to the March 5 event. If the report is dated March 7, the auditor's ethical and legal responsibility will be extended, although no audit procedures were applied after March 1 except for obtaining information about the fire. The auditor resolves this dilemma by dual dating the report, giving the completion of fieldwork as the basic date, but indicating a special later date for the footnote alone. The date on the report in this example would read: "March 1, 20XX, except for footnote XX as to which the date is March 7, 20XX."

If a subsequent event results in adjustment to the financial statements without disclosure of the event, the auditor's report should be dated as of the completion of fieldwork. Dual dating would not be appropriate.

The First Standard of Reporting States

The report shall state whether the financial statements are presented in accordance with GAAP.

Generally accepted accounting principles include the entire spectrum of accounting guidance provided by various bodies. In addressing accounting issues, the following hierarchy (from most authoritative to least authoritative) has been established:

- Officially established accounting principles (FASB Statements of Financial Accounting Standards and Interpretations, Accounting Principles Board Opinions, and AICPA Research Bulletins).
- Pronouncements of accounting standards–setting bodies that have been exposed for public comment (FASB Technical Bulletins, AICPA Industry Audit and Accounting Guides, AICPA Statements of Position).
- Pronouncements of accounting standards–setting bodies that have not been exposed for public comment (AICPA Accounting Standards Executive Committee Practice Bulletins, consensus positions of the FASB Emerging Issues Task Force).
- Recognized practices in a particular industry (AICPA Accounting Interpretations and Implementation Guides).
- Other guidance (FASB Statements of Financial Accounting Concepts, AICPA Issues Papers, etc.).

In order to indicate that financial statements are presented fairly in conformity with GAAP, the auditor must make certain judgments:

- The accounting principles selected and applied must have general acceptance by the profession.
- The accounting principles must be appropriate in the existing circumstances. Transactions must be recorded in accordance with their substance rather than their form.
- The financial statements, including their related notes, must be informative.
- The information presented in the financial statements must be classified and organized in a reasonable manner, neither too detailed nor too condensed.

- The financial statements must reflect the underlying events and transactions in a manner that presents the financial position, results of operations, and cash flows stated within a range of acceptable limits, reasonable and practicable to attain in financial statements.

When financial statements do not conform to GAAP, the auditor will normally issue either a qualified opinion or an adverse opinion, depending on the nature and materiality of the difference from GAAP.

If the financial statements contain a justified departure from authoritative pronouncements that, due to unusual circumstances, is necessary to prevent the financial statements from being misleading, an unqualified opinion may be issued with explanatory language added. This is an additional paragraph in the report describing the departure, its approximate effects, if practicable, and the reasons why compliance with the principle expressed in the pronouncement would result in a misleading statement. The explanatory paragraph may be placed either before or after the opinion paragraph.

The Second Standard of Reporting States

The report shall identify those circumstances in which such principles have not been consistently observed in the current period in relation to the preceding period.

The auditor's standard report implies that the comparability of financial statements between periods has not been affected by changes in accounting principles. No specific reference to consistency is contained within the standard report. Changes that affect consistency include:

- A change in accounting principle resulting from the adoption of a generally accepted accounting principle that is different from the one used previously for reporting purposes.
- A change in reporting entity, including changes in the members of a consolidated or combined group and changes among the cost, equity, and consolidation methods. A change in reporting entity does not relate to a situation where a company has acquired or disposed of a segment, but rather when the entity remains unchanged but the method of reporting on the individual units does change.
- A change from an accounting principle that is not generally accepted to one that is generally accepted, including the correction of a mistake in the application of a principle. Although the accounting treatment is that of a correction of errors, recognition is required as to consistency in the auditor's report.
- A change in an accounting principle that is inseparable from a change in an accounting estimate. Although the accounting treatment is that of a change in an accounting estimate, recognition is required as to consistency in the auditor's report.

There are also changes that do not affect consistency. These items may require disclosure or modification of the auditor's report related to issues other than consistency:

- A change in accounting estimate.
- A correction in an error not involving accounting principles, such as a mathematical error.
- A change in classification.

- Adoption of new or different accounting principles for transactions or events that are substantially different from those in which the client was involved previously.
- An accounting change that has no material effect in the current period. These changes require disclosure, but do not require recognition in the auditor's report.

If a change in accounting principles has occurred, and the effect of the change on comparability of the financial statements is material, the auditor should issue an unqualified opinion, but refer to the change in an explanatory paragraph, which must follow the opinion paragraph. Such explanatory paragraph should identify the nature of the change and refer the reader to the note in the financial statements that discusses the change in detail. A sample explanatory paragraph is as follows:

As discussed in Note X to the financial statements, the Company changed its method of computing depreciation in 20XX.

The auditor's concurrence with a change is implicit unless exception is taken to the change in expressing an opinion as to fair presentation of the financial statements in conformity with GAAP.

Even in a first audit of a client, the auditor must apply procedures so as to be satisfied regarding the consistency of application of accounting principles with the preceding year.

THE THIRD STANDARD OF REPORTING STATES

Informative disclosures in the financial statements are to be regarded as adequate unless otherwise stated in the report.

The auditor's standard report implies that all information essential for a fair presentation is set forth in the financial statements or related notes. If the financial statements, including accompanying notes, fail to disclose information that is required by GAAP, the auditor should express a qualified or adverse opinion because of the departure from those principles and should provide the information in the report, if practicable, in an explanatory paragraph preceding the opinion paragraph. An example of a report that is being qualified for inadequate disclosure is as follows:

[Standard introductory paragraph]

[Standard scope paragraph]

The company's financial statements do not disclose the issuance of debentures on January 15, 2005 in the amount of $10,000,000 for the purpose of financing plant expansion. In our opinion, disclosure of this information is required by U.S. GAAP.

In our opinion, except for the omission of the information discussed in the preceding paragraph, ... [Remainder is standard opinion paragraph].

If a company issues financial statements that purport to present financial position and results of operations, but omits the related statement of cash flows, the auditor will normally issue a qualified opinion. An example of such a report follows:

We have audited the accompanying balance sheet of XYZ Company as of December 31, 2005, and the related statements of income and retained earnings for the year then ended. These financial statements are the responsibility of XYZ Company's management. Our responsibility is to express an opinion on these financial statements based on our audit.

[Standard scope paragraph]

The Company declined to present a statement of cash flows for the year ended December 31, 2005. Presentation of such statement summarizing the company's operating, investing, and financing activities is required by U.S. GAAP.

In our opinion, except that the omission of a statement of cash flows results in an incomplete presentation as explained in the preceding paragraph, the financial statements referred to above present fairly, in all material respects, the financial position of XYZ Company as of December 31, 2005, and the results of its operations for the year then ended in conformity with U.S. GAAP.

It is not considered practicable for the auditor to attempt to prepare and present the statement of cash flows if the client has not done so.

THE FOURTH STANDARD OF REPORTING STATES

The report shall either contain an expression of opinion regarding the financial statements, taken as a whole, or an assertion to the effect that an opinion cannot be expressed. When an overall opinion cannot be expressed, the reasons therefore should be stated. In all cases where an auditor's name is associated with financial statements, the report should contain a clear-cut indication of the character of the auditor's examination, if any, and the degree of responsibility taken.

There are several significant features in the fourth reporting standard:

- Expression or disclaimer of opinion (opinion paragraph).
- The reasons for a disclaimer if one is made.
- Auditor association.
- Character of the examination (scope paragraph).
- Degree of responsibility being assumed (introductory paragraph).

When an auditor has consented to the use of his or her name in a report, document, or written communication containing financial statements, then the auditor is "associated with" the financial statements. An auditor is also associated with financial statements when he or she has submitted to the client, or to others, financial statements he or she has prepared or assisted in preparing, even if the auditor does not append his or her name to the statements.

Sometimes there will be a division of responsibility for the opinion. This occurs when the auditor is relying in part on the work of other auditors who have examined a significant portion of the evidence supporting the financial statements. A common example is the audit of a client that holds a controlling interest in another company, where other auditors have examined the subsidiary's financial statements. In such situations, the auditor must first determine which auditor is the principal auditor. Then, the principal auditor must determine whether the work of the other auditors can be relied upon. Before making this determination, the principal auditor should:

- Make inquiries about the professional reputation of the other auditors.
- Obtain representation from the other auditors that they are independent of the overall entity.
- Ascertain that the other auditors (1) are familiar with GAAP and GAAS, (2) are aware that the statements they have examined and their report will be used by the principal auditor, and (3) know that a review of intercompany transactions will be made by the principal auditor.

The principal auditor should next determine if he or she can take responsibility for the work of the other auditors. Steps to take in determining this may include:

- Visit the other auditors to discuss the audit.
- Review the audit program.
- Review the audit documents.
- Visit management of the component examined by the other auditors.
- Perform supplemental procedures on the component.

If the principal auditor decides to take responsibility for the work of the other auditors, then a standard report should be issued with no reference to the work of the other auditors. If the principal auditor decides to rely on the work of the other auditors but not take responsibility for that work, then an unqualified opinion should be issued with explanatory language added to the introductory, scope, and opinion paragraphs.

The introductory paragraph will indicate the relative significance of the work of the other auditors in terms of dollar amounts or percentages of assets, revenues, or other appropriate measures, and a clear indication of the reliance on their work. The scope paragraph should indicate that the auditor's work and that of the other auditors is believed to provide a reasonable basis for the opinion. The opinion paragraph should indicate the opinion is based on the principal auditor's work and that of the other auditors. This is not a qualification of the opinion, simply a division of responsibility for the opinion. An example of such a report is as follows:

We have audited the consolidated balance sheet of XYZ Company as of December 31, 2005, and the related consolidated statements of income, retained earnings, and cash flows for the year then ended. These financial statements are the responsibility of XYZ Company's management. Our responsibility is to express an opinion on these financial statements based on our audit. We did not audit the financial statements of Y Company, a wholly owned subsidiary, the statements of which reflect total assets and revenues constituting 20% and 22%, respectively, of the related consolidated totals. Those statements were audited by other auditors whose report has been furnished to us, and our opinion, insofar as it relates to the amounts included for Y Company, is based solely on the report of the other auditors.

We conducted our audit in accordance with U.S. GAAS. Those standards require that we plan and perform the audit to obtain reasonable assurance about whether the financial statements are free of material misstatement. An audit includes examining, on a test basis, evidence supporting the amounts and disclosures in the financial statements. An audit also includes assessing the accounting principles used and significant estimates made by management, as well as evaluating the overall financial statement presentation. We believe that our audit and the report of other auditors provide a reasonable basis for our opinion.

In our opinion, based on our audit and the report of other auditors, the consolidated financial statements referred to above present fairly, in all material respects, the financial position of XYZ Company as of December 31, 2005, and the results of its operations and its cash flows for the year then ended in conformity with U.S. GAAP.

The principal auditor should not name the other auditors unless they give permission and their report on the component is presented in the financial report.

UNCERTAINTIES

Uncertainties in financial reporting generally relate to contingent liabilities that are not susceptible to reasonable estimation at the date of the auditor's report. The appropriate method of handling these situations depends primarily on the likelihood of loss and management's discussion in the footnotes.

Even though the ultimate outcome of the uncertainty may not be known at the time of the audit, management is still responsible for estimating the effect of future events on the financial statements, or determining that a reasonable estimate cannot be made. Management must make all required disclosures in accordance with GAAP based on management's analysis of existing conditions. The auditor will then consider the existing conditions and available evidence and determine whether that evidence supports management's assertions regarding the uncertainty and the appropriate disclosures. If disclosure is considered adequate, then an unqualified opinion is appropriate.

GOING CONCERN ISSUES

One special form of uncertainty involves doubts about the entity's ability to continue as a going concern. Although there is no way to guarantee the continued existence of an entity, continuation will be assumed unless significant contradictory information exists. Ordinarily, such information relates to the inability of the entity to continue to meet its obligations as they become due without substantial disposition of assets outside the ordinary course of business, restructuring of debt, externally forced revisions of its operations, or similar actions. The auditor should pay attention to negative trends; defaults or restructuring of debt; internal difficulties, such as labor unrest and excessive dependence on the success of a particular project; and external matters such as legal proceedings, legislation, and the loss of a principal customer or supplier.

The auditor should evaluate such doubts as to the entity's ability to continue for a reasonable period of time, not to exceed one year beyond the date of the financial statements being audited. The auditor should obtain from management plans to deal with these doubts, and evaluate the likelihood that the plans can be implemented. If substantial doubt remains, the auditor should determine that adequate disclosure of these matters is made in the notes, and should provide explanatory language in the audit report (or, in extreme cases, disclaim an opinion). The explanatory paragraph, which should follow the opinion paragraph, might read as follows:

example

The accompanying financial statements have been prepared assuming that the company will continue as a going concern. As discussed in Note X to the financial statements, the company has suffered recurring losses from operations and has a net capital deficiency that raises substantial doubt about its ability to continue as a going concern. Management's plans in regard to these matters are also described in Note X. The financial statements do not include any adjustments that might result from the outcome of this uncertainty.

EMPHASIS OF A MATTER

The auditor may emphasize a matter regarding the financial statements solely at his or her discretion. Emphasis paragraphs are never required. The information to be emphasized should be presented in a separate paragraph either preceding or following the opinion paragraph. The following are examples of matters the auditor may wish to emphasize:

- That the entity is a component of a larger business enterprise.
- Significant related-party transactions.
- Unusually important subsequent events.
- Accounting matters affecting the comparability of the financial statements with that of the preceding period.

SCOPE LIMITATIONS

Restrictions on the scope of the audit, whether imposed by the client or by circumstances, such as the timing of the work, may require the auditor to qualify an opinion or to disclaim an opinion. Scope limitations should not be confused with uncertainties, because the latter deals with items that, by their nature, are not estimable, while the former involves the inability of the auditor to apply procedures that would have provided the information necessary to support dollar amounts or disclosures.

Common examples of scope limitations include the inability to observe physical inventories, prevention of confirmation of accounts receivable with debtors, and the unavailability of audited financial statements of a company in which the client has a significant long-term investment.

The auditor's decision to qualify or disclaim depends upon the assessment of the importance of the omitted procedure(s). Because of the implications, a restriction imposed by the client is more likely to lead to a disclaimer of opinion than one imposed by circumstances.

If the auditor concludes that a qualified opinion is appropriate, an explanatory paragraph should be placed before the opinion paragraph, and the scope and opinion paragraphs modified. An example follows:

[Standard introductory paragraph]

Except as discussed in the following paragraph, we... [Remainder is standard scope paragraph].

We were unable to obtain audited financial statements supporting the company's investment in a foreign affiliate stated at $1,000,000 at December 31, 2005, or its equity in earnings of that affiliate of $250,000, which is included in net income for the year then ended as described in Note X to the financial statements; nor were we able to satisfy ourselves as to the carrying value of the investment in the foreign affiliate or the equity in its earnings by other auditing procedures.

In our opinion, except for the effects of such adjustments, if any, as might have been determined to be necessary had we been able to examine evidence regarding the foreign affiliate investment and earnings, the financial statements referred to in the first paragraph above present fairly, in all material respects, the financial position of XYZ Company as of December 31, 2005, and the results of its operations and its cash flows for the year then ended in conformity with U.S. GAAP.

Notice that the qualification refers to the effects of the scope limitation and not to the limitation itself. An example of a disclaimer on the statements of income, retained earnings, and cash flows resulting from an inability to observe beginning inventories is provided in the section on comparative reports.

A scope limitation should not be confused with a limited reporting engagement, in which the auditor is asked to report on one basic financial statement and not on the others. As long as the auditor has full access to information required to support that statement, no limitation exists. An example of such a report on a balance sheet presented alone is as follows (this report assumes that the auditor has been satisfied regarding the consistency of application of accounting principles):

We have audited the accompanying balance sheet of XYZ Company as of December 31, 2005. This financial statement is the responsibility of XYZ Company's management. Our responsibility is to express an opinion on this financial statement based on our audit.

We conducted our audit in accordance with U.S. GAAS. Those standards require that we plan and perform the audit to obtain reasonable assurance about whether the balance sheet is free of material misstatement. An audit includes examining, on a test basis, evidence supporting the amounts and disclosures in the balance sheet. An audit also includes assessing the accounting principles used and significant estimates made by management, as well as evaluating the overall balance sheet presentation. We believe that our audit of the balance sheet provides a reasonable basis for our opinion.

In our opinion, the balance sheet referred to above presents fairly, in all material respects, the financial position of XYZ Company as of December 31, 2005, in conformity with U.S. GAAP.

Departures from GAAP

When financial statements are materially affected by a departure from GAAP, the auditor should express a qualified or adverse opinion. The proper treatment depends on the magnitude, significance, and pervasiveness of the departure(s).

When the auditor expresses a qualified opinion, the reasons should be disclosed in an explanatory paragraph preceding the opinion paragraph. An example of a qualified opinion is as follows:

[Standard introductory paragraph]

[Standard scope paragraph]

The company has excluded, from property and debt in the accompanying balance sheet, certain lease obligations that, in our opinion, should be capitalized in order to conform to U.S. GAAP. If these lease obligations were capitalized, property would be increased by $200,000, long-term debt by $180,000, and retained earnings by $20,000 as of December 31, 2005. Additionally, net income would be increased $10,000 and earnings per share would be increased by $1.50 for the year then ended.

In our opinion, except for the effects of not capitalizing certain lease obligations as discussed in the preceding paragraph, the financial statements referred to above present fairly, in all material respects, the financial position of XYZ Company as of December 31, 2005, and the results of its operations and its cash flows for the year then ended in conformity with U.S. GAAP.

If the pertinent facts are disclosed in a note to the financial statements, the explanatory paragraph might read as follows:

As more fully described in Note X to the financial statements, the company has excluded certain lease obligations from property and debt in the accompanying balance sheet. In our opinion, U.S. GAAP require that such obligations be included in the balance sheet.

Lack of Independence

When an auditor is not independent, a disclaimer must be issued stating that the auditor is not independent. No mention of the reason for the lack of independence or any audit procedures followed is to be given in the report. These circumstances might occur when the CPA firm has neglected to sell an equity interest in the client being audited.

Adverse Opinions

An adverse opinion states that the financial statements taken as a whole are not presented fairly. This is an understandably rare type of opinion, and requires a detailed explanation preceding the opinion that provides reasons for such an extreme conclusion. An example of such a report is:

[Standard introductory paragraph]

[Standard scope paragraph]

As discussed in Note X to the financial statements, the company carries its property, plant, and equipment accounts at appraisal values, and provides depreciation on the basis of such values. Further, the company does not provide for income taxes with respect to differences between financial income and taxable income arising because of the use, for income tax purposes, of the installment method of reporting gross profit from certain types of sales. U.S. GAAP require that property, plant, and equipment be stated at an amount not in excess of cost, reduced by depreciation based on such amount, and that deferred income taxes be provided.

Because of the departures from U.S. GAAP identified above, as of December 31, 2005, inventories have been increased $1,000,000 by inclusion in manufacturing overhead of depreciation in excess of that based on cost; property, plant, and equipment, less accumulated depreciation, is carried at $5,000,000 in excess of an amount based on the cost to the company; and deferred income taxes of $2,000,000 have not been recorded; resulting in an increase of $8,000,000 in retained earnings and in appraisal surplus of $6,000,000. For the year ended December 31, 2005, cost of goods sold has been increased $500,000, because of the effects of the depreciation accounting referred to above and deferred income taxes of $800,000 have not been provided, resulting in an increase in net income of $300,000.

In our opinion, because of the effects of the matters discussed in the preceding paragraphs, the financial statements referred to above do not present fairly, in conformity with U.S. GAAP, the financial position of XYZ Company as of December 31, 2005, or the results of its operations or its cash flows for the year then ended.

DISCLAIMER OF OPINION

A disclaimer of opinion is issued when an auditor is associated with the financial statements of a publicly held company without performing an audit or a review. In such circumstances, the accountant has no responsibility beyond reading the financial statements for obvious material misstatements.

Each page of the financial statements should be clearly marked as unaudited. The disclaimer will appear as follows:

The accompanying balance sheet of XYZ Company as of December 31, 2005, and the related statements of income, retained earnings, and cash flows for the year then ended were not audited by us and, accordingly, we do not express an opinion on them.

A disclaimer of opinion is rarely given in an audit engagement, but will be given when the auditor has not performed an audit sufficient in scope to enable an opinion to be formed on the financial statements. This may be the result of extreme uncertainty, scope limitations, or a discovery that the auditor lacks independence.

An example of a report disclaiming an opinion as a result of a severe scope limitation is as follows:

We were engaged to audit the accompanying balance sheet of XYZ Company as of December 31, 2005, and the related statements of income, retained earnings, and cash flows for the year then ended. These financial statements are the responsibility of XYZ Company's management.

The company did not make a count of its physical inventory in 2004, stated in the accompanying financial statements at $5,000,000 as of December 31, 2004. Further, evidence supporting the cost of property and equipment acquired prior to December 31, 2005 is no longer available. The company's records do not permit the application of other auditing procedures to inventories or property and equipment.

Because the company did not take physical inventories and we were not able to apply other auditing procedures to satisfy ourselves as to inventory quantities and the cost of property and equipment, the scope of our work was not sufficient to enable us to express, and we do not express, an opinion on these financial statements.

Notice that the introductory paragraph only expresses an engagement to audit rather than an audit itself, and the last sentence regarding the auditor's responsibility is omitted, as is the entire scope paragraph. It would be misleading to list any procedures that were applied, because this could overshadow the disclaimer.

COMPARATIVE FINANCIAL STATEMENTS

The auditor's reporting responsibility applies not only to the financial statements of the current period but also to those of one or more prior periods that are presented on a comparative basis with those of the current period. When a continuing auditor expresses an opinion on comparative financial statements, the opinion on the prior year(s) must be updated. This means that the auditor will expand the current report to cover both (all) years presented. An example of a standard report on comparative statements by a continuing auditor is as follows:

We have audited the accompanying balance sheets of XYZ Company as of December 31, 2005 and 2004, and the related statements of income, retained earnings, and cash flows for the years then ended. These financial statements are the responsibility of XYZ Company's management. Our responsibility is to express an opinion on these financial statements based on our audits.

We conducted our audits in accordance with U.S. GAAS. Those standards require that we plan and perform the audit to obtain reasonable assurance about whether the financial statements are free of material misstatement. An audit includes examining, on a test basis, evidence supporting the amounts and disclosures in the financial statements. An audit also includes assessing the accounting principles used and significant estimates made by management, as well as evaluating the overall financial statement presentation. We believe that our audits provide a reasonable basis for our opinion.

In our opinion, the financial statements referred to above present fairly, in all material respects, the financial position of XYZ Company as of December 31, 2005 and 2004, and the results of its operations and its cash flows for the years then ended in conformity with U.S. GAAP.

During the audit of the current-period financial statements, the auditor should be alert for circumstances or events that affect the prior-period financial statements presented or the adequacy of disclosures concerning those statements. In updating the audit report on the prior-period financial statements, the auditor should consider the effects of any such circumstances or events coming to his or her attention. If the opinion to be expressed on the prior-period statements is different from the one previously expressed on these statements, then an explanatory paragraph disclosing the reasons for the different opinion should be placed immediately preceding the opinion paragraph. For example, if the prior-period financial statements received an adverse opinion because of departures from GAAP, and the client has agreed to restate them properly in the comparative presentation with the current period, the explanatory paragraph preceding the now-unqualified opinion on the two years would read as follows:

> In our report dated March 1, 2006, we expressed an opinion that the 2004 financial statements did not present fairly financial position, results of operations, and cash flows in conformity with U.S. GAAP because of two departures from such principles: (1) the company carried its property, plant, and equipment at appraisal values, and provided for depreciation on the basis of such values, and (2) the company did not provide for deferred income taxes with respect to differences between income for financial reporting purposes and taxable income. As described in Note X, the company has changed its method of accounting for these items and restated its 2004 financial statements to conform with U.S. GAAP. Accordingly, our present opinion on the 2004 financial statements, as presented herein, is different from that expressed in our previous report.

It is not necessary to provide an explanatory paragraph for the resolution of an uncertainty that required explanatory language added to the prior-period audit report, because the opinion expressed would have been unqualified in both the prior and current reports. The auditor will simply omit any reference to the uncertainty.

The opinion expressed by the auditor in the current period may be different for the various financial statements included in the comparative report. For example, a qualification may result from a departure from GAAP that only affects the current-period financial statements. Such a report may be as follows:

> [Standard introductory paragraph]
>
> [Standard scope paragraph]
>
> The company has excluded, from property and debt in the accompanying 2005 balance sheet, certain lease obligations that were entered into in 2005 that, in our opinion, should be capitalized in order to conform with GAAP. If these lease obligations were capitalized, property would be increased by $200,000, long-term debt by $180,000, and retained earnings by $20,000 as of December 31, 2005, and net income and earnings per share would be increased by $20,000 and $3.00, respectively, for the year then ended.
>
> In our opinion, except for the effects on the 2005 financial statements of not capitalizing certain lease obligations as described in the preceding paragraph, the financial statements referred to above present fairly, in all material respects, the financial position of XYZ Company as of December 31, 2005 and 2004, and the results of its operations and its cash flows for the years then ended in conformity with U.S. GAAP.

Another example of differing opinions on the two years is a disclaimer relating to the statements of income, retained earnings, and cash flows for the prior period, resulting from an inability to observe the beginning inventory of that prior period. At the same time, it may be possible to express an unqualified opinion on the balance sheet of the prior period and on all financial statements of the current period. This is not a piecemeal opinion, which involves disclaiming or expressing an adverse opinion on a financial statement while giving an opinion on an item within the same statement. A report of this type, assuming the auditor is satisfied as to the consistency of application of accounting principles among the years presented, might read as follows:

[Standard introductory paragraph]

Except as explained in the following paragraph, we . . . [Remainder is standard scope paragraph].

We did not observe the taking of the physical inventory as of December 31, 2003, because that date was prior to our appointment as auditors for the company, and we were unable to satisfy ourselves regarding inventory quantities by means of other auditing procedures. Inventory amounts as of December 31, 2003, enter into the determination of net income and cash flows for the year ended December 31, 2004.

Because of the matter discussed in the preceding paragraph, the scope of our work was not sufficient to enable us to express, and we do not express, an opinion on the results of operations and cash flows for the year ended December 31, 2004.

In our opinion, the balance sheets of XYZ Company as of December 31, 2005 and 2004, and the related statements of income, retained earnings, and cash flows for the year ended December 31, 2005, present fairly, in all material respects, the financial position of XYZ Company as of December 31, 2005 and 2004, and the results of its operations and its cash flows for the year ended December 31, 2005, in conformity with U.S. GAAP.

If the financial statements of a prior period were previously examined by a predecessor auditor, and these statements are to be presented in comparative form with the current period financial statements, then the predecessor's report may be reissued and included along with the financial statements. Before agreeing to reissue the report, the predecessor should:

- Read the financial statements of the current period.
- Compare the prior-period financial statements that were reported on with the financial statements to be presented for comparative purposes.
- Obtain a letter of representation from the successor auditor, stating whether the successor's audit revealed any matters that might have a material effect on the financial statements reported on by the predecessor.

When reissuing an audit report, the predecessor should use the date of the previous report to avoid any implication of additional audit work beyond that date. If the predecessor needs to revise the original report or if the financial statements are restated as a result of information obtained by the successor and provided to the predecessor, then the predecessor auditor's report should be dual dated.

If consent is not given to present the predecessor auditor's report on the prior period along with the comparative financial statements, then the successor should indicate in the introductory paragraph:

- That the financial statements of the prior period were audited by another auditor (the successor must not name the predecessor).
- The date of the predecessor's report.
- The type of report issued.
- If the report was other than a standard report, the reasons therefore.

An example of a report modified to make reference to the work of a predecessor is as follows:

We have audited the balance sheet of XYZ Company as of December 31, 2005, and the related statements of income, retained earnings, and cash flows for the year then ended. These financial statements are the responsibility of XYZ Company's management. Our responsibility is to express an opinion on these financial statements based on our audit. The financial statements of XYZ Company as of December 31, 2004, were audited by other auditors whose report was dated March 1, 2005, and those statements included an explanatory paragraph that described the litigation discussed in Note X to the financial statements.

[Standard scope paragraph]

[Standard opinion paragraph, covering the 2005 statements only]

If the financial statements of the prior period have been restated, the introductory paragraph should indicate that a predecessor reported on the financial statements of the prior period before restatement. If the successor is personally satisfied as to the appropriateness of the restatement, the successor may include the following paragraph in the report:

We also reviewed the adjustments described in Note X that were applied to restate the 2004 financial statements. In our opinion, such adjustments are appropriate and have been properly applied.

Finally, if unaudited financial statements of the prior period are included in a report, they must be marked as "Unaudited." The audit report of the current year should be expanded to include a disclaimer on the prior-year financial statements. If the financial statements are contained in a document filed with the Securities and Exchange Commission, the audit report will not refer to the unaudited financial statements.

In summary, know that the following circumstances may result in unqualified opinions with additional explanatory language:

Circumstance	Introductory paragraph modified	Scope paragraph modified	Opinion paragraph modified	Explanatory paragraph added
Unqualified with Explanatory Language				
Other auditor	Yes	Yes	Yes	No
Justified GAAP departure	No	No	No	Yes
Going concern (may also require a disclaimer; see below)	No	No	No	Yes
Inconsistency	No	No	No	Yes
Report reissued	No	No	No	Yes
Required SEC quarterly data	No	No	No	Yes
Supplementary information	No	No	No	Yes
Other information	No	No	No	Yes
Emphasis of a matter	No	No	No	Yes
Predecessor report not reissued	Yes	No	No	No

These circumstances require an opinion other than an unqualified opinion:

Circumstance	Introductory paragraph modified	Scope paragraph modified	Opinion paragraph modified	Explanatory paragraph added
Qualified Opinion				
Departure from GAAP	No	No	Yes	Yes
Scope limitation	No	Yes	Yes	Yes
Disclaimer				
Going concern	Yes	Yes	Yes	Yes
Scope limitation	Yes	Omit	Yes	Yes
Lack of independence	One paragraph disclaimer issued			
Adverse				
Departure from GAAP	No	No	Yes	Yes

REPORTS ON INTERNAL CONTROL

PUBLIC COMPANIES

Section 404 of the Sarbanes-Oxley Act (SOX) requires auditors of public companies to perform a combined audit that results in a report on management's financial statements and a report on internal control over financial reporting. SOX requires management to assess the effectiveness of internal control over financial reporting as of the end of a company's fiscal year and to include management's conclusion about whether internal control is effective in the company's annual report to shareholders. The auditor's report on internal control will express an opinion on whether management's assertion regarding internal control is presented fairly, in all material respects, and another opinion as to whether the company maintained effective internal control over financial reporting. Therefore, the auditor must express two opinions in all reports on internal control over financial reporting—an opinion on management's assessment process and an opinion directly on the effectiveness of internal control.

An unqualified report is issued when the auditor has identified no material weaknesses in internal control. An adverse opinion must be issued when one or more material weaknesses exist. The relevant terms are:

- *Internal control*—a process designed by, or under the supervision of, the company's principal executive and principal financial officers, or persons performing similar functions, and affected by the company's board of directors, management, and other personnel, to provide reasonable assurance regarding the reliability of financial reporting and the preparation of financial statements for external purposes in accordance with GAAP.
- *Significant deficiency*—a deficiency that, alone or in combination with other deficiencies, adversely affects the ability to initiate, record, process, or report reliably in accordance with GAAP and, is *more than remotely likely* to cause a *more than inconsequential misstatement* that will not be prevented or detected.
- *Material weakness*—a significant deficiency that, alone or in combination with other deficiencies, is *more than remotely likely* to cause *a material misstatement* that will not be prevented or detected.

The basic elements of the auditor's standard report on internal controls over financial reporting would include the following:

- A title that includes the word *independent*.
- An identification of management's conclusion about the effectiveness of the company's internal control over financial reporting as of a specified date based on the control criteria [e.g., criteria established in *Internal Control—Integrated Framework* issued by the Committee of Sponsoring Organizations of the Treadway Commission (COSO)].
- An identification of the title of the management report that includes management's assessment.
- A statement that the assessment is the responsibility of management.
- A statement that the auditor's responsibility is to express an opinion on the assessment and an opinion on the company's internal control over financial reporting.

- A definition of internal control (defined above).
- A statement that the audit was conducted in accordance with the standards of the Public Company Accounting Oversight Board (PCAOB).
- A statement that the standards of PCAOB require that the auditor plan and perform the audit to obtain reasonable assurance about whether effective internal control over financial reporting was maintained in all material respects.
- A statement that an audit includes obtaining an understanding of internal control over financial reporting, evaluating management's assessment, testing and evaluating the design and operating effectiveness of internal control, and performing such other procedures as the auditor considered necessary.
- A statement that the auditor believes the audit provides a reasonable basis for his or her opinions.
- A paragraph regarding the inherent limitations of internal control.
- The auditor's opinion on whether management's assessment of the effectiveness of the company's internal control over financial reporting as of the specified date is fairly stated, in all material respects, based on the control criteria (COSO).
- The auditor's opinion on whether the company maintained, in all material respects, effective internal control over financial reporting as of the specified date, based on the control criteria (COSO).
- Firm signature.
- City and state (or city and country, in the case of non-U.S. auditors) from which the auditor's report has been issued.
- Date of the report.

An example of such a report follows:

Report of Independent Registered Public Accounting Firm

Board of Directors and Stockholders of XYZ Company

Introductory paragraph

We have audited management's assessment, included in the accompanying (*title of management's report*), that XYZ Company maintained effective internal control over financial reporting as of December 31, 2005, based on criteria established in *Internal Control—Integrated Framework* issued by the Committee of Sponsoring Organizations of the Treadway Commission (the COSO criteria). XYZ Company's management is responsible for maintaining effective internal control over financial reporting and for its assessment of the effectiveness of internal control over financial reporting. Our responsibility is to express an opinion on management's assessment and an opinion on the effectiveness of the company's internal control over financial reporting based on our audit.

Scope paragraph

We conducted our audit in accordance with the standards of the Public Company Accounting Oversight Board (United States). Those standards require that we plan and perform the audit to obtain reasonable assurance about whether effective internal control over financial reporting was maintained in all material respects. Our audit included obtaining an understanding of internal control over financial reporting, evaluating management's assessment, testing and evaluating the design and operating effectiveness of internal control, and performing such other procedures as we considered necessary in the circumstances. We believe that our audit provides a reasonable basis for our opinion.

Definition paragraph

A company's internal control over financial reporting is a process designed to provide reasonable assurance regarding the reliability of financial reporting and the preparation of financial statements for external purposes in accordance with GAAP. A company's internal control over financial reporting includes those policies and procedures that (1) pertain to the maintenance of records that, in reasonable detail, accurately and fairly reflect the transactions and dispositions of the assets of the company; (2) provide reasonable assurance that transactions are recorded as necessary to permit preparation of financial statements in accordance with GAAP, and that receipts and expenditures of the company are being made only in accordance with authorizations of management and directors of the company; and (3) provide reasonable assurance regarding prevention or timely detection of unauthorized acquisition, use, or disposition of the company's assets that could have a material effect on the financial statements.

Inherent limitations paragraph

Because of its inherent limitations, internal control over financial reporting may not prevent or detect misstatements. Also, projections of any evaluation of effectiveness to future periods are subject to the risk that controls may become inadequate because of changes in conditions, or that the degree of compliance with the policies or procedures may deteriorate.

Opinion paragraph

In our opinion, management's assessment that XYZ Company maintained effective internal control over financial reporting as of December 31, 2005, is fairly stated, in all material respects, based on the COSO criteria. Also, in our opinion, XYZ Company maintained, in all material respects, effective internal control over financial reporting as of December 31, 2005, based on the COSO criteria.

Explanatory paragraph

We have also audited, in accordance with the standards of the PCAOB, the (*specific financial statements*) of XYZ Company and our report dated (*date of report, which should be the same date as the report on the effectiveness of internal control*) expressed (*include nature of opinion*).

Signature

City and State (or Country)

Date

NONPUBLIC COMPANIES

The auditor's communication of material weaknesses and significant deficiencies is based on an examination of the internal control made as part of a GAAS audit. In some cases, management engages a practitioner to examine the effectiveness of an entity's internal control. This is considered an attestation engagement covered under the Statements on Standards for Attestation Engagements (SSAE). There are four types of engagements:

1. Engagement to examine the design and operating effectiveness of an entity's internal control.
2. Engagement to examine the design and operating effectiveness of a segment of an entity's internal control (for example, internal control over financial reporting of an entity's operating division or its accounts receivable).
3. Engagement to examine only the suitability of design of an entity's internal control (no assertion is made about the operating effectiveness of the internal control).
4. Engagement to examine the design and operating effectiveness of an entity's internal control based on criteria established by a regulatory agency.

Performing an examination of the effectiveness of an entity's internal control involves the following:

- Planning the engagement.
- Obtaining an understanding of internal control.
- Evaluating the design effectiveness of the controls.
- Testing and evaluating the operating effectiveness of the controls.
- Forming an opinion on the effectiveness of the entity's internal control, or the responsible party's assertion thereon, based on the control criteria.

The auditor's report expressing an opinion on management's assertion about the operating effectiveness of the internal control is shown below.

Independent Accountant's Report

We have examined the effectiveness of XYZ Company's internal control over financial reporting as of December 31, 2005, based on (*specific criteria*). XYZ Company's management is responsible for maintaining effective internal control over financial reporting. Our responsibility is to express an opinion on the effectiveness of internal control based on our examination.

Our examination was conducted in accordance with attestation standards established by the American Institute of Certified Public Accountants and, accordingly, included obtaining an understanding of the internal control over financial reporting, testing, and evaluating the design and operating effectiveness of the internal control, and performing such other procedures as we considered necessary in the circumstances. We believe that our examination provides a reasonable basis for our opinion.

Because of inherent limitations in any internal control, misstatements due to error or fraud may occur and not be detected. Also, projections of any evaluation of the internal control over financial reporting to future periods are subject to the risk that the internal control may become inadequate because of changes in conditions, or that the degree of compliance with the policies or procedures may deteriorate.

In our opinion, XYZ Company maintained, in all material respects, effective internal control over financial reporting as of December 31, 2005, based on (*specific criteria*).

The auditor's report on the effectiveness of a segment of an entity's internal control would be the same as the above report except that it would be modified to refer to the segment (for example, an entity's retail division).

The auditor's report on the suitability of design of an entity's internal control would differ from the above report in the following ways:

- The second paragraph would not refer to testing the operating effectiveness of the internal control.
- The fourth paragraph would express an opinion about whether the internal control was suitably designed (and not an opinion about whether the internal control was operating effectively).

The auditor's report on the design and operating effectiveness of an entity's internal control based on criteria established by a regulatory agency would differ from the above report in the following ways:

- The first paragraph would include the criteria established by the regulatory agency.
- The fourth paragraph would express the auditor's opinion based on the criteria established by the regulatory agency (and not the criteria considered by the client).
- A paragraph would be added to limit the distribution of the report to the client and the regulatory agency.

QUESTIONS: AUDIT OPINIONS

1. How are management's responsibility and the auditor's ~~report~~ responsibility represented in the standard auditor's report?

	Management's responsibility	Auditor's responsibility
A.	Explicitly	Implicitly
B.	Explicitly	Explicitly
C.	Implicitly	Explicitly
D.	Implicitly	Implicitly

   (B circled)

2. An auditor's report makes reference to the basic financial statements, which are customarily considered to be the balance sheet and the statements of:
   A. income, changes in retained earnings, and cash flows.
   B. income and cash flows.
   C. income and retained earnings.
   D. income, retained earnings, and cash flows.

   (A circled)

3. When audited financial statements are presented in a client's document containing other information, the auditor should:
   A. perform the appropriate substantive auditing procedures to corroborate the other information.
   B. perform inquiry and analytical procedures to ascertain whether the other information is reasonable.
   C. read the other information to determine that it is consistent with the audited financial statements.
   D. add an explanatory paragraph to the auditor's report without changing the opinion on the financial statements.

   (C circled)

4. When a qualified opinion results from a limitation on the scope of the audit, the situation should be described in an explanatory paragraph:
   A. preceding the opinion paragraph and referred to only in the scope paragraph of the auditor's report.
   B. following the opinion paragraph and referred to in both the scope and opinion paragraph of the auditor's report.
   C. preceding the opinion paragraph and referred to in both the scope and opinion paragraphs of the auditor's report.
   D. following the opinion paragraph and referred to only in the scope paragraph of the auditor's report.

   (C circled)

5. An auditor's report included an additional paragraph disclosing that there is a difference of opinion between the auditor and the client for which the auditor believed an adjustment to the financial statements should be made. The opinion paragraph of the auditor's report *most likely* expressed a(n):
   A. modified opinion.
   B. disclaimer of opinion.
   C. unqualified opinion.
   D. "except for" opinion.

6. When an independent CPA is associated with the financial statements of a publicly held entity but has not audited or reviewed such statements, the appropriate form of report to be issued must include a(an):
   A. report on pro forma financial statements.
   B. unaudited association report.
   C. regulation S-X exemption.
   D. disclaimer of opinion.

7. When a qualified opinion results from a limitation on the scope of the audit, the situation should be described in an explanatory paragraph:
   A. preceding the opinion paragraph and referred to only in the scope paragraph of the auditor's report.
   B. following the opinion paragraph and referred to in both the scope and opinion paragraphs of the auditor's report.
   C. preceding the opinion paragraph and referred to in both the scope and opinion paragraphs of the auditor's report.
   D. following the opinion paragraph and referred to only in the scope paragraph of the auditor's report.

8. An auditor includes a separate paragraph in an otherwise unmodified report to emphasize that the entity being reported on had significant transactions with related parties. The inclusion of this separate paragraph:
   A. necessitates a revision of the opinion paragraph to include the phrase "with the foregoing explanation."
   B. is appropriate and would not negate the unqualified opinion.
   C. violates GAAS if this information is already disclosed in footnotes to the financial statements.
   D. is considered an "except for" qualification of the opinion.

9. An auditor is confronted with an exception considered sufficiently material as to warrant some deviation from the standard unqualified auditor's report. If the exception relates to a departure from GAAP, the auditor must decide between expressing a(an):
   A. adverse opinion and a "special report."
   B. adverse opinion and a disclaimer of opinion.
   C. adverse opinion and an "except for" opinion.
   D. disclaimer of opinion and a "special report."

10. Which of the following will not result in modification of the auditor's report due to a scope limitation?
    A. Inability to obtain sufficient competent audit evidence.
    B. Restrictions imposed by the client.
    C. Reliance placed on the report of another auditor.
    D. Inadequacy in the accounting records.

11. When an auditor qualifies an opinion because of inadequate disclosure, the auditor should describe the nature of the omission in a separate explanatory paragraph and modify the:

	Introductory paragraph	Scope paragraph	Opinion paragraph
A.	No	No	Yes
B.	Yes	No	No
C.	Yes	Yes	No
D.	No	Yes	Yes

12. A company issues audited financial statements under circumstances which require the presentation of a statement of cash flows. If the company refuses to present a statement of cash flows, the independent auditor should:
    A. prepare a statement of cash flows and note in a middle paragraph of the report that this statement is auditor-prepared.
    B. qualify his opinion with an "except for" qualification and a description of the mission in a middle paragraph of the report.
    C. disclaim an opinion.
    D. prepare a statement of cash flows and disclose in a footnote that this statement is auditor-prepared.

13. An auditor concludes that there is a material inconsistency in the other information in an annual report to shareholders containing audited financial statements. If the auditor concludes that the financial statements do NOT require revision, but the client refuses to revise or eliminate the material inconsistency, the auditor may:
    A. disclaim an opinion on the financial statements after explaining the material inconsistency in a separate explanatory paragraph.
    B. consider the matter closed since the other information is not in the audited financial statements.
    C. issue an "except for" qualified opinion after discussing the matter with the client's board of directors.
    D. revise the auditor's report to include a separate explanatory paragraph describing the material inconsistency.

14. An auditor should disclose the substantive reasons for expressing an adverse opinion in an explanatory paragraph:
    A. following the opinion paragraph.
    B. within the notes to the financial statements.
    C. preceding the opinion paragraph.
    D. preceding the scope paragraph.

15. When financial statements contain a departure from GAAP because, due to unusual circumstances, the statements would otherwise be misleading, the auditor should explain the unusual circumstances in a separate paragraph and express an opinion that is:
    A. qualified.
    B. adverse.
    C. unqualified.
    D. qualified or adverse, depending on materiality.

16. When an auditor concludes there is substantial doubt about an entity's ability to continue as a going concern for a reasonable period of time, the auditor's responsibility is to:
    A. consider the adequacy of disclosure about the entity's possible inability to continue as a going concern.
    B. prepare prospective financial information to verify whether management's plans can be effectively implemented.
    C. issue a qualified or adverse opinion, depending upon materiality, due to the possible effects on the financial statements.
    D. project future conditions and events for a period of time not to exceed one year following the date of the financial statements.

17. In the first audit of a new client, an auditor was able to extend auditing procedures to gather sufficient evidence about consistency. Under these circumstances, the auditor should:
    A. state that the consistency standard does not apply.
    B. state that the accounting principles have been applied consistently.
    C. not report on the client's income statement.
    D. not refer to consistency in the auditor's report.

18. Reference in a principal auditor's report to the fact that part of the audit was performed by another auditor *most likely* would be an indication of the:
    A. lack of materiality of the portion of the financial statements audited by the other auditor.
    B. lack of materiality of the portion of the financial statements audited by the other auditor.
    C. different opinions the auditors are expressing on the components of the financial statements that each audited.
    D. divided responsibility between the auditors who conducted the audits of the components of the overall financial statements.

19. In which of the following circumstances would an auditor usually choose between issuing a qualified opinion or a disclaimer of opinion?
    A. Inability to obtain sufficient competent audit evidence
    B. Inadequate disclosure of accounting policies
    C. Departure from GAAP
    D. Inadequate disclosure of accounting policies

20. Grant Company's financial statements adequately disclose uncertainties that concern future events, the outcome of which are **NOT** susceptible to reasonable estimation. The auditor's report should include a(n):
    A. unqualified opinion.
    B. adverse opinion.
    C. "except for" qualified opinion.
    D. special report paragraph.

21. When a client will NOT permit inquiry of outside legal counsel, the audit report will ordinarily contain a(an):
    A. "except for" qualified opinion.
    B. referral opinion.
    C. disclaimer of opinion.
    D. unqualified opinion with a separate explanatory paragraph.

22. An auditor would express an unqualified opinion with an explanatory paragraph added to the auditor's report for:

	An unjustified accounting change	A material weakness in the internal control structure
A.	Yes	No
B.	No	No
C.	No	Yes
D.	Yes	Yes

23. Which paragraphs of an auditor's standard report on financial statements should refer to GAAS and GAAP in which paragraphs?

	GAAS	GAAP
A.	Opening	Scope
B.	Opening	Opinion
C.	Scope	Scope
D.	Scope	Opinion

24. When a client declines to make essential disclosures in the financial statements or in the footnotes, the independent auditor should:
    A. explain to the client that an adverse opinion must be issued.
    B. issue an unqualified report and inform the stockholders of the improper disclosure in an "unaudited" footnote.
    C. provide the necessary disclosures in the auditor's report and appropriately modify the opinion.
    D. issue an opinion "subject to" the client's lack of disclosure of supplementary information as explained in a middle paragraph of the report.

25. A limitation on the scope of an auditor's examination sufficient to preclude an unqualified opinion will always result when management:
    A. refuses to furnish a management representation letter to the auditor.
    B. engages the auditor after the year-end physical inventory count is completed.
    C. prevents the auditor from reviewing the audit documents of the predecessor auditor.
    D. fails to correct a material internal control weakness that had been identified during the prior year's audit.

26. An auditor may NOT issue a qualified opinion when:
    A. the auditor's report refers to the work of a specialist.
    B. a scope limitation prevents the auditor from completing an important audit procedure.
    C. the auditor lacks independence with respect to the audited entity.
    D. an accounting principle at variance with GAAP is used.

27. If information accompanying the basic financial statements in an auditor-submitted document has been subjected to auditing procedures, the auditor may include in the auditor's report on the financial statements an opinion that the accompanying information is fairly stated in:
    A. accordance with attestation standards expressing a conclusion about management's assertions.
    B. all material respects in relation to the basic financial statements taken as a whole.
    C. conformity with GAAP.
    D. accordance with GAAS.

28. Digit Co. uses the FIFO method of costing for its international subsidiary's inventory and LIFO for its domestic inventory. Under these circumstances, the auditor's report on Digit's financial statements should express an:
    A. unqualified opinion.
    B. opinion qualified because of a lack of consistency.
    C. opinion qualified because of a departure from GAAP.
    D. adverse opinion.

29. A limitation on the scope of an auditor's examination sufficient to preclude an unqualified opinion will usually result when management:
    A. states that the financial statements are not intended to be presented in conformity with GAAP.
    B. asks the auditor to report on the balance sheet and not on the other basic financial statements.
    C. presents financial statements that are prepared in accordance with the cash receipts and disbursements basis of accounting.
    D. does not make the minutes of the Board of Directors' meetings available to the auditor.

30. In determining the type of opinion to express, an auditor assesses the nature of the report qualifications and the materiality of their effects. Materiality will be the primary factor considered in the choice between a(an):
    A. adverse opinion and a disclaimer of opinion.
    B. "except for" opinion and an adverse opinion.
    C. "except for" opinion and a qualified opinion.
    D. qualified opinion and a piecemeal opinion.

31. Kane, CPA, concludes that there is substantial doubt about Lima Co.'s ability to continue as a going concern for a reasonable period of time. If Lima's financial statements adequately disclose its financial difficulties, Kane's auditor's report is required to include an explanatory paragraph that specifically uses the phrase(s):

	Possible discontinuance of operation	Reasonable period of time not to exceed one year
A.	Yes	No
B.	Yes	Yes
C.	No	No
D.	No	Yes

32. When an auditor expresses an adverse opinion, the opinion paragraph should include:
    A. the substantive reasons for the financial statements being misleading.
    B. the principal effects of the departure from GAAP.
    C. a direct reference to a separate paragraph disclosing the basis for the opinion.
    D. a description of the uncertainty or scope limitation that prevents an unqualified opinion.

33. Jones, CPA, is the principal auditor who is auditing the consolidated financial statements of his client. Jones plans to refer to another CPA's examination of the financial statements of a subsidiary company but does NOT wish to present the other CPA's audit report. Both Jones and the other CPA's audit reports have noted no exceptions to GAAP. Under these circumstances the opinion paragraph of Jones' consolidated audit report should express a(an):
    A. referral report.
    B. principal opinion.
    C. "except for" opinion.
    D. unqualified opinion.

34. Due to a scope limitation, an auditor disclaimed an opinion on the financial statements taken as a whole, but the auditor's report included a statement that the current asset portion of the entity's balance sheet was fairly stated. The inclusion of this statement is:
    A. not appropriate because it may tend to overshadow the auditor's disclaimer of opinion.
    B. not appropriate because the auditor is prohibited from reporting on only one basic financial statement.
    C. appropriate provided the statement is in a separate paragraph preceding the disclaimer of opinion paragraph.
    D. appropriate provided the auditor's scope paragraph adequately describes the scope limitations.

35. When the report of a principal auditor makes reference to the examination made by another auditor, the other auditor may be named if express permission to do so is given and the:
    A. principal auditor accepts responsibility for the work of the other auditor.
    B. other auditor is not an associate or correspondent firm whose work is done at the request of the principal auditor.
    C. report of the principal auditor names the other auditor in the opinion paragraph.
    D. report of the other auditor is presented together with the report of the principal auditor.

36. The introductory paragraph of an auditor's report contains the following sentences:

    We did not audit the financial statements of EZ Inc., a wholly-owned subsidiary, which statements reflect total assets and revenues constituting 27% and 29%, respectively, of the related consolidated totals. Those statements were audited by other auditors whose report has been furnished to us, and our opinion, insofar as it relates to the amounts included for EZ Inc., is based solely on the report of the other auditors.

    These sentences:
    A. assume responsibility for the other auditor.
    B. are an improper form of reporting.
    C. indicate a division of responsibility.
    D. require a departure from an unqualified opinion.

37. In connection with the examination of the consolidated financial statements of Mott Industries, Frazier, CPA, plans to refer to another CPA's examination of the financial statements of a subsidiary company. Under these circumstances Frazier's report must disclose:
    A. the name of the other CPA and the type of report issued by the other CPA.
    B. the nature of Frazier's review of the other CPA's work.
    C. the magnitude of the portion of the financial statements examined by the other CPA.
    D. in a footnote the portions of the financial statements that were covered by the examinations of both auditors.

38. Morgan, CPA, is the principal auditor for a multinational corporation. Another CPA has examined and reported on the financial statements of a significant subsidiary of the corporation. Morgan is satisfied with the independence and professional reputation of the other auditor, as well as the quality of the other auditor's examination. With respect to Morgan's report on the financial statements, taken as a whole, Morgan:
    A. must not refer to the examination of the auditor.
    B. may refer to the examination of the other auditor.
    C. must refer to the examination of the auditor.
    D. may refer to the examination of the other auditor, in which case Morgan must include, in the auditor's report on the consolidated financial statements, a qualified opinion with respect to the examination of the other auditor.

39. Jewel, CPA, audited Infinite Co.'s prior-year financial statements. These statements are presented with those of the current year for comparative purposes without Jewel's auditor's report, which expressed a qualified opinion. In drafting the current year's auditor's report, Crain, CPA, the successor auditor, should:

    I. not name Jewel as the predecessor auditor.
    II. indicate the type of report issued by Jewel.
    III. indicate the substantive reasons for Jewel's qualification.

    A. I, II, and III.
    B. I only.
    C. II and III only.
    D. I and II only.

40. A principal auditor decides not to refer to the audit of another CPA who audited a subsidiary of the principal auditor's client. After making inquiries about the other CPA's professional reputation and independence, the principal auditor *most likely* would:
    A. obtain written permission from the other CPA to omit the reference in the principal auditor's report.
    B. add an explanatory paragraph to the auditor's report indicating that the subsidiary's financial statements are not material to the consolidated financial statements.
    C. document in the engagement letter that the principal auditor assumes no responsibility for the other CPA's work and opinion.
    D. contact the other CPA and review the audit programs and audit documents pertaining to the subsidiary.

41. When unaudited financial statements of a nonpublic entity are presented in comparative form with audited financial statements in the subsequent year, the unaudited financial statements should be clearly marked to indicate their status and the:

    I. report on the unaudited financial statements should be released.
    II. report on the audited financial statements should include a separate paragraph describing the responsibility assumed for the unaudited financial statements.

    A. Both I and II.
    B. Either I or II.
    C. I only.
    D. II only.

42. Unaudited financial statements for the prior year presented in comparative form with audited financial statements for the current year should be clearly marked to indicate their status and the:

   I. report on the prior period should be reissued to accompany the current period report.
   II. report on the current period should include as a separate paragraph a description of the responsibility assumed for the prior period's financial statements.

   A. Either I or II.
   B. Both I and II.
   C. II only.
   D. I only.

43. In auditing the financial statements of Star Corp., Land discovered information leading Land to believe that Star's prior year's financial statements, which were audited by Tell, require substantial revisions. Under these circumstances, Land should:
   A. request Star to reissue the prior year's financial statements with the appropriate revisions.
   B. notify Star's audit committee and stockholders that the prior year's financial statements cannot be relied on.
   C. request Star to arrange a meeting among the three parties to resolve the matter.
   D. notify Tell about the information and make inquiries about the integrity of Star's management.

44. When reporting on comparative financial statements, which of the following circumstances ordinarily should cause the auditor to change the previously issued opinion on the prior year's financial statements?
   A. The prior year's financial statements are restated following a pooling of interests in the current year.
   B. A scope limitation caused a qualified opinion on the prior year's financial statements but the current year's opinion was properly unqualified.
   C. A change in accounting principle caused the auditor to make a consistency modification in the current year's auditor's report.
   D. A departure from GAAP caused an adverse opinion on the prior year's financial statements and those statements have been properly restated.

45. When reporting on comparative financial statements, an auditor ordinarily should change the previously issued opinion on the prior year's financial statements if the:
   A. prior year's opinion was unqualified and the opinion on the current year's financial statements is modified due to a lack of consistency.
   B. prior year's financial statements are restated to conform with GAAP.
   C. auditor is a predecessor auditor who has been requested by a former client to reissue the previously issued report.
   D. prior year's financial statements are restated following a pooling of interests in the current year.

46. In the first audit of a client, an auditor was not able to gather sufficient evidence about the consistent application of accounting principles between the current and the prior year, as well as the amounts of assets or liabilities at the beginning of the current year. This was due to the client's record retention policies. If the amounts in question could materially affect current operating results, the auditor would:
   A. withdraw from the engagement and refuse to be associated with the financial statements.
   B. specifically state that the financial statements are not comparable to the prior year due to an uncertainty.
   C. be unable to express an opinion on the current year's results of operations and cash flows.
   D. express a qualified opinion on the financial statements because of a client-imposed scope limitation.

47. How does an auditor make the following representations when issuing the standard auditor's report on comparative financial statements?

	Examination of evidence on a test basis	Consistent application of accounting principles
A.	Explicitly	Implicitly
B.	Implicitly	Implicitly
C.	Implicitly	Explicitly
D.	Explicitly	Explicitly

48. Comparative financial statements include the prior year's statements that were audited by a predecessor auditor whose report is not presented. If the predecessor's report was unqualified, the successor should:
   A. express an opinion on the current year's statements alone and make no reference to the prior year's statements.
   B. request the predecessor auditor to reissue the prior year's report.
   C. obtain a letter of representations from the predecessor concerning any matters that might affect the successor's opinion.
   D. indicate in the auditor's report that the predecessor auditor expressed an unqualified opinion.

49. Company B owns 77% of Company Y and prepares consolidated financial statements. The auditor of Company B examines the statements produced by Company B, and no material misstatements are noted. The auditor also has the consolidated financial statements but does not have the financial statements produced by Company Y. However, another independent auditor has provided an unqualified opinion on the financial statements of Company Y. The auditor of Company B should give an unqualified opinion on the consolidated financial statements.
   A. True.
   B. False.

STUDY MANUAL – AUDITING & ATTESTATION
CHAPTER 3

ANSWERS: AUDIT OPINIONS

1. **B** The auditor's standard report includes a statement that the financial statements are the responsibility of the Company's management and that the auditor's responsibility is to express an opinion on the financial statements based on his audit.

2. **D** These statements are required for complete presentation under GAAP.

3. **C** The auditor's report does not extend beyond the financial information identified in the report and the auditor has no obligation to perform any procedures to corroborate other information. However, the auditor should read the other information in a client's document that includes audited financial statements and consider whether such information is materially inconsistent with information appearing in the audited financial statements.

4. **A** If a client does not properly account for or disclose an illegal act, and as a result the financial statements are materially misstated, the auditor cannot issue an unqualified opinion. Because the auditor knows that the financial statements contain material departures from GAAP, the auditor should issue a qualified or adverse opinion.

5. **D** An adjustment represents a departure from GAAP. Thus an "except for" opinion is in order.

6. **D** AU 504 states that when an accountant is associated with financial statements of a public entity, but has not audited or reviewed such statements, the report to be issued is as follows:

    The accompanying balance sheet of X Company as of December 31, 20XX, and the related statements of income, retained earnings, and cash flows for the year then ended were not audited by us and, accordingly, we do not express an opinion on them. (Signature and date).

    This disclaimer of opinion is the means by which the accountant complies with the fourth standard of reporting when associated with unaudited financial statements in these circumstances. The disclaimer may accompany the unaudited financial statements or it may be placed directly on them. In addition, each page of the statements should be clearly and conspicuously marked as unaudited.

7. **C** Since the opinion resulted from a scope limitation, reference to the explanatory paragraph needs to be made in the scope paragraph. This is done by adding the phrase, "Except as discussed in the following paragraph, we conducted. . .," to the beginning of the scope paragraph. The opinion paragraph is also modified as follows: "In my opinion, except for. . ., the financial statements. . . ."

8. **B** The auditor may wish to emphasize a matter regarding the client's financial statements while expressing an unqualified opinion. Examples of matters that could be emphasized include the client entity being part of a larger business enterprise, an unusual subsequent event, or significant transactions with related parties.

9. **C** Deviations from GAAP result in either an "except for" qualification or an adverse opinion.

10. C   If the CPA relies on the work of another auditor, it does not constitute a scope limitation. The other answers constitute scope limitations.

11. A   The explanatory paragraph would be inserted between the scope paragraph and opinion paragraph. The opinion paragraph would refer to the explanatory paragraph as a basis for the qualification. The scope and introductory paragraph would not be modified.

12. B   The statement of cash flows is required by GAAP and its omission results in a qualified "except for" opinion. For reporting purposes, the statement of cash flows is considered the omission of a disclosure.

13. D   The auditor's responsibility with respect to information in an annual report does not extend beyond the financial information identified in his report. However, he should read the other information and consider whether it is materially inconsistent with information appearing in the financial statements. If he concludes that the other information is inconsistent and the client refuses to correct the inconsistency, the auditor should either revise his report to include an explanatory paragraph describing the material inconsistency, withhold the use of his report in the annual report, or withdraw from the engagement.

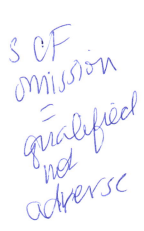

14. C   When the auditor expresses an adverse opinion, he should disclose in a separate explanatory paragraph preceding the opinion paragraph of his report all the substantive reasons for his adverse opinion and the principal effects of the subject matter of the adverse opinion on financial position, results of operations, and cash flows, if practicable.

15. C   Rule 203 of the AICPA Code of Professional Conduct states that an auditor shall not express an opinion that financial statements are presented in conformity with GAAP if such statements contain a departure from promulgated accounting principles. The rule provides, however, that if the statements contain such a departure from GAAP and the auditor can demonstrate that due to unusual circumstances the financial statements would otherwise have been misleading, the auditor can express an unqualified opinion but must describe the departure, its approximate effects, if practicable, and the reasons why compliance with the principle would result in a misleading statement. This type of situation is very rare. Typically, a departure from GAAP will result in a qualified or adverse opinion, depending on materiality. The other answers are incorrect in this case because an unqualified opinion would be appropriate.

16. A   The client has a responsibility to disclose in the financial statements concerns regarding the entity's ability to continue as a going concern. The auditor has a responsibility to consider whether the disclosure should be made and, if made, if it is adequate. If the auditor concludes that disclosure is not adequate, then the auditor should issue a qualified "except for" opinion.

17. D   The auditor's standard report implies that the auditor is satisfied that the comparability of financial statements between periods has not been materially affected by changes in accounting principles and that such principles have been consistently applied between periods. Therefore, if the auditor is able to gather sufficient evidence about consistency in the first audit of a new client or in a recurring audit, no reference to consistency would be made in the report.

18. D   When a principal auditor uses the work and reports of other auditors who conducted audits of components of the overall financial statements, he or she must decide whether to make reference to those other auditors. If the principal auditor decides to assume responsibility for the other auditor's work, no reference is made to the other auditor in the

principal auditor's audit report. If the principal auditor decides not to assume that responsibility, the principal auditor's report will refer to the other auditor and will indicate the division of responsibility between the principal and other auditors.

19. **A** Inadequate disclosure of accounting policies.

20. **A** An uncertainty exists when the outcome of future events that may affect the financial statements is not susceptible to reasonable estimation by management and it cannot be determined whether the financial statements should be adjusted or in what amount. Such uncertainties may require an explanatory paragraph in the auditor's report.

21. **C** When restrictions that significantly limit the scope of the audit are imposed by the client, ordinarily the auditor should disclaim an opinion on the financial statements. A letter of inquiry to the client's lawyer is the primary means of obtaining corroboration of the information furnished by management concerning litigation, claims, and assessments. Accordingly, the client not permitting the auditor to inquire of outside legal counsel is a significant scope limitation that would result in a disclaimer of opinion.

22. **B** If the auditor is not satisfied that management's justification for a change in accounting principle is justified, his opinion should be qualified for a departure from GAAP. Material weaknesses in internal control must be reported to the audit committee and affect the design of substantive tests, but are not noted in the auditor's opinion. The other answers are incorrect because an unqualified opinion would not be issued when there is a departure from GAAP, and an explanatory paragraph would not be added for internal control weaknesses.

23. **D** The auditor's standard report identifies the financial statements audited in an opening introductory paragraph. The nature of an audit, which is an examination in accordance with GAAS, is described in a scope paragraph. The auditor's conclusion regarding the fairness of the financial statements in accordance with GAAP is expressed in a separate opinion paragraph. The other answers are incorrect because GAAS is referred to in the scope paragraph and GAAP is referred to in the opinion paragraph.

24. **C** Disclosure is the third standard of reporting and thus failure to disclose would result in a qualified report. Explaining to the client that an adverse opinion must be issued is incorrect because a qualified report would be issued instead of an adverse opinion. The key is that this item was material to qualify, but not pervasive, which would result in an adverse opinion.

25. **A** Generally accepted auditing standards require the auditor to obtain written representations from management. Management's refusal to furnish those written representations, therefore, would always constitute a limitation on the scope of the auditor's examination which in turn would preclude an unqualified opinion.

26. **C** If the auditor lacks independence, the auditor should issue a disclaimer of opinion. A qualified opinion is expressed when there is a lack of sufficient competent audit evidence or there are restrictions on the scope of the audit, or when the auditor believes that the financial statements contain a material departure from GAAP.

27. **B** When an auditor submits a document containing audited financial statements to his client, he has a responsibility to report on all the information included in the document. If accompanying information is included, the auditor's report should describe clearly the degree of responsibility the auditor is taking, which is to evaluate the accompanying information in relation to the audited financial statements. The report, therefore, should

include either an opinion on whether the accompanying information is fairly stated in all material respects in relation to the basic financial statements taken as a whole or a disclaimer of opinion. Generally accepted auditing standards deal with how an audit is performed, not with the fairness of information presented. The accompanying information, some of which may come from sources outside the accounting system and therefore not be subject to accounting principles, is presented outside the financial statements and is not considered necessary for those statements to conform with GAAP. The auditor's responsibility regarding information that has been subjected to auditing procedures is addressed in the auditing standards, not the attestation standards.

28. A An auditor can issue an unqualified opinion when segments of an entity use different accounting methods if those methods are in accordance with GAAP, which they are in this case.

29. D The auditor will typically want the client to make all minutes of meetings of stockholders, directors and committees of directors available. If management does not make these minutes available to the auditor, this would be considered a scope restriction which could result in the auditor qualifying his opinion or disclaiming an opinion.

30. B "Except for" and "adverse" opinions are concerned with departures from GAAP. The difference in which opinion to render is determined by materiality and pervasiveness.

31. C If the auditor concludes that there is substantial doubt about an entity's ability to continue as a going concern for a reasonable period of time, the audit report should include an explanatory paragraph following the opinion paragraph to reflect that conclusion. The auditor's conclusion should be expressed through use of the phrase "substantial doubt about its (the entity's) ability to continue as a going concern" (or similar wording that includes the terms "substantial doubt" and "going concern"). The other answers are incorrect because the report is not required to include phrases such as "possible discontinuance of operations" or "reasonable period of time, not to exceed one year."

32. C When an adverse opinion is expressed, the opinion paragraph should include a direct reference to a separate paragraph preceding the opinion paragraph that discloses all the substantive reasons for the adverse opinion and the principal effects on the financial statements, if practicable.

33. D Part of the examination may be performed by another CPA with no effect on the principal auditor's opinion unless, of course, there is a problem that would normally require modification of the auditor's report.

34. A When an auditor disclaims an opinion or issues an adverse opinion on the financial statements as a whole, then he or she should not express any opinion on other identified items in the financial statements. Such piecemeal opinions would tend to overshadow or contradict a disclaimer or adverse opinion.

35. D When the other auditor is named, his report must be presented.

36. C When a principal auditor decides not to assume responsibility for the work of another auditor insofar as that work relates to the principal auditor's expression of an opinion on the financial statements as a whole, the principal auditor's report should make reference to the audit of the other auditor. In such a case, the introductory paragraph of the principal auditor's report should disclose the magnitude of the portion of the financial statements audited by the other auditor, as was done in this example.

37. C   When referring to another auditor's work, the principal auditor must disclose the scope of the second auditor's examination in relation to the total consolidated assets of both companies.

38. B   The principal auditor may or may not refer to the other auditor's examination. If he does, he is sharing the responsibility for his opinion. If he accepts full responsibility, no reference is made to the other auditor.

39. A   If the financial statements of a prior period have been audited by a predecessor auditor whose report is not presented, the successor auditor should indicate in the introductory paragraph of his report that the financial statements of the prior period were audited by another auditor, the date of his report, the type of report issued by the predecessor auditor, and, if the report was other than a standard report, the substantive reasons therefore.

40. D   If an auditor decides that he or she is the principal auditor and that he or she can use the other auditor's report, because the other auditor is reputable and independent, the principal auditor must decide whether or not to make reference to the other auditor. If the principal auditor decides not to refer to the other auditor, he or she should visit the other auditor, discuss the procedures followed, and review the audit program and audit documents of the other auditor.

41. B   When unaudited financial statements are presented in comparative form with audited financial statements, the financial statements that have not been audited should be clearly marked to indicate their status and either the report of the prior period should be reissued or the report on the current period should include as a separate paragraph an appropriate description of the responsibility assumed for the financial statements of the prior period.

42. A   When unaudited financial statements are presented in comparative form with audited financial statements in any document, other than in documents filed with the Securities and Exchange Commission, the financial statements that have not been audited should be clearly marked to indicate their status and either the report on the prior period should be reissued or the report on the current period should include as a separate paragraph an appropriate description of the responsibility assumed for the financial statements of the prior period.

43. C   If, during his audit, the successor auditor becomes aware of information that leads him to believe that financial statements reported on by the predecessor auditor may require revision, he should request his client to arrange a meeting among the three parties to discuss the information and to resolve the matter.

44. D   An auditor may update an opinion on prior period financial statements. An updated opinion means that an auditor may change (update) his opinion on previously issued financial statements because of new facts coming to the auditor's attention in the current period that affect a prior period. Such a situation is described in this question. The client departed from GAAP in the prior period; however, in the current period, the client wishes to restate the prior period financial statements to be in conformity with GAAP.

45. B   If, during the current audit, an auditor becomes aware of circumstances or events that affect the financial statements of a prior period, the auditor should consider such matters when updating his or her report on the financial statements of the prior period. For example, if a qualified or adverse opinion had been expressed on financial statements of a prior period because of a departure from GAAP, and those financial statements are

restated in the current period to conform with GAAP, the auditor's updated report should indicate that the financial statements have been restated and should express an unqualified opinion with respect to those restated financial statements.

46. **C** The results of operations (income statement) and cash flows (statement of cash flows) of financial statements are for a period of time, usually for a year. If the auditor is unable to establish a starting point (beginning of year), an opinion cannot be formed because the opening balances cannot be verified. Therefore, the audit may be able to establish ending balance but if the opening balance cannot be established, it is impossible to conclude on what transpired during the year.

47. **A** There is a specific statement in the audit report to examining evidence on a test basis. However, there is no reference to the consistent application of GAAP. The reference is implicit because the phrase, "presents fairly in accordance with GAAP," includes the fact that GAAP has been consistently applied.

48. **D** GAAS explicitly states that if the predecessor's report is not presented with the comparative financial statements, the current (successor) auditor's report must refer to the fact that the predecessor expressed an unqualified opinion on the prior year's financial statements. In order to do this the successor should modify the introductory paragraph of his report to include information about the prior year's audit.

49. **B** False. Without access to the actual financial statements of the subsidiary, the auditor of the consolidated financial statements cannot determine that the two sets of records were put together properly. Even if both sets of financial statements are presented fairly, the consolidated process must be examined. Without the financial statements of company Y, the auditor should give a scope qualification or a disclaimer on the consolidated statements. The auditor has not obtained sufficient, competent evidence on which to give an unqualified opinion.

COMPILATIONS AND REVIEWS

STUDY MANUAL – AUDITING & ATTESTATION
CHAPTER 4

Study Tip: Always focus on learning the essentials of each topic. The CPA exam rarely gets into much depth on any topic, but instead prefers to focus on testing a very broad range of questions. It is better to know the essentials about every topic than to know any topic in serious depth and detail.

COMPILATIONS

A compilation engagement is one where the accountant presents financial information that is the representation of management (owners), in the form of financial statements without undertaking to express any assurance on the financial statements. A compilation engagement may only be performed for a nonpublic client. In order to conduct such an engagement:

- The accountant must have or obtain an understanding of the accounting principles and practices of the industry in which the client operates.
- The accountant must have a general understanding of the nature of the entity's transactions, the form of its accounting records, the stated qualifications of its accounting personnel, the accounting basis on which the financial statements are to be presented, and the form and content of the financial statements.
- The accountant is not required to make inquiries or to perform other procedures for verification or review of the information supplied. If the accountant becomes aware of unusual circumstances, however, he or she must resolve the matter(s) to the auditor's satisfaction by making additional inquiries or by performing other verification or review procedures. If, upon performing such procedures, the accountant becomes aware that information is not presented in accordance with generally accepted accounting principles, the accountant should obtain additional or revised information. If the entity refuses to provide additional or revised information, the accountant should withdraw from the engagement.
- Before issuing a report, the accountant should read the financial statements to determine if they are free from obvious material errors, which include mistakes in compilation such as arithmetical or clerical mistakes, and mistakes in applying GAAP, such as inadequate disclosure.
- Each page of the financial statements should include the reference, "See Accountant's Compilation Report."

STANDARD COMPILATION REPORT

A compilation report should be dated as of the date of the completion of the compilation and be signed in the name of the firm. The following is a standard compilation report:

Date: [The date of completion of the compilation]

To: [There are no restrictions on the addressee]

We have compiled the accompanying balance sheet of XYZ Company as of December 31, 2005, and the related statements of income, retained earnings, and cash flows for the year then ended, in accordance with Statements on Standards for Accounting and Review Services issued by the American Institute of Certified Public Accountants.

A compilation is limited to presenting in the form of financial statements information that is the representation of management (owners). We have not audited or reviewed the accompanying financial statements and, accordingly, do not express an opinion or any other form of assurance on them.

[Signature of Accountant/CPA Firm]

An accountant may issue a compilation report when substantially all disclosures have been omitted, provided the omission was not intended to mislead users of the financial statements. If the financial statements omit substantially all disclosures, the accountant's report should include a third paragraph as follows:

Management has elected to omit substantially all of the disclosures (and the statement of cash flows) required by U.S. generally accepted accounting principles. If the omitted disclosures were included in the financial statements, they might influence the user's conclusions about the company's financial position, results of operations, and cash flows. Accordingly, these financial statements are not designed for those who are not informed about such matters.

An accountant may prepare a compilation report for financial statements of one period where substantially all disclosures have been omitted and for another period where all GAAP disclosures have been included. The accountant should not consent to the presentation of these statements in comparative form, however, because statements with disclosures are not comparable to those without them.

If the accountant is aware of any departures from generally accepted accounting principles in the financial statements or notes, a sentence is added to the end of the second paragraph stating, "We did become aware of a departure from GAAP that is explained in the following paragraph." A third paragraph of the report is then added to describe the matter.

If the financial statements are presented on a comprehensive basis of accounting other than GAAP, a paragraph should be added to the report such as the following:

These financial statements (including related disclosures) are presented in accordance with the cash basis of accounting, which differs from U.S. generally accepted accounting principles. Accordingly, these financial statements are not designed for those who are not informed about such differences.

Because compilations are not considered attest services, an accountant need not be independent to perform a compilation. When the accountant is not independent, the lack of independence should be disclosed in the report as follows: "We are not independent with respect to XYZ Company."

REVIEWS

A review engagement is one where the accountant performs inquiry and analytical procedures that provide the auditor with a reasonable basis for expressing limited assurance that there are no material modifications that should be made to the statements in order for them to be in conformity with generally accepted accounting principles.

A review is differentiated from a compilation in that it provides limited assurance as to the financial statements. A review also is differentiated from an audit in that it is not designed to provide a basis for expression of an opinion on the financial statements. A review does not contemplate:

- Tests of accounting records through inspection, observation, or confirmation
- Tests of controls
- Corroborating evidence in response to inquiries
- Application of other procedures ordinarily performed during an audit

Similar to an engagement calling for a compilation, there are certain requirements that the accountant must address in performing a review:

- The accountant should have knowledge sufficient to identify types of potential misstatements and to consider the likelihood of occurrence.
- The accountant should have knowledge sufficient to select inquiries and analytical procedures to provide a basis for communicating whether the auditor is aware of material modifications that should be made for the information to conform with GAAP.
- The accountant should perform procedures to update the accountant's knowledge of the business and its internal control to aid in determining appropriate review procedures:
    - The accountant must have or obtain an understanding of the accounting principles and practices of the industry in which the client operates.
    - The accountant should have an understanding of the client's business including an understanding of the entity's organization, its operating characteristics, and the nature of its assets, liabilities, revenues, and expenses. More specifically, the accountant should have general knowledge about the entity's production, distribution, and compensation methods; types of products and services; operating locations; and material transactions with related parties.
- The accountant's inquiry and analytical procedures should consist of the following:
    - Inquiries concerning the entity's accounting principles and practices and the methods followed in applying them
    - Inquiries concerning the entity's methods for recording, classifying, and summarizing transactions and accumulating information for financial statement disclosures

- Analytical procedures designed to identify relationships and unusual items, including comparisons with prior periods, comparisons with budgets, or other indications of anticipated results, and study of the relationships of elements of financial information that would be expected to conform to predictable patterns
- Inquiries concerning actions taken at meetings of stockholders, the board of directors, and committees
- Reading of the financial statements to determine if they appear to conform to generally accepted accounting principles
- Obtaining reports from other accountants, if any, who have been engaged to review the financial statements of significant components of the reporting entity, its subsidiaries, and other investees
- Inquiries of people having responsibility for financial and accounting matters concerning
  - whether the financial statements conform to generally accepted accounting principles,
  - changes in the entity's business activities or accounting principles or practices,
  - matters regarding which questions have arisen in performing the other inquiries and analytical procedures, and
  - events subsequent to the date of the financial statements that may have a material effect on the financial statements.
- If the accountant becomes aware of incorrect, incomplete, or otherwise unsatisfactory information in the financial statements, the accountant should perform any additional procedures considered necessary in order to issue a limited assurance report.
- No consideration of internal control is contemplated by a review of financial statements.
- The accountant must obtain a representation letter from a responsible person(s) within the client's organization, such as the owner, manager, chief executive officer, and chief financial officer.
- Each page of the financial statements reviewed by the accountant should include the reference, "See Accountant's Review Report."

STANDARD REVIEW REPORT

A review report should be dated as of the date of the completion of the review and be signed in the name of the firm. The following is a standard review report:

Date: [Completion of accountant's review procedures]

To: [There are no restrictions on the addressee]

We have reviewed the accompanying balance sheet of XYZ Company as of December 31, 2005, and the related statements of income, retained earnings, and cash flows for the year then ended, in accordance with Statements on Standards for Accounting and Review Services issued by the American Institute of Certified Public Accountants. All information included in these financial statements is the representation of the management (owners) of XYZ Company.

A review consists principally of inquiries of company personnel and analytical procedures applied to financial data. It is substantially less in scope than an audit in accordance with U.S. generally accepted auditing standards, the objective of which is the expression of an opinion regarding the financial statements taken as a whole. Accordingly, we do not express such an opinion.

Based on our review, we are not aware of any material modifications that should be made to the accompanying financial statements in order for them to be in conformity with U.S. generally accepted accounting principles.

[Signature of Accountant/CPA Firm]

If there is a departure from generally accepted accounting principles, the accountant should describe the matter in a fourth paragraph and modify the third paragraph of the report to read as follows:

Based on our review, with the exception of the matter(s) described in the following paragraph(s), we are not aware of any modifications that should be made to the accompanying financial statements in order for them to be in conformity with U.S. generally accepted accounting principles.

When current year financial statements have been reviewed and prior year financial statements were audited, the accountant may either reissue the audit report and issue a review report, or may refer to the audit in the review report. In referring to the audit in the review report, the CPA should indicate that the statements were audited, the date of the previous opinion, reasons for any departures from an unqualified form, and that no auditing procedures were performed after the date of the previous report. (When the current-year financial statements have been compiled, the same procedures are followed.)

When the current-year financial statements have been audited and prior year financial statements were reviewed; the audit report should include a statement indicating the type of service performed, the date of the report, a description of any material modifications noted in the report, and a statement that the service was less in scope than an audit and does not provide a basis for the expression of an opinion on the financial statements. (When prior year financial statements have been compiled, the same procedures are followed.)

Because reviews are attest services, an accountant must be independent to perform a review.

	Compilation and Review Report Summary	
	Compilation Report	Review Report
First paragraph	• A compilation has been performed in accordance with SSARS issued by the AICPA.	• A review was performed in accordance with SSARS issued by the AICPA. • All information included in the financial statements is the representation of management.
Second paragraph	• A compilation is limited to presenting in the form of financial statements information that is the representation of management. • I have not audited or reviewed the accompanying financial statements and, accordingly, do not express an opinion or any other form of assurance on them.	• A review consists principally of inquires of company personnel and analytical procedures applied to financial data. • It is substantially less in scope than an audit, the objective of which is the expression of an opinion regarding the financial statements taken as a whole.
Third paragraph	• [Standard report has only two paragraphs].	• We are not aware of any material modifications that should be made to the financial statements in order for them to be in conformity with GAAP.
Circumstances in which additional paragraphs are added	• Departures from GAAP. • Client omission of note disclosures. • Lack of independence.	• Departures from GAAP. • *Notes:* Client omission of disclosures is considered a departure from GAAP for a review. A CPA must be independent to perform a review.

STUDY MANUAL – AUDITING & ATTESTATION
CHAPTER 4

QUESTIONS: COMPILATIONS AND REVIEWS

1. During a review of the financial statements of a nonpublic entity, an accountant becomes aware of a lack of adequate disclosure that is material to the financial statements. If management refuses to correct the financial statement presentations, the accountant should:
   A. issue an "except for" qualified opinion.
   B. issue an adverse opinion.
   C. express only limited assurance on the financial statement presentations.
   D. disclose this departure from generally accepted accounting principles in a separate paragraph of the report.

2. Each page of the financial statements compiled by an accountant should include a reference such as:
   A. see accompanying accountant's footnotes.
   B. see accountant's compilation report.
   C. unaudited, see accountant's disclaimer.
   D. subject to compilation restrictions.

3. Which of the following procedures would *most likely* be included in a review engagement of a nonpublic entity?
   A. Assessing internal control.
   B. Inquiring about related party transactions.
   C. Preparing a bank transfer schedule.
   D. Performing cutoff tests on sales and purchases transactions.

4. Which of the following circumstances requires modification of the accountant's report on a review of interim financial information of a publicly held entity:

	An uncertainty	Inadequate disclosure
A.	No	Yes
B.	Yes	No
C.	Yes	Yes
D.	No	No

5. Financial statements of a nonpublic entity that have been reviewed by an accountant should be accompanied by a report stating that:
   A. a review is greater in scope than a compilation, the objective of which is to present financial statements that are free of material misstatements.
   B. a review includes examining, on a test basis, evidence supporting the amounts and disclosures in the financial statements.
   C. all information included in the financial statements is the representation of the management of the entity.
   D. the scope of the inquiry and analytical procedures performed by the accountant has not been restricted.

6. An accountant has been asked to compile the financial statements of a nonpublic company on a prescribed form that omits substantially all the disclosures required by generally accepted accounting principles. If the prescribed form is a standard preprinted form adopted by the company's industry trade association, and is to be transmitted only to such association, the accountant:
   A. should disclose the details of the omissions in separate paragraphs of the compilation report.
   B. need not advise the industry trade association of the omission of all disclosures.
   C. should express limited assurance that the financial statements are free of material misstatements.
   D. is precluded from issuing a compilation report when all disclosures are omitted.

7. An accountant should perform analytical procedures during an engagement to:

	Compile a nonpublic entity's financial statements	Review of a nonpublic entity's financial statements
A.	No	Yes
B.	Yes	Yes
C.	Yes	No
D.	No	No

8. Miller, CPA, is engaged to compile the financial statements of Web Co., a nonpublic entity, in conformity with the income tax basis of accounting. If Web's financial statements do not disclose the basis of accounting used, Miller should:
   A. withdraw from the engagement and provide no further services to Web.
   B. disclose the basis of accounting in the accountant's compilation report.
   C. issue a special report describing the effect of the incomplete presentation.
   D. clearly label each page "Distribution Restricted—Material Modifications Required."

9. When an independent CPA is associated with the financial statements of a publicly held entity, but has not audited or reviewed such statements, the appropriate form of report to be issued must include a(an):
   A. explanatory paragraph.
   B. negative assurance.
   C. compilation opinion.
   D. disclaimer of opinion.

10. The standard report issued by an accountant after reviewing the financial statements of a nonpublic entity states that:
    A. a review includes assessing the accounting principles used and significant estimates made by management.
    B. a review includes examining, on a test basis, evidence supporting the amounts and disclosures in the financial statements.
    C. the accountant is not aware of any material modifications that should be made to the financial statements.
    D. the accountant does not express an opinion or any other form of assurance on the financial statements.

11. Compiled financial statements should be accompanied by a report stating that
    A. the accountant has compiled the financial statements in accordance with standards established by the Auditing Standards Board.
    B. a compilation is substantially less in scope than a review or an audit in accordance with generally accepted auditing standards.
    C. a compilation is limited to presenting in the form of financial statements information that is the representation of management.
    D. the accountant does not express an opinion but expresses only limited assurance on the compiled financial statements.

12. Which of the following procedures ordinarily should be applied when an independent accountant conducts a review of interim financial information of a publicly held entity?
    A. Read the minutes of the board of directors' meetings.
    B. Perform cut-off tests for cash receipts and disbursements.
    C. Inspect the open purchase order file.
    D. Verify changes in key account balances.

13. The objective of a review of interim financial information is to provide an accountant with a basis for reporting whether:
    A. the financial statements are presented fairly in accordance with standards of interim reporting.
    B. a reasonable basis exists for expressing an updated opinion regarding the financial statements that were previously audited.
    C. the financial statements are presented fairly in accordance with generally accepted accounting principles.
    D. material modifications should be made to conform with generally accepted accounting principles.

14. A CPA who is associated with the financial statements of a public entity, but has NOT audited or reviewed such statements, should:
    A. insist that they be audited or reviewed before publication.
    B. read them to determine whether there are obvious material errors.
    C. state these facts in the accompanying notes to the financial statements.
    D. issue a compilation report.

15. Accepting an engagement to compile a financial projection for a publicly held company *most likely* would be inappropriate if the projection were to be distributed to:
    A. a bank with which the entity is negotiating for a loan.
    B. a labor union with which the entity is negotiating a contract.
    C. all stockholders of record as of the report date.
    D. the principal stockholder, to the exclusion of the other stockholders.

16. If compiled financial statements presented in conformity with the cash receipts and disbursements basis of accounting do **NOT** disclose the basis of accounting used, the accountant should:
    A. disclose the basis of accounting in the accountant's report.
    B. recompile the financial statements using generally accepted accounting principles.
    C. clearly label each page, "Unaudited."
    D. disclose the basis in the notes to the financial statements.

17. An accountant has been asked to issue a review report on the balance sheet of a nonpublic company but not to report on the other basic financial statements. The accountant may **NOT** do so:
    A. because compliance with this request would result in an incomplete review.
    B. if the review of the balance sheet discloses material departures from generally accepted accounting principles.
    C. because compliance with this request would result in a violation of the ethical standards of the profession.
    D. if the scope of the inquiry and analytical procedures has been restricted.

18. What type of analytical procedure would an auditor *most likely* use in developing relationships among balance sheet accounts when reviewing the financial statements of a nonpublic entity?
    A. Trend analysis.
    B. Ratio analysis.
    C. Regression analysis.
    D. Risk analysis.

19. Which of the following procedures is **NOT** usually performed by the accountant during a review engagement of a nonpublic entity?
    A. Reading the financial statements to consider whether they conform with generally accepted accounting principles.
    B. Issuing a report stating that the review was performed in accordance with standards established by the AICPA.
    C. Inquiring about actions taken at meetings of the board of directors that may affect the financial statements.
    D. Communicating any material weaknesses discovered during the consideration of internal control.

20. Baker, CPA, was engaged to review the financial statements of Hall Co., a nonpublic entity. During the engagement Baker uncovered a complex scheme involving client illegal acts and fraud that materially affect Hall's financial statements. If Baker believes that modification of the standard review report is **NOT** adequate to indicate the deficiencies in the financial statements, Baker should:
    A. issue an adverse opinion.
    B. issue a qualified opinion.
    C. withdraw from the engagement.
    D. disclaim an opinion.

21. A CPA should **NOT** submit unaudited financial statements of a nonpublic company to a client or others unless, as a minimum, the CPA complies with the provisions applicable to:
    A. statements on auditing standards.
    B. compilation engagements.
    C. review engagements.
    D. attestation standards.

22. The objective of a review of interim financial information of a public entity is to provide an accountant with a basis for reporting whether:
    A. material modifications should be made to conform with generally accepted accounting principles.
    B. the financial statements are presented fairly in accordance with generally accepted accounting principles.
    C. condensed financial statements or pro forma financial information should be included in a registration statement.
    D. a reasonable basis exists for expressing an updated opinion regarding the financial statements that were previously audited.

23. Davis, CPA, accepted an engagement to audit the financial statements of Tech Resources, a nonpublic entity. Before the completion of the audit, Tech requested Davis to change the engagement to a compilation of financial statements. Before Davis agrees to change the engagement, Davis is required to consider the:

	Additional audit effort necessary to complete the audit	Reason given for Tech's request
A.	Yes	Yes
B.	Yes	No
C.	No	No
D.	No	Yes

24. Performing inquiry and analytical procedures is the primary basis for an accountant to issue a(an):
    A. management advisory report prepared at the request of a client's audit committee.
    B. review report on comparative financial statements for a nonpublic entity in its second year of operations.
    C. compilation report on financial statements for a nonpublic entity in its first year of operations.
    D. internal accounting control report for a governmental agency in accordance with GAO standards.

25. An accountant who reviews the financial statements of a nonpublic entity should issue a report stating that a review:
    A. provides only limited assurance that the financial statements are fairly presented.
    B. provides negative assurance that internal control is functioning as designed.
    C. is substantially more in scope than a compilation.
    D. is substantially less in scope than an audit.

26. When compiling a nonpublic entity's financial statements, an accountant would be *least likely* to:
    A. omit substantially all of the disclosures required by generally accepted accounting principles.
    B. read the compiled financial statements and consider whether they appear to include adequate disclosure.
    C. perform analytical procedures designed to identify relationships that appear to be unusual.
    D. issue a compilation report on one or more, but not all, of the basic financial statements.

27. When providing limited assurance that the financial statements of a nonpublic entity require *no* material modifications to be in accordance with generally accepted accounting principles, the accountant should:
    A. test the accounting records that identify inconsistencies with the prior year's financial statements.
    B. understand the accounting principles of the industry in which the entity operates.
    C. understand the system of internal accounting control that the entity uses.
    D. develop audit programs to determine whether the entity's financial statements are fairly presented.

28. Which of the following procedures should an accountant perform during an engagement to review the financial statements of a nonpublic entity?
    A. Examining cash disbursements in the subsequent period for unrecorded liabilities.
    B. Sending bank confirmation letters to the entity's financial institutions.
    C. Obtaining a client representation letter from members of management.
    D. Communicating reportable conditions discovered during the assessment of control risk.

29. Which of the following inquiry or analytical procedures ordinarily is performed in an engagement to review a nonpublic entity's financial statements?
    A. Analytical procedures designed to test the accounting records by obtaining corroborating audit evidence.
    B. Inquiries of the entity's attorney concerning contingent liabilities.
    C. Analytical procedures designed to test management's assertions regarding continued existence.
    D. Inquiries concerning the entity's procedures for recording and summarizing transactions.

30. A CPA who is **NOT** independent may issue a:
    A. compilation report.
    B. qualified opinion.
    C. review report.
    D. comfort letter.

31. Financial statements of a nonpublic entity compiled without audit or review by an accountant should be accompanied by a report stating that:
    A. the scope of the accountant's procedures has not been restricted in testing the financial information that is the representation of management.
    B. the accountant does not express an opinion or any other form of assurance on the financial statements.
    C. a compilation consists principally of inquiries of entity personnel and analytical procedures applied to financial data.
    D. the accountant assessed the accounting principles used and significant estimates made by management.

32. When an accountant compiles a nonpublic entity's financial statements that omit substantially all disclosures required by generally accepted accounting principles, the accountant should indicate in the compilation report that the financial statements are:
    A. not to be given to financial institutions for the purpose of obtaining credit.
    B. restricted for internal use only by the entity's management.
    C. not designed for those who are uninformed about the omitted disclosures.
    D. compiled in conformity with a comprehensive basis of accounting other than generally accepted accounting principles.

33. An accountant's standard report on a compilation of a projection should NOT include a:
    A. disclaimer of responsibility to update the report for events occurring after the report's date.
    B. statement that the accountant expresses only limited assurance that the results may be achieved.
    C. separate paragraph that describes the limitations on the presentation's usefulness.
    D. statement that a compilation of a projection is limited in scope.

34. Which of the following accounting services may an accountant perform *without* being required to issue a compilation or review report under the Statements on Standards for Accounting and Review Services?

    I. Preparing a working trial balance.
    II. Preparing standard monthly journal entries.

    A. Both I and II.
    B. I only.
    C. Neither I nor II.
    D. II only.

35. If requested to perform a review engagement for a nonpublic entity in which an accountant has an immaterial direct financial interest, the accountant is:
    A. independent because the financial interest is immaterial and, therefore, may issue a review report.
    B. not independent and, therefore, may issue a review report, but may not issue an auditor's opinion.
    C. not independent, and therefore, may not issue a review report.
    D. not independent and, therefore, may not be associated with the financial statements.

36. When an accountant compiles projected financial statements, the accountant's report should include a separate paragraph that:
    A. identifies the accounting principles used by management.
    B. describes the limitations on the projection's usefulness.
    C. describes the differences between a projection and a forecast.
    D. expresses limited assurance that the actual results may be within the projection's range.

37. An accountant's compilation report on a financial forecast should include a statement that:
    A. there will usually be differences between the forecasted and actual results.
    B. the hypothetical assumptions used in the forecast are reasonable in the circumstances.
    C. the accountant expresses only limited assurance on the forecasted statements and their assumptions.
    D. the forecast should be read only in conjunction with the audited historical financial statements.

38. When an auditor performs a review of interim financial statements, which of the following steps would **NOT** be a part of the review?
    A. Inquiry of management.
    B. Reading the minutes of the stockholders' meetings.
    C. Review of ratios and trends.
    D. Review of computer controls.

39. Which of the following procedures is ordinarily performed by an accountant in a compilation engagement of a nonpublic entity?
    A. Applying analytical procedures designed to corroborate management's assertions that are embodied in the financial statement components.
    B. Obtaining written representations from management indicating that the compiled financial statements will not be used to obtain credit.
    C. Making inquiries of management concerning actions taken at meetings of the stockholders and the board of directors.
    D. Reading the financial statements to consider whether they are free of obvious mistakes in the application of accounting principles.

40. Smith, CPA, has been asked to issue a review report on the balance sheet of Cone Company, a nonpublic entity, and not on the other related financial statements. Smith may do so only if:
    A. Smith compiles and reports on the related statements of income, retained earnings, and cash flows.
    B. Smith is not aware of any material modifications needed for the balance sheet to conform with GAAP.
    C. the scope of Smith's inquiry and analytical procedures is not restricted.
    D. Cone is a new client and Smith accepts the engagement after the end of Cone's fiscal year.

41. Which of the following procedures is **NOT** included in a review engagement of a nonpublic entity?
    A. A study and evaluation of internal control.
    B. Inquiries regarding events subsequent to the balance sheet date.
    C. Inquiries of management.
    D. Any procedures designed to identify relationships among data that appear to be unusual.

Answers: Compilations and Reviews

1. **D** The accountant (CPA) must disclose the departure from GAAP in the review report. Issuing an adverse opinion and issuing an "except for" qualified opinion only apply to audit reports, not review reports. Expressing only limited assurance on the financial statement presentations is true about review reports. A review does express limited assurance, but this choice does not answer the question posed.

2. **B** Each page of the accountant's compilation report should contain a reference to the Compilation Report.

3. **B** A review consists primarily of analytical procedures and inquiry of the client personnel. The other answers are usually performed in an audit, not a review.

4. **A** There are only two reasons an auditor would modify a review report, and they are (1) departures from GAAP and (2) inadequate disclosure. Uncertainties would not require modification of a review report.

5. **C** All information included in the financial statements is the representation of the management of the entity.

6. **B** There is a presumption that the information required by a prescribed form is sufficient to meet the needs of the body that designed or adopted the form and that there is no need for that body to be advised of departures from generally accepted accounting principles required by the prescribed form or related instructions.

7. **A** A compilation is defined as presenting in the form of financial statements information that is the representation of management without undertaking to express any assurance on the statements. In a compilation, the accountant is not required to make inquiries or to perform other procedures to verify, corroborate, or review information supplied by the entity. A review is defined as performing inquiry and analytical procedures that provide the accountant with a reasonable basis for expressing limited assurance that there are no material modifications that should be made to the financial statements in order for them to be in conformity with GAAP, or, if applicable, with another comprehensive basis of accounting. Analytical procedures are required in a review engagement. Analytical procedures are not required in a compilation engagement.

8. **B** AR 100 states that if financial statements compiled in conformity with a comprehensive basis of accounting other than generally accepted accounting principles do not include disclosure of the basis of accounting used, the basis should be disclosed in the accountant's report.

9. **D** If the CPA has not audited he must disclaim an opinion.

10. **C** Statements on Standards for Accounting and Review Services require the accountant's review report for a nonpublic entity to state that a review is less in scope than an audit and that the accountant is not aware of any material modifications that should be made to the financial statements.

11. **C** Compiled financial statements should be accompanied by a report stating that: a compilation has been performed in accordance with Statements on Standards for Accounting and Review Services (SSARS) issued by the AICPA; a compilation is limited

to presenting in the form of financial statements information that is the representation of management; and the financial statements have not been audited or reviewed and, accordingly, the accountant does not express an opinion or any other form of assurance on them. Although it is true that a compilation is substantially less in scope than a review or audit in accordance with GAAS, the compilation report does not include such a statement. The accountant expresses no assurance on the compiled financial statements. The accountant follows SSARS issued by the AICPA Accounting and Review Services Committee, not Statements on Auditing Standards (SAS) or any other standards issued by the Auditing Standards Board.

12. A   Procedures for conducting a review of interim financial information are generally limited to inquiries and analytical procedures. Included in these procedures is reading the minutes of meetings of stockholders, the board of directors, and committees of the board of directors. A review does not typically include tests of balances and transactions such as those reflected in the other answers.

13. D   The objective of a review of interim financial information is to provide the accountant, based on objectively applying his knowledge of financial reporting practices to significant accounting matters of which he becomes aware through inquiries and analytical procedures, with a basis for reporting whether material modifications should be made for such information to conform with GAAP. A review does not provide a basis for the expression of an opinion regarding the financial statements.

14. B   For a nonpublic entity the type of service described would be a compilation. The only work the accountant must do for this service is described by the answer.

15. C   A report on a financial projection is identified as a "limited use" report, which means that the report is not for general distribution. Such a report is restricted to be used by only the parties named in the report. Since the stockholders could have changed from the report date it would be inappropriate to distribute a report on a financial projection to those individuals who are no longer stockholders.

16. A   The accountant may compile financial statements that omit all footnote disclosures. Normally, the footnotes to the financial statements would disclose the basis of accounting in preparing the financial statements. If all disclosures are omitted, then the CPA must disclose the basis of accounting followed in the compilation report.

17. D   An accountant may report (audit or review) on only one basic financial statement as long as he has access to all evidence and the scope of his procedures are not restricted.

18. B   Analytical procedures involve comparisons of recorded amounts, or ratios developed from recorded amounts, to expectations developed by the auditor. If the auditor wants to develop relationships among balance sheet accounts, he or she would calculate and evaluate financial statement ratios such as the current ratio and debt to equity ratio.

19. D   A review does not contemplate obtaining an understanding of internal control or assessing control risk. Accordingly, in a review engagement of a nonpublic entity, the accountant will not typically communicate material weaknesses discovered during the consideration of internal control. The other answers are examples of review procedures that should ordinarily be performed.

20. C   If the accountant believes that modification of his standard report is not adequate to indicate the deficiencies in the financial statements taken as a whole, he or she should withdraw from the review engagement and provide no further services with respect to those financial statements.

21. B   Since the CPA is associated with the financial statements (he is submitting them), he must indicate the degree of responsibility he is taking with respect to the statements. Since the statements are unaudited and the company is nonpublic, the appropriate standards are compilation standards.

22. A   The objective of a review is to provide the accountant, based on applying his or her knowledge of financial reporting practices to significant accounting matters of which he or she becomes aware through inquiries and analytical procedures, with a basis for reporting whether material modifications should be made for such information to conform with generally accepted accounting principles. A review, which does not provide assurance that the accountant will become aware of all significant matters that would be disclosed in audit, does not provide the basis for expressing or updating an audit opinion. A review does not provide a basis for reporting on whether certain information should or should not be included in a registration statement under the Securities Act of 1933.

23. A   A CPA who has been engaged to audit the financial statements of a nonpublic entity may, before the completion of the engagement, be requested to change the engagement to a compilation. Such a request may result from a change in circumstances affecting the client's requirement for an audit, a misunderstanding regarding the nature of an audit, or a restriction on the scope of the audit. Before agreeing to the change to a compilation, the CPA should consider the reason for the client's request, the additional audit effort required to complete the audit, and the estimated cost to complete the audit. The CPA is required to consider the additional audit effort necessary to complete the audit. The CPA is required to consider the reason given for the client's request, particularly the implications of a restriction on the scope of the audit, whether imposed by the client or by circumstances.

24. B   Inquiry and analytical procedures are the basis for a review engagement.

25. D   Financial statements of a nonpublic entity that are reviewed by an accountant should be accompanied by a report stating that a review is substantially less in scope than an audit.

26. C   Analytical procedures are performed in a review, not a compilation.

27. B   Understanding the accounting principles of the industry in which the entity operates is performed in a review engagement. All other answers are normally performed in an audit engagement.

28. C   AR 100 states that in an engagement to review the financial statements of a nonpublic entity, the accountant is required to obtain a representation letter from members of management whom the accountant believes are responsible for and knowledgeable, directly or through others in the organization, about the matters covered in the representation letter. Normally, the chief executive officer and chief financial officer should sign the representation letter. The other answers are incorrect because they are not performed during a review.

29. D   A review consists principally of inquiries of company personnel and analytical procedures applied to financial data. The review should ordinarily include inquiries concerning the entity's procedures for recording and summarizing transactions. A review does not contemplate tests of records and assertions and inquiries of non-company personnel, such as the entity's attorney.

30. **A** A CPA may issue a compilation report even though he is not independent, but his report must clearly state that he is not independent.

31. **B** Financial statements of a nonpublic entity compiled without audit or review by an accountant should be accompanied by a report stating that the financial statements have not been audited or reviewed, and, accordingly, the accountant does not express an opinion or any other form of assurance on them.

32. **C** When a nonpublic entity's financial statements that an accountant has compiled omit substantially all disclosures, a paragraph is added to the compilation report indicating that the financial statements are not designed for those who are not informed about the omitted disclosures. The accountant may compile such financial statements provided the omissions are not undertaken with the intention of misleading users of those statements. There is no requirement that these statements be restricted for internal use and no prohibition on giving them to financial institutions.

33. **B** The accountant's standard report on a compilation of prospective financial statements should include an identification of the financial statements, a statement that the accountant compiled the statements in accordance with AICPA standards, a statement that a compilation is limited in scope and does not enable the accountant to express an opinion or any other form of assurance, a caveat that the results may not be achieved, and a statement that the accountant assumes no responsibility to update the report for events and circumstances occurring after the date of the report. When the presentation is a projection, the report should include a separate paragraph that describes the limitations on the usefulness of the presentation.

34. **A** An accountant is required to issue a report whenever he compiles or reviews financial statements in accordance with Statements on Standards for Accounting and Review Services (SSARS). SSARS does not establish procedures for other accounting and bookkeeping services such as preparing a working trial balance and standard monthly journal entries.

35. **D** The CPA must be independent when performing a review service. Independence is considered impaired if the accountant had or was committed to acquire any direct or material indirect financial interest in the client.

36. **B** Projected financial statements present to the best of the responsible party's knowledge, given one or more hypothetical assumptions, an entity's expected financial position, results of operations, and cash flows. These projected statements are for the limited use of parties with whom the responsible party is dealing directly. When compiling projected financial statements, the accountant's report should include a paragraph that describes these limitations on the usefulness of the presentation. The accountant's report does not include references to the items in the other answers.

37. **A** AT 200 states that the following is the form of the accountant's standard report on the compilation of a forecast that does not contain a range:

"We have compiled the accompanying forecasted balance sheet, statements of income, retained earnings, and changes in financial position of XYZ Company as of December 31, 19XX, and for the year then ending, in accordance with standards established by the American Institute of Certified Public Accountants.

A compilation is limited to presenting in the form of a forecast information that is the representation of management and does not include evaluation of the support for the assumptions underlying the forecast. We have not examined the forecast and, accordingly, do not express an opinion or any other form of assurance on the accompanying statements or assumptions. Furthermore, there will usually be differences between the forecasted and actual results, because events and circumstances frequently do not occur as expected, and those differences may be material. We have no responsibility to update this report for events and circumstances occurring after the date of this report."

38. D During a review of a client's financial statements, a CPA will:

- Discuss with management the nature of the accounting system used to generate the financial statements (answer B)
- Perform an analytical review
- Read the minutes of meetings in order to determine if disclosure is adequate
- The CPA will not review any controls since this is associated with an audit.

39. D A compilation is the presentation in the form of financial statements information that is the representation of management without undertaking to express any assurance on the statements. Before issuing his or her compilation report, the accountant should read the compiled financial statements and consider whether such financial statements appear to be appropriate in form and free from obvious material errors, including mistakes in the application of accounting principles.

40. C A CPA may be asked to issue a review report on one financial statement, such as a balance sheet, and not on related financial statements such as statements of income, retained earnings, and cash flows. The CPA may do so if the scope of his or her inquiry and analytical procedures has not been restricted. The CPA can issue a review report on a balance sheet without reporting on other related financial statements. The CPA can issue a review report on a balance sheet that is modified to disclose a departure from GAAP. Whether the client is a new or continuing client, and whether the engagement is accepted before or after the end of the client's fiscal year are irrelevant. The CPA can issue a review report on a balance sheet for new or continuing clients, and for engagements accepted before or after fiscal year-end.

41. A A study and evaluation of internal control is associated with audit engagements, not review engagements.

Audit Risk

Study Manual – Auditing & Attestation
Chapter 5

Study Tip: After you qualify to take the CPA exam and sign up for a date, the examiners will send you all of the information they believe you need in advance. Read all of that material very carefully. They have studied the problems experienced by candidates in the past to determine what information is needed. They will expect you to have read the material and you should do so. The more you understand about the process, the more likely it is you will pass.

Risk

A. The *audit risk model*, which may be assessed *quantitatively* (e.g., a 20% risk of misstatement might be said to exist) or *nonquantitatively* (one account may be assessed as having *maximum* risk of misstatement, whereas another has *minimum* risk), consists of the following:

1. **Inherent risk**—the possibility that a material misstatement will occur within the client's accounting system.

    a. This risk differs by account and assertion. For example, cash is more susceptible to theft than an inventory of coal.

    b. This risk is assessed using various analytical techniques and available information on the company and its industry, as well as by using overall auditing knowledge.

2. **Control risk**—the possibility that a material misstatement will not be prevented or detected on a timely basis by the client's internal control.

    a. This risk is assessed using the results of tests of controls.

3. **Detection risk**—the possibility that an auditor's procedures lead to an improper conclusion that no material misstatement exists in an assertion, when in fact, such a misstatement does exist.

    a. The auditor's substantive tests are primarily relied upon to restrict detection risk.

B. For each group of accounts, the auditor is not satisfied until *audit risk is reduced to an acceptably low level*.

1. Acceptable audit risk is the amount of risk that the auditor is willing to assume and still provide reasonable assurance that no material misstatements exist.

2. The auditor estimates the severity of the inherent risk and control risk based on an assessment of the client and each particular group of accounts.

C. Certain factors increase the possibility that misstatements may have occurred and, therefore, impact the auditor's *judgment of inherent risk*.

1. It is a first audit.

2. It is a continuing audit in which misstatements were found in previous years.

3. Accounts exist with large balances or many transactions.

4. Significant balances are the result of estimations so that less objective evidence is available.

5. The accounting system is outdated, understaffed, or operated by individuals lacking training or experience.

6. Discovery is made during the performance of analytical procedures in the initial audit planning stages of client balances that vary significantly from the auditor's expectations.

D. Inherent risk and control risk differ from detection risk in that they exist independently of the audit, whereas detection risk relates to the effectiveness of the auditor's procedures.

1. If any risk increases, another must decrease to hold audit risk to the acceptable level, thus the relationship between inherent risk and/or control risk and detection risk is inverse.

2. Stated otherwise, if inherent risk and/or control risk are assessed as high, the auditor may have to reduce detection risk further than expected in order for overall audit risk to be acceptable.

3. Detection risk decreases whenever an auditor gathers more evidence or obtains evidence of a better quality. Evidence is considered to be of a better quality if:

    a. It is gathered closer to year-end.

    b. It is obtained by more experienced auditors.

    c. It is obtained by using more sophisticated techniques, such as statistical sampling rather than judgment sampling.

ERRORS AND FRAUD

A. An audit should be planned and performed to obtain reasonable assurance about whether the financial statements are free of material misstatements, whether *caused by error or fraud*.

   1. While both errors and fraud may result in misstatements or omissions in the financial statements, they differ in that fraud is intentional.

   2. An auditor may encounter two types of fraud.

      a. Fraudulent financial reporting results from manipulation of accounting records, misrepresentation of events in the financial statements, or intentional misapplication of accounting principles.

      b. Misappropriation of assets (also known as theft or defalcation) is the theft of assets, an action that causes the financial statements to be misstated.

B. During planning, the audit engagement team members should *brainstorm* as to where the financial statements might be susceptible to fraud, how management could perpetrate and conceal fraudulent reporting, and how assets could be stolen. This exercise should be repeated periodically during the audit and helps the auditor anticipate where special attention should be placed.

C. The "fraud triangle" consists of:

   1. **Incentive or pressure**—Management or other employees have an incentive to commit fraud or they are under pressures that provide them with a motivation to commit fraud.

   2. **Opportunity**—Circumstances exist (e.g., the absence of controls) that provide a person with a reasonable chance to commit fraud.

   3. **Rationalization or attitude**—Those individuals who could be involved in fraud are able to rationalize a fraudulent act as being consistent with their personal code of ethics.

D. Throughout the engagement, the auditor should be especially careful to look for fraud risk factors whenever concerns appear in the fraud triangle. The presence of one or more of these factors does not mean that fraud is actually present. However, it does alert the auditor that the risk of fraud is relatively high and should be investigated.

E. The following fraud risk factors are associated specifically with fraudulent financial reporting:

   1. Incentive or pressures on employees and/or management to attempt fraudulent financial reporting.

      a. The company's financial profitability or stability is being threatened:

- There is a high degree of competition.
- The company is vulnerable to rapid changes, such as changes in technology or product obsolescence.
- There has been a decline in customer demand and increasing business failures in either the industry or the overall economy.
- There have been significant or sustained operating losses making the threat of bankruptcy or foreclosure imminent.
- The company has recurring negative cash flows from operations while reporting positive earnings and earnings growth.
- There is rapid growth or unusual profitability, especially compared to that of other companies in the same industry.
- The company faces new accounting statutory or regulatory requirements.

b. Excessive pressure exists for management to meet the requirements or expectations of third parties due to the following:

- Profitability expectations of investment analysts, investors, or significant creditors.
- The need to obtain additional debt or equity financing to stay competitive.
- A marginal ability to meet debt repayment or other debt covenant requirements.

c. Information available indicates that management or the board of directors' personal financial situation is threatened by the entity's financial performance arising from the following:

- Significant financial interests in the entity.
- Significant portions of their compensation (e.g., bonuses or stock options) contingent upon achieving aggressive targets such as stock prices, reported income, or operating cash flows.
- Personal guarantees of the debts of the entity.

2. Opportunities of management and/or employees to carry out fraudulent financial reporting.

a. The nature of the industry or the company's operations can provide opportunities to engage in fraudulent financial reporting, such as the following:

- The company engages in significant related-party transactions not in the ordinary course of business.
- There is a strong financial presence or the ability to dominate a certain industry sector that allows the entity to dictate terms or conditions to suppliers or customers that may result in inappropriate transactions or transactions that are not at arm's length.
- The reporting of assets, liabilities, revenues, or expenses is based on significant estimates that involve subjective judgments which are difficult to corroborate.

- Significant, unusual, or highly complex transactions are reported, particularly those close to the end of the period, especially those where the substance may be difficult to ascertain.
- Significant operations are located or conducted across international borders in jurisdictions where differing business environments exist.
- Significant bank accounts or subsidiary operations are in tax-haven jurisdictions for which there appears to be no clear business justification.

b. There is ineffective monitoring of management as a result of the following:

- Domination of management by a single person or small group (in a nonowner managed business) without compensating controls.
- Ineffective board of directors or audit committee oversight.

c. There is a complex or unstable organizational structure, as evidenced by the following:

- Difficulty in determining the organization or individuals who have controlling interest in the entity.
- Overly complex organizational structure involving unusual legal entities or managerial lines of authority.
- High turnover of senior management, counsel, or board members.

d. Internal control components are deficient as a result of the following:

- Inadequate monitoring of controls.
- High turnover rates for accounting, internal audit, or information technology staff.
- Ineffective accounting and information systems in place.

3. Attitudes or possible rationalizations of management and/or employees who might carry out fraudulent financial reporting.

a. Management ineffectively communicates, implements, supports, or enforces the company's values or ethical standards.

b. Nonfinancial management has excessive participation in or preoccupation with the selection of accounting principles or the determination of significant estimates.

c. There is known history of violations of securities laws or claims against the entity, its senior management, or board members alleging fraud or violations of laws and regulations.

d. There is an excessive interest by management in maintaining or increasing the entity's stock price or earnings trend.

e. Management commits to achieve aggressive or unrealistic forecasts.

f. Management fails to correct known reportable conditions on a timely basis.

g. There are recurring attempts by management to justify marginal or inappropriate accounting on the basis of materiality.

h. The relationship between management and the auditor is strained, as exhibited by the following:

- Frequent disputes with the auditor on accounting, auditing, or reporting matters.
- Unreasonable demands on the auditor, such as unreasonable time constraints regarding the completion of the audit or the issuance of the auditor's report.
- Formal or informal restrictions on the auditor that inappropriately limit access to people or information or the ability to communicate effectively with the board of directors or audit committee.
- Domineering management behavior in dealing with the auditor, especially involving attempts to influence the scope of the auditor's work or the selection or continuance of personnel assigned to the audit engagement.

F. Fraud risk factors can also be associated with misappropriation (although it is not possible to completely separate fraud risk factors between fraudulent financial reporting and misappropriation).

1. Incentives or pressures on employees and/or management to misappropriate assets:

    a. Personal debts or other financial obligations.

    b. The existence of adverse relationships such as the following:

    - Known or anticipated future layoffs.
    - Known or anticipated changes to employee compensation or benefit plans.
    - Promotions, compensation, or other rewards inconsistent with expectations.

2. Opportunities of employees and/or management to misappropriate assets.

    a. Special circumstances:

    - Large amounts of cash are on hand or processed regularly.
    - Inventory items are small in size, of high value, or in high demand.
    - Easily convertible assets are present in the company, such as bearer bonds, diamonds, or computer chips.
    - Fixed assets are present that are small in size, marketable, or lacking observable identification of ownership.

    b. Inadequate internal control over assets:

    - Inadequate segregation of duties or independent checks.

- Inadequate management oversight of employees responsible for assets. (e.g., inadequate supervision or monitoring of operations at remote locations).
- Inadequate job applicant screening of employees with access to assets.
- Inadequate record keeping with respect to assets.
- Inadequate system of authorization and approval of transactions (e.g., in the purchasing cycle).
- Inadequate physical safeguards over cash, investments, inventory, or fixed assets.
- Lack of complete and timely reconciliations of assets.
- Lack of timely and appropriate documentation of transactions, (e.g., credits for merchandise returns).
- Lack of mandatory vacations for employees performing key control functions.
- Inadequate management understanding of information technology that could enable information technology employees to perpetrate a misappropriation.

3. Attitudes or rationalizations of employee and/or management that would allow them to justify misappropriations of assets are generally not susceptible to observation by the auditor. Nevertheless, the auditor who becomes aware of the following attitudes should consider them in identifying the risks of material misstatement arising from misappropriation of assets.

   a. Disregard for the need to monitor or reduce risks related to misappropriations of assets.

   b. Disregard for internal control over misappropriation of assets by overriding existing controls or by failing to correct known internal control deficiencies.

   c. Behavior indicating displeasure or dissatisfaction with the company or its treatment of employees.

   d. Changes in behavior or lifestyle.

G. If actual fraud risk factors are discovered, the auditor should respond in several ways:

   1. Auditors with specialized skills and experience should be assigned to the audit.

   2. Careful consideration should be given to all accounting principles adopted.

   3. Auditors should attempt to become more unpredictable in testing (do not always stick with a pattern that the client might come to anticipate).

   4. Actual testing procedures (either substantive testing or tests of controls) should be modified:

      a. Additional amounts of testing should be performed.

      b. Tests should be designed to gather more reliable evidence.

- Rely more on sources from outside of the client.
- Use more physical inspection.
- Use more computer-assisted audit techniques to gather information from within computers.

c. Increase testing at year-end, rather than relying on interim tests of controls.

d. Perform analytical procedures at more segregated levels of information (e.g., by store, rather than for the company as a whole).

H. If at any time during an audit, the auditor discovers evidence that indicates that a misstatement exists in the financial records, the auditor must assess whether the possible misstatement could be material.

1. If not, the auditor need only inform a member of management at least one level above those involved.

2. If so, the auditor must:

   a. Inform management because the statements are the responsibility of management.

   b. Inform the audit committee (even if the matter is resolved by management).

   c. Consider the need for a qualified or adverse opinion if the matter is not resolved.

NEW RISK ASSESSMENT STANDARDS

INTRODUCTION

Risk is the basic fundamental concept that underlies the audit process. It is the acceptance by auditors that there is some level of uncertainty in performing the audit function. The primary way that auditors handle risk in planning audit evidence is through the application of the **audit risk model.** The source of the audit risk model is SAS 39 (AU 350) on audit sampling and SAS 47 (AU 312) on materiality and risk.

A. Risk assessment for financial reporting is management's process for identifying, analyzing, and responding to risks relevant to the preparation of financial statements in conformity with GAAP.

B. Risks relevant to financial reporting include external and internal events and circumstances that may occur and adversely affect an entity's ability to initiate, authorize, record, process, and report financial data consistent with the assertions of management in the financial statements.

C. Risks can arise or change due to circumstances such as the following:

1. Changes in operating environment

2. New personnel

3. New or revamped information systems

4. Rapid growth

5. Management assertions

6. New technology

7. New business models, products, or activities

8. Corporate restructurings

9. Expanded foreign operations

10. New accounting pronouncements

D. The auditor should obtain sufficient knowledge of the entity's risk assessment process to understand how management considers risks relevant to financial reporting objectives and decides about actions to address those risks.

E. In evaluating the design and implementation of the entity's risk assessment process, the auditor should consider how management identifies business risks relevant to financial reporting, estimates the significance of the risks, assesses the likelihood of their occurrence, and decides upon actions to manage them.

F. Risk assessment involves considering threats to the organization's objectives in the areas of operations, financial reporting and compliance with laws and regulations.

G. Auditors perform risk assessment procedures to properly assess the risks of material misstatement and engagement risks.

RISK ASSESSMENT PROCESS

To properly assess the risks of material misstatement risk, auditors must perform risk assessment procedures. The auditor should obtain an understanding of management's objectives, strategies and business risks that may result in material misstatement of the financial statements.

A. To assess the risk of material misstatement, the auditor performs the following:

1. <u>Identify the risk</u>. Risks are identified throughout the process of obtaining an understanding of the entity and its environment

2. <u>Establish the significance of that risk</u>. Relates the identified risks to what can go wrong

3. <u>Assess the likelihood of the risk occurring</u>. Considers whether the risks are of a magnitude that could result in a material misstatement of the financial statements.

4. <u>Develop specific actions to reduce the risk to an acceptable level</u>. Considers the likelihood that the risks could result in a material misstatement of the financial statements.

B. The auditor should use information gathered by performing risk assessment procedures, including the audit evidence obtained in evaluating the design of controls and determining whether they have been implemented, as audit evidence to support the risk assessment.

C. The auditor should use the risk assessment to determine the nature, timing, and extent of further audit procedures to be performed.

D. In making risk assessments, the auditor should identify the controls that are likely to prevent or detect and correct material misstatements in specific relevant assertions.

RISK ASSESSMENT PROCEDURES

A. The auditor should perform the following risk assessment procedures to obtain an understanding of the entity and its environment, including its internal control:

1. Inquiries of management and others within the entity

2. Analytical procedures

3. Observation and inspection

B. The auditor's understanding of the entity and its environment consists of an understanding of the following aspects:

1. Industry, regulatory, and other external factors

2. Nature of the entity

3. Objectives and strategies and the related business risks that may result in a material misstatement of the financial statements

4. Measurement and review of the entity's financial performance

5. Internal control, which includes the selection and application of accounting policies

RISK ASSESSMENT STANDARDS

A. Auditing Standards Board (ASB) of the AICPA approved eight Statements on Auditing Standards –SASs, collectively referred to as Risk Assessment Standards.

B. The statements, SAS No. 104 through SAS No. 111 are effective for audits of non-issuer financial statements for periods beginning on or after December 15, 2006.

C. Three objectives of the Auditing Standards Board in developing the Risk Assessment Standards, as they relate to auditors:

   1. A more in-depth understanding of the audited entity and its environment, including internal control

   2. A more rigorous assessment of risks of where and how the financial statements could be materially misstated

   3. Improved linkage between the auditor's assessed risks and the nature, timing and extent of audit procedures performed in response to those risks

D. Risk Assessment Standards establish standards and provide guidance concerning

   1. The auditor's assessment of the risks of material misstatement whether caused by fraud or error

   2. The design and performance of tailored audit procedures to address assessed risks

   3. Audit risks and materiality

   4. Planning and supervision of an audit

   5. Audit Evidence

E. The eight Statements on Auditing Standards relating to the assessment of risk in an audit of financial statements:

   1. SAS No. 104, *Amendment to Statement on Auditing Standards No. 1, Codification of Auditing Standards and Procedures* ("Due Professional Care in the Performance of Work")

      a. Statement SAS No. 104 amends Statement on Auditing Standards (SAS) No. 1, *Codification of Auditing Standards and Procedures* ("Due Professional Care in the Performance of Work), to expand the definition of the term *reasonable assurance*.

      b. Statement SAS 104 wording: While exercising of due professional care, the auditor must plan and perform the audit to obtain sufficient appropriate audit evidence so that audit risk will be limited to a low level that is, in the auditor's professional judgment, appropriate for expressing an opinion on the financial statements.

   2. SAS No. 105, *Amendment to Statement on Auditing Standards No. 95, Generally Accepted Auditing Standards*

a. SAS No.105 amendment revises Statement on Auditing Standards (SAS) No. 95, *Generally Accepted Auditing Standards*, to expand the scope of the second standard of field work from "internal control" to "the entity and its environment, including its internal control."

b. SAS No. 105 amendment extends the purpose from "planning the audit" to "assessing the risk of material misstatement of the financial statements whether due to error or fraud."

c. The phrase "further audit procedures" replaces "tests to be performed" in recognition that audit procedures also are performed to obtain the understanding on which the auditor's risk assessments are based.

d. SAS No. 105 amendment revises the third standard of field work to eliminate references to specific audit procedures.

e. SAS No. 105 amendment replaces the terminology "audit evidence" with "audit evidence."

f. SAS No. 105 amendment revises the auditing standards to clarify the terminology used in SASs issued by the Auditing Standards Board in describing the professional requirements imposed on auditors.

- *General Standards:*
  - The audit *must* be performed by a person or persons having adequate technical training and proficiency as an auditor.
- *Standards of Field Work:*
  - The auditor *must* adequately plan *the work* and *must properly supervise any* assistants.
  - The auditor *must obtain a* sufficient understanding of *the entity and its environment, including its* internal control, to *assess the risk of material misstatement of the financial statements whether due to error or fraud,* and to *design* the nature, timing, and extent of *further audit procedures.*
  - The auditor *must obtain* sufficient *appropriate audit evidence* by performing *audit procedures* to afford a reasonable basis for an opinion regarding the financial statements under audit.

3. SAS No. 106, Audit Evidence *(Supersedes Statement on Auditing Standards No. 31, Audit Evidence.)*

   a. Statement SAS No. 106 provides guidance about concepts underlying the third standard of field work: "The auditor must obtain sufficient appropriate audit evidence by performing audit procedures to afford a reasonable basis for an opinion regarding the financial statements under audit."

   b. Statement SAS No. 106:

   - Defines *audit evidence*

- Defines *relevant assertions* and discusses their use in assessing risks and designing appropriate further audit procedures
- Discusses qualitative aspects that the auditor considers in determining the sufficiency and appropriateness of audit evidence
- Describes various audit procedures and discusses the purposes for which they may be performed.

4. SAS No. 107, Audit Risk and Materiality in Conducting an Audit

   a. SAS No. 107 provides guidance on the auditor's consideration of audit risk and materiality.

   b. Audit risk is recognized in the description of the responsibilities and functions of the independent auditor.

   c. The concept of materiality recognizes that some matters, either individually or in the aggregate, are important for fair presentation of financial statements in conformity with GAAP. In performing the audit, the auditor is concerned with matters that, either individually or in the aggregate, could be material to the financial statements.

5. SAS No. 108, Planning and Supervision

   a. SAS No. 108 establishes standards and provides guidance to the independent auditor conducting an audit in accordance with generally accepted auditing standards on the considerations and activities applicable to planning and supervision.

   b. Obtaining an understanding of the entity and its environment, including its internal control, is an essential part of planning and performing an audit in accordance with generally accepted auditing standards. The auditor **must** plan the audit so that it is responsive to the assessment of the risk of material misstatement based on the auditor's understanding of the entity and its environment, including its internal control.

   c. The auditor with final responsibility for the audit may delegate portions of the planning and supervision of the audit to other firm personnel. For purposes of SAS No.108 (*a*) firm personnel other than the auditor with final responsibility for the audit are referred to as *assistants* and (*b*) the term *auditor* refers to either the auditor with final responsibility for the audit or assistants.

6. SAS No. 109, Understanding the Entity and Its Environment and Assessing the Risks of Material Misstatement

   a. SAS No.109 establishes standards and provides guidance about implementing the second standard of field work, as follows:

   - The auditor must obtain a sufficient understanding of the entity and its environment, including its internal control, to assess the risk of material misstatement of the financial statements whether due to error or fraud, and to design the nature, timing, and extent of further audit procedures.

b. SAS No. 109 details the audit procedures that the auditor should perform to obtain the understanding of the entity and its environment, including its internal control (risk assessment procedures).

c. SAS No. 109 provides guidance to the auditor in understanding specified aspects of the entity and its environment, and components of its internal control, in order to identify and assess risks of material misstatement, and in designing and performing further audit procedures.

7. SAS No. 110, Performing Audit Procedures in Response to Assessed Risks and Evaluating the Audit Evidence Obtained

    a. SAS No. 110 provides guidance to the auditor in determining overall responses to address risks of material misstatement at the financial statement level and provides guidance on the nature of those responses.

    b. SAS No. 110 provides guidance to the auditor in designing and performing further audit procedures, including tests of the operating effectiveness of controls, where relevant or necessary, and substantive procedures, whose nature, timing, and extent are responsive to the assessed risks of material misstatement at the relevant assertion level.

    c. SAS No.110 includes matters the auditor should consider in determining the nature, timing, and extent of such further audit procedures.

    d. SAS No.110 provides guidance to the auditor in evaluating whether the risk assessments remain appropriate and to conclude whether sufficient appropriate audit evidence has been obtained.

8. SAS No. 111, *Amendment to Statement on Auditing Standards No. 39,* Audit Sampling

    a. SAS No. 111 amends Statement on Auditing Standards (SAS) No. 39, *Audit Sampling*, to move guidance from the Appendix into SAS No. 107, *Audit Risk and Materiality in Conducting an Audit*, and into the text of this Statement (SAS No. 111).

    b. SAS No. 111 amends SAS No. 39 to incorporate guidance from SAS No. 99, *Consideration of Fraud in a Financial Statement Audit*, and from SAS No. 110, *Performing Audit Procedures in Response to Assessed Risks and Evaluating the Audit Evidence Obtained*.

    c. SAS No.111 amends SAS No. 39 to enhance guidance relating the auditor's judgment about establishing tolerable misstatement for a specific audit procedure and on the application of sampling to tests of controls.

QUESTIONS: AUDIT RISK

1. In planning an audit, the auditor's knowledge about the design of relevant internal control policies and procedures should be used to:
   A. assess the operational efficiency of internal control.
   B. document the assessed level of control risk.
   C. determine whether controls have been circumvented by collusion.
   D. identify the types of potential misstatements that could occur.

2. An auditor uses the knowledge provided by the understanding of internal control and the final assessed level of control risk primarily to determine the nature, timing, and extent of the:
   A. tests of controls.
   B. compliance tests.
   C. substantive tests.
   D. attribute tests.

3. Which of the following auditor concerns *most likely* could be so serious that the auditor concludes that a financial statement audit CANNOT be conducted?
   A. The integrity of the entity's management is suspect.
   B. Procedures requiring segregation of duties are subject to management override.
   C. The entity has no formal written code of conduct.
   D. Management fails to modify prescribed controls for changes in conditions.

4. An auditor uses the knowledge provided by the understanding of internal control and the assessed level of control risk primarily to:
   A. ascertain whether the opportunities to allow any person to both perpetrate and conceal fraud are minimized.
   B. determine the nature, timing, and extent of substantive tests for financial statement assertions.
   C. determine whether procedures and records concerning the safeguarding of assets are reliable.
   D. modify the initial assessments of inherent risk and preliminary judgments about materiality levels.

5. In planning an audit of a new client, an auditor would *most likely* consider the methods used to process accounting information because such methods:
   A. determine the auditor's acceptable level of audit risk.
   B. affect the auditor's preliminary judgment about materiality levels.
   C. influence the design of internal control.
   D. assist in evaluating the planned audit objectives.

6. Which of the following is the basic fundamental concept that underlies the audit process?
   A. Skepticism.
   B. Materiality.
   C. Risk.
   D. Consistency.
   E. All of the above.

7. Risk assessment for financial reporting is management's process for identifying, analyzing, and responding to risks relevant to the preparation of financial statements in conformity with:
   A. Generally Accepted Auditing Standards.
   B. Generally Accepted Accounting Standards.
   C. PCAOB Auditing Standards.
   D. Generally Accepted Accounting Principles.

8. Risks relevant to financial reporting include the basic internal events and circumstances that may occur and adversely affect an entity's ability to initiate, authorize, record, process, and report financial data consistent with the assertions of management in the financial statements.
   A. True.
   B. False.

9. Risk affecting the preparation of financial statements can arise or change due to circumstances such as:
   A. Corporate restructurings.
   B. Rapid growth.
   C. New accounting pronouncements.
   D. Ownership & rights.
   E. All of the above.

10. Auditors perform risk assessment procedures to properly assess the risks of which of the following:
    A. Misstatements and fraud.
    B. Misstatement and engagement risks.
    C. Fraud and Misappropriation of assets.
    D. Material errors and fraud.

11. The auditor should obtain sufficient knowledge of the entity's risk assessment process to understand how management considers risks relevant to financial reporting.
    A. True.
    B. False.

12. Risk assessment involves considering threats to the organization's objectives in the areas of:
    A. Operations, financial reporting and compliance with laws and regulations.
    B. Marketing, financial reporting and compliance.
    C. Financial reporting, performance and marketing.
    D. Compliance with laws and regulations, operations and performance.

13. In evaluating the design and implementation of the entity's risk assessment process, the auditor should consider how management identifies business risks relevant to financial reporting and decides upon actions to manage them.
    A. True.
    B. False.

14. The auditor should use the risk assessment to determine:
    A. Whether to accept the engagement.
    B. The type of 'opinion' to issue in the Audit Report.
    C. The size of the audit team.
    D. The nature, timing, and extent of further audit procedures to be performed.

15. In making risk assessments, the auditor should identify the controls that are likely to prevent or detect and correct material misstatements in specific relevant assertions.
    A. True.
    B. False.

16. To obtain an understanding of the entity and its environment, including its internal control, the auditor should perform each of the following risk assessment procedures EXCEPT:
    A. Inquiries of management and others within the entity.
    B. Attribute Sampling.
    C. Analytical procedures.
    D. Observation and inspection.

17. Auditing Standards Board (ASB) of the AICPA issued eight Statements on Auditing Standards –SASs, collectively referred to as Risk Assessment Standards applicable to all private and publicly trading companies.
    A. True.
    B. False.

18. The Risk Assessment Statements (SAS No. 104 through SAS No. 111) are effective for audits of non-issuer financial statements for periods beginning on or after December 15, 2006.
    A. True.
    B. False.

19. Risk Assessment SAS No. 104 amends Statement on Auditing Standards (SAS) No. 1, *Codification of Auditing Standards and Procedures* ("Due Professional Care in the Performance of Work), to expand the definition of the term:
    A. Reasonable assurance.
    B. Due professional care.
    C. Risk Assessment.
    D. All of the above.

20. In accordance with SAS No.105, which revises Statement on Auditing Standards (SAS) No. 95, *Generally Accepted Auditing Standards*, to expand the scope of the second standard of field work from "internal control" to:
    A. The entity and management assertions, including internal control.
    B. The entity and its environment, including its internal control.
    C. The entity and its business model, including internal control.
    D. The entity, including internal control.

21. In accordance with SAS No. 105 amendment replaces the terminology "audit evidence" with "audit evidence."
    A. True.
    B. False.

22. Risk Assessment SAS No. 105 amendment extends the purpose from "planning the audit" to "assessing the risk of material misstatement of the financial statements due to error."
    A. True.
    B. False.

23. Risk Assessment SAS No. 105 amendment extends the purpose from "planning the audit" to "assessing the risk of material misstatement of the financial statements due to fraud."
    A. True.
    B. False.

24. Risk Assessment SAS No. 105 amendment extends the purpose from "planning the audit" to "assessing the risk of material misstatement of the financial statements whether due to error or fraud."
    A. True.
    B. False.

25. In accordance with Risk Assessment SAS No. 105, which of the following correctly denotes the revised wording of the first General Standard of auditing?
    A. The audit must is to be performed by a person or persons with a college degree in accounting.
    B. The audit must is to be performed by a person or persons who are partners in a CPA firm.
    C. The audit must is to be performed by a person or persons having adequate technical training and proficiency as an auditor.
    D. The audit should is to be performed by a person or persons having adequate technical training and proficiency as an auditor.

26. In accordance with Risk Assessment SAS No. 105, which of the following correctly denotes the revised wording of the first Field Work Standard of auditing?
   A. The auditor needs to adequately plan the work and properly supervise any assistants.
   B. The auditor should adequately plan the work and properly supervise any assistants.
   C. The auditor must properly plan the work and must adequately supervise any assistants.
   D. The auditor must adequately plan the work and must properly supervise any assistants.

27. The auditor *must* obtain sufficient appropriate audit evidence by performing audit procedures to afford a (an) _____ basis for an opinion regarding the financial statements under audit.
   A. Accurate
   B. Correct
   C. Reasonable
   D. Justifiable

28. In performing the audit, the auditor is concerned with matters that, either individually or in the aggregate, could be material to the financial statements.
   A. True.
   B. False.

29. The auditor *must* plan the audit so that it is responsive to the assessment of the risk of material misstatement based on the auditor's understanding of the entity and its environment, including its internal control.
   A. True.
   B. False.

ANSWERS: AUDIT RISK

1. **D** The auditor should obtain an understanding of a client's internal control, including knowledge about the design of relevant policies, procedures and records, and whether they have been placed in operation by the entity. In planning the audit, such knowledge should be used to identify types of material misstatements, consider factors that affect the risk of material misstatements, and design substantive tests.

2. **C** Substantive tests are audit tests performed to substantiate the fairness of presentation of each account on the financial statements. The nature, timing, and extent of substantive tests is determined by the auditor's assessment of control risk.

3. **A** The auditor's understanding of an entity and its internal control may raise doubts about the auditability of that entity's financial statements. For example, concerns may arise about the integrity of the entity's management. These concerns may be so serious as to cause the auditor to conclude that the risk of management misrepresentations in the financial statements is such that an audit cannot be conducted.

4. **B** The second standard of field work states that, "The auditor should obtain a sufficient understanding of internal control to plan the audit and determine the nature, timing, and extent of tests to be performed." These tests are the substantive tests for financial statement assertions. The auditor does not use the knowledge provided by the understanding of internal control and the assessed level of control risk to determine the reliability of procedures to safeguard assets and opportunities to perpetrate and conceal fraud; instead, the safeguarding of assets and minimization of fraud affect the understanding of the control structure and assessment of control risk. Inherent risk, which is the susceptibility of a balance or transaction to an error, and materiality judgments are not directly affected by the control structure.

5. **C** AU 311 states that the auditor should consider the methods the entity uses to process accounting information because such methods influence the design of internal control. The extent to which computer processing is used in accounting applications, as well as the complexity of that processing, may also influence the nature, timing, and extent of audit procedures. The other answer choices are incorrect because materiality, audit objectives, and acceptable levels of audit risk are not based on the methods used to process accounting information.

6. **C** Risk is the basic fundamental concept that underlies the audit process. It is the acceptance by auditors that there is some level of uncertainty in performing the audit function.

7. **D** Financial statements are always prepared in conformity with Generally Accepted Accounting Principles (GAAP).

8. **B** False. Risks relevant to financial reporting include both external and internal events and circumstances that may occur and adversely affect an entity's ability to initiate, authorize, record, process, and report financial data consistent with the assertions of management in the financial statements.

9. E Risks relevant to financial reporting include external and internal events and circumstances that may occur and adversely affect an entity's ability to initiate, authorize, record, process, and report financial data consistent with the assertions of management in the financial statements.

10. B Auditors perform risk assessment procedures to properly assess the risks of material misstatement and engagement risks.

11. A True. The auditor should obtain sufficient knowledge of the entity's risk assessment process to understand how management considers risks relevant to financial reporting objectives and decides about actions to address those risks.

12. A Risk assessment involves considering threats to the organization's objectives in the areas of operations, financial reporting and compliance with laws and regulations.

13. B False. In evaluating the design and implementation of the entity's risk assessment process, the auditor should consider (1) how management identifies business risks relevant to financial reporting, (2) estimates the significance of the risks, (3) assesses the likelihood of their occurrence, and (4) decides upon actions to manage them.

14. D The auditor should use the risk assessment to determine the nature, timing, and extent of further audit procedures to be performed.

15. A True. This is the fundamental 'Test of Controls.' Yes, the auditor should identify the controls that are likely to prevent or detect and correct material misstatements in specific relevant assertions.

16. B Attribute sampling frequently used in performing test of controls when the auditor is looking for a 'rate', in most cases an error rate.

17. B False. The Auditing Standards Board (ASB) of the AICPA statements and pronouncements are applicable to non-issuers, private entities. The PCAOB is the authoritative source for publicly trading entities.

18. A True. The statements, SAS No. 104 through SAS No. 111 are effective for audits of non-issuer financial statements for periods beginning on or after December 15, 2006.

19. A Statement SAS No. 104 amends Statement on Auditing Standards (SAS) No. 1, Codification of Auditing Standards and Procedures ("Due Professional Care in the Performance of Work), to expand the definition of the term reasonable assurance.

20. B SAS No.105 amendment revises Statement on Auditing Standards (SAS) No. 95, Generally Accepted Auditing Standards, to expand the scope of the second standard of field work from "internal control" to "the entity and its environment, including its internal control."

21. A True. SAS No. 105 amendment replaces the terminology "audit evidence" with "audit evidence."

22. B False. SAS No. 105 amendment extends the purpose from "planning the audit" to "assessing the risk of material misstatement of the financial statements whether due to error or fraud."

23. B False. SAS No. 105 amendment extends the purpose from "planning the audit" to "assessing the risk of material misstatement of the financial statements whether due to error or fraud."

24. A True. SAS No. 105 amendment extends the purpose from "planning the audit" to "assessing the risk of material misstatement of the financial statements whether unintentional (error) or fraud (intentional)."

25. C SAS No. 105 amendment revises the auditing standards to clarify the terminology used in SASs issued by the Auditing Standards Board in describing the professional requirements imposed on auditors.

   General Standards #1: The audit must is to be performed by a person or persons having adequate technical training and proficiency as an auditor.

26. D SAS No. 105 amendment revises the auditing standards to clarify the terminology used in SASs issued by the Auditing Standards Board in describing the professional requirements imposed on auditors.

   Field Work Standard #2: The auditor must adequately plan the work and must properly supervise any assistants.

27. C The auditor must obtain sufficient appropriate audit evidence by performing audit procedures to afford a reasonable basis for an opinion regarding the financial statements under audit.

28. A True. The concept of materiality recognizes that some matters, either individually or in the aggregate, are important for fair presentation of financial statements in conformity with GAAP. In performing the audit, the auditor is concerned with matters that, either individually or in the aggregate, could be material to the financial statements.

29. A True. Obtaining an understanding of the entity and its environment, including its internal control, is an essential part of planning and performing an audit in accordance with generally accepted auditing standards. The auditor must plan the audit so that it is responsive to the assessment of the risk of material misstatement based on the auditor's understanding of the entity and its environment, including its internal control.

EVIDENCE GATHERING

STUDY MANUAL – AUDITING & ATTESTATION
CHAPTER 6

Study Tip: The more you know about the CPA exam, the more chance you have for success. Before you get too far into your preparation, go to ww.cpa-exam.org and read the official "Candidate Bulletin."

INTRODUCTION

The entire financial statement audit may be described as a process of evidence accumulation and evaluation. This process enables the auditor to formulate an informed opinion as to whether the financial statements are presented fairly in accordance with U.S. generally accepted accounting principles.

A. **Audit Evidence.** The third standard of fieldwork states: Sufficient competent audit evidence is to be obtained through inspection, observation, inquiries, and confirmations to afford a reasonable basis for an opinion regarding the financial statements under examination.

  1. *Audit evidence* is defined as all the underlying accounting data and all corroborating information that support the financial statements and that are available to the auditor.

     a. However, the books of original entry (journals), the general and subsidiary ledgers, related accounting manuals, and such informal and memorandum records as worksheets supporting cost allocations, reconciliations, and other computations are necessary, but not sufficient, support for the financial statements.

     b. The auditor must obtain corroborating or confirming evidence.

     c. This type of evidence includes documentary material such as checks, invoices, contracts, and minutes of meetings; confirmations and other written representation by knowledgeable people; information obtained by the auditor from inquiry, observation, inspection, and physical examination; and other information developed by or made available to the auditor.

  2. Competence (quality) of audit evidence. Competent audit evidence has two characteristics:

     a. *Relevance.* The relevance of audit evidence is a function of its usefulness in attaining audit objectives. If the audit evidence contributes to the attainment of audit objectives, it is relevant or useful.

b. *Validity.* The validity of audit evidence is based on the auditor's judgment, which is influenced by the source of the evidence. Three presumptions relate to the validity of evidence:

- Evidence from independent sources provides more assurance than evidence secured solely from within the entity.
- Information from direct personal knowledge is more persuasive than information obtained indirectly.
- Assertions developed under effective internal control are more reliable than those developed in the absence of internal control.

3. There are four broad sources of information and each has a different level of validity implied. They are:

   a. Evidence that has been developed and processed by the entity. This evidence has a low level of validity. Its basic validity is a function of the level of internal control for developing and processing the data (e.g., sales invoice).

   b. Evidence that has been developed by independent parties outside the entity, but which has been processed by the entity. This evidence has a moderate level of validity. Its validity is a function of the level of internal accounting control for processing such data (e.g., vendor's invoice).

   c. Evidence that has been developed by independent parties outside the entity and communicated directly to the auditor. This evidence has a high level of validity (e.g., attorney's letter).

   d. Evidence that has been obtained directly by the auditor through physical examination, observation, computation, and inspection. This evidence has the highest level of validity (e.g., observation of physical inventory).

4. Sufficiency (quantity) of audit evidence. Sufficiency, the amount of evidence necessary, depends upon the form of accountant association (examination, review, agreed-upon procedures, compilation) and is a matter of professional or experienced judgment.

   a. An auditor uses professional judgment to determine the extent of tests necessary to obtain sufficient evidence. In exercising this professional judgment, an auditor considers both the materiality of the item in question as well as the inherent risk of the item.

   b. In the greatest majority of cases, the auditor finds it necessary to rely on evidence that is persuasive rather than convincing.

   c. An acceptable level of audit risk does not indicate that all uncertainty be eliminated for sufficient evidence to have been gathered.

   d. The auditor must be able to form an opinion within a reasonable length of time, at a reasonable cost.

e. However, the difficulty or expense involved in testing a particular item is not in itself a valid reason for omitting a test.

f. Sufficient evidence has been gathered when audit risk is considered to be at an acceptable level.

5. Overall approach for substantive testing. The audit risk model decomposes audit risk (AR) into three components: inherent risk (IR), control risk (CR), and detection risk (DR). The audit risk model looks like this:

$$AR = IR \times CR \times DR$$

a. Based on the desired exposure, an auditor will establish a predetermined level of audit risk.

- The level of audit risk should generally be established at low levels.
- After considering the susceptibility of the account balance to misstatement, the auditor will assess inherent risk.
- Inherent risk represents the susceptibility of the account balance to misstatement.
- If an account balance is more highly susceptible to misstatement, the auditor would assess inherent risk at higher levels (and vice versa).

b. After obtaining an understanding of internal control, control risk is assessed.

- Control risk represents the risk that the client's internal control will fail to prevent and/or detect errors.
- As the internal control is judged to be more effective, control risk should be assessed at lower levels (and vice versa).

c. At this point, the auditor can "solve" the audit risk model for detection risk.

- Detection risk is the risk that the auditor's substantive testing procedures will fail to detect material financial statement misstatements.
- The auditor will establish his or her substantive tests (detection risk) at a level to reduce audit risk to the desired level.
- The table below displays how substantive tests relate to the necessary level of detection risk.

	Lower detection risk	*Higher detection risk*
Nature	Gather more competent forms of evidence	Gather less competent forms of evidence
Timing	Perform tests after year-end	Perform tests before year-end (at an interim date)
Extent	Examine a larger number of transactions or components	Examine a smaller number of transactions or components

- It is important to note that the auditor cannot totally eliminate substantive testing procedures for significant account balances or classes of transactions, regardless of the effectiveness of the client's internal control.
- Some level of substantive tests must be performed for significant account balances.
- The auditor's substantive tests may, however, be appropriately limited for lower levels of control risk.

6. Types of evidence

    a. *Corroborating evidence* is the supporting documentation that is the basis for a transaction being recorded in the journals and ledgers.

    b. The following is a list of types of corroborating evidence. Recall the list by using the mnemonic AICPAS.

        - **A**—Authoritative documents
        - **I**—Interrelationships
        - **C**—Calculations
        - **P**—Physical existence
        - **A**—Authoritative statements
        - **S**—Subsequent events

    c. *Authoritative documents*, such as truck titles, vendor invoices, etc., support ownership and transaction occurrence.

    d. *Interrelationships* within the data, such as interest expense and accrued interest payable, unusual items, etc., provide assurance as to the reasonableness of items and the absence of material misstatements due to errors.

    e. *Calculations* by the auditor, such as calculation of depreciation expense, tax liabilities, etc., support the application of GAAP.

    f. *Physical existence* is determined by the auditor's observation and count.

    g. *Authoritative statements* by a client provide support for the treatment of certain items in the recording and aggregation of transaction data. Authoritative statements by third parties, such as confirmations, provide evidence concerning the existence of transactions with third parties.

    h. *Subsequent events* confirm the status of estimates and assertions at the financial statement date. For example, subsequent collection of receivables gives evidence as to their valuation and collectibility. Court award of a lawsuit pending at year-end is evidence of the year-end payable or receivable.

B. Audit Programs

1. *Audit programs* are detailed lists of the audit procedures to be performed in gathering audit evidence.

a. Audit programs also provide evidence of audit planning, and indicate the nature, timing, and extent of the audit procedures to be performed.

b. Ultimately it is by way of the audit program that the auditor manages detection risk and audit risk.

c. The auditor will follow a three-step process in developing a plan of substantive audit procedures or an audit program for each account and transaction class to be examined:

- Determine and evaluate the specific assertions being made by management.
- Determine the audit objectives based on those assertions made by management.
- Determine the appropriate audit procedures to perform, which will depend on the types of audit evidence available for examination.

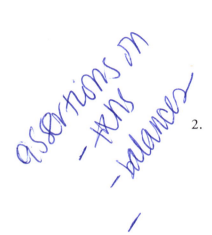

2. *Management assertions* are the representations by management that are implicitly or explicitly expressed in the financial statement components.

a. In general, the assertions fall into five broad categories.

b. The mnemonic PERCV may help you remember the assertions:

- **P**—Presentation and disclosure
- **E**—Existence or occurrence
- **R**—Rights and obligations
- **C**—Completeness
- **V**—Valuation or allocation

3. *Presentation and disclosure.* The various components of the financial statements are properly classified, described, and disclosed.

a. The presentation and disclosure assertion involves various issues related to different accounts.

b. Some examples include:

- If liabilities are classified as long term, management is indicating that these liabilities will *not* mature during the coming year.
- When assets are presented on the balance sheet, a presumption exists that these assets are available for management's use. Therefore, any restrictions or limitations on the use of assets (e.g., compensating balances for cash accounts; accounts receivable and inventory pledged as collateral; and liens on property, plant, and equipment) should be properly disclosed in the footnotes accompanying the financial statements.
- Significant accounting policies and procedures (method of accounting for inventories, depreciation methods, etc.) should be disclosed in the footnotes accompanying the financial statements.

4. *Existence or occurrence.* The assets and liabilities exist as of a given date and the recorded transactions have occurred during a given period.

   a. Because of the nature of assets and revenues, the auditor is more concerned about the assertion of existence or occurrence for these accounts than for liabilities and expenses.

   b. That is, entities are more likely to overstate assets and revenues intentionally than they would be to overstate liabilities and expenses.

      - For inventories presented on the balance sheet, management is indicating that the related inventory items actually exist.
      - For accounts receivable presented on the balance sheet, management indicates that the sales transactions giving rise to the accounts receivable actually occurred.

5. *Rights and obligations.* The assets are the rights of the entity and liabilities are the obligations of the entity as of a given date. For example:

   a. Recorded items of property, plant, and equipment are owned by the entity.

   b. Recorded liabilities represent obligations incurred on the part of the entity.

6. *Completeness.* The accounts and transactions reflected in the financial statements represent all of the accounts and transactions for the period.

   a. Simply stated, the completeness assertion indicates that all transactions have been recorded.

      - Recorded accounts receivable represent all sales made to customers on account during the period for which payment has not been received.
      - Recorded accounts payable represent all purchases made from vendors on account during the period for which payment has not been remitted.

   b. Because of the nature of liabilities and expenses, the auditor is more concerned with the completeness assertion for these accounts.

   c. One of the auditor's major types of substantive tests for liabilities is the search for unrecorded liabilities.

7. *Valuation or allocation.* The accounts have been included in the financial statements at the appropriate amounts, including appropriate allocations between balance sheet and income statement accounts.

   a. Cash has been recognized in the balance sheet at the proper dollar amount.

   b. The balance in long-term liabilities reflects all transactions at the proper dollar amounts.

8. *Audit objectives.* An audit plan will be based on the auditor's evaluation of the specific assertions made by management in the particular situation. Based on that evaluation, the auditor will establish the specific audit objectives to achieve during the audit.

   a. These objectives will differ for different account types and transaction classes.

   b. For example, with regard to assets, the auditor is more concerned with **actual** existence and ownership of the assets included in the financial statements.

   c. With respect to liabilities the auditor is more concerned that everything is included.

   d. The approach to audit objectives can be summarized best as follows:

Assets

Presentation and disclosure	Assets are appropriately classified, described, and disclosed in the financial statements.
Existence or occurrence	The reported assets actually exist.
Rights and obligations	The entity really owns and has clear title to the reported assets.
Completeness	There are no other undisclosed assets.
Valuation or allocation	The assets are valued appropriately and accurately.

Liabilities

Presentation and disclosure	Liabilities are appropriately classified, described, and disclosed in the financial statements.
Existence or occurrence	The reported liabilities actually exist.
Rights and obligations	The entity really owes the reported liabilities.
Completeness	There are no other undisclosed liabilities.
Valuation or allocation	The liabilities are valued appropriately and accurately.

Shareholders' Equity

Presentation and disclosure	Shareholders' equity balances and capital transactions have been properly classified, described, and disclosed in the financial statements.
Existence or occurrence	All recorded classifications within shareholders' equity are proper and all recorded changes in capital actually took place and were properly authorized.
Rights and obligations	Recorded equity balances pertain to the classes of stockholders indicated and the company and its stockholders were really parties to the capital transactions recorded.

Completeness	There are no omissions in the recording of equity classifications or capital transactions.
Valuation or allocation	Equity balances have been properly valued and capital transactions appropriately measured.

Income Components

Presentation and disclosure	The income components are appropriately classified, described, and disclosed in the financial statements.
Existence or occurrence	The reported transactions really occurred.
Rights and obligations	The entity, and not some other person or entity, was a party to the reported transaction.
Completeness	There are no other undisclosed transactions.
Valuation or allocation	The income components are measured appropriately and accurately in the correct period.

9. *Audit procedures.* After establishing the audit objectives, the auditor will determine the audit procedures that are appropriate for attaining the audit objectives. These procedures are referred to as substantive tests.

   a. There is not necessarily a one-to-one relationship between audit objectives and audit procedures. In some cases, a single procedure may accomplish more than one objective, whereas in other cases, it may require a combination of procedures to accomplish a single objective.

   b. The audit objectives do not change based on the methods used to process information, whether manual, mechanical, electronic, or a combination. The audit procedures, however, may be affected by the methods used to process data.

   c. The nature, timing, and extent of the audit procedures is a matter of professional judgment based on the particular circumstances. In making such judgments, the auditor must be assured that the audit objectives are attained.

   d. It may be difficult or impossible to access information without using information technology. The use of information technology may make it impractical for the auditor to reduce detection risk to an acceptable level by only performing substantive tests. It may be necessary to perform tests of controls in order to assess control risk.

   e. In some organizations significant accounting data may only be available in electronic form. Furthermore, the evidence may only be available for a limited period of time. Therefore, the nature, timing, and extent of the substantive tests and the tests of controls may be affected by a client's use of electronic data.

   f. *Substantive testing procedures* should be clearly distinguished from *tests of controls procedures.*

- As noted previously, tests of controls are used by the auditor to determine whether the client's internal control is functioning as intended. For example, by examining vendor invoices for initials, the auditor is verifying that client personnel checked these invoices for arithmetical accuracy.
- Substantive tests are concerned with whether transactions and components of the client's account balance are recorded according to generally accepted accounting principles. An example of a substantive test related to a vendor invoice would be comparing the amount of the vendor invoice with the journal entry representing the recording of that invoice.

g. The eight substantive testing procedures summarized in the following section can be classified into two categories.

- The first seven audit procedures are referred to as *tests of details of transactions*.
- These procedures require the auditor to examine evidence related to specific transactions or components of the account balance.

h. In contrast, *analytical procedures* are *tests of balances* and evaluate the account balance on an overall basis without examining specific components.

10. The Statement on Attestation Standards suggests two basic types of evidence collection procedures: (1) search and verification, and (2) internal inquiries and comparisons.

   a. Search and verification procedures include procedures such as inspecting assets, confirming receivables, and observing the counting of inventory.

   b. Internal inquiry and comparison procedures include discussions with firm representatives and analytical procedures such as ratio analysis.

   c. Audit procedures are undertaken by the auditor to obtain the corroborating evidence discussed above.

   d. Immediately following is a list of frequently used terms that represent distinct audit procedures.

11. Types of audit procedures

   a. *Confirmations.* Confirmations represent direct communication by the auditor with third parties. Some instances when confirmation may be useful include:

   - Accounts receivable (confirm with customers)
   - Cash (confirm with banks)
   - Accounts payable (confirm with vendors)
   - Inventory (confirm with parties holding inventory for sale)
   - Property, plant, and equipment (confirm with lessees for operating leases)

b. *Inspection.* The primary form of evidence supporting most transactions is some sort of authoritative documentary evidence that can be inspected. These authoritative documents include:

- Canceled checks and deposit slips (for cash)
- Sales invoices prepared by the client (for accounts receivable)
- Vendor invoices (for inventory)
- Vendor invoices, board of directors' minutes, contracts, leases, and amortization schedules (for property, plant, and equipment)

c. *Recalculation.* Recalculation involves the auditor mathematically verifying account balances or components that are determined through calculations. These include:

- Bad debt expense or allowance for bad debts
- Unrealized gain or loss on marketable securities
- Interest expense or revenue
- Depreciation expense or accumulated depreciation
- Premium or discount on bonds payable

d. *Observation and physical examination.* Physical existence can be determined by observation and count. The auditor can observe the items representing the account balance. These include:

- Cash
- Inventory
- Property, plant, and equipment
- Bonds and notes payable

e. *Inquiries.* The auditor will frequently make inquiries of management regarding various aspects of accounts. Some examples include:

- The existence of compensating balances or other restrictions on the use of cash (for cash)
- Methods used to identify delinquent accounts (for accounts receivable)
- Slow-moving or obsolete inventory items (for inventory)
- Management's intent with respect to holding various marketable securities (for investments)
- Contingent liabilities, such as potential litigation, commitments to purchase or sell inventory at a fixed price, and guarantees of debt for other parties (for liabilities)
- The existence of related parties and transactions with those parties

f. *Vouch.* Vouch from recorded entry to supporting documentation.

g. *Trace.* Trace from supporting documentation to recorded entry.

h. *Analytical procedures.* Analytical procedures involve comparisons of the relationships among financial and nonfinancial data. The auditor can perform procedures such as the following:

- Compare current accounts receivable to accounts receivable from one or more prior year(s).
- Evaluate the reasonableness of interest expense based on the balance in long-term liabilities.

12. Performing audit procedures. The following are frequently tested examples of the substantive testing procedures defined above:

   a. *Confirmations* involve a process in which the auditor obtains and evaluates information directly from third parties regarding financial statement assertions.

      - The process includes:
         - Selecting items for confirmation
         - Designing the confirmation request
         - Communicating the request to the appropriate third parties
         - Obtaining responses from the third parties
         - Evaluating the information and its reliability, or the lack of response from third parties, as appropriate
      - Confirmation provides a form of evidence that is highly reliable. The auditor will assess inherent and control risk, will determine the acceptable level of detection risk, and will design an audit program with the objective of minimizing audit risk.
      - It is generally accepted that evidence obtained from independent sources outside of the entity provides greater assurance than that obtained from within the entity. As a result, the degree of inherent and control risk will be a factor in determining whether or not the audit program should include the use of confirmations.
         - The greater the combined assessed level of inherent and control risk, the greater the assurance required from substantive testing and the greater the likelihood the auditor will use confirmation procedures.
         - The lower the combined assessed level of inherent and control risk, the less assurance required from substantive testing and the lower the likelihood the auditor will use confirmation procedures.
      - Properly designed confirmations can be used to support some or all of the financial statement assertions related to existence or occurrence, completeness, rights and obligations, valuation or allocation, or presentation and disclosure. Confirmations do not, however, address all assertions equally well and the auditor must consider what other procedures are necessary to provide the appropriate level of satisfaction.
         - Confirmations of goods held on consignment would be effective for the assertions related to existence and rights and obligations.
         - Accounts receivable confirmations relate to the assertion of existence.
         - Accounts payable confirmations can provide information about the assertion of completeness.
         - Bank confirmations may be used to provide information about the assertion of valuation or allocation.
      - The auditor should consider the assertions being addressed and factors that may affect the reliability of the confirmations, such as prior experience on the audit or similar engagements, the nature of the

information being confirmed, and the third party to whom the confirmation is addressed in determining the form of confirmation request to be used.
- There are two basic methods of confirmation: positive and negative.
  - *Positive*—Request that the debtor review the account balance indicated and respond to the auditor whether the amount is correct or incorrect. This method of confirmation is appropriate when the individual account balances are large, when a substantial number of accounts are expected to be incorrect due to errors or fraud, or when the auditor suspects that there is a disagreement between the client and customers. If positive confirmations are used, the auditor is expected to send second and sometimes third requests to nonrespondents. In any event, for each confirmation that is not returned, the auditor must obtain satisfactory evidence by examining various alternative sources of evidence such as subsequent cash receipts, cash remittance advices, and sales and shipping documents.
  - *Negative*—Request that the debtor respond to the auditor only if the requested information is incorrect. This method of confirmation is appropriate when the individual account balances are small, when the internal control is effective, and when there is no reason to believe that the receiving party will not return the confirmation request if necessary. This method is also used for confirmation of liabilities. The risk inherent in using this method is that the auditor may draw the wrong conclusion as a result of the lack of responses (i.e., that a lack of responses appears to indicate that balances are correct when the fact may be that the recipients ignored the confirmation requests). Generally, if negative confirmations are used, the number of requests sent is greater than for positive confirmations.
- When performing confirmation procedures, the auditor should maintain control over the confirmation requests and the responses. When confirmation responses are in some form other than written (such as in the form of a fax), the auditor should try to minimize the risk that the responses are not valid. The auditor may verify the source and contents, for example, in a phone call to the respondent.
- When an auditor does not receive a response to a confirmation, alternative procedures generally should be applied. It would be appropriate to decide not to apply alternative procedures if either there is no unusual pattern to the nonresponses (such as they all relate to transactions near year-end) or nonresponses in the aggregate would not have a material effect on the auditor's judgment relative to the assertion being tested. In the absence of a returned confirmation, an auditor could perform the following alternative procedures:
  - Review subsequent cash collections or disbursements.
  - Review sales invoices.
  - Review shipping documents.
- Alternative procedures will vary according to the circumstances. Examination of subsequent collections, for example, would be an appropriate procedure to provide evidence about the existence of accounts receivable. Likewise, examination of subsequent cash disbursements will provide evidence about accounts payable.

- Another use of confirmation involves a standard bank confirmation request. This is a communication sent directly from the bank to the auditor. A bank confirmation addresses two issues. First, it confirms the cash account balance as of the requested date (usually year end), and second it confirms loans on which the client is directly liable to the bank.
- If the auditor is prevented by the client or by circumstances from sending confirmations, the auditor should consider whether the scope limitation warrants a qualified opinion or a disclaimer. The outcome is based upon the auditor's professional judgment concerning significance.

b. *Observation.* Observation of inventories is a generally accepted auditing procedure. An auditor who issues an audit opinion without observing the inventories must be prepared to justify the opinion expressed.

- If the *periodic approach* to inventory is used, physical counts of inventories are to be made as of the balance sheet date or as of a single date within a reasonable time before or after the balance sheet date. The auditor is to observe such counts to determine that the inventory-taking procedures are sufficient to result in an accurate count of the inventory, to make test counts, to make inquiries concerning the inventory, to obtain shipping and receiving cut-off information, and to obtain direct information concerning the condition of the inventory.
- If the *perpetual record approach* to inventory is used, the perpetual record may be periodically compared by the client to the physical counts. In such cases, the auditor's observation procedures may be performed either during or after the end of the period under audit, assuming that the client maintains an effective internal control over inventory.
- Auditors may be engaged to examine financial statements covering the current period and other periods for which they did not observe or make physical counts of the inventory. As long as auditors are satisfied as to the current inventory, they are not precluded from issuing an unqualified opinion on the financial statements assuming that they are satisfied about the inventories for each of the other periods. Alternative auditing procedures, such as testing prior transactions, reviewing records of prior counts, and applying gross profit tests, may satisfy auditors about opening inventory balances.
- If the auditors cannot satisfy themselves by means of other auditing procedures with respect to opening inventories, a scope limitation exists and they should either disclaim an opinion or qualify the opinion on the statements of income, retained earnings, and cash flows, depending on the degree of materiality of the amount involved. An unqualified opinion may be issued on the balance sheet.
- If the auditor is prevented by the client or by circumstances from observing inventories, the auditor should consider whether the scope limitation warrants a qualified opinion or a disclaimer. The outcome is based upon the auditor's professional judgment concerning significance.
- If inventories are in the hands of outside parties, the usual audit procedure is to obtain direct written confirmations of those goods from the custodians. If the inventory in the hands of outside parties is a significant proportion of the current or total assets, the auditor is to apply at least one of the following procedures:

- Review and test the owner's control procedures for investigating the warehouseman and evaluating the warehouseman's performance.
- Obtain an independent accountant's report on the warehouseman's internal control relevant to custody of goods and, if applicable, pledging of receipts, or apply alternative procedures at the warehouse to gain reasonable assurance that information received from the warehouseman is reliable.
- Observe physical counts of goods, if practicable and reasonable.
- If warehouse receipts have been pledged as collateral, confirm with lenders pertinent details of the pledged receipts (on a test basis, if appropriate).

c. *Analytical procedures.* Analytical procedures consist of evaluations of financial information made by a study of plausible relationships (ratios and comparisons) among both financial and nonfinancial data. A basic premise underlying the application of analytical procedures is that relationships among data may reasonably be expected to exist and continue in the absence of known conditions to the contrary.

- Analytical procedures are used for the following purposes:
    - To assist the auditor in planning the nature, timing, and extent of other auditing procedures (required)
    - As a substantive test to obtain audit evidence about particular assertions related to account balances or classes of transactions (recommended)
    - As an overall review of the financial information in the final review stage of the audit (required)
- Analytical procedures involve comparisons of recorded amounts to expectations developed by the auditor. Some examples of sources of information for developing expectations:
    - Financial information for comparable prior periods giving consideration to known changes
    - Anticipated results from budgets, forecasts, or extrapolation of interim data
    - Relationships among elements of financial information within the period
    - Information regarding the industry in which the client operates, such as gross profit percentages
    - Relationships between financial information and relevant nonfinancial information
- The steps involved in using analytical procedures are generally as follows:
    - Select audit area and analytical procedure.
    - Develop and document an expectation.
    - Determine materiality parameters—the amount of difference from the expectation that can be accepted without investigation.
    - Perform the analytical procedure.
    - Compare the result of the analytical procedure with the expectation.

- Explain/propose adjustment for and document material differences between the result and the expectation.
- When developing an expectation, the auditor must attempt to identify plausible relationships. These expectations may be derived from:
  - The information itself in prior periods
  - Anticipated results such as budgets and forecasts
  - The relationship among elements of financial information within the period
  - Industry information
  - Relevant nonfinancial information
- Analytical procedures applied in planning the audit should focus on enhancing the auditor's understanding of the client's business and the transactions and events that have occurred since the last audit date, and identifying areas of high risk.
- Analytical procedures used as substantive tests will be designed to test specific assertions in the financial statements, and to identify potential misstatements in individual accounts and classes of transactions. The effectiveness and efficiency of applying analytical procedures depends upon:
  - The nature of the assertion
  - The plausibility and predictability of the relationship
  - The availability and reliability of the data used to develop the expectation
  - The precision of the expectation
- The more predictable the relationships among data, the more effective analytical procedures will be when used as substantive tests. Relationships in a stable environment are more predictable than in a dynamic or unstable environment. Relationships among income statement accounts represent transactions over a period of time and are more reliable than those among balance sheet accounts because they represent items as of a point in time. In addition, relationships involving transactions subject to management discretion may be less predictable.
- In planning the analytical procedures as a substantive test, the auditor should consider the amount of difference from the expectation that can be accepted without further investigation, based on materiality and relative risk considerations. The auditor should evaluate significant unexpected differences. Inquiry of management may assist in this regard, but this should be corroborated with other audit evidence.
- Analytical procedures are used in the overall review to assist the auditor in assessing the conclusions reached and in the evaluation of the overall financial statement presentation. The overall review would generally include reading the financial statements and notes and considering:
  - The adequacy of evidence gathered in response to unusual or unexpected balances identified in planning the audit or in the course of the audit
  - Unusual or unexpected balances or relationships in the financial statements or notes that were not previously identified

C. Audit Documents

1. The auditor prepares audit documents to document all audit procedures performed during an audit in order to:

    a. Aid the auditor in the conduct and supervision of the examination.

    b. Provide support for the auditor's opinion.

    c. Support the auditor's representation as to compliance with generally accepted auditing standards.

2. Various factors will determine the quantity, type, and content of audit documents:

    a. The nature of the engagement

    b. The nature of the auditor's report

    c. The nature of the financial statements, schedules, or other information being reported on

    d. The nature and condition of the client's records

    e. The degree of reliance on internal control and the assessed level of control risk

    f. The needs for supervision and review dictated by the circumstances surrounding the engagement

3. The auditor's documents normally contain sufficient information so that supplemental oral explanations are not required. The contents of the audit documents should demonstrate, as a minimum, that:

    a. The financial statements or other information reported on agrees with or has been reconciled to the accounting records.

    b. The work has been adequately planned and supervised.

    c. There has been a consideration of internal control and an assessment of control risk to determine the degree to which internal control may be relied upon and substantive testing restricted.

    d. Sufficient, competent audit evidence has been obtained and that the procedures applied and the tests performed have provided sufficient evidence to afford a reasonable basis for an opinion.

4. The Sarbanes-Oxley Act requires that registered firms must maintain audit documentation for each audit report for seven years. Documents related to an

audit generally will be maintained in two separate files, the current audit file and the permanent file.

a. Current audit file—includes information relative to the current audit that will not be of general use in future audits, other than to serve as guidelines for the work to be performed in the subsequent period.

b. Permanent file—includes all audit documents that are useful in the current audit and will have continuing usefulness in future engagements. They generally include:

- A copy of the engagement letter
- Copies of flowcharts of the client's accounting system
- Copies of, or abstracts from, the articles of incorporation
- Minutes of meetings of the board of directors, committees, and stockholders
- Major leases, agreements, bond trust indenture agreements, contracts, and preferred stock agreements
- Schedules of depreciation, amortization, depletion, and temporary differences for long-term assets and liabilities
- Other information that the auditor believes will be useful in future dealings with the client

Questions: Evidence Gathering

1. Which of the following procedures would an auditor *most likely* perform in obtaining evidence about subsequent events?
    A. Inquire about payroll checks that were recorded before year-end but cashed after year-end.
    B. Investigate changes in long-term debt occurring after year-end.
    C. Recompute depreciation charges for plant assets sold after year-end.
    D. Determine that changes in employee pay rates after year-end were properly authorized.

2. The permanent (continuing) file of an auditor's audit documents *most likely* would include copies of the:
    A. attorney's letters.
    B. debt agreements.
    C. lead schedules.
    D. bank statements.

3. When using the work of a specialist, an auditor may refer to and identify the specialist in the auditor's report if the:
    A. auditor expresses an adverse opinion as a result of the specialist's findings.
    B. auditor wishes to indicate a division of responsibility.
    C. specialist is not independent of the client.
    D. specialist's work provides the auditor greater assurance of reliability.

4. Audit programs should be designed so that:
    A. the auditor can make constructive suggestions to management.
    B. most of the required procedures can be performed as interim work.
    C. the audit evidence gathered supports the auditor's conclusions.
    D. most of the required procedures can be performed as interim work.

5. An auditor issued an audit report that was dual dated for a subsequent event occurring after the completion of fieldwork but before issuance of the auditor's report. The auditor's responsibility for events occurring subsequent to the completion of fieldwork was:
    A. Extended to subsequent events occurring through the date of issuance of the report.
    B. Extended to include all events occurring since the completion of fieldwork.
    C. Limited to include only events occurring up to the date of the last subsequent event referenced.
    D. Limited to the specific event referenced.

6. Analytical procedures used in the overall review stage of an audit generally include:
   A. retesting control procedures that appeared to be ineffective during the assessment of control risk.
   B. performing tests of transactions to corroborate management's financial statement assertions.
   C. considering unusual or unexpected account balances that were not previously identified.
   D. gathering evidence concerning account balances that have not changed from the prior year.

7. The date of the management representation letter should coincide with the date of the:
   A. latest related party transaction.
   B. auditor's report.
   C. latest interim financial information.
   D. balance sheet.

8. The audit document that reflects the major components of an amount reported in the financial statements is the:
   A. interbank transfer schedule.
   B. supporting schedule.
   C. carryforward schedule.
   D. lead schedule.

9. An auditor should examine minutes of board of directors' meetings
   A. on a test basis.
   B. through the date of the financial statements.
   C. only at the beginning of the audit.
   D. through the date of his report.

10. Which of the following factors *most likely* would affect an auditor's judgment about the quantity, type, and content of the auditor's audit documents?
    A. The content of the management representation letter.
    B. The likelihood of a review by a second (concurring) partner.
    C. The assessed level of control risk.
    D. The number of personnel assigned to the audit.

11. An auditor's decision either to apply analytical procedures as substantive tests or to perform tests of transactions and account balances usually is determined by the:
    A. relative effectiveness and efficiency of the tests.
    B. auditor's familiarity with industry trends.
    C. availability of data aggregated at a high level.
    D. timing of tests performed after the balance sheet date.

12. In using the work of a specialist, an understanding should exist among the auditor, the client, and the specialist as to the nature of the specialist's work. The documentation of this understanding should cover the:
    A. auditor's disclaimer as to whether the specialist's findings corroborate the representations in the financial statements.
    B. specialist's understanding of the auditor's corroborative use of the specialist's findings.
    C. conditions under which a division of responsibility may be necessary.
    D. auditor's disclaimer as to whether the specialist's findings corroborate the representations in the financial statements.

13. Which of the following statements concerning audit evidence is correct?
    A. An effective internal control contributes little to the reliability of the evidence created within the entity.
    B. The cost of obtaining evidence is not an important consideration to an auditor in deciding what evidence should be obtained.
    C. A client's accounting data cannot be considered sufficient audit evidence to support the financial statements.
    D. Competent evidence supporting management's assertions should be convincing rather than merely persuasive.

14. To obtain audit evidence about control risk, an auditor selects tests from a variety of techniques including:
    A. inquiry.
    B. analytical procedures.
    C. confirmation.
    D. calculation.

15. Which of the following auditing procedures *most likely* would assist an auditor in identifying related party transactions?
    A. Reviewing accounting records for nonrecurring transactions recognized near the balance sheet date.
    B. Inspecting communications with law firms for evidence of unreported contingent liabilities.
    C. Sending second requests for unanswered positive confirmations of accounts receivable.
    D. Retesting ineffective internal control procedures previously reported to the audit committee.

16. Which of the following statements is correct concerning an auditor's use of the work of a specialist?
    A. The work of a specialist who is related to the client may be acceptable under certain circumstances.
    B. If there is a material difference between a specialist's findings and the assertions in the financial statements, only an adverse opinion may be issued.
    C. The work of a specialist who is related to the client may be acceptable under certain circumstances.
    D. An auditor may not use a specialist in the determination of physical characteristics relating to inventories.

17. The audit program usually **CANNOT** be finalized until the:
    A. engagement letter has been signed by the auditor and the client.
    B. consideration of the entity's internal control has been completed.
    C. reportable conditions have been communicated to the audit committee of the board of directors.
    D. consideration of the entity's internal control has been completed.

18. Which of the following presumptions is correct about the reliability of audit evidence?
    A. To be reliable, audit evidence should be convincing rather than persuasive.
    B. An effective internal control provides more assurance about the reliability of audit evidence.
    C. Reliability of audit evidence refers to the amount of corroborative evidence obtained.
    D. Information obtained indirectly from outside sources is the most reliable audit evidence.

19. Analytical procedures used in the overall review stage of an audit generally include:
    A. gathering evidence concerning account balances that have not changed from the prior year.
    B. considering unusual or unexpected account balances that were not previously identified.
    C. performing tests of transactions to corroborate management's financial statement assertions.
    D. retesting control procedures that appeared to be ineffective during the assessment of control risk.

20. An auditor searching for related party transactions should obtain an understanding of each subsidiary's relationship to the total entity because:
    A. intercompany transactions may have been consummated on terms equivalent to arm's-length transactions.
    B. this may permit the audit of intercompany account balances to be performed as of concurrent dates.
    C. this may reveal whether particular transactions would have taken place if the parties had not been related.
    D. the business structure may be deliberately designed to obscure related party transactions.

21. Of the following which is the *least* persuasive type of audit evidence?
    A. Copies of sales invoices inspected by the auditor.
    B. Documents mailed by outsiders to the auditor.
    C. Computations made by the auditor.
    D. Correspondence between auditor and vendors.

22. Which of the following audit procedures would *most likely* assist an auditor in identifying conditions and events that may indicate there could be substantial doubt about an entity's ability to continue as a going concern?
    A. Confirmation of bank balances.
    B. Confirmation of accounts receivable from principal customers.
    C. Review compliance with the terms of debt agreements.
    D. Reconciliation of interest expense with debt outstanding.

23. Which of the following documentation is required for an audit in accordance with generally accepted auditing standards?
    A. A client engagement letter.
    B. A client representation letter.
    C. A planning memorandum or checklist.
    D. An internal control questionnaire.

24. An auditor would *least likely* initiate a discussion with a client's audit committee concerning:
    A. the methods used to account for significant unusual transactions.
    B. indications of fraud and illegal acts committed by a corporate officer that were discovered by the auditor.
    C. the maximum dollar amount of misstatements that could exist without causing the financial statements to be materially misstated.
    D. disagreements with management as to accounting principles that were resolved during the current year's audit.

25. An entity's income statements were misstated due to the recording of journal entries that involved debits and credits to an unusual combination of expense and revenue accounts. The auditor *most likely* could have detected this fraud by:
    A. performing analytical procedures designed to disclose differences from expectations.
    B. investigating the reconciliations between controlling accounts and subsidiary records.
    C. evaluating the effectiveness of internal control policies and procedures.
    D. tracing a sample of journal entries to the general ledger.

26. A written client representation letter *most likely* would be an auditor's *best* source of corroborative information of a client's plans to:
    A. settle an outstanding lawsuit for an amount less than the accrued loss contingency.
    B. terminate an employee pension plan.
    C. make a public offering of its common stock.
    D. discontinue a line of business.

27. Before reissuing the prior year's auditor's report on the financial statements of a former client, the predecessor auditor should obtain a letter of representations from the:
    A. former client's attorney.
    B. former client's board of directors.
    C. successor auditor.
    D. former client's management.

28. An auditor performs interim work at various times throughout the year. The auditor's subsequent events work should be extended to the date of:
    A. the next scheduled interim visit.
    B. a postdated footnote.
    C. the final billing for audit services rendered.
    D. the auditor's report.

29. Which of the following statements ordinarily is included among the written client representations obtained by the auditor?
   A. Management acknowledges responsibility for illegal actions committed by employees.
   B. Compensating balances and other arrangements involving restrictions on cash balances have been disclosed.
   C. Sufficient audit evidence has been made available to permit the issuance of an unqualified opinion.
   D. Management acknowledges that there are no material weaknesses in the internal control.

30. The third standard of fieldwork states that sufficient competent audit evidence is to be obtained through inspection, observation, inquiries, and confirmations to afford a reasonable basis for an opinion regarding the financial statements under audit. The substantive audit evidence required by this standard may be obtained, in part, through:
   A. analytical procedures.
   B. proper planning of the audit engagement.
   C. flowcharting internal control.
   D. auditor audit documents.

31. Which of the following types of audit evidence is the most persuasive?
   A. Client representation letter.
   B. Prenumbered client purchase order forms.
   C. Bank statements obtained from the client.
   D. Client worksheets supporting cost allocations.

32. After issuing a report, an auditor has *no* obligation to make continuing inquiries or perform other procedures concerning the audited financial statements, unless:
   A. information about an event that occurred after the end of fieldwork comes to the auditor's attention.
   B. information, which existed at the report date and may affect the report, comes to the auditor's attention.
   C. final determinations or resolutions are made of contingencies that had been disclosed in the financial statements.
   D. management of the entity requests the auditor to reissue the auditor's report.

33. Which of the following statements is correct about an auditor's required communication with an entity's audit committee?
   A. Weaknesses in internal control previously reported to the entity's audit committee are required to be communicated to the audit committee after each subsequent audit until the weaknesses are corrected.
   B. Any matters communicated to the entity's audit committee also are required to be communicated to the entity's management.
   C. Disagreements with management about the application of accounting principles are required to be communicated in writing to the entity's audit committee.
   D. The auditor is required to inform the entity's audit committee about significant errors discovered by the auditor and subsequently corrected by management.

34. To which of the following matters would materiality limits NOT apply in obtaining written management representations?
   A. The availability of minutes of stockholders' and directors' meetings.
   B. The disclosure of compensating balance arrangements involving related parties.
   C. Losses from purchase commitments at prices in excess of market value.
   D. Reductions of obsolete inventory to net realizable value.

35. Analytical procedures are:
   A. substantive tests designed to evaluate a system of internal control.
   B. compliance tests designed to evaluate the reasonableness of financial information.
   C. compliance tests designed to evaluate the validity of management's representation letter.
   D. substantive tests designed to evaluate the reasonableness of financial information.

36. To help plan the nature, timing, and extent of substantive auditing procedures, preliminary analytical procedures should focus on:
   A. applying ratio analysis to externally generated data such as published industry statistics or price indices.
   B. comparing recorded financial information to the results of other tests of transactions and balances.
   C. enhancing the auditor's understanding of the client's business and events that have occurred since the last audit date.
   D. developing plausible relationships that corroborate anticipated results with a measurable amount of precision.

37. A basic premise underlying the application of analytical procedures is that:
   A. statistical tests of financial information may lead to the discovery of material errors in the financial statements.
   B. plausible relationships among data may reasonably be expected to exist and continue in the absence of known conditions to the contrary.
   C. the study of financial ratios is an acceptable alternative to the investigation of unusual fluctuations.
   D. these procedures cannot replace tests of balances and transactions.

38. An auditor's audit documents serve mainly to:
   A. monitor the effectiveness of the CPA firm's quality control procedures.
   B. satisfy the auditor's responsibilities concerning the Code of Professional Conduct.
   C. provide the principal support for the auditor's report.
   D. document the level of independence maintained by the auditor.

39. Which of the following pairs of accounts would an auditor *most likely* analyze on the same audit document?
   A. Accrued interest receivable and accrued interest payable.
   B. Interest income and interest expense.
   C. Notes payable and notes receivable.
   D. Notes receivable and interest income.

40. Which of the following procedures would an auditor *most likely* perform in planning a financial statement audit?
    A. Comparing the financial statements to anticipated results.
    B. Inquiring of the client's legal counsel concerning pending litigation.
    C. Examining computer generated exception reports to verify the effectiveness of internal controls.
    D. Searching for unauthorized transactions that may aid in detecting unrecorded liabilities.

41. Which of the following would NOT be considered an analytical procedure?
    A. Computing accounts receivable turnover by dividing credit sales by the average net receivables.
    B. Projecting an error rate by comparing the results of a statistical sample with the actual population characteristics.
    C. Estimating payroll expense by multiplying the number of employees by the average hourly wage rate and the total hours worked.
    D. Developing the expected current-year sales based on the sales trend of the prior five years.

42. Which of the following material events occurring subsequent to the balance sheet date would require an adjustment to the financial statements before they could be issued?
    A. Loss of a plant as a result of a flood.
    B. Sale of long-term debt or capital stock.
    C. Major purchase of a business which is expected to double the sale volume.
    D. Settlement of litigation, in excess of the recorded liability.

43. In determining whether transactions have been recorded, the direction of the audit testing should be from the:
    A. general journal entries.
    B. adjusted trial balance.
    C. original source documents
    D. general ledger balances.

44. One reason why the independent auditor makes an analytic review of the client's operations is to identify:
    A. improper separation of accounting and other financial duties.
    B. unusual transactions.
    C. noncompliance with prescribed control procedures.
    D. weaknesses of a material nature in the system of internal control.

45. Which of the following statements is correct about the auditor's use of the work of a specialist?
    A. The auditor should obtain an understanding of the methods and assumptions used by the specialist.
    B. The client should not have an understanding of the nature of the work to be performed by the specialist.
    C. The auditor is required to perform substantive procedures to verify the specialist's assumptions and findings.
    D. The specialist should not have an understanding of the auditor's corroborative use of the specialist's findings.

46. An auditor ordinarily uses a working trial balance resembling the financial statements without footnotes, but containing columns for:
    A. reclassifications and adjustments.
    B. reconciliations and tickmarks.
    C. audit objectives and assertions.
    D. cash flow increases and decreases.

47. Which of the following presumptions does NOT relate to the competence of audit evidence?
    A. The more effective internal control, the more assurance it provides about the accounting data and financial statements.
    B. An auditor's opinion, to be economically useful, is formed within reasonable time and based on evidence obtained at a reasonable cost.
    C. Evidence obtained from independent sources outside the entity is more reliable than evidence secured solely within the entity.
    D. The independent auditor's direct personal knowledge, obtained through observation and inspection, is more persuasive than information obtained indirectly.

48. Which of the following procedures would an auditor *most likely* perform in auditing the statement of cash flows?
    A. Vouch all bank transfers for the last week of the year and first week of the subsequent year.
    B. Reconcile the amounts included in the statement of cash flows to the other financial statements' balances and amounts.
    C. Compare the amounts included in the statement of cash flows to similar amounts in the prior year's statement of cash flows.
    D. Reconcile the cutoff bank statements to verify the accuracy of the year-end bank balances.

49. Which of the following matters is an auditor required to communicate to an entity's audit committee?
    I. Disagreements with management about matters significant to the entity's financial statements that have been satisfactorily resolved.
    II. Initial selection of significant accounting policies in emerging areas that lack authoritative guidance.
    A. I only.
    B. II only.
    C. Both I and II.
    D. Neither I nor II.

50. What is an auditor's responsibility for supplementary information, such as segment information, which is outside the basic financial statements, but required by the FASB?
    A. The auditor's only responsibility for required supplementary information is to determine that such information has not been omitted.
    B. The auditor should apply tests of details of transactions and balances to the required supplementary information, and report any material misstatements in such information.
    C. The auditor has no responsibility for required supplementary information as long as it is outside the basic financial statements.
    D. The auditor should apply certain limited procedures to the required supplementary information, and report deficiencies in, or omissions of, such information.

51. In evaluating an entity's accounting estimates, one of an auditor's objectives is to determine whether the estimates are:
    A. based on objective assumptions.
    B. not subject to bias.
    C. reasonable in the circumstances.
    D. consistent with industry guidelines.

52. When an auditor does NOT receive replies to positive requests for year-end accounts receivable confirmations, the auditor *most likely* would:
    A. increase the assessed level of detection risk for the valuation and completeness assertions.
    B. increase the assessed level of inherent risk for the revenue cycle.
    C. ask the client to contact the customers to request that the confirmations be returned.
    D. inspect the allowance account to verify whether the accounts were subsequently written off.

53. Cooper, CPA, believes there is substantial doubt about the ability of Zero Corp. to continue as a going concern for a reasonable period of time. In evaluating Zero's plans for dealing with the adverse effects of future conditions and events, Cooper *most likely* would consider, as a mitigating factor, Zero's plans to:
    A. postpone expenditures for research and development projects.
    B. purchase production facilities currently being leased from a related party.
    C. discuss with lenders the terms of all debt and loan agreements.
    D. strengthen internal controls over cash disbursements.

54. Six months after issuing an unqualified opinion on audited financial statements, an auditor discovered that the engagement personnel failed to confirm several of the client's material accounts receivable balances. The auditor should first:
    A. request the permission of the client to undertake the confirmation of accounts receivable.
    B. inquire whether there are persons currently relying, or likely to rely, on the unqualified opinion.
    C. perform alternative procedures to provide a satisfactory basis for the unqualified opinion.
    D. assess the importance of the omitted procedures to the auditor's ability to support the previously expressed opinion.

55. When a CPA is approached to perform an audit for the first time, the CPA should make inquiries of the predecessor auditor. This is a necessary procedure because the predecessor may be able to provide the successor with information that will assist the successor in determining whether:
    A. the company follows the policy of rotating its auditors.
    B. the engagement should be accepted.
    C. the predecessor's work should be utilized.
    D. in the predecessor's opinion, internal control of the company has been satisfactory.

56. Which of the following procedures would an auditor *most likely* perform in searching for unrecorded liabilities?
    A. Trace a sample of accounts payable entries recorded just before year-end to the unmatched receiving report file.
    B. Vouch a sample of cash disbursements recorded just after year-end to receiving reports and vendor invoices.
    C. Compare a sample of purchase orders issued just after year-end with the year-end accounts payable trial balance.
    D. Scan the cash disbursements entries recorded just before year-end for indications of unusual transactions.

57. In creating lead schedules for an audit engagement, a CPA often uses automated audit document software. What client information is needed to begin this process?
    A. Specialized journal information such as the invoice and purchase order numbers of the last few sales and purchases of the year.
    B. Interim financial information such as third quarter sales, net income, and inventory and receivables balances.
    C. General ledger information such as account numbers, prior-year account balances, and current-year unadjusted information.
    D. Adjusting entry information such as deferrals and accruals, and reclassification journal entries.

58. "There are no violations or possible violations of laws or regulations whose effects should be considered for disclosure in the financial statements or as a basis for recording a loss contingency."
    The foregoing passage *most likely* is from a(an):
    A. report on compliance with laws and regulations.
    B. attestation report on an internal control.
    C. client engagement letter.
    D. management representation letter.

59. Because of the risk of material misstatement, an audit of financial statements in accordance with generally accepted auditing standards should be planned and performed with an attitude of:
    A. objective judgment.
    B. independent integrity.
    C. professional skepticism.
    D. impartial conservatism.

60. An auditor concludes that the omission of a substantive procedure considered necessary at the time of the examination may impair the auditor's present ability to support the previously expressed opinion. The auditor need not apply the omitted procedure if the:
    A. results of other procedures that were applied tend to compensate for the procedure omitted.
    B. results of the subsequent period's tests of controls make the omitted procedure less important.
    C. auditor's opinion was qualified because of a departure from generally accepted accounting principles.
    D. risk of adverse publicity or litigation is low.

61. Which of the following types of audit evidence is the *least* persuasive?
    A. Correspondence from the client's attorney about litigation.
    B. Test counts of inventory performed by the auditor.
    C. Bank statements obtained from the client.
    D. Prenumbered purchase order forms.

62. The accuracy of information included in footnotes that accompany the audited financial statements of a company whose shares are traded on a stock exchange is the primary responsibility of the:
    A. stock exchange officials.
    B. company's management.
    C. independent auditor.
    D. Securities and Exchange Commission.

63. Which of the following factors would *least* likely affect the quantity and content of an auditor's audit documents?
    A. The nature of the auditor's report.
    B. The content of the representation letter.
    C. The assessed level of control risk.
    D. The condition of the client's records.

64. Auditors try to identify predictable relationships when using analytical procedures. Relationships involving transactions from which of the following accounts *most likely* would yield the highest level of evidence?
    A. Interest expense.
    B. Accounts payable.
    C. Accounts receivable.
    D. Travel and entertainment expense.

65. Which of the following matters would an auditor *most likely* include in a management representation letter?
    A. Plans to acquire or merge with other entities in the subsequent year.
    B. Communications with the audit committee concerning weaknesses in the internal control structure.
    C. The completeness and availability of minutes of stockholders' and directors' meetings.
    D. Management's acknowledgment of its responsibility for the detection of employee fraud.

66. When auditing related party transactions, an auditor places primary emphasis on:
    A. confirming the existence of the related parties.
    B. ascertaining the rights and obligations of the related parties.
    C. verifying the valuation of the related party transactions.
    D. evaluating the disclosure of the related party transactions.

67. Which of the following statements would *least likely* appear in an auditor's engagement letter?
    A. Our engagement is subject to the risk that material errors or fraud, including fraud and defalcations, if they exist, will not be detected.
    B. After performing our preliminary analytical procedures we will discuss with you the other procedures we consider necessary to complete the engagement.
    C. During the course of our audit we may observe opportunities for economy in, or improved controls over, your operations.
    D. Fees for our services are based on our regular per diem rates, plus travel and other out-of-pocket expenses.

68. Which of the following documentation is **NOT** required for an audit in accordance with generally accepted auditing standards?
    A. An indication that the accounting records agree or reconcile with the financial statements.
    B. A written audit program setting forth the procedures necessary to accomplish the audit's objectives.
    C. The basis for the auditor's conclusions when the assessed level of control risk is below the maximum level.
    D. A client engagement letter that summarizes the timing and details of the auditor's planned fieldwork.

69. Which of the following procedures would an auditor *most likely* perform to obtain evidence about the occurrence of subsequent events?
    A. Investigating changes in stockholders' equity occurring after year-end.
    B. Recomputing a sample of large-dollar transactions occurring after year-end for arithmetic accuracy.
    C. Confirming bank accounts established after year-end.
    D. Inquiring of the entity's legal counsel concerning litigation, claims, and assessments arising after year-end.

70. An auditor's analytical procedures *most likely* would be facilitated if the entity:
    A. develops its data from sources solely within the entity.
    B. corrects material weaknesses in internal control before the beginning of the audit.
    C. uses a standard cost system that produces variance reports.
    D. segregates obsolete inventory before the physical inventory count.

71. Which of the following procedures would an auditor *least* likely perform before the balance sheet date?
    A. Confirmation of accounts payable.
    B. Observation of merchandise inventory.
    C. Identification of related parties.
    D. Assessment of control risk.

72. Which of the following matters is an auditor required to communicate to an entity's audit committee?
    A. The auditor's preliminary judgments about materiality levels.
    B. The process used by management in formulating sensitive accounting estimates.
    C. The basis for assessing control risk below the maximum.
    D. The justification for performing substantive procedures at interim dates.

73. In evaluating the reasonableness of an accounting estimate, an auditor *most likely* would concentrate on key factors and assumptions that are:
    A. consistent with prior periods.
    B. similar to industry guidelines.
    C. deviations from historical patterns.
    D. objective and not susceptible to bias.

74. Which of the following conditions or events *most likely* would cause an auditor to have substantial doubt about an entity's ability to continue as a going concern?
    A. Significant related party transactions are pervasive.
    B. Stock dividends replace annual cash dividends.
    C. Research and development projects are postponed.
    D. Cash flows from operating activities are negative.

75. Which of the following procedures is *least likely* to be performed before the balance sheet date?
    A. Search for unrecorded liabilities.
    B. Confirmation of receivables.
    C. Observation of inventory.
    D. Testing of internal control over cash.

76. A successor auditor *most likely* would make specific inquiries of the predecessor auditor regarding:
    A. specialized accounting principles of the client's industry.
    B. disagreements with management as to auditing procedures.
    C. the competency of the client's internal audit staff.
    D. the uncertainty inherent in applying sampling procedures.

77. Which of the following is **NOT** a typical analytical review procedure?
    A. Comparison of recorded amounts of major disbursements with budgeted amounts.
    B. Comparison of recorded amounts of major disbursements with appropriate invoices.
    C. Comparison of financial information with similar information regarding the industry in which the entity operates.
    D. Study of relationships of financial information with relevant nonfinancial information.

78. In using the work of a specialist, an auditor referred to the specialist's findings in the auditor's report. This would be an appropriate reporting practice if the:
    A. auditor, as a result of the specialist's findings, decides to indicate a division of responsibility with the specialist.
    B. client is not familiar with the professional certification, personal reputation, or particular competence of the specialist.
    C. auditor, as a result of the specialist's findings, adds an explanatory paragraph emphasizing a matter regarding the financial statements.
    D. client understands the auditor's corroborative use of the specialist's findings in relation to the representations in the financial statements.

79. Which of the following procedures would an auditor ordinarily perform first in evaluating management's accounting estimates for reasonableness?
    A. Obtain an understanding of how management developed its estimates.
    B. Consider the appropriateness of the key factors or assumptions used in preparing the estimates.
    C. Develop independent expectations of management's estimates.
    D. Test the calculations used by management in developing the estimates.

80. Which of the following circumstances *most likely* would cause an auditor to consider whether material misstatements exist in an entity's financial statements?
    A. Reportable conditions previously communicated to management are not corrected.
    B. Management places little emphasis on meeting earnings projections.
    C. The board of directors makes all major financing decisions.
    D. Transactions selected for testing are not supported by proper documentation.

81. The primary objective of analytical procedures used in the final review stage of an audit is to:
    A. satisfy doubts when questions arise about a client's ability to continue in existence.
    B. obtain evidence from details tested to corroborate particular assertions.
    C. assist the auditor in assessing the validity of the conclusions reached.
    D. identify areas that represent specific risks relevant to the audit.

82. The permanent file of an auditor's audit documents generally would NOT include (a):
    A. flowchart of internal control.
    B. working trial balance.
    C. lease agreements.
    D. bond indenture agreements.

83. Hill, CPA, has been retained to audit the financial statements of Monday Co. Monday's predecessor auditor was Post, CPA, who has been notified by Monday that Post's services have been terminated. Under these circumstances, which party should initiate the communications between Hill and Post?
    A. Hill, the successor auditor.
    B. Monday's controller or CFO.
    C. The chairman of Monday's board of directors.
    D. Post, the predecessor auditor.

84. Soon after Boyd's audit report was issued, Boyd learned of certain related party transactions that occurred during the year under audit. These transactions were not disclosed in the notes to the financial statements. Boyd should:
    A. determine whether the lack of disclosure would affect the auditor's report.
    B. ask the client to disclose the transactions in subsequent interim statements.
    C. recall all copies of the audited financial statements.
    D. plan to audit the transactions during the next engagement.

85. Which of the following circumstances is *most likely* to cause an auditor to consider whether a material misstatement exists?
    A. The turnover of senior accounting personnel is exceptionally low.
    B. Management places little emphasis on meeting earnings projections.
    C. Transactions selected for testing are not supported by proper documentation.
    D. Operating and financing decisions are dominated by several persons.

86. An auditor should obtain sufficient knowledge of an entity's accounting system to understand the:
    A. safeguards used to limit access to computer facilities.
    B. policies used to detect the concealment of fraud.
    C. procedures used to assure proper authorization of transactions.
    D. process used to prepare significant accounting estimates.

87. As a result of analytical procedures, the independent auditor determines that the gross profit percentage has declined from 30% in the preceding year to 20% in the current year. The auditor should:
   A. express an opinion which is qualified due to inability of the client company to continue as a going concern.
   B. consider the possibility of an error in the financial statements.
   C. evaluate management's performance in causing this decline.
   D. require footnote disclosure.

ANSWERS: EVIDENCE GATHERING

1. **B** The auditor is concerned with subsequent events, which occur subsequent to the balance-sheet date but prior to the issuance of the auditor's report, that may have a material effect on the financial statements and therefore require adjustment or disclosure in the statements. Because changes in long-term debt occurring after year-end may require disclosure to keep the financial statements from being misleading, the auditor should investigate such changes. The procedures described in the other answers would not likely reveal events that could have a material effect on the current financial statements.

2. **B** The permanent file of an auditor's audit documents contains information and documents of continuing interest. Examples of such items are debt agreements, the corporate charter and bylaws, contracts such as leases and royalty agreements, and continuing schedules of accounts whose balances are carried forward for several years. The other answers relate to the current year under audit and would be included in the current file of an auditor's audit documents.

3. **A** If the auditor decides to give an adverse opinion as a result of the report or findings of a specialist, reference to and identification of the specialist may be made if it will facilitate an understanding of the reason for the modified opinion. When expressing an unqualified opinion, the auditor should not refer to the work or findings of a specialist, whether or not the specialist's work provided reliable evidence or the specialist is independent of the client. Such a reference might be misunderstood to be a qualification of the auditor's opinion or a division of responsibility, neither of which is intended.

4. **C** AU 339 states that the purpose of a financial statement audit is to express an opinion regarding the presentation of the statements. The quantity, type, and content of audit documents vary with the circumstances, but they should be sufficient to show that the accounting records agree or reconcile with the financial statements or other information reported on and that the applicable standards of fieldwork have been observed. Audit documents ordinarily should include documentation showing that:

   - The work has been adequately planned and supervised, indicating observance of the first standard of fieldwork.
   - A sufficient understanding of internal control has been obtained to plan the audit and to determine the nature, timing, and extent of tests to be performed.
   - The audit evidence obtained, the auditing procedures applied, and the testing performed have provided *sufficient competent audit evidence* to afford a reasonable basis for an opinion.

5. **D** AU 530 states that the independent auditor has two methods available for dating the report when a subsequent event disclosed in the financial statements occurs after completion of fieldwork but before issuance of the report. He may use "dual dating," for example, "February 16, 19??, except for Note ?, as to which the date is March 1, 19??" or he may date the report as of the later date. In the former instance, the responsibility for events occurring subsequent to the completion of fieldwork is limited to the specific event referred to in the note or otherwise disclosed. In the latter instance, the independent auditor's responsibility for subsequent events extends to the date of the report and, accordingly, the subsequent events procedures should be extended to that date.

6. **C** The objective of analytical procedures in the final overall review stage of the audit is to assist the auditor in assessing the conclusions reached and in the evaluation of the overall financial statement presentation. The overall review would generally include considering unusual or unexpected balances or relationships that were not previously identified.

7. **B** Because the auditor is concerned with events occurring through the date of the auditor's report that may require adjustment to or disclosure in the financial statements, the representations included in the management representation letter should be dated as of the date of the auditor's report. The dates listed in the other answers are incorrect.

8. **D** The lead schedule is the audit document that reflects the major components of an amount reported in the financial statements.

9. **D** The review of corporate minutes is a standard part of work done in the subsequent period.

10. **C** Factors affecting the auditor's judgment about the quantity, type, and content of the audit documents for a particular engagement include: the nature of the engagement, the nature of the auditor's report, the nature of the financial statements on which the auditor is reporting, the nature and condition of the client's records, the assessed level of control risk, and the needs in the particular circumstances for supervision and review of the work.

11. **A** Substantive tests, which are comprised of analytical procedures and tests of details (transactions and account balances), must be performed to substantiate the financial statement assertions. The decision about which procedures to use to achieve a particular audit objective is based on the auditor's judgment on the expected effectiveness and efficiency of the available procedures.

12. **B** The understanding among the auditor, the client, and the specialist should be documented and should cover: the specialist's understanding of the auditor's corroborative use of the specialist's findings, the objectives and scope of the specialist's work, the specialist's relationship to the client, the methods or assumptions to be used, a comparison of the methods and assumptions to those used in the preceding period, and the form and content of the specialist's report.

13. **C** In planning the audit, the auditor should consider his preliminary judgment about materiality levels. In some situations, this is done before the financial statements under audit have been prepared. In such a situation, the auditor's preliminary judgment about materiality might be based on the entity's annualized interim statements, or financial statements of one or more prior annual periods. The other answers are incorrect because the auditor's preliminary judgment about materiality levels is considered in planning the audit, before sample sizes and substantive tests are planned, and before internal control questionnaires and management representation letters are prepared.

14. **A** AU 319 states that when the auditor assesses control risk at below the maximum level, he should obtain sufficient audit evidence to support that assessed level. The type of audit evidence, its source, its timeliness, and the existence of other audit evidence related to the conclusion to which it leads, all bear on the degree of assurance audit evidence provides. These characteristics influence the nature, timing, and extent of the tests of controls that the auditor applies to obtain audit evidence about control risk. The auditor selects such tests from a variety of techniques such as inquiry, observation, inspection, and reperformance of a policy or procedure that pertains to an assertion. No one specific test of controls is always necessary, applicable, or equally effective in every circumstance. The other answer choices are incorrect because they are direct tests of financial statement balances (substantive tests), and not tests of controls which provide evidence about control risk.

15. A   The auditor should test material transactions with parties related to the entity being audited to determine that the financial statements adequately disclose these related party transactions. Among the procedures an auditor would follow to identify these transactions is to review accounting records for large, unusual, or nonrecurring transactions or balances, paying particular attention to transactions recognized at or near the end of the reporting period.

16. C   Ordinarily, the auditor should attempt to obtain a specialist who is unrelated to the client. However, when the circumstances so warrant, work of a specialist who has a relationship with the client may be acceptable.

17. D   An audit program sets forth the audit procedures the auditor believes are necessary to accomplish the objectives of the audit. Audit procedures consist of tests of controls and substantive tests. The audit program cannot be finalized until the auditor completes his review of internal control because substantive tests are designed using the knowledge obtained from understanding internal control.

18. B   AU 326 states that to be competent, evidence must be both valid and relevant. The more effective internal control, the more assurance it provides about the reliability of accounting data and financial statements. The validity of audit evidence is so dependent on the circumstances under which it is obtained that generalizations about the reliability of various types of evidence are subject to important exceptions. If the possibility of important exceptions is recognized, however, the following presumptions, which are not mutually exclusive, about the validity of audit evidence in auditing have some usefulness:

    - When audit evidence can be obtained from independent sources outside an entity, it provides greater assurance of reliability for the purposes of an independent audit than that secured solely within the entity.
    - The more effective internal control, the more assurance it provides about the reliability of the accounting data and financial statements.
    - The independent auditor's direct personal knowledge, obtained through physical examination, observation, computation, and inspection, is more persuasive than information obtained indirectly.

19. B   The overall review would generally include reading the financial statements and notes and considering the adequacy of evidence gathered in response to unusual or unexpected balances identified in planning the audit or in the course of the audit, and unusual or unexpected balances or relationships that were not previously identified.

20. D   In determining the scope of work to be performed with respect to possible transactions with related parties, the auditor should obtain an understanding of management responsibilities and the relationship of each component to the total entity. Normally, the business structure is based on the abilities of management, tax and legal considerations, product diversification, and geographical location. Experience has shown, however, that business structure may be deliberately designed to obscure related party transactions. Therefore, when searching for related party transactions the auditor should obtain an understanding of each subsidiary's relationship to the total entity.

21. A   The competency (reliability) of evidence depends upon the degree of control exercised over the evidence by the client. The client does not have any control in the other answer choices. The client does have control over sales invoices and, thus, it is the least competent.

22. **C** Review of compliance with terms of debt and loan agreements is an audit procedure that may identify conditions and events that indicate there could be substantial doubt about an entity's ability to continue as a going concern for a reasonable period of time. Default on such agreements may indicate possible financial difficulty. The audit procedures listed in the other answers would be less likely to identify information about an entity's ability to continue as a going concern.

23. **B** There is a requirement that the independent auditor obtain certain written representations from management as a part of an examination made in accordance with generally accepted auditing standards. The documentation listed in the other answers is not required by auditing standards. An internal control questionnaire is one of several approaches to documenting the auditor's understanding of internal control. Auditors are encouraged to obtain an engagement letter to eliminate misunderstandings. An audit program is required; a planning memorandum is not.

24. **C** The auditor is required to communicate certain matters to those having responsibility for oversight of the financial reporting process, which is typically the audit committee. Generally the auditor must report items that relate to the scope and results of the audit process that may assist the audit committee with its oversight responsibility. Because materiality judgments made by the auditor do not directly affect the audit committee's responsibility, they are not typically communicated to that committee.

25. **A** AU 329 states that analytical procedures used in planning the audit generally use data aggregated at a high level. An unusual combination of expense and revenue accounts in a journal entry might result in unusual aggregate information.

26. **D** In some cases, the corroborating information that can be obtained by the application of auditing procedures other than inquiry is limited. When a client plans to discontinue a line of business, for example, the auditor may not be able to obtain information through other auditing procedures to corroborate the plan or intent. Accordingly, the auditor should obtain a written representation to provide confirmation of management's intent. The client's plans included in the other answers, in comparison to the plans to discontinue a line of business, could be more readily corroborated by other evidence.

27. **C** AU 508 states that before reissuing (or consenting to the reuse of) a report previously issued on the financial statements of a prior period, a predecessor auditor should consider whether his previous report on those statements is still appropriate. Either the current form or manner of presentation of the financial statements of the prior period or one or more subsequent events might make a predecessor auditor's previous report inappropriate. Consequently, a predecessor auditor should:

    - read the financial statements of the current period, compare the prior-period financial statements that he reported on with the financial statements to be presented for comparative purposes, and
    - obtain a letter from the successor auditor. The letter of representations should state whether the successor's audit revealed any matters that in the successor's opinion might have a material effect on, or require disclosure in, the financial statements reported on by the predecessor auditor.

28. **D** The auditor's subsequent events work extends through the date of his audit report.

29. B   The auditor is required to obtain written representations from management. The specific written representations ordinarily confirm oral representations given to the auditor and relate to management knowledge and intent. They ordinarily include disclosure of compensating balance or other arrangements involving restrictions on cash balances, and disclosure of line-of-credit or similar arrangements.

30. A   Substantive audit procedures include test of balances and analytical procedures. The objectives of analytical procedures are to gather evidence concerning the completeness of the items included in the financial statements, and to indicate unusual fluctuations in account balances that may require more detailed substantive audit procedures.

31. C   Evidence generated by external parties, such as a bank, is more competent, and therefore more persuasive, than evidence generated internally by the client. A bank statement, even if obtained from the client rather than directly from the bank, is more persuasive than internally-generated evidence. The other answers are examples of internally-generated documents, worksheets and letters, which are less persuasive than a bank statement.

32. B   An auditor has no responsibility to perform any additional auditing procedures after the audit report is issued except in the following two situations:

   1. The auditor omitted an auditing procedure that should have been performed, for example, obtaining a client representation letter, and

   2. Information that comes to the auditor's attention that existed at the report date, and this information, if known, may have affected the auditor's report.

33. D   Items that are usually communicated to the audit committee include significant accounting policies, management's process involved in determining significant accounting estimates, significant audit adjustments, disagreements with management and their resolution, consultation with other accountants, and difficulties encountered in the audit. Significant errors discovered by the auditor and subsequently corrected by management would fall under the items listed above.

34. A   A typical management representation letter refers to the completeness and availability of all minutes of meetings of stockholders, directors and committees of directors. Materiality does not apply to these minutes of meetings. The management representation letter typically also refers to the matters listed in the other answers, but materiality limits could apply to losses from purchase commitments, related party disclosures, and inventory reductions.

35. D   analytical procedures are substantive tests.

36. C   The purpose of applying analytical procedures in planning the audit is to assist in planning the nature, timing, and extent of auditing procedures that will be used to obtain audit evidence for specific account balances or classes of transactions. To accomplish this, the analytical procedures used in planning the audit should focus on enhancing the auditor's understanding of the client's business and the transactions and events that have occurred since the last audit date, and identifying areas that may represent specific risks relevant to the audit.

37. B   The application of analytical procedures to financial statements is based upon the presumption that plausible relationships exist among data (for example, that a company consistently marks up its products to earn a 30% gross profit). An auditor applying analytical procedures would then expect the gross profit percentage to be approximately 30%.

38. C   Audit documents are records kept by the auditor of the procedures applied, the tests performed, the information obtained, and the pertinent conclusions reached in an engagement. Audit documents serve mainly to provide the principal support for the auditor's report and to aid the auditor in the conduct and supervision of the engagement. Because audit documents are prepared for individual engagements, they do not address all of the broader issues raised by the other answers. For example, audit documents do not address contingent fees, which are dealt with in the Code of Conduct; hiring practices, which are part of CPA firm quality controls; and spousal ownership of client stock, which is an independence issue.

39. D   The interest income account should reflect interest earned during the period under audit. In analyzing interest income, the auditor would also analyze accounts, such as notes receivable, that affect the balance in the interest income account. The other answers list accounts that are independent of each other; that is, activity in the first account listed has no effect on the second account listed.

40. B   As part of planning, an auditor is required to use analytical procedures to enhance the auditor's understanding of the client's business and to identify areas that may represent specific risks relevant to the audit. Analytical procedures involve comparisons of financial statement amounts to expectations developed by the auditor. Anticipated results, such as budgets and forecasts, is one source for developing such expectations. Other sources include prior period information, current period relationships within the financial statements, industry information, and relevant nonfinancial information. Examining computer generated exception reports to verify the effectiveness of internal controls is a test of controls, not a planning procedure.

41. A   Analytical procedures consist of evaluations of financial information made by a study of plausible relationships among both financial and nonfinancial data, and involve comparisons of recorded amounts, or ratios developed from recorded amounts, to expectations developed by the auditor. Projecting error rates based on sample results relates more to tests of controls rather than to analytical procedures.

42. D   There are two types of subsequent events. 1. Requires disclosure of events of importance subsequent to the balance sheet date but prior to issuance of the report. The important point here is the amounts on the statements are correct as of year-end. 2. Requires a change in the amount previously determined as of the balance sheet date. New information is available that sheds new light on amounts previously estimated. The other answers are type 1, and the correct answer is type 2.

43. C   When testing to determine that transactions have been recorded, which relates to the completeness assertion, the auditor would select original source documents, such as sales invoices, and trace them to the records, such as the sales journal. The other answers could be starting points if the auditor wanted to determine that all recorded transactions were valid, which is the existence assertion. To test existence or occurrence, the auditor would start with ledger balances, an adjusted trial balance, or journal entries and vouch them back to source documents.

44. B   Comparison, trend and ratios are analytical tools used by the auditor to detect unusual transactions.

45. A AU 336 states that an understanding should exist among the auditor, the client, and the specialist as to the nature of the work to be performed by the specialist. Preferably, the understanding should be documented and should cover the following:

- The objectives and scope of the specialist's work.
- The specialist's representations as to his relationship, if any, to the client.
- The methods or assumptions to be used.
- A comparison of the methods or assumptions to be used with those used in the preceding period.
- The specialist's understanding of the auditor's corroborative use of the specialist's findings in relation to the representations in the financial statements.

Although the appropriateness and reasonableness of methods or assumptions used and their application are the responsibility of the specialist, the auditor should obtain an understanding of the methods or assumptions used by the specialist to determine whether the findings are suitable for corroborating the representations in the financial statements. The auditor should consider whether the specialist's findings support the related representations in the financial statements and make appropriate tests of accounting data provided by the client to the specialist.

46. A AU 329 states that the auditor's working trial balance includes the balances in the client's accounts which will become the final financial statement balances. To produce those final figures, the initial figures are reclassified to the correct accounts and adjusted to the correct balances required by generally accepted accounting principles. This is done with reclassification and adjustment columns in the working trial balance.

47. B There should be a rational relationship between the cost of obtaining evidence and the usefulness of the information obtained. However, when considering competency of evidence, time and cost are not relevant. The three presumptions made about the competency of evidence are presented in the other answers.

48. B The statement of cash flows presents amounts for financing and investing activities, which come from changes in balance sheet accounts, and operating activities, which come from income statement accounts. Therefore, the auditor, in auditing the statement of cash flows, would reconcile the amounts shown in that statement to the other financial statements.

49. C An auditor is required to ensure that the audit committee receives information regarding the scope and results of the audit. Included in the matters to be communicated are disagreements with management about significant matters (whether or not resolved) and the initial selection of and changes in significant accounting policies.

50. D Although the auditor has no responsibility to audit information outside the basic financial statements, he or she does have some responsibility regarding such information. The extent of such responsibility varies with the nature of the information. If the supplementary information is required by the FASB or GASB, the auditor should apply certain limited procedures and should report deficiencies in, or omission of, such information.

51. **C** The auditor's objective when evaluating accounting estimates is to obtain sufficient competent audit evidence to provide reasonable assurance that all accounting estimates that could be material to the financial statements have been developed; those accounting estimates are reasonable in the circumstances; and the accounting estimates are presented in conformity with applicable accounting principles and are properly disclosed.

52. **C** When the auditor has not received replies to positive accounts receivable confirmation requests, he or she should apply alternative procedures such as examining subsequent cash receipts. Before applying alternative procedures, the auditor would typically mail a second request and ask the client to encourage the customer to respond.

53. **A** If the auditor believes there is substantial doubt about the ability of an entity to continue as a going concern for a reasonable period of time, the auditor should consider management's plans for dealing with the adverse effects of the conditions and events that gave rise to the substantial doubt. The auditor's considerations relating to management's plans may include plans to dispose of assets, plans to borrow money or restructure debt, plans to reduce or delay expenditures, and plans to increase ownership equity. Postponing expenditures for research and development projects would be a way of delaying expenditures, which could mitigate the effects of conditions or events that gave rise to the auditor's substantial doubt.

54. **D** Before undertaking any audit procedures, the auditor would determine whether omitted procedures constitute the ability to issue an opinion. If the omitted procedures were deemed to be necessary to support the opinion issued, the auditor would attempt to perform such procedures.

55. **B** This is a major consideration for the successor CPA to determine whether to accept the engagement. "The successor auditor should make specific and reasonable inquiries of the predecessor regarding matters that the successor believes will assist him in determining whether to accept the engagement."

56. **B** An auditor searches for unrecorded liabilities to determine if there are liabilities that were not recorded in the year being audited that should be recorded in that year. A procedure performed to find these unrecorded liabilities is to vouch a sample of cash disbursements recorded just after year-end to receiving reports and vendor invoices. If the payment was for goods or services received before year-end, the auditor would review the details of accounts payable and other liabilities to determine that a liability is properly recorded as of year-end.

57. **C** Lead schedules are audit documents that contain unadjusted general ledger amounts for all accounts. In order to prepare these schedules, the names, account numbers, and unadjusted general ledger amounts must be determined. A typical lead schedule would appear as follows:

Client Name

Account Name and Number

Audit Date

Prior Year Balance	Current Year Balance	Adjustments Dr.	Cr.	Audited Balance
XXXX	YYY	ZZZ		YYYZZZ

58. D AU 317 states that the auditor ordinarily obtains written representations from management concerning the absence of violations or possible violations of laws or regulations whose effects should be considered for disclosure in the financial statements or as a basis for recording a loss contingency.

59. C An audit of financial statements in accordance with generally accepted auditing standards should be planned and performed with an attitude of professional skepticism, which means that the auditor neither assumes that management is dishonest nor assumes unquestioned honesty. The auditor attributes of objectivity, independence, integrity, impartiality, and conservatism presented in the other answers are desirable, but not specifically required in planning and performing an audit.

60. A When an auditor concludes that an auditing procedure considered necessary at the time of the examination was omitted from his examination of financial statements, he should assess the importance of the omitted procedure to his present ability to support his previously expressed opinion. A review of his audit documents, discussion of the circumstances, and a reevaluation of the overall scope of the examination may be helpful in making this assessment. For example, the results of other procedures that were applied may tend to compensate for the one omitted or make its omission less important. Also, subsequent examinations may provide audit evidence in support of the previously expressed opinion.

61. D Internal evidence, consisting of documents such as purchase orders that are produced within the client's system, is generally considered low in competence and therefore the least persuasive.

62. B The auditor is responsible for his report only; management is responsible for the statements and disclosures.

63. B AU 339 states that the factors affecting the auditor's judgment about the quantity, type, and content of the audit documents for a particular engagement include the:

- nature of the engagement,
- nature of the auditor's report,
- nature of the financial statements, schedules, or other information on which the auditor is reporting,
- nature and condition of the client's records,
- assessed level of control risk, and
- needs in the particular circumstances for supervision and review of the work.

64. A When using analytical procedures to identify predictable relationships, higher levels of evidence will be obtained when those relationships are most predictable. Relationships involving income statement accounts, such as interest expense, tend to be more predictable than relationships involving only balance sheet accounts, because income statement accounts represent transactions over a period of time rather than a point in time. Also, interest expense, which can be related to debt, is more predictable than the travel and entertainment expense, which is more subject to management discretion.

65. C Although the specific representations obtained by the auditor in a management representation letter will depend on the circumstances of the engagement and the nature and basis of presentation of the financial statements, they ordinarily include the completeness and availability of all minutes of meetings of stockholders, directors, and committees of directors.

66. **D** Established accounting principles ordinarily do not require transactions with related parties to be accounted for on a basis different from that which would be appropriate if the parties were not related. Therefore, the auditor should view related party transactions within the framework of existing pronouncements, placing primary emphasis on the adequacy of disclosure of such transactions. Because transactions with related parties are more likely to raise questions as to their economic substance, the auditor is more concerned with evaluating the disclosure of those transactions than with determining the rights of related parties, confirming the existence of related parties, or verifying the valuation of related party transactions.

67. **B** An engagement letter sets forth the terms of the engagement and the level of responsibility the auditor is assuming in the engagement. Typical points covered include the type of service to be performed, dates covered, professional standards to be followed, description of procedures to be employed, limited responsibility for detection of fraud, report on control deficiencies, other work to be performed, client assistance, and fees. The engagement letter does not typically include statements regarding future discussions about audit procedures after analytical procedures are performed.

68. **D** AU 311 states that an engagement letter is not normally required by GAAS. However, it would be foolish these days to operate without one. It focuses on the overall goals of the engagement, records to be provided by the client, and the type of report, the scope of the engagement, the timing of the fieldwork, a fraud disclaimer, and the set fee.

69. **D** The auditor should inquire of the entity's legal counsel regarding any events occurring after year-end as part of the auditor's search for subsequent events, which are events or transactions that occur subsequent to the balance sheet date but prior to the issuance of the auditor's report that have a material effect on the financial statements and therefore require adjustment or disclosure in the statements.

70. **C** The purpose of analytical procedures is to identify unusual fluctuations in data. Analytical procedures involve comparisons of recorded amounts or ratios developed from recorded amounts to expectations developed by the auditor. There are various sources of information, such as anticipated results reflected in budgets, for developing these auditor expectations. Since a standard cost system that produces variance reports is based on budgets, analytical procedures would be facilitated when such a system is used.

71. **A** Confirming accounts payable is the least likely procedure, of those listed, that the auditor would perform prior to the balance sheet date. The auditor would prefer to perform payables confirmation work as of year-end because, when auditing payables, the auditor is most concerned with the completeness of payables at the year-end balance sheet date.

72. **B** AU 380 states that accounting estimates are an integral part of the financial statements prepared by management and are based upon management's current judgments. Those judgments are normally based on knowledge and experience about past and current events and assumptions about future events. Certain accounting estimates are particularly sensitive because of their significance to the financial statements and because of the possibility that future events affecting them may differ markedly from management's current judgments. The auditor should determine that the audit committee is informed about the process used by management in formulating particularly sensitive accounting estimates and about the basis for the auditor's conclusions regarding the reasonableness of those estimates. The other answers are incorrect because they deal with the auditor's judgment and no explanation is needed to the committee.

73. **C** AU 342 states that the auditor should consider the historical experience of the entity in making past estimates as well as the auditor's experience in the industry. However, changes in facts, circumstances, or the entity's procedures may cause factors different from those in the past to become significant to the accounting estimate. In evaluating the reasonableness of an estimate, the auditor concentrates on key factors that are:

    - Significant to the accounting estimate
    - Sensitive to variations
    - Deviations from historical patterns
    - Subjective and susceptible to misstatement and bias

74. **D** AU 341 states that in performing audit procedures the auditor may identify information about certain conditions or events that, when considered in the aggregate, indicate there could be substantial doubt about the entity's ability to continue as a going concern for a reasonable period of time. The significance of such conditions and events will depend on the circumstances, and some may have significance only when viewed in conjunction with others. The following are examples of such conditions and events:

    - Negative trends—for example, recurring operating losses, working capital deficiencies, negative cash flows from operating activities, adverse key financial ratios.
    - Other indications of possible financial difficulties: default on loan or similar agreements, arrearages in dividends, denial of usual trade credit from suppliers, restructuring of debt, noncompliance with statutory capital requirements, need to seek new sources or methods of financing or to dispose of substantial assets.
    - Internal matters: work stoppages or other labor difficulties, substantial dependence on the success of a particular project, uneconomic long-term commitments, need to significantly revise operations. External matters that have occurred—for example, legal proceedings, legislation, or similar matters that might jeopardize an entity's ability to operate; loss of a key franchise, license, or patent; loss of a principal customer or supplier; uninsured or underinsured catastrophe such as a drought, earthquake, or flood.

75. **A** The auditor is concerned with unrecorded liabilities as of the balance sheet date (completeness assertion), thus audit procedures performed to identify unrecorded liabilities before the balance sheet date would be meaningless. Accounts receivable may be confirmed prior to the balance sheet date if the auditor concludes internal controls surrounding accounts receivable are effective. Inventory counts may be observed prior to year-end if the client maintains perpetual inventory records and the controls surrounding those records are effective.

76. **B** A successor auditor is required to make inquiries of the predecessor auditor regarding matters that the successor believes will assist him in determining whether he should accept a new audit engagement. The inquiries, which focus on the integrity of management and the reasons for the change in auditors, should include specific questions regarding disagreements with management as to accounting principles, auditing procedures, or other similarly significant matters.

77. **B** analytical procedures are designed to discover unusual relationships. The other answers are examples of analytical procedures.

78. **C** When expressing an unqualified opinion, the auditor should not refer to the work of a specialist because such a reference may be misunderstood. However, if as a result of the specialist's work, the auditor decides to depart from an unqualified opinion or to add a paragraph describing an uncertainty, a going concern issue, or an emphasis of a matter, the auditor may refer to the specialist in the auditor's report.

79. **A** The auditor is responsible for evaluating the reasonableness of accounting estimates made by management and, as a first step, should obtain an understanding of how management developed its estimates. Based on that understanding, the auditor should develop an independent expectation of the estimates, and/or review and test the process used by management to develop the estimates, and/or review subsequent events or transactions occurring prior to the completion of fieldwork.

80. **D** AU 316 states that if a condition or circumstance differs adversely from the auditor's expectation, the auditor needs to consider the reason for such a difference. For example:

    - Analytical procedures disclose significant differences from expectations.
    - Significant unreconciled differences between reconciliations of a control account and subsidiary records.
    - Confirmation requests disclose significant differences or yield fewer responses than expected.
    - Transactions selected for testing are not supported by proper documentation.
    - Supporting records or files that should be readily available are not promptly produced when requested.
    - Audit tests detect errors that apparently were known to client personnel, but were not voluntarily disclosed.
    - When such conditions exist, the planned scope of audit procedures should be reconsidered. As the differences from expectations increase, the auditor should consider whether the assessment of the risk of material misstatement of the financial statements made in the planning stage of the engagement is still appropriate.

81. **C** The objective of analytical procedures used in the overall review stage of the audit is to assist the auditor in assessing the conclusions reached and in the evaluation of the overall financial statement presentation.

82. **B** The permanent file would include information of continuing accounting significance, so that the auditor could refer to it year after year. This information could include a schedule of accumulated depreciation, an analysis of contingencies, bond and lease agreements which will be in effect in future years, and a flowchart of internal control. The trial balance is for a particular period and part of the current year audit documents.

83. **A** AU 315 states that the initiative in communicating rests with the successor auditor. The communication may be either written or oral. Both the predecessor and successor auditors should hold in confidence information obtained from each other. This obligation applies whether or not the successor accepts the engagement. Before contacting the predecessor, the successor auditor must have the permission from the client to do so.

84. **A.** If the auditor becomes aware of facts that existed at the report date, he should determine whether the facts would have affected the audit report. If they would have affected his report and people are currently relying on the report, the auditor should advise the client to make appropriate disclosures of the facts and their impact.

85. C If transactions are not supported by proper documentation, it may indicate that the transactions are fictitious. If so, the financial statements would be materially misstated.

86. D The auditor should obtain sufficient knowledge of the accounting system to understand the classes of transactions in the entity's operations that are significant to the financial statements; how those transactions are initiated; the accounting records, supporting documents, and specific accounts involved in processing and reporting transactions; the accounting processes involved from the initiation of a transaction to its inclusion in the financial statements, including how the computer is used; and the financial reporting process used to prepare financial statements, including significant estimates and disclosures. The process to prepare significant estimates is thus part of the accounting system, which consists of the methods and records established to identify, assemble, analyze, classify, record, and report an entity's transactions and to maintain accountability for the related assets and liabilities.

87. B analytical procedures are designed to detect unusual fluctuations in financial statement account balances. They are not conclusive evidence in the same respect as confirmation or documentation. The results of these analytical procedures should be investigated, however, if unusual relationships are revealed.

INTERNAL CONTROL

STUDY MANUAL – AUDITING & ATTESTATION
CHAPTER 7

Study Tip: No matter how busy you get preparing for the CPA exam, make time to exercise several times each week. Even 15 minutes of walking around your neighborhood every other day will help you release tension and keep your mind clear. Candidates often try to study every minute they are awake and then do not understand why they make careless mistakes and cannot concentrate. Get enough exercise so you can maximize the efficiency of your study time.

INTRODUCTION

The second standard of fieldwork states that a sufficient understanding of the internal control is to be obtained to plan the audit and to determine the nature, timing, and extent of tests to be performed.

Definition: An entity's internal control is a process effected by an entity's board of directors, management, and other personnel, and consists of the policies and procedures established to provide reasonable assurance that specific entity objectives will be achieved in the following categories: reliability of financial reporting, effectiveness and efficiency of operations, and compliance with applicable laws and regulations.

The standard and the definition point to an important inverse relationship between the effectiveness of internal control and the extent of detailed audit procedures. Therefore, the more effective an entity's internal control, the fewer detailed audit procedures are necessary. This relationship is based in the logic that the auditor is able to rely upon effective systems of internal control and is not able to rely upon ineffective systems of internal control.

THE ELEMENTS OF INTERNAL CONTROL

An entity's internal control consists of five elements: (1) control environment, (2) risk assessment, (3) control activities, (4) information and communication, and (5) monitoring. These five components provide a useful framework for analyzing the impact of internal controls on an audit.

A. **Control Environment.** The control environment reflects the overall attitude, awareness, and actions of the board of directors, management, owners, and others concerning the importance of control. The following seven control environment factors set the tone of an organization, influencing the control consciousness of its people.

1. Integrity and ethical values.

2. Commitment to competence.

3. Board of directors or audit committee participation.

4. Management's philosophy and operating style.

5. Organizational structure.

6. Assignment of authority and responsibility.

7. Human resource policies and practices.

B. **Risk Assessment.** Risk assessment for financial reporting purposes consists of an entity's identification, analysis, and management of risks relevant to the preparation of financial statements in conformity with GAAP. The following are considered risks that may affect an entity's ability to properly record, process, summarize, and report financial data:

1. Changes in the operating environment (e.g., increased competition).

2. New personnel.

3. New information systems.

4. Rapid growth.

5. New technology.

6. New lines, products, or activities.

7. Corporate restructuring.

8. Foreign operations.

9. Accounting pronouncements.

C. **Control Activities.** Control activities are those policies and procedures management has established to provide reasonable assurance that necessary actions are taken to address risks to specific entity objectives. These policies and procedures include the following:

1. *Performance reviews*—controls that should include the comparison of actual versus budgeted performance, as well as the procedures to ensure that corrective actions are performed in a timely manner.

2. *Information processing*—controls that check the accuracy, completeness, and proper authorization of transactions. They are classified into the two following groups:

a. General controls, which are procedures over:

- Development of new programs and systems.
- Revisions to existing programs and systems.
- Computer operations.
- Access to programs and data.

b. Application controls, which are procedures over the processing of the accounting data that are designed to ensure the accuracy, validity, completeness of processing, and proper authorization of the data.

3. *Physical controls*—controls that ensure that unauthorized access to the company's assets is restricted. These controls are particularly important for assets highly susceptible to theft or misappropriation, such as cash. Examples include depositing cash receipts intact and daily, preparing receiving reports upon receipt of the inventory, and preparing remittance listings to provide control over the initial receipt of cash. Additionally, the procedures should include frequent comparisons involving the account balances. These comparisons include the following:

a. Comparing the recorded balance to the physical asset (inventory).

b. Comparing the recorded balance to an external recording of that balance (bank reconciliations).

c. Comparing the subsidiary accounts to the control total (accounts receivable and accounts payable).

4. *Segregation of duties*—assigning the responsibilities of authorization, recording, custody, and comparison to different people.

D. **Information and Communication.**

1. Information and communication consist of the information systems that are relevant to the financial reporting objectives. These include the methods and records established to record, process, summarize, and report transactions and to maintain accountability for the related assets, liabilities, and equity. To be effective, the information and communication system must accomplish the following goals for transactions:

a. Identify and record all valid transactions.

b. Describe on a timely basis.

c. Measure the value properly.

d. Record in the proper time period.

e. Properly present and disclose.

f. Communicate responsibilities to employees.

2. The auditor should obtain a sufficient understanding of the information system relevant to the financial reporting to understand:

    a. The classes of transactions significant to the financial statements.

    b. How the transactions are initiated.

    c. The accounting records supporting the financial statements.

    d. The accounting processing involved, including the use of computers.

    e. The processes used to prepare the financial statements.

E. **Monitoring.** Monitoring consists of management's procedures to determine whether controls are functioning as intended and/or whether the controls should be modified. The monitoring may be accomplished in various ways, including the use of internal and/or external auditors. The auditor should obtain sufficient knowledge about the types of activities used by the client to monitor its controls.

F. **Additional Considerations.**

1. *Management responsibility.* Management is responsible for the establishment of the internal control and for ongoing supervision to determine if it is operating as intended and if it needs to be modified for changes in conditions.

2. *The Foreign Corrupt Practices Act.* This is a law passed by Congress in 1977 that amended the Securities and Exchange Act of 1934 to:

    a. Require every corporation registered under the Securities Exchange Act of 1934 to maintain a system of internal control sufficient to provide reasonable assurance that internal control objectives are met.

    b. Require every corporation registered under the Securities Exchange Act of 1934 to maintain accurate books and records.

    c. Make it illegal for individuals or business entities to make payments to foreign officials to secure business.

3. *Reasonable assurance.* There should be reasonable (not absolute) assurance that the objectives of the internal control system are being accomplished and that the costs of the controls do not exceed the benefits to be derived from them (cost-benefit relationship).

4. *Limitations.* Even the best internal control has inherent limitations due to:

    a. Faulty human judgment in decision making.

b. Human failures, such as errors from misunderstandings, mistakes, personal carelessness, and distraction or fatigue.

c. Circumvention of controls by collusion.

d. Management override of controls.

e. Cost constraints.

f. Failure of custom, culture, and the corporate governance system that may inhibit fraud, but cannot be an absolute deterrent.

5. *Applicability.* The applicability and importance of specific controls should be considered in the context of:

   a. The entity's size (small and midsized clients tend to have less formal systems than larger clients).

   b. Its organizational and ownership characteristics.

   c. The nature of its business.

   d. The diversity and complexity of its operations.

   e. Its methods of processing data.

   f. Its applicable legal and regulatory requirements.

6. *The Sarbanes-Oxley Act of 2002 (SOX).* As indicated earlier, SOX created a variety of new regulations and eliminated a significant portion of the accounting profession's system of self-regulation. Three particularly relevant sections are the following:

   a. **Section 302:** Makes officers responsible for maintaining effective internal control and requires the principal executive and financial officers to disclose all significant internal control deficiencies to the company's auditors and audit committee.

   b. **Section 404:** Requires management to acknowledge its responsibility for establishing adequate internal control over financial reporting and provide an assessment in the annual report of the effectiveness of internal control. It also requires auditors to attest to management's report on internal control as part of the audit of the financial statements.

   c. **Section 906:** Requires management to certify that reports filed with the SEC (primarily annual 10-K and quarterly 10-Qs) comply with the relevant securities laws and also fairly present, in all material respects, the financial condition and results of operations of the company.

7. *Internal auditors.* Internal auditing is performed by employees of the entity, rather than by an independent auditor. Internal auditors report to upper levels of management, the board of directors, or the audit committee about the effectiveness, efficiency, and accuracy of certain aspects of the entity. The higher the level to which the internal audit staff reports, the more independent the staff will be in performing its internal audit functions. Reporting to the audit committee provides the greatest atmosphere of organizational independence.

Although the work of internal auditors cannot be substituted for the work of the independent auditor, such work can affect the nature, timing, and extent of the independent auditor's work. Before relying on a client's internal auditors, the competence and objectivity of the internal auditors must be considered, and an evaluation of their work must be performed.

a. A determination as to the competence of internal auditors can be made through inquiries about their qualifications and the client's practices for hiring, training, and supervising the internal audit staff.

b. In considering the objectivity of the internal audit staff, the independent auditor should consider the organizational level to which it reports the results of its work, whether it has access to the audit committee, and whether there are policies preventing internal auditors from auditing areas where relatives are employed or the audit staff itself will be subsequently assigned. (One method for testing objectivity is to review the recommendations in internal audit reports.)

c. An independent auditor may evaluate the work of internal auditors by examining, on a test basis, documentary evidence of work performed. The independent auditor should consider the scope of the work, the adequacy of audit programs, the adequacy of audit documents, the appropriateness of conclusions reached, and the consistency of reports prepared with the work performed. The independent auditor should also perform tests of some of the work of the internal auditors, by either re-examining specific items examined by the internal auditors or by retesting populations tested by the internal auditors, and comparing the independent audit results with the internal audit results.

d. The independent auditor should keep in mind that the internal auditors are often concerned with details relating to the operations of the company that are not always relevant to the independent auditor.

When work of internal auditors is expected to be significant to the independent auditor's consideration of the internal control, the internal auditors should be informed of the reports and audit documents needed. With proper supervision and review, the independent auditor may use the internal auditors to assist in the performance of substantive tests or tests of controls. When the independent auditor considers the work of internal auditors or uses their direct assistance, any judgments as to the effectiveness of the internal control, sufficiency of tests performed, materiality of transactions, and other matters affecting the report on the financial statements must be the judgments of the independent auditor.

THE AUDITOR'S CONSIDERATION OF INTERNAL CONTROL

The auditor has two primary purposes for understanding internal control. The first is to determine the nature, timing, and extent of substantive tests (plan the audit), and the second is to assess control risk. In obtaining this understanding, the auditor will perform the following procedures required by GAAS:

- Obtain an understanding of internal control.
- Document the understanding of internal control.
- Form and document a preliminary assessment of control risk.
- Perform tests of controls.
- Determine the level of detection risk.
- Document the risk assessment.
- Communicate with the audit committee, if applicable.

A. **Obtain an Understanding of Internal Control.**

1. The auditor should obtain and document a sufficient understanding of each of the five elements of the entity's internal control to plan the audit of the entity's financial statements. The objectives of this knowledge are to:

    a. Identify types of potential misstatements.

    b. Consider factors that affect the risk of material misstatement.

    c. Design tests of controls when applicable.

    d. Design substantive tests.

2. The auditor is interested in determining what controls have been placed in operation. The auditor does not need to determine the operating effectiveness of the controls to obtain a proper understanding of the internal control.

3. If the auditor intends to rely on the client's internal control, tests of the operating effectiveness of internal control may be performed in conjunction with obtaining an overall understanding of the internal control. However, tests of controls are not required to be performed as the auditor obtains the overall understanding of the client's internal control.

    a. *Control environment.* In gaining an understanding of the control environment, the auditor must obtain sufficient knowledge to understand management's and the board of directors' attitude, awareness, and actions concerning the control environment. In other words, the substance of the policies, procedures, and actions is more important than the form. For example, the fact that a client has established a code of conduct does not mean it is being followed; nor does the establishment of an elaborate reporting system demonstrate the reports are being read.

b. *Risk assessment.* The auditor must obtain a sufficient knowledge to understand how management considers risks relevant to financial reporting objectives and decides about actions to address those risks. This knowledge generally includes obtaining an understanding of how management identifies risks, estimates the significance of risks, assesses the likelihood of their occurrence, and relates them to financial reporting.

c. *Control activities.* The auditor should obtain an understanding of those control activities relevant to planning the audit. While obtaining an understanding of the other components of internal control, the auditor obtains knowledge about some control activities. For example, while obtaining an understanding of accounting for cash disbursements, an auditor is likely to become aware of whether bank accounts are reconciled.

d. *Information and communication.* In gaining an understanding of the accounting system, the auditor should obtain sufficient knowledge to understand the following:

- The classes of transactions that are significant to the financial statements.
- How those transactions are initiated.
- The accounting records and support.
- The accounting manner of processing transactions.
- The financial reporting process used to prepare financial statements.
- The means the entity uses to communicate financial reporting roles and responsibilities.

e. *Monitoring.* The auditor should obtain sufficient knowledge of the major types of monitoring activities the entity uses to monitor internal control over financial reporting, including how those activities are used to initiate corrective action.

4. In gaining an understanding of the control policies and procedures, the auditor should recognize that the procedures followed to gain an understanding of the control environment and accounting system may provide sufficient understanding of the control policies and procedures to plan the audit, without additional effort. The auditor does not need an understanding of the control procedures related to each account balance, transaction class, and disclosure component in the financial statements. The understanding of the five elements of the internal control will come from various procedures, including:

   a. Previous experience with the entity.

   b. Inquiries of management and employees.

   c. Inspection of documents and records.

   d. Observation of activities and operations.

5. At this point in the audit, these procedures are performed primarily to help the auditor to understand the design and whether the controls have been placed in

operation. An auditor should distinguish between determining that controls are placed in operations versus evaluating their operating effectiveness. In determining whether controls have been placed in operation, the auditor determines that the entity is using them.

6. In evaluating operating effectiveness, the auditor goes further and considers:

   a. How the control was applied.

   b. The consistency with which it was applied.

   c. Who applied the control.

7. Tests of controls address the effectiveness of the design and operation of a control. Tests of controls are necessary to assess control risk below the maximum level.

B. **Document the Understanding of Internal Control.**

1. The documentation of an auditor's understanding of internal control for purposes of planning the audit is influenced by the size and complexity of the entity, as well as the nature of the entity's internal control. For a small client, a narrative may be sufficient. For a larger client, flowcharts, questionnaires, and decision tables may be needed. The more complex the internal control and the more extensive the procedures performed by the auditor, the more documentation is required. The types of documentation generally used include:

   a. An *internal control questionnaire*—a tool frequently used for obtaining and documenting an understanding of the internal control. The questionnaire will consist of questions to be asked of management. It will often be designed such that a negative response would indicate a weakness in internal control.

   b. A *narrative*—a written description (memorandum) of the entity's internal control.

   c. *Flowcharts*—charts that use symbols to depict the entity's internal control in pictorial form. Flowcharts are advantageous in that the auditor can quickly review the entity's entire internal control.

   d. *Decision tables*—graphic methods of describing the logic of decisions. Various combinations of conditions are matched to one of several actions. In an internal control setting, the various important controls are reviewed and, based on the combination of answers received, an action is taken, perhaps a decision on whether to perform tests of controls. For example:

	Rules						
Conditions	1	2	3	4	5	6	7
1. Segregation of function adequate	Y	Y	Y	Y	N	N	N
2. Adequate documents	Y	Y	N	N	Y	Y	N
3. Independent checks on performance	Y	N	Y	N	Y	N	–
Actions							
1. Perform all relevant tests of controls	X						
2. Perform limited tests of controls		X	X		X		
3. Perform no tests of controls				X		X	X

Note: In decision rule 7, because the first two conditions have received a no it doesn't matter what the third condition is, tests of controls will not be used. Also, while a decision table is an efficient means of describing the logic of an internal control process, it does not provide an analysis of document flow as does a flowchart.

C. **Form and Document a Preliminary Assessment of Control Risk.**

1. Assessing control risk is the process of evaluating the effectiveness of an entity's internal control in preventing or detecting material misstatements in the financial statements. This assessment is organized in terms of financial statement assertions, often by transaction cycle. After documenting an understanding of internal control, the auditor determines a planned assessed level of control risk for the various financial statement assertions.

2. For controls known to be *ineffective*, the planned assessed level of control risk will necessarily be established at the maximum level, and no tests of controls will be performed because no purpose is served by testing controls already known to be ineffective.

3. A decision must be made for controls that appear *effective*.

   a. First an auditor may establish the planned assessed level of control risk at the *maximum*. This may be the case when:

      - Internal control policies or procedures are unlikely to pertain to financial statement assertions.

- Internal control policies or procedures are unlikely to be effective.
- Evaluating the effectiveness of internal control polices or procedures is not efficient or cost effective (extensive substantive testing would be more efficient and less costly).
- No evidence on the operating effectiveness of the controls need then be gathered; that is, no tests of controls will be performed.

  b. Alternatively, when controls appear effective, the planned assessed level of control risk may be assessed *below the maximum level*. This may be the case when the auditor believes that a combination of tests of controls and a decreased scope of substantive tests is likely to be more efficient and cost effective than performing extensive substantive tests. Supporting such an assessment involves identifying specific internal control policies and procedures that are likely to prevent or detect material misstatements in specific financial statement assertions.

4. At this point in the audit, the auditor will have obtained the understanding of internal control necessary to plan the audit. During this process, the effectiveness of some controls may have been tested. If these controls justify an assessed level of control risk at the planned level, no more tests of controls need to be performed. Thus, there are three circumstances in which additional tests of controls will not be performed subsequent to obtaining an understanding to plan the audit.

   a. Controls are believed to be ineffective, and therefore, control risk is to be assessed at the maximum level.

   b. Controls are believed to be effective, but testing them is not efficient and cost effective. Therefore, control risk is to be assessed at the maximum level.

   c. Controls are believed to be effective, and evidence already obtained is adequate to support a planned assessed level of control risk that is below the maximum level. In most circumstances, though, the testing of the controls effectiveness will have been quite limited to this point, and the planned level will often not have been met. Therefore, additional tests of controls will be required.

D. **Perform Tests of Controls.**

1. When assessing control risk below the maximum level, the auditor should perform tests of controls to evaluate the operating effectiveness of these policies and procedures. Tests of controls are audit procedures directed toward either the effectiveness of the design or operation of an internal control policy or procedure. Approaches include:

   a. Inquiries of appropriate personnel.

   b. Inspection of documents and reports.

   c. Observation of the application of controls.

d. Reenactment of the control by the auditor.

2. As a result of the performance of tests of controls, the auditor should be able to determine if the identified control policies and procedures are actually in place. The auditor should also determine if they appear effective in the prevention or detection of material misstatements. If so, control risk may be assessed at a level below maximum.

3. For reasons of efficiency and practicality, auditors often perform tests of controls at a date prior to year end. Also, pertaining to observation, note that for many situations, only a limited number of observations of individuals performing controls are practical. The auditor must realize that generalizing the results of tests of controls beyond the period sampled is risky. It is for this reason that auditors must consider whether additional tests should be performed over untested periods to provide assurance that controls functioned over the entire period. Additionally, while auditors may consider audit evidence obtained from prior audits, they should obtain audit evidence in the current period to determine whether changes have occurred in internal control.

E. **Determine the Level of Detection Risk.**

1. The auditor uses the assessed level of control risk together with the assessed level of inherent risk to determine the acceptable level of detection risk for financial statement assertions. The lower the assessed level of control risk, the greater the acceptable level of detection risk. Thus, there is an inverse relationship between the assessed level of control risk and detection risk. The auditor uses the acceptable level of detection risk to determine the nature, timing, and extent of the substantive tests to be used to detect material misstatements in the financial statement assertions.

2. As the *assessed level of control risk decreases*, the auditor may modify the nature, timing, and extent of substantive tests. If the auditor assesses control risk at some level less than the maximum, the auditor has determined that control procedures are operating effectively and can be relied upon to prevent or detect material misstatements. Therefore, the nature of substantive tests may be changed to a less effective test; the timing of tests may be moved to interim periods rather than at year end; and selecting a smaller sample size may decrease the extent of substantive tests. It is important to emphasize that, to choose this approach, the auditor must perform tests of the operating effectiveness of internal control policies and procedures.

3. Conversely, if the auditor assesses control risk at the *maximum level*, the auditor has determined that control procedures are not operating effectively and cannot be relied upon to prevent or detect material misstatements. Therefore, the auditor will require more effective tests, generally performed at year end, using larger sample sizes.

F. **Document the Risk Assessment.**

1. The auditor needs to document assertions in which the assessed level of control risk is at the maximum level, but not the basis for the conclusion. For those assertions where the assessed level of control risk is below the maximum, the auditor should document the basis for this conclusion and the design and operation of internal control that supports that assessed level.

G. **Communicating With the Audit Committee.**

   1. The existence of an audit committee is a factor in the control environment. An audit committee is a group of outside directors whose functions typically include:

      a. Nominating and terminating independent auditors.

      b. Negotiating audit fees.

      c. Discussing broad, general matters concerning the type, scope, and timing of the audit with the independent auditor.

      d. Reviewing the financial statements and the public accounting firm's audit report.

      e. Working with the company's internal auditors.

   2. Auditors communicate with the audit committee on a variety of matters. Fraud and illegal acts must be communicated to the audit committee. Auditors are also required to communicate reportable conditions to the audit committee. A *reportable condition* is a significant deficiency in the design or operation of internal control that could adversely affect the organization's ability to record, process, summarize, and report financial data consistent with the assertions of management.

   3. The auditor's objective in an audit of financial statements is to form an opinion on the entity's financial statements as a whole. The auditor is not obligated to search for reportable conditions. The auditor may, however, become aware of these conditions as a by-product of audit work.

   4. These reportable conditions may be communicated orally (with the discussion documented in the audit documents), but is preferably written. The written report should:

      a. Indicate that the purpose of the audit was to report on the financial statements and not to provide assurance on the internal control.

      b. Include the definition of reportable conditions.

      c. State that it is intended solely for the use of the audit committee, management, and others in the organization (unless requirements established by governmental authorities require such reports, in which case the report may be provided).

5. A reportable condition may be so significant as to be considered a material weakness in internal control. A *material weakness* is a condition that does not reduce to a relatively low level the risk that material misstatements might occur and not be detected within a timely period by employees in the normal course of performing their assigned functions. Unless a different arrangement is made with the client, auditors are not required to classify reportable conditions as being material weaknesses.

6. The auditor may choose to communicate significant matters during the course of the audit or after it is concluded, as seems appropriate. If no reportable conditions were noted during the audit, then no written communication should occur. There is great potential for misunderstanding when the auditor issues a written report that indicates that no reportable conditions were found.

7. Finally, the following communications are required on SEC engagements, as well as engagements of other companies with active audit committees or boards of directors:

   a. Auditor responsibility under GAAS.

   b. Material audit adjustments.

   c. Uncorrected misstatements determined by management to be immaterial.

   d. Auditor responsibility for other information in documents containing audited financial statements.

   e. Significant accounting policies.

   f. Important management judgments and accounting estimates.

   g. Quality of accounting principles (only required for SEC registrant clients).

   h. Disagreements with management.

   i. Management consultation with other accountants.

   j. Major issues discussed with management prior to retention.

   k. Difficulties encountered in performing the audit.

   l. Materially misstated interim information that has been filed with, or is about to be filed with, a regulatory agency such as the SEC and on which management fails to take proper corrective action.

INTERNAL CONTROL IN OPERATING CYCLES

INTRODUCTION

A. After obtaining and documenting an understanding of a client's internal control, the auditor may deem it efficient to test control procedures to attempt to justify a significant reduction in control risk. The steps the auditor will accordingly take are as follows:

1. Select a cycle.

2. Identify the specific objectives for the cycle.

3. Review the client's stated internal control procedures for the cycle.

4. Design tests of control procedures for the cycle.

5. Perform tests of controls.

6. Evaluate the test results.

7. Determine control risk for the cycle.

B. An accounting information system (AIS) consists of a series of subsystems or operating cycles. The typical operating cycles are:

1. Sales, receivables, and cash receipts.

2. Purchases, payables, and cash disbursements.

3. Inventories and production.

4. Personnel and payroll.

5. Financing.

6. Investing.

C. In each operating cycle, certain internal control considerations must be incorporated to provide reasonable assurance that the objectives of the accounting information system are being achieved. Specific objectives apply to each subsystem within the system, and procedures can be prescribed to increase the likelihood that the objectives will be met. These objectives include control procedures which help ensure:

1. Validity of transactions.

2. Proper authorization (general or specific) of transactions.

3. Complete recording of transactions.

4. Proper valuation of transactions.

5. Proper classification of transactions.

6. Proper timing of transactions.

7. Proper inclusion of transactions in subsidiary records.

8. Safeguarding of assets and records.

D. These objectives can be achieved if the organization incorporates some or all of the following characteristics:

1. There is an organization chart complete with job descriptions.

2. There is adequate segregation of duties.

3. There are independent checks on performance.

4. Financial reports are prepared for management on a regular basis and allow for comparison of actual amounts to projected amounts.

5. There are proper procedures for authorization.

6. Operating budgets and cash budgets are being utilized.

7. There are adequate documents and records.

8. There is an independent internal audit function.

9. There are physical controls over assets and financial and accounting records.

10. The board of directors has regular meetings in which policies and objectives are established and the performance of the entity is reviewed.

11. There is a proper chart of accounts.

12. Established policies and procedures are written and communicated properly.

13. There are regular book-to-physical-asset reconciliations.

14. Individuals handling cash, securities, or other liquid assets are subject to background investigations and are bonded.

15. Transactions are initiated on prenumbered documents, whenever appropriate, with timely accountability of the numerical sequence.

SALES, ACCOUNTS RECEIVABLE, AND CASH RECEIPTS

A. The sales, accounts receivable, and cash receipts cycle consists of the basic functions of marketing and sales (including order taking and processing), credit management, inventory or warehousing, shipping, billing and collection, and accounting (accounts receivable and cash receipts).

B. There are various key documents (multiple copy form) that evolve during the sales, accounts receivable, and cash receipts cycle:

1. Customer purchase order.

2. Sales order.

3. Bill of lading.

4. Sales invoice.

5. Cash receipt remittance.

6. Advice remittance listing.

7. Bank deposit slip.

8. Bank reconciliation.

C. If accounting controls are not adequate in the sales, accounts receivable, and cash receipts cycle, there could be:

1. Unauthorized acceptance of orders.

2. Shipments to unauthorized customers.

3. Violations of pricing policies.

4. Negligent handling of returned sales.

5. Improper write-offs of customer accounts.

6. Improper distribution of sensitive information to competitors or other parties internal or external to the entity.

7. Misappropriation of assets.

D. The basic process for the sales, accounts receivable, and cash receipts cycle is:

1. The customer submits a purchase order.

2. The sales or order processing department prepares a sales order.

3. Credit approval is then obtained from the credit department.

4. The inventory is checked to determine if the goods are available for sale or whether they will have to be back-ordered through production or purchasing.

5. If the sale goods are in inventory, they will be identified as sold.

6. The sales order is transmitted to the warehouse.

7. The goods are transferred to shipping, which identifies the appropriate carrier based on the customer's instructions.

8. A shipping document (e.g., bill of lading) is prepared.

9. The goods are transferred to the carrier.

10. The billing department prepares the sales invoice and sends it to the customer.

11. Sales invoice information is used to post to the sales journal, the general ledger, and the accounts receivable subsidiary ledger.

12. The customer pays the account and a remittance advice is enclosed to describe which invoice the customer is paying.

13. As a preventative control, two individuals open the mail, list the checks, and send them to a cashier.

14. The cashier receives the customer's cash receipt (e.g., cash, check, credit card), prepares a deposit slip, and makes the deposit.

15. The cash receipt information (cash receipt remittance advice) is transmitted to accounts receivable for updating of the cash receipts journal, the general ledger, and the accounts receivable subsidiary ledger.

E. The important control procedures for the sales, accounts receivable, and cash receipts cycle are summarized below.

1. Authorization of transactions.

    a. Authorized price listings should be used in preparing sales invoices.

    b. Credit should be granted by the credit department.

    c. Approval of sales on account should be evidenced by preparation of a sales order or other form of authorization.

    d. Sales returns should be presented to the receiving clerk who prepares a receiving report that supports prenumbered credit memos.

e. Approval of adjustments to write-off or credit accounts receivable for discounts or allowances should be approved by management that is independent of the recordkeeping responsibility.

2. Recording of transactions.

   a. Prenumbered, multiple-part documents should be used for recording transactions related to the sales, accounts receivable, and cash receipts cycle.

3. Custody of assets.

   a. A shipping document, shipping advice, or bill of lading should be prepared to provide evidence of the quantities shipped. This document should be dated after the approval of the sale.

   b. A receipt for any goods sent through an external carrier should be obtained.

   c. Cash receipts received in the mail should be listed by individuals with no record-keeping responsibility. The cash goes to the cashier and the remittance advice goes to accounting.

   d. Checks received through the mail should be restrictively endorsed.

   e. Over-the-counter cash receipts should be controlled using cash register tapes.

   f. Cash should be deposited daily.

   g. Employees handling cash should be bonded.

   h. If possible and practical, a lockbox (a post office box controlled by the company's bank) should be used for receipt of customer remittances. The bank collects customer remittances, immediately credits the cash to the company's bank account, and forwards the remittance advices to the company. A lockbox system is considered an extremely effective control because company employees have no access to cash and bank employees have no access to company accounting records.

4. Comparison.

   a. Subsidiary ledgers should be reconciled to the general ledger monthly.

   b. An individual independent of receivable posting should review monthly statements before sending them to customers.

   c. Monthly statements should be sent to customers. Any differences between the monthly statements and the recorded accounts receivable reported by customers should be investigated.

   d. The quantities from the shipping advice or bill of lading should be compared to the quantities listed on the sales invoice.

e. Client personnel should recalculate the footings and extensions on sales invoices.

f. Remittance advices should be reconciled to remittance listings.

g. Upon receipt of monthly bank statements, an individual independent of cash receipts recordkeeping should reconcile the bank statements.

h. An individual independent of recordkeeping responsibilities should periodically account for the numerical sequence of all prenumbered documents.

5. Segregation of functions.

a. The functions of authorizing sales on account, authorizing credits to accounts receivable (sales discounts, sales returns, sales allowances, or write-offs), recording accounts receivable, and having custody of cash receipts should be segregated.

b. Persons responsible for reconciling cash balances should not have access to cash receipts or recordkeeping responsibility related to cash.

PURCHASES, ACCOUNTS PAYABLE, AND CASH DISBURSEMENTS CYCLE

A. Another major subsystem of the accounting information system is the purchases, accounts payable, and cash disbursements cycle, which consists of the basic functions of purchasing, receiving, warehousing, accounts payable, and cash disbursements.

B. There are various key documents and records that evolve during the purchases, accounts payable, and cash disbursements cycle:

1. Purchase requisition.

2. Purchase order.

3. Receiving report.

4. Inspection report.

5. Inventory record.

6. Purchase invoice.

7. Payment voucher.

8. Purchases journal.

9. Voucher register.

10. Vendor statement.

11. Check.

12. Check register.

13. Cash disbursements journal.

14. Bank statement.

15. Bank reconciliation.

C. If accounting controls are not adequate in the purchases, accounts payable, and cash disbursements cycle, there could be:

1. Purchases from unauthorized vendors.

2. Acceptance of unauthorized orders.

3. Violations of pricing policies.

4. Negligent handling of purchase returns.

5. Improper write-offs of inventory.

6. Improper distribution of sensitive information to competitors or other parties internal or external to the entity.

D. The basic process for the purchases, accounts payable, and cash disbursements cycle is:

1. A purchase requisition is sent by the department in need of the supplies to the purchasing department.

2. The purchasing department determines the proper quantity and vendor for the purchase and prepares a purchase order.

3. Copies of the purchase order are sent to the vendor and to the receiving department.

4. When the goods are received, a receiving report is prepared by the receiving department and forwarded to the accounting department.

5. A vendor's invoice is received by the accounting department.

6. The accounting department matches the vendor invoice with the receiving report and the purchase order and approves the payment.

7. A check and remittance advice is subsequently sent to the vendor in accordance with the terms of the sale.

8. The purchase order, receiving report, and vendor's invoice are stamped paid to prevent duplicate payments.

E. The important control procedures for the purchases, accounts payable, and cash disbursements cycle are summarized below.

1. Authorization of transactions.

    a. Purchases on account should be authorized through the preparation of prenumbered purchase orders.

    b. A separate purchasing department should make purchases.

    c. Payments for purchases on account should be authorized through the preparation of a voucher.

    d. Authorized signatures should be required on checks—two for large check amounts.

    e. Checks only should be signed with appropriate support.

2. Recording of transactions.

    a. Prenumbered, multiple-part documents (purchase requisitions, purchase orders, receiving reports, vouchers, and checks) should be used for recording transactions related to the purchases, accounts payable, and cash disbursements cycle.

    b. Separate documentation should be used for goods accepted or released on consignment.

    c. Voided checks should be mutilated, retained, and accounted for.

3. Custody of assets.

    a. A perpetual inventory system should be used to record purchases and sales of inventory.

    b. Receiving reports should be prepared upon receipt of the inventory.

    c. Access to inventories should be safeguarded and protected from loss due to fire and other natural disasters.

    d. Adequate insurance coverage should be maintained against losses for its inventories.

    e. All disbursements, except those from petty cash, should be made by check.

    f. Supplies of unused checks should be properly safeguarded by the client.

g. Checks should be mailed immediately after signing and not handled by others who participated in the check-preparation process.

h. Supporting documentation should be canceled or marked as "paid" to prevent duplicate payments.

i. Checks should be prepared using a mechanical check protector.

j. If a check-signing machine is used, the key to the machine or signature plate should be secured.

4. Comparisons.

   a. Quantities of inventory on hand should be periodically reconciled to perpetual inventory records.

   b. Information from vendor invoices (quantities, prices, and descriptions of goods) should be compared to similar information on purchase orders and receiving reports.

   c. The footings and extensions on vendor invoices should be recalculated.

   d. Statements from vendors should be reconciled to accounts payable records.

   e. The subsidiary accounts payable records should be reconciled to the control total of accounts payable.

   f. Upon receipt of monthly bank statements, an individual independent of cash disbursements record keeping should reconcile the bank statements.

   g. An individual independent of record keeping responsibilities should periodically account for the numerical sequence of all prenumbered documents.

5. Segregation of functions.

   a. Purchasing personnel should be independent of receiving and record keeping.

   b. Accounts payable personnel should be independent of purchasing, receiving, and disbursements.

   c. Persons responsible for reconciling cash balances should not have access to cash receipts or record-keeping responsibility related to cash.

INVENTORIES AND PRODUCTION CYCLE

A. Inventories and production fit under the first two cycles. However, due to the unique nature of inventories, separate coverage is warranted. The primary objectives of internal control for this cycle are to provide assurance that transactions are properly executed and recorded and custody of raw materials, work-in-process, and finished goods inventories is properly maintained. Two cases will be considered: a nonmanufacturing firm and a manufacturing firm.

B. Some of the key documents and records that may result from this area are:

1. Sales order.

2. Production order.

3. Bill of materials.

4. Materials requisition routing sheet.

5. Job cost sheet.

6. Production status report.

C. If accounting controls are not adequate in the inventories and production cycle, there could be:

1. Production of unauthorized products or quantities in excess of authorized levels.

2. Untimely processing of inventory or production transactions.

3. Reduction in safeguards over assets.

4. Unauthorized release of production orders.

5. Incorrect accounting distributions.

D. The basic process for the inventories and production cycle for a nonmanufacturing firm is as follows:

1. As in the purchases, accounts payable, and cash disbursements cycle, purchase requisitions and purchase orders are used and controlled to purchase the inventory items that are of a "finished goods" nature. Likewise, when ordered goods are received, personnel in the receiving department fill out a receiving report. When the vendor's invoice is received, it flows through the cash disbursements cycle described above.

2. Perpetual inventory records are maintained for all or large items.

3. When quantities on hand reach the reorder points and quantities previously calculated by the entity, a purchase requisition is prepared and sent to the purchasing department that places the order.

4. At the end of the year, a physical inventory is taken during which items on hand are counted and compared to the perpetual inventory records. For items without perpetual records, the total on hand is used to adjust the cost of goods sold at

year-end (i.e., beginning inventory + purchases – ending inventory = cost of goods sold).

E. The basic process for the inventories and production cycle for a manufacturing firm is as follows:

1. A customer order is received.

2. The customer order is approved through the preparation of a sales order.

3. Based on the approved quantities from the sales order, along with any additional production required to maintain inventory at desired levels, a production order is prepared to authorize the commencement of production.

4. After production has been authorized, a bill of materials is prepared to schedule the quantity and type of materials required for the particular job.

5. The materials requisition (direct materials) and routing sheet (labor and overhead) are prepared to allow production to obtain inputs that will be used in the production process. Supplies and raw material are purchased from suppliers in much the same manner as described above.

6. As materials, labor, and overhead costs are incurred in production, these costs are accumulated with inventory through the use of a job cost sheet.

7. The production status report is used to document the transfer of inventory costs as the items move through the various stages of the production process. They are transferred at their cost to finished goods.

8. Finally, when the goods are sold, the entry is to credit finished goods and to debit cost of goods sold.

F. The important control procedures for the inventories and production cycle are summarized below.

1. Authorization of transactions.

    a. Sales to customers on account should be authorized through the preparation of a sales order.

    b. Production orders should be prepared to authorize the commencement of production.

    c. A bill of materials (written inventory requisitions) should be prepared to authorize the release of materials to the production department.

2. Recording of transactions.

    a. Prenumbered, multiple-part documents (sales orders, production orders, bills of materials, materials requisitions, routing sheets, and job cost sheets) should be used for recording transactions related to the inventories and production cycle.

    b. Adequate documentation (production status reports) should be used to monitor the status of inventory and transfer the costs of inventory as it moves through various stages of the production process.

3. Custody of assets.

    a. A perpetual inventory system should be used to record inventory transactions.

    b. Secured storage areas should be used for inventory (materials, inventory in process, and finished goods inventory).

    c. Materials, labor, and overhead (facilities) inputs should not be released for use in production without materials requisitions and routing sheets.

    d. There should be physical controls to prevent theft.

4. Comparisons.

    a. Quantities of inventory on hand should be periodically reconciled to perpetual inventory records.

    b. Quantities of inventory from production orders should be periodically reconciled with information on production status reports.

    c. Quantities and prices of direct materials from the materials requisitions should be compared to similar information on job cost sheets.

    d. Direct materials prices on materials requisitions should be compared to prices from vendor invoices or perpetual inventory records.

    e. Departmental overhead rates used in production should be reviewed and overhead charges to production costs on job cost sheets should be recalculated.

    f. Direct labor costs from job cost sheets should be compared with payroll accounting records.

    g. Information relating to direct labor and overhead costs from routing sheets should be compared to similar information on job cost sheets.

    h. Summary totals from job cost sheets should be compared and production status reports should be compared to accounting records.

    i. Actual production costs should be compared to standard production costs and any significant variances should be investigated.

j. An individual independent of record-keeping responsibilities should periodically account for the numerical sequence of all prenumbered documents.

5. Segregation of functions.

    a. Individuals having custody of materials, work-in-process, or finished goods inventory should not have any record-keeping or authorization responsibilities with respect to inventories.

PERSONNEL AND PAYROLL CYCLE

A. Another major subsystem of an accounting information system is the personnel and payroll cycle. This cycle may be considered as a subset of the purchases, accounts payable, and cash disbursements cycle and the inventories and production cycle. Therefore, it is not assigned to any one operating cycle. This cycle involves manpower planning, fringe benefits administration, compensation administration, and government compliance.

B. Some of the key documents and records that evolve from personnel and payroll processing are:

  1. Hiring and deduction forms.

  2. Time cards.

  3. Job time cards.

  4. Payroll register.

  5. Payroll checks.

  6. Payroll cost distribution report.

C. If accounting controls are not adequate in the personnel and payroll cycle, there could be:

  1. Incorrect payments to employees.

  2. Payments to fictitious employees.

  3. Incorrect statement of labor expenses.

  4. Violations of government regulations and laws.

  5. Hiring of unqualified persons.

D. The basic process for the personnel and payroll cycle is as follows:

1. The appropriate employee is hired.

2. Once hired, several hiring and deduction forms are prepared. These forms contain information about level of education, experience, authorized pay rates, and payroll deductions. These forms are used to establish the employee's personnel file.

3. Employees use a time clock to record hours on time cards (for general hours worked) and on job time cards (to distribute hours worked over particular jobs).

4. Salaried and other employees fill out weekly time summaries indicating hours worked.

5. These records are then approved by the employee's supervisor and sent to the accounting department.

6. Payroll is then calculated based on information from the time cards and the employees' personnel files.

7. Based on the calculation of payroll, a payroll register (or payroll summary) is prepared. The payroll register summarizes the gross pay, deductions, and net pay for each employee.

8. Payroll cost distribution reports are prepared to allow direct labor costs to be associated with specific jobs or batches of inventory.

9. Unsigned payroll checks are prepared.

10. The payroll checks are signed by the appropriate authorized signatory.

11. The checks are distributed by a person independent of other payroll functions.

E. The important control procedures for the personnel and payroll cycle are summarized below.

1. Authorization of transactions.

   a. Employee payroll information should be authorized through hiring and deduction forms.

   b. Changes to employee payroll information (pay rates, deductions, etc.) should be properly authorized.

   c. Employee time cards and job time cards should be authorized by the employee's supervisor.

   d. The personnel department should promptly send termination notices to the payroll department.

2. Recording of transactions.

a. Prenumbered payroll checks should be used.

b. Time clocks should be used by employees to record hours worked on time cards and job time cards.

3. Custody of assets.

    a. Paychecks should be signed by a person independent of other payroll functions.

    b. Paychecks should be distributed by a person independent of other payroll functions.

    c. Adequate control should be maintained over unclaimed paychecks.

    d. The payroll register should be scanned for recently terminated employees to ensure that these employees have been removed.

    e. The client should use a separate (imprest) bank account for payroll transactions.

    f. Unclaimed payroll checks should be controlled by someone otherwise independent of the payroll function (locked up and eventually voided if not claimed).

    g. Unclaimed pay should be deposited into a special bank account.

4. Comparisons.

    a. Information from authorized hiring documents (pay rates, deductions, etc.) should be compared with information in the payroll register.

    b. Hours worked from approved time cards and job time cards should be compared with the payroll register.

    c. Periodically, the gross wages, deductions, and net pay should be recalculated for selected employees.

    d. Information from the payroll cost distribution reports should be compared to the accounting records for the inventory produced.

    e. Upon receipt of monthly bank statements, an individual independent of personnel and payroll should reconcile the payroll bank account.

    f. An individual independent of record-keeping responsibilities should periodically account for the numerical sequence of all payroll checks.

5. Segregation of functions.

a. The functions of personnel (authorization), timekeeping (recording), and payroll disbursement (custody) should be segregated.

PROPERTY, PLANT, AND EQUIPMENT CYCLE

A. The property, plant, and equipment subsystem is part of the purchases, accounts payable, and cash disbursements cycle.

B. Some of the key documents and records that evolve from the property, plant, and equipment cycle are:

1. Purchase requisition.

2. Authorization (from board of directors).

3. Inspection report.

4. Vendor invoice.

C. The basic process for the property, plant, and equipment cycle is as follows:

1. A purchase requisition and a purchase order are prepared. Unlike inventory or supplies, purchases of property, plant, and equipment are normally authorized by top management or the board of directors.

2. Upon receipt, the requesting department should inspect the property, plant, and equipment for quality and prepare an inspection report. This report parallels the receiving report prepared in the purchases, accounts payable, and cash disbursements cycle.

3. The item is recorded as an addition when purchase authorization, a vendor's invoice, and a receiving report are present.

4. When the vendor invoice is received, the control procedures used are identical to those used in the purchases, accounts payable, and cash disbursements cycle and are not repeated here.

5. The purchases of property, plant, and equipment may involve special forms of financing, such as issuances of debt or equity securities.

6. The company selects an appropriate life and depreciation method.

7. Depreciation entries are made in the general journal.

D. Many of the control procedures for property, plant, and equipment were previously discussed in the purchases, accounts payable, and cash disbursements cycle. Additional control procedures over property, plant, and equipment transactions include:

1. Authorization of transactions.

    a. Purchases of property, plant, and equipment should be authorized by top management or the board of directors.

    b. Written policies should exist regarding the capitalization versus expensing decisions, classification of leases, and determination of depreciation methods, useful lives, and salvage values.

    c. Disposals of property, plant, and equipment should be authorized through the use of prenumbered retirement work orders.

2. Recording of transactions.

    a. Prenumbered, multiple-part documents (purchase requisitions, purchase orders, and inspection reports) should be used.

    b. Detailed records should be available for property assets and accumulated depreciation.

    c. Depreciation should be properly calculated.

3. Custody of assets.

    a. Access to property, plant, and equipment should be safeguarded against theft.

    b. Adequate insurance coverage against losses for property, plant, and equipment should be maintained.

    c. Property, plant, and equipment should be inspected for quality upon receipt through the preparation of an inspection report.

    d. Budgets should be used to monitor and control acquisitions and retirements of property, plant, and equipment.

    e. Repair and maintenance expense should be reviewed to ensure that capitalized items are not inappropriately expensed.

    f. Asset retirements are recorded by removing the asset and accumulated depreciation from the general ledger; a gain (loss) may occur on the transaction.

4. Comparisons.

    a. Information from purchase orders, inspection reports, and vendor's invoices should be reconciled and compared to the accounting records.

    b. Property, plant, and equipment should be physically inspected and reconciled to recorded amounts at reasonable intervals.

c. A subsidiary ledger for property, plant, and equipment should be maintained and reconciled to the control total.

d. The footings and extensions on vendor invoices should be recalculated.

e. An individual independent of record-keeping responsibilities should periodically account for the numerical sequence of all prenumbered documents.

5. Segregation of functions.

a. The functions of authorizing purchases of property, plant, and equipment; inspecting property, plant, and equipment; and recording property, plant, and equipment should be segregated.

FINANCING CYCLE

A. This cycle includes issuance and repurchase of debt (bank loans, leases, mortgage, bonds payable) and capital stock and payment of interest and dividends. Debt and capital stock transactions should be authorized by the board of directors. Often an independent trustee issues bonds, monitors company compliance with the provisions of the debt agreement, and pays interest.

B. For capital stock transactions, corporations may either employ an independent stock registrar and a stock transfer agent, or handle their own transactions. Normally, internal control is stronger when a stock registrar and a stock transfer agent are utilized. A stock registrar's primary responsibility is to verify that stock is issued in accordance with the authorization of the board of directors and the articles of incorporation; the stock transfer agent's primary responsibility is maintaining detailed stockholder records and carrying out transfers of stock ownership.

C. The important control procedures for the financing cycle are summarized below.

1. Debt and equity transactions should be properly approved by the board of directors.

2. Transactions should be executed in the company's name.

3. There should be periodic reviews of debt agreement compliance.

4. There should be adequate records of collateral.

5. An independent trustee should handle bond transactions.

6. A stock registrar and a stock transfer agent should handle capital stock transactions.

7. Canceled stock certificates should be defaced to prevent their reissuance.

INVESTING CYCLE

A. This cycle includes investments in the debt and equity of other organizations. Investments may be categorized as marketable securities and long-term investments. Purchases are recorded at cost and reported at the lower of cost or market.

B. The important control procedures for the investing cycle are summarized below.

1. An independent agent such as a stockbroker, bank, or trust company should be used to maintain custody of securities.

2. The custodian should be bonded.

3. Securities not in the custody of an independent agent should be maintained in a bank safe-deposit box under the joint control of the treasurer and one other company official; both individuals must be present to gain access. Visits to the safe-deposit box should be recorded.

4. Securities should be registered in the name of the company.

5. Detailed records should be maintained for all securities and the related revenue (interest and dividends), and reconciled with the control accounts.

6. There should be a periodic physical inspection of securities by individuals with no responsibility for the authorization, custody, or record keeping of investments.

MANAGEMENT ASSERTIONS AND CONTROL POLICIES AND PROCEDURES

A. As stated previously, management is expressing (or implying) many assertions (or claims) when it prepares financial statements. These assertions can be subdivided into five major categories:

1. *Presentation and disclosure.* The various components of the financial statements are properly classified, described, and disclosed.

2. *Existence or occurrence.* The assets and liabilities did exist as of a given date, and the recorded transactions did occur during the identified period.

3. *Rights and obligations.* The assets are the rights of the entity and liabilities are the obligations of the entity as of a given date.

4. *Completeness.* The accounts and transactions reflected in the financial statements represent all of the accounts and transactions for the period. Simply stated, all transactions have been recorded.

5. *Valuation or allocation.* The accounts have been included in the financial statements at the appropriate amounts, including appropriate allocations between balance sheet and income statement accounts.

B. While these assertions will be addressed again and in more detail in our discussion of audit evidence (see Chapter 7), it is important to note that the control policies and procedures established by management are intended to address these assertions. In gathering evidence, the auditor generally follows these procedures:

1. Identify important assertions for the account balance or class of transactions.

2. Identify control policies and procedures that relate to those assertions.

3. Test the operating effectiveness of control policies and procedures related to management assertions.

4. Based on the results of the tests of operating effectiveness, design substantive tests to gather evidence regarding management assertions.

C. The table in Figure 6.1 provides a summary of how the five major categories of control procedures relate to management assertions. It is important to note that this is general information and other control procedures may differ slightly, depending on the circumstances.

D. The CPA exam frequently requires candidates to identify deficiencies in the internal control of a hypothetical entity. These deficiencies are identified based on examining a flowchart of an entity's internal control or a written narrative of that internal control. In each of these types of questions, the candidate can identify internal control deficiencies by recalling the control procedures introduced above.

E. In responding to questions requesting the candidate to identify internal control deficiencies, it is normally best to assume that each step in a flowchart or each description in a narrative contains some type of deficiency.

Figure 1: Control procedures and related management assertions

Authorization of transactions	Existence or occurrence	If transactions are properly authorized by management, it is unlikely that fictitious transactions will be recorded.
Recording of transactions	Completeness	By using prenumbered documents and accounting for the numerical sequence of these documents, the company will identify transactions that should have been recorded.
Custody of assets	Completeness, existence or occurrence, rights and obligations	If strong controls exist relating to custody of assets, employees would be unable to participate in a defalcation scheme and cover their theft by failing to record transactions (completeness) or recording a fictitious transaction (existence or occurrence). In addition, this would ensure that the entity truly had rights to the assets over which controls have been implemented.
Comparisons	Valuation or allocation, completeness, existence or occurrence	Comparisons allow the company to ensure that transactions are recorded at the proper dollar amounts (e.g., recalculating sales invoices). In addition, by comparing different documents, the company can determine that (1) a particular transaction was recorded (completeness) and (2) a recorded transaction actually occurred (existence or occurrence).
Segregation of functions	Completeness, existence or occurrence, rights and obligations	The primary benefit provided by segregation of functions is not allowing employees to individually participate in a defalcation scheme. Therefore, the assertions addressed by this category are similar to those for custody.

F. The candidate will need a basic understanding of common flowcharting symbols. Some of the more common symbols tested on the CPA exam are shown in Figure 2.

Figure 2: Some Common Flowchart Symbols

QUESTIONS: INTERNAL CONTROL

1. The ultimate purpose of assessing control risk is to contribute to the auditor's evaluation of the risk that:
   A. entity policies may be overridden by senior management.
   B. tests of controls may fail to identify procedures relevant to assertions.
   C. material misstatements may exist in the financial statements.
   D. specified controls requiring segregation of duties may be circumvented by collusion.

2. After obtaining an understanding of an entity's internal control and assessing control risk, an auditor may next:
   A. evaluate whether internal control policies and procedures detected material misstatements in the financial statements.
   B. perform tests of controls to verify management's assertions that are embodied in the financial statements.
   C. apply analytical procedures as substantive tests to validate the assessed level of control risk.
   D. consider whether audit evidence is available to support a further reduction in the assessed level of control risk.

3. On the basis of audit evidence gathered and evaluated, an auditor decides to increase the assessed level of control risk from that originally planned. To achieve an overall audit risk level that is substantially the same as the planned audit risk level, the auditor would:
   A. decrease detection risk.
   B. increase inherent risk.
   C. decrease substantive testing.
   D. increase materiality levels.

4. Which of the following statements is correct concerning an auditor's assessment of control risk?
   A. The basis for an auditor's conclusions about the assessed level of control risk need not be documented unless control risk is assessed at the maximum level.
   B. Assessing control risk may be performed concurrently during an audit with obtaining an understanding of the entity's internal control.
   C. The lower the assessed level of control risk, the less assurance the evidence must provide that the control procedures are operating effectively.
   D. Evidence about the operation of control procedures in prior audits may not be considered during the current year's assessment of control risk.

5. After obtaining an understanding of internal control and assessing control risk, an auditor decided to perform tests of controls. The auditor *most likely* decided that:
   A. additional evidence to support a further reduction in control risk is not available.
   B. there were many internal control weaknesses that could allow errors to enter the accounting system.
   C. it would be efficient to perform tests of controls that would result in a reduction in planned substantive tests.
   D. an increase in the assessed level of control risk is justified for certain financial statement assertions.

6. An auditor assesses control risk because it:
   A. determines whether sampling risk is sufficiently low.
   B. affects the level of detection risk the auditor may accept.
   C. indicates where inherent risk may be the greatest.
   D. includes the aspects of nonsampling risk that are controllable.

7. As the acceptable level of detection risk decreases, the assurance directly provided from:
   A. tests of controls should increase.
   B. tests of controls should decrease.
   C. substantive tests should decrease.
   D. substantive tests should increase.

8. An auditor assesses control risk because it:
   A. affects the level of detection risk that the auditor may accept.
   B. indicates to the auditor where inherent risk may be the greatest.
   C. provides assurance that the auditor's materiality levels are appropriate.
   D. is relevant to the auditor's understanding of the control environment.

9. As the acceptable level of detection risk decreases, an auditor may:
   A. postpone the planned timing of substantive tests from interim dates to the year end.
   B. eliminate the assessed level of inherent risk from consideration as a planning factor.
   C. reduce substantive testing by relying on the assessments of inherent risk and control risk.
   D. lower the assessed level of control risk from the maximum level to below the maximum.

10. The acceptable level of detection risk is inversely related to the:
    A. preliminary judgment about materiality levels.
    B. assurance provided by substantive tests.
    C. risk of misapplying auditing procedures.
    D. risk of failing to discover material misstatements.

11. The ultimate purpose of assessing control risk is to contribute to the auditor's evaluation of the risk that:
    A. tests of controls may fail to identify procedures relevant to assertions.
    B. specified controls requiring segregation of duties may be circumvented by collusion.
    C. material misstatements may exist in the financial statements.
    D. entity policies may be overridden by senior management.

12. To which of the following matters would materiality limits NOT apply when obtaining written client representations?
    A. Losses from sales commitments.
    B. Fraud involving management.
    C. Unasserted claims and assessments.
    D. Noncompliance with contractual agreements.

13. Which of the following characteristics *most likely* would heighten an auditor's concern about the risk of intentional manipulation of financial statements?
    A. Insiders recently purchased additional shares of the entity's stock.
    B. The rate of change in the entity's industry is slow.
    C. Turnover of senior accounting personnel is low.
    D. Management places substantial emphasis on meeting earnings projections.

14. The existence of audit risk is recognized by the statement in the auditor's standard report that the auditor:
    A. assesses the accounting principles used and also evaluates the overall financial statement presentation.
    B. realizes some matters, either individually or in the aggregate, are important while other matters are not important.
    C. obtains reasonable assurance about whether the financial statements are free of material misstatement.
    D. is responsible for expressing an opinion on the financial statements, which are the responsibility of management.

15. Which of the following audit risk components may be assessed in nonquantitative terms?

	Control	Detection	Inherent risk
A.	Yes	Yes	Yes
B.	No	Yes	Yes
C.	Yes	Yes	No
D.	Yes	No	Yes

16. Which of the following statements about internal control is CORRECT?
    A. The establishment and maintenance of the internal control is an important responsibility of the internal auditor.
    B. The cost-benefit relationship is a primary criterion that should be considered in designing an internal control.
    C. An exceptionally strong internal control is enough for the auditor to eliminate substantive tests on a significant account balance.
    D. A properly maintained internal control reasonably ensures that collusion among employees cannot occur.

17. The primary objective of procedures performed to obtain an understanding of internal control is to provide an auditor with:
    A. information necessary to prepare flowcharts.
    B. knowledge necessary to plan the audit.
    C. a basis from which to modify tests of controls.
    D. audit evidence to use in reducing detection risk.

18. Which of the following components of an entity's internal control includes the development of personnel manuals documenting employee promotion and training policies?
    A. Control environment.
    B. Accounting system.
    C. Control procedures.
    D. Quality control system.

19. Proper segregation of duties reduces the opportunities to allow persons to be in positions to both:
    A. journalize entries and prepare financial statements.
    B. establish internal controls and authorize transactions.
    C. perpetuate and conceal errors and fraud.
    D. record cash receipts and cash disbursements.

20. Each of the following might, by itself, form a valid basis for an auditor to decide to omit a test EXCEPT the:
    A. relative risk involved.
    B. degree of reliance on the relevant internal controls.
    C. relationship between the cost of obtaining evidence and its usefulness.
    D. difficulty and expense involved in testing a particular item.

21. Which of the following statements concerning material weaknesses and reportable conditions is CORRECT?
    A. An auditor should report immediately material weaknesses and reportable conditions discovered during an audit.
    B. All reportable conditions are material weaknesses.
    C. All material weaknesses are reportable conditions.
    D. An auditor should identify and communicate material weaknesses separately from reportable conditions.

22. In assessing the competence and objectivity of an entity's internal auditor, an independent auditor least likely would consider information obtained from:
    A. the results of analytical procedures.
    B. previous experience with the internal auditor.
    C. external quality reviews of the internal auditor's activities.
    D. discussions with management personnel.

23. Reportable conditions are matters that come to an auditor's attention that should be communicated to an entity's audit committee because they represent:
    A. material fraud or illegal acts perpetrated by high-level management.
    B. significant deficiencies in the design or operation of internal control.
    C. disclosures of information that significantly contradict the auditor's going concern assumption.
    D. manipulation or falsification of accounting records or documents from which financial statements are prepared.

24. In obtaining an understanding of an entity's internal control policies and procedures that are relevant to audit planning, an auditor is required to obtain knowledge about the:
    A. consistency with which the policies and procedures are currently being applied.
    B. effectiveness of the policies and procedures that have been placed in operation.
    C. control procedures related to each principal transaction class and account balance.
    D. design of the policies and procedures pertaining to internal control elements.

25. When considering the objectivity of internal auditors, an independent auditor should:
    A. test a sample of the transactions and balances that the internal auditors examined.
    B. determine the organizational level to which the internal auditors report.
    C. evaluate the quality control program in effect for the internal auditors.
    D. examine documentary evidence of the work performed by the internal auditors.

26. After obtaining an understanding of an entity's internal control, an auditor may assess control risk at the maximum level for some assertions because the auditor:
    A. identifies internal control policies and procedures that are likely to prevent material misstatements.
    B. determines that the pertinent internal control elements are not well documented.
    C. performs tests of controls to restrict detection risk to an acceptable level.
    D. believes the internal control policies and procedures are unlikely to be effective.

27. The objective of tests of details of transactions performed as tests of controls is to:
    A. detect material misstatements in the account balances of the financial statements.
    B. determine whether internal control policies and procedures have been placed in operation.
    C. evaluate whether internal control procedures operated effectively.
    D. monitor the design and use of entity documents such as prenumbered shipping forms.

28. Which of the following statements is correct concerning an auditor's required communication of reportable conditions?
    A. An auditor's report on reportable conditions should include a restriction on the distribution of the report.
    B. An auditor should perform tests of controls on reportable conditions before communicating them to the client.
    C. A reportable condition previously communicated during the prior year's audit that remains uncorrected causes a scope limitation.
    D. An auditor should communicate reportable conditions after tests of controls, but before commencing substantive tests.

29. Tests of controls are concerned primarily with each of the following questions EXCEPT:
    A. Were the necessary procedures performed?
    B. How were the procedures performed?
    C. By whom were the procedures performed?
    D. Why were the procedures performed?

30. The likelihood of assessing control risk too high is the risk that the sample selected to test controls:
    A. contains proportionately fewer monetary errors or deviations from prescribed internal control policies or procedures than exist in the balance or class as a whole.
    B. does not support the auditor's planned assessed level of control risk when the true operating effectiveness of the control structure justifies such an assessment.
    C. contains misstatements that could be material to the financial statements when aggregated with misstatements in other account balances or transactions classes.
    D. does not support the tolerable error for some or all of management's assertions.

31. An internal auditor's work would *most likely* affect the nature, timing, and extent of an independent CPA's auditing procedures when the internal auditor's work relates to assertions about the:
    A. valuation of intangible assets.
    B. existence of contingencies.
    C. existence of fixed asset additions.
    D. valuation of related party transactions.

32. Tests of controls are performed in order to determine whether or not:
    A. material dollar errors exist.
    B. controls are functioning as designed.
    C. incompatible functions exist.
    D. necessary controls are absent.

33. During an audit, an internal auditor may provide direct assistance to an independent CPA in:

	Obtaining an understanding of internal control	Performing test of controls	Performing substantive tests
A.	No	No	No
B.	Yes	Yes	No
C.	Yes	No	No
D.	Yes	Yes	Yes

34. An auditor's primary consideration regarding an entity's internal control policies and procedures is whether the policies and procedures:
    A. affect the financial statement assertions.
    B. prevent management override.
    C. reflect management's philosophy and operating style.
    D. relate to the control environment.

35. After assessing control risk at below the maximum level, an auditor desires to seek a further reduction in the assessed level of control risk. At this time, the auditor would consider whether:
    A. it would be efficient to obtain an understanding of the entity's accounting system.
    B. the entity's internal control policies and procedures have been placed in operation.
    C. additional audit evidence sufficient to support a further reduction is likely to be available.
    D. the entity's internal control policies and procedures pertain to any financial statement assertions.

36. In assessing control risk, an auditor ordinarily selects from a variety of techniques, including:
    A. comparison and confirmation.
    B. reperformance and observation.
    C. inspection and verification.
    D. inquiry and analytical procedures.

37. When obtaining an understanding of an entity's internal control procedures, an auditor should concentrate on the substance of the procedures rather than their form because:
    A. the procedures may be so inappropriate that no reliance is contemplated by the auditor.
    B. the procedures may be operating effectively, but may not be documented.
    C. management may implement procedures whose costs exceed their benefits.
    D. management may establish appropriate procedures, but not enforce compliance with them.

38. Which of the following is a management control method that could *most likely* improve management's ability to supervise company activities effectively?
    A. Establishing budgets and forecasts to identify variances from expectations.
    B. Supporting employees with the resources necessary to discharge their responsibilities.
    C. Limiting direct access to assets by physical segregation and protective devices.
    D. Monitoring compliance with internal control requirements imposed by regulatory bodies.

39. Which of the following would *most likely* not be considered an inherent limitation of the potential effectiveness of an entity's internal control?
    A. Incompatible duties.
    B. Management override.
    C. Mistakes in judgment.
    D. Collusion among employees.

40. The overall attitude and awareness of an entity's board of directors concerning the importance of internal control usually is reflected in its:
    A. system of segregation of duties.
    B. safeguards over access to assets.
    C. computer-based controls.
    D. control environment.

41. An auditor's purpose for performing tests of controls is to provide reasonable assurance that:
    A. transactions are executed in accordance with management's authorization and access to assets is limited by a segregation of functions.
    B. the risk that the auditor may unknowingly fail to modify the opinion on the financial statements is minimized.
    C. the controls on which the auditor plans to rely are being applied as perceived during the preliminary evaluation.
    D. transactions are recorded as necessary to permit the preparation of the financial statements in conformity with generally accepted accounting principles.

42. It is important for the CPA to consider the competence of the audit clients' employees because their competence bears directly and importantly upon the:
    A. comparison of recorded accountability with assets.
    B. achievement of the objectives of the system of internal control.
    C. timing of the tests to be performed.
    D. cost/benefit relationship of the system of internal control.

43. Which of the following statements is **CORRECT** concerning an auditor's communication of internal control related matters (reportable conditions) noted in an audit?
    A. Reportable conditions should be recommunicated each year even if the audit committee has acknowledged its understanding of such efficiencies.
    B. The auditor may issue a written report to the audit committee representing that no reportable conditions were noted during the audit.
    C. Reportable conditions may not be communicated in a document that contains suggestions regarding activities that concern other topics such as business strategies or administrative efficiencies.
    D. The auditor may choose to communicate significant internal control related matters either during the course of the audit or after the audit is concluded.

44. Which of the following is a step in an auditor's decision to assess control risk at below the maximum?
    A. Identify specific internal control policies and procedures that are likely to detect or prevent material misstatements.
    B. Document that the additional audit effort to perform tests of controls exceeds the potential reduction in substantive testing.
    C. Perform tests of details of transactions and account balances to identify potential errors and fraud.
    D. Apply analytical procedures to both financial data and nonfinancial information to detect conditions that may indicate weak controls.

45. After obtaining an understanding of internal control and assessing control risk, an auditor decided not to perform additional tests of controls. The auditor *most likely* concluded that the:
    A. internal control was properly designed and justifiably may be relied on.
    B. additional evidence to support a further reduction in control risk was not cost beneficial to obtain.
    C. assessed level of inherent risk exceeded the assessed level of control risk.
    D. evidence obtainable through tests of controls would not support an increased level of control risk.

46. Which of the following types of evidence would an auditor *most likely* examine to determine whether internal control policies and procedures are operating as designed?
    A. Gross margin information regarding the client's industry.
    B. Anticipated results documented in budgets or forecasts.
    C. Confirmations of receivables verifying account balances.
    D. Client records documenting the use of I.T. programs.

47. Which of the following controls would a company *most likely* use to safeguard marketable securities when an independent trust agent is not employed?
    A. The investment committee of the board of directors periodically reviews the investment decisions delegated to the treasurer.
    B. The internal auditor and the controller independently trace all purchases and sales of marketable securities from the subsidiary ledgers to the general ledger.
    C. Two company officials have joint control of marketable securities, which are kept in a bank safe-deposit box.
    D. The chairman of the board verifies the marketable securities, which are kept in a bank safe-deposit box, each year on the balance sheet date.

48. When an entity uses a trust company as custodian of its marketable securities, the possibility of concealing fraud most likely would be reduced if the:
    A. trust company has no direct contact with the entity employees responsible for maintaining investment accounting records.
    B. securities are registered in the name of the trust company, rather than the entity itself.
    C. trust company places the securities in a bank safe-deposit vault under the custodian's exclusive control.
    D. interest and dividend checks are mailed directly to an entity employee who is authorized to sell securities.

49. Management philosophy and operating style would *most likely* have a significant influence on entity's control environment when:
    A. accurate management job descriptions delineate specific duties.
    B. management is dominated by one individual.
    C. the audit committee actively oversees the financial reporting process.
    D. the internal auditor reports directly to management.

50. An auditor's flowchart of a client's accounting system is a diagrammatic representation that depicts the auditor's:
    A. identification of weaknesses in the system.
    B. understanding of the system.
    C. assessment of the control environment's effectiveness.
    D. assessment of control risk.

51. A flowchart is most frequently used by an auditor in connection with the:
    A. documentation of the client's internal control procedures.
    B. performance of analytical procedures of account balances.
    C. preparation of generalized computer audit programs.
    D. use of statistical sampling in performing an audit.

52. Which of the following **BEST** describes the principal advantage of the use of flowcharts in reviewing internal control?
    A. Standard flowcharts are available and can be effectively used for describing most company internal operations.
    B. Flowcharting is the most efficient means available for summarizing internal control.
    C. Flowcharts aid in the understanding of the sequence and relationships of activities and documents.
    D. Audit documents are not complete unless they include flowcharts as well as memoranda on internal control.

53. An auditor's flowchart of a client's accounting system is a diagrammatic representation that depicts the auditor's:
    A. documentation of the study and evaluation of the system.
    B. understanding of the types of fraud that are probable, given the present system.
    C. program for tests of controls.
    D. understanding of the system.

54. Independent internal verification of inventory occurs when employees who:
    A. issue raw materials obtain material requisitions for each issue and prepare daily totals of materials issued.
    B. compare records of goods on hand with physical quantities do not maintain the records or have custody of the inventory.
    C. obtain receipts for the transfer of completed work to finished goods prepare a completed production report.
    D. are independent of issuing production orders update records from completed job cost sheets and production cost reports on a timely basis.

55. Tracing selected items from the payroll register to employee time cards that have been approved by supervisory personnel provides evidence that:
    A. internal controls relating to payroll disbursements were operating effectively.
    B. payroll checks were signed by an appropriate officer independent of the payroll preparation process.
    C. only bona fide employees worked and their pay was properly computed.
    D. employees worked the number of hours for which their pay was computed.

56. Which of the following control procedures is **NOT** usually performed in the vouchers payable department?
    A. Determining the mathematical accuracy of the vendor's invoice.
    B. Having an authorized person approve the voucher.
    C. Controlling the mailing of the check and remittance advice.
    D. Matching the receiving report with the purchase order.

57. The most likely result of ineffective internal control policies and procedures in the revenue cycle is that:
    A. fraud in recording transactions in the subsidiary accounts could result in a delay in goods shipped.
    B. omission of shipping documents could go undetected, causing an understatement of inventory.
    C. final authorization of credit memos by personnel in the sales department could permit an employee defalcation scheme.
    D. fictitious transactions could be recorded, causing an understatement of revenues and overstatement of receivables.

58. Proper authorization procedures in the revenue cycle usually provide for the approval of bad debt write-offs by an employee in which of the following departments?
    A. Treasurer.
    B. Sales.
    C. Billing.
    D. Accounts receivable.

59. The objectives of the internal control for a production cycle are to provide assurance that transactions are properly executed and recorded, and that:
    A. independent internal verification of activity reports is established.
    B. transfers to finished goods are documented by a completed production report and a quality control report.
    C. production orders are prenumbered and signed by a supervisor.
    D. custody of work in process and of finished goods is properly maintained.

60. Effective internal control procedures over the payroll function may include:
    A. reconciliation of totals on job time tickets with job reports by employees responsible for those specific jobs.
    B. verification of agreement of job time tickets with employee clock card hours by a payroll department employee.
    C. preparation of payroll transaction journal entries by an employee who reports to the supervisor of the personnel department.
    D. custody of rate authorization records by the supervisor of the payroll department.

61. Which of the following controls would be most effective in assuring that the proper custody of assets in the investing cycle is maintained?
    A. Direct access to securities in the safety deposit box is limited to only one corporate officer.
    B. Personnel who post investment transactions to the general ledger are not permitted to update the investment subsidiary ledger.
    C. The purchase and sale of investments are executed on the specific authorization of the board of directors.
    D The recorded balances in the investment subsidiary ledger are periodically compared with the contents of the safety deposit box by independent personnel.

62. An auditor would consider a cashier's job description to contain compatible duties if the cashier receives remittances from the mailroom and also prepares the:
    A. prelist of individual checks.
    B. monthly bank reconciliation.
    C. daily deposit slip.
    D. remittance advices.

63. Which of the following most likely would be an internal control procedure designed to detect errors and fraud concerning the custody of inventory?
    A. Periodic reconciliation of work in process with job cost sheets.
    B. Segregation of functions between general accounting and cost accounting.
    C. Independent comparisons of finished goods records with counts of goods on hand.
    D. Approval of inventory journal entries by the storekeeper.

64. Sound internal control procedures dictate that defective merchandise returned by customers should be presented initially to the:
    A. sales clerk.
    B. purchasing clerk.
    C. receiving clerk.
    D. inventory control clerk.

65. The primary responsibility of a bank acting as registrar of capital stock is to:
    A. ascertain that dividends declared do not exceed the statutory amount allowable in the state of incorporation.
    B. account for stock certificates by comparing the total shares outstanding to the total in the shareholders' subsidiary ledger.
    C. act as an independent third party between the board of directors and outside investors concerning mergers, acquisitions, and the sale of treasury stock.
    D. verify that stock is issued in accordance with the authorization of the board of directors and the articles of incorporation.

66. Mailing disbursement checks and remittance advices should be controlled by the employee who:
    A. approves the vouchers for payment.
    B. matches the receiving reports, purchase orders, and vendors' invoices.
    C. maintains possession of the mechanical check-signing device.
    D. signs the checks last.

67. The safeguarding of inventory most likely includes:
    A. comparison of the information contained on the purchase requisitions, purchase orders, receiving reports, and vendors' invoices.
    B. periodic reconciliation of detailed inventory records with the actual inventory on hand by taking a physical count.
    C. analytical procedures for raw materials, goods in process, and finished goods that identify unusual transactions, theft, and obsolescence.
    D. application of established overhead rates on the basis of direct labor hours or direct labor costs.

68. The purpose of segregating the duties of hiring personnel and distributing payroll checks is to separate the:
    A. authorization of transactions from the custody of related assets.
    B. operational responsibility from the record-keeping responsibility.
    C. human resources function from the controllership function.
    D. administrative controls from the internal accounting controls.

69. Immediately upon receipt of cash, a responsible employee should:
    A. record the amount in the cash receipts journal.
    B. prepare a remittance listing.
    C. update the subsidiary accounts receivable records.
    D. prepare a deposit slip in triplicate.

70. Which of the following controls most likely would be effective in offsetting the tendency of sales personnel to maximize sales volume at the expense of high bad debt write-offs?
    A. Employees responsible for authorizing sales and bad debt write-offs are denied access to cash.
    B. Shipping documents and sales invoices are matched by an employee who does not have authority to write off bad debts.
    C. Employees involved in the credit-granting function are separated from the sales function.
    D. Subsidiary accounts receivable records are reconciled to the control account by an employee independent of the authorization of credit.

71. In meeting the control objective of safeguarding of assets, which department should be responsible for:

	Distribution of paychecks	Custody of unclaimed paychecks
A.	Treasurer	Treasurer
B.	Payroll	Treasurer
C.	Treasurer	Payroll
D.	Payroll	Payroll

72. An entity with a large volume of customer remittances by mail could most likely reduce the risk of employee misappropriation of cash by using:
    A. employee fidelity bonds.
    B. independently prepared mailroom prelists.
    C. daily check summaries.
    D. a bank lockbox system.

73. For effective internal control, the accounts payable department generally should:
    A. obliterate the quantity ordered on the receiving department copy of the purchase order.
    B. establish the agreement of the vendor's invoice with the receiving report and purchase order.
    C. stamp, perforate, or otherwise cancel supporting documentation after payment is mailed.
    D. ascertain that each requisition is approved as to price, quantity, and quality by an authorized employee.

74. When the shipping department returns nonconforming goods to a vendor, the purchasing department should send to the accounting department the:
    A. unpaid voucher.
    B. debit memo.
    C. vendor invoice.
    D. credit memo.

75. Which of the following procedures most likely would be considered a weakness in an entity's internal controls over payroll?
    A. A voucher for the amount of the payroll is prepared in the general accounting department based on the payroll department's payroll summary.
    B. Payroll checks are prepared by the payroll department and signed by the treasurer.
    C. The employee who distributes payroll checks returns unclaimed payroll checks to the payroll department.
    D. The personnel department sends employees' termination notices to the payroll department.

76. Which of the following controls would an entity most likely use in safeguarding against the loss of marketable securities?
    A. An independent trust company that has no direct contact with the employees who have record-keeping responsibilities has possession of the securities.
    B. The internal auditor verifies the marketable securities in the entity's safe each year on the balance sheet date.
    C. The independent auditor traces all purchases and sales of marketable securities through the subsidiary ledgers to the general ledger.
    D. A designated member of the board of directors controls the securities in a bank safe-deposit box.

77. Which of the following most likely would be the result of ineffective internal control policies and procedures in the revenue cycle?
    A. Final authorization of credit memos by personnel in the sales department could permit an employee defalcation scheme.
    B. Fictitious transactions could be recorded, causing an understatement of revenues and an overstatement of receivables.
    C. Fraud in recording transactions in the subsidiary accounts could result in a delay in goods shipped.
    D. Omission of shipping documents could go undetected, causing an understatement of inventory.

78. The authority to accept incoming goods in receiving should be based on a(an):
    A. vendor's invoice.
    B. materials requisition.
    C. bill of lading.
    D. approved purchase order.

79. Mailing disbursement checks and remittance advices should be controlled by the employee who:
    A. matches the receiving reports, purchase orders, and vendors' invoices.
    B. signs the checks last.
    C. prepares the daily voucher summary.
    D. agrees the check register to the daily check summary.

80. Sound internal control procedures dictate that defective merchandise returned by customers should be presented initially to the:
    A. accounts receivable supervisor.
    B. receiving clerk.
    C. shipping department supervisor.
    D. sales clerk.

81. Which of the following internal control procedures most likely would justify a reduced assessed level of control risk concerning plant and equipment acquisitions?
    A. Periodic physical inspection of plant and equipment by the internal audit staff.
    B. Comparison of current-year plant and equipment account balances with prior-year actual balances.
    C. The review of prenumbered purchase orders to detect unrecorded trade-ins.
    D. Approval of periodic depreciation entries by a supervisor independent of the accounting department.

82. Which of the following procedures most likely would give the greatest assurance that securities held as investments are safeguarded?
    A. There is no access to securities between the year-end and the date of the auditor's security count.
    B. Proceeds from the sale of investments are received by an employee who does not have access to securities.
    C. Investment acquisitions are authorized by a member of the Board of Directors before execution.
    D. Access to securities requires the signatures and presence of two designated officials.

83. Which of the following internal control procedures is not usually performed in the treasurer's department?
    A. Verifying the accuracy of checks and vouchers.
    B. Controlling the mailing of checks to vendors.
    C. Approving vendors' invoices for payment.
    D. Canceling payment vouchers when paid.

84. The objectives of the internal control for a production cycle are to provide assurance that transactions are properly executed and recorded, and that:
    A. production orders are prenumbered and signed by a supervisor.
    B. custody of work in process and of finished goods is properly maintained.
    C. independent internal verification of activity reports is established.
    D. transfers to finished goods are documented by a completed production report and a quality control report.

85. In a well-designed internal control, employees in the same department most likely would approve purchase orders, and also:
    A. reconcile the open invoice file.
    B. inspect goods upon receipt.
    C. authorize requisitions of goods.
    D. negotiate terms with vendors.

86. The purpose of segregating the duties of hiring personnel and distributing payroll checks is to separate the:
    A. human resources function from the controllership function.
    B. administrative controls from the internal accounting controls.
    C. authorization of transactions from the custody of related assets.
    D. operational responsibility from the record-keeping responsibility.

87. Which of the following departments most likely would approve changes in pay rates and deductions from employee salaries?
    A. Personnel.
    B. Treasurer.
    C. Controller.
    D. Payroll.

88. Which question would an auditor most likely include on an internal control questionnaire for notes payable?
    A. Are assets that collateralize notes payable critically needed for the entity's continued existence?
    B. Are two or more authorized signatures required on checks that repay notes payable?
    C. Are the proceeds from notes payable used for the purchase of noncurrent assets?
    D. Are direct borrowings on notes payable authorized by the board of directors?

89. Which of the following internal control procedures most likely would assure that all billed sales are correctly posted to the accounts receivable ledger?
    A. Daily sales summaries are compared to daily postings to the accounts receivable ledger.
    B. Each sales invoice is supported by a prenumbered shipping document.
    C. The accounts receivable ledger is reconciled daily to the control account in the general ledger.
    D. Each shipment on credit is supported by a prenumbered sales invoice.

90. An auditor most likely would assess control risk at the maximum if the payroll department supervisor is responsible for:
    A. examining authorization forms for new employees.
    B. comparing payroll registers with original batch transmittal data.
    C. authorizing payroll rate changes for all employees.
    D. hiring all subordinate payroll department employees.

91. In a properly designed internal control, the same employee most likely would match vendors' invoices with receiving reports and also:
    A. post the detailed accounts payable records.
    B. recompute the calculations on vendors' invoices.
    C. reconcile the accounts payable ledger.
    D. cancel vendors' invoices after payment.

92. Which of the following internal control procedures most likely would prevent direct labor hours from being charged to manufacturing overhead?
    A. Periodic independent counts of work in process for comparison to recorded amounts.
    B. Comparison of daily journal entries with approved production orders.
    C. Use of time tickets to record actual labor worked on production orders.
    D. Reconciliation of work-in-process inventory with periodic cost budgets.

93. Which of the following internal control procedures most likely would be used to maintain accurate inventory records?
    A. Perpetual inventory records are periodically compared with the current cost of individual inventory items.
    B. A just-in-time inventory ordering system keeps inventory levels to a desired minimum.
    C. Requisitions, receiving reports, and purchase orders are independently matched before payment is approved.
    D. Periodic inventory counts are used to adjust the perpetual inventory records.

94. Upon receipt of customers' checks in the mailroom, a responsible employee should prepare a remittance listing that is forwarded to the cashier. A copy of the listing should be sent to the:
    A. internal auditor to investigate the listing for unusual transactions.
    B. treasurer to compare the listing with the monthly bank statement.
    C. accounts receivable bookkeeper to update the subsidiary accounts receivable records.
    D. entity's bank to compare the listing with the cashier's deposit slip.

95. Proper authorization of write-offs of uncollectible accounts should be approved in which of the following departments?
    A. Accounts receivable.
    B. Credit.
    C. Accounts payable.
    D. Treasurer.

96. Which of the following procedures most likely would not be an internal control procedure designed to reduce the risk of errors in the billing process?
    A. Comparing control totals for shipping documents with corresponding totals for sales invoices.
    B. Using computer programmed controls on the pricing and mathematical accuracy of sales invoices.
    C. Matching shipping documents with approved sales orders before invoice preparation.
    D. Reconciling the control totals for sales invoices with the accounts receivable subsidiary ledger.

97. Which of the following internal control procedures is not usually performed in the vouchers payable department?
    A. Matching the vendor's invoice with the related receiving report.
    B. Approving vouchers for payment by having an authorized employee sign the vouchers.
    C. Indicating the asset and expense accounts to be debited.
    D. Accounting for unused prenumbered purchase orders and receiving reports.

98. Which question would an auditor *least likely* include on an internal control questionnaire concerning the initiation and execution of equipment transactions?
    A. Are requests for major repairs approved at a higher level than the department initiating the request?
    B. Are prenumbered purchase orders used for equipment and periodically accounted for?
    C. Are requests for purchases of equipment reviewed for consideration of soliciting competitive bids?
    D. Are procedures in place to monitor and properly restrict access to equipment?

99. Sound internal control procedures dictate that immediately upon receiving checks from customers by mail, a responsible employee should:
    A. add the checks to the daily cash summary.
    B. verify that each check is supported by a prenumbered sales invoice.
    C. prepare a duplicate listing of checks received.
    D. record the checks in the cash receipts journal.

100. To provide assurance that each voucher is submitted and paid only once, an auditor most likely would examine a sample of paid vouchers and determine whether each voucher is:
    A. supported by a vendor's invoice.
    B. stamped "paid" by the check signer.
    C. prenumbered and accounted for.
    D. approved for authorized purchases.

101. Which of the following internal controls most likely would reduce the risk of diversion of customer receipts by an entity's employees?
    A. A bank lockbox system.
    B. Prenumbered remittance advices.
    C. Monthly bank reconciliations.
    D. Daily deposit of cash receipts.

102. Which of the following is a control procedure that most likely could help prevent employee payroll fraud?
    A. The personnel department promptly sends employee termination notices to the payroll supervisor.
    B. Employees who distribute payroll checks forward unclaimed payroll checks to the absent employees' supervisors.
    C. Salary rates resulting from new hires are approved by the payroll supervisor.
    D. Total hours used for determination of gross pay are calculated by the payroll supervisor.

103. In assessing control risk, an auditor ordinarily selects from a variety of techniques, including:
    A. inquiry and analytical procedures.
    B. reperformance and observation.
    C. comparison and confirmation.
    D. inspection and verification.

104. For effective internal control, the accounts payable department generally should:
    A. stamp, perforate, or otherwise cancel supporting documentation after payment is mailed.
    B. ascertain that each requisition is approved as to price, quantity, and quality by an authorized employee.
    C. obliterate the quantity ordered on the receiving department copy of the purchase order.
    D. establish the agreement of the vendor's invoice with the receiving report and purchase order.

105. A weakness in internal control over recording retirements of equipment may cause an auditor to:
    A. inspect certain items of equipment in the plant and trace those items to the accounting records.
    B. review the subsidiary ledger to ascertain whether depreciation was taken on each item of equipment during the year.
    C. trace additions to the "other assets" account to search for equipment that is still on hand but no longer being used.
    D. select certain items of equipment from the accounting records and locate them in the plant.

106. Which of the following circumstances most likely would cause an auditor to suspect an employee payroll fraud scheme?
    A. There are significant unexplained variances between standard and actual labor cost.
    B. Payroll checks are disbursed by the same employee each payday
    C. Employee time cards are approved by individual departmental supervisors.
    D. A separate payroll bank account is maintained on an imprest basis.

Answers: Internal Control

1. **C** AU 319 states that the ultimate purpose of assessing control risk is to contribute to the auditor's evaluation of the risk that material misstatements exist in the financial statements. The process of assessing control risk (together with assessing inherent risk) provides audit evidence about the risk that such misstatements may exist in the financial statements. The auditor uses this audit evidence as part of the reasonable basis for an opinion.

2. **D** After the auditor assesses control risk, he/she may desire a further reduction in the assessed level of control risk for some assertions. The auditor would then decide if it is likely that additional audit evidence could be obtained to support a lower assessed level of control risk for these assertions. If yes, and it is likely to be efficient to obtain such audit evidence, the auditor would then perform additional tests of controls. Next, whether the auditor performed additional tests of controls or not, the auditor would document the basis for conclusions about the assessed level of control risk and design substantive tests.

3. **A** AU 312 states that detection risk should bear an inverse relationship to inherent and control risk. The less the inherent and control risk the auditor believes exists, the greater the acceptable level of detection risk. Conversely, when the inherent and control risk increases, the auditor must decrease the detection risk. These components of audit risk may be assessed in quantitative terms such as percentages or in non-quantitative terms that range, for example, from a minimum to a maximum.

4. **B** The objective of procedures performed to understand internal control is to provide the auditor with knowledge necessary for audit planning. The objective of tests of controls is to provide the auditor with evidence to use in assessing control risk. Because procedures performed to achieve one of these objectives may also pertain to the other objective, understanding internal control and assessing control risk may be performed concurrently in an audit.

5. **C** If the controls appear to be effective, the auditor would test the controls and if they were found to be effective, the auditor would assess control risk below the maximum and reduce the extent of substantive testing. These tests of controls should only be performed when it is efficient to do so. It would be efficient if less time and effort would be spent testing controls than could be saved in substantive tests due to the lower control risk assessment.

6. **B** Detection risk is the risk that the auditor's procedures are not sufficiently extensive to discover an error or an fraud should one exist in an account. Detection risk is minimized by selecting a large sample size. Control risk is the risk that the client's internal controls are not sufficient to prevent, detect, and correct errors and fraud in the normal course of business. Thus, when control risk is high, the auditor would choose a large sample size in order to minimize detection risk.

7. **D** When detection risk decreases, the auditor will accept a smaller chance of not detecting an error; therefore, the auditor would test more transactions. That is, the auditor would increase the scope of substantive testing.

8. **A** Using the audit risk model (audit risk = inherent risk × control risk × detection risk), acceptable detection risk can be calculated as a function of allowable audit risk, inherent risk, and control risk. In order to determine his/her acceptable level of detection risk, the auditor must therefore assess control risk.

9. **A** Detection risk is the risk that the auditor will not detect a material misstatement that exists in an assertion. As the acceptable level of detection risk decreases, the assurance provided from substantive tests should increase. Since applying substantive tests as of an interim date rather than as of the year end potentially increases the risk that misstatements that may exist will not be detected, if the auditor wants to decrease detection risk, he or she may decide to perform substantive tests at year end, rather than at an interim date.

10. **B** Detection risk is the risk that the auditor's procedures will not detect an error in an account when in fact one exists. As the auditor's assurance that there are no errors in an account balance by applying substantive procedures is increased, the auditor's detection risk by definition may decrease.

11. **C** Control risk is defined as the risk that a material misstatement that could occur in an assertion will not be prevented or detected on a timely basis by an entity's internal control policies or procedures. The auditor assesses control risk as part of his overall evaluation of the risk that material misstatements may exist in the financial statements.

12. **B** Fraud are intentional misstatements or omissions of amounts or disclosures in financial statements. A typical client representation letter states that there have been no fraud involving management or employees who have significant roles in internal control.

13. **D** Material misstatements, including intentional manipulation of financial statements, are more likely to occur when management places undue emphasis on meeting earnings projections, especially if compensation is affected by meeting earnings targets. Another management characteristic that increases the risk of intentional manipulation is high turnover of senior accounting personnel, not low turnover. Similarly, a rapid rate of change in an entity's industry would heighten an auditor's concern rather than a slow rate of change. The auditor may be more concerned if insiders are selling stock, rather than purchasing stock.

14. **C** Audit risk precludes giving a guarantee; auditors can only provide reasonable assurance that financial statement assertions are free of material misstatement. Assessment of accounting principles and evaluation of overall financial statement presentation go to the basis of whether reasonable assurance is obtained. Relative importance is embodied in the concept of materiality, not audit risk. It is the fact that the client produces its financial statements, not audit risk, that makes them the responsibility of management.

15. **A** Audit risk consists of inherent risk, control risk, and detection risk. These risks represent the susceptibility of an item to misstatement, the likelihood that the internal control will not prevent or detect the misstatement, and the risk that the audit procedures will not detect it, respectively. All of these may be assessed in either quantitative or nonquantitative terms.

16. **B** An inherent limitation of internal control is that procedures which depend on segregation of functions can be overridden by collusion. The maintenance of an internal control is the responsibility of management. Internal control can never be relied upon so heavily as to entirely eliminate substantive testing. One of the constraints in designing an internal control is that the benefits of the system should exceed the costs.

17. **B** The second standard of fieldwork states, "The auditor should obtain a sufficient understanding of internal control to plan the audit and to determine the nature, timing, and extent of tests to be performed."

18. **A** The entity's internal control consists of the control procedures, the control environment and the accounting system. The control environment consists of management's and the board of directors' philosophy, operating style, attitude to work controls, the entity's organizational structure, and personnel policies and procedures. The accounting system consists of the methods and records used to identify, assemble, classify, and record transactions. The control procedures are the policies and procedures established to provide reasonable assurance that specific control objectives are met and include segregation of duties, authorization methods, and independent checks on performance. The organization's personnel manuals would be part of the control environment.

19. **C** AU 319 states that control procedures are those policies and procedures, in addition to the control environment and accounting system, that management has established to provide reasonable assurance that specific entity objectives will be achieved. Control procedures have various objectives and are applied at various organizational and data processing levels. They may also be integrated into specific components of the control environment and the accounting system. Generally, they may be categorized as procedures that pertain to the following:

    - Proper authorization of transactions and activities.
    - Segregation of duties that reduce the opportunities to both perpetrate and conceal fraud, assigning different people the responsibilities of authorizing transactions, recording transactions, and maintaining custody of assets.
    - Design and use of adequate documents and records to help ensure the proper recording of transactions and events, such as monitoring the use of prenumbered shipping documents.

20. **D** The auditor's objective is to obtain sufficient competent audit evidence to provide him with a reasonable basis for forming an opinion. There should be a rational relationship between the cost of obtaining that evidence and the usefulness of the information obtained. In determining the usefulness of evidence, relative risk may properly be given consideration. Also, the auditor's understanding and evaluation of internal control affects the nature, timing, and extent of testing. The matter of difficulty and expense involved in testing a particular item is not in itself a valid basis for omitting the test.

21. **C** A material weakness is a condition where control procedures are not suitably designed or operating effectively to prevent or detect an error or fraud in the normal course of business by employees performing their assigned duties. Therefore, accounting records and financial statements may be incorrect. A reportable condition is a situation in the control structure that may be designed ineffectively or not operating properly, but the deficiency has no effect on the timely recording and summarizing accounting transactions. According to GAAS, both situations, a material weakness and a reportable condition, are reportable conditions, but a reportable condition may not be a material weakness.

22. **A** AU 322 states that in assessing competence and objectivity, the auditor usually considers information obtained from previous experience with the internal audit function, from discussions with management personnel, and from a recent external quality review, if performed, of the internal audit function's activities. The auditor may also use professional internal auditing standards as criteria in making the assessment. If the

auditor determines that the internal auditors are sufficiently competent and objective, the auditor should then consider how the internal auditors' work may affect the audit. The other choices are all considered by the auditor as per above and therefore incorrect.

23. **B** AU 325 states that during the course of an audit, the auditor may become aware of matters relating to internal control that may be of interest to the audit committee. The matters that this section requires for reporting to the audit committee are referred to as reportable conditions. Specifically, these are matters coming to the auditor's attention that should be communicated to the audit committee because they represent significant deficiencies in the design or operation of internal control, which could adversely affect the organization's ability to record, process, summarize, and report financial data consistent with the assertions of management in the financial statements.

24. **D** The auditor should obtain an understanding of each of internal control elements to plan the audit. The understanding should include knowledge about the design of relevant policies, procedures, and records and whether they have been placed in operation by the entity.

25. **B** Objectivity refers to the potential biasness of the internal auditor. Objectivity is enhanced by having the internal auditor report to a level of management sufficiently removed from the accounting function (preferably the board of directors). The other answers relate to the quality of the internal auditor's work rather than the objectivity of the internal auditors.

26. **D** Control risk is the risk that the client's internal control will not be effective in preventing, detecting, and correcting errors and fraud in the normal course of business. Thus, if the auditor assesses control risk at the maximum, the auditor has determined that risk of errors and fraud being present in account balances is very likely.

27. **C** AU 319 states that the substantive tests that the auditor performs consist of tests of details of transactions and balances and analytical procedures. In assessing control risk, the auditor may also use tests of details of transactions as tests of controls. The objective of tests of details of transactions performed as substantive tests is to detect material misstatements in the financial statements. The objective of tests of details of transactions performed as tests of controls is to evaluate whether an internal control policy or procedure operated effectively. Although these objectives are different, both may be accomplished concurrently through performance of a test of details on the same transaction. The auditor should recognize, however, that careful consideration should be given to the design and evaluation of such tests to ensure that both objectives will be accomplished.

28. **A** AU 325 states that the report should state that the communication is intended solely for the information and the use of the audit committee, management, and others within the organization. When there are requirements established to furnish such reports, specific reference to such regulatory authorities may be made. Any report on reportable conditions should:

- Indicate that the purpose of the audit was to report on the financial statements and not to provide assurance on internal control.
- Include the definition of reportable conditions.
- Include the restriction on distribution.

29. D The question deals with the primary questions asked in testing controls. The auditor is least concerned with why. The auditor performs the procedures because he/she is concerned with control that centers primarily on how, where, and who, as opposed to why (this is answered in the understanding of the system).

30. B AU 350 states that the risk of incorrect rejection and the risk of assessing control risk too high relate to the efficiency of the audit. If the auditor's evaluation of a sample leads him to unnecessarily assess control risk too high for an assertion, he would ordinarily increase the scope of substantive tests to compensate for the perceived ineffectiveness of internal control policy or procedure. Although the audit may be less efficient in these circumstances, the audit is, nevertheless, effective.

31. C In making judgments about the extent of the effect of an internal auditor's work on the CPA's auditing procedures, the CPA should consider the materiality of financial statement amounts, the risk of material misstatement, and the degree of subjectivity involved in the evaluation of the audit evidence gathered in support of the assertions. Work done by internal auditors related to assertions about fixed asset additions, because such assertions involve a low degree of subjectivity and may have a lower risk of material misstatement, will likely affect the CPA's auditing procedures. The other answers deal with contingencies, valuation, and related-party transactions, which are examples of assertions that might have high risk or involve a high degree of subjectivity.

32. B Tests of controls are designed to determine whether the control procedures prescribed by the client are actually functioning. An example of a test of controls is to examine purchase orders for proper authorization.

33. D In performing an audit, the CPA may request direct assistance from internal auditors. For example, internal auditors may assist the independent CPA in obtaining an understanding of internal control or in performing tests of controls or substantive tests.

34. A Internal control policies and procedures relevant to an audit are those that pertain to an entity's ability to record, process, summarize, and report financial data consistent with management's assertions. The auditor's primary concern is the effect those policies and procedures have on the financial statement assertions.

35. C After obtaining the understanding of internal control and assessing control risk, the auditor may desire to seek a further reduction in the assessed level of control risk for certain assertions. In such cases, the auditor considers whether additional audit evidence sufficient to support a further reduction is likely to be available, and whether it would be efficient to perform tests of controls to obtain that audit evidence.

36. B In assessing control risk, the auditor may perform tests of controls directed toward the effectiveness of the design or operation of an internal control policy or procedure. These tests include inquiries, inspection of documents and reports, observation, and reperformance of the application of the policy or procedure by the auditor. The other answers are incorrect because analytical procedures, comparison and confirmation, and verification are examples of substantive tests, not tests of controls used to assess control risk.

37. D The auditor should concentrate on the substance of management's policies, procedures, and related actions rather than their form, because management may establish appropriate policies and procedures but not act on them.

38. A Management control methods is a control environment factor that affects management's ability to effectively supervise overall company activities. These methods include establishing systems that set forth management's plans and the results of actual performance, establishing methods that identify variances from budgets and forecasts, and using methods to investigate variances.

39. A Segregating incompatible duties is a typical control procedure. Thus, the existence of incompatible duties is a weakness in control procedures, not an inherent limitation of internal control. Even if control policies and procedures are placed in operation, the potential effectiveness of an entity's internal control is subject to inherent limitations. Mistakes in the application of policies and procedures may arise from such causes as mistakes in judgment, as well as personal carelessness, fatigue, and distraction. Also, policies and procedures that require segregation of duties can be circumvented by management override or collusion among internal or external parties.

40. D An entity's internal control consists of five components: the control environment, risk assessment, the accounting information and communication system, control activities, and monitoring. The control environment reflects the overall attitude, awareness, and actions of the board of directors, management, owners, and others concerning the importance of control and its emphasis in the entity. The other answers are examples of control procedures.

41. C The purpose of tests of controls is to provide reasonable assurance that internal controls are being applied as determined by the auditor during the review of internal control.

42. B One of the basic elements of an adequate system of internal control is competent personnel with clear lines of authority and responsibility.

43. D Because timely communication may be important, the auditor may choose to communicate significant matters during the course of the audit rather than after the audit is completed. The decision on whether interim communication should be issued would be influenced by the relative significance of the matters noted and the urgency of corrective follow-up action.

44. A AU 319 states that the auditor may make a preliminary assessment of control risk at less than a high level only when the auditor is able to identify policies and procedures of the accounting and internal control systems relevant to specific assertions that are likely to prevent or detect material misstatements in the financial statements; and plans to perform tests of control to support the assessment.

45. B After obtaining an understanding of internal control and assessing control risk, the auditor may desire a further reduction in the assessed level of control risk for certain assertions. In such cases, the auditor considers whether additional audit evidence sufficient to support a further reduction is likely to be available, and whether it would be cost efficient to perform tests of controls to obtain that audit evidence. If the auditor decides not to perform additional tests it is likely the auditor concluded that additional evidence to support a further reduction in control risk was not likely to be available or was not cost beneficial to obtain, which is the answer in this case.

46. D An examination of client records of the use of I.T. programs is appropriate for determining whether internal control is operating as designed. The types of evidence presented in the other choices are the types obtained in the performance of substantive tests.

47. C   Dual custody is a desirable control over marketable securities when an independent trust agent is not employed. Neither the review of the investment decisions nor the tracking of sales and purchases safeguard securities already acquired. The annual verification of securities by the chairman of the board is too infrequent to be an adequate control.

48. A   The probability of fraud involving marketable securities would be heightened if the individual having access to the securities also maintains the accounting records related to those securities. The potential for fraud can be reduced if the trust company has no direct contact with employees responsible for maintaining investment accounting records.

49. B   Management is responsible for the establishment and ongoing supervision of the internal control. When management is dominated by one individual, the credibility of the internal control is impaired. The other choices do not relate directly to management philosophy and operating style.

50. B   The auditor must document the understanding of a client's internal control. Such documentation may include flowcharts, questionnaires, decision tables, or memoranda. Flowcharts, which are diagrams that show a sequence of operations or processes, would not typically be used to describe or depict other work done by the auditor in meeting the second standard of fieldwork regarding internal control. Thus, although the auditor would perform the activities listed in the other answers, he/she would probably use means other than flowcharts to document the work that was done.

51. A   The auditor may document his understanding of the client's internal control through the use of a narrative, internal control questionnaire or flowchart, or any other appropriate means. Therefore, documentation of the client's internal control procedures is the correct answer.

52. C   A flowchart is a diagram showing by means of symbols and interconnecting lines (1) the structure and general sequence of operations of a program (program flowchart) or (2) a system of processing (system flowchart). Accordingly, a system flowchart would be the best means in the understanding of the sequence and relationships of activities and documents.

53. D   There are three common methods the auditor uses to document his/her understanding of internal control (control environment, accounting system, control procedures) in the audit documents—narrative, flowchart, and internal control questionnaire.

54. B   Inventory can be verified when perpetual records of goods on hand are compared to physical counts. If this is performed by an individual within the entity who neither maintains the records nor has custody of the inventory, such as an internal auditor, it is considered independent internal verification.

55. D   When an auditor selects items from the payroll register for examination, he is selecting from a population consisting of all payments made to employees. By tracing these selected items to time cards that have been approved by a supervisor, the auditor is verifying that the employees did work the hours that they were paid for. This is only one aspect of internal control related to payroll disbursements and would probably not be sufficient to reach a conclusion as to the effectiveness of internal controls. The auditor would trace the items to the cancelled payroll checks to determine if they were signed by an appropriate officer and would trace the items to personnel records to make certain that the payees were bona fide employees and that the rates of pay were proper.

56. C   The vouchers payable department prepares vouchers to authorize check issuances. Verifying the accuracy of vendor's invoices would be one step performed before preparing the voucher, as would having an authorized person approve the voucher, and matching the receiving report with the purchase order. Custody of assets such as checks would be incompatible with the authorization and recording functions represented by the vouchers payable department.

57. C   Subsidiary accounts are updated following shipment, so fraud in these accounts should not delay shipping. Omission of shipping documents would cause an overstatement of inventory because of the failure to decrease inventory for the goods shipped out. Final authorization of credit memos by personnel in the sales department could permit the personnel to pocket cash and eliminate unrecorded collections with credit memos. Fictitious transactions would increase reported revenues.

58. A   Bad debt write-offs should be authorized by an officer who is not involved in accounting. The treasurer could be that officer. The sales department deals directly with customers and could pocket payments, covering the unrecorded collection by authorizing a bad debt write-off. The billing and receivables departments are involved in clerical recordkeeping and should not be involved in a high level authorization function.

59. D   If transactions are properly executed and recorded then there is no supplementary concern about the activity reports, documentation of transfers, and production orders, since these are parts of those objectives. In addition to ensuring reliable records, there is a concern for safeguarding of assets, which includes proper custody of work-in-process and finished goods inventories.

60. B   Reconciliations should not be performed by employees involved in the records being compared. Job time tickets and clock card hours may be reconciled by the payroll department, which is independent of both records. The personnel department is involved in authorization and execution and should not be involved in accounting. The payroll department calculates payroll amounts and should not have influence over the authorization function.

61. D   Periodic reconciliation of securities with records by an independent party is a useful procedure. Direct access to securities being limited to one officer without such periodic reconciliation is less effective, and it might be reasonable to require two employees to be present when the securities are accessed. Postings to subsidiary and general ledger accounts both are record-keeping activities so segregation does little to protect custody of assets. The authorization of purchases and sales by the board does not address the problem of custody over the securities.

62. C   A cashier who is receiving remittances is engaged in a custody function and may properly engage in activities related to the custody of cash and check remittances, including the preparation of the daily deposit slip to accompany the transfer of those remittances to the bank. The cashier should not be involved in accounting or recording functions involving cash, such as preparation of a schedule of individual checks received, the monthly bank reconciliation, or remittance advices.

63. C   A comparison of physical counts with accounting records provides a useful independent check of quantities on hand, and may assist in the identification of missing inventory. Reconciliation of work-in-process with job cost sheets would only be of limited valued in determining proper custody of inventory, since job cost sheets include labor and overhead items that cannot be proven by examination of physical units, as well as costs for quantities that may have been spoiled. Segregation between two different accounting

functions is pointless, since internal control over custody requires segregation of custody functions from accounting functions. Approval of inventory journal entries by the storekeeper would constitute a weakness in internal control, since one employee is participating in both custody and accounting functions.

64. C For proper control, all merchandise received by a company should be delivered to the same location, the receiving department. Receipt of goods by any other department represents a failure to properly limit access to assets.

65. D The bank registrar of capital stock keeps track of stock issuances, primarily to ensure that such issuances do not exceed the authorization granted by the state of incorporation and the directives of the board of directors, which must approve all such issuances. The registrar does not determine the appropriateness of dividend declarations. Accounting for stock certificates is a task for the transfer agent, not the registrar. The registrar is not a participant in mergers, acquisitions, and sales of treasury stock, and is only involved in the issuances of stock.

66. D Once a check is finally signed, it becomes equivalent to cash and must be controlled by the person who created it who should also take final responsibility for it. No other person can take adequate responsibility for mailing checks, nor would such a separation of duties add to controlling cash transactions.

67. B Periodic reconciliations of recorded amounts to physical counts of inventory are necessary to identify and pursue possible wrongful inventory shortages on a timely basis. Comparing only paper records without addressing the physical inventory fails to address the reality of actual inventory quantities. Analytical procedures similarly fail to address actual inventory quantities, as do cost accounting overhead rate applications.

68. A Hiring personnel is an authorization function, whereas distribution of payroll checks involves custody of a resulting asset. These two functions should be segregated. While hiring personnel relates to operational responsibility, distribution of payroll checks is not a form of record keeping. While hiring personnel is a human resources function, distribution of payroll checks is not a controllership function which relates to the accounting records. There is no general need to separate administrative controls from internal accounting controls.

69. B Cash must be closely controlled as it is qualitatively material and relatively risky. As soon as it is received, a remittance listing of cash items must be prepared, before recording, posting, or deposit.

70. C If credit granting is separate from the sales function, sales on credit could not be made without approval from someone performing the credit granting function. This would prevent sales personnel from making sales to individuals with questionable credit that could result in high bad debt write-offs. Denying employees access to cash avoids thefts of cash, but does not prevent sales being made to individuals who are not creditworthy. Matching shipping documents to sales invoices occurs after sales have been made. Likewise, reconciliation of the accounts receivable records to the control account would occur after sales have been made. Neither would prevent selling to customers who are not creditworthy.

71. A The control objective of safeguarding of assets can best be met by limiting access to assets to a minimum number of individuals. Since the treasurer is responsible for the company's cash, cash can best be safeguarded if the treasurer is the only one with access to it. This will include access to signed checks, and can be accomplished if the treasurer distributes paychecks and retains custody of unclaimed paychecks.

72. D With a bank lockbox system, a company can limit employees' access to cash, reducing the risk of misappropriation. Independently prepared mailroom prelists and daily check summaries improve the probability of detection, while employee fidelity bonds will improve likelihood of recovery.

73. B Before making a payment, a vendor's invoice should be matched with a purchase order to make certain that the goods invoiced were ordered, and with a receiving report to make certain that the goods were received. The other controls mentioned are all valid controls, but are not directly related to the accounts payable function.

74. B When nonconforming goods are returned to a vendor, the purchasing department should make certain that the goods are not paid for. Overpayment can be avoided if a debit memo is sent by the purchasing department to the accounting department.

75. C Once checks have been signed, they are equivalent to cash. As a result, unclaimed payroll checks should not be returned to the payroll department as they should be segregated from the handling of cash. A voucher for the amount of payroll should be prepared in the general accounting department to make certain that an appropriate transfer of funds is made to the payroll account. Payroll checks are normally prepared by the payroll department and signed by the treasurer, and the payroll department must be notified of terminations so that they do not prepare payroll checks for terminated employees.

76. A By having an independent trust company retain possession of securities, the custody and record keeping functions for the securities are segregated. Verifying the securities in the safe each year verifies their existence, while tracing purchases and sales verifies that transactions have been properly recorded. Having a member of the board of directors control the securities in a bank safe-deposit box could be an effective way to safeguard against loss, but not as effective as the use of an independent trust company.

77. A If personnel in sales were able to authorize credit memos, they could take possession of cash receipts and simultaneously reduce the customer's account so that the misappropriation of funds would not be detected. If fictitious transactions were recorded, both revenues and accounts receivable would be overstated. Shipping goods to customers is entirely separate from the recording of transactions in the subsidiary ledger. Finally, an omission of shipping documents would result in an overstatement of inventory.

78. D A vendor's invoice and a bill of lading are both documents that are prepared by the vendor and would not be useful in verifying that goods received were properly ordered. A materials requisition may initiate the acquisition process, but the order is placed by completing and approving a purchase order.

79. B Once checks are signed, it is virtually equivalent to cash and should be handled by as few people as possible. As a result, the employee who signs a check would be the best person to mail it.

80. B The receiving clerk should receive all merchandise, including goods shipped from a vendor and goods being returned by a customer. If received by the accounts receivable supervisor, they could retain the goods and write off the account as if they had never been

returned. If received by the shipping department supervisor, detection of shipments of defective merchandise could go undetected. If received by the sales clerk, shipments that were not supported by valid sales could go undetected.

81. A Periodic inspection of plant and equipment by the internal audit staff would result in the detection of changes which could be checked against records for proper authorization and recording. Such a procedure would indicate a reduced level of control risk.

    Comparing current-year and prior-year balances would only address recorded transactions. Reviewing prenumbered purchase orders would not provide information about disposals, and approval of depreciation does not provide any safeguards over either the plant and equipment or the recording of acquisitions or disposals.

82. D If access to securities required the signatures and presence of two designated officials, misappropriation of the securities would require collusion.

83. C The treasurer's duties relate to processing and sending cash disbursements. Thus, the treasurer's department would verify the accuracy of checks and vouchers, mail checks to vendors, and cancel payment vouchers. The accounts payable department would approve vendors' invoices for payment.

84. B If transactions are properly executed and recorded, there is no supplementary concern about the activity reports, documentation of transfers, and production orders, since these are components of the objectives of executing and recording transactions. In addition to ensuring reliable records, there is concern for safeguarding of assets, which includes proper custody of work-in-process and finished goods inventories.

85. D A well designed internal control should separate the functions of authorization, custody, and reconciliation. The department approving purchase orders should not reconcile the open invoice file (reconciliation) or inspect the goods upon receipt (custody). Also, in a well designed internal control, the purchase order should be approved by a department other than that requesting the purchase. Therefore, the department approving the purchase order would not ordinarily authorize the requisition of goods. In approving purchase orders, it is customary for the department to select vendors and negotiate terms with the selected vendors.

86. C Hiring personnel is an authorization function, whereas distribution of payroll checks involves custody of a resulting asset. These two functions should be segregated. While hiring personnel is a human resources function, distribution of payroll checks is not a controllership function relating to the accounting records. There is no general need to separate administrative controls from internal accounting controls. While hiring personnel relates to an operational responsibility, distribution of payroll checks is not a form of record keeping.

87. A The controller is responsible for the preparation of accounting records, the treasurer is responsible for the paychecks, and payroll will apply the appropriate pay rates to hours worked in computing paychecks. For adequate segregation of duties, the personnel department should be responsible for authorizing pay rate and deduction changes.

88. D In studying and evaluating the client's internal control over notes payable, the auditor would be most interested in verifying that all borrowings are properly authorized by the board of directors. Controls related to the use of authorized signatures on checks would be of more concern in the audit of the spending cycle. Issues such as the

collateral for notes payable and the use of the proceeds from notes payable are operating matters that are not ordinarily of concern in the auditor's study and evaluation of the internal control.

89. A Comparing daily sales summaries to postings in the accounts receivable ledger would provide evidence that all billed sales are correctly posted to the accounts receivable ledger. Examining shipping documents supporting sales invoices provides evidence that all billed sales represent actual shipments made by the client. Reconciling the accounts receivable subsidiary ledger to the control total establishes the agreement between these amounts, but does not provide evidence about the timely posting of sales. Verifying that each shipment is supported by a sales invoice provides the auditor with assurance that all shipments have been invoiced by the client.

90. C The payroll department is primarily responsible for the recording function. Accordingly, they should not perform any duties related to authorization, custody of assets, or comparisons. Authorization forms for new employees are normally processed by the personnel department. If so, no problem occurs when the payroll supervisor merely examines these forms. In a computerized accounting environment, the payroll register should be compared with the original data for reasonableness to ensure accurate processing. Finally, the payroll department supervisor should initiate hiring employees under his or her supervision but should not authorize payroll rate changes for these employees.

91. B The process of matching receiving reports and vendors' invoices represents the comparison (independent checks on performance) control procedure. The employee performing this function would also logically recompute the calculations of the vendors' invoices.

92. C Using time tickets to record actual labor worked on production orders would prevent direct labor hours from being incorrectly charged to manufacturing overhead, since the actual recording of direct labor costs is evaluated. Comparing counts of work-in-process to recorded amounts verifies that the physical inventory agrees with the accounting records. Comparing daily journal entries with approved production orders provides assurance that all production activity is recorded. Reconciling work-in-process inventory with periodic cost budgets provides some evidence that the overall inventory balances are reasonably stated. However, none of these final three control procedures explicitly evaluate the recording of direct labor costs.

93. D Accurate inventory records will be maintained if periodic inventory counts are used to adjust the perpetual inventory records. This procedure ensures that the accounting records agree with the inventory maintained by the client.

94. C Remittance listings represent a record of cash received from the organization's customers for sales made on account. This document contains the customer's account number along with the amount of cash received from the customer. One copy of the remittance listing should be used by the accounts receivable bookkeeper to update the subsidiary accounts receivable records.

95. D For effective segregation of duties, the write-off of uncollectible accounts receivable should be authorized by an individual who has no other responsibilities with respect to accounts receivable. Since the accounts receivable department records accounts receivable transactions and the credit department authorizes sales to customers on account, neither of these departments should approve write-offs. The treasurer would normally approve write-offs.

96. D Comparing control totals for shipping documents and invoices will assist in determining that all goods shipped have been billed. Using computer controls to verify the mathematical accuracy of sales invoices will assist in detecting errors on billings. Matching shipping documents with approved sales orders will assist in determining that all goods shipped were based on authorized sales. All of these procedures enable a company to detect errors in the billing process. Reconciling control totals for sales invoices with the accounts receivable subsidiary ledger enables the company to determine that all invoices have been recorded, but this does not relate to errors in the billing process.

97. D In examining invoices received from vendors, the vouchers payable department will match the invoice with the receiving report and approve the invoice for payment. Once the invoice has been examined, the account distribution could also be provided on the voucher itself to assist in record keeping. In contrast, unused prenumbered purchase orders and receiving reports would be accounted for in purchasing and receiving, the departments that issue these documents.

98. D Restricting access to equipment relates to safeguarding of assets, but does not concern the initiation and execution of equipment transactions. The approval of major repairs, use of prenumbered purchase orders, and solicitation of competitive bids are all related to the initiation of equipment transactions.

99. C Upon receipt of checks from customers by mail, a remittance listing should be prepared by a responsible employee. Following the preparation of the remittance listing, client employees would add the checks to the daily cash summary and record the checks in the cash receipts journal. The individual opening the mail would verify that checks were supported by a remittance advice, not a sales invoice.

100. B Stamping vouchers as "paid" provides assurance that each voucher is only paid once. Determining that vouchers are supported by a vendor's invoice ensures that vouchers are prepared only for items billed by vendors. The use of prenumbered vouchers and accounting for the numerical sequence of those vouchers provides evidence that all vouchers have been recorded. Finally, ascertaining that vouchers are prepared for authorized purchases provides evidence that vouchers are not prepared for payment to fictitious vendors.

101. A The use of a lockbox prevents employees from having access to cash receipts and, therefore, is superior to the other choices.

102. A The notification of the payroll supervisor by the personnel department of terminated employees allows the payroll supervisor to remove the terminated employee from the payroll to prevent a check from being issued.

103. B Reperformance and observation are audit procedures commonly used in tests of controls. The other choices represent audit procedures more commonly associated with substantive tests.

104. D Agreeing the vendor's invoice with the receiving report insures that the company is only billed for what it receives. Agreeing the vendor's invoice with the purchase order insures that the company was billed for what it ordered. After establishing agreement, a voucher is prepared and submitted for payment.

105.D By vouching assets recorded in the accounting records to the actual assets, the auditor would gather evidence concerning failure to record retirements (a weakness in internal control over retirements). Inspecting equipment and tracing it to plant asset records will not detect failures to record retirement, because the population being sampled does not include any retired assets. If an asset is in the subsidiary ledger, even though it may have actually been retired, depreciation is normally taken on the asset. The most likely scenario for equipment which is unused, but still on hand, is to leave it in the plant asset records. It is not likely that unused assets would be transferred to other assets.

106.A Analytical procedures revealing a large difference between actual labor costs and standard labor costs would alert the auditor to possible employee payroll fraud. All other choices consist of standard payroll procedures.

ACCOUNTS RECEIVABLE AND REVENUE

STUDY MANUAL – AUDITING & ATTESTATION
CHAPTER 8

Study Tip: Keep a diary of your study time. Each day, write down the amount of time you spend and what you get accomplished. People often tend to overestimate their study hours and, thus, quit too soon. A diary will help you monitor whether you are investing an adequate amount of time so that you can take remedial action if necessary.

INTRODUCTION

As noted in earlier, financial statements that purport to be in conformity with generally accepted accounting principles contain certain assertions: presentation and disclosure, existence or occurrence, rights and obligations, completeness, and valuation or allocation. Auditors gather evidence to form an opinion with respect to these assertions. The experienced auditor should be able to prepare an audit program for an audit area (e.g., receivables) to test whether these assertions are supportable. The process is one in which specific audit objectives are developed based on the assertions being made in the financial statements. Finally, audit procedures to meet these audit objectives are formulated and listed in an audit program. For purposes of the CPA exam, consider two possible approaches for auditing an account: tests of balances and tests of details.

A. Tests of Balances and Tests of Details.

1. *Direct tests of ending balance (tests of balances)*. This approach requires the auditor to identify specific components of an account balance. For example, the cash account can be broken down into cash on hand and cash on deposit in the client's various bank accounts. Under this approach, the auditor will select and verify a sample of components of the account balance. Accounts that are normally examined via this approach are high turnover accounts such as cash, accounts receivable, inventory, and accounts payable.

2. *Tests of inputs and outputs during the year (tests of details)*. This approach requires the auditor to verify individual transactions comprising an account balance or class of transactions. This approach focuses on the individual transactions occurring during the year and not the final account balance. Accounts normally examined via this approach are lower turnover accounts, such as investments; property, plant and equipment; notes and bonds payable; and shareholders' equity.

3. Many audit procedures provide support for *multiple management assertions*. For example, cut-off procedures provide support for rights and obligations as well as for

existence and completeness. The following are typical procedures included in a substantive audit program:

a. To support presentation and disclosure:

- Review disclosures for compliance with GAAP.
- Inquire about disclosures.

b. To support existence or occurrence:

- Confirmation.
- Observation—always consider whether you can observe the item itself and/or legal documents representing the item.
- Trace/vouch transactions.

c. To support rights and obligations:

- Cutoffs—consider whether transactions have been reported in the proper period.
- Authorization—consider whether there are transactions that require specific authorization.

d. To support completeness:

- Analytical procedures.
- Omissions—consider how transactions could improperly have been omitted from the account.

e. To support valuation:

- Foot and cross-foot schedules (total them across and down).
- Agree the account balances on schedules to the general ledger.
- Agree financial statement balances to account balances on schedules.
- Consider valuation methods and whether they have been properly applied.
- Consider related accounts (e.g., accounts receivable and bad debt expense; long-term debt and interest expense; fixed assets and repair and maintenance expense; and fixed assets and depreciation expense).

B. Auditing Receivables.

1. The auditor's primary substantive testing procedure related to accounts receivable involves confirming accounts receivable with customers. Auditors are to confirm receivables unless the receivables are immaterial, the procedure would be ineffective, or the combined assessment of inherent and control risk is low and that assessment with other substantive evidence is sufficient to reduce audit risk to an acceptably low level.

2. *When no reply is received to the negative form of confirmation*, the assumption is made that the debtor agrees with the amount and that evidence as to the existence

assertion has been collected. *When no reply is received to a positive confirmation*, a second request is normally mailed to the debtor; if no reply to the second request is received, the auditor normally performs alternative procedures, such as verifying individual sales invoices or shipping documents and examining subsequent cash receipts affecting the account.

3. Confirmation of accounts receivable may reveal a defalcation scheme known as lapping.

   a. Lapping occurs when cash received from a customer is not deposited and the account of the customer is not credited for payment.

   b. Subsequent cash receipts are recorded as credits to the account of the original customer, which leaves the account of the subsequent customer overstated.

   c. Lapping most frequently occurs when one individual has responsibility for both record keeping and custody of cash.

4. In addition, the auditor should also evaluate the client's provision for bad debt expense and the allowance for doubtful accounts.

5. The table below details the typical substantive audit procedures performed for accounts receivable.

Type of audit procedure	Audit procedure	Management assertion(s)
Confirmation	Confirm selected amounts receivables with customers.	Existence or occurrence
Observe	Physically examine notes receivable.	Existence or occurrence; rights and obligations
Recalculation	Obtain an aged analysis of accounts receivables and recalculate the client's provision for bad debt expense and the allowance for doubtful accounts.	Rights and obligations; valuation or allocation
Recalculation	Recalculate interest revenue on notes receivable.	Valuation or allocation
Recalculation	Foot the subsidiary ledger. Reconcile the subsidiary ledger to the general ledger	Valuation or allocation
Inspect documents	Review cash collections of accounts receivable which occur subsequent to year-end.	Existence or occurrence; valuation or allocation

Type of audit procedure	Audit procedure	Management assertion(s)
Inspect documents	Perform cutoff procedures by reviewing sales invoices, shipping documents, and credit memos near year-end.	Completeness; rights and obligations
Inspect documents	Review correspondence files, minutes of the board of directors' meetings, attorney letters, loan agreements, and other documentation for evidence of accounts pledged, factored, or assigned.	Rights and obligations
Inspect documents	For confirmation exceptions and confirmations with no response, examine sales invoices and evidence of subsequent cash receipts.	Existence or occurrence
Inspect documents	Review the listing of accounts receivable to identify amounts due from officers and employees.	Presentation and disclosure
Inspect documents	Review disclosures for compliance with GAAP.	Presentation and disclosure
Inquiry	Inquire about accounts receivable pledged, factored, or assigned.	Rights and obligations
Inquiry	Inquire about the reasonableness of accounts written off during the current period and the adequacy of the allowance for doubtful accounts.	Valuation or allocation
Inquiry	Inquire about accounts receivable due from officers and employees.	Presentation and disclosure
Analytical procedures	Calculate accounts receivable turnover ratios for reasonableness.	Valuation or allocation; completeness
Analytical procedures	Compare sales activity for the current period with expectations based on economic conditions, the industry, activity, and prior periods.	Valuation or allocation; completeness

Type of audit procedure	Audit procedure	Management assertion(s)
Analytical procedures	Evaluate the reasonableness of the client's provision for bad debt expense and allowance for doubtful accounts.	Valuation and allocation; completeness

eval bad debt exp estimate

QUESTIONS: ACCOUNTS RECEIVABLE AND REVENUE

1. Proper authorization procedures in the revenue cycle usually provide for the approval of bad debt write-offs by an employee in which of the following departments?
   A. Treasurer.
   B. Sales.
   C. Billing.
   D. Accounts receivable.

2. Which of the following controls *most likely* would help ensure that all credit sales transactions of an entity are recorded?
   A. The billing department supervisor sends copies of approved sales orders to the credit department for comparison to authorized credit limits and current customer account balances.
   B. The accounting department supervisor independently reconciles the accounts receivable subsidiary ledger to the accounts receivable control account monthly.
   C. The accounting department supervisor controls the mailing of monthly statements to customers and investigates any differences reported by customers.
   D. The billing department supervisor matches prenumbered shipping documents with entries in the sales journal.

3. Which of the following internal control procedures *most likely* would assure that all billed sales are correctly posted to the accounts receivable ledger?
   A. Daily sales summaries are compared to daily postings to the accounts receivable ledger.
   B. Each sales invoice is supported by a prenumbered shipping document.
   C. The accounts receivable ledger is reconciled daily to the control account in the general ledger.
   D. Each shipment on credit is supported by a prenumbered sales invoice.

4. Upon receipt of customers' checks in the mailroom, a responsible employee should prepare a remittance listing that is forwarded to the cashier. A copy of the listing should be sent to the:
   A. Internal auditor to investigate the listing for unusual transactions.
   B. Treasurer to compare the listing with the monthly bank statement.
   C. Accounts receivable bookkeeper to update the subsidiary accounts receivable records.
   D. Entity's bank to compare the listing with the cashier's deposit slip.

5. Proper authorization of write-offs of uncollectible accounts should be approved in which of the following departments?
   A. Accounts receivable.
   B. Credit.
   C. Accounts payable.
   D. Treasurer.

6. Which of the following procedures *most likely* would NOT be an internal control procedure designed to reduce the risk of errors in the billing process?
   A. Comparing control totals for shipping documents with corresponding totals for sales invoices.
   B. Using computer programmed controls on the pricing and mathematical accuracy of sales invoices.
   C. Matching shipping documents with approved sales orders before invoice preparation.
   D. Reconciling the control totals for sales invoices with the accounts receivable subsidiary ledger.

7. Which of the following tests of controls *most likely* would help assure an auditor that goods shipped are properly billed?
   A. Scan the sales journal for sequential and unusual entries.
   B. Examine shipping documents for matching sales invoices.
   C. Compare the accounts receivable ledger to daily sales summaries.
   D. Inspect unused sales invoices for consecutive prenumbering.

8. To reduce the risks associated with accepting e-mail responses to requests for confirmation of accounts receivable, an auditor *most likely* would:
   A. Request the senders to mail the original forms to the auditor.
   B. Examine subsequent cash receipts for the accounts in question.
   C. Consider the e-mail responses to the confirmations to be exceptions.
   D. Mail second requests to the e-mail respondents.

ANSWERS: ACCOUNTS RECEIVABLE AND REVENUE

1. **A** Authorization for write-off of bad debts rests with the credit manager. The credit manager, organizationally, reports to the treasurer.

2. **D** A sale typically occurs and should be recorded when goods are shipped. Matching prenumbered shipping documents with sales journal entries is a good control to ensure that all sales are recorded. All the shipping documents should be accounted for as either resulting in a journal entry or having been voided.

3. **A** If an entity wants to be sure that all billed sales are correctly posted to the accounts receivable subsidiary ledger, an internal control procedure that compares invoices or billings to the subsidiary ledger entries should be designed. Thus, comparing daily summaries of billed sales to daily postings to the receivables ledger will provide the necessary assurance. Answers (b) and (d), which compare invoices and shipments, do not include any comparisons with postings to the accounts receivable ledger. Answer (c), which compares general and subsidiary ledgers, does not include comparisons to billings or invoices.

4. **C** A copy of the remittance listing is sent to the accounts receivable clerk and posted to the subsidiary records. Accounting for assets is a function that should be separated from the custody of those assets. The accounts receivable bookkeeper maintains records of the balance owed by each customer, while the cashier has custody of the cash. The cashier does not have an opportunity to cover a shortage of cash by using checks received on account because the AR ledger would indicate a different balance than that owed. There is no need to send copies to the internal auditor, the treasurer, or the bank, because the goal is to establish accountability for the asset.

5. **D** The treasurer has responsibility for custody of assets; therefore, authorizing the write-off of a receivable (an asset) is the responsibility of the treasurer. Choice (a) is incorrect because A/R is an accounting function that should be separated from the custody of the asset. Choice (b) is incorrect because the credit department authorized credit to customers and they should not be in the position of writing-off what they authorized. Choice (c) is incorrect because the accounts payable department has nothing to do with receivables.

6. **D** The reconciliation provides evidence that sales which have been invoiced are recorded in the accounts receivable subsidiary ledger but does not reduce the risk of errors in billing. Choice (a) is incorrect because it reduces the risk of errors in the billing process by providing evidence that all items shipped were included in the sales invoices. Choice (b) is incorrect because it reduces the risk of errors in the billing process by controlling the mathematical accuracy of the computations on the sales invoices. Choice (c) is incorrect because matching shipping documents with sales orders reduces the risk of errors in the billing process by providing evidence that approved sales orders were shipped before being invoiced.

7. **B** The auditor is looking for evidence to prove that goods shipped are properly billed. To accomplish the completeness of the billing process for all goods shipped, it is necessary to sample from a population that includes all goods shipped by examining a sample of shipping documents and tracing them to matching sales invoices.

8. A The problem with e-mail responses to audit confirmation requests is that the origin of the e-mail is not secure. That means that someone other than the recipient of the confirmation request may respond. By requesting a "hard copy" of the confirmation, the auditor may place greater reliance on the communication.

STATISTICAL SAMPLING

STUDY MANUAL – AUDITING & ATTESTATION
CHAPTER 9

Study Tip: Do not dwell on whether you are going to pass or fail the CPA exam. That is pure speculation and can harm your chances. Your only goal is to add a point or two to your score every day. That is a reasonable goal and one that will bring you success faster than you might think possible.

Audit sampling is the application of an audit procedure (tests of control or substantive testing) to less than 100%t of the items within an account balance or class of transactions for the purpose of drawing a general conclusion about the account balance or the entire group of transactions based on the characteristics detected in the sample. Sampling allows an auditor to draw conclusions about transactions or balances without incurring the time and cost of examining every transaction.

STATISTICAL AND NONSTATISTICAL SAMPLING

Audit sampling can take one of two forms:

1. Statistical sampling applies the laws of probability theory to assist the auditor in designing a sampling plan and subsequently evaluating the results of the sample.

2. Nonstatistical sampling (also referred to as *judgmental sampling*) is based solely on the auditor's judgment.

Statistical sampling is permitted in the examination of financial statements, but it is not required. The use of statistical sampling as opposed to nonstatistical sampling will have no effect on the substance of the audit procedures, the competency of the evidence gathered, or the ultimate audit conclusions based on sampled items. In other words, either statistical or nonstatistical sampling can provide sufficient audit evidence in accordance with the third standard of fieldwork.

The use of statistical sampling provides certain advantages over the use of nonstatistical sampling in that it provides a means of mathematically evaluating the outcome of a sampling plan by applying the laws of probability to measure the likelihood that sample results are representative of the population. It also provides a means to design an efficient sampling plan. An auditor can determine the exact sample size required to achieve the objectives of the test to which it is applied.

A disadvantage to statistical sampling is that an auditor can overvalue the evidence it provides. The use of statistical sampling does not replace the need for a healthy skepticism. Another disadvantage of statistical sampling could be its cost. It can be more costly to train auditors to use statistical sampling and more costly to design samples.

APPLICATIONS OF SAMPLING IN THE AUDIT

ATTRIBUTE SAMPLING

When studying and evaluating the client's internal control, the auditor will perform tests of controls on control policies and procedures. The use of sampling for compliance testing is referred to as attribute (qualitative characteristic) sampling.

When performing attribute sampling, the auditor attempts to estimate the rate of occurrence of some attribute in the population. In this case, the auditor attempts to estimate the rate at which internal control policies and procedures are not being followed by client personnel.

The auditor's decision based on performing attribute sampling will be either:

- To rely on the client's internal control as planned and not modify the planned extent of substantive tests.
- To reduce reliance on internal control and increase the planned extent of substantive tests.

VARIABLES SAMPLING

The auditor will also utilize sampling when performing substantive tests on the client's account balances. This type of sampling is referred to as variables (quantitative characteristic) sampling. Variables sampling attempts to estimate either:

- A numerical amount such as the balance in an account or class of transactions.
- The dollar error in an account or class of transactions.

The auditor's decision based on performing variables sampling will be either:

- To accept the client's account balance as fairly stated.
- To reject the client's account balance and conclude that material misstatement exists in the account balance.

AUDIT RISK

Audit risk is a combination of the risk that a material misstatement will occur and the risk that the auditor will not detect it. It consists of the risk (inherent and control) that the balance or class and related assertions contain misstatements that could be material when aggregated with other misstatements, and the risk (detection) that the auditor will not detect such misstatement.

NONSAMPLING RISK

Nonsampling risk includes all aspects of audit risk that are not due to sampling. It is controlled by adequate planning and supervision of audit work and proper adherence to quality control standards. The following are examples of nonsampling risk:

- The failure to select appropriate audit procedures.
- The failure to recognize misstatements in documents examined.
- Misinterpreting the results of audit tests.

SAMPLING RISK

Sampling risk is the risk that the auditor's sample is not representative of the population. Stated another way, sampling risk is the risk that the auditor's conclusion, based on a sample, might be different from the conclusion that would be reached if the test were applied in the same way to the entire population.

Matrix of Alternative Audit Conclusions

	True but Unknown Population	
Conclusion based on audit sample	Rely on internal control/ no material misstatements	Reduce reliance on internal control/material misstatements exist
Rely on internal control/ no material misstatements	Correct conclusion	Overreliance/incorrect acceptance
Reduce reliance on internal control/material misstatements exist	Underreliance/incorrect rejection	Correct conclusion

Sampling Risk in Attribute Sampling.

Considering the possible outcomes in the auditor's study and evaluation of internal control, the sampling risks faced by auditors in performing attribute sampling are summarized below:

- *Risk of underreliance* (or risk of assessing control risk too high). The auditor decides not to rely on internal control when, in fact, the auditor should rely on the internal control. Therefore, the auditor will perform more effective levels of substantive testing resulting in a loss of efficiency.
- *Risk of overreliance* (or risk of assessing control risk too low). The auditor decides to rely on internal control when it is not appropriate. As reliance on internal control is increased, the auditor will perform insufficient levels of substantive tests resulting in a loss of effectiveness.

Sampling Risk in Variables Sampling.

The outcomes in the auditor's use of variables sampling are summarized below:

- *Risk of incorrect rejection.* The auditor's sample indicates that the account balance is materially misstated even though it is fairly stated. Because the auditor's initial reaction when an account appears to be materially misstated is to gather additional evidence. This results in a loss of efficiency.
- *Risk of incorrect acceptance.* The auditor's sample indicates that the account balance is fairly stated even though the account balance is materially misstated. Therefore, the auditor accepts a misstated account balance. This results in a loss of effectiveness.

The risks above are all caused by nonrepresentative samples. In addition to a nonrepresentative sample, incorrect decisions can be made by the auditor for other reasons such as human error in failure to recognize exceptions, in sample selection, in evaluation, and in the use of inappropriate audit procedures.

PRECISION AND RELIABILITY

When discussing the overall sampling procedure used by the auditor for attribute and variables sampling, there are two important concepts to consider:

1. *Precision* (or the allowance for sampling risk) represents the closeness of the auditor's sample estimate to the true (but unknown) population value. In sampling for attributes, the auditor's objective is to determine whether the rate of compliance deviations is less than a specified tolerable rate of occurrence. The tolerable rate is a matter of audit judgment and is the maximum rate of deviations from a prescribed control procedure that the auditor would be willing to tolerate without reducing planned reliance on the control. In sampling for variables, precision is expressed as a dollar amount. Here the auditor's objective is to determine whether the error is less than the tolerable error. Tolerable error is related to the auditor's estimate of materiality and is the maximum amount of error that may exist without causing a material misstatement.

2. *Reliability* (or level of confidence) is the probability that the auditor's sample provides a sample estimate that is of a specified precision.

The concepts of precision and reliability are used together in evaluating audit evidence. For example, assume that the auditor has performed tests of controls and determined a deviation rate of 5% in his or her sample. If precision is 2% and the reliability is 90%, the auditor's conclusion would be as follows:

There is a 90% probability that the true deviation rate in the population is between 3% (5% − 2%) and 7% (5% + 2%).

DEVELOPING A SAMPLING PLAN

ATTRIBUTE SAMPLING (USED IN TESTS OF CONTROLS)

In developing an attribute sampling plan, the auditor would perform the following steps:

1. Determine the controls to be tested (those controls on which the auditor intends to rely). Some of the attributes or controls to be tested may include:

   - All transactions have proper supporting documentation.
   - All valid transactions are recorded without omissions.
   - All transactions are authorized.
   - Dollar amounts and quantities are correctly calculated.
   - All transactions are properly classified and allocated.
   - There is a proper cutoff for all transactions.

2. Determine the objectives of the test. An auditor should identify characteristics that would indicate operation of the internal control procedures.

3. Define the deviation conditions. A deviation is a departure from the prescribed internal control policy or procedure.

4. Define the population in a manner consistent with the audit objectives. For tests of controls, the population is the class of transactions being tested. Conclusions based on sample results can be projected only to the population from which the sample was selected. There are three steps involved in defining the population:

   a. Define the period covered by the test. Ideally, tests of controls should be applied to transactions executed during the entire period under audit. In some cases, it is most efficient to test transactions at an interim date and use supplemental procedures to obtain reasonable assurance regarding the remaining period.

   b. Define the sampling unit. The sampling unit is one of the individual elements constituting the population.

   c. Consider the completeness of the population.

5. Determine the method of selecting the sample. The sample should be representative of the population; all items in the population should have an opportunity to be selected. Methods will be discussed later.

6. Determine the sample size.

   - Consider the acceptable risk of assessing control risk too low. Because the auditor uses the results of tests of controls as the source of evidence for assessing control risks at levels below the maximum, a low allowable risk is normally selected.
   - Determine the tolerable rate, which is the maximum error rate that would not require a revision in the plan for substantive testing.
   - Determine the expected population deviation rate that will be a matter of professional judgment and will be based largely on the auditor's past experience. This is used only to determine sample size and not to evaluate sample results, so the estimate need not be exact.

- The auditor should select extra sample items so that voided, unused, or inapplicable documents can be excluded from the sample and be replaced.

Attributes Sampling Summary of Relationships to Sample Size	
Increase in:	*Effect on sample size:*
Risk of assessing control risk too low	Decrease
Tolerable rate	Decrease
Expected population deviation rate	Increase
Population	Increase (slightly for large samples)

- Fixed versus sequential sample size approach. Audit samples may be designed using either a fixed or a sequential sample size approach. Supplementing traditional attributes (fixed size) sampling approaches are:
  - Discovery sampling is a form of sampling for attributes that can be used when the expected rate of occurrence is either zero or very low. In applying discovery sampling, the auditor will determine the rate of deviations that is acceptable for continuing to rely on the control. The auditor then determines the reliability for the sample. Using these, the auditor selects a sample size large enough so that at least one deviation would most likely show up in the sample if the overall rate of occurrence in the population exceeded the tolerable rate. If no deviations occur in the sample, the auditor will conclude that the rate of occurrence is acceptably low, and will rely on the control. If even one deviation occurs, the auditor will conclude that the deviation rate exceeds the tolerable rate and will not rely on the control.
  - Another approach to attribute sampling is sequential (or stop-and-go) sampling. Sequential sampling provides the auditor with the potential to reduce his sample size by only selecting a large number of items for examination when some question exists as to the effectiveness of the internal control procedure. The basic procedure for using sequential sampling is:
    - Select an initial sample of items for examination. This initial sample will be smaller than that selected under traditional attribute sampling methods.
    - Evaluate the initial sample for deviations. Based on the results, the auditor's decision will be one of the following:
    - Rely on the internal control without further testing.
      - Reduce reliance on the internal control without further testing.
      - Select additional items.
        — If additional items are selected, the above step is repeated until the auditor can make a clear decision.

Study Manual – Auditing & Attestation
Chapter 9

7. Examine the sample using the appropriate audit procedure. If an auditor is unable to examine a selected item (e.g., a document has been misplaced), it should be considered a deviation for evaluation purposes. Furthermore, the auditor should consider the reasons for this limitation and its implications for the audit. In some cases, the auditor may find enough deviations early in the sampling process to indicate that a control cannot be relied upon. The auditor need not continue the tests in such circumstances.

8. Evaluate the sample results. Once audit procedures have been performed on all sample items, the sample results must be evaluated and projected to the entire population from which the sample was selected using the following steps:

    a. Calculate the sample deviation rate (deviation rate = number of observed deviations / sample size). The deviation rate is the auditor's best estimate of the true but unknown deviation rate in the population.

    b. Given the auditor's judgment of the risk of assessing control risk too low, determine the upper deviation limit. (Upper deviation limit is also called upper occurrence limit or achieved upper precision limit.) The auditor uses the number of deviations noted, and the appropriate sampling table (not presented here) to calculate the upper deviation limit. This upper deviation limit represents the sample deviation rate plus an allowance for sampling risk.

    c. Compare the upper deviation limit to the tolerable rate specified in designing the sample. If the upper deviation limit is less than or equal to the tolerable rate, the sample results support reliance on the control procedure tested.

Example:

Assume the auditor established the following criteria for an attributes sampling plan:

Population size: over 5,000 units.

Allowable risk of assessing control risk too low: 5%.

Tolerable deviation rate: 6%.

Estimated population deviation rate: 2.5%.

By referencing the appropriate sample size table (not presented here), the auditor determined that the required sample size was 150 units. The auditor applied the appropriate audit procedures to the 150 sample units and found eight deviations. Therefore, the sample deviation rate is 5.3% (8 / 150).

The upper deviation limit found from the table (not presented here) for a 5% risk of assessing control risk too low and eight deviations is 9.5%.

The allowance for sampling risk is 4.2% (9.5% – 5.3%).

The conclusion is that there is a 5% chance of the true population deviation rate being greater than or equal to 9.5%. Because the upper deviation limit of 9.5% exceeds the tolerable deviation rate of 6%, the sample results indicate that control risk for the control procedure being tested is higher than planned, and, therefore, the scope of resulting substantive tests must be increased.

    d. In addition to the frequency of deviations found, the auditor should consider the qualitative aspects of each deviation. For example, are the deviations due to a misunderstanding of instructions or to carelessness? The possible relationship of the deviations to other phases of the audit should be considered.

9. Draw logical conclusions as to whether to accept or reject the perceived reliance on internal control. If all evidence obtained, including sample results, supports the auditor's planned assessed level of control risk, the auditor generally does not need to modify planned substantive tests. If the planned level is not supported, the auditor will test other related controls or modify the related substantive tests to reflect increased control risk assessment.

10. Document the sampling procedures and conclusion.

VARIABLES SAMPLING

In developing a variable estimation sampling plan, the auditor would perform the following steps:

1. Define the problem, which will generally be to determine if the account balance is reasonably stated.

2. Determine the audit objectives which would include some or all of the following:

   - Representative sampling to learn about the population based upon the sample.
   - Corrective sampling to correct as many errors as possible by selecting sample areas with the highest probability of errors.
   - Protective sampling to guard against missing material errors involving the wide coverage of large dollar items.
   - Preventive sampling involving keeping client personnel uncertain about which items are to be examined to prevent manipulation of data by client employees.

3. Determine the appropriate audit procedures to be applied.

4. Define the population consistent with the audit objectives. The population consists of the items constituting the account balance of class of transactions of interest. Three areas need to be considered:

       a. Define the sampling unit. The sampling unit is any of the individual elements that constitute the population.

      b. Consider the completeness of the population.

      c. Identify individually significant items. Items that are individually significant for which sampling risk is not justified should be tested separately and not be subjected to sampling. These are items in which potential misstatements could individually equal or exceed tolerable misstatement.

5. Select an audit sampling technique. Either nonstatistical or statistical sampling may be used. If statistical sampling is used, either probability-proportional-to-size sampling (PPS) or classical variables techniques (discussed later) are appropriate.

6. Determine the sample size. Five items need to be considered:

      a. Variation within the population. Increases in variation (standard deviation in classical sampling) result in increases in sample size.

      b. Acceptable level of risk. The risk of incorrect acceptance is related to audit risk. The auditor may also control the risk of incorrect rejection so as to allow an efficiently performed audit. Increases in these risks result in decreases in sample size.

      c. Tolerable misstatement (error). An estimate of the maximum monetary misstatement that may exist in an account balance or class of transactions, when combined with misstatements in other accounts, without causing the financial statements to be materially misstated. As tolerable misstatement increases, sample size decreases.

      d. Expected amount of misstatement (error). Expected misstatement is estimated using an understanding of the business, prior-year information, a pilot sample, and/or the results of the review and evaluation of internal control. As expected misstatement increases, a larger sample size is required.

e. Population size. Sample size increases as population size increases.

Variable Sampling Summary of Relationships to Sample Size	
Increase in:	*Effect on sample size:*
Risk—incorrect acceptance	Decrease
Risk—incorrect rejection	Decrease
Tolerable misstatement (error)	Decrease
Expected misstatement (error)	Increase
Population	Increase
Variation (standard deviation)	Increase

7. Determine the method of selecting the sample. The sample should be representative of the population; all items in the population should have an opportunity to be selected. Methods will be discussed later.

8. Examine the sample.

9. Evaluate the sample results. The auditor should project the results of the sample to the population. The total projected misstatement, after any adjustments made by the entity, should be compared with the tolerable misstatement and the auditor should consider whether the risk of misstatement in excess of the tolerable amount is at an acceptably low level. Also, qualitative factors (such as the nature of the misstatements and their relationship to other phases of the audit) should be considered.

10. Draw logical conclusions as to whether to accept or reject the balance in the account or financial statement area.

11. Document the sampling procedures and conclusion.

SAMPLE SELECTION METHODS

The selection of a representative sample may be accomplished by various methods of sample selection. Some of the techniques are explained as follows:

- *Random-number sampling.* The auditor may equate items in the population with random numbers and, using computer-generated random numbers or a random-number table, select the sample.

- *Systematic sampling.* Under a systematic approach the auditor will select a random starting point and select every *n*th item from a random start point until the appropriate number of items has been selected.
  - A potential problem associated with systematic samples is that when the information is prepared in a systematic fashion, the randomness of the sample may be destroyed. More than one random starting point may be selected to offset systematic recording to some degree.
  - An advantage of systematic sampling, as compared to random-number sampling, is that the population items do not have to be consecutively numbered.
- *Haphazard sampling.* This is a sample consisting of units selected without any conscious bias, that is, without any special reason for including or omitting items from the sample. It is not scientifically random, but is an acceptable selection technique. *Haphazard* or *unsystematic* does not mean careless. This method is not used for statistical sampling.
- *Block sampling.* The auditor may use block or cluster sampling where the data is grouped by dates (say month) or pages. The auditor will randomly select an appropriate number of months or pages for testing and test each item within that group. Block sampling generally will not provide a representative sample because it is unlikely that at least one of each type of transaction occurring during a fiscal period will be selected for examination. For this reason, it is the least desirable method.

STRATIFICATION

In populations having wide variability, the overall sample size can often be reduced by stratification of the population. The objective of using a stratified sample is to enhance audit efficiency. In a stratified sample:

- The population is divided into smaller groups of items. Each group is referred to as a stratum.
- Within each stratum, items should be as similar to one another as possible, meaning that the range of values within each stratum would be narrow.
- The items within one stratum should be fairly dissimilar to items in other strata.
- A sample will be taken for each stratum. The total of the items in all the samples will generally be less than that for the overall population.

PROBABILITY-PROPORTIONATE-TO-SIZE

SAMPLING

Probability-proportionate-to-size (PPS) sampling is a method of sampling that can be used in testing for attributes and in variable estimation sampling. It enables an auditor to draw conclusions from a test on the basis of the dollar amounts affected by errors, not simply on the numerical frequency with which errors occur. There are numerous versions of PPS including combined-attributes-variables (CAV) sampling, cumulative-monetary-amount (CMA) sampling, and dollar-unit sampling (DUS).

PPS is a stratified sampling plan that places a higher significance on items with a larger dollar amount. As a result, the auditor is more likely to select items for the sample that have a large dollar amount. In addition, the auditor can quantify the dollar impact of an error rather than simply measure the frequency of the error.

The major advantage to PPS, however, is that it does not require the assumption as to the normal distribution as do all of the classical statistical methods.

There are some disadvantages to the use of PPS.

- The method is relatively conservative, resulting in a higher probability of incorrect rejection.
- PPS measures overstatements, but is not effective at measuring understatements.
- When it appears that there is a material overstatement, it is difficult to expand a dollar-unit sample unless the sample is computer generated.

As a result of the advantages and disadvantages, PPS should be used when

- Very few or no errors are expected.
- The risk of overstatement is the greatest risk of error.

PPS should not generally be used when:

- Many errors are expected.
- The auditor has no real basis for estimating the expected frequency of errors.
- There is a risk of understatement as well as overstatement.

PPS Samples

In selecting a sample under PPS, the auditor will select a sample interval, expressed in terms of a dollar amount. The auditor will also select a random starting point. The random starting point should be some dollar amount between zero and the sample interval. The auditor will then view the population in terms of the total number of dollars it represents.

AUDITING & ATTESTATION

Example:

An auditor is examining certain sales with a total dollar value of $5,000,000 and a total of 2,500 invoices. The average invoice amount is $2,000 per sale ($5,000,000 ÷ 2,500), although actual sales range from parts selling for as low as $100 to machines selling for as high as $250,000. The first ten invoices might be:

Invoice Number	Amount	Cumulative Amount
1	200	200
2	7,000	7,200
3	15,000	22,200
4	90,000	112,200
5	300	112,500
6	3,400	115,900
7	160,000	275,900
8	1,500	277,400
9	200	277,600
10	3,900	281,500

Assume that the tolerable error is $225,000. The risk factor is determined by a table similar to the one provided (in part) below. The risk of incorrect acceptance is computed by subtracting the desired reliability from 1:

Reliability Factors for Errors of Overstatement						
Reliability	99%	95%	93%	90%	85%	80%
Risk of incorrect acceptance	1%	5%	7%	10%	15%	20%
Estimated number of overstatement errors –0	4.61	3.00	2.66	2.30	1.90	1.61
Estimated number of overstatement errors – 1	6.64	4.74	4.33	3.89	3.37	2.99

If we assume that we have set a desired reliability of 95% or an acceptable risk of incorrect acceptance at 5%, and if we expect one error, we would compute the sample interval by dividing the tolerable error by the risk factor provided by the table. In this case it would be:

$225,000 / 4.74 = $47,468

The auditor will select a random starting point, (assume the number selected from a random number table is 19,853) and add 47,468 to that number over and over again. As a result, the following strata will be selected:

1st	19,853
2nd	67,321
3rd	114,789
4th	162,257
5th	209,725
6th	257,193
7th	304,661

This will continue until the auditor reaches a number that is within 47,468 of the total amount, $5,000,000. The sample size can be determined by dividing the population total by the sample interval as follows:

$5,000,000 / $47,468 = 105

This indicates that there will be a total of 105 selections. Note from our first ten invoices above, however, that the same invoice can be selected more than once. Using the starting point and sample interval determined, the items selected would be:

- 1st selection will be the third invoice.
- 2nd selection will be the fourth invoice.
- 3rd selection will be the sixth invoice.
- 4th, 5th, and 6th selections will be the seventh invoice; 7th selection will be some invoice after the tenth.

The selection is made on the basis of the cumulative dollar amounts and the sample interval. As a result, four of the first ten invoices will be selected. The auditor will examine the invoices and compare the audited amounts to the recorded amounts. Assume the results are as follows:

Invoice Number	Recorded Amount	Audited Amount	Sample Error
3	15,000	13,500	1,500
4	90,000	85,500	4,500
6	3,400	2,500	900
7	160,000	160,000	0

The auditor will then evaluate the results of the test. This will be done by comparing the book value of items in the sample to the sampling interval. Note that every item that has a recorded value in excess of the sampling interval must be tested under this approach. For those items, the actual error can be measured.

For items that are lesser in amount than the sampling interval, a "tainting percentage" or "tainting factor" is determined by taking the amount of the overstatement divided by the book value. A projected error is determined for these items by multiplying the tainting factor times the sampling interval.

In the sample referred to above, assume that the only errors found were those in the first ten invoices. Although this is not likely, remember that we were examining a sample of items where the expected number of errors was one in total.

Invoice 4 is for an amount in excess of the sampling frequency. As a result, the effect of the error will be taken at 100%. Invoices 3 and 6 are for less than the sampling interval so a tainting percentage is computed and used to determine the projected error

Invoice Number	Recorded Amount	Audited Amount	Sample Error	Tainting Factor	Sampling Interval	Projected Error
3	15,000	13,500	1,500	10.0%	47,468	4,747
4	90,000	85,500	4,500	—*	—	4,500
6	3,400	2,500	900	26.5%	47,468	12,579
TOTAL						21,826

* Not applicable: book value larger than sampling interval.

As a result, the projected error will be computed at 21,826.

Questions: Statistical Sampling

1. If a CPA selects a random sample for which he specified a confidence level of 99% and upper precision limit of 5% and subsequently changes the confidence level to 90%, the sample will produce an estimate which is:
   A. less reliable and more precise.
   B. more reliable and less precise.
   C. more reliable and more precise.
   D. less reliable and less precise.

2. If a CPA wishes to select a random sample which must have a 90% confidence level and an upper precision limit of 10%, the size of the sample he must select will decrease as his estimate of the:
   A. reliability of the sample decreases.
   B. occurrence rate increases.
   C. occurrence rate decreases.
   D. population size increases.

3. As the specified reliability is increased in a discovery sampling plan for any given population and maximum occurrence rate, the required sample size:
   A. remains the same.
   B. increases.
   C. decreases.
   D. cannot be determined.

4. What is an auditor's evaluation of a statistical sample for attributes when a test of 100 documents results in 4 deviations if tolerable rate is 5%, the expected population deviation rate is 3%, and the allowance for sampling risk is 2%?
   A. Modify planned reliance on the control because the sample deviation rate plus the allowance for sampling risk exceeds the tolerable rate.
   B. Accept the sample results as support for planned reliance on the control because the sample deviation rate plus the allowance for sampling risk exceeds the tolerable rate.
   C. Modify planned reliance on the control because the tolerable rate plus the allowance for sampling risk exceeds the expected population deviation rate.
   D. Accept the sample results as support for planned reliance on the control because the tolerable rate less the allowance for sampling risk equals the expected population deviation rate.

5. Which of the following statements is *correct* concerning statistical sampling in tests of controls?
   A. There is an inverse relationship between the expected population deviation rate and the sample size.
   B. As the population size increases, the sample size should increase proportionately.
   C. In determining tolerable rate, an auditor considers detection risk and the sample size.
   D. Deviations from specific internal control procedures at a given rate ordinarily result in misstatements at a lower rate.

6. A CPA who believes the occurrence rate of a certain characteristic in a population being examined is 3% and who has established a maximum acceptable occurrence rate at 5% should use a (an):
   A. stratified sampling plan.
   B. attribute sampling plan.
   C. discovery sampling plan.
   D. variable sampling plan.

7. An auditor who uses statistical sampling for attributes in testing internal controls should reduce the planned reliance on a prescribed control when the:
   A. sample rate of deviation plus the allowance for sampling risk equals the tolerable rate.
   B. sample rate of deviation is less than the expected rate of deviation used in planning the sample.
   C. sample rate of deviation plus the allowance for sampling risk exceeds the tolerable rate.
   D. tolerable rate less the allowance for sampling risk exceeds the sample rate of deviation.

8. Which of the following factors is generally **NOT** considered in determining the sample size for a test of controls?
   A. Tolerable rate.
   B. Expected population deviation rate.
   C. Risk of overreliance.
   D. Population size.

9. Which of the following courses of action would an auditor *most likely* follow in planning a sample of cash disbursements if the auditor is aware of several unusually large cash disbursements?
   A. Continue to draw new samples until all the unusually large disbursements appear in the sample.
   B. Stratify the cash disbursements population so that the unusually large disbursements are selected.
   C. Increase the sample size to reduce the effect of the unusually large disbursements.
   D. Set the tolerable rate of deviation at a lower level than originally planned.

10. The sample size of a test of controls varies inversely with:

	Expected population deviation rate	Tolerable rate
A.	No	Yes
B.	No	No
C.	Yes	No
D.	Yes	Yes

11. Precision is a statistical measure of the maximum likely difference between the sample estimate and the true but unknown population total, and is directly related to:
    A. relative risk.
    B. reliability of evidence.
    C. materiality.
    D. cost benefit analysis.

12. While performing a test of details during an audit, an auditor determined that the sample results supported the conclusion that the recorded account balance was materially misstated. It was, in fact, not materially misstated. This situation illustrates the risk of:
    A. assessing control risk too high.
    B. incorrect acceptance.
    C. incorrect rejection.
    D. assessing control risk too low.

13. Auditors who prefer statistical to judgmental sampling believe that the principal advantage of statistical sampling flows from its unique ability to:
    A. promote a more legally defensible procedural approach.
    B. provide a mathematical measurement of uncertainty.
    C. establish conclusive audit evidence with decreased audit effort.
    D. define the precision required to provide audit satisfaction.

14. In the evaluation of the results of a sample of a specified reliability and precision, the fact that the occurrence rate in the sample was the same as the estimated occurrence rate would cause the reliability of the sample estimate to:
    A. decrease.
    B. become indeterminate.
    C. increase.
    D. remain the same.

15. An auditor makes separate compliance and substantive tests in the accounts payable area which has good internal control. If the auditor uses statistical sampling for both of these tests, the confidence level established for the substantive tests is normally:
    A. totally independent of that for tests of compliance.
    B. the same as that for tests of compliance.
    C. less than that for tests of compliance.
    D. greater than that for tests of compliance.

16. How would increases in tolerable misstatement and assessed level of control risk affect the sample size in a substantive test of details?

	Increase in tolerable misstatement	Increase in assessed level of control risk
A.	Decrease sample size	Increase sample size
B.	Increase sample size	Increase sample size
C.	Decrease sample size	Decrease sample size
D.	Increase sample size	Decrease sample size

17. In the evaluation of the results of a sample of a specified reliability and precision, the fact that the occurrence rate in the sample was 2% rather than the estimated occurrence rate of 4% would cause the required sample size to:
    A. increase.
    B. decrease.
    C. remain the same.
    D. become indeterminate.

18. If all other factors specified in a sampling plan remain constant, changing the specified precision from 8% to 12% would cause the required sample size to
    A. increase.
    B. become indeterminate.
    C. remain the same.
    D. decrease.

19. As the acceptable level of detection risk decreases, an auditor may change the:
    A. timing of tests of controls by performing them at several dates rather than at one time.
    B. nature of substantive tests from a less effective to a more effective procedure.
    C. timing of substantive tests by performing them at an interim date rather than at year-end.
    D. assessed level of inherent risk to a higher amount.

20. Approximately 5% of the 10,000 homogeneous items included in Barletta's finished-goods inventory are believed to be defective. The CPA examining Barletta's financial statements decides to test this estimated 5% defective rate. He learns that by sampling without replacement that a sample of 284 items from the inventory will permit specified reliability (confidence level) of 95% and specified precision (confidence interval) of .025. If specified precision is changed to .05, and specified reliability remains 95%, the required sample size is:
    A. 436.
    B. 335.
    C. 1,543.
    D. 72.

21. In confirming a client's accounts receivable in prior years, an auditor found that there were many differences between the recorded account balances and the confirmation replies. These differences, which were not misstatements, required substantial time to resolve. In defining the sampling unit for the current year's audit, the auditor *most likely* would choose:
    A. individual invoices.
    B. large account balances.
    C. small account balances.
    D. individual overdue balances.

22. In planning a statistical sample for a test of controls, an auditor increased the expected population deviation rate from the prior year's rate because of the results of the prior year's test of controls and the overall control environment. The auditor would then *most likely* increase the planned:
    A. allowance for sampling risk.
    B. risk of assessing control risk too low.
    C. sample size.
    D. tolerable rate.

23. An example of sampling for attributes would be estimating the:
    A. quantity of specific inventory items.
    B. dollar value of accounts receivable.
    C. percentage of overdue accounts receivable.
    D. probability of losing a patent infringement case.

24. When assessing the tolerable rate, the auditor should consider that, while deviations from control procedures increase the risk of material errors, such deviations do not necessarily result in errors. This explains why:
    A. a recorded disbursement that is properly authorized may nevertheless be a transaction that contains a material error.
    B. deviations from pertinent control procedures at a given rate ordinarily would be expected to result in errors at a higher rate.
    C. deviations would result in errors in the accounting records only if the deviations and the errors occurred on different transactions.
    D. a recorded disbursement that does not show evidence of required approval may nevertheless be a transaction that is properly authorized and recorded.

25. In connection with his test of the accuracy of inventory counts, a CPA decides to use discovery sampling. Discovery sampling may be considered a special case of:
    A. sampling for attributes.
    B. judgmental sampling.
    C. stratified sampling.
    D. sampling for variables.

26. The purpose of tests of controls is to provide reasonable assurance that the accounting control procedures are being applied as prescribed. The sampling method that is *most* useful when testing for compliance is:
    A. unrestricted random sampling with replacement.
    B. attribute sampling.
    C. stratified random sampling.
    D. judgment sampling.

27. An auditor who uses statistical sampling for attributes in testing internal controls should reduce the planned reliance on a prescribed control when the:
    A. sample rate of deviation plus the allowance for sampling risk equals the tolerable rate.
    B. sample rate of deviation is less than the expected rate of deviation used in planning the sample.
    C. tolerable rate less the allowance for sampling risk exceeds the sample rate of deviation.
    D. sample rate of deviation plus the allowance for sampling risk exceeds the tolerable rate.

28. Which of the following *best* describes what the auditor means by the rate of occurrence in an attribute sampling plan?
    A. The dollar range within which the true population total can be expected to fall.
    B. The degree of confidence that the sample is representative of the population.
    C. The frequency with which a certain characteristic occurs within a population.
    D. The number of errors that can reasonably be expected to be found in a population.

29. There are many kinds of statistical estimates that an auditor may find useful, but basically every accounting estimate is either of a quantity or of an error rate. The statistical terms that roughly correspond to "quantities" and "error rate," respectively, are:
    A. constants and variables.
    B. constants and attributes.
    C. variables and attributes.
    D. attributes and variables.

30. The risk of incorrect acceptance and the likelihood of assessing control risk too low relate to the:
    A. effectiveness of the audit.
    B. efficiency of the audit.
    C. preliminary estimates of materiality levels.
    D. allowable risk of tolerable misstatement.

31. As a result of tests of controls, an auditor overrelied on internal control and decreased substantive testing. This overreliance occurred because the true deviation rate in the population was:
    A. more than the risk of overreliance on the auditor's sample.
    B. more than the deviation rate in the auditor's sample.
    C. less than the deviation rate in the auditor's sample.
    D. less than the risk of overreliance on the auditor's sample.

32. The auditor's failure to recognize an error in an amount or an error in an internal-control data-processing procedure is described as a:
    A. statistical error.
    B. sampling error.
    C. nonsampling error.
    D. standard error of the mean.

33. In performing a review of his client's cash disbursements, a CPA uses systematic sampling with a random start. The primary *disadvantage* of systematic sampling is that population items:
    A. may occur twice in the sample.
    B. must be reordered in a systematic pattern before the sample can be drawn.
    C. must be replaced in the population after sampling to permit valid statistical inference.
    D. may occur in a systematic pattern, thus negating the randomness of the sample.

34. Which of the following sampling methods would be used to estimate a numerical measurement of a population, such as a dollar value?
    A. Attributes sampling.
    B. Variables sampling.
    C. Random-number sampling.
    D. Stop-or-go sampling.

ANSWERS: STATISTICAL SAMPLING

1. **A** Decreasing the confidence level (reliability) will make the estimate less reliable but more precise.

2. **C** An increase in sample size varies directly with an increase in the estimated occurrence rate, all other factors remaining the same.

3. **B** Increasing reliability in any kind of a sampling plan, including discovery, while the other elements stay the same, will always cause the required sample size to increase.

4. **A** The tolerable rate is the maximum population rate of deviation from a prescribed control procedure that the auditor will tolerate without modifying the planned reliance on the control procedure. The sample deviation rate is the rate of deviation found in the sample. The allowance for sampling risk is a measure of the difference between a sample result and the corresponding population characteristic. The auditor adds the allowance for sampling risk to the sample deviation rate to estimate the population deviation rate. Since the rate of deviation found in this sample (4 deviation in a test of 100 documents = 4%) plus an allowance for sampling risk (2%) results in a population rate (6%) which exceeds the tolerable rate (5%), the auditor would modify planned reliance on the control.

5. **D** AU 350 states that in assessing the tolerable rate of deviations, the auditor should consider that, while deviations from pertinent control structure policies or procedures increase the risk of material misstatements in the accounting records, such deviations do not necessarily result in misstatements. For example, a recorded disbursement that does not show evidence of required approval may nevertheless be a transaction that is properly authorized and recorded. Deviations would result in misstatements in the accounting records only if the deviations and the misstatements occurred on the same transactions. Deviations from pertinent control procedures at a given rate ordinarily would be expected to result in misstatements at a lower rate. Population size has no effect on sample size when testing for compliance, unless the population is really small. There is a direct relationship between expected population and sample size. The tolerable rate is the maximum rate of deviation the auditor is willing to accept without changing his level of risk.

6. **B** Occurrence rates and maximum acceptable occurrence rates are always an indication of an attribute sampling plan. There is no maximum acceptable occurrence rate applicable to discovery sampling plans. Stratified sampling and variable sampling apply to the estimation of some dollar amount.

7. **C** In a test of controls, the auditor takes a sample, determines the sample deviation rate, compares this rate to the maximum rate he can tolerate and still rely on the control, and decides whether to rely on the control as planned or not. When sampling, the auditor runs the risk that the sample is not representative of the population. Statistical sampling, which in a test of controls is termed statistical sampling for attributes, can measure that risk by computing an allowance for sampling risk. This allowance is added to the sample deviation rate to compute a statistical estimate of the maximum population deviation rate, based on that sample result. If this population deviation rate exceeds the tolerable deviation rate for the control, the auditor should reduce the planned reliance on the control. If the sample deviation rate plus the allowance for sampling risk is less than or equal to the tolerable deviation rate, the test results support the auditor's planned reliance on the control. The expected rate of deviation is used to determine sample size, not to evaluate the results of a sample.

8. **D** Population size has little or no effect on sample size except for very small populations. Tolerable rate and risk of overreliance are inversely related to sample size, resulting in larger samples when these factors are set low. The expected population deviation rate has a direct relationship with sample size, resulting in a larger sample when this factor is set high.

9. **B** An auditor would normally select 100% of unusually large cash disbursements and a lower percentage of smaller cash disbursements because the larger disbursements are more material to the financial statements. Stratified sampling divides the population into strata, or groups of transactions that possess the same characteristics. The auditor would select 100% of the items in the category that includes the unusually large disbursements and a smaller percentage of the other categories. Rate of deviation relates to tests of controls and not substantive tests. The auditor selects the sample so that 100 % of the larger disbursements are selected. You can't increase more than 100%. You don't continue to draw new samples since you already have 100%.

10. **A** In determining sample size for a test of controls, the auditor will consider the expected population deviation rate and tolerable rate. If, based on prior experience with the client or a preliminary sample, the auditor expects to find few deviations from a control, the expected population deviation rate would be low and sample size would be small. Thus, there is a direct relationship between the expected population deviation rate and sample size, not an inverse relationship. The tolerable rate is the maximum rate of deviation from a prescribed control that an auditor is willing to accept without altering the planned reliance on internal control. If the auditor can tolerate a higher rate, he will test a smaller sample. Thus, tolerable rate varies inversely with sample size. Sample size does not vary inversely with the expected population deviation rate. Sample size does vary inversely with tolerable rate.

11. **C** Precision or confidence interval represents the range of values within which the true but unknown population total will fall, and this is directly related to materiality.

12. **C** Incorrect rejection occurs when the auditor concludes, based on a sample, that a recorded account balance is materially misstated when it is not materially misstated. As a result, the auditor rejects an acceptable balance. Assessing control risk too high or too low refers to risks associated with tests of controls, not substantive tests of details. Incorrect acceptance occurs when the auditor concludes, based on a sample, that a recorded account balance is not materially misstated when it is, resulting in the auditor accepting an incorrect balance.

13. **B** Statistical sampling is preferable to judgmental sampling in that it provides a mathematical measurement of uncertainty.

14. **D** Evaluation of sample results in attribute sampling would use the table at the same reliability level, and, accordingly, it would remain the same.

15. **D** A confidence level of 95% indicates that a good system of internal control has been determined by means of a sample. Having met that test, the auditor could place much less reliance on the substantive tests.

16. **A** If the auditor can tolerate a larger misstatement in an account, the auditor would need less assurance from a sample that the account is fairly stated in all material respects; thus, sample size would decrease. If the auditor assesses a higher control risk, there is a greater likelihood that accounts are misstated. As a result, the extent of substantive testing, and thus sample sizes in substantive tests, will increase. An increase in tolerable misstatement results in a decrease in sample size, and an increase in assessed level of control risk results in an increase in sample size.

17. C   Evaluation of sample results in attribute sampling does not use the estimated occurrence rate, and, accordingly, there is no effect on sample size.

18. D   Widening the precision range from 8% to 12% will cause a decrease in sample size.

19. B   Detection risk is defined as the risk that the auditor's procedures will not detect any error or fraud when one exists in the account being audited. As planned detection risk is decreased, the auditor will (1) select a greater sample size of items to be tested, (2) change the audit tests (substantive procedures) to more effective procedures, and (3) change the timing of substantive tests to perform them at year-end rather than at an interim date.

20. D   This is an example of an attribute sampling plan. A sample of 284 items was determined based on a reliability of 95% and a specified precision of plus or minus 0.025. If the specified precision is made wider to plus or minus 0.05 and the reliability stays the same, the required sample size will be smaller, and 72 would be the only possible answer.

21. A   A sampling unit is any of the individual elements, as defined by the auditor, that constitute the population. In the case of accounts receivable, each customer's account balance could be defined as the sampling unit. If confirming these balances is inefficient because of the time needed to resolve differences, the auditor could decide to define the sampling unit as a smaller part of the population, such as individual invoices. The auditor can then confirm and test invoices rather than balances. The other answers are account balances; choosing any of them as the sampling unit would not eliminate the difficulties that were encountered.

22. C   There is a direct relationship between expected population deviation rate and sample size. If the auditor expects to find more deviations from a control, he must test a larger sample. Tolerable rate and allowance for sampling risk are factors affecting sample size and are not affected by the expected population deviation rate. Risk of assessing control risk too low is an aspect of sampling risk and has nothing to do with the expected deviation rate.

23. C   Attribute sampling always deals with the rate of occurrence, and, accordingly, the percentage of overdue accounts receivable would be one type of application. Quantity of specific inventory items and dollar value of accounts receivable are examples of variable sampling. Probability of losing a patent infringement case, of course, is not related to sampling.

24. D   The question states that a deviation from a control procedure does not necessarily mean there will be an error in the account balance.

25. A   Discovery sampling is a type of attribute sampling. However, the objective is not one of estimation of a specific occurrence rate. Rather, the basic objective of discovery sampling is to provide a sample size large enough that we will have a prescribed chance of seeing at least one example of some designated attribute.

26. B   Testing for compliance is always related to attribute sampling.

27. D   In a test of controls, the auditor takes a sample, determines the sample deviation rate, compares this rate to the maximum rate he can tolerate and still rely on the control, and decides whether to rely on the control or not. When sampling, the auditor runs the risk that the sample is not representative of the population. Statistical sampling, which in a test of controls is termed statistical sampling for attributes, can measure that risk by computing an allowance for sampling risk. This allowance is added to the sample

deviation rate to give a statistically sound estimate of the true population rate. If this population deviation rate exceeds the tolerable deviation rate for the control, the auditor should not rely on the control.

28. **C** The frequency with which a certain characteristic occurs within a population.

29. **C** The statistical terms that roughly correspond to "quantities" and "error rate," respectively, are variables and attributes.

30. **A** When sampling, the auditor runs the risk that the sample is unrepresentative of the population. As a result, the auditor may reach the wrong conclusion. When the auditor performs substantive tests, he runs the risk of incorrect acceptance, which is the risk of accepting a balance as fairly stated when, in fact, the balance is not fairly stated. When the auditor performs tests of controls, he runs the risk of assessing control risk too low, which is the risk of deciding, based on the sample, that the controls are operating effectively when, in fact, they are not. These risks relate to the effectiveness of the audit because these erroneous conclusions, based on sampling, could cause the auditor to issue the wrong audit opinion and therefore be ineffective. Allowable risk of tolerable misstatement and estimated materiality levels, which relate to the auditor's judgments about how much risk he is willing to take that the financial statements are materially misstated, are judgments the auditor makes in planning a sample. The risk of incorrect acceptance and the risk of assessing control risk too low are related to evaluating the results of a sample. Efficiency of the audit is related to the sampling risk of incorrect rejection, which occurs when the sample results cause the auditor to reject a balance when it is fairly stated, and the risk of assessing control risk too high, which occurs when the auditor's sample results cause the auditor to assess control risk higher than it really is. As a result, the auditor is inefficient because he performs additional unnecessary testing.

31. **B** The purpose of a test of controls is to determine if the client is adequately following the prescribed controls. The auditor assesses the maximum rate of deviations from a prescribed control that he would be willing to accept and still rely on the control (tolerable deviation rate). The auditor then tests a sample, computes a sample deviation rate and projects that sample result to the population. If he decides to rely on the control, he runs the risk that the true deviation rate in the population is more than the deviation rate in the sample. In such a case, the auditor will have overrelied on the control.

32. **C** Failing to recognize an error in an amount or error in an internal control data processing procedure is not related to statistical sampling and therefore would be characterized as a nonsampling error.

33. **D** Systematic sampling is one in which every *n*th item in a population is selected as a sample. Its disadvantage, however, is that the items selected may occur in a systematic pattern which would negate the randomness of the sample.

34. **B** Variables sampling estimates numerical measures of a population, such as the quantity of units or a dollar value. Attributes sampling is used when testing internal control and estimates the percentage of items in the population that possess a desired attribute, not a dollar value. Stop-or-go sampling continues to select additional sample items until a desired level of assurance has been obtained. Random-number sampling is a technique used to select items and assure that each population item has an equal chance of being selected for the sample.

INVENTORY AND ACCOUNTS PAYABLE

STUDY MANUAL – AUDITING & ATTESTATION
CHAPTER 10

Study Tip: Before you get too involved in studying for the CPA exam, make sure you know exactly why you want to pass this exam. It is much easier to do the necessary work if you have a clear understanding of why you want pass.

INTRODUCTION

As noted earlier, financial statements that purport to be in conformity with generally accepted accounting principles contain certain assertions: presentation and disclosure, existence or occurrence, rights and obligations, completeness, and valuation or allocation. Auditors gather evidence to form an opinion with respect to these assertions. The experienced auditor should be able to prepare an audit program for an audit area (e.g., receivables) to test whether these assertions are supportable. The process is one in which specific audit objectives are developed based on the assertions being made in the financial statements. Finally, audit procedures to meet these audit objectives are formulated and listed in an audit program. For purposes of the CPA exam, consider two possible approaches for auditing an account: tests of balances and tests of details.

A. Tests of Balances and Tests of Details.

1. *Direct tests of ending balance (tests of balances).* This approach requires the auditor to identify specific components of an account balance. For example, the cash account can be broken down into cash on hand and cash on deposit in the client's various bank accounts. Under this approach, the auditor will select and verify a sample of components of the account balance. Accounts that are normally examined via this approach are high turnover accounts such as cash, accounts receivable, inventory, and accounts payable.

2. *Tests of inputs and outputs during the year (tests of details).* This approach requires the auditor to verify individual transactions comprising an account balance or class of transactions. This approach focuses on the individual transactions occurring during the year and not the final account balance. Accounts normally examined via this approach are lower turnover accounts, such as investments; property, plant and equipment; notes and bonds payable; and shareholders' equity.

3. Many audit procedures provide support for *multiple management assertions*. For example, cut-off procedures provide support for rights and obligations as well as for existence and completeness. The following are typical procedures included in a substantive audit program:

a. To support presentation and disclosure:

- Review disclosures for compliance with GAAP.
- Inquire about disclosures.

b. To support existence or occurrence:

- Confirmation.
- Observation—always consider whether you can observe the item itself and/or legal documents representing the item.
- Trace/vouch transactions.

c. To support rights and obligations:

- Cutoffs—consider whether transactions have been reported in the proper period.
- Authorization—consider whether there are transactions that require specific authorization.

d. To support completeness:

- Analytical procedures.
- Omissions—consider how transactions could improperly have been omitted from the account.

e. To support valuation:

- Foot and cross-foot schedules (total them across and down).
- Agree the account balances on schedules to the general ledger.
- Agree financial statement balances to account balances on schedules.
- Consider valuation methods and whether they have been properly applied.
- Consider related accounts (e.g., accounts receivable and bad debt expense; long-term debt and interest expense; fixed assets and repair and maintenance expense; and fixed assets and depreciation expense).

B. Auditing Inventories.

1. Observation by the auditor of the client's counting of inventory is a generally accepted auditing procedure and departure from it must be justified.

2. During the counting of inventory, the auditor will obtain an inventory listing from the client.

3. The auditor will perform test counts (quantity) from the list to the floor and from the floor to the list.

4. The auditor will account for inventory tags and client count sheets.

5. The auditor will select vendor invoices or other records of cost (prices) and vouch them to the list.

6. The auditor will also mathematically verify the inventory listing.

7. In addition to inventory observation procedures, the auditor will perform cutoff tests to ensure that inventory transactions are recorded in the proper accounting period.

8. The table below details the typical substantive audit procedures performed for inventories.

Type of audit procedure	Audit procedure	Management assertion(s)
Confirmation	Confirm agreements for inventory pledged under loan agreements with lenders.	Presentation and disclosure
Observation	Observe physical inventory counts. Perform test counts. Account for all inventory tags and count sheets.	Existence or occurrence; rights and obligations; completeness
Observation	Examine inventory quality (salable conditions).	Valuation or allocation
Recalculation	Mathematically verify the accuracy of the client's inventory listing and compare the total to the general ledger balance.	Valuation or allocation
Recalculation	Obtain information about the market value of inventory. Perform a lower of cost or market calculation and verify the need for a valuation allowance.	Valuation or allocation
Inspect documents	Examine vendor invoices for purchased inventory.	Valuation or allocation; rights and obligations
Inspect documents	Examine the accumulation of direct materials, direct labor, and overhead costs for manufactured inventory.	Valuation or allocation
Inspect documents	If physical inventories are taken at an interim date, examine the perpetual inventory records for activity occurring between the inventory date and year-end.	Existence or occurrence

Type of audit procedure	Audit procedure	Management assertion(s)
Inspect documents	Perform cutoff procedures by examining documents representing purchases and sales of inventory near year-end.	Rights and obligations; valuation and allocation; completeness
Inspect documents	Review disclosures for compliance with GAAP.	Presentation and disclosure
Inquiry	Inquire about the existence of purchase and sales commitments related to the inventory.	Valuation or allocation; presentation and disclosure
Inquiry	Inquire about pledging of inventory.	Presentation and disclosure
Inquiry	Inquire about consigned inventory.	Presentation and disclosure
Inquiry	Inquire about possible obsolete inventory.	Valuation or allocation
Analytical procedures	Examine variances between standard and actual costs.	Valuation or allocation
Analytical procedures	Examine an analysis of inventory turnover.	Valuation or allocation
Analytical procedures	Review industry experience and trends.	Valuation or allocation
Analytical procedures	Examine the relationship between inventory balances and recent purchasing, sales, and/or production activity.	Valuation or allocation; completeness

C. Auditing Accounts Payable and Accrued Liabilities.

1. When examining the client's accounts payable and accrued liabilities, the auditor's attention focuses on the completeness assertion.

2. The primary objective is to ensure that the client records all liabilities that exist as of year-end.

3. The auditor will perform a series of procedures to search for unrecorded liabilities.

4. Accounts payable confirmations with vendors are sometimes omitted due to the availability of externally generated evidence and due to the inability of confirmations to adequately address the completeness assertions (an auditor cannot confirm a payable which has been omitted from the payables listing).

A/P - focus on completeness

Study Manual – Auditing & Attestation
Chapter 10

5. Accounts payable confirmations are most frequently used in circumstances involving bad internal control, bad financial position, and situations when vendors do not send month-end statements.

6. The table below details the typical substantive audit procedures performed for accounts payable and accrued liabilities.

Type of audit procedure	Audit procedure	Management assertion(s)
Confirmation	Confirm recorded accounts payable with vendors.	Existence or occurrence
Confirmation	Confirm accounts payable with vendors with whom the client normally does business.	Completeness
Recalculation	Mathematically verify the total of the accounts payable listing and compare the total to the general ledger.	Existence of occurrence; valuation or allocation
Recalculation	Recalculate interest expense.	Valuation or allocation
Recalculation	Recalculate accrued payroll at year-end.	Valuation or allocation
Recalculation	Recalculate other accrued liabilities at year-end.	Valuation or allocation
Inspect documents	Vouch payables—examine purchase order, purchase invoices, receiving reports, and payment vouchers. Verify that the goods and services represented by these purchases are for the benefit of the entity.	Existence or occurrence; valuation or allocation; rights and obligations
Inspect documents	Perform cutoff tests to determine that transactions occurring at or near year-end are recorded in the proper period.	Rights and obligations; completeness
Inspect documents	Perform a search for unrecorded liabilities—inspect payments made to vendors after year-end and inspect unpaid vendor invoices or unmatched receiving reports.	Completeness
Inspect documents	Review disclosures for compliance with GAAP.	Presentation and disclosure

©2007 Kaplan CPA Review

Type of audit procedure	Audit procedure	Management assertion(s)
Inspect documents	Inspect copies of notes and note agreements.	Existence or occurrence
Inquiry	Inquire about the appropriateness of valuation accounts for purchase discounts, returns, and allowances.	Valuation or allocation
Inquiry	Inquire about purchase commitments.	Presentation and disclosure
Inquiry	Inquire of management as to completeness.	Completeness
Analytical procedures	Evaluate the reasonableness of rations and relationships involving accounts payable, inventory, and other expenses.	Valuation or allocation

QUESTIONS: INVENTORY AND ACCOUNTS PAYABLE

1. For effective internal control purposes, the vouchers payable department generally should:
   A. ascertain that each requisition is approved as to price, quantity, and quality by an authorized employee.
   B. establish the agreement of the vendor's invoice with the receiving report and purchase order.
   C. stamp, perforate, or otherwise cancel supporting documentation after payment is mailed.
   D. obliterate the quantity ordered on the receiving department copy of the purchase order.

2. An auditor selected items for test counts while observing a client's physical inventory. The auditor then traced the test counts to the client's inventory listing. This procedure *most likely* obtained evidence concerning management's assertion of:
   A. existence or occurrence.
   B. rights and obligations.
   C. valuation.
   D. completeness.

3. An auditor *most likely* would make inquiries of production and sales personnel concerning possible obsolete or slow-moving inventory to support management's financial statement assertion of:
   A. presentation and disclosure.
   B. rights and obligations.
   C. valuation or allocation.
   D. existence or occurrence.

4. An auditor generally tests the segregation of duties related to inventory by:
   A. personal inquiry and observation.
   B. document inspection and reconciliation.
   C. analytical procedures and invoice recomputation.
   D. test counts and cutoff procedures.

5. Which of the following auditing procedures *most likely* would provide assurance about a manufacturing entity's inventory valuation?
   A. Reviewing shipping and receiving cutoff procedures for inventories.
   B. Tracing test counts to the entity's inventory listing.
   C. Testing the entity's computation of standard overhead rates.
   D. Obtaining confirmation of inventories pledged under loan agreements.

6. Which of the following internal control procedures *most likely* addresses the completeness assertion for inventory?
   A. Employees responsible for custody of finished goods do not perform the receiving function.
   B. Receiving reports are prenumbered and periodically reconciled.
   C. Work in process account is periodically reconciled with subsidiary records.
   D. There is a separation of duties between payroll department and inventory accounting personnel.

7. Internal control procedures are strengthened when the quantity of merchandise ordered is omitted from the copy of the purchase order sent to the:
   A. accounts payable department.
   B. purchasing agent.
   C. receiving department.
   D. department that initiated the requisition.

8. When goods are received, the receiving clerk should match the goods with the:
   A. purchase order and the requisition form.
   B. vendor's invoice and the receiving report.
   C. receiving report and the vendor's shipping document.
   D. vendor's shipping document and the purchase order.

9. To gain assurance that all inventory items in a client's inventory listing schedule are valid, an auditor *most likely* would trace:
   A. items listed in the inventory listing schedule to inventory tags and the auditor's recorded count sheets.
   B. inventory tags noted during the auditor's observation to items listed in receiving reports and vendors' invoices.
   C. inventory tags noted during the auditor's observation to items listed in the inventory listing schedule.
   D. items listed in receiving reports and vendors' invoices to the inventory listing schedule.

10. In a properly designed internal control system, the same employee *most likely* would match vendors' invoices with receiving reports and also:
    A. post the detailed accounts payable records.
    B. recompute the calculations on vendors' invoices.
    C. reconcile the accounts payable ledger.
    D. cancel vendors' invoices after payment.

11. To *best* ascertain that a company has properly included merchandise that it owns in its ending inventory, the auditor should review and test the:
    A. contractual commitments made by the purchasing department.
    B. terms of the open purchase orders.
    C. purchase invoices received on or around year-end.
    D. purchase cut-off procedures.

12. Which of the following audit procedures is *best* for identifying unrecorded trade accounts payable?
    A. Reconciling vendors' statements to the file of receiving reports to identify items received just prior to the balance sheet date.
    B. Examining unusual relationships between monthly accounts payable balances and recorded cash payments.
    C. Reviewing cash disbursements recorded subsequent to the balance sheet date to determine whether the related payables apply to the prior period.
    D. Investigating payables recorded just prior to and just subsequent to the balance sheet date to determine whether they are supported by receiving reports.

13. When using confirmations to provide evidence about the completeness assertion for accounts payable, the appropriate population *most likely* would be:
    A. vendors with whom the entity has previously done business.
    B. invoices filed in the entity's open invoice file.
    C. amounts recorded in the accounts payable subsidiary ledger.
    D. payees of checks drawn in the month after the year-end.

14. In order to efficiently establish the correctness of the accounts payable cutoff, an auditor will be *most likely* to:
    A. coordinate mailing of confirmations with cutoff tests.
    B. compare cutoff reports with purchase orders.
    C. compare vendors' invoices with vendors' statements.
    D. coordinate cutoff tests with physical inventory observation.

15. To determine whether accounts payable are complete, an auditor performs a test to verify that all merchandise received is recorded. The population of documents for this test consists of all:
    A. vendor's invoices.
    B. canceled checks.
    C. receiving reports.
    D. purchase orders.

16. In assessing control risk for purchases, an auditor vouches a sample of entries in the voucher register to the supporting documents. Which assertion would this test of controls *most likely* support?
    A. Rights and obligations.
    B. Existence or occurrence.
    C. Valuation or allocation.
    D. Completeness.

17. Which of the following audit procedures is *best* for identifying unrecorded trade accounts payable?
    A. Investigating payables recorded just prior to and just subsequent to the balance sheet date to determine whether they are supported by receiving reports.
    B. Examining unusual relationships between monthly accounts payable balances and recorded cash payments.
    C. Reconciling vendors' statements to the file of receiving reports to identify items received just prior to the balance sheet date.
    D. Reviewing cash disbursements recorded subsequent to the balance sheet date to determine whether the related payables apply to the prior period.

18. An auditor *most likely* would analyze inventory turnover rates to obtain evidence concerning management's assertions about:
    A. rights and obligations.
    B. existence or occurrence.
    C. valuation or allocation.
    D. presentation and disclosure.

19. To measure how effectively an entity employs its resources, an auditor calculates inventory turnover by dividing average inventory into:
    A. gross sales.
    B. net sales.
    C. cost of goods sold.
    D. operating income.

ANSWERS: INVENTORY AND ACCOUNTS PAYABLE

1. **B** The vouchers payable department approves vendors' invoices for payment. Before approval, the invoice should be compared with supporting documents. The other answers are desirable internal control procedures, but they are typically performed by other departments—cash disbursements and purchasing.

2. **D** Assertions about completeness deal with whether all accounts and transactions that should be presented in the financial statements are so included. If an auditor test counts selected items while observing a client's physical inventory and then traces those counts to the client's inventory listing, the auditor is obtaining evidence that all inventory items that should be included in the listing, which becomes the basis for the financial statement amounts, are so included. The assertions presented in the other answers are not tested by this procedure. If an inventory item is test counted and on the listing, the client may not have the rights to that item. In order to test existence, the auditor would compare the listing to the actual items on hand instead of comparing the test counts to the listing. Valuation of inventory includes tests of lower of cost and market, not just quantities obtained during test counts.

3. **C** Assertions about valuation or allocation deal with whether asset, liability, revenue, and expense components have been included in the financial statements at appropriate amounts. Inquiries and other tests designed to determine if inventory is obsolete or slow-moving will help provide assurance that inventory, which should be adjusted to lower of cost or market, is properly valued on the financial statements.

4. **A** Some internal control procedures, such as the segregation of duties, may not generate an audit trail of documents that the auditor can inspect. The auditor can test this type of control procedure by making inquiries of client personnel and observing who performs what duties.

5. **C** Evidence about the valuation assertion that inventories are properly stated at cost (except when market is lower) is provided by:

    - Examining paid vendors' invoices.
    - Reviewing direct labor rates.
    - Testing the computation of standard overhead rates.
    - Examining analyses of purchasing and manufacturing variances.

6. **B** The completeness assertion made by management in the form of financial statements means that no transactions that should be recorded on the books of the entity have been omitted. By having the receiving reports prenumbered, the reconciliation process will include determining the status of each receiving report as being matched with a vendor invoice and recorded, awaiting matching, voided, or unmatched and thus unrecorded.

7. **C** The receiving department copy of the purchase order should be "blind" (i.e., quantities omitted). This ensures that the receiving department personnel count the incoming merchandise. Thus the company will end up paying only for what was received, which may not be what was billed by the vendor.

8. **D** When goods are received, they should be examined for quantity to determine agreement with the amount ordered (purchase order) and the amount the vendor claims to have shipped (vendor's shipping document). The receiving clerk prepares a receiving report

which indicates the quantity received. Agreement of quantity on receiving report with quantity on vendor's invoice is usually determined before payment, not at time of receipt of the goods.

9. **A** In order to determine that items on an inventory listing are valid and in fact exist at physical inventory date, the auditor would select items on that listing and trace them to inventory tags and count sheets that were prepared during the physical inventory count.

10. **B** The accounts payable, or vouchers payable, department has the responsibility to prepare vouchers for payment. As part of that process, an employee in that department should check vendors' invoices for mathematical accuracy by recomputing calculations and extensions, and should match the vendors' invoices with receiving reports and purchase orders for quantities, prices, and terms.

11. **D** Purchase cutoff procedures are designed to determine that items actually received in inventory have been included in the proper period.

12. **C** The question concerns unrecorded accounts payable at the balance date. In reviewing subsequent cash disbursements the auditor would review whether an invoice paid in the current period actually was received in the prior period.

13. **A** AU 330 states that confirmation requests can be designed to elicit evidence that addresses the completeness assertion: that is, if properly designed, confirmations may provide evidence to aid in assessing whether all transactions and accounts that should be included in the financial statements are included. Their effectiveness in addressing the completeness assertion depends in part on whether the auditor selects from an appropriate population for testing. For example, when using confirmations to provide evidence about the completeness assertion for accounts payable, the appropriate population might be a list of vendors rather than the amounts recorded in the accounts payable subsidiary ledger.

14. **D** Cutoff tests are used to determine whether items have been recorded in the proper period. By coordinating cutoff tests with the physical inventory, auditors can determine if the items are physically present.

15. **C** The question is concerned with the completeness of the accounts payable balance, i.e., whether everything that should be recorded as a payable is in fact included in the balance. To test the completeness of an item in the financial statements, the auditor would draw a sample from the population that represents the source documents. In this case, the source document is the receiving report which indicates the *date* the company received the merchandise and thus, depending on the shipping terms, when the title passes and a liability recognized.

16. **B** AU 326 states that assertions about existence or occurrence deal with whether assets or liabilities of the entity exist at a given date and whether recorded transactions have occurred during a given period. For example, management asserts that finished goods inventories in the balance sheet are available for sale, or management asserts that sales in the income statement represent the exchange of goods or services with customers for cash or other consideration.

17. **D** The auditor reviews cash disbursements recorded in the period subsequent to the balance sheet date to determine if they represent payments for goods and/or services received during the period ending on the balance sheet date. If so, the auditor would then

determine whether or not they have been properly recorded in the period prior to the balance sheet date. This review of subsequent payments is designed to identify unrecorded trade accounts payable and other unrecorded liabilities.

18. **C** Assertions about valuation or allocation deal with whether asset, liability, revenue, and expense components have been included in the financial statements at appropriate amounts. An auditor would look at inventory turnover rates to determine if the inventory amount on the balance sheet and the cost of goods sold amount on the income statement are reasonable, in relation to each other.

19. **C** Inventory turnover, which is an operations ratio that calculates how many times inventory is sold during a period of time such as a year, is calculated by dividing average inventory into cost of goods sold. The other answers are incorrect because inventory is divided into cost of goods sold, not into net sales, operating income, or gross sales.

AUDITING AND TECHNOLOGY

STUDY MANUAL – AUDITING & ATTESTATION
CHAPTER 11

Study Tip: Don't make any sudden changes in your sleeping or eating habits right before you take the CPA exam. Keep life as normal as possible so that there is not any unnecessary stress on you. The CPA exam is a challenge; don't make your body and your mind have to adapt to new circumstances at this critical juncture.

COMPUTER SYSTEMS AND INFORMATION TECHNOLOGY

Computers have become the primary means used to process financial accounting information and have resulted in a situation in which auditors must be able to use and understand current information technology to audit a client's financial statements. Accordingly, knowledge of computer terminology, computer systems, and related audit procedures is tested both on the Business Environment & Comments section and on the Auditing and Attestation section of the CPA exam.

The auditor's consideration of internal control includes an assessment of how an entity's use of information technology (IT) and manual procedures may affect controls relevant to the audit. IT encompasses automated means of originating, processing, storing, and communicating information, and includes recording devices, communication systems, computer systems (including hardware and software components and data), and other electronic devices. Also, audit procedures may include computerized and manual procedures for considering internal control and for performing substantive tests.

Generally accepted auditing standards and the concepts and objectives of internal control are the same for manual, mechanical, and computerized systems. The technical training and proficiency required of an auditor depends on the methods used by the entity to process transactions.

When performing an audit on the financial statements of a client using IT, the auditor should have both a general knowledge of IT and knowledge about the client's specific system.

- The auditor should be familiar with computer hardware (equipment), its uses, and its capabilities.
- The auditor should have a broad knowledge of file organization, process flow, and system design as well as various methods for safeguarding computer files.
- The auditor should understand the fundamentals of computer programming and be able to prepare specifications for and supervise the preparation of a computer program.

- The auditor should understand the relationship of software (input and output) to operations and should understand the role of the operator.
- The auditor should be able to supervise the performance of computer audit programs.
- The auditor should understand the different patterns of organization, supervision, and division of duties, as well as the duties that should be appropriately segregated to enhance internal accounting control.
- The auditor should understand the documentation practices inherent in the system and should be able to follow system flowcharts, record layouts, and error listings.
- The auditor should be familiar with the various IT controls used, the types of errors expected, and the methods of detecting, handling and correcting them. Controls fall into various categories including: controls relative to equipment malfunctions or improper internal handling of data; controls over input and output; program controls over processing of data; and safeguarding of records and files.
- The auditor should understand audit techniques that do not make use of the computer and how to obtain the records necessary for implementing these procedures.
- The auditor should be able to use computer-assisted audit techniques (CAAT) in conducting the audit.

In determining whether specialized information technology skills are needed to design and perform the audit, the auditor considers factors such as:

- The complexity of the entity's systems and information technology controls
- The significance of changes made to existing systems, or implementation of new systems
- The extent to which data is shared among systems
- The extent of the entity's participation in electronic commerce
- The entity's use of emerging technologies
- The significance of audit evidence available only in electronic form

Procedures an auditor may assign to a professional possessing information technology skills include:

- Inquiring of the entity's information technology personnel on how data and transactions are initiated, recorded, processed, and reported and how information technology controls are designed
- Inspecting systems documentation
- Observing operation of information technology controls
- Planning and performing of tests of information technology controls

If a client uses a computer to process significant accounting data relevant to the audit, the consideration of the internal control must include a review of the computer processing system. Also, the auditor may use the computer in the audit to obtain data, perform analyses, test to evaluate data, select samples for tests of control or substantive tests, or compare audit evidence obtained from physical counts.

An organization's computer data processing system consists of the following elements:

- Computer hardware (central processing unit, storage devices, input/output devices, printing devices)

- System software (operating systems, compilers)
- Generalized utility software (programs that handle common tasks such as sorting)
- Personnel (systems analysts, programmers, operators, librarians, control clerks)
- General operating procedures and controls
- Applications (specific programs and procedures for each application)
- Data (organized as files used by single applications or as databases used by several applications)

Information technology provides potential benefits of effectiveness and efficiency because it enables the entity to:

- Consistently apply predefined business rules and perform complex calculation on large volumes of transactions.
- Enhance timeliness, availability, and accuracy of information.
- Facilitate the additional analysis of information.
- Enhance the ability to monitor the performance of the entity's activities and its policies and procedures.
- Reduce risk that controls will be circumvented.
- Enhance ability to achieve effective segregation of duties by implementing security controls in applications, databases, and operating systems.

The computer system used by the client may use a number of approaches to processing. The more common approaches to processing are: batch processing; online processing; online, real-time processing; and distributed processing.

- *Batch processing.* Data from a number of transactions are grouped or batched for processing at the same time. Batch processing is periodic and may be at predetermined times (payroll processing) or sporadic (inventory updating). Batch processing may be either sequential or random.
- *Online processing.* Data are entered directly by the originators and output is sent directly to the user without passing through other processes or people. Master files and programs are directly accessed by the central processing unit and a data set may be accessible by different application programs. Files are not updated immediately as the data is entered into the system.
- *Online, real-time processing.* A real-time system must be an online system, but an online system is not necessarily a real-time system. An online, real-time system is the same as an online system except that as the data is entered it is processed immediately, and is up to date and available for use by the users. The response is quick enough to control the activity being monitored such as the work of air traffic controllers, airline reservation clerks, and perpetual inventory clerks.
- *Distributed processing.* Information processing systems may distribute processing capabilities to user locations rather than to concentrate them in a central processing center. Distributed processing may take many forms, depending on which capabilities are dispersed. Some examples are: local, independent computers in several locations; local computers that are part of a network controlled by a central computer; remote job-entry stations that process input of data and handle output; and small computers (microcomputers) dedicated to a few uses or a few users.

Those attributes that distinguish processing through computerized systems from processing through manual systems include:

- *Transaction or audit trails.* Input documents may exist only for short periods of time or only in computer-readable form. Also, the information is recorded on media (tape, disk, drum) that are invisible to the human eye, which increases the opportunity for undetected errors and frauds.
- *Uniform processing of transactions.* Each transaction will be processed by the processing instructions in exactly the same way (higher level of reliability). Human or clerical errors due to such factors as carelessness or fatigue will be eliminated or reduced.
- *Segregation of functions.* To detect or prevent errors and fraud, manual systems rely heavily on organizational factors such as alertness, judgment, acceptance of responsibility, and segregation of functions. A computerized system reduces the number of humans involved in processing transactions and concentrates activities within a single function (IT department). Therefore, computer processing reduces the controls based on segregation of duties and human alertness and judgment, and thereby increases the potential for an individual who has access to IT facilities to perform incompatible functions. Controls may be established in a computerized system that attains the same basic objectives as those established in manual systems. Some of the alternative controls are preprogrammed validity or reasonableness tests, segregation of incompatible functions within the IT function, segregation of the IT function from other functional areas, establishment of control groups, and use of password control procedures.
- *Potential for errors and fraud.* Due to the reduction in the human factor there are fewer opportunities to observe errors and fraud. Also, in a computerized system, there is a greater potential for gaining access to data and assets without visible evidence. Undetected system and application design errors or fraud can remain undetected for long periods of time.
- *Dependence of other controls on controls over computer processing.* Computer processing may produce reports and other output, such as error listings and access logs, that are used in performing manual control procedures. The effectiveness of the manual control procedures depends on the effectiveness of the controls over the completeness and accuracy of computer processing. For example, if an error is not reported, no follow-up can or will occur.

The methods used by an entity to process accounting information do influence the design of the accounting system and the nature of the internal control procedures. Therefore, the auditor should consider the methods of processing data when planning the audit engagement, such as:

- The extent to which the computer is used in each significant accounting application
- The complexity of the entity's computer operations, including the use of an outside service bureau or center
- The organizational structure of the computer processing activities
- The availability of data. Input documents may exist only for short periods of time or only in computer-readable form. An entity's data retention policies may require that the auditor make special arrangements for data retention. In some systems, input documents may not exist because data is entered directly into the system at the time of the initial recognition of the transaction. As a result of a computerized system, certain data or management analyses may be available that would not be practical to develop in a manual system.
- The use of computer-assisted audit techniques to increase the efficiency of performing audit procedures. In some cases, the auditor may be able to perform

procedures to an entire population of accounts or transactions. In other cases, the auditor may not obtain certain data without computer assistance.

When computer processing is used in significant accounting applications, internal control activities related to IT are categorized into two types: general controls and application controls.

GENERAL CONTROLS

General controls are policies and procedures that apply to many applications and support the effective functioning of application controls. There are four areas of general controls:

1. Controls over data center and network operations

2. System software acquisition and maintenance

3. Access security

4. Application system acquisition, development, and maintenance

Information technology poses specific risks to internal control, including:

- Systems or programs that inaccurately process information
- Unauthorized access to data that leads to destruction of data or inappropriate changes to data
- Unauthorized changes to data in master files
- Unauthorized changes to systems or programs
- Failure to make necessary changes to systems or programs
- Inappropriate manual intervention
- Potential loss of data

DEVELOPMENT OF NEW PROGRAMS AND SYSTEMS AND CHANGES TO EXISTING PROGRAMS AND SYSTEMS

Controls over the development of new programs and systems and controls over changes to existing programs and systems include:

- Documentation describing purposes and objectives of the application
- A complete set of flowcharts
- A program source code listing
- A compiled program listing
- Computer operating instructions for the computer operations group
- Program testing documentation such as tests run and results of tests
- Samples and layouts of all program inputs and outputs
- Approvals for initial applications or systems and approvals for any subsequent changes

COMPUTER OPERATIONS

Control over computer operations encompasses controls such as the following:

- Organization and operation of the IT department includes proper segregation of the various functions within the IT department.
    - A systems analyst analyzes the requirements for information, evaluates the existing application system and designs new or improved data processing procedures, outlines the new application system and prepares specifications that guide the programmer, and develops implementation plan and procedure manuals.
    - A programmer determines the logic of the computer programs required by the overall system designed by the systems analyst, codes the logic in the computer program language, debugs the resulting program, and prepares documentation.
    - A data entry operator prepares data for machine processing by entering it using a keyboard into a device that will either record data on machine-readable media or enter it directly into the computer for processing.
    - A computer operator operates the computer according to the operating procedures for the installation and the detailed, written procedures for each program.
    - A librarian maintains the library of all data and program files, releases the files and follows up on their return in accordance with established policy, and may be responsible for maintaining a library of all documentation.
    - A control clerk controls, and may schedule, all data entering the data processing system, reviews output, performs control balancing, distributes reports coming from the system, and maintains error logs.
- IT hardware controls are designed by the computer manufacturers to detect equipment failures or malfunctions. The auditor's concern in this area is with the client's procedures for identifying and correcting data processed by the faulty hardware because he or she is concerned with the accuracy of IT-generated information. These hardware controls include the following:
    - Parity check
    - Read after write
    - Dual read check

Hardware controls include physical controls over the IT installation such as protection against water damage, fire, or vandalism, which generally involve physically locating the computer center in a climate-controlled building or floor level where such risks are reduced. Such controls also include insurance coverage. These controls also involve backup (includes off-site storage of copies of computer files) and recovery procedures (procedures to recreate individual files from backup copies such as use of a grandparent-parent-child concept for magnetic-tape systems). A disk-file system does not produce a backup copy automatically; a special copying procedure must be used to create a backup copy. Also, updating a disk file alters the old record and results in destruction of the previous records.

ACCESS TO PROGRAMS AND DATA

Controls over access to programs and data are those controls designed to restrict entry to all IT facilities, records, and files. These controls involve physical controls such as:

- Door locks
- Uniformed guards
- Terminal access such as locking devices and passwords
- Central processing unit access such as passwords
- File or database access such as passwords used as file protection codes
- Other program and data controls:
    - File protection rings are devices related to magnetic tape files. If the ring is removed from a tape, the computer will not erase or write over the data on the tape.
    - Internal labels are labels readable by the computer. These are used so that the computer can determine if the proper data has been placed on the computer for processing before any actual processing is performed.
    - External labels stick on the outside casing of files or disks, indicating such identifying information as the file name and the date created. These labels are visible and provide a means for humans to identify the contents of a file or disk; labeling is part of the librarian function.
    - Boundary protection is the means of separating different files of data that may be included on the same tape or disk. It prevents the computer from going into another field of data when updating a specific item.

APPLICATION CONTROLS

Application controls apply to the processing of individual applications, and relate to the use of IT to initiate, record, process, and report transactions and other financial data.

Application controls usually are categorized into three classifications:

1. Input

2. Processing

3. Output

INPUT CONTROLS

The four general objectives of input controls are to ensure that:

1. All data processed is properly authorized.

2. All data is properly converted into machine-readable form.

3. No data is lost, added, or altered during transmission for processing.

4. Rejected data is properly controlled and resubmitted.

Input controls include:

- Verification in which data that is converted into machine-readable form is checked to make certain that the conversion was accurate.
- Check digit or self-checking number in which the final digit, or any other digit in a consistent position, of a number is derived by some formula based on the other digits in the number. If the other digits in the number are transposed, or some other error occurs in transcribing the number, the formula will not derive the proper check digit and the computer will detect the error in the number.
- File labels.

Additional application controls are used to check the input data itself for validity. Several controls are used for this purpose:

- Valid code checks
- Valid character checks
- Valid field size, sign, and composition checks
- Valid transaction checks
- Valid combination checks
- Missing data checks
- Sequence tests
- Limit or reasonableness tests in which the computer tests data to determine if it is within an acceptable range of values for that particular type of data

Control totals may also be used in the control of input. Control totals are numbers entered into the computer for comparison with the data processed to make certain that all data has been processed. There are several types of control totals in use:

- Financial totals in which a total of certain monetary items, such as sales, are calculated by the computer operator or other clerk, and the total is compared to the computer's total to make certain that they agree
- Hash totals in which a field of data that has no meaning by itself, such as invoice numbers, is added together; the computer also computes a total of this field, and the two are compared to make certain that all data has been processed
- Document or record counts in which the number of documents being input is counted and the number is compared to the number processed by the computer to make certain that all data has been processed

PROCESSING CONTROLS

Processing controls are designed to ensure that:

- All data submitted was processed correctly as authorized.
- No data was added or omitted.

Processing controls include:

- Limit and reasonableness tests in which the results of an operation are compared to predetermined limits to make certain that the results are reasonable
- Cross-footing tests in which totals generated by programs are footed and cross-footed to determine their correctness
- Control procedures similar to those included as input controls can also be used.

OUTPUT CONTROLS

The general objectives of output controls are to:

- Ensure the accuracy of processing results.
- Restrict output to authorized personnel.

Output controls include:

- Review of output by the control clerk and user department for accuracy and reasonableness
- "Files control." There are two basic types of computer files:

  1. *Transaction files* contain information of a temporary nature, such as daily sales transactions actions.

  2. *Master files* contain information that is of a more permanent nature, such as customer number, name, address, credit limit, and terms. Information generated by applications is heavily dependent upon the accuracy of the basic information that is stored in the master files. The auditor wants reasonable assurance that the data stored in the master files remains authorized, accurate, and complete. Master files are revised in two ways: (a) updating through the processing of normal transactions (update accounts receivable master file from processing sales or cash receipts transactions), and (b) updating outside the processing of normal transactions or master file maintenance (adding data on a new customer or deleting data on an old customer).

- Major controls in the files area are reports on the components in a file, such as an aged trial balance of accounts receivable; user department review of a listing of all changes to the master file; balancing the number of records and dollar amounts in the master file to other records; and adequate library procedures including internal and file-labeling procedures.
- The effectiveness of application controls is heavily dependent upon the general controls. In most cases, if the general controls are unsatisfactory, the application controls will be unsatisfactory automatically.

CONTINUITY OF CONTROLS

One concern of the auditor relative to controls in a computer or manual environment is whether the controls have been in place and have been effective throughout the period under consideration. The continuity of use problem is more a problem in computerized systems than manual systems because the execution of a number of procedures in computerized systems, such as reasonableness tests, does not leave a visible trail of evidence if there are no exceptions. For computerized systems, the auditor may test for consistency of controls by testing program control procedures throughout the period or by testing controls over the maintenance and processing of such programs. In such cases, the auditor may use computer-assisted audit techniques or may reprocess the data and compare the audited results with the original results.

APPROACHES TO AUDITING COMPUTER SYSTEMS

Auditing around the computer is a manual approach in which the auditor selects a sample of source documents, manually determines processing results, and compares the results of the manual processing with the computer printouts. The auditor would not be able to obtain any information about the effectiveness of the processing controls or techniques used by the client except that the outputs do or do not appear reasonable in comparison with the inputs.

Auditing through the computer involves using the computer to test whether hardware and software controls are operating as designed. There are a number of computer-assisted audit techniques that may be useful and in some cases may be required because manual tests may be impractical (input documents are nonexistent where data is entered online; the system does not produce a visible audit trail of transactions processed by computer; or detailed output reports are not produced by the system, only summaries).

Techniques for Program Analysis

- *Program code checking.* The auditor manually reads program code or uses automatic computer-generated flowcharts to determine that programs perform as documented and as authorized.
- *Comparison programs.* These programs allow the auditor to compare computerized files.
- *Flowcharting software.* Flowcharting software is used to produce a flowchart of a program's logic and may be used both in mainframe and microcomputer environments.
- *Program tracing and mapping.* Program tracing is a technique in which each instruction executed is listed along with control information affecting that instruction. Program mapping identifies sections of code that can be "entered" and thus are executable. These techniques allow an auditor to recognize logic sequences or dormant sections of code that may be a potential source of abuse.
- *Snapshot.* This technique, in essence, takes a picture of the status of program execution, intermediate results, or transaction data at specified processing points in the program processing. The technique helps an auditor analyze the processing logic of specific programs.

Techniques for Program Testing

- *Test data.* The auditor prepares test data that simulates both valid and invalid transactions. The test data is processed on the client's computer system. The auditor then compares the computer system output and reported exception conditions to the output expected based on the auditor's knowledge of the test data. The auditor determines the test data and controls the processing of the test data. The auditor needs to develop techniques to be assured that the client programs being used for

testing are the same programs that the client used for processing transactions throughout the audit period, and that any test data processed does not contaminate the files or data of the client.
- *Parallel simulation.* The auditor creates or obtains a set of computer programs that simulate or duplicate the major processing activities of the client's programs. Actual or test data are processed by the auditor's computer programs and by the client's computer programs. The auditor compares the results from his or her programs with those from the client's programs and forms a conclusion about the reliability of the controls in the client's programs. This really is nothing more than a computerized version of "auditing around the computer." This is, however, an improvement over the manual approach to auditing around the computer because the auditor controls the processing and can process a larger mass of data.
- *Integrated test facility (ITF).* The auditor submits test data along with actual data into the client's actual processing system. If processed properly, the data should end up in a file established by the auditor to represent a dummy division or subsidiary. This provides for a direct test of the client's system. A major problem is that the auditor's data may contaminate the client's actual data files. This technique is usually used with online, real-time (OLRT) systems.
- *Controlled reprocessing.* Controlled reprocessing, a variation of parallel simulation, processes actual client data through a copy of the client's application program. As with parallel simulation, this method uses actual transactions and the auditor compares the output obtained with output obtained from the client.

Techniques for Continuous or Concurrent Testing

- *Transaction tagging.* The auditor "marks" or "tags" selected client input data using a data field that is not used in regular processing. Tagged data then result in special reports indicating all files affected by the tagged item and the effect of the transaction on those files. This technique is used only on online, real-time systems and requires that the tagging capability be programmed into the client's system at the time that it is designed.
- *Embedded audit modules and audit hooks.* Embedded audit modules are programmed routines incorporated into an application program that are designed to perform an audit function such as a calculation, or logging activity. Because embedded audit modules require that the auditor be involved in system design of the application to be monitored, this approach is often not practical. An audit hook is an exit point in an application program that allows an auditor to subsequently add an audit module (or particular instructions) by activating the hook to transfer control to an audit module.
- *Systems control audit review files (SCARF).* A SCARF is a log, usually created by an embedded audit module, used to collect information for subsequent review and analysis. The auditor determines the appropriate criteria for review and the SCARF selects that type of transaction, dollar limit, or other characteristic.
- *Extended records.* This technique attaches additional data that would not otherwise be saved to regular historic records and thereby helps to provide a more complicated audit trail. The extended record information may subsequently be analyzed.

Techniques for Review of Operating Systems and Other Systems Software

- *Job accounting data/operating systems logs.* These logs, created by either the operating system itself or additional software packages that track particular functions, include reports of the resources used by the computer system. Because these logs provide a record of the activity of the computer system, the auditor may be able to use them to review the work processed, to determine whether unauthorized applications were processed, and to determine that authorized applications were processed properly.
- *Library management software.* This software logs changes in programs, program modules, job control language, and other processing activities. Auditors may review these logs.
- *Access control and security software.* This software supplements the physical and control measures relating to the computer and is particularly helpful in online environments or in systems with data communications because of difficulties of physically securing computers. Access control and security software restricts access to computers to authorized personnel through techniques such as only allowing certain users with "read-only" access or through use of encryption. An auditor may perform tests of the effectiveness of the use of such software.

THE USE OF COMPUTERIZED AUDIT TOOLS IN PERFORMING AN AUDIT

A variety of computerized audit tools is available for administering, planning, performing, and reporting of an audit. The major types are:

- Custom-designed audit software programs are written to perform audit tasks in the system of one client. This technique is useful, but the development costs are very high.
- Generalized audit software (GAS) packages have been developed that have the capability of performing a wide variety of useful audit tasks on systems with a wide variety of hardware and file formats. These programs use very-high-level programming languages and typically are sequential file manipulation tools. They perform such routine tasks as:
  - Extracting records that meet certain criteria, such as accounts receivable balances over the credit limit, inventory items with negative quantities or unreasonably large quantities, uncosted inventory items, and transactions with related parties
  - Sorting
  - Summarization, such as by customer account number, inventory turnover statistics, and duplicate sales invoices
  - Field statistics, such as net value, total of all debt, number of records, average value, maximum or minimum value, and standard deviation
  - File comparison, such as payroll details with personnel records or current and prior period inventory files
  - Gap detection/duplicate detection to find missing or duplicate records
  - Sampling
  - Calculation
  - Exportation
- Electronic spreadsheets are often included in GAS and may be used for applications such as analytical procedures and performing mathematical procedures. Also, auditors

often use microcomputer electronic spreadsheets to prepare working trial balances, lead sheets, and other schedules.
- Automated audit document software is generally microcomputer based and is increasingly being used by auditors. Originally used to generate trial balances, lead schedules, and other audit documents, advances in computer technology (e.g., improvements in scanning) make possible an electronic audit document environment. Ordinarily, this type of software is easy to use and inexpensive. The primary disadvantage is the time required to enter the data for the first year being audited.
- Database management systems may be used to perform analytical procedures, mathematical calculation, generation of confirmation requests, and to prepare customized automated audit documents. An auditor may, for example, download relevant client files into a database and analyze the data as desired. Advantages of this approach include a great opportunity for the auditor to rearrange, edit, analyze, and evaluate a data file in a manner well beyond that possible to be performed manually and the ability to download client data without time-consuming data entry. Disadvantages include auditor training and the need for adequate client documentation of applications.
- Text retrieval software (also referred to as text database software) enables access to such databases as the AICPA professional standards and various FASB and SEC pronouncements. This software allows an auditor to research technical issues quickly and requires minimal training. Disadvantages include the fact that some training is required and that some professional literature is not currently available in software form.
- Public databases may be used to obtain accounting information related to particular companies and industries as well as other publicly available information on, for example, electronic bulletin boards that an auditor may use. Current developments for companies and their industries may be obtained from the Internet. The Internet provides online access to newspaper and journal articles. In addition, many companies and industry associations have World Wide Web home pages that describe current developments and statistics.
- Word processing software is used by auditors in a variety of communication-related manners, including the consideration of internal control, developing audit programs, and reporting.

REPORTS ON THE PROCESSING OF TRANSACTIONS BY SERVICE ORGANIZATIONS

In many cases, the computer processing of a client's transactions occurs at a location physically separate from the client organization. This occurs when one organization (known as the service organization) provides some form of processing services to the client organization (known as the user organization). The problem introduced in this situation is that internal control policies and procedures that affect the client's financial statements are being implemented physically and operationally separate from the client's premises.

In order to evaluate internal control procedures that exist at a service organization, the client's auditor (known as the user auditor) can either apply tests of controls at the service organization or obtain a report from the auditor of the service organization (known as the service auditor). In many instances, it is more efficient to obtain a report from the service auditor. Two types of reports may be obtained from the service auditor.

- A report on policies and procedures placed in operation includes the following major components:
- A description of the service organization's policies and procedures that may affect the user organization's internal control
- An opinion on whether the description of the service organization's policies and procedures is fairly presented
- An opinion on whether the service organization's policies and procedures are designed to provide reasonable assurance of achieving the objectives of the internal control at the service organization

Note that the report on policies and procedures placed in operation does not address the operating effectiveness of the service organization's internal control. In addition to the components listed above, a report on the operating effectiveness of the internal control includes:

- A description of tests of controls performed by the service auditor
- An opinion on the operating effectiveness of the internal control policies and procedures tested by the service auditor

The type of report obtained from the service auditor depends upon the user auditor's assessment of control risk and the importance of internal control policies and procedures implemented at the service organization. The user auditor should obtain a report on the operating effectiveness of the internal control when

- the overall control risk assessment is less than maximum, and
- control procedures serve as the basis for the assessment of control risk.

QUESTIONS: AUDITING AND TECHNOLOGY

1. Which of the following computer-assisted auditing techniques allows fictitious and real transactions to be processed together without client operating personnel being aware of the testing process?
    A. Test data approach.
    B. Parallel simulation.
    C. Integrated test facility.
    D. Generalized audit software programming.

2. An auditor who is testing IT controls in a payroll system would *most likely* use test data that contain conditions such as:
    A. overtime not approved by supervisors.
    B. time tickets with invalid job numbers.
    C. payroll checks with unauthorized signatures.
    D. deductions not authorized by employees.

3. An auditor *most likely* would introduce test data into a computerized payroll system to test internal controls related to the:
    A. discovery of invalid employee I.D. numbers.
    B. existence of unclaimed payroll checks held by supervisors.
    C. proper approval of overtime by supervisors.
    D. early cashing of payroll checks by employees.

4. Which of the following computer documentation would an auditor *most likely* utilize in obtaining an understanding of internal control?
    A. Record layouts.
    B. Record counts.
    C. Program listings.
    D. Systems flowcharts.

5. 'An auditor *most likely* would test for the presence of unauthorized IT program changes by running a:
    A. check digit verification program.
    B. source code comparison program.
    C. program with test data.
    D. program that computes control totals.

6. To obtain evidence that user identification and password controls are functioning as designed, an auditor would *most likely*:
    A. attempt to sign on to the system using invalid user identifications and passwords.
    B. examine statements signed by employees stating that they have not divulged their user identifications and passwords to any other person.
    C. extract a random sample of processed transactions and ensure that the transactions were appropriately authorized.
    D. write a computer program that simulates the logic of the client's access control software.

7. Misstatements in a batch computer system caused by incorrect programs or data may not be detected immediately because:
   A. there are time delays in processing transactions in a batch system.
   B. the identification of errors in input data typically is not part of the program.
   C. the processing of transactions in a batch system is not uniform.
   D. errors in some transactions may cause rejection of other transactions in the batch.

8. In a computerized payroll system environment, an auditor would be *least likely* to use test data to test controls related to:
   A. agreement of hours per clock cards with hours on time tickets.
   B. missing employee numbers.
   C. proper approval of overtime by supervisors.
   D. time tickets with invalid job numbers.

9. Daylight Corporation's organization chart provides for a controller and an IT manager, both of whom report to the financial vice-president. Internal control would **NOT** be strengthened by:
   A. providing for maintenance of input data controls by an independent control group which reports to the controller.
   B. providing for review and distribution of computer output by an independent control group which reports to the controller.
   C. rotating periodically among machine operators the assignments of individual application runs.
   D. assigning the programming and operating of the computer to an independent control group which reports to the controller.

10. Which of the following *most likely* represents a weakness in internal control of an IT system?
    A. The accounts payable clerk prepares data for computer processing and enters the data into the computer.
    B. The systems analyst reviews output and controls the distribution of output from the IT department.
    C. The control clerk establishes control over data received by the IT department and reconciles control totals after processing.
    D. The systems programmer designs the operating and control functions of programs and participates in testing operating systems.

11. When an accounting application is processed by computer, an auditor cannot verify the reliable operation of programmed control procedures by:
    A. periodically submitting auditor-prepared test data to the same computer process and evaluating the results.
    B. constructing a processing system for accounting applications and processing actual data from throughout the period through both the client's program and the auditor's program.
    C. manually comparing detail transaction files used by an edit program to the program's generated error listings to determine that errors were properly identified by the edit program.
    D. manually reperforming, as of a point in time, the processing of input data and comparing the simulated results to the actual results.

12. Lake, CPA, is auditing the financial statements of Gill Co. Gill uses the IT Service Center, Inc. to process its payroll transactions. IT's financial statements are audited by Cope, CPA, who recently issued a report on IT's internal control. Lake is considering Cope's report on IT's internal control in assessing control risk on the Gill engagement. What is Lake's responsibility concerning making reference to Cope as a basis, in part, for Lake's own opinion?
    A. Lake may refer to Cope only if Lake's report indicates the division of responsibility.
    B. Lake may refer to Cope only if Lake relies on Cope's report in restricting the extent of substantive tests.
    C. Lake may not refer to Cope under the circumstances above.
    D. Lake may refer to Cope only if Lake is satisfied as to Cope's professional reputation and independence.

13. When an auditor tests a computerized accounting system, which of the following is true of the test data approach?
    A. Test data are processed by the client's computer programs under the auditor's control.
    B. Test data must consist of all possible valid and invalid conditions.
    C. Several transactions of each type must be tested.
    D. The program tested is different from the program used throughout the year by the client.

14. Which of the following client information technology (IT) systems generally can be audited without examining or directly testing the IT computer programs of the system?
    A. A system that performs relatively complicated processing and produces very little detailed output.
    B. A system that performs relatively uncomplicated processes and produces detailed output.
    C. A system that updates a few essential master files and produces no printed output other than final balances.
    D. A system that affects a number of essential master files and produces a limited output.

15. Which of the following is **NOT** a major reason why an accounting audit trail should be maintained for a computer system?
    A. Monitoring purposes.
    B. Deterrent to fraud.
    C. Analytical procedures.
    D. Query answering.

16. Which of the following employees in a company's information technology department should be responsible for designing new or improved data processing procedures?
    A. Programmer.
    B. Control-group supervisor.
    C. Systems analyst.
    D. Flowchart editor.

17. Data Corporation has just completely computerized its billing and accounts receivable record keeping. You want to make maximum use of the new computer in your audit of Data Corporation. Which of the following audit techniques could not be performed through a computer program?
    A. Examining sales invoices for completeness, consistency between different items, valid conditions, and reasonable amounts.
    B. Selecting on a random number basis accounts to be confirmed.
    C. Tracing audited cash receipts to accounts receivable credits.
    D. Resolving differences reported by customers on confirmation requests.

18. Computer systems are typically supported by a variety of utility software packages that are important to an auditor because they:
    A. are very versatile programs that can be used on hardware of many manufacturers.
    B. may enable unauthorized changes to data files if not properly controlled.
    C. are written specifically to enable auditors to extract and sort data.
    D. may be significant components of a client's application programs.

19. Which of the following types of evidence would an auditor *most likely* examine to determine whether internal control policies and procedures are operating as designed?
    A. Client records documenting the use of IT programs.
    B. Anticipated results documented in budgets or forecasts.
    C. Confirmations of receivables verifying account balances.
    D. Gross margin information regarding the client's industry.

20. Which of the following is an example of a validity check?
    A. As the computer corrects errors and data are successfully resubmitted to the system, the causes of the errors are printed out.
    B. After data for a transaction are entered, the computer sends certain data back to the terminal for comparison with data originally sent.
    C. The computer flags any transmission for which the control field value did not match that of an existing file record.
    D. The computer ensures that a numerical amount in a record does not exceed some predetermined amount.

21. A technique for controlling identification numbers (part number, man number, etc.) is:
    A. parity control.
    B. echo checks.
    C. file protection.
    D. self-checking digits.

22. Using microcomputers in auditing may affect the methods used to review the work of staff assistants because:
   A. documenting the supervisory review may require assistance of consulting services personnel.
   B. audit document documentation may not contain readily observable details of calculations.
   C. the audit fieldwork standards for supervision may differ.
   D. supervisory personnel may not have an understanding of the capabilities and limitations of microcomputers.

23. When an auditor tests a computerized accounting system, which of the following is true of the test data approach?
   A. The program tested is different from the program used throughout the year by the client.
   B. Several transactions of each type must be tested.
   C. Test data are processed by the client's computer programs under the auditor's control.
   D. Test data must consist of all possible valid and invalid conditions.

24. Computer Services Company (CSC) processes payroll transactions for schools. Drake, CPA, is engaged to report on CSC's policies and procedures placed in operation as of a specific date. These policies and procedures are relevant to the schools' internal control, so Drake's report will be useful in providing the schools' independent auditors with information necessary to plan their audits. Drake's report expressing an opinion on CSC's policies and procedures placed in operation as of a specific date should contain a(an):
   A. description of the scope and nature of Drake's procedures.
   B. statement that CSC's management has disclosed to Drake all design deficiencies of which it is aware.
   C. paragraph indicating the basis for Drake's assessment of control risk.
   D. opinion on the operating effectiveness of CSC's policies and procedures.

25. Which of the following control procedures *most likely* could prevent IT personnel from modifying programs to bypass programmed controls?
   A. Segregation of duties within IT for computer programming and computer operations.
   B. Participation of user department personnel in designing and approving new systems.
   C. Physical security of IT facilities in limiting access to IT equipment.
   D. Periodic management review of computer utilization reports and systems documentation.

ANSWERS: AUDITING AND TECHNOLOGY

1. **C** An integrated test facility is a method of testing programmed controls by creating a small subsystem within the regular IT system. Dummy files and records are appended to existing client files, and fictitious test transactions, specifically coded to correspond with the dummy files and records, are introduced into a system together with actual real transactions. Parallel simulation is an approach which involves reprocessing actual company data using auditor-controlled programs. Test data approach is an approach which involves dummy transactions prepared and processed by the auditor using the client's computer program.

2. **B** IT controls can be tested by processing test data using the client's program. The auditor's test data must include valid and invalid transactions in order to determine if the programs will react correctly to the different kinds of data. In a test of the payroll system, the auditor would want to determine that the programs are processing time tickets and other data correctly and would, therefore, include in his test data time tickets with invalid job numbers. The other answers refer primarily to authorizations, not to data processing.

3. **A** Auditors may run test data, which simulate actual transactions, on a client's computerized system to determine if the controls related to processing those transactions are operating effectively. The types of controls that can be tested in this manner are control procedures that can be programmed, such as discovering invalid employee I.D. numbers. The auditor could introduce simulated payroll data that have invalid I.D. numbers to determine if the computerized payroll system detects the error. The other answers are not programmable controls, which exist in a computerized payroll system, that can be tested using test data. Control over the existence of unclaimed payroll checks held by supervisors is outside of the computer system and could be tested through inquiry and observation. Control over early cashing of payroll checks is outside the computer system and could be tested by inquiry, observation and examination of canceled checks. Control over approval of overtime by supervisors is typically outside the computer system and can be tested by examining timecards or other documentation for authorization.

4. **D** A systems flowchart is a pictorial representation of the processing steps in moving an item through processing. The question deals with understanding internal control. Therefore, a flowchart would aid the auditor in understanding the flow of the system.

5. **B** If the auditor wants to discover unauthorized changes to an IT program, he could compare the authorized program's source code with the unauthorized program's source code. The other answers are programs that are designed primarily to test a client's application programs and programmed controls, not controls over unauthorized program changes.

6. **A** This will provide the auditor with the most competent evidence that the user identification and password controls are functioning as designed. The other answers do not relate directly to actual system access; they refer to programming, authorization and written statements.

7. **A** Misstatements may not be detected immediately because a batch computer system processes transactions in a batch or group, instead of individually. Therefore, there is a delay between the transaction and the processing while the transactions are accumulated. An error in one transaction will not cause the rejection of other transactions but rather the rejection of the entire batch until

the errors are corrected. Input controls typically are designed into the system to reduce the chance of errors being introduced when the transactions are entered. Processing of transactions in a batch is intended to be uniform since all are processed at the same time by the same program.

8. **C** A department supervisor would indicate approval of overtime by signing the employee's time card. Visual inspection of the time card by the auditor would determine whether or not total hours worked were properly approved.

9. **D** The assignment of programmers and the operation of a computer are the prime responsibilities of an IT manager. An independent control group should function between the user department and the IT department. The other answers are good examples of internal control within an IT system.

10. **B** A data control group should review output and control the distribution of output from the IT department. The systems analyst designs and evaluates systems and prepares program specifications for programmers. These two functions should be separated. The accounts payable clerk preparing data for computer processing and entering the data into the computer may be acceptable, especially in an on-line system. The other answer choices describe appropriate functions of a programmer and a control clerk.

11. **D** An auditor can verify the reliable operation of programmed control procedures by auditing around the computer, comparing the results from manually reperforming the processing of input data with the actual results; however, doing this as of a *point* in time will not determine if the controls are operating reliably over the period of time affected by the programmed control procedures.

12. **C** When an entity uses a service organization to process certain transactions, part of its accounting system and internal control are not internal. Such an entity is referred to as a user organization and its auditor is referred to as the user auditor. In this situation, the user auditor may consider work done by the service auditor, which is the term used to describe the auditor of the service organization, in evaluating internal control and assessing control risk. If a report by the service auditor on the service organization's internal control is considered, the user auditor should not make reference to the report of the service auditor as a basis for his or her opinion on the user organization's financial statements. Since the service auditor is not responsible for examining any portion of the user organization's financial statements, there cannot be a division of responsibility for the audit of the user organization's financial statements. The user auditor, Lake, would not consider the report of the service auditor, Cope, if the service auditor were not reputable and independent. The user auditor cannot refer to the service auditor in his or her report.

13. **A** The test data approach tests computer controls by processing the auditor's test data, which consist of valid and invalid transactions, using the client's program. The basic concept of test data is that a computer program will handle every transaction exactly the same way, therefore only one transaction of each type has to be tested. The auditor needs only to prepare a limited number of simulated transactions to determine whether controls are operating. The test data are processed with the client program that is supposed to have been used during the period under audit.

14. **B** A system that, for instance, debits, credits and computes the balances of customer accounts receivable subsidiary ledger, but also printed out all the entries made plus the beginning and ending balances, could be audited without directly testing it because external documentation is provided as evidence of each transaction.

15. C Analytical procedures are substantive audit tests, not a reason why an accounting audit trail should be maintained for a computer system. An audit trail is a chain of evidence connecting account balances and other summary results with original transaction data. The trail is used by management to monitor the system, to respond to inquiries, and to deter misuse. Auditors use the accounting audit trail to vouch and trace transactions.

16. C A systems analyst has the primary responsibility for the design of new and improved data processing procedures.

17. D Resolving differences reported by customers on confirmation request would have to be done manually.

18. B Utility programs perform common data processing tasks such as copying, sorting, merging, reorganizing data in a file, and printing. They can also be used to enter and change data. Utility software packages are important to the auditor because if not properly controlled, unauthorized changes to data files may occur.

19. A In a computerized environment, there are general controls that are pervasive in their effect and relate to all computerized accounting activities. Control over access to information technology (IT) programs is an example of a general control. In order to test control over access, the auditor would most likely examine client records documenting the use of IT programs. The other answers are examples of substantive tests, not tests of controls.

20. D Validity checks are computer-programmed routines that determine whether or not a particular character is legitimate. An example of a validity check would be a comparison of input data fields to existing file records to determine if the characters being entered are valid. If the validity check is operating properly, the computer will flag any transmissions for which the control field value (input data) did not match that of an existing file record.

21. D One method for controlling identification numbers is to include an appended check digit as part of the number which is a result of some mathematical process that is applied to each digit in the number. The additional digit created is the result of this mathematical process.

22. B Work performed by assistants should be reviewed to determine whether it was adequately performed and to evaluate whether the results are consistent with the conclusions to be presented in the auditor's report. Audit documentss, which may be in the form of data stored on tapes or other media, are used to document procedures applied, tests performed, information obtained, and conclusions reached by the audit staff. Examples of audit documents are audit programs, analyses, memoranda, letters, abstracts of documents, and schedules or commentaries. When prepared manually, audit document documentation would typically contain readily observable details of calculations. This may not be true when using microcomputers since audit document documentation may be in the form of computer files. The fieldwork standard for planning and supervision is the same whether or not microcomputers are used in the audit. Audit supervisors should be able to document their review of staff assistants' work and should understand the capabilities and limitations of microcomputers.

23. C The purpose of a test data approach is to validate the processing of accounting data by the client's IT equipment. The test data has a known outcome and this known outcome is compared with the processing outcome to validate the processing of data.

24. **A** A service auditor's report expressing an opinion on a description of policies and procedures placed in operation at a service organization should contain a description of the scope and nature of the service auditor's procedures. The report should also contain a reference to applications, services, products, or other aspects of the service organization covered; identification of the party specifying the control objectives; an indication of the purpose of the service auditor's engagement; a disclaimer of opinion on the operating effectiveness of the policies and procedures; the service auditor's opinion on whether the policies and procedures are suitably designed to provide reasonable assurance that stated control objectives would be achieved if the control policies and procedures were complied with satisfactorily; a statement of inherent limitations; and identification of the parties for whom the report is intended. The other answers are incorrect because the service auditor's report expressing an opinion on a description of policies and procedures placed in operation at a service organization does not indicate that management of the user service organization disclosed design deficiencies to the service auditor; does not give an opinion on operating effectiveness, which is a different type of report that a service auditor can provide; and does not indicate the basis for the service auditor's assessment of control risk.

25. **A** In order to prevent unauthorized program modification, the duties of analysts, programmers and operators should be segregated. Specifically, systems analysts and computer operators should not do the technical programming and should not have access to the programmer's work. Review of utilization reports and system documentation may detect control problems but will not prevent control problems, such as IT personnel modifying programs. Designing new systems is unrelated to preventing program changes. Limiting physical access to equipment may not prevent modification of programs if programs can be accessed from off-site.

FLOWCHARTING

STUDY MANUAL – AUDITING & ATTESTATION
CHAPTER 12

Study Tip: Before you go to bed each night, write down what exam preparation you plan to accomplish the following day and when you will do it. In that way, you begin each day with an organized plan and do not have to waste time determining what to do as the day progresses.

MANAGEMENT ASSERTIONS AND CONTROL POLICIES AND PROCEDURES

A. As stated previously, management is expressing (or implying) many assertions (or claims) when it prepares financial statements. These assertions can be subdivided into five major categories:

1. *Presentation and disclosure.* The various components of the financial statements are properly classified, described, and disclosed.

2. *Existence or occurrence.* The assets and liabilities did exist as of a given date, and the recorded transactions did occur during the identified period.

3. *Rights and obligations.* The assets are the rights of the entity and liabilities are the obligations of the entity as of a given date.

4. *Completeness.* The accounts and transactions reflected in the financial statements represent all of the accounts and transactions for the period. Simply stated, all transactions have been recorded.

5. *Valuation or allocation.* The accounts have been included in the financial statements at the appropriate amounts, including appropriate allocations between balance sheet and income statement accounts.

B. While these assertions will be addressed again and in more detail in our discussion of audit evidence, it is important to note that the control policies and procedures established by management are intended to address these assertions. In gathering evidence, the auditor generally follows these procedures:

1. Identify important assertions for the account balance or class of transactions.

2. Identify control policies and procedures that relate to those assertions.

3. Test the operating effectiveness of control policies and procedures related to management assertions.

4. Based on the results of the tests of operating effectiveness, design substantive tests to gather evidence regarding management assertions.

C. The table in Figure 1 provides a summary of how the five major categories of control procedures relate to management assertions. It is important to note that this is general information and other control procedures may differ slightly, depending on the circumstances.

D. The CPA exam frequently requires candidates to identify deficiencies in the internal control of a hypothetical entity. These deficiencies are identified based on examining a flowchart of an entity's internal control or a written narrative of that internal control. In each of these types of questions, the candidate can identify internal control deficiencies by recalling the control procedures introduced above.

E. In responding to questions requesting the candidate to identify internal control deficiencies, it is normally best to assume that each step in a flowchart or each description in a narrative contains some type of deficiency.

Figure 1: Control Procedures and Related Management Assertions

Authorization of transactions	Existence or occurrence	If transactions are properly authorized by management, it is unlikely that fictitious transactions will be recorded.
Recording of transactions	Completeness	By using prenumbered documents and accounting for the numerical sequence of these documents, the company will identify transactions that should have been recorded.
Custody of assets	Completeness, existence or occurrence, rights and obligations	If strong controls exist relating to custody of assets, employees would be unable to participate in a defalcation scheme and cover their theft by failing to record transactions (completeness) or recording a fictitious transaction (existence or occurrence). In addition, this would ensure that the entity truly had rights to the assets over which controls have been implemented.
Comparisons	Valuation or allocation, completeness, existence or occurrence	Comparisons allow the company to ensure that transactions are recorded at the proper dollar amounts (e.g., recalculating sales invoices). In addition, by comparing different documents, the company can determine that (1) a particular transaction was recorded (completeness) and (2) a recorded transaction actually occurred (existence or occurrence).
Segregation of functions	Completeness, existence or occurrence, rights and obligations	The primary benefit provided by segregation of functions is not allowing employees to individually participate in a defalcation scheme. Therefore, the assertions addressed by this category are similar to those for custody.

F. The candidate will need a basic understanding of common flowcharting symbols. Some of the more common symbols tested on the CPA exam are shown in Figure 2.

Figure 2: Some Common Flowchart Symbols

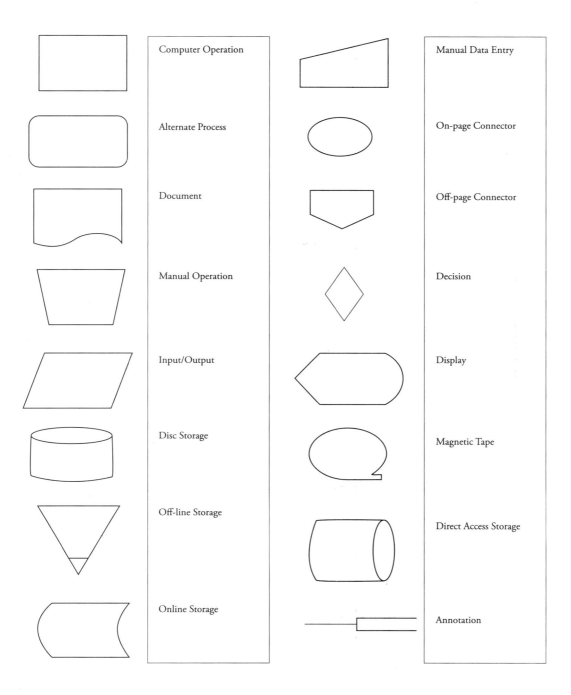

Cash Receipts and Cash Balances

Study Manual – Auditing & Attestation
Chapter 13

Study Tip: Many CPA exam candidates complain that they do not have a sufficient amount of time to study. It is important to learn to study at times that would otherwise be wasted. Study at lunch or while exercising or while waiting for the bus. If candidates can make use of these wasted moments, they usually discover that they do have enough time to adequately prepare.

INTRODUCTION

As noted earlier, financial statements that purport to be in conformity with generally accepted accounting principles contain certain assertions: presentation and disclosure, existence or occurrence, rights and obligations, completeness, and valuation or allocation. Auditors gather evidence to form an opinion with respect to these assertions. The experienced auditor should be able to prepare an audit program for an audit area (e.g., receivables) to test whether these assertions are supportable. The process is one in which specific audit objectives are developed based on the assertions being made in the financial statements. Finally, audit procedures to meet these audit objectives are formulated and listed in an audit program. For purposes of the CPA exam, consider two possible approaches for auditing an account: tests of balances and tests of details.

A. Tests of Balances and Tests of Details.

1. *Direct tests of ending balance (tests of balances)*. This approach requires the auditor to identify specific components of an account balance. For example, the cash account can be broken down into cash on hand and cash on deposit in the client's various bank accounts. Under this approach, the auditor will select and verify a sample of components of the account balance. Accounts that are normally examined via this approach are high turnover accounts such as cash, accounts receivable, inventory, and accounts payable.

2. *Tests of inputs and outputs during the year (tests of details)*. This approach requires the auditor to verify individual transactions comprising an account balance or class of transactions. This approach focuses on the individual transactions occurring during the year and not the final account balance. Accounts normally examined via this approach are lower turnover accounts, such as investments; property, plant and equipment; notes and bonds payable; and shareholders' equity.

3. Many audit procedures provide support for *multiple management assertions*. For example, cut-off procedures provide support for rights and obligations as well as for existence and completeness. The following are typical procedures included in a substantive audit program:

   a. To support presentation and disclosure:

   - Review disclosures for compliance with GAAP.
   - Inquire about disclosures.

   b. To support existence or occurrence:

   - Confirmation.
   - Observation—always consider whether you can observe the item itself and/or legal documents representing the item.
   - Trace/vouch transactions.

   c. To support rights and obligations:

   - Cutoffs—consider whether transactions have been reported in the proper period.
   - Authorization—consider whether there are transactions that require specific authorization.

   d. To support completeness:

   - Analytical procedures.
   - Omissions—consider how transactions could improperly have been omitted from the account.

   e. To support valuation:

   - Foot and cross-foot schedules (total them across and down).
   - Agree the account balances on schedules to the general ledger.
   - Agree financial statement balances to account balances on schedules.
   - Consider valuation methods and whether they have been properly applied.
   - Consider related accounts (e.g., accounts receivable and bad debt expense; long-term debt and interest expense; fixed assets and repair and maintenance expense; and fixed assets and depreciation expense).

B. Auditing Cash.

   1. The auditor will confirm the cash on deposit in the client's various bank accounts, and verify the bank reconciliation prepared by the client (corroborate the various reconciling items appearing on that bank reconciliation). The auditor may count cash on hand if it is significant.

2. Additionally, because of potential defalcation schemes, the auditor will investigate the possibility of kiting by requesting a cutoff bank statement directly from the bank and preparing a bank transfer schedule.

   a. Kiting is a form of fraud that overstates cash by causing it to be simultaneously included in two or more bank accounts.

   b. Kiting is possible because a check takes several days to clear the bank on which it is drawn (the "float period").

   c. When funds are transferred from one bank account to another near the end of the year, the auditor should investigate the possibility of kiting.

   d. When examining the cutoff bank statement, the auditor will determine that deposits-in-transit listed on the client's bank reconciliation actually exist and are properly recorded.

   e. The auditor will also verify that all outstanding checks are included in the client's bank reconciliation and are properly recorded.

3. The table below details the typical substantive audit procedures performed for cash.

Type of audit procedure	Audit procedure	Management assertion(s)
Confirmation	Confirm bank balances	Existence or occurrence; rights and obligations; valuation or allocation
Observation	Count cash on hand	Existence or occurrence; rights and obligations; valuation or allocation
Recalculation	Examine the client's bank reconciliation. Recalculate lists of deposits in transit, outstanding checks, and miscellaneous items. Recalculate the bank reconciliation itself	Valuation or allocation; completeness
Recalculation	Foot summary schedules.	Valuation or allocation
Recalculation	Reconcile summary schedules to general ledger.	Presentation and disclosure; rights and obligations
Inquiry	Inquire about compensating balances and restrictions.	Presentation and disclosure; rights and obligations
Inspect documents	Review bank statements.	Existence or occurrence; rights and obligations; completeness; valuation or allocation

Type of audit procedure	Audit procedure	Management assertion(s)
Inspect documents	Obtain a cutoff bank statement directly from the bank.	Existence or occurrence; rights and obligations; completeness; valuation or allocation
Inspect documents	Prepare a bank transfer schedule.	Existence or occurrence; rights and obligations; completeness; valuation or allocation
Inspect documents	Review disclosures for compliance with GAAP	Presentation and disclosure
Analytical procedures	Compare balances to budget	Valuation or allocation; completeness

Questions: Cash Receipts and Cash Balances

1. In testing controls over cash disbursements, an auditor *most likely* would determine that the person who signs checks also:
   A. reviews the monthly bank reconciliation.
   B. is denied access to the supporting documents.
   C. returns the checks to accounts payable.
   D. is responsible for mailing the checks.

2. Mailing disbursement checks and remittance advices should be controlled by the employee who:
   A. matches the receiving reports, purchase orders, and vendors' invoices.
   B. approves the vouchers for payment.
   C. maintains possession of the mechanical check-signing device.
   D. signs the checks last.

3. Which of the following internal controls *most likely* would reduce the risk of diversion of customer receipts by an entity's employees?
   A. Monthly bank reconciliations.
   B. Prenumbered remittance advices.
   C. Daily deposit of cash receipts.
   D. A bank lockbox system.

4. Upon receipt of customers' checks in the mailroom, a responsible employee should prepare a remittance listing that is forwarded to the cashier. A copy of the listing should be sent to the:
   A. treasurer to compare the listing with the monthly bank statement.
   B. accounts receivable bookkeeper to update the subsidiary accounts receivable records.
   C. entity's bank to compare the listing with the cashier's deposit slip.
   D. internal auditor to investigate the listing for unusual transactions.

5. Sound internal control procedures dictate that immediately upon receiving checks from customers by mail, a responsible employee should:
   A. record the checks in the cash receipts journal.
   B. prepare a duplicate listing of checks received.
   C. verify that each check is supported by a prenumbered sales invoice.
   D. add the checks to the daily cash summary.

6. Internal control over cash receipts is weakened when an employee who receives customer mail receipts also:
   A. records credits to individual accounts receivable.
   B. prepares bank deposit slips for all mail receipts.
   C. prepares initial cash receipts records.
   D. maintains a petty cash fund.

7. The usefulness of the standard bank confirmation request may be limited because the bank employee who completes the form may:
   A. not believe that the bank is obligated to verify confidential information to a third party.
   B. sign and return the form without inspecting the accuracy of the client's bank reconciliation.
   C. be unaware of all the financial relationships that the bank has with the client.
   D. not have access to the client's cutoff bank statement.

Answers: Cash Receipts and Cash Balances

1. **D** The individual who signs checks should also mail the checks to reduce the likelihood of others accessing and misusing checks.

2. **D** Once the checks have been signed, they should not be returned to any employee involved in the disbursement cycle of the entity. The other answers represent tasks performed by individuals in the disbursement cycle. Therefore, these individuals should not be responsible for mailing the disbursement checks.

3. **D** When a bank lockbox system is used, customers, in effect, send their remittances directly to the bank, thus eliminating the possibility of employees misappropriating those cash receipts. The other answers are internal control procedures that involve employees. In addition to using prenumbered remittance advices, an employee would have to account for their sequence to determine if any have been returned, but the accompanying cash not properly recorded. A reconciliation of cash per bank and cash per books will not detect cash receipts that have not been properly recorded and not deposited in the bank. Depositing cash receipts daily will not, by itself, reduce the risk of misappropriated cash receipts.

4. **B** A copy of the remittance listing is sent to the accounts receivable clerk and posted to the subsidiary records. Accounting for assets is a function that should be separated from the custody of those assets. The accounts receivable bookkeeper maintains records of the balance owed by each customer, while the cashier has custody of the cash. The cashier does not have an opportunity to cover a shortage of cash by using checks received on account because the AR ledger would indicate a different balance than that owed. There is no need to send copies to the internal auditor, the treasurer, or the bank, because the goal is to establish accountability for the asset.

5. **B** The initial task in the cash receipts cycle is to establish immediate control over incoming cash receipts. This control is achieved by having the employee who is responsible for opening the mail prepare listings of checks received.

6. **A** There is a control weakness because the employee has both custody of an asset, cash, and the accounting record (accounts receivable subsidiary ledgers).

7. **C** The AICPA Standard Form to Confirm Account Balance Information With Financial Institutions is designed to substantiate information that is stated on the confirmation request. If the bank employee who completes the form is unaware of all financial relationships that the bank has with the client, the response may not provide information beyond that which is specifically requested. This limits the usefulness of the standard bank confirmation request.

Special Reports and Other Reports

Study Manual – Auditing & Attestation
Chapter 14

Study Tip: The biggest enemy that any CPA exam candidate faces is procrastination. Adequate preparation requires a significant number of hours. It is easy to put off doing the studying that is necessary. There is always something that absolutely has to be done prior to studying: paying the bills, washing the dishes, taking out the garbage, mowing the grass, etc. Eventually, the dishes get washed but the candidate never manages to get around to studying. Study first so you can avoid procrastination.

Operational Audits

An operational audit is a review of any part of an organization's operating policies, procedures, and methods for the purposes of (1) assessing performance, (2) identifying opportunities for improvement, and (3) developing recommendations for improvement or further action. These audits generally involve the issues of effectiveness (doing the right things), efficiency (doing the right things correctly), and economy (doing the right things with the minimum waste of time).

The accomplishment of the purposes involves activities such as:

- Reviewing and appraising the soundness, adequacy, and application of accounting, financial, and other operating controls, and promoting effective control at reasonable cost
- Ascertaining the appropriateness of policies, procedures, and methods in meeting the goals and objectives of the organization
- Ascertaining the extent of compliance with established policies, plans, and procedures
- Ascertaining the extent to which company assets are accounted for and safeguarded from losses
  of all kinds
- Ascertaining the reliability of management data developed within the organization
- Appraising the quality of performance in carrying out assigned responsibilities
- Recommending operating improvements

Operational auditing may be performed by independent or external auditors, but in many organizations, the function is performed by internal auditors.

DOWNGRADING AN ENGAGEMENT

In some circumstances, a client may request a change in an engagement from an audit to a compilation or a review. Before accepting a changed engagement, the accountant should consider:

- The reason for the client's request, especially the implications of a scope limitation imposed by the client or by circumstances
- The additional audit effort and estimated additional cost required to complete the examination

If the accountant determines that a change is appropriate under the circumstances, the accountant should perform the changed engagement and issue a normal review or compilation report. The accountant should not refer to the original engagement or any audit procedures that may have been performed, nor to any scope limitations that resulted in the changed engagement.

REPORTING ON INFORMATION ACCOMPANYING AUDITED FINANCIAL STATEMENTS

There are three categories of "information" that may be presented with the audited financial statements and the auditor's report. The auditor has no responsibility to audit information outside the basic financial statements. However, the auditor does have certain responsibilities for the information provided outside the basic financial statements. The nature of that responsibility varies with the nature of both the information and the document containing the financial statements.

1. *Category I: Other information in documents containing audited financial statements.* Information may be provided by the client and published or distributed with the audited basic financial statements and the auditor's report. Examples include the president's annual letter to stockholders, product information, and graphs depicting trends.

2. *Category II: Required supplementary information.* Information may be required by the FASB, which the FASB considers an essential part of financial reporting for certain entities and provides guidelines for measurement and presentation of the information. This information is not part of the basic financial statements. An example would be disclosures of oil and gas reserves.

3. *Category III: Other information in auditor submitted documents.* Information may be included in a document submitted by the auditor that is in addition to the basic financial statements and the auditor's standard report. Examples include additional details or explanations, consolidating information, historical summaries of data, or statistical information.

CATEGORY I: OTHER INFORMATION IN DOCUMENTS CONTAINING AUDITED FINANCIAL STATEMENTS

The auditor has the responsibility to read the other information to determine if its content or presentation is materially misstated or inconsistent with the information that appears in the audited financial statements.

If there are material inconsistencies, the auditor should determine whether the "other information" is inconsistent or whether the information in the basic financial statements is inconsistent. The auditor should request that the client revise the inconsistent information. If the client refuses to revise the inconsistent information, the auditor should consider such actions as revising the audit report to include an explanatory paragraph describing the material inconsistency, withholding the use of the auditor's report in the document, or withdrawing from the engagement.

If there are material misstatements of fact that are not material inconsistencies, the auditor should discuss the matter with the client. The auditor should consider that the issue may be outside the auditor's area of expertise or that there is a difference of judgment or opinion. In such cases, the auditor should encourage the client to obtain outside expertise or assistance, such as the client's legal counsel. If the auditor continues to conclude that there is a material misstatement of fact, the auditor should consider notifying the client in writing of the auditor's views concerning the information and then consult the legal counsel.

In those cases where another auditor is involved in the audit engagement, the principal auditor should consider having the other auditor read the other information for material inconsistencies and misstatements of fact.

Note that in this category the auditor has a reading responsibility, but has no reporting responsibilities unless there are material inconsistencies or misstatements of facts. Reading, with no other audit procedures applied, is not an adequate basis for expressing an opinion on information.

CATEGORY II: REQUIRED SUPPLEMENTARY INFORMATION

Information required by the FASB or the GASB (Government Accounting Standards Board), which the FASB or GASB considers an essential part of financial reporting for certain entities and provides guidelines for measurement and presentation of the information, is not part of the basic financial statements and is not covered by the standard auditor's report.

Certain review procedures should be applied to information that is required by the FASB or the GASB, but is presented outside the basic financial statements. The first procedure is to determine if the information is required by the FASB or the GASB. If such information is required, the auditor will apply limited procedures to the information and report deficiencies in, or omission of, the information.

The auditor's reporting responsibilities with respect to supplemental information required by the FASB or GASB is one of "exception reporting." An auditor should report on supplemental information required by the FASB or GASB when:

- Supplemental information that the FASB or GASB requires to be presented in the circumstances is omitted. (The auditor need not provide the missing information.)
- The auditor has concluded that the measurement or presentation of the supplemental information departs materially from guidelines prescribed by the FASB or GASB.
- The auditor is unable to complete the prescribed procedures listed above.

Because the supplemental information generally is reported outside the basic financial statements, there is no effect on the fair presentation of the basic financial statements. However, if the client implies an examination or opinion on the supplemental information when none occurred, the audit report should be expanded to include a disclaimer on such information. If the supplemental information is reported with the audited information, it should be clearly identified as "unaudited," and, if it is not, the auditor should modify his or her audit report to disclaim an opinion on the supplemental information.

CATEGORY III: OTHER INFORMATION IN AUDITOR SUBMITTED DOCUMENTS

Information included in a document submitted by the auditor that is in addition to the basic financial statements and the auditor's standard report is not part of the basic financial statements and is not covered by the standard auditor's report. Unlike the supplemental information previously discussed, the following applies to information in auditor-prepared documents.

When an auditor submits a document containing audited basic financial statements and supplemental information, the auditor has no responsibility to examine or review the other supplemental information, but the auditor does have a responsibility to report on all the information included in the document including the basic financial statements and the supplemental information. The reporting responsibility for the supplemental information is the same as that for the audited basic financial statements in that there must be a clear indication of the character of the examination and the degree of responsibility being assumed.

When reporting on the supplemental information included in the auditor-prepared document, the auditor should:

- State that an examination has been performed for the purpose of forming an opinion on the basic financial statements taken as a whole.
- Identify the supplementary information, either by descriptive title or page number.
- State that the supplementary information is presented for purposes of analysis and is not a part of the basic financial statements.
- Include either an opinion on the accompanying information or a disclaimer of opinion. The auditor may express an opinion on part of the supplemental information and disclaim on the remainder.
- The report on the supplemental information may be part of the auditor's standard report (modified) on the basic financial statements or may be a separate report. As in the case

of a combined report, if a separate report is issued, both reports must reflect the character of the examination and the degree of responsibility being assumed.

SEGMENT INFORMATION

According to generally accepted accounting principles, financial statements of publicly held companies must disclose segment information as well as certain information about products and services, geographic areas, and major customers. These disclosures are an integral part of the basic financial statements.

The objective of the auditing procedures to be applied to segment information is to determine whether or not the segment information is presented in conformity with GAAP. The auditor will apply auditing procedures to the segment information relative to the financial statements taken as a whole, not relative to a separate opinion on the segment information unless the issuance of a separate opinion is intended. Therefore, if no separate opinion is expected, the materiality criteria for the segment information will be the same as that for the financial statements taken as a whole.

GAAP requires that the management approach be used to identify and measure the financial information disclosed about operating segments. This approach focuses on the financial information that the entity's chief operating decision maker (CODM) uses internally to evaluate the performance of segments. The CODM could be the chief executive officer, chief operating officer, or another individual who exercises decision-making authority.

In planning the audit engagement, the auditor should consider the following:

- An understanding of who performs the function of CODM
- How management organizes the entity into operating segments
- The nature and extent of differences between the information systems used to generate data used by the CODM and the information systems that generate data for external reporting purposes

The auditor should apply certain audit procedures to evaluate whether the entity identified its reportable operating segments in accordance with GAAP:

- Inquire of management concerning its methods of determining segment information, and evaluate the reasonableness of those methods.
- Review corroborating evidence, such as information used by the CODM to assess performance, minutes and materials from board of directors meetings, and information that management provides for management's discussion and analysis (MD&A), for consistency with financial statement disclosures.
- Assess whether the entity has applied aggregation criteria and quantitative thresholds appropriately to determine its reportable operating segments.
- Obtain management's written representation that operating segments are appropriately identified and disclosed in accordance with GAAP.

The auditor should consider applying the following procedures to obtain additional evidence about segment disclosures:

- Perform analytical procedures on the information about segments to identify relationships and items that appear to be unusual and may indicate misstatements.
- Evaluate the adequacy of disclosures with regard to general information; information about reported segment profit or loss, segment assets, and the basis of measurement; and reconciliations required by GAAP for totals of segment revenues, profit or loss, and assets to corresponding enterprise information.
- Assess whether restatements of prior-period segment information is in accordance with GAAP.

The auditor's standard report will apply to segment information unless the information is marked as unaudited. The report, however, will not refer to the segment information unless there is a misstatement or omission, or a change in accounting principle, relating to the segment information that is material in relation to the financial statements taken as a whole, or the auditor is unable to apply to segment information auditing procedures he or she considers necessary under the circumstances. Materiality is to be viewed both quantitatively and qualitatively:

- A misstatement in segment information requires a qualification of the auditor's report due to nonconformity with generally accepted accounting principles.
- An omission of part or all required segment information will require a qualification of the auditor's report due to inadequate disclosure and the report should describe the type of information omitted. The report is not required to provide the omitted information.

When segment information has been omitted, the report may be modified as follows:

[Standard introductory paragraph]

Except as explained in the following paragraph, we . . . [Remainder is standard scope paragraph].

The company has not developed the information we consider necessary to reach a conclusion as to whether the presentation of segment information concerning the company's operations in different industries, its foreign operations and export sales, and its major customers is necessary to conform with Statement No. 131 of the Financial Accounting Standards Board.

- In our opinion, except for the possible omission of segment information, the financial statements referred to above present fairly . . . [Remainder is standard opinion paragraph].

REVIEW OF INTERIM (QUARTERLY) FINANCIAL STATEMENTS

An auditor may be asked to perform a review of interim (quarterly) financial statements. The review form of association discussed above is also appropriate for companies wishing to have their interim (quarterly) financial information reviewed.

The objective of a review of interim financial information is to provide the accountant with a basis for communicating whether he or she is aware of any material modifications that should be made to the interim financial information for it to conform with GAAP.

KNOWLEDGE OF INTERNAL CONTROL

During a review of interim financial information, the accountant needs to obtain sufficient knowledge of the client's internal control. This knowledge should enable the accountant to:

- Identify the types of potential misstatements and to consider the likelihood of occurrence.
- Select the inquiries and analytical procedures that may enable the accountant to determine whether material modifications should be made to the interim financial information.

If the accountant has performed the audit of the client's annual financial statements, a sufficient knowledge of internal control would ordinarily exist without performing additional procedures. If the accountant has not audited the client's annual financial statements, the accountant should perform procedures to obtain the necessary knowledge related to internal control.

NATURE OF PROCEDURES

Procedures relating to a review of interim financial information will consist primarily of inquiries and analytical procedures.

- Inquiries are made concerning the accounting system and any significant changes in internal control.
- Minutes are read to identify actions that may affect the interim financial information.
- The interim financial information is read to determine if it conforms with generally accepted accounting principles.
- Reports are obtained from other accountants, if any, who have been engaged to review interim financial information of components of the reporting entity, its subsidiaries, and other investees.
- Inquiries are made of officers and executives as to whether interim financial information has been prepared in conformity with generally accepted accounting principles, changes in activities or accounting practices of the entity, matters that arose when performing analytical procedures, and subsequent events information.
- Written representations are obtained from management regarding management's responsibility for the interim financial information, completeness of the minutes, subsequent events, and other matters the accountant believes to be significant.

TIMING OF PROCEDURES

The adequate planning of the interim review procedures is important. The accountant should plan the performance of the work during the interim period as well as at the fiscal year-end so that the work will be carried out efficiently and will be completed at an early date.

There are two aspects that are significant in relationship to timing.

1. One issue relates to getting information to users more promptly than on an annual basis. Consequently, there is a greater reliance on estimates during a review of interim financial information than during an audit.

2. The other aspect of timing relates to the fact that an interim period is considered an integral part of the annual period and items such as tax rates will be computed based on annual estimates.

EXTENT OF PROCEDURES

The extent of the procedures to be applied to the interim financial information will depend on various factors. These include:

- The accountant's knowledge of the client's accounting and reporting practices
- The accountant's knowledge, from the annual audit, of weaknesses in the client's internal control
- The existence of accounting records at multiple locations
- The accountant's knowledge of changes in the nature or volume of the client's activity or any accounting changes
- The issuance of any new pronouncements or new applications of existing accounting pronouncements that may affect the client's reporting
- Questions that may be raised as a result of other procedures that are performed by the accountant

Review procedures should be modified as the accountant takes into consideration the results of auditing procedures applied in performing an examination in accordance with generally accepted auditing standards.

STANDARD INTERIM REVIEW REPORT

An interim review report should be dated as of the date of the completion of the review and be signed in the name of the firm. The following is a standard review report:

Independent Accountant's Report

Date: [Completion of accountant's review procedures]

To: [There are no restrictions on the addressee]

We have reviewed the accompanying [*describe the interim financial information*] of XYZ Company as of September 30, 2005, and for the three-month and nine-month periods then ended. This interim financial information is the responsibility of the company's management.

We conducted our review in accordance with standards established by the American Institute of Certified Public Accountants. A review of interim financial information consists principally of applying analytical procedures and making inquiries of persons responsible for financial and

accounting matters. It is substantially less in scope than an audit conducted in accordance with U.S. generally accepted auditing standards, the objective of which is the expression of an opinion regarding the financial statements taken as
a whole. Accordingly, we do not express such an opinion.

Based on our review, we are not aware of any material modifications that should be made to the accompanying interim financial information in order for it to be in conformity with U.S. generally accepted accounting principles.

[Signature of Accountant/CPA Firm]

Certain circumstances may call for a modification from the standard report on interim financial information:

In the case of a departure from generally accepted accounting principles, the nature of the departure should be stated along with, if practicable, the effects.

In the case of inadequate disclosure, if practicable, missing information should be provided.

In the above circumstances, "if practicable" means that the data is readily available from the client's records, and by providing such information the auditor does not become a preparer of information.

In an annual presentation, interim financial information may be presented as supplemental information or as a note to audited financial statements.

When interim financial information is presented in a note to audited financial statements, no special mention need be made in the auditor's report on the financial statements provided that the interim financial information is clearly marked as unaudited.

An auditor's report on audited financial statements should be modified if the scope of the review on interim financial information was restricted or if interim financial information presented does not appear to be in conformity with generally accepted accounting principles. The auditor's report should likewise be expanded if the financial statements do not clearly indicate that the interim financial information is unaudited.

SPECIAL REPORTS

An auditor prepares special reports when called upon to report on:

- Financial statements prepared in accordance with a comprehensive basis of accounting other than generally accepted accounting principles (e.g., cash basis or tax basis)
- Specified elements, accounts, or items of a financial statement
- Compliance with aspects of contractual agreements related to audited financial statements
- Financial presentations to comply with a contractual agreement
- A printed form or schedule prescribing the wording of the auditor's report

A Comprehensive Basis of Accounting Other Than GAAP

Examples include:

- A basis of accounting that the reporting entity uses to comply with the requirements or financial reporting provisions of a government regulatory agency to whose jurisdiction the entity is subject
- A basis of accounting that the reporting entity uses or expects to use to file its income tax return for the period covered by the financial statements
- The cash receipts and disbursements basis of accounting, and modifications of the cash basis having substantial support, such as recording depreciation on fixed assets
- A definitive set of criteria having substantial support that is applied to all material items appearing in financial statements, such as the price-level basis of accounting

When preparing a report on financial statements prepared in accordance with a comprehensive basis of accounting other than generally accepted accounting principles, the auditor should include:

- A title that includes the word *independent*
- A paragraph identifying the financial statements audited, indicating that the financial statements are the responsibility of management, and that the auditor's responsibility is to express an opinion based on the audit
- A paragraph stating whether the audit was made in accordance with U.S. GAAS, the auditor's need to obtain reasonable assurance regarding material misstatements, the definition of an audit, and that the audit performed provides a reasonable basis for the opinion
- A paragraph that states: the basis of presentation and refers to the note to the financial statements that describes the basis of presentation and how the basis of presentation differs from GAAP; and that the basis of presentation is a comprehensive basis of accounting other than GAAP
- A paragraph that expresses the auditor's opinion (or disclaims an opinion) on whether the financial statements are presented fairly in conformity with the basis of accounting described in the note to the financial statement
- A signature
- The date as of the last day of fieldwork

An example of such a report follows:

Independent Auditor's Report

Board of Directors of XYZ Company

We have audited the accompanying statements of assets and liabilities arising from cash transactions of XYZ Company as of December 31, 2005, and the related statement of revenue collected and expenses paid for the year then ended. These financial statements are the responsibility of XYZ Company's management. Our responsibility is to express an opinion on these financial statements based on our audit.

We conducted our audit in accordance with U.S. generally accepted auditing standards. Those standards require that we plan and perform the audit to obtain reasonable assurance about whether the financial statements are free of material misstatement. An audit includes examining, on a test basis, evidence supporting the amounts and disclosures in the financial statements. An audit also includes assessing the accounting principles used and significant estimates made by management, as well as evaluating the overall financial statement presentation. We believe that our audit provides a reasonable basis for our opinion.

As described in Note X, these financial statements were prepared on the basis of cash receipts and disbursements, which is a comprehensive basis of accounting other than U.S. generally accepted accounting principles.

In our opinion, the financial statements referred to above present fairly, in all material respects, the assets and liabilities arising from cash transactions of XYZ Company as of December 31, 2005, and its revenue collected and expenses paid during the year then ended, on the basis of accounting described in Note X.

[Signature of Accountant/CPA Firm]

[Date of last day of fieldwork]

If the auditor concludes that the financial statements are not presented fairly on the basis of accounting described, he or she should disclose all the substantive reasons for that conclusion in an additional explanatory paragraph of his or her report and should include in the opinion paragraph appropriate modifying language and a reference to the explanatory paragraph.

SPECIFIED ELEMENTS, ACCOUNTS, OR ITEMS OF A FINANCIAL STATEMENT

When an auditor is called upon to prepare a report expressing an opinion on one or more specified elements, accounts, or items of a financial statement, the examination will be more extensive than if the same information were being considered in conjunction with an examination of the financial statements taken as a whole.

The auditor is not to express an opinion on specified elements, accounts, or items that are included in financial statements on which the auditor has expressed an adverse opinion or disclaimed an opinion if the opinion could be construed to be a piecemeal opinion. When the auditor is able to express an opinion on the specified elements, accounts, or items, the report should:

- Identify the specified elements, accounts, or items examined.
- State whether the examination was made in accordance with generally accepted auditing standards and, if applicable, that it was made in conjunction with an examination of financial statements.
- Identify the basis on which the specified elements, accounts, or items are presented and, when applicable, any agreements specifying such basis.
- Describe and indicate the source of significant interpretations made by the client in the course of the engagement relating to the provisions of a relevant agreement.

- Indicate whether in the auditor's opinion the specified elements, accounts, or items are presented fairly on the basis indicated.

APPLICATION OF AGREED UPON PROCEDURES

An agreed upon procedure engagement is one in which a practitioner is engaged by a specified party to issue a report of findings based on specific procedures performed on subject matter (e.g., agreed upon procedures to an entity's internal control over financial reporting, compliance with various laws and regulations, or on a schedule of statistical production data). The engagement may be accepted by the practitioner provided:

- The practitioner is independent.
- The party that wishes to engage the practitioner is responsible for subject matter, or has a reasonable basis for providing a written assertion about the subject matter, or is not responsible for the subject matter but is able to provide the auditor with evidence of a third party's responsibility for the subject matter.
- The parties have a clear understanding of the procedures to be performed.
- The specified parties take responsibility for sufficiency of procedures.
- The subject matter involved is subject to reasonably consistent measurement.
- The procedures applied are expected to result in reasonably consistent findings using the criteria.
- audit evidence is expected to provide a reasonable basis for expressing findings.
- The practitioner and the specified party agree on materiality limits.
- Distribution of the report is to be restricted to named parties involved.

Ordinarily the practitioner will meet with the parties involved to discuss the procedures to be performed. If this is not practicable, the parties can obtain the necessary understanding by applying one or more of the following procedures:

- Discussing the procedures to be applied with legal counsel or other appropriate representatives of the parties involved
- Reviewing relevant correspondence from the parties
- Comparing the procedures to be applied to written requirements of a supervisory agency
- Distributing a draft of the report or a copy of the client's engagement letter to the parties involved with a request for their comments before the report is issued

The report on the results of applying the agreed-upon procedures should:

- Include the word *independent* in the title
- Identify the specified parties
- Identify the subject matter and character of the engagement
- Indicate that the subject matter is the responsibility of the specified party
- Indicate that the procedures performed were agreed to by the specified parties
- State that the engagement was conducted in accordance with attestation standards established by the AICPA
- Indicate that the sufficiency of procedures performed is the responsibility of the specified parties
- List the procedures performed and the related findings

- Describe the agreed upon materiality limits
- Disclaim an opinion with respect to the subject matter
- Include a statement restricting the use of the report to the specified parties
- Be signed by the auditor
- Be dated as of the completion of the agreed upon procedures

COMPLIANCE WITH A CONTRACTUAL AGREEMENT

An auditor may be called upon to furnish a report indicating a client's compliance with a contractual agreement, such as a bond indenture or loan agreement, or regulatory requirements, for example, certain sections of the Internal Revenue Code. The auditor will generally satisfy the request by giving negative assurance relative to the applicable covenants. The assurance may be given in a separate report or as a separate paragraph of the auditor's report on the financial statements, but may not be given at all unless the auditor has examined the financial statements to which the contractual agreements or regulatory requirements relate.

REPORTS ON A PRINTED FORM

An auditor may be called upon to prepare a report on a printed form or schedule, prescribing the wording of the auditor's report. If a printed form calls upon the auditor to make an assertion that the auditor believes is not justified, the auditor would reword the form or attach a separate report.

REPORTING ON TRANSACTIONS

An accountant, other than the continuing accountant engaged to report on financial statements, may be asked to prepare a written report:

- Related to the application of accounting principles to a completed or proposed transaction.
- Related to the type of opinion that may be issued on an entity's financial statements.
- To intermediaries related to the application of accounting principles to hypothetical transactions.

In addition to meeting the appropriate general standards and standards of fieldwork, the accountant should consider who is requesting the report, the circumstances under which the request is made, the purpose of the request, and the intended use of the report.

The procedures that the accountant should follow include:

- Obtaining an understanding of the form and substance of the transaction
- Reviewing applicable generally accepted accounting principles
- Consulting with other professionals or experts, if appropriate
- Determining, through research or other procedures, if there are creditable precedents or analogies, if appropriate

In either of the latter two types of reporting engagements, the accountant should consult with the continuing accountant to ascertain all of the relevant facts. The continuing accountant may be able to provide information about:

- The form and substance of the transaction
- How accounting principles have been applied to similar transactions
- Whether there is a dispute with the continuing accountant as to the application of accounting principles
- Whether the continuing accountant has reached a different conclusion as to the application of accounting principles or the type of opinion that should be issued

The accountant's report will include:

- A description of the nature of the engagement and a statement that it was performed in accordance with AICPA standards
- A description of the transaction; the relevant facts, circumstances, and assumptions; and a statement about the source of the information
- Identification of principals to specific transactions
- A statement indicating the responsibility of the financial statement preparers for the proper accounting
- A statement that a change in facts, circumstances, or assumptions may change the report

PROSPECTIVE FINANCIAL STATEMENTS

The "statement" that deals with prospective financial statements is neither a Statement on Auditing Standards nor a Statement on Standards for Accounting Review Services. It is a Statement on Standards for Attestation Engagements (SSAE) issued by the AICPA.

The statement provides that a practitioner who either submits to his or her clients or others prospective financial statements that he or she has assembled or assisted in assembling, or reports on prospective financial statements, should either compile, examine, or apply agreed-upon procedures (practitioners do not perform reviews on prospective information) to the prospective financial statements if those statements are, or reasonably might be, expected to be used by another (third) party. The statement also applies to partial presentations that present prospective financial information that excludes certain items required under minimum presentation guidelines (discussed below).

The statement does not apply to an engagement involving prospective financial statements that are used solely in connection with litigation support services.

MINIMUM PRESENTATION GUIDELINES

Partial presentations are prospective financial statement presentations that do not meet the minimum presentation guidelines, and, therefore, are not appropriate for general use. The minimum presentation guidelines are based on the premise that prospective financial statements should be in the format of the historical financial statements that would be issued for the period(s) covered.

Prospective financial statements may take the form of complete basic financial statements or may be limited to the following minimum items (an item derivable from the information presented is not considered to be an omission):

- Group 1:
  - Sales or gross revenues
  - Gross profit or cost of sales
  - Unusual or infrequently occurring items
  - Provision for income taxes
  - Discontinued operations
  - Extraordinary items
  - Income from continuing operations
  - Net income
  - Basic and diluted earnings per share
  - Significant changes in financial position
- Group 2 (Background information):
  - A description of what management intends the prospective financial statements to present
  - A statement that the assumptions are based on information about circumstances and conditions existing at the time the prospective financial information was prepared
  - A statement that the prospective results may not be achieved
- Group 3
  - A summary of significant assumptions
  - A summary of significant accounting policies

Note: Omission of Group 1 items creates a partial presentation not considered in the statement. Omission of Group 2 items in the presence of Group 1 items results in a presentation subject to the provisions of the statement. The accountant should not compile or examine statements lacking disclosure of assumptions (Group 3).

The "preparer" of prospective financial statements generally is management—the party responsible for the assumptions underlying the prospective financial statements.

Prospective financial statements are either financial forecasts or financial projections including the summaries of significant assumptions and accounting policies.

- Financial forecasts—prospective financial statements that present an entity's expected financial position, results of operations, and cash flows. It is based on the responsible party's assumptions reflecting conditions it expects to exist and the course of action it expects to take. It may use single point or range estimates.
- Financial projections—prospective financial statements that present, given one or more hypothetical assumptions, an entity's expected financial position, results of operations, and cash flows. It is based on the responsible party's assumptions reflecting conditions it expects would exist and the course of action it expects would be taken given one or more hypothetical assumptions. It may use single point or range estimates. A hypothetical assumption is a condition or course of action that is not necessarily expected to occur.

Prospective financial statements are for either general use or limited use.

- *General use* refers to the use of the statements by persons with whom the responsible party is not negotiating directly, persons who are unable to ask the responsible party directly about the presentation. Only a financial forecast is appropriate for general use unless the financial projection is used as a supplement to a financial forecast.
- *Limited use* refers to the use of the statements by the responsible party alone or by the responsible party and third parties with whom the responsible party is negotiating directly. The user parties can ask questions of and negotiate directly with the responsible party. Either a financial forecast or financial projection is appropriate for limited use.

An accountant should not be associated with forecasts/projections that do not disclose assumptions.

COMPILATION OF PROSPECTIVE FINANCIAL STATEMENTS

A compilation is a professional service that involves:

- Assembling the prospective financial statements based on the responsible party's assumptions
- Performing the required compilation procedures
- Issuing a compilation report

A practitioner need not be independent to perform a compilation. In a compilation, the practitioner does not express an opinion or any form of assurance on the prospective financial statements or assumptions underlying those statements. The practitioner's report on a compilation of a financial forecast is shown below:

We have compiled the accompanying forecasted balance sheet, statements of income, retained earnings, and cash flows of XYZ Company as of December 31, 2005, and for the year then ending, in accordance with standards established by the American Institute of Certified Public Accountants.

A compilation is limited to presenting, in the form of a forecast, information that is the representation of management and does not include evaluation of the support for the assumptions underlying the forecast. We have not examined the forecast and, accordingly, do not express an opinion or any other form of assurance on the accompanying statements or assumptions. Furthermore, there will usually be differences between the forecasted and actual results, because events and circumstances frequently do not occur as expected, and those differences may be material. We have no responsibility to update this report for events and circumstances occurring after the date of this report.

[Signature of Accountant/CPA Firm]

[Date of last day of fieldwork]

Circumstances resulting in a departure from the standard compilation report:

- Presentation deficiencies or disclosure omissions, other than a significant assumption

- Comprehensive basis statements that do not disclose the basis used
- Summary of significant accounting policies omitted

EXAMINATION OF PROSPECTIVE FINANCIAL STATEMENTS

An examination of prospective financial statements is a professional service that involves:

- Evaluating the preparation of the prospective financial statements
- Evaluating the support underlying the assumptions
- Obtaining a written representation letter
- Evaluating the presentation of the prospective financial statements for conformity with AICPA
  presentation guidelines
- Issuing an examination report
- The person(s) performing the examination is to be independent with respect to the entity, have adequate technical training and proficiency to examine prospective financial statements, adequately plan and supervise the engagement, and obtain sufficient evidence to provide a reasonable basis for the examination report.

Examination procedures include:

- Prepare an engagement letter that confirms the understanding concerning the services to be provided.
- Accumulate sufficient evidence to limit attestation risk to a level that is appropriate for the level of assurance that is provided in the examination report. The only assurance given is that the prospective financial statements are in conformity with AICPA presentation guidelines and that the assumptions by the responsible party provide a reasonable basis for the forecast, or for the projection given the hypothetical assumptions. There is no assurance concerning achievability of the prospective results.
- Assess inherent and control risk and restrict detection risk.
- Assess the nature and materiality of the information as it relates to the prospective financial statements taken as a whole.
- Evaluate the support for the assumptions.
- Evaluate the preparation and presentation of the prospective financial statements to ascertain that:
  - The presentation reflects identified assumptions.
  - Computations made to translate the assumptions into financial statements are mathematically correct.
  - Assumptions are internally consistent.
  - Accounting principles used are consistent with the accounting principles expected to be used during the prospective period.
  - The presentation conforms to AICPA guidelines.
  - Assumptions are adequately disclosed based on AICPA guidelines.
- Consider revisions in prospective financial statements due to mathematical errors, unreasonable or internally inconsistent assumptions, inappropriate or incomplete presentation, or inadequate disclosure.

- Obtain written representations from the responsible party, which indicates that the responsible party is responsible for both the presentation and the underlying assumptions.

EXAMINATION REPORTS ON PROSPECTIVE FINANCIAL STATEMENTS

The issues addressed in the above report are similar to those in reports prepared by an auditor for examination engagements. The major contents of an examination report are as follows:

- A title that includes the word *independent*
- Identification of the prospective financial statements
- Identification of the responsible party
- The practitioner's responsibility to express an opinion on the prospective financial information
- A statement that an examination was conducted in accordance with AICPA standards
- A statement that the examination provides a reasonable basis for the opinion
- An opinion on whether the subject matter follows the criteria
- A statement indicating that prospective results may not be achieved
- A statement that the practitioner assumes no responsibility to update the report for events and circumstances occurring after the date of the report
- If the presentation is a projection, a separate paragraph that describes the limitations on the usefulness of the presentation
- A signature
- Date of the report

In an examination engagement, the practitioner expresses his or her opinion that the prospective financial statements are presented in conformity with AICPA presentation guidelines and the assumptions provide a reasonable basis for the prospective statements. (Note that the practitioner is not expressing an opinion on the fairness or the reasonableness of the prospective financial statements.) The practitioner's report on an examination of a forecast is shown below:

We have examined the accompanying forecasted balance sheet, statements of income, retained earnings, and cash flows for XYZ Company as of December 31, 2005, and for the year then ended. XYZ Company's management is responsible for the forecast. Our responsibility is to express an opinion on the forecast based on our examination.

Our examination was conducted in accordance with attestation standards established by the American Institute of Certified Public Accountants and, accordingly, included such procedures that we considered necessary to evaluate both the assumptions used by management and the preparation and presentation of the forecast. We believe that our examination provides a reasonable basis for our opinion.

In our opinion, the accompanying forecast is presented in conformity with guidelines for presentation of a forecast established by the American Institute of Certified Public Accountants, and the underlying assumptions provide a reasonable basis for management's forecast. However, there will usually be differences between the forecasted and actual results because events and circumstances frequently do not occur as expected, and those differences may be material. We have no responsibility to update this report for events and circumstances occurring after the date of this report.

APPLYING AGREED-UPON PROCEDURES TO PROSPECTIVE FINANCIAL STATEMENTS

An engagement to apply agreed-upon procedures to prospective financial statements is appropriate provided that:

- The practitioner is independent.
- The specified users involved have participated in establishing the nature and scope of the engagement and take responsibility for the adequacy of the procedures to be performed.
- The prospective financial statements include a summary of significant assumptions.
- The prospective financial statements to which the procedures are applied are subject to reasonably consistent estimation or measurement.
- Criteria to be used are agreed upon between the practitioner and the specified users.
- Procedures are expected to result in reasonably consistent findings using the criteria.
- audit evidence to which the procedures are applied is expected to exist to provide a reasonable basis for expressing the findings in the practitioner's report.
- Where applicable, there is agreement on any materiality limits.
- Distribution of the report is restricted to the specified users involved.

The issues addressed in the above report are similar to those in reports prepared by a practitioner for agreed-upon procedure engagements. The major contents of an agreed-upon procedures report are as follows:

- A title that includes the word *independent*
- Identification of specified parties
- Identification of the prospective financial statements and the character of the engagement
- A statement that the procedures were agreed to by the specified parties
- Identification of the responsible party
- A reference to attestation standards established by the AICPA
- A statement that the sufficiency of the procedures is the responsibility of the specified parties and a disclaimer of responsibility for sufficiency of those procedures
- A list of procedures performed and related findings
- Where applicable, a description of any agreed-upon materiality limits
- A statement indicating that the accountant did not perform an examination of prospective financial statements; a disclaimer of opinion
- A statement of restriction on the use of the report
- A caveat that prospective results may not be achieved
- A statement that the practitioner assumes no responsibility to update the report
- A signature
- Date of the report

LETTERS FOR UNDERWRITERS

Underwriters are encumbered with the responsibility of performing an investigation of a company issuing a registration statement under the Securities Act of 1933. In meeting their responsibilities, they will call on an independent auditor to provide "comfort" on the financial and accounting data in the prospectus that is not covered by an accountant's report of some form (e.g., an audit report on the financial statements). The accountant's reasonable investigation must be premised upon an audit; it cannot be accomplished without an audit.

The auditor, in addition to issuing a report on the audited financial data, will issue a letter to the underwriter, often referred to as a comfort letter, which will provide positive assurance that the auditor is independent and that his or her audit followed SEC standards. The auditor will provide negative assurance or a summary of findings on various types of accounting-related matters, such as the following: unaudited condensed and summarized interim information, pro forma financial information, change subsequent to the balance sheet date, and on various tables of data.

In preparing the letter to an underwriter, the auditor will work along with the underwriter to make certain that the work performed conforms to the needs of the underwriter. The procedures to be followed by the accountants are to be clearly set forth in the comfort letter, in both draft and final form, so that there will be no misunderstanding about the basis upon which the accountant's comments have been made, and so that the underwriter can decide whether the procedures performed are sufficient. The underwriter assumes full responsibility for the sufficiency of the procedures.

The comfort letter will have characteristics that differ from other types of reports by accountants and will generally refer to one or more of the following subjects:

- The independence of the accountants (explicitly stated)
- Compliance in form in all material respects of the audited financial statements and schedules included in the registration statement with the applicable accounting requirements of the Securities Act of 1933 and the published rules and regulations thereunder (explicitly stated)
- Unaudited financial statements, condensed financial statements, or capsule information included in the registration statements (negative assurance)
- Changes in selected financial statement items during a period subsequent to the date and period of the latest financial statements included in the registration statement (negative assurance)
- Tables, statistics, and other financial information or supplementary disclosures included in the registration statement (negative assurance)

FILING UNDER FEDERAL SECURITIES STATUTES

The Securities and Exchange Commission has stated that management has the responsibility for the accuracy of the information filed with the SEC regardless of the use of outside experts such as independent accountants.

The Securities Act of 1933 (as amended) imposes a responsibility for false or misleading statements if the accountant or any other expert has consented to having his or her name associated with statements in the registration statement.

The defenses against lawsuits regarding false or misleading statements are:

- The accountant or expert can prove that he or she conducted a "reasonable investigation" that provided the accountant with reasonable grounds to believe and he or she did believe at the effective date of the registration that the statements were true and disclosures were adequate.
- The part of the registration statement that was not true was because the information was not taken accurately from his or her report.

The "standard of reasonableness" is that required of a prudent person in the management of his or her own property.

A "reasonable investigation" includes a request that the client keep the accountant informed about the progress of registration proceedings, and the extension of audit procedures with respect to subsequent events from the date of the audit report up to the effective date of the registration or as close to the effective date as is reasonable and practicable. In addition to performing those procedures recommended for subsequent events, the auditor should:

- Read the entire prospectus and other pertinent sections of the registration statement.
- Make inquiries of and obtain written representations from officers and other executives responsible for financial and accounting matters about whether any events have occurred that have a material effect on the audited financial statements in the registration statement or that should be disclosed in order to keep those statements from being misleading.

If the independent accountant concludes that unaudited financial statements or unaudited interim financial statements do not conform to GAAP, the auditor should insist on appropriate revision. If the client refuses and a report has been issued on the statements, the auditor should follow the procedures for the subsequent discovery of facts existing at the date of the report. If a report has not been issued, the auditor should modify the report to disclose the departure from GAAP. In both cases, the auditor should consider (with advice of legal counsel) withholding his or her consent to have the report on the audited financial statements included in the registration statement.

A predecessor auditor also has subsequent event responsibility and should:

- Read the entire prospectus and other pertinent sections of the registration statements.
- Obtain a letter of representation from the successor auditor regarding whether the successor auditor's examination revealed any matters that would have a material effect on the financial statements reported on by the predecessor auditor or would require disclosure thereto.

An independent accountant's report on the interim review of financial statements is not a report or part of the registration statement as defined by the Securities Act of 1933.

Therefore, the accountant does not have the same statutory responsibility with respect to such reports.

REPORTING ON CONDENSED FINANCIAL STATEMENTS AND SELECTED FINANCIAL DATA

Condensed financial statements do not contain sufficient detail to present financial position, results of operations, or cash flows in conformity with GAAP. Therefore:

- They should be read in conjunction with the entity's most recent financial statements that include all the disclosures for conformity with GAAP.
- The auditor should report on the condensed financial statements in a different manner than he or she reports on complete financial statements.
- The auditor's report on condensed financial statements should indicate:
    - That the auditor has audited and expressed an opinion on the complete financial statements
    - The date of the auditor's report on the complete financial statements
    - The type of opinion expressed
    - Whether the information set forth in the condensed financial statements is fairly stated in all material respects in relation to the complete financial statements from which they were derived

Condensed financial statements derived from audited financial statements of a public entity may be presented on a comparative basis with interim financial statements that have been reviewed. The auditor's report for each set of data should reflect the level of service provided.

A client might prepare a document that names the auditor and indicates that condensed financial statements were derived from audited financial statements. If the audited financial statements are included in the document or are incorporated by reference to information filed with a regulatory agency, there is no concern on the part of the auditor. However, if the audited financial statements are not included in the client-prepared document or there is no incorporating reference, the auditor should request that his or her name not be included in the document or that the document include the auditor's report on the condensed financial statements.

If the auditor is engaged to report on the selected financial data, his or her report should be limited to data that are derived from audited financial statements. If the selected financial data that are presented in the client-prepared document are based on audited and unaudited financial information, the auditor's report should specifically identify the data on which he or she is reporting.

The auditor's report on selected financial data should indicate:

- That the auditor has audited and expressed an opinion on the complete financial statements
- The type of opinion expressed

- Whether the data set forth in the selected financial data is fairly stated in all material respects in relation to the complete financial statements from which it has been derived

A client might prepare a document that names the auditor and indicates that selected financial data was derived from audited financial statements. If the audited financial statements are included in the document or are incorporated by reference to information filed with a regulatory agency, there is no concern on the part of the auditor.

However, if the audited financial statements are not included in the client-prepared document or there is no incorporating reference, the auditor should request that his or her name not be included in the document or he or she should issue a disclaimer on the selected financial data and request that the client include the disclaimer in the document.

REPORTING ON FINANCIAL STATEMENTS PREPARED FOR USE IN OTHER COUNTRIES

Before reporting on financial statements prepared in conformity with accounting principles of another country, the auditor should have a clear understanding of, and obtain written representations from management regarding, the purpose and uses of such financial statements. If the auditor uses the standard report of another country and the financial statements will have general distribution in that country, the auditor should determine whether there are additional legal responsibilities being assumed due to legal, custom, or cultural differences in interpreting certain terminology or uses of terminology.

The auditor has a responsibility to be informed about accounting and auditing practices in the other country. The auditor should consider engaging a specialist if the auditor is inexperienced concerning the auditing and accounting practices of the other country. The auditor should follow the general and fieldwork standards of U.S. GAAS and those of the other country.

If the financial statements are to be generally distributed (as opposed to limited use) in the United States and the other country based on the respective GAAP of each country, the auditor may need to issue two reports: one conforming to the report form and GAAP in the United States and the other conforming to the report form and GAAP of the other country. The auditor may want to include in the one or both reports a statement that another report has been issued on the financial statements for the entity that have been prepared in accordance with accounting principles generally accepted in another country.

GOVERNMENTAL AUDITING

Standards for audits of government organizations, programs, activities and functions, and of government assistance received by contractors, nonprofit organizations, and other nongovernment organizations are contained in what is known as "The Yellow Book." These standards are often referred to as government auditing standards or generally accepted government auditing standards (GAGAS). They are issued from the U.S. Government Accountability Office (GAO) by the Comptroller General of the United States.

GAGAS is to be followed by auditors and audit organizations when required by law, regulation, agreement, contract, or policy. Further, the Single Audit Act of 1984 (as amended in 1996) requires that these standards be followed in audits of state and local government that receive federal financial assistance. Other federal policies and regulations such as OMB (Office of Management and Budget) Circular A-133 require that these standards be followed in audits of institutions of higher education and other nonprofit organizations that receive federal financial assistances.

There are three types of government audits:

1. Financial audits.

2. Attestation engagements.

3. Performance audits.

FINANCIAL AUDITS

Financial audits include financial statement audits and financial-related audits:

1. *Financial statement audits* provide reasonable assurance about whether statements follow GAAP.

2. *Financial-related audits* include determining whether the entity:

    - Presented financial information in accordance with established criteria.
    - Adhered to financial compliance requirements.
    - Designed and implemented suitable internal control over financial reporting and/or safeguarding assets to achieve the control objectives.

GENERAL STANDARDS FOR FINANCIAL AUDITS

The general standards of GAGAS relate to the personal qualifications of the auditor and audit organizations. There are four general standards:

1. In all matters relating to audit work, audit organization and the individual auditor, whether government or public, should be free both in fact and appearance from personal, external, and organizational impairments to independence.

2. Professional judgment should be used in planning and performing audits and attestation engagements, and in reporting the results.

3. The staff assigned to perform the audit or attestation engagement should collectively possess adequate professional competence for the tasks required.

4. Each audit organization performing audits and/or attestation engagements in accordance with GAGAS should have an appropriate internal quality control system in place and should undergo an external peer review.

FIELDWORK STANDARDS FOR FINANCIAL AUDITS

For financial statement audits, GAGAS incorporates the three AICPA standards of fieldwork and prescribes five additional standards. The additional standards are:

1. Auditors should communicate information regarding the nature, timing, and extent of planned testing and reporting, and the level of assurance provided to officials of the audited entity and to the individuals contracting for or requesting the audit.

2. Auditors should consider the results of previous audits and attestation engagements and follow up on known significant findings and recommendations that directly relate to the objectives of the audit being undertaken.

3a. Auditors should design the audit to provide reasonable assurance of detecting material misstatements resulting from violations of provisions of contracts or grant agreements that have a direct and material effect on the determination of financial statement amounts or other financial data significant to the audit objectives. If specific information comes to the auditors' attention that provides evidence concerning the existence of possible violations of provisions of contracts or grant agreements that could have a material indirect effect on the determination of financial statement amounts or other financial data significant to the audit objectives, auditors should apply audit procedures specifically directed to ascertain whether violations of provisions of contracts or grant agreements have occurred or are likely to have occurred.

3b. Auditors should be alert to situations or transactions that could be indicative of abuse, and if indications of abuse exist that could significantly affect the financial statement amounts or other financial data, auditors should apply audit procedures specifically directed to ascertain whether abuse has occurred and the effect on the financial statement amounts or other financial data.

4. Audit findings, such as deficiencies in internal control, fraud, illegal acts, violations of provisions of contracts or grant agreements, and abuse, have often been regarded as containing the elements of criteria, condition, and effect, plus cause when problems are found.

5. Audit documentation related to planning, conducting, and reporting on the audit should contain sufficient information to enable an experienced auditor, who has had no previous connection with the audit, to ascertain from the audit documentation the evidence that supports the auditors' significant judgments and conclusions. Audit documentation should contain support for findings, conclusions, and recommendations before auditors issued their report.

REPORTING STANDARDS FOR FINANCIAL AUDITS

For financial statement audits, GAGAS incorporates the four AICPA standards of reporting and prescribes six additional standards. The additional standards are:

1. Audit reports should state that the audit was performed in accordance with GAGAS.

2. When providing an opinion or a disclaimer on financial statements, auditors should include in their report on the financial statements either (1) a description of the scope of the auditors' testing of internal control over financial reporting and compliance with laws, regulations, and provisions of contracts or grant agreements and the results of those tests or an opinion, if sufficient work was performed; or (2) reference to the separate reports(s) containing that information. If auditors report separately, the opinion or disclaimer should contain a reference to the separate report containing this information and state that the separate report is an integral part of the audit and should be considered in assessing the results of the audit.

3. For financial audits, including audits of financial statements in which the auditor provides an opinion or disclaimer, auditors should report as applicable to the objectives of the audit: (1) deficiencies in internal control considered to be reportable conditions as defined in AICPA standards, (2) all instances of fraud and illegal acts unless clearly inconsequential, and (3) significant violations of provisions of contracts or grant agreements and abuse. In some circumstances, auditors should report fraud, illegal acts, violations of provisions of contracts or grant agreements, and abuse directly to parties external to the audited entity.

4. If the auditors' report discloses deficiencies in internal control, fraud, illegal acts, violations of provisions of contracts or grant agreements, or abuse, auditors should obtain and report the views of responsible officials concerning the findings, conclusions, and recommendations, as well as planned corrective actions.

5. If certain pertinent information is prohibited from general disclosure, the audit report should state the nature of the information omitted and the requirement that makes the omission necessary.

6. Government auditors should submit audit reports to the appropriate officials of the audited entity and to appropriate officials of the organizations requiring or arranging for the audits, including external funding organizations such as legislative bodies, unless legal restrictions prevent it. Auditors should also send copies of the reports to other officials who have legal oversight authority or who may be responsible for acting on audit findings and recommendations and to others authorized to receive such reports. Unless the report is restricted by law or regulation or contains privileged and confidential information, auditors should clarify that copies are made available for public inspection. Nongovernment auditors should clarify report distribution responsibilities with the party contracting for the audit and follow the agreements reached.

MOST COMMON FINANCIAL AUDITS

- Reporting on financial statements under GAGAS.
- Compliance auditing in audits of governmental entities and other entities that receive federal financial assistance conducted in accordance with GAS.

- Engagements covered by the Single Audit Act.

Governmental Auditing Standards.

These audits are required for certain organizations that receive federal financial assistance. Whether a governmental organization is so required depends upon requirements of the federal financial assistance programs in which it participates and whether it is required to have a Single Audit (described below).

The audit responsibilities in an audit conducted under governmental auditing standards are identical to that in a GAAS audit with respect to studying and evaluating internal control, and testing compliance with laws and regulations. However, the auditor has increased reporting responsibility in each of these areas. Thus, there are three required reports: (1) a report on the financial statements, the "audit report," (2) a report on internal control, and (3) a report on compliance with laws and regulations.

These reporting requirements may be met by issuing one combined report, two reports (internal control and compliance are combined), or three separate reports.

The report on the financial statements is similar to the standard audit report, but also includes a number of modifications:

- The scope paragraph indicates that the audit was conducted in accordance with GAAS and GAS.
- Paragraph 4 refers to issuance of another report on internal control over financial reporting and tests of compliance.
- Paragraph 5 states that the audit was performed for the purpose of forming an opinion on the basic financial statements.
- Paragraph 5 indicates that the accompanying required supplementary information is not a required part of the basic financial statements.
- Paragraph 6 indicates that the accompanying required supplementary information has been subjected to auditing procedures applied in the audit of the basic financial statements and in the auditor's opinion, is fairly stated, in all material respects, in relation to the basic financial statements taken as a whole.

The auditor will also report on the client's internal control. This report will include:

- An indication that the audit was conducted in accordance with GAAS and GAS.
- A statement that the auditor considered the internal control to determine the audit procedures for expressing an opinion on the financial statements and not to provide assurance on the internal control.
- Any reportable conditions and material weaknesses noted by the auditor.

The auditor will report on compliance with laws and regulations. The report will include:

- An indication that the audit was conducted in accordance with GAAS and GAS
- A statement that providing an opinion on compliance with laws and regulations was not an objective of the audit and accordingly no opinion is expressed
- A summary of the findings of the engagement, including material instances of noncompliance

If material instances of noncompliance or an illegal act that could result in criminal prosecution is noted, the auditor should modify the report and issue a qualified or adverse opinion, depending on the severity. This is true even if the misstatements are corrected. If instances of noncompliance that are not material are noted, the auditor will normally communicate these separately to the client.

Compliance Auditing

In a GAAS audit, a major consideration in the examination of a governmental entity is considering the effect of laws and regulations on that entity's financial statements. While this is done for all clients in GAAS audits, the activities and financial statements of governmental entities are particularly subject to the effect of laws and regulations.

The auditor will focus on instances where noncompliance with laws and regulations has a material effect on the governmental entity's financial statements. Some of the more important activities that should be performed by the auditor include:

- Requesting that management identify the laws and regulations that affect its financial statements.
- Obtaining an understanding of the effect of laws and regulations on the governmental entity's financial statements.
- Evaluating internal control policies and procedures designed to prevent or detect instances of noncompliance with laws and regulations having a material effect on the financial statements.
- Performing tests of compliance on laws and regulations having a material effect on the financial statements.
- Obtaining written representations from management indicating that management is responsible for compliance with laws and regulations and all laws and regulations having a direct and material effect on the financial statements have been disclosed to the auditor.

It is important to note that the auditor's reporting responsibility is unchanged. That is, he would issue a report on the conformity of the governmental entity's financial statements with GAAP (or other basis of accounting). No report on compliance with laws and regulations is issued in a GAAS audit.

The Single Audit Act

State and local governments that receive, directly or indirectly, federal financial assistance may be required to have an audit performed in accordance with the Single Audit Act. The Single Audit Act requires that the auditor under a GAAS audit issue reports and that the audit be conducted in accordance with GAS. Therefore, the auditor will issue three required reports: (1) a report on the financial statements—the "audit report," (2) a report on internal control, and (3) a report on compliance with laws and regulations.

In addition, the Single Audit Act includes requirements that supplement the GAS audit procedures. It requires the auditor to issue reports on compliance with the laws and regulations of each federal assistance program. Two types of requirements are identified by the Single Audit Act—specific requirements and general requirements.

Specific requirements represent requirements that relate to individual federal financial assistance programs. While these requirements vary from program to program, the major categories of specific requirements are:

- The types of goods or services that entities may purchase with federal financial assistance.
- The eligibility of individuals or groups to whom the entity may provide assistance.
- The amount of funds that entities must contribute from their own resources toward projects for which financial assistance is provided.
- Additional reports that must be filed related to the federal financial assistance.
- Other provisions of federal financial assistance programs.

General requirements are requirements that apply to all federal financial assistance programs. These requirements include:

- Prohibiting the use of funds for partisan political activity.
- Prohibiting the use of funds to violate another party's civil rights.
- Minimizing the time elapsing between the receipt and disbursement of federal funds.
- Providing a drug-free workplace to employees.

The auditor's responsibility differs depending on the amount of expenditures associated with the particular federal financial assistance program being examined. Major programs are those programs that account for a large percentage of the total expenditures made by a governmental entity. In contrast, nonmajor programs account for a relatively small percentage of the total expenditures made by a governmental entity.

When examining compliance with specific requirements for major programs, the auditor is required to plan the audit to detect instances of material noncompliance with these specific requirements. In doing so, the auditor should specifically select and test expenditures for compliance with the specific requirements of that program. Thus, the audit responsibility is expanded compared to GAAS and GAS audits. In selecting expenditures, materiality should be defined based on the federal financial assistance program and not the financial statements taken as a whole.

The auditor's report for compliance with specific requirements for major programs includes:

- An opinion on the entity's compliance with specific requirements.
- A reference to a separate schedule of any immaterial instances of noncompliance with specific requirements.
- A description of any material instances of noncompliance with specific requirements (in these cases, a qualified or adverse opinion will be issued).

In testing compliance with specific requirements for nonmajor programs, the auditor is not required to select expenditures to test for compliance with these requirements. If transactions are selected in connection with the audit of the financial statements or study of the internal control, the auditor should also test for compliance with the specific requirements noted earlier. The requirements that are of most interest relate to whether the program expenditure is allowable and the eligibility of the individuals or groups to whom assistance is provided.

In some cases, the auditor may not select any expenditures from nonmajor programs in connection with the audit of the financial statements or study of the internal control. If so, a report on compliance with these requirements would not be issued.

The requirements for examining compliance with general requirements are not distinguished between major and nonmajor programs. Auditors are required to select items to examine compliance with these requirements for each federal financial assistance program (both major and nonmajor). The auditor's report on compliance with these requirements includes:

- An opinion on the entity's compliance with general requirements.
- A reference to a separate schedule of any immaterial instances of noncompliance with general requirements.
- A description of any material instances of noncompliance with general requirements.

The auditor's responsibility for financial audits is summarized below:

	Testing	*Reporting*
Compliance with laws and regulations	Same as GAAS	Opinion on compliance
internal control	Same as GAAS	Reportable conditions and material weakness
Compliance with specific requirements (major programs)	Specifically select expenditures and test for compliance	Opinion on compliance
Compliance with specific requirements (nonmajor programs)	Same as GAAS	Summary of findings
Compliance with general requirements	Specifically select expenditures and test for compliance	Summary of findings

ATTESTATION ENGAGEMENTS

Attestation engagements concern examining, reviewing, or performing agreed-upon procedures on a subject matter or an assertion about a subject matter and reporting on the results. Possible subjects of attestation engagements include reporting on the following:

- An entity's internal control over financial reporting.
- An entity's compliance with requirements of specified laws, regulations, rules, contracts, or grants.
- The effectiveness of an entity's internal control over compliance with specified requirements, such as those governing the bidding for, accounting for, and reporting on grants and contracts.
- Management's discussion and analysis (MD&A) presentation.
- Prospective financial statements or pro forma financial information.
- The reliability of performance measures.
- Final contract cost.
- What is allowable and reasonable for proposed contract amounts and specific procedures performed (agreed-upon procedures).

PERFORMANCE AUDITS

Performance audits entail an objective and systematic examination of evidence to provide an independent assessment of the performance and management of a program against objective criteria as well as assessments that provide a prospective focus or that synthesize information on best practices or cross-cutting issues.

Performance audits encompass a wide variety of objectives, including objectives related to assessing program effectiveness and results; economy and efficiency; internal control; compliance with legal or other requirements; and objectives related to providing prospective analyses, guidance, or summary information.

Performance audits may entail a broad or narrow scope of work and apply a variety of methodologies; involve various levels of analysis, research, or evaluation; generally provide findings, conclusions, and recommendations; and result in the issuance of a report.

Examples of performance audits include the following:

- The extent to which legislative, regulatory, or organizational goals and objectives are being achieved.
- The relative ability of alternative approaches to yield better program performance or eliminate factors that inhibit program effectiveness.
- The relative cost and benefits or cost effectiveness of program performance.
- Whether a program produced intended results or produced effects that were not intended by the program's objectives.
- The extent to which programs duplicate, overlap, or conflict with other related programs.
- Whether the audited entity is following sound procurement practices.
- The validity and reliability of performance measures concerning program effectiveness and results, or economy and efficiency.
- The reliability, validity, or relevance of financial information related to the performance of a program.

General Standards for Performance Audits

These are the same as for financial audits.

Fieldwork Standards for Performance Audits

1. Work is to be adequately planned.

2. Staff members are to be properly supervised.

3. Sufficient, competent, and relevant evidence is to be obtained to provide a reasonable basis for the auditors' findings and conclusions.

4. Auditors should prepare and maintain audit documentation. Audit documentation related to planning, conducting, and reporting on the audit should contain sufficient information to enable an experienced auditor, who has had no previous connection with the audit, to ascertain from the audit documentation the evidence that supports the auditors' significant judgments and conclusions. Audit documentation should contain support for findings, conclusions, and recommendations before auditors issue their report.

Reporting Standards for Performance Audits

1. Auditors should prepare audit reports communicating the results of each audit.

2. The audit report should include the objectives, scope, and methodology; the audit results, including findings, conclusions, and recommendations, as appropriate; a reference to compliance with generally accepted government auditing standards; the views of responsible officials; and, if applicable, the nature of any privileged and confidential information omitted.

3. The report should be timely, complete, accurate, objective, convincing, clear, and as concise as the subject permits.

4. Government auditors should submit audit reports to the appropriate officials of the audited entity and to appropriate officials of the organizations requiring or arranging for the audits, including external funding organizations such as legislative bodies, unless legal restrictions prevent it. Auditors should also send copies of the reports to other officials who have legal oversight authority or who may be responsible for acting on audit findings and recommendations and to others authorized to receive such reports. Unless the report is restricted by law or regulation or contains privileged and confidential information, auditors should clarify that copies are made available for public inspection. Nongovernment auditors should clarify report distribution responsibilities with the party contracting for the audit and follow the agreements reached.

QUESTIONS: SPECIAL REPORTS AND OTHER REPORTS

1. When providing limited assurance that the financial statements of a nonpublic entity require *no* material modifications to be in accordance with generally accepted accounting principles, the accountant should:
   A. develop audit programs to determine whether the entity's financial statements are fairly presented.
   B. confirm with the entity's lawyer that material loss contingencies are disclosed.
   C. understand the accounting principles of the industry in which the entity operates.
   D. assess the risk that a material misstatement could occur in a financial statement assertion.

2. Kell engaged March, CPA, to submit to Kell a written personal financial plan containing unaudited personal financial statements. March anticipates omitting certain disclosures required by GAAP because the engagement's sole purpose is to assist Kell in developing a personal financial plan. For March to be exempt from complying with the requirements of SSARS 1, Compilation and Review of Financial Statements, Kell is required to agree that the:
   A. financial statements will not be disclosed to a non-CPA financial partner.
   B. financial statements will not be used to obtain credit.
   C. omitted disclosures required by GAAP are not material.
   D. financial statements will not be presented in comparative form with those of the prior period.

3. When making a review of interim financial information the auditor's work consists primarily of:
   A. scanning and reviewing client-prepared, internal financial statements.
   B. confirming and verifying significant account balances at the interim date.
   C. studying and evaluating limited amounts of documentation supporting the interim financial information.
   D. making inquiries and performing analytical procedures concerning significant accounting matters.

4. The objective of a review of the interim financial information of a publicly held company is to:
   A. provide the accountant with a basis for the expression of an opinion.
   B. provide the accountant with a basis for reporting to the board of directors or stockholders.
   C. obtain corroborating audit evidence through inspection, observation and confirmation.
   D. estimate the accuracy of financial statements based upon limited tests of accounting records.

5. When third party use of prospective financial statements is expected, an accountant may NOT accept an engagement to:
   A. apply agreed-upon procedures.
   B. perform an examination.
   C. perform a review.
   D. perform a compilation.

6. When reporting on financial statements prepared on the same basis of accounting used for income tax purposes, the auditor should include in the report a paragraph that:
   A. refers to the authoritative pronouncements that explain the income tax basis of accounting being used.
   B. states that the income tax basis of accounting is a comprehensive basis of accounting other than generally accepted accounting principles.
   C. emphasizes that the financial statements are not intended to have been examined in accordance with generally accepted auditing standards.
   D. justifies the use of the income tax basis of accounting.

7. An examination of a financial forecast is a professional service that involves:
   A. evaluating the preparation of a financial forecast and the support underlying management's assumptions.
   B. assuming responsibility to update management on key events for one year after the report's date.
   C. compiling or assembling a financial forecast that is based on management's assumptions.
   D. limiting the distribution of the accountant's report to management and the board of directors.

8. An auditor's report on financial statements prepared on the cash receipts and disbursements basis of accounting should include all of the following EXCEPT a(an):
   A. opinion as to whether the financial statements are presented fairly in conformity with the cash receipts and disbursements basis of accounting.
   B. reference to the note to the financial statements that describes the cash receipts and disbursements basis of accounting.
   C. statement that the cash receipts and disbursements basis of accounting is not a comprehensive basis of accounting.
   D. statement that the audit was conducted in accordance with generally accepted auditing standards.

9. Which of the following is a prospective financial statement for general use upon which an accountant may appropriately report?
   A. Financial projection
   B. Partial presentation
   C. Pro forma financial statement
   D. Financial forecast

10. In reporting on an entity's internal control over financial reporting, a practitioner should include a paragraph that describes the:
    A. changes in internal control since the prior report.
    B. inherent limitations of any internal control.
    C. potential benefits from the practitioner's suggested improvements.
    D. documentary evidence regarding the control environment factors.

11. An auditor's report on financial statements prepared in accordance with another comprehensive basis of accounting should include all of the following EXCEPT:
    A. reference to the note to the financial statements that describes the basis of presentation.
    B. an opinion as to whether the financial statements are presented fairly in conformity with the other comprehensive basis of accounting.
    C. a statement that the basis of presentation is a comprehensive basis of accounting other than generally accepted accounting principles.
    D. an opinion as to whether the basis of accounting used is appropriate under the circumstances.

12. Snow, CPA, was engaged by Master Co. to examine and report on management's written assertion about the effectiveness of Master's internal control over financial reporting. Snow's report should state that:
    A. the purpose of the engagement is to enable Snow to plan an audit and determine the nature, timing, and extent of tests to be performed.
    B. because of inherent limitations of any internal control, errors or fraud may occur and not be detected.
    C. management's assertion is based on criteria established by the American Institute of Certified Public Accountants.
    D. the results of Snow's tests will form the basis for Snow's opinion on the fairness of Master's financial statements in conformity with GAAP.

13. Which of the following statements concerning prospective financial statements is correct?
    A. Only a financial forecast would normally be appropriate for limited use.
    B. Any type of prospective financial statements would normally be appropriate for general use.
    C. Any type of prospective financial statements would normally be appropriate for limited use.
    D. Only a financial projection would normally be appropriate for general use.

14. An accountant's report on a review of pro forma financial information should include a:
    A. disclaimer of opinion on the financial statements from which the pro forma financial information is derived.
    B. reference to the financial statements from which the historical financial information is derived.
    C. statement that the entity's internal control was not relied on in the review.
    D. caveat that it is uncertain whether the transaction or event reflected in the pro forma financial information will ever occur.

15. Which of the following representations should **NOT** be included in a report on internal control related matters noted in an audit?
    A. There are no significant deficiencies in the design or operation of internal control.
    B. Corrective follow-up action is recommended due to the relative significance of material weaknesses discovered during the audit.
    C. The auditor's consideration of internal control would not necessarily disclose all reportable conditions that exist.
    D. Reportable conditions related to internal control design exist, but none is deemed to be a material weakness.

16. When an accountant examines a financial forecast that fails to disclose several significant assumptions used to prepare the forecast, the accountant should describe the assumptions in the accountant's report and issue a(an):
    A. "subject to" qualified opinion.
    B. unqualified opinion with a separate explanatory paragraph.
    C. "except for" qualified opinion.
    D. adverse opinion.

17. In connection with a proposal to obtain a new client, an accountant in public practice is asked to prepare a written report on the application of accounting principles to a specific transaction. The accountant's report should include a statement that:
    A. nothing came to the accountant's attention that caused the accountant to believe that the accounting principles violated GAAP.
    B. the guidance provided is for management use only and may not be communicated to the prior or continuing auditors.
    C. any difference in the facts, circumstances, or assumptions presented may change the report.
    D. the engagement was performed in accordance with Statements on Standards for Consulting Services.

18. When an accountant examines projected financial statements, the accountant's report should include a separate paragraph that:
    A. disclaims an opinion on whether the assumptions provide a reasonable basis for the projection.
    B. states that the accountant is responsible for events and circumstances up to one year after the report's date.
    C. provides an explanation of the differences between an examination and an audit.
    D. describes the limitations on the usefulness of the presentation.

19. The party responsible for assumptions identified in the preparation of prospective financial statements is usually:
    A. a third-party lending institution.
    B. the client's management.
    C. the client's independent auditor.
    D. the reporting accountant.

20. An auditor is reporting on cash-basis financial statements. These statements are *best* referred to in his opinion by which one of the following descriptions?
    A. Balance sheet and income statement resulting from cash transactions
    B. Assets and liabilities arising from cash transactions, and revenue collected and expenses paid
    C. Financial position and results of operations arising from cash transactions
    D. Cash balance sheet and the source and application of funds

21. Comfort letters ordinarily are signed by the client's:
    A. underwriter of securities.
    B. senior management.
    C. independent auditor.
    D. audit committee.

22. A CPA's report on a forecast should include all of the following EXCEPT a(an):
    A. statement that the CPA assumes no responsibility to update the report for events occurring after the date of the report.
    B. caveat as to the ultimate attainment of the forecasted results.
    C. opinion as to whether the forecast is fairly presented.
    D. description of what the forecast information is intended to represent.

23. Which of the following statements is a standard applicable to financial statement audits in accordance with Government Auditing Standards?
    A. An auditor should assess whether the entity has reportable measures of economy and efficiency that are valid and reliable.
    B. An auditor should briefly describe in the auditor's report the method of statistical sampling used in performing tests of controls and substantive tests.
    C. An auditor should determine the extent to which the entity's programs achieve the desired level of results.
    D. An auditor should report on the scope of the auditor's testing of internal controls.

24. In auditing compliance with requirements governing major federal financial assistance programs under the Single Audit Act, the auditor's consideration of materiality differs from materiality under generally accepted auditing standards. Under the Single Audit Act, materiality is:
    A. determined separately for each major federal financial assistance program.
    B. calculated in relation to the financial statements taken as a whole.
    C. decided in conjunction with the auditor's risk assessment.
    D. ignored, because all account balances, regardless of size, are fully tested.

25. When reporting on an entity's internal control under Government Auditing Standards, an auditor should issue a written report that includes a:
    A. statement of negative assurance that nothing came to the auditor's attention that caused the auditor to believe reportable conditions were present.
    B. description of the scope of the auditor's work in obtaining an understanding of internal control and in assessing control risk.
    C. statement of positive assurance that the results of tests indicate that internal control either can, or cannot, be relied on to reduce control risk to an acceptable level.
    D. description of the weaknesses considered to be reportable conditions and the strengths that the auditor can rely on in reducing the extent of substantive testing.

26. Wolf is auditing an entity's compliance with requirements governing a major federal financial assistance program in accordance with Government Auditing Standards. Wolf detected noncompliance with requirements that have a material effect on the program. Wolf's report on compliance should express:
    A. no assurance on the compliance tests.
    B. reasonable assurance on the compliance tests.
    C. a qualified or adverse opinion.
    D. an adverse or disclaimer of opinion.

27. An auditor notes reportable conditions in a financial statement audit conducted in accordance with Government Auditing Standards. In reporting on internal control, the auditor should state that:
    A. expressing an opinion on the entity's financial statements provides no assurance on internal control.
    B. the auditor obtained an understanding of the design of relevant policies and procedures, and determined whether they have been placed in operation.
    C. the specified government funding or legislative body is responsible for reviewing internal control as a condition of continued funding.
    D. the auditor has not determined whether any of the reportable conditions described in the report are so severe as to be material weaknesses.

28. Hill, CPA, is auditing the financial statements of Helping Hand, a not-for-profit organization that receives financial assistance from governmental agencies. To detect misstatements in Helping Hand's financial statements resulting from violations of laws and regulations, Hill should focus on violations that:
    A. have a direct and material effect on the amounts in the organization's financial statements.
    B. could result in criminal prosecution against the organization.
    C. involve reportable conditions to be communicated to the organization's trustees and the funding agencies.
    D. demonstrate the existence of material weaknesses in the organization's internal control.

29. Which of the following bodies promulgates standards for audits of federal financial assistance recipients?
    A. Governmental Accounting Standards Board
    B. Financial Accounting Standards Board
    C. Governmental Auditing Standards Board
    D. Government Accountability Office

30. Which of the following statements represents a quality control requirement under government auditing standards?
    A. A CPA seeking to enter into a contract to perform an audit should provide the CPA's most recent external quality control review report to the party contracting for the audit.
    B. An external quality control review of a CPA's practice should include a review of the audit documents of each government audit performed since the prior external quality control review.
    C. A CPA who conducts government audits may not make the CPA's external quality control review report available to the public.
    D. A CPA who conducts government audits is required to undergo an annual external quality control review when an appropriate internal quality control system is not in place.

31. Although the scope of audits of recipients of federal financial assistance in accordance with federal audit regulations varies, these audits generally have which of the following elements in common?
    A. The materiality levels are lower and are determined by the government entities that provided the federal financial assistance to the recipient.
    B. The auditor should obtain written management representations that the recipient's internal auditors will report their findings objectively without fear of political repercussion.
    C. The auditor is to determine whether the federal financial assistance has been administered in accordance with applicable laws and regulations.
    D. The auditor is required to express both positive and negative assurance that illegal acts that could have a material effect on the recipient's financial statements are disclosed to the inspector general.

32. In reporting on compliance with laws and regulations during a financial statement audit in accordance with Government Auditing Standards, an auditor should include in the auditor's report:
    A. a statement of assurance that all controls over fraud and illegal acts were tested.
    B. the materiality criteria used by the auditor in considering whether instances of noncompliance were significant.
    C. an opinion on whether compliance with laws and regulations affected the entity's goals and objectives.
    D. material instances of fraud and illegal acts that were discovered.

Answers: Special Reports and Other Reports

1. **C** A review of a nonpublic entity's financial statements provides limited assurance that there are no material modifications that should be made to the statements in order for them to be in conformity with generally accepted accounting principles. The accountant, in order to perform the inquiry and analytical procedures required in a review engagement, should possess a level of knowledge of the accounting principles and practices of the industry in which the entity operates and an understanding of the entity's business.

2. **B** An accountant may submit a written personal financial plan containing unaudited financial statements to a client without complying with SSARS 1 when the client agrees that the financial statements will be used solely to assist the client and the client's advisors to develop the client's personal financial goals and objectives, and will not be used to obtain credit or for any purposes other than developing these goals and objectives.

3. **D** Review engagements, whether for a public or non-public company, include, among other procedures, an analytical review and inquiries of company personnel.

4. **B** The CPA has not audited. The CPA does not report on accuracy. A limited review provides a basis for reporting to the Board of Directors.

5. **C** Statements on Standards for Accountants' Reports on Prospective Financial Information do not permit the CPA performing reviews of such information.

6. **B** Financial statements prepared on the income tax basis of accounting are a type of special report as defined by auditing standards. Those standards state that the income tax basis of accounting is "a comprehensive basis of accounting other than GAAP." In writing a report on such a basis, the auditor must expand the standard report to include a separate paragraph that states the income tax basis of accounting is a comprehensive basis of accounting other than GAAP.

7. **A** An accountant may be engaged to examine, compile, or apply agreed-upon procedures to financial forecasts or other prospective financial statements. An examination of a financial forecast involves evaluating the preparation of the forecasted statements, evaluating the support underlying the assumptions used in preparing the statements, evaluating the presentation of the statements for conformity with AICPA guidelines, and issuing an examination report.

8. **C** Generally accepted auditing standards are applicable when an auditor conducts an audit of and reports on any financial statements, including those prepared in conformity with an Other Comprehensive Basis Of Accounting (OCBOA). The cash receipts and disbursements basis is an OCBOA, and the auditor's report would include a statement to that effect. The report should also include a reference to the note that describes the OCBOA; an opinion on whether the financial statements are fairly presented in conformity with the OCBOA; and a standard scope paragraph that refers to generally accepted auditing standards.

9. **D** A financial forecast is defined by Statements on Standards for Accountants' Reports on Prospective Financial Information as a *general use* financial statement.

10. **B** A practitioner's report on an examination of management's assertion about the effectiveness of the entity's internal control should include a paragraph stating that, because of inherent limitations of any internal control, errors or fraud may occur and not be detected. In addition, the report should include a title with the word "independent," identify management's assertion, state that the examination was made in accordance with AICPA standards, and include the practitioner's opinion. The report would not include the statements presented in the other answers.

11. **D** The other answers include information that would be included in the auditor's report on financial statements prepared in accordance with another comprehensive basis of accounting other than GAAP. It would be inappropriate to justify the basis of accounting used in the auditor's report. The method of accounting does not have to be justified in the auditor's report.

12. **B** AT 400.50 states that when management presents its assertion in a separate report that will accompany the practitioner's report, the practitioner's report should include:

    - A title that includes the word "independent"
    - An identification of management's assertion about the effectiveness of the entity's internal control over financial reporting
    - A statement that the examination was made in accordance with standards established by the AICPA and, accordingly, that it included obtaining an understanding of internal control over financial reporting, testing and evaluating the design and operating effectiveness of internal control, and performing other such procedures as the practitioner considered necessary in the circumstances. In addition, the report should include a statement that the practitioner believes the examination provides a reasonable basis for his or her opinion.
    - A paragraph stating that because of inherent limitations of any internal control, errors or fraud may occur and not be detected. In addition, the paragraph should state that projections of any evaluation of internal control over financial reporting to future periods are subject to the risk that internal control may become inadequate because of changes in conditions, or that the degree of compliance with the policies or procedures may deteriorate.
    - The practitioner's opinion on whether management's assertion about the effectiveness of the entity's internal control over financial reporting as of the specified date is fairly stated, in all material respects, based on the control criteria.

13. **C** According to the "Statements on Standards for Prospective Financial Information," there are two types of prospective financial information: forecasts and projections. Forecasts are appropriate for "general use," meaning the CPA's report does not have to name a specific user. Projections are appropriate only for "limited use," meaning the CPA's report must specify a named user. Both a forecast and a projection can be issued and specify a named user, thus "limited use."

14. **A** The objective of pro forma financial information is to show what the significant effects on historical financial information might have been had a consummated or proposed transaction occurred at an earlier date. An accountant can be engaged to examine or review pro forma financial information. In a review report, the accountant should identify the pro forma information, refer to the financial statements from which the historical information is derived and state whether such financial statements were audited or reviewed, state that the review was in accordance with AICPA standards, explain the objective of pro forma information and its limitations, and provide negative assurance regarding the pro forma information.

15. A — During an audit, if the auditor discovers "reportable conditions," which are significant deficiencies in the design or operation of internal control, he should communicate them to the audit committee. If no significant deficiencies are found, the auditor should not issue a written report representing that no reportable conditions were noted because of the potential for misinterpretation.

16. D — An accountant should not examine a presentation that omits *all* disclosures of assumptions. If the presentation fails to disclose assumptions that appear to be significant, the accountant should describe the assumptions in his report and issue an adverse opinion.

17. C — Accountants in public practice are sometimes engaged to report on the application of accounting principles to specific transactions and financial products. When providing such a service, in connection with a proposal to obtain a new client or otherwise, the accountant should follow AICPA guidance, which includes reporting guidelines. The written report should include a description of the nature of the engagement; a description of the transaction; a statement describing the appropriate accounting treatment; a statement that the responsibility for proper accounting rests with the financial statement preparers; and a statement that any difference in the facts, circumstances, or assumptions presented may change the report. An engagement to report on the application of accounting principles is performed in accordance with AICPA standards, not with Statements on Standards for Consulting Services. There is generally no restriction on distribution of the report. The accountant's report includes a statement that describes the appropriate accounting principles to be applied instead of negative assurance.

18. D — Financial projections are prospective financial statements that are based on one or more hypothetical assumptions. Projected financial statements should be distributed only to those who are negotiating directly with the party responsible for those financial statements because the negotiating parties are able to ask the responsible party directly about the presentation; specifically, the hypothetical assumptions. Thus, when an accountant examines a projection, his report should include a separate paragraph that describes the limitations on the usefulness of the presentation. That paragraph states that the projection and the accountant's report were prepared for a special purpose and should not be used for any other purpose.

19. B — As with all financial information, the client's management is responsible for the assertions in the information, not the user or the CPA reporting on the information.

20. B — Statements upon which the CPA reports that are not GAAP representations but rather "special reports" should not use the terms "Balance Sheet," "Income Statement," etc. Such terms are associated with GAAP and should not be used with statements that are not GAAP.

21. C — The services of independent auditors include audits of financial statements and schedules contained in registration statements filed with the Securities and Exchange Commission. In connection with this type of service, they are often called upon to perform other services, including the issuance of letters to underwriters, commonly called comfort letters.

22. D — *Statements on Standards for Accountant's Services on Prospective Financial Information* states that forecasts take the form of historical financial statements. Thus, there is no need to explain what the information is since the forecast represents financial statements. The other answers are part of the accountant's report.

23. **D** Government Auditing Standards include additional reporting standards for financial statement audits. One of those standards requires that the report on the financial statements describe the scope of the auditor's testing of compliance with laws and regulations and internal controls.

24. **A** In an audit of an entity's financial statements conducted in accordance with generally accepted auditing standards, the auditor considers materiality in relation to the financial statements. In auditing an entity's compliance with requirements governing each major federal financial assistance program in accordance with the Single Audit Act, the auditor considers materiality in relation to each such program. When reaching a conclusion as to whether the effect of noncompliance is material to a major federal financial assistance program, an auditor ordinarily should consider the nature of the noncompliance and the amount affected by the noncompliance in relation to the nature and amount of the major federal financial assistance program under audit.

25. **B** Government Auditing Standards requires a written report on internal control in all audits. Those standards also require description of any reportable conditions noted, identification of the categories of internal control, description of the scope of the auditor's work in obtaining an understanding of internal control and in assessing control risk, and description of deficiencies in internal control not considered significant enough to be reportable conditions. If the auditor notes no reportable conditions during an audit he may so state, rather than give negative assurance. The report does not include the comments about reliable controls and strengths.

26. **C** AU 801 states that when the audit of an entity's compliance with requirements governing a major federal financial assistance program detects noncompliance with those requirements which the auditor believes have a material effect on that program, the auditor should express a qualified or adverse opinion. The auditor should state the basis for such an opinion in the report.

27. **B** When the auditor has noted reportable conditions in a financial statement audit conducted in accordance with Government Auditing Standards, the auditor's report on internal control should contain a description of the scope of the auditor's work, stating that the auditor obtained an understanding of the design of relevant policies and procedures, determined whether these policies and procedures have been placed in operation, and assessed control risk.

28. **A** The auditor should design the audit to provide reasonable assurance that the financial statements are free of material misstatements resulting from violations of laws and regulations that have a direct and material effect on the determination of financial statement amounts. This responsibility exists for all audits conducted in accordance with generally accepted auditing standards. The auditor undertakes the same responsibility in an audit, in accordance with Government Auditing Standards, of financial statements of a not-for-profit organization that accepts financial assistance from a governmental entity.

29. **D** The Government Accountability Office performs the audit function for Congress and has published Standards for Audits of Governmental Organizations, Programs, Activities, and Functions. The Governmental Accounting Standards Board (GASB) and the Financial Accounting Standards Board (FASB) establish accounting standards, not auditing standards. The Governmental Auditing Standards Board does not exist.

30. **A** Government auditing standards include a general standard stating that each audit organization conducting government audits should have an appropriate internal quality control system in place and participate in an external quality control review program. A

CPA seeking to enter into a contract to perform an audit subject to government auditing standards should provide the CPA's most recent external quality review report to the party contracting for the audit.

31. C   The audit of recipients of federal financial assistance is conducted under the Generally Accepted Governmental Auditing Standards. Because the recipient has a legal obligation to spend monies in accordance with applicable laws and regulations, the auditor has the responsibility to audit and report on compliance.

32. D   Government Auditing Standards include additional reporting standards for financial statement audits. One of those standards requires the report on the financial statements to describe the scope of the auditors' testing of compliance with laws and regulations and internal controls and present the results of those tests. The standard goes on to state that in presenting the results of those tests, auditors should report fraud, illegal acts, and other material noncompliance. Discoveries of fraud, which is a type of illegal act involving the obtaining of something of value through willful misrepresentation, would also be reported.

LONG-TERM LIABILITIES AND CONTINGENCIES

STUDY MANUAL – AUDITING & ATTESTATION
CHAPTER 15

Study Tip: When you are studying a complicated subject such as the equity method of accounting, it is good to remind yourself that you do not need to be perfect. There is no need to shoot for a grade of 100. You only have to make a grade of 75 in order to pass the CPA exam and that means that you can miss a lot of questions and still pass. That is quite different from school where teachers write most tests looking for students who can answer all of the questions. On the CPA exam, any grade above 75 indicates that the candidate studied too hard.

INTRODUCTION

As noted earlier, financial statements that purport to be in conformity with generally accepted accounting principles contain certain assertions: presentation and disclosure, existence or occurrence, rights and obligations, completeness, and valuation or allocation. Auditors gather evidence to form an opinion with respect to these assertions. The experienced auditor should be able to prepare an audit program for an audit area (e.g., receivables) to test whether these assertions are supportable. The process is one in which specific audit objectives are developed based on the assertions being made in the financial statements. Finally, audit procedures to meet these audit objectives are formulated and listed in an audit program. For purposes of the CPA exam, consider two possible approaches for auditing an account: tests of balances and tests of details.

A. Tests of Balances and Tests of Details.

1. *Direct tests of ending balance (tests of balances)*. This approach requires the auditor to identify specific components of an account balance. For example, the cash account can be broken down into cash on hand and cash on deposit in the client's various bank accounts. Under this approach, the auditor will select and verify a sample of components of the account balance. Accounts that are normally examined via this approach are high turnover accounts such as cash, accounts receivable, inventory, and accounts payable.

2. *Tests of inputs and outputs during the year (tests of details)*. This approach requires the auditor to verify individual transactions comprising an account balance or class of transactions. This approach focuses on the individual transactions occurring during the year and not the final account balance. Accounts normally examined via this approach are lower turnover accounts, such as investments; property, plant and equipment; notes and bonds payable; and shareholders' equity.

3. Many audit procedures provide support for *multiple management assertions*. For example, cut-off procedures provide support for rights and obligations as well as for existence and completeness. The following are typical procedures included in a substantive audit program:

   a. To support presentation and disclosure:

      - Review disclosures for compliance with GAAP.
      - Inquire about disclosures.

   b. To support existence or occurrence:

      - Confirmation.
      - Observation—always consider whether you can observe the item itself and/or legal documents representing the item.
      - Trace/vouch transactions.

   c. To support rights and obligations:

      - Cutoffs—consider whether transactions have been reported in the proper period.
      - Authorization—consider whether there are transactions that require specific authorization.

   d. To support completeness:

      - Analytical procedures.
      - Omissions—consider how transactions could improperly have been omitted from the account.

   e. To support valuation:

      - Foot and cross-foot schedules (total them across and down).
      - Agree the account balances on schedules to the general ledger.
      - Agree financial statement balances to account balances on schedules.
      - Consider valuation methods and whether they have been properly applied.
      - Consider related accounts (e.g., accounts receivable and bad debt expense; long-term debt and interest expense; fixed assets and repair and maintenance expense; and fixed assets and depreciation expense).

B. Auditing Long-Term Liabilities.

   1. Despite the fact that this account's turnover rate is low, considerable analysis is performed on its ending balance.

   2. Confirmations are frequently used; when the debt is owed to banks, confirmation is obtained with the standard bank confirmation.

3. In addition, minutes of the board of directors and/or stockholders' meetings will be reviewed to determine whether new borrowings have been properly authorized.

4. The proceeds of any new borrowings are traced to the cash receipts journal, deposit slips, and bank statements.

5. Repayments are traced to the cash disbursements journal, canceled checks, and canceled notes.

6. The table below details the typical substantive audit procedures performed for long-term liabilities.

Type of audit procedure	Audit procedure	Management assertion(s)
Confirmation	Confirm long-term liabilities with the issuer or trustee.	Existence or occurrence
Confirmation	Obtain a letter from the client's attorney regarding any long-term liabilities and contingencies.	Completeness
Confirmation	Review the standard bank confirmation to determine that all long-term liabilities confirmed by banks are included in the financial statements.	Completeness
Recalculation	Mathematically verify the total of the long-term liability listing and compare the total to the general ledger.	Valuation or allocation
Recalculation	Mathematically recalculate the client's interest expense and accrued interest payable.	Valuation or allocation
Recalculation	Recalculate the amount of the premium or discount and the related amortization.	Valuation or allocation
Recalculation	Recalculate the amount of the gain/loss on the early retirement of debt.	Valuation or allocation
Inspect documents	Trace cash proceeds from the issuance of debt to journals, bank deposit slips, and entries on bank statements.	Existence or occurrence; valuation or allocation

Type of audit procedure	Audit procedure	Management assertion(s)
Inspect documents	Examine various accounts to ensure that liabilities and any accruals are eliminated for all retirements of long-term liabilities.	Valuation or allocation
Inspect documents	Review minutes of meetings of committees, board of directors, and/or shareholders for proper authorization.	Existence or occurrence; completeness
Inspect documents	Review disclosures for compliance with GAAP	Presentation and disclosure
Inspect documents	Examine the debt agreement and note important characteristics (face amount, interest rate, maturity dates, important covenants, pledging, and events causing defaults).	Existence or occurrence; presentation and disclosure
Inquiry	Ask management about the existence and disclosure of any sinking funds used to retire long-term liabilities.	Presentation and disclosure
Inquiry	Ask management about the possible need to reclassify long-term liabilities for violations of covenants.	Presentation and disclosure
Inquiry	Inquire of management as to completeness.	Completeness
Inquiry	Inquire about pledging of assets.	Presentation and disclosure
Analytical procedures	Analyze the reasonableness of interest expense based on outstanding long-term debt.	Completeness

Questions: Long-Term Liabilities and Contingencies

1. An auditor *most likely* would inspect loan agreements under which an entity's inventories are pledged to support management's financial statement assertion of:
   A. presentation and disclosure.
   B. completeness.
   C. existence or occurrence.
   D. valuation or allocation.

2. Which of the following is an audit procedure that an auditor *most likely* would perform concerning litigation, claims, and assessments?
   A. Examine the legal documents in the client's lawyer's possession concerning litigation, claims, and assessments to which the lawyer has devoted substantive attention.
   B. Discuss with management its policies and procedures adopted for evaluating and accounting for litigation, claims, and assessments.
   C. Confirm directly with the client's lawyer that all litigation, claims, and assessments have been recorded or disclosed in the financial statements.
   D. Request the client's lawyer to evaluate whether the client's pending litigation, claims, and assessments indicate a going concern problem.

3. The primary reason an auditor requests letters of inquiry be sent to a client's attorneys is to provide the auditor with:
   A. corroboration of the information furnished by management about litigation, claims, and assessments.
   B. a description and evaluation of litigation, claims, and assessments that existed at the balance sheet date.
   C. the attorneys' opinions of the client's historical experiences in recent similar litigation.
   D. the probable outcome of asserted claims and pending or threatened litigation.

4. In auditing long-term bonds payable, an auditor would *most likely*:
   A. confirm the existence of individual bond-holders at year end.
   B. examine documentation of assets purchased with bond proceeds for liens.
   C. compare interest expense with the bond payable amount for reasonableness.
   D. perform analytical procedures on the bond premium and discount accounts.

5. An auditor would *most likely* inspect loan agreements under which an entity's inventories are pledged to support management's financial statement assertion of:
   A. completeness.
   B. existence or occurrence.
   C. valuation or allocation.
   D. presentation and disclosure.

6. In an audit of contingent liabilities, which of the following procedures would be *least* effective?
   A. Reviewing a bank confirmation letter.
   B. Reading the minutes of the board of directors.
   C. Examining invoices for professional services.
   D. Examining customer confirmation replies.

7. The scope of an audit is not restricted when an attorney's response to an auditor as a result of a client's letter of audit inquiry limits the response to:
   A. the attorney's opinion of the entity's historical experience in recent similar litigation.
   B. matters to which the attorney has given substantive attention in the form of legal representation.
   C. an evaluation of the likelihood of an unfavorable outcome of the matters disclosed by the entity.
   D. the probable outcome of asserted claims and pending or threatened litigation.

8. Auditors should request that an audit client send a letter of inquiry to those attorneys who have been consulted concerning litigation, claims, or assessments. The primary reason for this request is to provide:
   A. an estimate of the dollar amount of the probable loss.
   B. an expert opinion as to whether a loss is possible, probable, or remote.
   C. corroborative audit evidence.
   D. information concerning the progress of cases to date.

9. An auditor's purpose in reviewing the renewal of a note payable shortly after the balance sheet date *most likely* is to obtain evidence concerning management's assertions about:
   A. presentation and disclosure.
   B. valuation or allocation.
   C. completeness.
   D. existence or occurrence.

ANSWERS: LONG-TERM LIABILITIES AND CONTINGENCIES

1. **A** Assertions about presentation and disclosure deal with whether particular components of the financial statements are properly classified, described, and disclosed. An auditor would inspect loan agreements regarding pledged inventories to determine that management has adequately disclosed the security arrangements.

2. **B** Since the events or conditions that should be considered in the accounting for and reporting of litigation, claims, and assessments are matters within the direct knowledge of management of an entity, management is the primary source about such matters. Accordingly, the auditor should inquire of and discuss with management the policies and procedures adopted for identifying, evaluating, and accounting for litigation, claims, and assessments.

3. **A** AU 337 states that a letter of audit inquiry to the client's lawyer is the auditor's primary means of obtaining corroboration of the information furnished by management concerning litigation, claims, and assessments.

4. **C** AU 8502 states that auditors commonly use inquiries and analytical procedures to provide evidence concerning loans when control risk is low. These procedures would include:

   - Obtain from management a schedule of loans payable and determine if the total agrees with the trial balance.
   - Inquire whether there are any loans where management has not complied with provisions of the loan agreement and inquire as to management's actions and if appropriate adjustments have been made in the F/S.
   - Consider the reasonableness of interest expense in relation to loan balances.
   - Inquire whether loans payable are secured.
   - Inquire whether loans payable have been classified between noncurrent and current.

5. **D** Assertions about presentation and disclosure deal with whether particular components of the financial statements are properly classified, described, and disclosed. An auditor would inspect loan agreements regarding pledged inventories to determine that management has adequately disclosed the security arrangements.

6. **D** A primary objective when auditing liabilities is to determine that they are all properly included. Accordingly, the auditor has to search for liabilities that exist as of balance sheet date. In searching for contingent liabilities, the auditor will typically review bank confirmation letters for any indication of direct or contingent liabilities, examine invoices for professional services especially from attorneys who may be working on pending litigation, and read minutes of the board of directors for indications of lawsuits or other contingencies.

7. **B** During the audit of financial statements, the auditor is required to send a letter of audit inquiry to the client's legal counsel concerning claims, litigation and assessments. It is reasonable to assume that an attorney would be responsible to respond concerning only those items to which he has given substantive attention. He would not be able to respond to items to which he has not given substantive attention (the attorney has no knowledge). Therefore, such a limited response on the part of an attorney would not be considered a scope limitation.

8. **C** A letter of audit inquiry to the client's lawyer is the auditor's primary means of obtaining corroboration of the information furnished by management concerning litigation, claims, and assessments. The matters included in the other answers could be covered in a letter of audit inquiry but the primary reason for the request is to provide corroborative audit evidence.

9. **A** The presentation and disclosure assertion relates to the fact that the financial statements should reflect all pertinent information necessary to reach an informed decision concerning the company. By reviewing the renewal of a note payable after year-end the auditor will be able to determine whether the year-end financial statements include all pertinent information such as due date, interest rate and collateral, if any.

PAYROLL

STUDY MANUAL – AUDITING & ATTESTATION
CHAPTER 16

Study Tip: A key to passing the CPA exam is to break each topic into learnable segments. Normally, each topic is composed of several different specific steps. Break the topic into those steps and then learn each one individually. Passing the CPA exam becomes quite difficult when a candidate attempts to learn a major topic as a single whole. That is similar to trying to eat a watermelon without cutting it into pieces. People come to understand the topic better when they are faced with a segment of information that is small enough to be learnable.

INTRODUCTION

As noted earlier, financial statements that purport to be in conformity with generally accepted accounting principles contain certain assertions: presentation and disclosure, existence or occurrence, rights and obligations, completeness, and valuation or allocation. Auditors gather evidence to form an opinion with respect to these assertions. The experienced auditor should be able to prepare an audit program for an audit area (e.g., receivables) to test whether these assertions are supportable. The process is one in which specific audit objectives are developed based on the assertions being made in the financial statements. Finally, audit procedures to meet these audit objectives are formulated and listed in an audit program. For purposes of the CPA exam, consider two possible approaches for auditing an account: tests of balances and tests of details.

A. Tests of Balances and Tests of Details.

1. *Direct tests of ending balance (tests of balances)*. This approach requires the auditor to identify specific components of an account balance. For example, the cash account can be broken down into cash on hand and cash on deposit in the client's various bank accounts. Under this approach, the auditor will select and verify a sample of components of the account balance. Accounts that are normally examined via this approach are high turnover accounts such as cash, accounts receivable, inventory, and accounts payable.

2. *Tests of inputs and outputs during the year (tests of details)*. This approach requires the auditor to verify individual transactions comprising an account balance or class of transactions. This approach focuses on the individual transactions occurring during the year and not the final account balance. Accounts normally examined via this approach are lower turnover accounts, such as investments; property, plant and equipment; notes and bonds payable; and shareholders' equity.

3. Many audit procedures provide support for *multiple management assertions*. For example, cut-off procedures provide support for rights and obligations as well as for existence and completeness. The following are typical procedures included in a substantive audit program:

   a. To support presentation and disclosure:

      - Review disclosures for compliance with GAAP.
      - Inquire about disclosures.

   b. To support existence or occurrence:

      - Confirmation.
      - Observation—always consider whether you can observe the item itself and/or legal documents representing the item.
      - Trace/vouch transactions.

   c. To support rights and obligations:

      - Cutoffs—consider whether transactions have been reported in the proper period.
      - Authorization—consider whether there are transactions that require specific authorization.

   d. To support completeness:

      - Analytical procedures.
      - Omissions—consider how transactions could improperly have been omitted from the account.

   e. To support valuation:

      - Foot and cross-foot schedules (total them across and down).
      - Agree the account balances on schedules to the general ledger.
      - Agree financial statement balances to account balances on schedules.
      - Consider valuation methods and whether they have been properly applied.
      - Consider related accounts (e.g., accounts receivable and bad debt expense; long-term debt and interest expense; fixed assets and repair and maintenance expense; and fixed assets and depreciation expense).

A. When auditing payroll balances, the auditor should be aware of several potential problems. Because money is being removed from the company, theft is the biggest concern. Overpayment can occur for several reasons.

   1. Payment may be for more hours than the employee actually worked or for a higher rate than the employee actually earned.

   2. Extra deductions may be taken from one employee in order to increase another employee's paycheck.

3. Paychecks may be issued in the name of false employees or individuals who are no longer employed. These checks are stolen and then cashed.

B. The client company should have a well-designed payroll system to ensure that records are correct and payments are appropriate.

1. The Human Resources Department hires employees and sets up a personnel file to accumulate information for computing payroll.

    a. A W-4 form lists marital status and number of dependents.

    b. Any employee or union contract gives pay rates and terms of fringe benefits.

    c. Deduction authorizations are signed by the employee as approval for deducting money for medical insurance, savings bonds, union fees, donations, etc.

    d. Human Resources department prepares a payroll input record for each pay period giving a list of employees, marital status, pay rate, deductions, etc. A copy is sent to the payroll department so that wages can be computed.

2. For employees paid an hourly rate, the number of hours worked is maintained by the **timekeeping department.** Clock cards or some other system is used to determine the exact time spent at work.

3. Where applicable, employees keep records of their work own **time tickets** (or job order cards). This information can be used in determining labor costs charged to each job.

4. The employee's supervisor reviews the number of hours being reported and provides authorization. Since overtime hours are usually paid at a higher rate, a special authorization may e necessary.

5. The **Payroll department** computes each employee's gross wages, deductions, and net pay based on hours worked and information from the payroll input records.

    a. Salary information is recorded for each employee in a payroll register. Totals are forwarded to general accounting for reporting purposes.

    b. A second employee verifies all figures and computations and provides authorization.

6. The **Payroll register** is sent to the cash disbursements department in the treasurer's office. It is reviewed and approved unless discrepancies are apparent.

7. Paychecks are written on a separate payroll bank account which has no money in it except when payroll is issued. Use of a separate payroll account reduces the chance and potential amount of theft.

8. A second employee compares the paychecks to to the register and signs his/her approval.

9. The **Paymaster** distributes the checks to employees, but only after they provide proper identification.

10. Unclaimed paychecks are recorded by the paymaster and given to an independent party for follow up.

C. A number of substantive testing procedures should be performed to verify the five assertions made by client about payroll.

1. **Analytical procedures** should be carried out, such as comparing expense to previous years, budgeted figures, and number of employees. The auditor may want to compare expense from month to month to note any unusual amounts.

2. Select a sample of employees and trace payroll information from personnel file to payroll input form to clock cards to payroll register to general ledger account to canceled check.

3. Vouch a sample of payroll checks to find supporting documentation.

4. Verify mathematical computation of individual paychecks, including all deductions.

5. Verify extensions and footings in payroll register.

6. Recompute year-end accrual of any unpaid salaries.

7. Observe paymaster's distribution of checks to verify that each employee has proper identification. Investigate the handling of any unclaimed checks.

QUESTIONS: PAYROLL

1. An auditor *most likely* would assess control risk at the maximum if the payroll department supervisor is responsible for:
   A. examining authorization forms for new employees.
   B. comparing payroll registers with original batch transmittal data.
   C. authorizing payroll rate changes for all employees.
   D. hiring all subordinate payroll department employees.

2. An auditor *most likely* would extend substantive tests of payroll when:
   A. payroll expense is substantially higher than in the prior year.
   B. employees complain to management about too much overtime.
   C. payroll is extensively audited by the state government.
   D. overpayments are discovered in performing tests of details.

3. An auditor vouched data for a sample of employees in a payroll register to approved clock card data to provide assurance that:
   A. payments to employees are computed at authorized rates.
   B. employees work the number of hours for which they are paid.
   C. internal controls relating to unclaimed payroll checks are operating effectively.
   D. segregation of duties exist between the preparation and distribution of the payroll.

4. Which of the following circumstances *most likely* would cause an auditor to suspect an employee payroll fraud scheme?
   A. There are significant unexplained variances between standard and actual labor cost.
   B. A separate payroll bank account is maintained on an imprest basis.
   C. Employee time cards are approved by individual departmental supervisors.
   D. Payroll checks are disbursed by the same employee each payday.

5. When control risk is assessed as low for assertions related to payroll, substantive tests of payroll balances *most likely* would be limited to applying analytical procedures and:
   A. recalculating payroll accruals.
   B. footing and crossfooting the payroll register.
   C. observing the distribution of paychecks.
   D. inspecting payroll tax returns.

6. An auditor would consider internal control over a client's payroll procedures to be ineffective if the payroll department supervisor is responsible for:
   A. having custody over unclaimed paychecks.
   B. hiring subordinate payroll department employees.
   C. updating employee earnings records.
   D. applying pay rates to time tickets.

7. An effective system of control procedures over the payroll function would include:
   A. custody of rate authorization records by the supervisor of the payroll department.
   B. preparation of payroll transaction journal entries by an employee who reports to the supervisor of the personnel department.
   C. reconciliation of totals on job time tickets with job reports by employees responsible for those specific jobs.
   D. verification of agreement of job time tickets with employee clock card hours by a payroll department employee.

8. Which of the following is a control procedure that *most likely* could help prevent employee payroll fraud?
   A. Salary rates resulting from new hires are approved by the payroll supervisor.
   B. The personnel department promptly sends employee termination notices to the payroll supervisor.
   C. Employees who distribute payroll checks forward unclaimed payroll checks to the absent employees' supervisors.
   D. Total hours used for determination of gross pay are calculated by the payroll supervisor.

9. Which of the following *best* describes proper internal control over payroll?
   A. The confidentiality of employee payroll data should be carefully protected to prevent fraud.
   B. The payment of cash to employees should be replaced with payment by checks.
   C. The duties of hiring, payroll computation, and payment to employees should be segregated.
   D. The preparation of the payroll must be under the control of the personnel department.

10. Which of the following internal control activities *most likely* would prevent direct labor hours from being charged to manufacturing overhead?
    A. Use of time tickets to record actual labor worked on production orders.
    B. Reconciliation of work-in-process inventory with periodic cost budgets.
    C. Periodic independent counts of work in process for comparison to recorded amounts.
    D. Comparison of daily journal entries with approved production orders.

11. In determining the effectiveness of an entity's policies and procedures relating to the existence or occurrence assertion for payroll transactions, an auditor *most likely* would inquire about, and:
    A. recompute the payroll deductions for employee fringe benefits.
    B. inspect evidence of accounting for prenumbered payroll checks.
    C. verify the preparation of the monthly payroll account bank reconciliation.
    D. observe the segregation of duties concerning personnel responsibilities and payroll disbursement.

12. Which of the following departments should have the responsibility for authorizing payroll rate changes?
    A. Treasurer.
    B. Timekeeping.
    C. Payroll.
    D. Personnel.

13. An example of an internal control weakness is to assign to a department supervisor the responsibility for:
    A. authorizing payroll checks for terminated employees.
    B. distributing payroll checks to subordinate employees.
    C. initiating requests for salary adjustments for subordinate employees.
    D. reviewing and approving time reports for subordinate employees.

14. In auditing payroll, an auditor *most likely* would:
    A. observe entity employees during a payroll distribution.
    B. trace individual employee deductions to entity journal entries.
    C. verify that checks representing unclaimed wages are mailed.
    D. compare payroll costs with entity standards or budgets.

15. Which of the following procedures *most likely* would be considered a weakness in an entity's internal controls over payroll?
    A. The employee who distributes payroll checks returns unclaimed payroll checks to the payroll department.
    B. The personnel department sends employees' termination notices to the payroll department.
    C. Payroll checks are prepared by the payroll department and signed by the treasurer.
    D. A voucher for the amount of the payroll is prepared in the general accounting department based on the payroll department's payroll summary.

16. It would be appropriate for the payroll accounting department to be responsible for which of the following functions?
    A. Maintenance of records of employment, discharges, and pay increases.
    B. Preparation of periodic governmental reports as to employees' earnings and withholding taxes.
    C. Distribution of paychecks to employees.
    D. Approval of employee time records.

17. The auditor may observe the distribution of paychecks to ascertain whether:
    A. payrate authorization is properly separated from the operating function.
    B. deductions from gross pay are calculated correctly and are properly authorized.
    C. employees of record actually exist and are employed by the client.
    D. paychecks agree with the payroll register and the time cards.

ANSWERS: PAYROLL

1. **C** Authorization and recording are incompatible functions that should be assigned to different individuals. In this case, authorization of payroll changes, which is typically the responsibility of the human resources department, should be segregated from recording payroll, which is the responsibility of the payroll department. If the payroll department supervisor is responsible for these two functions, the entity's internal control may be inadequate to prevent or detect material misstatements in the payroll area. Thus, the auditor would assess control risk at the maximum.

2. **D** If overpayments are discovered by the auditor, this suggests that errors and/or fraud exist. Accordingly, the auditor would extend substantive tests of payroll.

3. **B** An auditor examines approved clock card data to determine the number of hours an employee worked. Comparing the payroll register to clock data provides assurance that the number of hours used to compute the payroll is the number of hours worked. The other answers are incorrect because looking at clock card data will not provide information regarding pay rates, segregation of duties, or controls over unclaimed payroll checks.

4. **A** Standard labor cost is based on expectations and budgets. If actual labor cost is significantly different from standard labor cost, the resultant variances should be analyzed by the auditor. If these variances are not readily explainable, the auditor may suspect payroll fraud. The other answers are desirable controls that reduce the likelihood of payroll fraud. Payroll checks can be distributed by the same employee each pay day, particularly if that individual is associated with the treasury or cash disbursements function. Employee time cards should be approved by supervisors. Using a separate payroll account that is reimbursed from other general bank accounts provides additional control over payroll disbursements.

5. **A** When the auditor determines that internal control is effective and thus the control risk is assessed as low, the auditor may alter the nature, timing, and extent of substantive tests performed. In the case of assertions related to payroll, the auditor may decide to limit substantive tests to performing analytical procedures, which would evaluate the reasonableness of payroll-related amounts for the year, and recalculating payroll accruals, which would provide some assurance that the year-end adjustments are proper.

6. **D** The payroll accounting department has a recording responsibility and as such it should not have custody of unclaimed payroll checks (custody of an asset). If the payroll accounting department had custody of payroll checks, its employees could add a fictitious employee to the payroll and subsequently obtain the check.

7. **D** Control procedures over the payroll function include the reconciliation of job time tickets to employee clock card hours.

8. **B** Payroll fraud could involve fictitious employees and/or fictitious salary rates. In order to prevent these frauds, new hires, terminations of employees, and salary rates should be approved by the personnel department, which in turn should keep the payroll department and employee supervisors informed on a timely basis.

9. **C** The authorization of transactions, record keeping, and custodial functions should be segregated.

10. A   Time tickets should be designed to keep track of hours worked, by whom, and on what production orders. After approval by a production supervisor, time tickets provide the information on number of hours worked directly on specific production orders. If time tickets are properly used to record actual hours worked on orders, approval and/or review of these cards should prevent direct labor hours from being incorrectly charged to manufacturing overhead.

11. D   Assertions about existence or occurrence deal with whether assets or liabilities of the entity exist at a given date and whether recorded transactions occurred during a given period. Segregating payroll-related duties such as authorizing new hires and wage rates, as is done by a personnel department, and disbursing payroll checks, as is done by the treasurer, reduces the likelihood that fictitious payroll transactions that did not occur will get recorded. The auditor, therefore, inquires about and observes the segregation of payroll-related duties.

12. D   In an organizational structure, the personnel department is delegated the authorization power over pay rates.

13. B   Department supervisor authorizes payroll and should not be responsible for distribution (custodial function-custody of checks).

14. D   AU 8012 states that auditors commonly use analytical procedures to provide evidence concerning payroll when control risk is low. Analytical procedures include comparison of financial information with:

- Comparable information for a prior period or periods.
- Anticipated results, such as budgets or forecasts.
- Similar industry information, such as a comparison of the entity's ratio of sales to accounts receivable with industry averages or with other entities of comparable size in the same industry.
- Study relationships among elements of financial information that would be expected to conform to a predictable pattern based on the entity's experience, such as a study of gross margin percentage.
- Study relationships between financial information and relevant non-financial information, such as a study of payroll costs to number of employees.

15. A   Documents should not flow back through a system. If checks are returned to a record keeping department, such as the payroll department as in this case, they may be misallocated or may represent unauthorized or invalid payments, such as payments to fictitious or terminated employees in this case. The other choices are examples of internal control strengths.

16. B   This department has access to the records necessary to prepare payroll tax reports.

17. C   The other answers are incorrect because the auditor can ascertain that these controls are in place by other means through records available within the company. However, in order to determine whether a given employee actually exists, the auditor must observe the actual distribution of checks and would usually include the employee providing some form of personal identification.

Land, Buildings, and Equipment

Study Manual – Auditing & Attestation
Chapter 17

Study Tip: Forget the past. People often approach the CPA exam talking about previous failures, either on the exam itself or in school. "I was never a very good student" is a common refrain. The past is not important. If you use good, quality preparation materials and are willing to invest a sufficient amount of time studying, you can pass. Do not let something that occurred in the past hold you back from success today.

Introduction

As noted earlier, financial statements that purport to be in conformity with generally accepted accounting principles contain certain assertions: presentation and disclosure, existence or occurrence, rights and obligations, completeness, and valuation or allocation. Auditors gather evidence to form an opinion with respect to these assertions. The experienced auditor should be able to prepare an audit program for an audit area (e.g., receivables) to test whether these assertions are supportable. The process is one in which specific audit objectives are developed based on the assertions being made in the financial statements. Finally, audit procedures to meet these audit objectives are formulated and listed in an audit program. For purposes of the CPA exam, consider two possible approaches for auditing an account: tests of balances and tests of details.

A. Tests of Balances and Tests of Details.

1. *Direct tests of ending balance (tests of balances)*. This approach requires the auditor to identify specific components of an account balance. For example, the cash account can be broken down into cash on hand and cash on deposit in the client's various bank accounts. Under this approach, the auditor will select and verify a sample of components of the account balance. Accounts that are normally examined via this approach are high turnover accounts such as cash, accounts receivable, inventory, and accounts payable.

2. *Tests of inputs and outputs during the year (tests of details)*. This approach requires the auditor to verify individual transactions comprising an account balance or class of transactions. This approach focuses on the individual transactions occurring during the year and not the final account balance. Accounts normally examined via this approach are lower turnover accounts, such as investments; property, plant and equipment; notes and bonds payable; and shareholders' equity.

3. Many audit procedures provide support for *multiple management assertions*. For example, cut-off procedures provide support for rights and obligations as well as for

existence and completeness. The following are typical procedures included in a substantive audit program:

a. To support presentation and disclosure:

- Review disclosures for compliance with GAAP.
- Inquire about disclosures.

b. To support existence or occurrence:

- Confirmation.
- Observation—always consider whether you can observe the item itself and/or legal documents representing the item.
- Trace/vouch transactions.

c. To support rights and obligations:

- Cutoffs—consider whether transactions have been reported in the proper period.
- Authorization—consider whether there are transactions that require specific authorization.

d. To support completeness:

- Analytical procedures.
- Omissions—consider how transactions could improperly have been omitted from the account.

e. To support valuation:

- Foot and cross-foot schedules (total them across and down).
- Agree the account balances on schedules to the general ledger.
- Agree financial statement balances to account balances on schedules.
- Consider valuation methods and whether they have been properly applied.
- Consider related accounts (e.g., accounts receivable and bad debt expense; long-term debt and interest expense; fixed assets and repair and maintenance expense; and fixed assets and depreciation expense).

B. **Auditing Property, Plant, and Equipment.**

1. The reasonableness of the entire account balance must be audited in detail for a client that has not previously been audited.

    a. When a predecessor auditor exists, the successor will normally review that auditor's documents.

    b. For a continuing audit client, the audit of property, plant, and equipment consists largely of an analysis of the year's acquisitions and disposals as "tests of details of transactions."

c. The auditor should also evaluate the client's depreciation expense and accumulated depreciation.

2. A property, plant, and equipment acquisition may be improperly recorded in the repair and maintenance expense accounts.

   a. Therefore, an analysis of repairs and maintenance may detect an understatement of property, plant, and equipment.

   b. Alternatively, an analysis of property, plant, and equipment may disclose repairs and maintenance that have improperly been capitalized, thereby resulting in an overstatement of property, plant, and equipment.

3. Disposals may occur due to retirements or thefts of property, plant, and equipment items.

   a. Simple retirements of equipment are often difficult to detect because no journal entry may have been recorded to reflect the event.

   b. Unrecorded or improperly recorded retirements (and thefts) may be discovered through examination of changes in insurance policies, consideration of the purpose of recorded acquisition, examination of property tax files, discussions, observation, or through an examination of debits to accumulated depreciation and of credits to miscellaneous revenue accounts.

   c. Inquiry of the plant manager may disclose unrecorded retirements and/or obsolete equipment.

   d. The table below details the typical substantive audit procedures performed for property, plant, and equipment.

Type of audit procedure	Audit procedure	Management assertion(s)
Confirmation	Confirm property, plant, and equipment held by others under operating lease agreements.	Existence or occurrence; rights and obligations
Observation	Observe property, plant, and equipment held by the client, especially additions.	Existence or occurrence; rights and obligations
Recalculation	Recalculate depreciation expense.	Valuation or allocation
Recalculation	Recalculate the gain/loss on disposals.	Valuation or allocation

Type of audit procedure	Audit procedure	Management assertion(s)
Recalculation	Mathematically verify the accuracy of the client's schedule of property, plant, and equipment. Agree the balance to the general ledger.	Valuation or allocation
Inspect documents	Vouch purchases to invoices.	Existence or occurrence; valuation or allocation
Inspect documents	Review titles, registration, property tax notices, and insurance policies.	Rights and obligations
Inspect documents	Review the minutes of the meetings of the shareholders or the board of directors to determine if any liens or claims exist against property, plant, and equipment, and for approval of additions.	Rights and obligations
Inspect documents	Review disclosures for compliance with GAAP.	Presentation and disclosure
Inspect documents	Examine insurance policies to determine if any liens exist against property, plant, and equipment.	Rights and obligations
Inspect documents	Vouch repairs and maintenance expenses to determine if expenditures should be capitalized.	Completeness
Inspect documents	Review loan agreements for liens and restrictions	Presentation and disclosure
Inspect documents	Review lease agreements for proper accounting (capital versus operating).	Presentation and disclosure; existence or occurrence
Inspect documents	Perform a search for unrecorded disposals.	Existence or occurrence
Inquiry	Inquire about the existence of liens and restrictions on property, plant, and equipment.	Presentation and disclosure; rights and obligations
Inquiry	Inquire about the existence of operating lease agreements between the client and lessees.	Completeness

Type of audit procedure	Audit procedure	Management assertion(s)
Inquiry	Inquire about the client's policy for capitalizing property, plant, and equipment.	Completeness
Inquiry	Inquire of the appropriateness of estimated lives, estimated salvage values, and the method used to depreciate property, plant, and equipment.	Valuation or allocation
Inquiry	Inquire about disposals.	Existence or occurrence
Analytical procedures	Evaluate the reasonableness of depreciation expense based on the balance in property, plant, and equipment or depreciation expense from previous years.	Valuation or allocation

QUESTIONS: LAND, BUILDINGS, AND EQUIPMENT

1. When there are numerous property and equipment transactions during the year, an auditor who plans to assess control risk at a low level usually performs:
   A. analytical procedures for current year property and equipment transactions.
   B. analytical procedures for property and equipment balances at the end of the year.
   C. tests of controls and limited tests of current year property and equipment transactions.
   D. tests of controls and extensive tests of property and equipment balances at the end of the year.

2. When there are numerous property and equipment transactions during the year, an auditor who plans to assess control risk at a low level usually performs:
   A. analytical procedures for current year property and equipment transactions.
   B. tests of controls and extensive tests of property and equipment balances at the end of the year.
   C. analytical procedures for property and equipment balances at the end of the year.
   D. tests of controls and limited tests of current year property and equipment transactions.

3. Which of the following combinations of procedures would an auditor *most likely* perform to obtain evidence about fixed asset additions?
   A. Inspecting documents and physically examining assets.
   B. Observing operating activities and comparing balances to prior period balances.
   C. Confirming ownership and corroborating transactions through inquiries of client personnel.
   D. Recomputing calculations and obtaining written management representations.

4. Determining that proper amounts of depreciation are expensed provides assurance about management's assertions of valuation or allocation and
   A. presentation and disclosure.
   B. rights and obligations.
   C. completeness.
   D. existence or occurrence.

5. In testing plant and equipment balances, an auditor examines new additions listed on an analysis of plant and equipment. This procedure *most likely* obtains evidence concerning management's assertion of:
   A. completeness.
   B. existence or occurrence.
   C. valuation or allocation.
   D. presentation and disclosure.

6. Which of the following audit procedures would be *least likely* to lead the auditor to find unrecorded fixed asset disposals?
   A. Review of property tax files.
   B. Examination of insurance policies.
   C. Scanning of invoices for fixed asset additions.
   D. Review of repairs and maintenance expense.

7. A weakness in internal control over recording retirements of equipment may cause an auditor to:
   A. trace additions to the "other assets" account to search for equipment that is still on hand but no longer being used.
   B. review the subsidiary ledger to ascertain whether depreciation was taken on each item of equipment during the year.
   C. select certain items of equipment from the accounting records and locate them in the plant.
   D. inspect certain items of equipment in the plant and trace those items to the accounting records.

8. Which of the following explanations *most likely* would satisfy an auditor who questions management about significant debits to the accumulated depreciation accounts?
   A. The estimated remaining useful lives of plant assets were revised upward.
   B. Overhead allocations were revised at year-end.
   C. The prior year's depreciation expense was erroneously understated.
   D. Plant assets were retired during the year.

9. Which of the following questions would an auditor *least likely* include on an internal control questionnaire concerning the initiation and execution of equipment transactions?
   A. Are requests for purchases of equipment reviewed for consideration of soliciting competitive bids?
   B. Are procedures in place to monitor and properly restrict access to equipment?
   C. Are requests for major repairs approved at a higher level than the department initiating the request?
   D. Are prenumbered purchase orders used for equipment and periodically accounted for?

10. In testing for unrecorded retirements of equipment, an auditor *most likely* would:
    A. select items of equipment from the accounting records and then locate them during the plant tour.
    B. scan the general journal for unusual equipment additions and excessive debits to repairs and maintenance expense.
    C. inspect items of equipment observed during the plant tour and then trace them to the equipment subsidiary ledger.
    D. compare depreciation journal entries with similar prior-year entries in search of fully depreciated equipment.

11. An auditor analyzes repairs and maintenance accounts primarily to obtain evidence in support of the audit assertion that all:
    A. expenditures for property and equipment have been recorded in the proper period.
    B. noncapitalizable expenditures for repairs and maintenance have been properly charged to expense.
    C. expenditures for property and equipment have not been charged to expense.
    D. noncapitalizable expenditures for repairs and maintenance have been recorded in the proper period.

12. In performing a search for unrecorded retirements of fixed assets, an auditor *most likely* would:
    A. tour the client's facilities, and then analyze the repair and maintenance account.
    B. inspect the property ledger and the insurance and tax records, and then tour the client's facilities.
    C. analyze the repair and maintenance account, and then tour the client's facilities.
    D. tour the client's facilities, and then inspect the property ledger and the insurance and tax records.

Answers: Land, Buildings, and Equipment

1. **C** An auditor assesses control risk to determine the acceptable detection risk and extent of substantive tests to perform. When an auditor plans to assess control risk at a low level, he must identify specific policies and procedures that are likely to prevent or detect material misstatements, and he must perform tests of controls to evaluate the effectiveness of such policies and procedures. If, based on the tests of controls, the control risk is assessed at a low level, the auditor may limit the extent of substantive testing.

2. **D** An auditor assesses control risk to determine acceptable detection risk and the nature, extent and timing of substantive tests to perform. When an auditor plans to assess control risk at a low level, the auditor must identify specific policies and procedures that are likely to prevent or detect material misstatements, and he or she must perform tests of controls to evaluate the effectiveness of such policies and procedures. If, based on tests of controls, the control risk is assessed at a low level, the auditor may limit the extent of substantive testing.

3. **A** The auditor wants to determine that the addition exists, is properly valued, and is owned by the client. Physical examination by the auditor provides competent evidence of existence. Inspection of purchase and title documents by the auditor provides evidence regarding amounts and ownership.

4. **A** AU 326 states that assertions about valuation or allocation deal with whether asset, liability, revenue, and expense components have been included in the financial statements at appropriate amounts. For example, management asserts that property is recorded at historical cost and that such cost is systematically allocated to appropriate accounting periods. Similarly, management asserts that trade A/R included in the balance sheet are stated at net realizable value. Determining that proper amounts of depreciation are expensed provides assurance about the assertions of valuation or allocation amounts and presentation such as an expense on the I/S. The other assertions relate to balance sheet items rights and obligations or to transactions about completeness or existence.

5. **B** Management's assertion of existence or occurrence deals with whether assets of the entity, such as plant and equipment, exist at a given date and whether recorded transactions, such as plant and equipment additions, have occurred during a given period. If the auditor physically examines new additions listed on an analysis of plant and equipment, the auditor is obtaining evidence about the existence or occurrence assertion. The assertions presented in the other answers are not tested by this procedure. The auditor would test in the opposite direction for completeness. That is, the auditor would select items of plant and equipment or transactions involving plant and equipment and determine if they have been properly included in the plant and equipment balance rather than working from the account balance back to the physical item or transaction documentation. The presentation and disclosure assertion deals with whether particular components of the financial statements are properly classified, described and disclosed, not whether additions to an account exist or occurred. Valuation and allocation of plant and equipment deal with whether plant and equipment have been included in the financial statements at appropriate amounts. The auditor would test initial valuation at cost and the allocation of that cost to periods benefited, through depreciation.

6. **D** The question deals with fixed asset disposals. The auditor examines repairs and maintenance accounts to find unrecorded fixed asset additions.

7. **C** A weakness in controls over recording equipment retirements increases the risk that equipment which is removed from the plant is not removed from the accounting records. When the auditor selects items in the accounting records and tries to locate them in the plant, he may discover retired equipment that is still in the accounting records.

8. **D** When a plant asset, such as equipment, is retired, the asset account is credited and the related accumulated depreciation account is debited. Therefore, an acceptable explanation for significant debits to the accumulated depreciation accounts would be that plant assets were retired during the year.

9. **B** An internal control questionnaire concerning the initiation and execution of equipment transactions would not be concerned with equipment that is owned and in place because it is not part of the current transactions.

10. **A** The auditor can test for unrecorded retirements of equipment by selecting items of equipment listed in the accounting records and trying to physically locate them. If the item of equipment has been retired, it will not exist in the client's plant and the auditor will not be able to locate it.

11. **C** AU 326 states that an auditor who is analyzing the repairs and maintenance accounts is testing transactions that have been recorded in the accounts. Sampling from transactions that have been recorded provides evidence in support of the presentation and disclosure assertion. Assertions about presentation and disclosure deal with whether particular components of the financial statements are properly classified, described, and disclosed. For example, management asserts that obligations classified as long-term liabilities in the balance sheet will not mature within one year. Or management asserts that amounts presented as extraordinary items in the income statement are properly classified and described. The auditor is obtaining evidence that transactions recorded in repairs and maintenance accounts do represent expenditures properly charged to expense, not assets which should be capitalized. The cost of capitalized assets is allocated to the periods benefited in a systematic and rational manner, depreciated, depleted, or amortized, not expensed in the period incurred. The other choices would not constitute the primary purpose because the auditor should be selecting from expenditures that did occur, not from the expenditures that were recorded in the repairs and maintenance accounts.

12. **B** In searching for unrecorded retirements of fixed assets, the auditor would select items included in the property ledger and other records and then, by touring the client's facilities, look to see if they are on hand. A fixed asset that is not on hand but is included in the records may indicate that a retirement was not recorded.

INVESTMENTS

STUDY MANUAL – AUDITING & ATTESTATION
CHAPTER 18

Study Tip: Believe in yourself. Thousands of people just like you pass the CPA exam each year. They are no smarter and no better educated. They just use good quality materials and they put in the time and the energy. You can do it also. The CPA exam is challenging, but it is certainly not impossible. People will constantly tell you that you cannot pass. Tell them to go away. There is nothing more important that you can bring to the CPA exam than a belief that you can do the work and make it happen.

INTRODUCTION

As noted earlier, financial statements that purport to be in conformity with generally accepted accounting principles contain certain assertions: presentation and disclosure, existence or occurrence, rights and obligations, completeness, and valuation or allocation. Auditors gather evidence to form an opinion with respect to these assertions. The experienced auditor should be able to prepare an audit program for an audit area (e.g., receivables) to test whether these assertions are supportable. The process is one in which specific audit objectives are developed based on the assertions being made in the financial statements. Finally, audit procedures to meet these audit objectives are formulated and listed in an audit program. For purposes of the CPA exam, consider two possible approaches for auditing an account: tests of balances and tests of details.

A. Tests of Balances and Tests of Details.

1. *Direct tests of ending balance (tests of balances)*. This approach requires the auditor to identify specific components of an account balance. For example, the cash account can be broken down into cash on hand and cash on deposit in the client's various bank accounts. Under this approach, the auditor will select and verify a sample of components of the account balance. Accounts that are normally examined via this approach are high turnover accounts such as cash, accounts receivable, inventory, and accounts payable.

2. *Tests of inputs and outputs during the year (tests of details)*. This approach requires the auditor to verify individual transactions comprising an account balance or class of transactions. This approach focuses on the individual transactions occurring during the year and not the final account balance. Accounts normally examined via this approach are lower turnover accounts, such as investments; property, plant and equipment; notes and bonds payable; and shareholders' equity.

3. Many audit procedures provide support for *multiple management assertions*. For example, cut-off procedures provide support for rights and obligations as well as for

existence and completeness. The following are typical procedures included in a substantive audit program:

a. To support presentation and disclosure:

- Review disclosures for compliance with GAAP.
- Inquire about disclosures.

b. To support existence or occurrence:

- Confirmation.
- Observation—always consider whether you can observe the item itself and/or legal documents representing the item.
- Trace/vouch transactions.

c. To support rights and obligations:

- Cutoffs—consider whether transactions have been reported in the proper period.
- Authorization—consider whether there are transactions that require specific authorization.

d. To support completeness:

- Analytical procedures.
- Omissions—consider how transactions could improperly have been omitted from the account.

e. To support valuation:

- Foot and cross-foot schedules (total them across and down).
- Agree the account balances on schedules to the general ledger.
- Agree financial statement balances to account balances on schedules.
- Consider valuation methods and whether they have been properly applied.
- Consider related accounts (e.g., accounts receivable and bad debt expense; long-term debt and interest expense; fixed assets and repair and maintenance expense; and fixed assets and depreciation expense).

B. Auditing investments.

1. Evidence related to investments is obtained by inspecting any securities that are held by a client (often in a safe-deposit box) and by confirming securities held by custodians (e.g., a bank or trust company).

2. It is important to note that the auditor must also evaluate the classification of investment securities, the market value of investment securities, and the disposition of unrealized holding gains and losses on investment securities.

3. The table below details the typical substantive audit procedures performed for investments.

Type of audit procedure	Audit procedure	Management assertion(s)
Confirmation	Confirm securities held by third parties.	Existence or occurrence; rights and obligations
Observation	Physically inspect investment securities.	Existence or occurrence; rights and obligations
Recalculation	Recalculate the market value for investment securities and the need for recognizing an unrealized holding gain or loss.	Valuation or allocation
Recalculation	Test amortization of premiums and discounts	Valuation or allocation
Recalculate	Recalculate any realized gains or losses from the disposal of investment securities.	Valuation or allocation
Recalculate	Recalculate any dividends and/or interest received from investment securities. Reconcile dividends received to published records.	Completeness
Recalculate	Mathematically verify the accuracy of a schedule of investments. Agree the schedule with the ledger. Vouch the list to available documents.	Valuation or allocation; existence or occurrence
Inspect documents	Examine and count documents such as broker advices and bank or trust company advices and trace to the schedule of investments.	Existence or occurrence; rights and obligations
Inspect documents	Review minutes of meetings of shareholders or the board of directors and loan agreements to determine if any liens or claims exist against securities.	Presentation and disclosure; rights and obligations

Type of audit procedure	Audit procedure	Management assertion(s)
Inspect documents	Review minutes of meetings of shareholders or the board of directors to determine that purchases and disposals of investment securities are authorized.	Completeness
Inspect documents	Perform cutoff procedures by examining documents representing purchases and sales of securities at or near year-end.	Rights and obligations
Inspect documents	Review disclosures for compliance with GAAP.	Presentation and disclosure
Inspect documents	Review audited financial statements of major investees.	Valuation or allocation
Inquiry	Inquire as to management's intent for investment securities in order to determine that securities are properly classified.	Presentation and disclosure
Inquiry	Inquire about whether any investment securities have been pledged as collateral.	Rights and obligations
Analytical procedures	Analyze investment revenue accounts based on the recorded investments.	Completeness; valuation or allocation

review f/s of major investees

QUESTIONS: INVESTMENTS

1. In confirming with an outside agent, such as a financial institution, that the agent is holding investment securities in the client's name, an auditor *most likely* gathers evidence in support of management's financial statement assertions of existence or occurrence and:
   A. completeness.
   B. presentation and disclosure.
   C. valuation or allocation.
   D. rights and obligations.

2. Which of the following controls would an entity *most likely* use in safeguarding against the loss of marketable securities?
   A. The internal auditor verifies the marketable securities in the entity's safe each year on the balance sheet date.
   B. An independent trust company that has no direct contact with the employees who have record keeping responsibilities has possession of the securities.
   C. A designated member of the board of directors controls the securities in a bank safe-deposit box.
   D. The independent auditor traces all purchases and sales of marketable securities through the subsidiary ledgers to the general ledger.

3. In establishing the existence and ownership of a long-term investment in the form of publicly traded stock, an auditor should inspect the securities or:
   A. determine that the investment is carried at the lower of cost or market.
   B. confirm the number of shares owned that are held by an independent custodian.
   C. inspect the audited financial statements of the investee company.
   D. correspond with the investee company to verify the number of shares owned.

4. Which of the following controls would a company *most likely* use to safeguard marketable securities when an independent trust agent is **NOT** employed?
   A. The internal auditor and the controller independently trace all purchases and sales of marketable securities from the subsidiary ledgers to the general ledger.
   B. The chairman of the board verifies the marketable securities, which are kept in a bank safe-deposit box, each year on the balance sheet date.
   C. Two company officials have joint control of marketable securities, which are kept in a bank safe-deposit box.
   D. The investment committee of the board of directors periodically reviews the investment decisions delegated to the treasurer.

5. An auditor would *most likely* verify the interest earned on bond investments by:
   A. recomputing the interest earned on the basis of face amount, interest rate, and period held.
   B. confirming the bond interest rate with the issuer of the bonds.
   C. vouching the receipt and deposit of interest checks.
   D. testing the internal controls over cash receipts.

6. A client has a large and active investment portfolio that is kept in a bank safe-deposit box. If the auditor is unable to count the securities at the balance sheet date, the auditor *most likely* will:
   A. request the client to have the bank seal the safe-deposit box until the auditor can count the securities at a subsequent date.
   B. count the securities at a subsequent date and confirm with the bank whether securities were added or removed since the balance sheet date.
   C. examine supporting evidence for transactions occurring during the year.
   D. request the bank to confirm to the auditor the contents of the safe-deposit box at the balance sheet date.

7. A company starts investing in securities this year. At the end of the year, the company holds both trading securities and available for sale securities but both portfolios are reported at historical cost. The auditor explains that fair market value must be used and company officials immediately make the proper adjustment which is a material amount. The company had never held securities before and officials did not understand the rule. The auditor does not expect such problems to reappear in the future. The auditor must disclose this event to the audit committee of the board of directors.
   A. True.
   B. False.

ANSWERS: INVESTMENTS

1. **D** Assertions about rights and obligations deal with whether assets are the rights of the entity and liabilities are the obligations of the entity at a given date. Assertions about existence or occurrence deal with whether assets or liabilities of the entity exist at a given date and whether recorded transactions have occurred during a given period. Confirming that an outside agent is holding investment securities in the client's name provides evidence that the securities exist at a given date and that they are owned by the client on that date.

2. **B** A basic control procedure is to separate custody of assets from the record keeping for those assets. Using an independent trust company to hold securities is a very common procedure.

3. **B** AU 332 states that audit evidence about the existence, ownership, and cost of long-term investments includes accounting records and documents of the investor relating to acquisition. In the case of investments in the form of securities (such as stocks, bonds, and notes), this audit evidence should be corroborated by inspection of the securities, or in appropriate circumstances, by written confirmation from an independent custodian of securities on deposit, pledged, or in safekeeping.

4. **C** Keeping marketable securities in a bank safe-deposit box and assigning joint control to two officials should reduce the likelihood of those securities being misappropriated. These physical security and access controls are likely to be used to safeguard marketable securities when an independent trust agent is not employed. The other answers are incorrect because the listed controls will not physically safeguard and prevent the misuse of marketable securities. Reviewing investment decisions will not determine if securities have been misappropriated. Comparing subsidiary and general ledgers will not necessarily prevent securities from being stolen, nor detect transactions that have not entered the accounting system. Annual physical verification by the chairman of the board is not a timely control and has limited effectiveness.

5. **A** The amount of interest earned is based on face amount, interest rate, and time period. Since this is a bond investment, the auditor can examine the actual bond instrument and recompute the interest earned. Such evidence, obtained directly by the auditor's recalculation, is very competent.

6. **A** Physically counting securities is a common audit procedure designed to test existence of an investment portfolio at balance sheet date and to assure the auditor that the securities are not used to cover cash shortages. If the auditor is unable to count securities that are kept in a bank safe-deposit box on the balance sheet date, the auditor would want the bank to secure the box until such time as the auditor could perform the count.

7. **A** True. The auditor is required to inform the audit committee of any problems encountered that had a significant effect on the financial statements. Company officials can then explain to the committee why they were not aware of the appropriate generally accepted accounting principle.

OTHER ISSUES IN AUDITING

STUDY MANUAL – AUDITING & ATTESTATION
CHAPTER 19

Study Tip: Learn to study when other candidates are not studying. Get up early and study for an hour in the morning or study on Friday evening rather than going out. Study at lunch or on holidays. On each part of the exam, roughly 40% to 45% of the candidates are going to pass. If you can find time to study when others are not, it will help you get into that top 40% to 45%.

INTRODUCTION

As noted earlier, financial statements that purport to be in conformity with generally accepted accounting principles contain certain assertions: presentation and disclosure, existence or occurrence, rights and obligations, completeness, and valuation or allocation. Auditors gather evidence to form an opinion with respect to these assertions. The experienced auditor should be able to prepare an audit program for an audit area (e.g., receivables) to test whether these assertions are supportable. The process is one in which specific audit objectives are developed based on the assertions being made in the financial statements. Finally, audit procedures to meet these audit objectives are formulated and listed in an audit program. For purposes of the CPA exam, consider two possible approaches for auditing an account: tests of balances and tests of details.

A. Tests of Balances and Tests of Details.

1. *Direct tests of ending balance (tests of balances)*. This approach requires the auditor to identify specific components of an account balance. For example, the cash account can be broken down into cash on hand and cash on deposit in the client's various bank accounts. Under this approach, the auditor will select and verify a sample of components of the account balance. Accounts that are normally examined via this approach are high turnover accounts such as cash, accounts receivable, inventory, and accounts payable.

2. *Tests of inputs and outputs during the year (tests of details)*. This approach requires the auditor to verify individual transactions comprising an account balance or class of transactions. This approach focuses on the individual transactions occurring during the year and not the final account balance. Accounts normally examined via this approach are lower turnover accounts, such as investments; property, plant and equipment; notes and bonds payable; and shareholders' equity.

3. Many audit procedures provide support for *multiple management assertions*. For example, cut-off procedures provide support for rights and obligations as well as for

existence and completeness. The following are typical procedures included in a substantive audit program:

a. To support presentation and disclosure:

- Review disclosures for compliance with GAAP.
- Inquire about disclosures.

b. To support existence or occurrence:

- Confirmation.
- Observation—always consider whether you can observe the item itself and/or legal documents representing the item.
- Trace/vouch transactions.

c. To support rights and obligations:

- Cutoffs—consider whether transactions have been reported in the proper period.
- Authorization—consider whether there are transactions that require specific authorization.

d. To support completeness:

- Analytical procedures.
- Omissions—consider how transactions could improperly have been omitted from the account.

e. To support valuation:

- Foot and cross-foot schedules (total them across and down).
- Agree the account balances on schedules to the general ledger.
- Agree financial statement balances to account balances on schedules.
- Consider valuation methods and whether they have been properly applied.
- Consider related accounts (e.g., accounts receivable and bad debt expense; long-term debt and interest expense; fixed assets and repair and maintenance expense; and fixed assets and depreciation expense).

B. Auditing stockholders' equity.

1. Clients use one of two approaches for capital stock transactions.

2. First, a stock certificate book may be used which summarizes shares issued through the use of "stubs" which remain after a certificate has been removed.

   a. The certificates for outstanding shares are held by the stockholders; canceled certificates (for repurchased stock or received when a change in stock ownership occurs) are held by the client.

b. When a stock certificate book is used, auditors reconcile outstanding shares, par value, etc., with the "stubs" in the book. Confirmations are sometimes sent to stockholders.

3. The second approach, typically used by large clients, is to engage a registrar and a stock transfer agent to manage the company's stock transactions.

   a. The primary responsibility of the registrar is to verify that stock that is issued is properly authorized.

   b. Stock transfer agents maintain detailed stockholder records and carry out transfers of stock ownership.

   c. The number of shares authorized, issued, and outstanding will usually be confirmed to the auditor directly by the registrar and stock transfer agent.

4. Little effort will be exerted in auditing the retained earnings of a continued client.

   a. The audit procedures for dividends will allow the auditor to verify the propriety of that debit to retained earnings.

   b. The entry to record the year's net income (loss) is readily available.

   c. Finally, the nature of any prior period adjustments is examined to determine whether they meet the criteria for an adjustment to retained earnings.

   d. Recall that the type of adjustment typically encountered is a correction of prior years' income.

5. The table below details the typical substantive audit procedures performed for stockholders' equity.

Type of audit procedure	Audit procedure	Management assertion(s)
Confirmation	Confirm year-end balances and transactions occurring in stockholders' equity during the year with the registrar and transfer agent.	Existence or occurrence
Observation	Inspect share subs, unissued certificates, and canceled certificates for issuances and retirements of stock during the year if there is not registrar or transfer agent.	Existence or occurrence; completeness
Recalculation	Recalculate the distribution of proceeds between legal capital (par value) and additional paid in-capital.	Valuation or allocation

Type of audit procedure	Audit procedure	Management assertion(s)
Recalculation	Review declarations of dividends (both cash and other) to determine that they were properly recorded and valued.	Valuation or allocation
Recalculation	Mathematically verify the total of stockholder equity schedules and compare the total to the general ledger.	Valuation or allocation
Inspect documents	Inspect advices from brokers, the registrar, and transfer agents for capital transactions.	Existence or occurrence
Inspect documents	Review the minutes of meetings of committees, board of directors, and/or stockholders for proper authorization.	Rights and obligations
Inspect documents	Review the articles of incorporation and bylaws to determine the requirements for issuing stock, redeeming or acquiring stock, and declaring dividends.	Rights and obligations; existence or occurrence
Inspect documents	Vouch new issuances or repurchases of stock to cash receipts and disbursements records.	Existence or occurrence; valuation or allocation
Inspect documents	Review disclosures for compliance with GAAP.	Presentation and disclosure
Inspect documents	Review information on stock options and dividend restrictions.	Presentation and disclosure
Inspect documents	Inspect Treasury stock certificates.	Completeness
Inspect documents	Vouch dividend payments.	Valuation or allocation
Inquiry	Inquire about management's intent with respect to repurchased shares of its stock.	Presentation and disclosure
Inquiry	Inquire of legal counsel on legal issues.	Rights and obligations

C. Revenue.

1. Most revenue accounts are verified in conjunction with the audit of a related asset or liability account. For example:

Balance sheet account	Revenue account
Accounts receivable	Sales
Notes receivable	Interest
Investments	Interest, dividends, gains on sales
Property, plant, and equipment	Rent, gains on sales

2. Most frequently, sales are recorded during the period in which title has passed, or services have been rendered to customers who have made firm enforceable commitments to purchase such goods or services. SEC Staff Accounting Bulletin 101 provides a more specific, helpful overall set of criteria for revenue recognition:

   a. Persuasive evidence of an arrangement exists.

   b. Delivery has occurred or services have been rendered.

   c. The seller's price to the buyer is fixed or determinable.

   d. Collectibility is reasonably assured.

3. The table below details the typical substantive audit procedures performed for revenue.

Type of audit procedure	Audit procedure	Management assertion(s)
Analytical procedures	Evaluate the reasonableness of ratios and relationships involving revenues.	Valuation or allocation
Analytical procedures	Obtain or review analyses of selected revenue accounts.	Valuation or allocation
Inspect documents	Vouch selected transactions and determine that they represent proper revenue for the period.	Valuation or allocation

D. Expenses.

1. Most expense accounts are verified in conjunction with the audit of a related asset or liability account. For example

Balance sheet account	Revenue account
Accounts receivable	Uncollectible accounts
Inventories	Purchases, cost of goods sold, and payroll
Property, plant, and equipment	Depreciation, repairs, and maintenance
Accrued liabilities	Commissions, fees, and product warranty expenses

2. The table below details the typical substantive audit procedures performed for expenses.

Type of audit procedure	Audit procedure	Management assertion(s)
Analytical procedures	Evaluate the reasonableness of ratios and relationships involving expenses.	Valuation or allocation
Analytical procedures	Obtain or review analyses of expense revenue accounts.	Valuation or allocation
Inspect documents	Vouch selected transactions and determine that they represent proper expenses for the period.	Valuation or allocation

E. Client representation letters.

1. Management makes various representations to the auditor, both oral and written, in the form of answers to inquiries as well as in the form of the financial statements themselves.

2. Written representations confirm the oral representations, indicate and document the continuing appropriateness of the representations, and reduce the possibility of misunderstandings concerning the subject matter of the representations.

3. The representation letter should be:

    a. Addressed to the auditor and dated no earlier than the date of the auditor's report.

    b. Signed by the chief executive officer and the chief financial officer.

c. Obtained for all periods being reported upon, even if management was not present during all of those periods.

4. The auditor must obtain written representations from management to complement other auditing procedures. The written representations are not a substitute for the application of those auditing procedures necessary to provide a reasonable basis for an opinion on the financial statements.

5. Although written representations will vary from engagement to engagement, they generally will include some or all of the following acknowledgments from management:

   a. Responsibility for the fair presentation of the financial statements in conformity with generally accepted accounting principles. (Small, privately owned companies with little or no knowledge of GAAP may state that they have engaged their auditor to advise them on GAAP.)

   b. All financial records and related data were made available to the auditor.

   c. All minutes of meetings of stockholders, directors, and committees of directors were made available in their entirety to the auditors.

   d. The financial statements are free from error and all transactions have been properly recorded.

   e. All related-party transactions and related amounts receivable or payable have been disclosed.

   f. Noncompliance with aspects of contractual agreements that may affect the financial statements has been disclosed.

   g. All information concerning subsequent events that may affect the financial statements has been disclosed.

   h. All fraud involving management or employees have been disclosed.

   i. Communications from regulatory agencies concerning noncompliance with, or deficiencies in, financial reporting practices have been disclosed.

   j. Plans or intentions that may affect the carrying value or classification of assets or liabilities have been disclosed.

   k. All compensating balance arrangements or other arrangements involving restrictions on cash balances, and disclosure of lines-of-credit or similar arrangements have been disclosed.

   l. All appropriate reductions of excess or obsolete inventories to net realizable value have been made.

   m. Losses from sales commitments have been disclosed.

n. Satisfactory title to assets, liens on assets, and assets pledged as collateral has been disclosed.

o. Agreements to repurchase assets previously sold have been disclosed.

p. Losses from purchase commitments for inventory quantities in excess of requirements or at prices in excess of market have been disclosed.

q. Violations or possible violations of laws or regulations whose effects should be considered for disclosure in the financial statements or as a basis for recording a loss contingency have been disclosed.

r. Other liabilities and gain or loss contingencies that are required to be accrued have been disclosed.

s. Unasserted claims or assessments that the client's lawyer has advised are probable of assertion have been disclosed.

t. Capital stock repurchase options or agreements or capital stock reserved for options, warrants, conversions, or other requirements have been disclosed.

6. If a representation made by management is contradicted by other audit evidence, the auditor should investigate the circumstances and consider the reliability of the representations made.

7. Management's representations may be limited to matters that are considered either individually or collectively material to the financial statements, provided that management and the auditor have reached an understanding on the limits of materiality for this purpose.

8. Such limitations do not apply to those representations that are not directly related to amounts included in the financial statements such as availability of all financial records and related data and fraud involving management or employees.

9. If management refuses to provide a written representation of items that the auditor believes to be essential, this constitutes a scope limitation and precludes an unqualified opinion. Generally, this results in a disclaimer, although a qualified opinion may be appropriate in some circumstances.

F. Accounting estimates.

1. An accounting estimate is an approximation of a financial statement element, item, or account. Examples include allowances for uncollectible accounts and declines in inventory prices, revenues from long-term contracts accounted for by the percentage-of-completion method, and estimated warranty expenses.

2. Management is responsible for establishing a process for preparation of accounting estimates.

3. The auditor's role is to obtain reasonable assurance that:

a. All accounting estimates that could be material to the financial statements have been developed.

b. Those accounting estimates are reasonable in the circumstances.

c. The accounting estimates are presented in conformity with applicable accounting principles and are properly disclosed.

4. In determining the reasonableness of accounting estimates, the auditor may apply one or more of the following procedures:

a. Ascertain the process used by management to develop the estimate, decide whether or not the methodology is reasonable, and test management's process.

b. Develop an independent expectation of the estimate and compare it to management's. (This may involve the use of a specialist.)

c. Review subsequent events or transactions occurring prior to completion of fieldwork which bear on the estimate.

G. Specialists.

1. The services of a specialist will be engaged when the auditor encounters a matter that is potentially material to the fair presentation of the financial statements and requires special knowledge beyond the scope of the technical training of the auditor.

2. Auditors are increasingly finding it necessary to use the work of specialists in situations such as postemployment and postretirement benefits, environmental cleanup obligations, and fair value disclosures and derivatives, as well as in more traditional areas such as the valuation of inventory (e.g., diamonds).

3. In general, an auditor may seek the services of a specialist in the following areas:

a. Determination of the valuation of special items.

b. Determination of physical characteristics relating to quantity on hand or condition.

c. Determination of amounts derived by using specialized techniques or methods.

d. Interpretation of technical requirements, regulations, or agreements.

e. Application of computers.

4. In selecting the specialist, the auditor must be satisfied as to the specialist's qualifications and will consider:

a. The specialist's professional certification or license.

b. The specialist's reputation, experience, or other recognition in the type of work under consideration.

c. The relationship, if any, of the specialist to the client.

5. The auditor should document the understanding with the specialist of the nature of the work to be performed. The document should include:

    a. The objective and scope of the work.

    b. The specialist's relationship to the client.

    c. The methods or assumptions to be used and a comparison to those used in the preceding period.

    d. The specialist's understanding of the auditor's corroborative use of findings in relation to representations in the financial statements.

    e. The form and content of the specialist's report.

6. The auditor is not required to have the ability to perform the specialist's tasks.

    a. However, he or she should be able to supervise and evaluate the work of the specialist.

    b. The auditor should test the data provided by the client to the specialist and consider if any other tests are necessary to be performed on the specialist's assumptions, methods, or findings to determine if the findings are reasonable.

7. The auditor should never refer to the work of a specialist in a standard (unmodified) opinion.

    a. In an opinion modified as a result of the report of the specialist, reference to the work of the specialist and identification of the specialist will be appropriate if it facilitates an understanding of the reason for the modification.

    b. A modified opinion may include a modification to an unqualified opinion, a qualified opinion, or an adverse opinion.

H. Inquiry of a client's lawyer.

1. The client's lawyer is the primary source of corroboration of information obtained from the client concerning loss contingencies.

    a. Therefore, the client prepares a list and describes claims, litigation, assessments, and unasserted claims pending against the firm.

b. This information is sent by the auditor to the attorney who is to review it and provide additional input, if possible.

2. Refusal of the lawyer to reply is a scope limitation that may affect the audit report.

3. If the lawyer is unable to estimate the effect of litigation, claims, and assessments on the financial statements, it may result in an uncertainty that would also have an effect on the audit report.

4. In the case of unasserted claims that the client has not disclosed, the lawyer is not required to note them in the reply to the auditor.

5. However, the lawyer is generally required to inform the client of the omission and to consider withdrawing if the client fails to inform the auditor.

I. Fair value.

1. Generally accepted accounting principles require companies to use "fair value" for measuring, presenting, and disclosing various accounts (e.g., investments, intangible assets, impaired assets, derivatives). Fair value is generally considered to be the amount at which an asset could be bought or sold in a current transaction between willing parties.

2. The determination of fair value is easiest when there are published price quotations in an active market (e.g., stock exchange).

3. Determining fair value is more difficult when an active market does not exist for items such as various investment properties or complex derivative financial instruments. In such circumstances, fair value may be calculated through the use of a valuation model (e.g., a model based on forecasts and discounting of future cash flows).

4. Auditing fair values is similar to that of other estimates described above in that a combination of three approaches is often used:

a. Review and test management's process.

b. Independently develop an estimate.

c. Review subsequent events.

5. When reviewing management's process, the auditors consider whether the assumptions used by management are reasonable, whether the valuation model seems appropriate, and whether management has used relevant information that is reasonably available.

6. Developing one's own estimate offers the advantage of allowing the auditors to compare that estimate with that developed by management.

7. Reviewing subsequent events allows the auditors to use information obtained subsequent to year-end to help evaluate the reasonableness of management's estimate.

8. Often auditors will use a combination of the approaches.

9. Regardless of the approach(es) followed, the auditors should evaluate whether the disclosures of fair values required by generally accepted accounting principles have been properly presented.

J. Related-party transactions.

1. Material related-party transactions must be disclosed in the footnotes. Related parties include affiliates of the company, substantial owners, management and their immediate families, and anyone who exerts significant influence over the company.

2. The main issue with related-party transactions concerns the price at which a transaction occurs. The price must be one that would have resulted from an "arm's-length transaction."

3. The disclosures required include:

    a. The nature of the relationship(s).

    b. A description of transaction(s).

    c. The dollar amount of transaction(s).

    d. The amounts due to/from related parties, including terms.

4. Because financial statements must reflect the economic substance of transactions, rather than their legal form, the existence of related-party transactions may require additional investigation by the auditor.

5. The auditor will need to determine whether the recording of the transactions does in fact represent the economic substance. The following transactions may be indicative of related-party transactions:

    a. Borrowing or lending at interest rates above or below the market rate.

    b. Selling real estate at a price significantly different from its appraised value.

    c. Exchanging property for similar property in a nonmonetary transaction.

    d. Making loans with no scheduled repayment terms.

6. An auditor must consider the possibility of the existence of related-party transactions in designing the audit procedures to be performed. In determining the scope of work to be performed, the auditor should obtain an understanding of

management responsibilities and the relationship of each component of the entity. The auditor must also be aware that business structure and operating style, on occasion, are deliberately designed to obscure related-party transactions. Certain conditions should alert the auditor to the possibility that related-party transaction are likely:

  a. Lack of sufficient working capital or credit to continue the business.

  b. An urgent desire for favorable earnings trends.

  c. Overly optimistic earnings forecast.

  d. Dependence on a few products, customers, or transactions.

  e. Declining industry profitability.

  f. Excess capacity.

  g. Significant litigation.

  h. Significant obsolescence.

7. The following audit procedures may be used to determine the existence of related parties:

  a. Evaluate the client's procedures for identifying and properly accounting for related-party transactions.

  b. Ask the client for names of all related parties and whether there have been any transactions with these parties.

  c. Review SEC filings.

  d. Determine the names of officers of all employee trusts.

  e. Review the stockholder listings of closely held companies.

  f. Review prior audit documents for the names of related parties.

  g. Inquire of the predecessor and/or principal auditors.

  h. Review material investment transactions.

8. If there are related-party relationships in existence or if the auditor believes that there are related-party relationships in existence, the following audit procedures may identify material related-party transactions:

  a. Provide audit personnel with related party names.

  b. Review the board of directors' minutes.

c. Review SEC filings.

d. Review the client's "conflict of interest" statements obtained by the company from management.

e. Review the nature of transactions with major customers, suppliers, etc.

f. Consider whether unrecorded transactions exist.

g. Review accounting records for large, nonrecurring transactions.

h. Review confirmations of compensating balances for indications that balances are maintained for or by related parties.

i. Review legal invoices.

j. Review confirmations of loans receivable and payable for guarantees.

9. When related-party transactions are identified, the auditor should apply audit procedures to the identified related-party transactions considering the purpose, nature, and extent of these transactions and their effect on the financial statements. Procedures may include:

   a. Obtain an understanding of the business purpose of the transactions. The auditor needs to understand the business sense of material transactions in order to complete his or her examination.

   b. Examine invoices, executed copies of agreements, contracts, and other pertinent documents, such as receiving reports and shipping documents.

   c. Determine whether the transaction has been approved by the board of directors or other appropriate officials.

   d. Test for reasonableness the compilation of amounts to be disclosed, or considered for disclosure, in the financial statements.

   e. Arrange for the audits of intercompany account balances to be performed as of concurrent dates, even if the fiscal years differ, and for the examination of specified, important, and representative related-party transactions by the auditors for each of the parties, with an appropriate exchange of relevant information.

   f. Inspect or confirm and obtain satisfaction as to the transferability and value of the collateral.

   g. Confirm transaction amounts and terms, including guarantees and other significant data, with the other party or parties to the transaction.

   h. Inspect evidence in possession of the other party or parties to the transaction.

i. Confirm or discuss significant information with intermediaries, such as banks, guarantors, agents, or attorneys to obtain a better understanding of the transaction.

j. Refer to financial publications, trade journals, credit agencies, and other information sources when there is reason to believe that unfamiliar customers, suppliers, or other business enterprises with which material amounts of business have been transacted may lack substance.

k. With respect to material uncollected balances, guarantees, and other obligations, obtain information as to the financial capability of the other party or parties to the transaction.

10. The auditor must make a determination as to whether the related-party transaction has been adequately disclosed. Disclosure of related-party transactions should include the following:

    a. The nature of the relationship.

    b. A description of the transactions, whether or not there are transaction amounts for each period for which income statements are presented, and such other information as deemed necessary to an understanding of the effects on the financial statements.

    c. The dollar amounts of transactions and the effects of any change in the method of establishing terms from that used in the preceding period.

    d. Amounts due from or to related parties as of the date of each balance sheet presented and, if not otherwise apparent, the terms and manner of settlement.

11. Except for routine transactions, it is difficult to determine if a transaction would have occurred if the parties had not been related. Therefore, it is difficult to determine if the transaction was consummated on a basis similar to an arm's-length transaction.

12. If related-party transactions are presented (implicitly or explicitly) in the financial statements as being arm's-length transactions, management has the duty to substantiate that representation.

13. If management does not substantiate the representation that the transactions are arm's-length transactions, there is a departure from generally accepted accounting principles (full disclosure), and the auditor should express a qualified or adverse opinion.

14. Whether the opinion would be qualified or adverse would depend on qualitative and quantitative materiality considerations.

K. Going concern considerations.

1. The use of accruals by generally accepted accounting principles relies on an assumption that an entity will continue indefinitely as a going concern. For example, capitalizing assets and depreciating them over future periods is justified on the basis that the costs will be "matched" against future revenues.

2. While audits do not contain specific procedures to test the appropriateness of this going concern assumption, procedures performed for other objectives may identify conditions and events indicating substantial doubt as to whether an entity will remain a going concern. These procedures include:

    a. Analytical procedures.

    b. The review of subsequent events.

    c. Review of compliance with debt agreements.

    d. Reading of minutes.

    e. Inquiry of legal counsel.

    f. Confirmation of arrangements with various organizations to maintain financial support.

3. Some of the indicators of possible going concern problems are:

    a. Recurring losses.

    b. Negative cash flows from operations.

    c. Negative working capital position.

    d. Restructuring of debt.

    e. Default on loans.

    f. Lawsuits.

    g. Unpaid dividends.

    h. Loss of key customers.

4. When procedures indicate that substantial doubt may exist as to whether an entity will remain a going concern, the auditor must obtain management's plans for dealing with the situation and assess the likelihood that these plans can be implemented.

    a. If the auditor is not satisfied with management's plans, an explanatory paragraph is added after the opinion paragraph to warn readers that substantial doubt exists as to whether the company can remain as a going concern.

    b.   Alternatively, an auditor may issue a disclaimer.

L.   Subsequent events.

    1.   Subsequent events are events or transactions that occur subsequent to the balance sheet date, but prior to issuance of the financial statements and auditor's report. These events have a material effect on the financial statements and require adjustment or disclosure in the statements.

    2.   There are two types of subsequent events that require consideration by the auditor:

        a.   *Additional information about events that existed at the balance sheet date.* This type of subsequent event is an event that provides additional information with respect to conditions that existed at the date of the balance sheet and affect the estimates and judgments inherent in the process of preparing the financial statements. These events generally will require adjustment of the financial statements. Examples are:

- Events that make large portions of assets worthless not caused by events that occurred after the balance sheet date.
- Settlement of litigation that existed at the balance sheet date.
- Notification of the bankruptcy or pending bankruptcy of a customer not caused by any event occurring after the balance sheet date.
- Filings of litigation claims based on events that existed at the balance sheet date.

        b.   *Events that occur after the balance sheet date but affect the interpretation or usefulness of the financial statements.* This type of subsequent event is an event that provides evidence with respect to conditions that did not exist at the date of the balance sheet being reported on, but arose subsequent to that date. These events do not require adjustment to the financial statements, but may require disclosure because they may affect the positive or negative interpretation or usefulness of the financial statements. Examples of this type of event may include:

- Sale of a bond or capital stock issue.
- Purchase of a business.
- Settlement of litigation, when the event giving rise to the claim took place subsequent to the balance sheet date.
- Loss of plant or inventories as a result of fire or flood.
- Losses on receivables resulting from conditions arising subsequent to the balance sheet date.

    3.   The period beginning on the first day after the balance sheet date and extending until the date of the auditor's report is referred to as the subsequent period. Certain specific procedures that require the exercise of professional and

experienced judgment and knowledge of the facts and circumstances generally are applied to the subsequent period, including:

    a. Examination of data to ensure that proper cutoffs have been made.

    b. Examination of data that provide information to aid the auditor in his or her evaluation of the assets and liabilities as of the balance sheet date.

4. Additional procedures should be applied during the subsequent period to ascertain if any subsequent events have occurred. These procedures, performed at or near the completion of the field work, will include:

    a. Read the latest available interim financial statements, compare them with the financial statements being reported upon, and make any other comparisons considered appropriate in the circumstances.

    b. Inquire of and discuss with officers and other executives having responsibility for financial and accounting matters as to:

- Whether any substantial contingent liabilities or commitments existed at the date of the balance sheet being reported on or at the date of the inquiry.
- Whether there were any significant changes in the capital stock, long-term debt, or working capital to the date of the inquiry.
- The current status of items in the financial statements being reported on that were accounted for on the basis of tentative, preliminary, or inconclusive data.
- Whether any unusual adjustments had been made during the period from the balance sheet date to the date of the inquiry.

    c. Read the available minutes of meetings of stockholders, directors, and appropriate committees. As to meetings for which minutes are not available, inquire about matters dealt with at such meetings.

    d. Inquire of the client's legal counsel concerning litigation, claims, and assessments.

    e. Obtain a letter of representation, dated as of the date of the auditor's report, from appropriate officials (generally CEO and CFO) as to whether any events occurred subsequent to the date of the financial statements being reported on by the independent auditor that, in the officer's opinion, would require adjustment or disclosure in the statements.

    f. Make such additional inquiries or perform such procedures as are considered necessary and appropriate to dispose of questions that arise in carrying out the foregoing procedures, inquiries, and discussions.

M. Subsequent discovery of facts existing at the date of the auditor's report.

1. Once an auditor has issued a report on audited financial statements, the auditor has no further obligation to perform additional audit procedures with respect to the audited financial statements covered by the report unless new information that may affect the report comes to the auditor's attention.

2. If the auditor becomes convinced that the information is reliable and existed at the date of the auditor's report, certain procedures should be applied.

3. These procedures will be applied only if the auditor believes that the report would have been affected if the information had been known at the date of the report and had not been reflected in the financial statements, and the auditor believes there are persons, who would attach importance to the information, currently relying or likely to rely on the financial statements.

4. If the auditor determines that action should be taken to prevent further reliance on the report, the auditor should advise the client to make appropriate disclosure of the newly discovered facts.

5. Various alternatives in the method of disclosing the facts will be selected based on the circumstances.

    a. If the effect of the information on the financial statements and auditor's report can be promptly determined, revised financial statements and a revised report should be issued.

    b. If financial statements for a subsequent period, along with an auditor's report, are to be issued imminently, the disclosure may be in the new financial statements.

    c. If the effect of the information will require investigation, persons known to be, or thought to be, relying on the financial statements and auditor's report should be informed that they are not to be relied upon and that revised financial statements and the related report will be issued upon completion of the investigation.

6. If the client refuses to make proper disclosure of the newly discovered facts, the auditor should take certain steps to prevent further reliance on the report.

    a. Notify the client, including each member of the board of directors, that the auditor's report must no longer be associated with the financial statements.

    b. Notify regulatory agencies, including stock exchanges, if any, having jurisdiction over the client that the auditor's report should no longer be relied upon.

    c. Notify each person known to the auditor to be relying on the financial statements that his or her report should no longer be relied upon.

N. Omitted procedures detected after the report date.

1. This situation is not the same as the subsequent discovery of facts after the issuance of an audit report; it is when necessary audit procedure was not performed.

2. If, as a result of a postissuance review of an engagement (internal review procedure or peer review), an auditor should discover that a necessary audit procedure was not performed, the auditor should evaluate the effect of the omission on the sufficiency and competency of the evidence underlying the audit report that was issued, and whether or not the audit report is reliable.

3. If the auditor determines that the performance of other audit procedures adequately compensated for the omission of the particular audit procedure, no further work would be necessary.

4. If the auditor determines, however, that the performance of other audit procedures do not adequately compensate for the omission of the particular audit procedure, the auditor would perform the omitted procedure.

5. If after performing the omitted audit procedure the auditor determines that the audit report continues to be reliable, no further work or action would be necessary.

6. If after performing the omitted audit procedure the auditor determines that the audit report is no longer reliable, the auditor then would invoke the procedures listed above for the subsequent discovery of facts existing at the date of the auditor's report.

QUESTIONS: OTHER ISSUES IN AUDITING

1. Of the following which is the least persuasive type of audit evidence?
   A. Documents mailed by outsiders to the auditor.
   B. Correspondence between auditor and vendors.
   C. Copies of sales invoices inspected by the auditor.
   D. Computations made by the auditor.

2. A CPA auditing an electric utility wishes to determine whether all customers are being billed. The CPA's *best* direction of test is from the:
   A. Meter department records to the billing (sales) register.
   B. Billing (sales) register to the meter department records.
   C. Accounts receivable ledger to the billing (sales) register.
   D. Billing (sales) register to the accounts receivable ledger.

3. Which of the following audit procedures is most effective in testing credit sales for understatement?
   A. Age accounts receivable.
   B. Confirm accounts receivable.
   C. Trace sample of initial sales slips through summaries to recorded general ledger sales.
   D. Trace sample of recorded sales, from general ledger to initial sales slip.

4. An auditor is testing sales transactions. One step is to trace a sample of debit entries from the accounts receivable subsidiary ledger back to the supporting sales invoices. What would the auditor intend to establish by this step?
   A. All sales have been recorded.
   B. Debit entries in the accounts receivable subsidiary ledger are properly supported by sales invoices.
   C. All sales invoices have been properly posted to customer accounts.
   D. Sales invoices represent bona fide sales.

5. As part of an audit, a CPA must request a representation letter from his client. Which one of the following is **NOT** a valid purpose of such a letter?
   A. To provide audit evidence.
   B. To emphasize to the client his responsibility for the correctness of the financial statements.
   C. To satisfy himself by means of other auditing procedures when certain customary auditing procedures are not performed.
   D. To provide possible protection to the CPA against a charge of knowledge in cases where fraud is subsequently discovered to have existed in the accounts.

6. As a result of analytical proceduress, the independent auditor determines that the gross profit percentage has declined from 30% in the preceding year to 20% in the current year. The auditor should:
   A. Express an opinion which is qualified due to inability of the client company to continue as a going concern.
   B. Evaluate management's performance in causing this decline.
   C. Require footnote disclosure.
   D. Consider the possibility of an error in the financial statements.

7. Which of the following procedures would an auditor ordinarily perform during the review of subsequent events?
   A. Review the cut-off bank statements for the period after the year-end.
   B. Inquire of the client's legal counsel concerning litigation.
   C. Investigate reportable conditions previously communicated to the client.
   D. Analyze related party transactions to discover possible fraud.

8. Which of the following *most likely* would be detected by an auditor's review of a client's sales cut-off?
   A. Unrecorded sales for the year.
   B. Lapping of year-end accounts receivable.
   C. Excessive sales discounts.
   D. Unauthorized goods returned for credit.

9. Auditors should request that an audit client send a letter of inquiry to those attorneys who have been consulted concerning litigation, claims, or assessments. The primary reason for this request is to provide:
   A. Information concerning the progress of cases to date.
   B. Corroborative audit evidence.
   C. An estimate of the dollar amount of the probable loss.
   D. An expert opinion as to whether a loss is possible, probable, or remote.

10. A written client representation letter *most likely* would be an auditor's *best* source of corroborative information of a client's plans to:
    A. Terminate an employee pension plan.
    B. Make a public offering of its common stock.
    C. Settle an outstanding lawsuit for an amount less than the accrued loss contingency.
    D. Discontinue a line of business.

11. An auditor searching for related party transactions should obtain an understanding of each subsidiary's relationship to the total entity because:
    A. This may permit the audit of intercompany account balances to be performed as of concurrent dates.
    B. Intercompany transactions may have been consummated on terms equivalent to arm's-length transactions.
    C. This may reveal whether particular transactions would have taken place if the parties had not been related.
    D. The business structure may be deliberately designed to obscure related party transactions.

12. Soon after Boyd's audit report was issued, Boyd learned of certain related party transactions that occurred during the year under audit. These transactions were not disclosed in the notes to the financial statements. Boyd should:
    A. Plan to audit the transactions during the next engagement.
    B. Recall all copies of the audited financial statements.
    C. Determine whether the lack of disclosure would affect the auditor's report.
    D. Ask the client to disclose the transactions in subsequent interim statements.

13. When using the work of a specialist, an auditor may refer to and identify the specialist in the auditor's report if the:
    A. Auditor wishes to indicate a division of responsibility.
    B. Specialist's work provides the auditor greater assurance of reliability.
    C. Auditor expresses an adverse opinion as a result of the specialist's findings.
    D. Specialist is not independent of the client.

14. Which of the following documentation is required for an audit in accordance with generally accepted auditing standards?
    A. An internal control questionnaire.
    B. A client engagement letter.
    C. A planning memorandum or checklist.
    D. A client representation letter.

15. Tracing bills of lading to sales invoices provides evidence that:
    A. Shipments to customers were invoiced.
    B. Shipments to customers were recorded as sales.
    C. Recorded sales were shipped.
    D. Invoiced sales were shipped.

16. The scope of an audit is not restricted when an attorney's response to an auditor as a result of a client's letter of audit inquiry limits the response to:
    A. Matters to which the attorney has given substantive attention in the form of legal representation.
    B. An evaluation of the likelihood of an unfavorable outcome of the matters disclosed by the entity.
    C. The attorney's opinion of the entity's historical experience in recent similar litigation.
    D. The probable outcome of asserted claims and pending or threatened litigation.

17. Cutoff tests designed to detect credit sales made before the end of the year that have been recorded in the subsequent year provide assurance about management's assertion of:
    A. Presentation.
    B. Completeness.
    C. Rights.
    D. Existence.

18. If the objective of a test of details is to detect overstatements of sales, the auditor should trace transactions from the:
    A. Cash receipts journal to the sales journal.
    B. Sales journal to the cash receipts journal.
    C. Source documents to the accounting records.
    D. Accounting records to the source documents.

19. In using the work of a specialist, an understanding should exist among the auditor, the client, and the specialist as to the nature of the specialist's work. The documentation of this understanding should cover:
    A. A statement that the specialist assumes no responsibility to update the specialist's report for future events or circumstances.
    B. The conditions under which a division of responsibility may be necessary.
    C. The specialist's understanding of the auditor's corroborative use of the specialist's findings.
    D. The auditor's disclaimer as to whether the specialist's findings corroborate the representations in the financial statements.

20. Which of the following factors *most likely* would affect an auditor's judgment about the quantity, type, and content of the auditor's audit documents?
    A. The assessed level of control risk.
    B. The likelihood of a review by a concurring (second) partner.
    C. The number of personnel assigned to the audit.
    D. The content of the management representation letter.

21. Which of the following *most likely* would indicate the existence of related parties?
    A. Writing down obsolete inventory just before year end.
    B. Failing to correct previously identified internal control deficiencies.
    C. Depending on a single product for the success of the entity.
    D. Borrowing money at an interest rate significantly below the market rate.

22. Which of the following procedures would an auditor *most likely* perform to obtain evidence about the occurrence of subsequent events?
    A. Recomputing a sample of large-dollar transactions occurring after year end for arithmetic accuracy.
    B. Investigating changes in stockholders' equity occurring after year end.
    C. Inquiring of the entity's legal counsel concerning litigation, claims, and assessments arising after year end.
    D. Confirming bank accounts established after year end.

23. In evaluating an entity's accounting estimates, one of an auditor's objectives is to determine whether the estimates are:
    A. Not subject to bias.
    B. Consistent with industry guidelines.
    C. Based on objective assumptions.
    D. Reasonable in the circumstances.

24. In using the work of a specialist, an auditor referred to the specialist's findings in the auditor's report. This would be an appropriate reporting practice if the:
    A. Client is not familiar with the professional certification, personal reputation, or particular competence of the specialist.
    B. Auditor, as a result of the specialist's findings, adds an explanatory paragraph emphasizing a matter regarding the financial statements.
    C. Client understands the auditor's corroborative use of the specialist's findings in relation to the representations in the financial statements.
    D. Auditor, as a result of the specialist's findings, decides to indicate a division of responsibility with the specialist.

25. Which of the following auditing procedures *most likely* would assist an auditor in identifying related party transactions?
    A. Retesting ineffective internal control procedures previously reported to the audit committee.
    B. Sending second requests for unanswered positive confirmations of accounts receivable.
    C. Reviewing accounting records for nonrecurring transactions recognized near the balance sheet date.
    D. Inspecting communications with law firms for evidence of unreported contingent liabilities.

26. During the annual audit of Ajax Corp., a publicly held company, Jones, CPA, a continuing auditor, determined that illegal political contributions had been made during each of the past seven years, including the year under audit. Jones notified the board of directors about the illegal contributions, but they refused to take any action because the amounts involved were immaterial to the financial statements.

    Jones should reconsider the intended degree of reliance to be placed on the:
    A. Letter of audit inquiry to the client's attorney.
    B. Prior years' audit programs.
    C. Management representation letter.
    D. Preliminary judgment about materiality levels.

27. An entity's income statements were misstated due to the recording of journal entries that involved debits and credits to an unusual combination of expense and revenue accounts. The auditor *most likely* could have detected this fraud by:
    A. Tracing a sample of journal entries to the general ledger.
    B. Evaluating the effectiveness of internal control policies and procedures.
    C. Investigating the reconciliations between controlling accounts and subsidiary records.
    D. Performing analytical procedures designed to disclose differences from expectations.

28. Which of the following documentation is **NOT** required for an audit in accordance with generally accepted auditing standards?
    A. A written audit program setting forth the procedures necessary to accomplish the audit's objectives.
    B. An indication that the accounting records agree or reconcile with the financial statements.
    C. A client engagement letter that summarizes the timing and details of the auditor's planned field work.
    D. The basis for the auditor's conclusions when the assessed level of control risk is below the maximum level.

29. In performing tests concerning the granting of stock options, an auditor should:
    A. Confirm the transaction with the Secretary of State in the state of incorporation.
    B. Verify the existence of option holders in the entity's payroll records or stock ledgers.
    C. Determine that sufficient treasury stock is available to cover any new stock issued.
    D. Trace the authorization for the transaction to a vote of the board of directors.

30. "There are no violations or possible violations of laws or regulations whose effects should be considered for disclosure in the financial statements or as a basis for recording a loss contingency." The foregoing passage *most likely* is from a(an):
    A. Client engagement letter.
    B. Report on compliance with laws and regulations.
    C. Management representation letter.
    D. Attestation report on an internal control.

31. Which of the following statements is correct about the auditor's use of the work of a specialist?
    A. The specialist should not have an understanding of the auditor's corroborative use of the specialist's findings.
    B. The auditor is required to perform substantive procedures to verify the specialist's assumptions and findings.
    C. The client should not have an understanding of the nature of the work to be performed by the specialist.
    D. The auditor should obtain an understanding of the methods and assumptions used by the specialist.

32. The primary reason an auditor requests letters of inquiry be sent to a client's attorneys is to provide the auditor with:
    A. The probable outcome of asserted claims and pending or threatened litigation.
    B. Corroboration of the information furnished by management about litigation, claims, and assessments.
    C. The attorneys' opinions of the client's historical experiences in recent similar litigation.
    D. A description and evaluation of litigation, claims, and assessments that existed at the balance sheet date.

33. After determining that a related party transaction has, in fact, occurred, an auditor should:
    A. Add a separate paragraph to the auditor's standard report to explain the transaction.
    B. Perform analytical procedures to verify whether similar transactions occurred, but were not recorded.
    C. Obtain an understanding of the business purpose of the transaction.
    D. Substantiate that the transaction was consummated on terms equivalent to an arm's-length transaction.

34. Which of the following factors would *least likely* affect the quantity and content of an auditor's audit documents?
    A. The condition of the client's records.
    B. The assessed level of control risk.
    C. The nature of the auditor's report.
    D. The content of the representation letter.

35. Which of the following matters is an auditor required to communicate to an entity's audit committee?
    A. The basis for assessing control risk below the maximum.
    B. The process used by management in formulating sensitive accounting estimates.
    C. The auditor's preliminary judgments about materiality levels.
    D. The justification for performing substantive procedures at interim dates.

36. The audit program usually cannot be finalized until the:
    A. Consideration of the entity's internal control has been completed.
    B. Engagement letter has been signed by the auditor and the client.
    C. Reportable conditions have been communicated to the audit committee of the board of directors.
    D. Search for unrecorded liabilities has been performed and documented.

37. Tracing shipping documents to prenumbered sales invoices provides evidence that:
    A. No duplicate shipments or billings occurred.
    B. Shipments to customers were properly invoiced.
    C. All goods ordered by customers were shipped.
    D. All prenumbered sales invoices were accounted for.

38. When an auditor does not receive replies to positive requests for year-end accounts receivable confirmations, the auditor *most likely* would:
    A. Inspect the allowance account to verify whether the accounts were subsequently written off.
    B. Increase the assessed level of detection risk for the valuation and completeness assertions.
    C. Ask the client to contact the customers to request that the confirmations be returned.
    D. Increase the assessed level of inherent risk for the revenue cycle.

39. Which of the following statements is correct concerning an auditor's use of the work of a specialist?
    A. The work of a specialist who is related to the client may be acceptable under certain circumstances.
    B. If an auditor believes that the determinations made by a specialist are unreasonable, only a qualified opinion may be issued.
    C. If there is a material difference between a specialist's findings and the assertions in the financial statements, only an adverse opinion may be issued.
    D. An auditor may not use a specialist in the determination of physical characteristics relating to inventories.

40. In using the work of a specialist, an auditor may refer to the specialist in the auditor's report if, as a result of the specialist's findings, the auditor:
    A. Becomes aware of conditions causing substantial doubt about the entity's ability to continue as a going concern.
    B. Desires to disclose the specialist's findings, which imply that a more thorough audit was performed.
    C. Is able to corroborate another specialist's earlier findings that were consistent with management's representations.
    D. Discovers significant deficiencies in the design of the entity's internal control that management does not correct.

41. The refusal of a client's attorney to provide information requested in an inquiry letter generally is considered:
    A. Grounds for an adverse opinion.
    B. A limitation on the scope of the audit.
    C. Reason to withdraw from the engagement.
    D. Equivalent to a reportable condition.

42. Which of the following procedures would an auditor *most likely* perform in obtaining evidence about subsequent events?
    A. Determine that changes in employee pay rates after year end were properly authorized.
    B. Recompute depreciation charges for plant assets sold after year end.
    C. Inquire about payroll checks that were recorded before year end but cashed after year end.
    D. Investigate changes in long-term debt occurring after year end.

43. The date of the management representation letter should coincide with the date of the:
    A. Balance sheet.
    B. Latest interim financial information.
    C. Auditor's report.
    D. Latest related party transaction.

44. When auditing related party transactions, an auditor places primary emphasis on:
    A. Ascertaining the rights and obligations of the related parties.
    B. Confirming the existence of the related parties.
    C. Verifying the valuation of the related party transactions.
    D. Evaluating the disclosure of the related party transactions.

45. Which of the following procedures would an auditor ordinarily perform first in evaluating management's accounting estimates for reasonableness?
    A. Develop independent expectations of management's estimates.
    B. Consider the appropriateness of the key factors or assumptions used in preparing the estimates.
    C. Test the calculations used by management in developing the estimates.
    D. Obtain an understanding of how management developed its estimates.

46. Which of the following procedures would an auditor *least likely* perform before the balance sheet date?
    A. Confirmation of accounts payable.
    B. Observation of merchandise inventory.
    C. Assessment of control risk.
    D. Identification of related parties.

47. An auditor *most likely* would limit substantive audit tests of sales transactions when control risk is assessed as low for the existence or occurrence assertion concerning sales transactions and the auditor has already gathered evidence supporting:
    A. Opening and closing inventory balances.
    B. Cash receipts and accounts receivable.
    C. Shipping and receiving activities.
    D. Cutoffs of sales and purchases.

48. Which of the following statements is correct concerning an auditor's use of the work of a specialist?
    A. The auditor need not obtain an understanding of the methods and assumptions used by the specialist.
    B. The auditor may not use the work of a specialist in matters material to the fair presentation of the financial statements.
    C. The reasonableness of the specialist's assumptions and their applications are strictly the auditor's responsibility.
    D. The work of a specialist who has a contractual relationship with the client may be acceptable under certain circumstances.

49. Which of the following is an audit procedure that an auditor *most likely* would perform concerning litigation, claims, and assessments?
    A. Request the client's lawyer to evaluate whether the client's pending litigation, claims, and assessments indicate a going concern problem.
    B. Examine the legal documents in the client's lawyer's possession concerning litigation, claims, and assessments to which the lawyer has devoted substantive attention.
    C. Discuss with management its policies and procedures adopted for evaluating and accounting for litigation, claims, and assessments.
    D. Confirm directly with the client's lawyer that all litigation, claims, and assessments have been recorded or disclosed in the financial statements.

50. Which of the following procedures would an auditor *most likely* perform to obtain evidence about the occurrence of subsequent events?
    A. Confirming a sample of material accounts receivable established after year end.
    B. Comparing the financial statements being reported on with those of the prior period.
    C. Investigating personnel changes in the accounting department occurring after year end.
    D. Inquiring as to whether any unusual adjustments were made after year end.

51. Which of the following matters would an auditor *most likely* include in a management representation letter?
    A. Communications with the audit committee concerning weaknesses in internal control.
    B. The completeness and availability of minutes of stockholders' and directors' meetings.
    C. Plans to acquire or merge with other entities in the subsequent year.
    D. Management's acknowledgment of its responsibility for the detection of employee fraud.

52. Which of the following auditing procedures *most likely* would assist an auditor in identifying related party transactions?
    A. Inspecting correspondence with lawyers for evidence of unreported contingent liabilities.
    B. Vouching accounting records for recurring transactions recorded just after the balance sheet date.
    C. Reviewing confirmations of loans receivable and payable for indications of guarantees.
    D. Performing analytical procedures for indications of possible financial difficulties.

53. The permanent (continuing) file of an auditor's audit documents *most likely* would include copies of the:
    A. Lead schedules.
    B. Attorney's letters.
    C. Bank statements.
    D. Debt agreements.

54. Which of the following events occurring after the issuance of an auditor's report *most likely* would cause the auditor to make further inquiries about the previously issued financial statements?
    A. An uninsured natural disaster occurs that may affect the entity's ability to continue as a going concern.
    B. A contingency is resolved that had been disclosed in the audited financial statements.
    C. New information is discovered concerning undisclosed lease transactions of the audited period.
    D. A subsidiary is sold that accounts for 25% of the entity's consolidated net income.

STUDY MANUAL – AUDITING & ATTESTATION
CHAPTER 19

ANSWERS: OTHER ISSUES IN AUDITING

1. **C** The competency (reliability) of evidence depends upon the degree of control exercised over the evidence by the client. The client does not have any control in answers (a), (b) and (d). The client does have control over sales invoices and, thus, it is the least competent.

2. **A** Trace from source documents to records to ensure all items have been billed.

3. **C** Source document to accounting records.

4. **B** The client is not inflating sales or accounts receivable by making fictitious entries.

5. **C** Client representations in any form (written or oral) must be supported by other audit evidence.

6. **D** analytical procedures are designed to detect unusual fluctuations in financial statement account balances. They are not conclusive evidence in the same respect as confirmation or documentation. The results of these analytical procedures should be investigated, however, if unusual relationships are revealed.

7. **B** GAAS requires that the auditor must obtain an attorney's letter date as of the last day of field work (audit report date). Information received from the client's attorney may be the basis for an adjustment of the financial statement as of year end or the basis for financial statement disclosures of events occurring during the subsequent period.

8. **A** An auditor reviews a client's sales cut-off to determine if year-end sales are being recorded in the correct period. Sales records are compared with shipping documents. If, assuming title passes at time of shipment, goods were shipped before year end and no sale was recorded as of year end, the auditor will have detected unrecorded sales. Similarly, if a sale was recorded as of year end, but goods were not shipped until the following year, sales would be overstated.

9. **B** A letter of audit inquiry to the client's lawyer is the auditor's primary means of obtaining corroboration of the information furnished by management concerning litigation, claims, and assessments. The matters included in answers (a), (c) and (d) could be covered in a letter of audit inquiry but the primary reason for the request is to provide corroborative audit evidence.

10. **D** In some cases, the corroborating information that can be obtained by the application of auditing procedures other than inquiry is limited. When a client plans to discontinue a line of business, for example, the auditor may not be able to obtain information through other auditing procedures to corroborate the plan or intent. Accordingly, the auditor should obtain a written representation to provide confirmation of management's intent. The client's plans included in the other answers, in comparison to the plans to discontinue a line of business, could be more readily corroborated by other evidence.

11. **D** In determining the scope of work to be performed with respect to possible transactions with related parties, the auditor should obtain an understanding of management responsibilities and the relationship of each component to the total entity. Normally, the business structure is based on the abilities of management, tax and legal considerations, product diversification, and geographical location. Experience has shown, however, that

business structure may be deliberately designed to obscure related party transactions. Therefore, when searching for related party transactions the auditor should obtain an understanding of each subsidiary's relationship to the total entity.

12. C If the auditor becomes aware of facts that existed at the report date, he should determine whether the facts would have affected the audit report. If they would have affected his report and people are currently relying on the report, the auditor should advise the client to make appropriate disclosures of the facts and their impact. Answer (a) does not address what the auditor should do regarding the current year's audit. Answers (b) and (d) would be considered only after the auditor determined that the lack of footnote disclosure affected his report.

13. C If the auditor decides to give an adverse opinion as a result of the report or findings of a specialist, reference to and identification of the specialist may be made if it will facilitate an understanding of the reason for the modified opinion. When expressing an unqualified opinion, the auditor should not refer to the work or findings of a specialist-regardless of whether or not the specialist's work provided reliable evidence [answer (b)] or the specialist is independent of the client [answer (d)]. Such a reference might be misunderstood to be a qualification of the auditor's opinion or a division of responsibility [answer (a)], neither of which is intended.

14. D There is a requirement that the independent auditor obtain certain written representations from management as a part of an examination made in accordance with generally accepted auditing standards. The documentation listed in the other answers is not required by auditing standards. An internal control questionnaire is one of several approaches to documenting the auditor's understanding of internal control. Auditors are encouraged to obtain an engagement letter to eliminate misunderstandings. An audit program is required, a planning memorandum is not.

15. A By tracing bills of lading to sales invoices, the auditor will confirm that all shipments have been invoiced, that is, that each shipment resulted in a sales invoice being prepared. Answer (b) is incorrect because the auditor would have to trace sales invoices to the sales journal to prove that all shipments were recorded as sales. Answers (c) and (d) are incorrect because the direction of the test will not prove that recorded sales were shipped or that invoiced sales were shipped because the auditor's starting point is what has been shipped, not with what has been recorded.

16. A During the audit of financial statements, the auditor is required to send a letter of audit inquiry to the client's legal counsel concerning claims, litigation and assessments. It is reasonable to assume that an attorney would be responsible to respond concerning only those items that he has given substantive attention. He would not be able to respond to items he has not given substantive attention (the attorney has no knowledge). Therefore, such a limited response on the part of an attorney would not be considered a scope limitation.

17. B The completeness assertion means that nothing has been omitted from the financial statements that should be recorded during a particular period. By performing a cutoff test the auditor is searching for items that have been omitted from the financial statements of the current period.

18. D The objective is to test whether recorded sales are valid (not overstated). The auditor is answering the question, "Is this recorded sale a valid transaction?" In order to answer that question, the auditor would start with the recorded sales and look for documentation corroborating its validity.

19. C The understanding among the auditor, the client, and the specialist should be documented and should cover: the specialist's understanding of the auditor's corroborative use of the specialist's findings, the objectives and scope of the specialist's work, the specialist's relationship to the client, the methods or assumptions to be used, a comparison of the methods and assumptions to those used in the preceding period, and the form and content of the specialist's report.

20. A Factors affecting the auditor's judgment about the quantity, type, and content of the audit documents for a particular engagement include; the nature of the engagement, the nature of the auditor's report, the nature of the financial statements on which the auditor is reporting, the nature and condition of the client's records, the assessed level of control risk, and the needs in the particular circumstances for supervision and review of the work. Although answers (b) and (c) could be related to supervision and review, answer (a) is the best choice because it is specifically included above as a factor. The content of the letter referred to in answer (d) is determined by the auditor; it does not affect the auditor's judgment about audit documents.

21. D Borrowing or lending on an interest-free basis or at a rate of interest significantly above or below market rates prevailing at the time of the transaction would be an example of a transaction which, because of its very nature, may be indicative of the existence of related parties. A borrowing between unrelated parties should be at or near the market rate of interest.

22. C The auditor should inquire of the entity's legal counsel regarding any events occurring after year end as part of the auditor's search for subsequent events, which are events or transactions that occur subsequent to the balance sheet date but prior to the issuance of the auditor's report that have a material effect on the financial statements and therefore require adjustment or disclosure in the statements. Answer (b) is a good choice since the auditor would inquire of officers as to whether there was any change in capital stock. The reference to "investigating" in answer (b), however, results in answer (c) being the better choice. An auditor would also review large-dollar transaction after year-end to determine if they are recorded in the proper period, not for arithmetic accuracy as noted in answer (a). Answer (d) has no direct impact on the current financial statements.

23. D The auditor's objective when evaluating accounting estimates is to obtain sufficient competent audit evidence to provide reasonable assurance that all accounting estimates that could be material to the financial statements have been developed; those accounting estimates are reasonable in the circumstances; and the accounting estimates are presented in conformity with applicable accounting principles and are properly disclosed. Answers (a) and (c) are incorrect because estimates are based on subjective as well as objective factors and may involve biased judgments made by management. Answer (b) presents a procedure the auditor would perform to determine whether the estimates are reasonable. In addition to consistency with industry data, the auditor would evaluate consistency with other supporting and relevant historical data.

24. B When expressing an unqualified opinion, the auditor should not refer to the work of a specialist because such a reference may be misunderstood. However, if as a result of the specialist's work, the auditor decides to depart from an unqualified opinion or to add a paragraph describing an uncertainty, a going concern issue, or an emphasis of a matter, the auditor may refer to the specialist in the auditor's report. Answers (a) and (c) would have no effect on the auditor's report. The auditor, not the client, should consider the specialist's certification, reputation and competency before using the specialist's work. Also, an understanding should exist among the auditor, client and specialist regarding the

work to be performed by the specialist. Answer (d) is incorrect because the auditor is responsible for the audit opinion and the evidence-gathering procedures followed in the audit. The auditor can not share responsibility with a specialist.

25. C   The auditor should test material transactions with parties related to the entity being audited to determine that the financial statements adequately disclose these related party transactions. Among the procedures an auditor would follow to identify these transactions is to review accounting records for large, unusual, or nonrecurring transactions or balances, paying particular attention to transactions recognized at or near the end of the reporting period. Answer (a) is incorrect because retesting the effectiveness of control procedures will not help the auditor identify related-party transactions. Answer (b) is a procedure that is followed when customers do not respond to confirmation requests, which is less likely to be the case if the customer is a related party. Answer (d) is incorrect because inquiry of lawyers may provide information about litigation, claims and assessments, not about related party transactions.

26. C   AU 317 states that the auditor may conclude that withdrawal is necessary when the client does not take the remedial action that the auditor considers necessary in the circumstances, even when the illegal act is not material to the financial statements. Factors that should affect the auditor's conclusion include the implications of the failure to take remedial action, which may affect the auditor's ability to rely on management representations, and the effects of continuing association with the client.

27. D   AU 329 states that analytical procedures used in planning the audit generally use data aggregated at a high level. An unusual combination of expense and revenue accounts in a journal entry might result in unusual aggregate information. Choice (a) is incorrect because tracing proves completeness and would not detect unusual relationships between the numbers. Choices (b) and (c) are incorrect because evaluating the effectiveness of the system of internal control or reconciling controlling accounts to the subsidiary ledger would not detect unusual relationships between the numbers.

28. C   AU 311 states that an engagement letter is normally required by GAAS. However, it would be foolish these days to operate without one. It focuses on the overall goals of the engagement, records to be provided by the client, and the type of report, the scope of the engagement, the timing of the field work, a fraud disclaimer, and the set fee. Choice (a) is incorrect because in planning the audit, the auditor should consider the nature, extent, and timing of work to be performed and should prepare a written audit program. An audit program aids in instructing assistants in the work to be done. It should set forth in reasonable detail the audit procedures that the auditor believes are necessary to accomplish the objectives of the audit. Choice (b) is incorrect because the content of audit documents should be sufficient to show that the accounting records agree or reconcile with the financial statements or other information reported on and that the applicable standards of field work have been observed. Choice (d) is incorrect because the auditor should document his conclusion for assessing control risk below the max. However, for those assertions where control risk is assessed at the maximum level, the auditor should document that control risk is at the maximum level but need not document the basis for that conclusion.

29. D   The auditor would normally determine that a stock option was authorized by tracing the authorization to the minutes of the board of directors. Choice (a) is incorrect because the Secretary of State would have no knowledge of a stock option granted by a corporation. Choice (b) is incorrect because options might be issued to people or other entities that do

not currently own stock in the corporation and who do not work for the corporation. Choice (c) is incorrect because stock options may be distributed from authorized common stock instead of using treasury shares to fulfill the options.

30. C   AU 317 states that the auditor ordinarily obtains written representations from management concerning the absence of violations or possible violations of laws or regulations whose effects should be considered for disclosure in the financial statements or as a basis for recording a loss contingency.

31. D   AU 336 states that an understanding should exist among the auditor, the client, and the specialist as to the nature of the work to be performed by the specialist. Preferably, the understanding should be documented and should cover the following:

- The objectives and scope of the specialist's work.
- The specialist's representations as to his relationship, if any, to the client.
- The methods or assumptions to be used.
- A comparison of the methods or assumptions to be used with those used in the preceding period.
- The specialist's understanding of the auditor's corroborative use of the specialist's findings in relation to the representations in the financial statements.

Although the appropriateness and reasonableness of methods or assumptions used and their application are the responsibility of the specialist, the auditor should obtain an understanding of the methods or assumptions used by the specialist to determine whether the findings are suitable for corroborating the representations in the financial statements. The auditor should consider whether the specialist's findings support the related representations in the financial statements and make appropriate tests of accounting data provided by the client to the specialist. Choices (a) and (c) are incorrect because an understanding should exist between the auditor, the client, and the specialist as per above. Choice (b) is incorrect because the auditor should consider performing substantive procedures to verify the specialist findings only if the specialist is related to the client.

32. B   AU 337 states that a letter of audit inquiry to the client's lawyer is the auditor's primary means of obtaining corroboration of the information furnished by management concerning litigation, claims, and assessments. Choice (a) is incorrect because the primary source of this information is management. Choice (c) is incorrect because the attorney's opinion is secondary. Choice (d) is incorrect because the attorney is asked to comment on management's description and evaluate litigation claims that exist at the balance sheet date.

33. C   AU 334 states that after identifying related party transactions, the auditor should apply the procedures necessary to obtain satisfaction concerning the purpose, nature, and extent of these transactions and their effect on the financial statements. The procedures should be directed toward obtaining and evaluating sufficient competent audit evidence and should extend beyond inquiry of management. Procedures that should be considered include:

- Obtain an understanding of the business purpose of the transaction.
- Examine invoices, executed copies of agreements, contracts, and other pertinent documents, such as receiving reports and shipping documents.
- Determine whether the transaction has been approved by the board of directors or other appropriate officials.
- Test for reasonableness the compilation of amounts to be disclosed, or considered for disclosure, in the financial statements.

Choice (a) is incorrect because while an extra paragraph is added, related party transactions are generally disclosed in the footnotes. Choice (b) is incorrect because analytical procedures are not effective to identify related party transactions. Choice (d) is incorrect because it is difficult to validate that the transactions were consummated on terms equivalent to other arm's-length transactions.

34. D AU 339 states that the factors affecting the auditor's judgment about the quantity, type, and content of the audit documents for a particular engagement include:

- the nature of the engagement,
- the nature of the auditor's report,
- the nature of the financial statements, schedules, or other information on which the auditor is reporting,
- the nature and condition of the client's records,
- the assessed level of control risk, and
- the needs in the particular circumstances for supervision and review of the work.

35. B AU 380 states that accounting estimates are an integral part of the financial statements prepared by management and are based upon management's current judgments. Those judgments are normally based on knowledge and experience about past and current events and assumptions about future events. Certain accounting estimates are particularly sensitive because of their significance to the financial statements and because of the possibility that future events affecting them may differ markedly from management's current judgments. The auditor should determine that the audit committee is informed about the process used by management in formulating particularly sensitive accounting estimates and about the basis for the auditor's conclusions regarding the reasonableness of those estimates. Choices (a), (c), and (d) are incorrect because they deal with the auditor's judgment and no explanation is needed to the committee.

36. A An audit program sets forth the audit procedures the auditor believes are necessary to accomplish the objectives of the audit. Audit procedures consist of tests of controls and substantive tests. The audit program cannot be finalized until the auditor completes his review of internal control because substantive tests are designed using the knowledge obtained from understanding internal control. Answers (b), (c) and (d) are incorrect because finalization of the audit program does not depend on signing an engagement letter, which typically occurs at the very beginning of the audit; or communicating reportable conditions, which can occur during or at the end of the audit; or searching for unrecorded liabilities, which is one of the last audit procedures performed by the auditor.

37. B By tracing shipping documents to sales invoices, the auditor will obtain evidence that all shipments have been invoiced; that is, that each shipment resulted in a sales invoice being prepared. Answer (a) is incorrect because tracing shipping documents to invoices will not detect duplicate shipments if both a shipping document and invoice were prepared for the duplicate shipment. Answer (c) is incorrect because the auditor would have to trace customer orders to shipping documents to determine if all orders have been shipped. Answer (d) is incorrect because if the auditor wants to account for all invoices, he should start his test with invoices, not shipping documents.

38. C When the auditor has not received replies to positive accounts receivable confirmation requests, he or she should apply alternative procedures such as examining subsequent cash receipts. Before applying alternative procedures, the auditor would typically mail a second request and ask the client to encourage the customer to respond. Answer (a) is incorrect because the auditor, through confirmations, is testing the existence of the receivable at year-end. Writing off an account after year-end provides no evidence that it was a valid

asset. Answer (b) is incorrect because the auditor must obtain sufficient evidence regarding the existence assertion and cannot trade off one assertion with others. Answer (d) is incorrect because inherent risk would not be reassessed due to lack of response to confirmation requests.

39. **A** Ordinarily, the auditor should attempt to obtain a specialist who is unrelated to the client. However, when the circumstances so warrant, work of a specialist who has a relationship with the client may be acceptable. Answers (b) and (d) are incorrect because the auditor would apply additional procedures if the specialist's determinations are unreasonable or if the specialist's findings do not support the financial statement assertions, and, depending on the results of those additional procedures, the auditor would issue the appropriate report. Answer (d) is incorrect because a specialist, which is a person or firm that possesses skills in fields other than accounting and auditing, can be used to evaluate inventory characteristics that fall outside the auditor's expertise.

40. **A** If the auditor, as a result of the report or findings of a specialist, decides to add explanatory language to the auditor's report regarding a going concern issue, he or she may refer to and identify the specialist in that auditor's report. Answers (b), (c) and (d) are incorrect because the auditor should only refer to the specialist if, as a result of the specialist's work, the auditor decides to add explanatory language to his or her report or depart from an unqualified opinion. Otherwise, such a reference may be misunderstood to be a qualification of the auditor's opinion or a division of responsibility, neither of which is intended. Further, there may be an inference that the auditor making such reference performed a more thorough audit than an auditor not making such a reference.

41. **B** A lawyer's refusal to furnish the information requested in an inquiry letter would be a limitation on the scope of the audit. Such an inability to obtain sufficient competent evidence may require the auditor to qualify the opinion or disclaim an opinion. An adverse opinion, answer (a), is issued when the financial statements are not fairly stated, not when there is inadequate evidence. An auditor does not typically withdraw from an engagement, answer (c), unless the client refuses to accept an auditor's report. A reportable condition, answer (d), is a deficiency in internal control, which is unrelated to legal letters.

42. **D** The auditor is concerned with subsequent events, which occur subsequent to the balance-sheet date but prior to the issuance of the auditors's report, that may have a material affect on the financial statements and therefore require adjustment or disclosure in the statements. Because changes in long-term debt occurring after year end may require disclosure to keep the financial statements from being misleading, the auditor should investigate such changes. The procedures described in answers (a), (b) and (c) would not likely reveal events that could have a material affect on the current financial statements.

43. **C** Because the auditor is concerned with events occurring through the date of the auditor's report that may require adjustment to or disclosure in the financial statements, the representations included in the management representation letter should be dated as of the date of the auditor's report. The dates listed in answers (a), (b) and (d) are incorrect.

44. **D** Established accounting principles ordinarily do not require transactions with related parties to be accounted for on a basis different from that which would be appropriate if the parties were not related. Therefore, the auditor should view related party transactions within the framework of existing pronouncements, placing primary emphasis on the adequacy of disclosure of such transactions. Because transactions with related parties are more likely to raise questions as to their economic substance, the auditor is more

concerned with evaluating the disclosure of those transactions than with determining the rights of related parties, answer (a), confirming the existence of related parties, answer (b), or verifying the valuation of related party transactions, answer (c).

45. **D** The auditor is responsible for evaluating the reasonableness of accounting estimates made by management and, as a first step, should obtain an understanding of how management developed its estimates. Based on that understanding, the auditor should develop an independent expectation of the estimates, as indicated in answer (a), and/or review and test the process used by management to develop the estimates, as reflected in answers (b) and (c), and/or review subsequent events or transactions occurring prior to the completion of fieldwork.

46. **A** Confirming accounts payable is the least likely procedure, of those listed, that the auditor would perform prior to the balance sheet date. The auditor would prefer to perform payables confirmation work as of year end because, when auditing payables, the auditor is most concerned with the completeness of payables at the year end balance sheet date. Answer (b) is incorrect because inventory observation is often done at an interim date, partly because of practical business reasons such as the time needed to compile the physical inventory results. Answers (c) and (d) are procedures that are typically performed at the earliest stages of the audit as they affect the planning of other audit procedures.

47. **B** If the control risk for the existence or occurrence assertion regarding sales transactions is assessed as low, there is a reduced likelihood that sales are overstated. Substantive tests of sales would be limited as a result. If, in addition, the auditor has already gathered evidence regarding cash receipts and accounts receivable, which are the debit sides of the credits to the sales account, the auditor has already obtained some evidence about sales and would therefore limit any additional testing of sales transactions. Answer (a) is incorrect because the inventory balances are not directly related to the sales account. Answers (c) and (d) are incorrect because, although shipping activities and cutoffs of sales relate to sales transactions, receiving activities and cutoffs of purchases do not.

48. **D** The work of a specialist who has a relationship with the client may be acceptable under certain circumstances. If the specialist has a relationship with the client, the auditor should assess the risk that the specialist's objectivity might be impaired. If the auditor believes the relationship might impair the specialist's objectivity, the auditor should perform additional procedures to determine that the specialist's findings are not unreasonable or should engage another specialist for that purpose. Answer (a) is incorrect because the auditor should obtain an understanding of the methods and assumptions used by the specialist. Answer (b) is incorrect because the auditor may use the specialist's work in material matters. Answer (c) is incorrect because the appropriateness and reasonableness of methods and assumptions used and their application are the responsibility of the specialist, not the auditor.

49. **C** Since the events or conditions that should be considered in the accounting for and reporting of litigation, claims, and assessments are matters within the direct knowledge of management of an entity, management is the primary source about such matters. Accordingly, the auditor should inquire of and discuss with management the policies and procedures adopted for identifying, evaluating, and accounting for litigation, claims, and assessments. Answer (a) is incorrect because the auditor, not the client's lawyer, has the responsibility to evaluate whether a going concern problem exists. Answer (b) is incorrect because the auditor is not responsible for examining documents in the lawyer's possession. Answer (d) is incorrect because proper recording and disclosure are accounting and auditing issues, not legal issues.

50. **D** The auditor should perform auditing procedures with respect to the period after the balance-sheet date for the purpose of ascertaining the occurrence of subsequent events that may require adjustment or disclosure. Included in those auditing procedures is inquiring of and discussing with officers and other executives having responsibility for financial and accounting matters as to whether any unusual adjustments had been made during the period from the balance-sheet date to the date of inquiry. Answer (a) is incorrect because confirmation of receivables is done before year-end. Answer (b) is incorrect because this is an analytical review procedure that is done at the beginning of the audit as part of audit planning. Answer (c) is incorrect because personnel changes in the accounting department after year-end do not typically relate to subsequent events that could affect the financial statements.

51. **B** Although the specific representations obtained by the auditor in a management representation letter will depend on the circumstances of the engagement and the nature and basis of presentation of the financial statements, they ordinarily include the completeness and availability of all minutes of meetings of stockholders, directors, and committees of directors. Answer (a) is incorrect because communications with the audit committee concerning weaknesses in controls is the auditor's responsibility, not management's. Answer (c) is incorrect because plans to acquire or merge with other entities in the future do not affect the current period's financial statements. Answer (d) is incorrect because the management representation letter, which does include reference to fraud involving management or employees, does not indicate that management is responsible for detecting employee fraud.

52. **C** The auditor performs various procedures to identify material transactions with parties known to be related and for identifying material transactions that may be indicative of the existence of previously undetermined relationships. One such procedure is reviewing confirmations of loans receivable and payable for indications of guarantees. When guarantees are indicated, the auditor should determine their nature and the relationships, if any, of the guarantors to the reporting entity. Answers (a), (b) and (d) are incorrect because they do not focus on and may not identify related party transactions; rather, they focus on discovering contingent liabilities, evaluating subsequent events, and determining if there are going concern problems.

53. **D** The permanent file of an auditor's audit documents contains information and documents of continuing interest. Examples of such items are debt agreements, the corporate charter and bylaws, contracts such as leases and royalty agreements, and continuing schedules of accounts whose balances are carried forward for several years. Answers (a), (b) and (c) relate to the current year under audit and would be included in the current file of an auditor's audit documents.

54. **C** When the auditor becomes aware of information that relates to financial statements previously reported on by the auditor, but which was not known to the auditor at the date of the auditor's report and which is of such a nature that the auditor would have investigated it had it come to the auditor's attention during the course of the audit, the auditor should make further inquiries about the previously issued financial statements. New information concerning undisclosed lease transactions of the audited period would lead the auditor to make further inquiries to determine if the new information is reliable and whether the facts existed at the date of the auditor's report. Answers (a) and (d) are events that did not exist at the date of the auditor's report and would not require any additional investigation by the auditor about the previously issued financial statements. Answer (b), which resolves a contingency that had been properly accounted for, would not cause the auditor to reevaluate the previously issued financial statements.

Cram Essentials: Contents

Study Manual – Auditing & Attestation

Overview of Audit Function 455

Sarbanes-Oxley Act of 2002 458

Audit Opinions 461

Use of Report of Another Auditor 464

Comparative Financial Statements 465

Compilations and Reviews 466

Audit Risk 471

Evidence Gathering 479

Internal Control 488

Accounts Receivable and Revenues 492

Statistical Sampling 495

Inventory and Accounts Payable 499

Auditing and Technology 502

Flowcharting 506

Cash Receipts and Cash Balances 508

Special Reports and Other Reports 510

Long-Term Liabilities and Contingencies 514

Payroll 516

Land, Buildings, and Equipment 518

Investments 519

CRAM ESSENTIALS

STUDY MANUAL – AUDITING & ATTESTATION

OVERVIEW OF AUDIT FUNCTION

A. An independent audit is made up of two separate steps.

  1. First step is the examination of a set of financial statements that have been produced by the management of the reporting entity.

      a. Purpose of examination is to gather sufficient, competent evidence on which to form an opinion as to the fair presentation of the statements in accordance with generally accepted accounting principles (GAAP).

      b. For each group of accounts and for the statements taken as a whole, management makes five assertions.

      - **Valuation:** all accounts are shown at proper amounts based on generally accepted accounting principles.
      - **Existence or occurrence:** all reported assets and liabilities actually exist; all other balances did occur. The account is not overstated.
      - **Presentation and disclosure:** all accounts are properly classified, and all relevant information is disclosed.
      - **Completeness:** all transactions and accounts have been included within the financial statements. The account is not understated.
      - **Obligations and rights:** all assets and liabilities are those of the reporting entity.

      c. Auditor attempts to corroborate these assertions in order to provide reasonable assurance that no material misstatements exist in any of the assertions.

      - The term "**material**" means anything of a size or type that would influence the judgment of a reasonable person relying on the information. A preliminary judgment of the size component of materiality is set at the beginning of an audit but is continuously reassessed as new information is gathered. The materiality of a misstatement should be judged based on the likely total amount of misstatement and not on the amount actually discovered by the CPA.
      - A **misstatement** is an **error** (an unintentional mistake), **fraud** (an intentional act that results in a material misstatement in financial

statements), or a **direct illegal act** (one that has an immediate effect on the financial statement figures).

2. Second step is the report of the findings to outside parties, primarily to stockholders and other parties outside of the reporting entity. The report is intended to add credibility to the financial information being distributed.

B. All of the auditor's work must follow generally accepted auditing standards (GAAS), which are currently established by means of Statements of Auditing Standards produced by the Auditing Standards Board.

1. Statements on Standards for Accounting and Review Services provide rules for work done for a nonpublic company that is less than an audit engagement.

2. Statements on Standards for Attestation Engagements provide rules when a conclusion is expressed about an assertion (compliance with a contract, for example).

C. There are ten basic, generally accepted auditing standards that provide the basis for an auditing engagement.

1. General Standards

a. The audit is to be performed by a person or persons having adequate technical training and proficiency as an auditor. The auditor should have sufficient education and experience in (1) auditing, (2) accounting, and (3) the industry in which the client operates in order to make the decisions necessary to evaluate whether any material misstatements exist in any of the management's five assertions.

b. In all matters relating to the assignment, independence in mental attitude is to be maintained by the auditor.

- The degree of independence varies according to the individual in question. A **covered member** is anyone on the engagement team and anyone who can influence the engagement or the members of the engagement team (such as the person in the firm who sets the salary levels). The firm itself, as a separate legal entity, is also a covered member. A covered member can have no direct financial interest (such as ownership of stocks or bonds) in an attestation client.
- A covered member's immediate family is defined as the spouse or spousal equivalent and any dependent. The independence rules are the same for this group as for the individual covered member except that the family member can work for the client as long as the person is not in a position to influence the client's financial statements.
- The covered member's close relatives are defined as a parent, sibling, or nondependent child. A close relative cannot hold a key employment position with the client where there is a significant relationship to the accounting or financial reporting function. In addition, the close relative

- cannot hold a financial interest in the client that is viewed as material to the close relative.
- Any partner of the firm or professional employee who is not a covered employee for a particular engagement can hold equity shares in the client but not more than 5% of the outstanding stock.
- To ensure independence, auditor cannot render an opinion on statements of one year until all fees from the prior year's audit have been paid.
- To emphasize independence from management, auditor is usually appointed by audit committee of the board of directors.

c. Due professional care is to be exercised in the performance of the audit and preparation of the report.

- Auditor must do at least what any average auditor would do and never less.

2. Standards of Fieldwork

a. The work is to be adequately planned, and assistants, if any, are to be properly supervised.

- Audit program is developed before substantive testing to ensure that adequate planning has occurred.
- All evidence is recorded within the audit documentation, which is reviewed by qualified personnel to ensure proper supervision. Even a partner other than the partner in charge of the engagement should review the audit documentation.

b. A sufficient understanding of internal control is to be obtained to help determine the nature, extent, and timing of the substantive testing to be performed.

- Assessment is made of control risk. If that risk is high, the auditor will have to gather more evidence than anticipated or a better quality of evidence.

c. Sufficient, competent audit evidence is to be obtained through inspection, observation, inquiries, confirmations, and the like to afford a reasonable basis for an opinion regarding the financial statements under audit.

- Evidence gathering is sometimes called **substantive testing.** Any testing that confirms the ending balance of an account is known as a test of a balance. Evidence gathered to support an account by looking at the various transactions that have affected it during the period is called a test of details.
- The actual amount and quality of evidence to be gathered depends on the judgment of the auditor.

3. Standards of Reporting

a. The report shall state whether the financial statements are presented in accordance with generally accepted accounting principles. (This assurance is stated explicitly.)

- The determination of what specific generally accepted accounting principle (GAAP) applies to a situation can be difficult because various sources can give conflicting guidelines. A **GAAP Hierarchy** has been established with five levels of authority. The higher levels have highest priority. In the top level (for businesses) are FASB Statements and Interpretations, APB Opinions, and AICPA Accounting Research Bulletins.

b. The report shall identify those circumstances in which such principles have not been consistently observed in the current period in relation to the preceding period. (Assurance of consistency is implied.)

c. Informative disclosures in the financial statements are to be regarded as reasonably adequate unless otherwise stated in report. (Assurance of adequate disclosure is implied.)

d. The report shall either contain an expression of opinion regarding the financial statements, taken as a whole, or an assertion to the effect that an opinion cannot be expressed. When an overall opinion cannot be rendered, the reasons should be stated. A clear-cut indication of the character of the auditor's work should be included along with the degree of responsibility that the auditor is taking.

SARBANES-OXLEY ACT OF 2002

A. The Sarbanes-Oxley Act of 2002 was passed by Congress as a major reform in independent auditing, but only in connection with the audit of publicly traded companies.

1. Created the Public Company Accounting Oversight Board (PCAOB) which is discussed in more detail below.

2. Prohibits certain services from being provided by an independent auditor to an audit client. These prohibited services include:

   a. Financial information system design and implementation.

   b. Internal auditing.

   c. Bookkeeping.

   d. Valuation services.

   e. Actuarial services.

  f. Human resource functions.

  g. Brokerage or investment services.

  h. Legal and expert services unrelated to the audit.

3. Requires that the audit committee of the board of directors must be independent from management and must hold the responsibility for appointment, compensation, and retention of the company's independent auditors.

4. Requires independent auditor to report to audit committee rather than to the management of the reporting company.

5. Requires independent auditing firm to rotate the lead partner off each audit engagement every five years at a minimum.

6. Requires CEO and CFO of each publicly traded company to sign a statement certifying the appropriateness of the financial statements and that those statements and disclosures fairly present, in all material respects, the operations and financial condition of the reporting company.

7. Establishes that non-U.S. public accounting firms that prepare audit reports with respect to any U.S. public companies are subject to the rules of the PCAOB.

8. Section 404 of the Act requires the management of each public company to report in each annual report its assessment of internal control over financial reporting. The independent auditor must attest to this assessment made by management and this attestation must also be included in the annual report.

B. The Public Company Accounting Oversight Board (PCAOB) was created by the Sarbanes-Oxley Act to enforce auditing, quality control, and independence standards in connection with the independent audit of publicly traded companies.

 1. The PCAOB is an independent, not-for-profit agency that was created to function under the authority of the Securities and Exchange Commission (SEC).

 2. The PCAOB is comprised of five members who are appointed by the SEC. Only two of the members can be CPAs.

 3. The PCAOB is funded by fees charged to the publicly traded companies as well as their independent audit firms.

 4. An "issuer" is any company that issues securities. Any auditing firm that prepares, issues, or participates in the preparation of an audit report for an issuer must register with the PCAOB.

 5. The PCAOB gathers considerable information through this registration process.

  a. All clients who are issuers.

b. All of the firm's accountants who participate in the audit process of an issuer.

c. Fees from each issuer, divided between audit services and nonaudit services.

d. Information about criminal, civil, or administrative actions that are pending.

e. Disagreements with any issuer.

6. The PCAOB periodically carries out an inspection of each registered auditing firm.

   a. An annual inspection is performed if the firm does 100 or more audits of issuers each year.

   b. Otherwise, the inspection is carried out every three years.

   c. Special inspections can be authorized by the PCAOB or requested by the SEC at any time if problems occur.

7. The PCAOB has considerable power over the registered CPA firms.

   a. Can suspend or revoke their registration.

   b. Can assess fees of up to $15 million for registered firms and up to $750,000 for individuals.

   c. Can require additional training or continuing professional education.

   d. Deficiencies uncovered through inspection can be made public.

8. PCAOB—Auditing Standard No. 1. In the audit report for an issuer, the scope paragraph must indicate that the audit was conducted in accordance with the standards of the PCAOB. For a company that is not an issuer, the CPA will continue to state that the audit was conducted in accordance with generally accepted auditing standards.

9. PCAOB—Auditing Standard No. 2. In an audit of the financial statements of an issuer, the CPA must evaluate management's assessment of internal control over financial reporting and also make an independent assessment of the effectiveness of this internal control. Thus, the auditor must express two opinions in all reports on internal control: one on the management's assessment process and another on the actual effectiveness of the internal control over financial reporting.

10. PCAOB—Auditing Standard No. 3. In an audit, the documentation for what was done and what was uncovered should be able to stand on its own with no need for oral or written description. Should indicate clearly the work that was performed, who carried out the work, when the work was completed, who reviewed the work, and the date that it was reviewed. All audit documentation must be completed within 45 days after the auditor's report is issued. Any subsequent changes must be clearly

explained and the original documentation retained. Audit documentation should be kept for a minimum of seven years.

AUDIT OPINIONS

A. An unqualified opinion (also called a standard auditor's report) is given when auditor's examination provides sufficient evidence that statements are presented fairly in accordance with GAAP. It provides the users of financial statements with reasonable assurance that no material misstatements exist in any of the five assertions made by management.

B. A standard unqualified opinion should contain several specific elements.

1. The heading should state, "Independent Auditor's Report."

2. The report is normally dated as of the final day of the auditor's fieldwork and can never be dated prior to the final day of fieldwork. Under normal circumstances, this concludes the auditor's responsibility for any type of evidence gathering.

    a. If an account has to be changed or a footnote added after the conclusion of the audit, management can request that the auditor return and audit that particular change. If that is done, the report must be dual dated ("March 22, 2004 except for Note Y as of April 2, 2004") to indicate that the auditor's work and responsibility have been extended for that one item.

3. The first paragraph is called the introductory paragraph.

    a. Indicates that an audit has been carried out (and not a preparation) of the financial statements.

    b. Identifies the financial statements by name, by name of the company, and by the dates.

    - Balance sheet is for a particular date; statements of income, retained earnings, and cash flows are for a period of time.

    c. Specifies that the statements are the responsibility of the company's management.

    d. States that the auditor's responsibility is to express an opinion on statements based on audit.

4. The second paragraph is called the scope paragraph.

    a. Specifies that the audit was conducted according to the auditing standards generally accepted in the United States.

    b. Indicates that audit was planned and performed to obtain reasonable assurance that the statements were free from material misstatements. Perfect assurance is not given for many reasons: not every transaction is examined; human error might occur in audit; fraud and illegal acts might be hidden; etc.

    c. Explains that evidence supporting amounts and disclosures has been examined but only on a test basis.

- This statement shows that not every transaction was examined.
- Stresses reliance on auditor's judgment.

    d. Indicates that an assessment was made of accounting principles, significant estimations, and statement presentation.

    e. States the belief that audit provides a reasonable basis for the opinion.

5. The third paragraph is called the opinion paragraph.

    a. Starts with the phrase "in our opinion" to show that this is not a guarantee but only an expert judgment.

    b. Says that statements present fairly in all material respects the financial position, operations, and cash flows.

    c. States that financial statements conform to accounting principles generally accepted in the United States.

C. An explanatory fourth paragraph should be added in several specific instances. In these cases, the extra paragraph is placed after the opinion paragraph and does not affect the wording of the other three paragraphs.

1. Emphasis of a matter—the paragraph is added to draw attention to a matter of particular importance, such as significant related party transactions or a subsequent event.

2. Lack of consistency—the paragraph is added to draw attention to a footnote that explains a change in accounting principle. The paragraph mentions change but does not provide any judgment of it.

    a. If auditor does not concur that change is appropriate, the opinion should be qualified rather than relying on this explanatory paragraph.

3. Going concern problem—the paragraph is added if substantial doubt exists as to company's ability to stay in business for 12 months from the date of the balance sheet. In this case, auditor does have the option to disclaim an opinion instead of adding an extra paragraph.

4. Other information attached to audited financial statements—auditor is required to read all information attached to financial statements to determine if it is consistent with the information presented in the financial statements. If inconsistency is discovered and the financial statements are judged to be fairly

presented, an extra paragraph is added to describe the problem. A qualified opinion is not rendered because the problem lies outside of the financial statements.

D. If a problem arises and an unqualified opinion cannot be given, the appropriate wording depends on the type of problem. In each case, an additional paragraph is added to describe the problem, but it always comes before the opinion paragraph.

1. There can be a qualification because of a scope limitation; the auditor fails to follow one or more of the generally accepted auditing standards. Frequently, the auditor is unable to obtain sufficient, competent evidence to provide reasonable assurance that a material misstatement does not exist in one of the assertions made by management.

    a. Introductory paragraph does not change, but scope paragraph indicates that GAAS was followed "except as discussed below" in the explanatory paragraph. As indicated above, explanatory paragraph describes problem and may direct the reader to a footnote where more information is provided.

    b. Opinion paragraph says that statements are fairly presented "except for adjustments, if any, that might have been found had we been able to…"

    c. If the lack of evidence is so material that auditor cannot add any credibility to financial statements, disclaimer (no opinion) should be given rather than a scope qualification.

       - For a disclaimer, the last sentence in introductory paragraph about auditor's responsibility is removed.
       - Scope paragraph is omitted completely.
       - Opinion paragraph reiterates problem identified in explanatory paragraph and indicates that "the scope of our work was not sufficient to enable us to express, and we do not express, an opinion on these statements."
       - Even in a disclaimer, auditor must spell out any GAAP problems that were discovered.
       - If independence is lacking, auditor always issues a disclaimer but never gives the specific reason for the problem. In this case, the disclaimer is often just a single sentence: "I am not independent; I have no opinion."

2. Statements can contain a departure from GAAP. For example, disclosure might not be adequate, or a balance might not be capitalized properly. If the problem is material but some credibility can be given to the statements as a whole, the auditor issues an opinion qualification.

    a. The introductory and scope paragraphs are both left with standard wording. As always, an explanatory paragraph is added before opinion paragraph.

    b. In opinion paragraph, the wording is changed to warn of the problem: "In our opinion, except for the effects of…"

c. In severe cases, a departure from GAAP can have such an impact that the entire statements cannot be viewed as fairly presented in any capacity. An adverse opinion is appropriate. Again, the first two paragraphs are standard and the explanatory paragraph is added. The opinion paragraph states that "because of the effects...the financial statement referred to above does not present fairly..."

3. Auditor can give different opinions for different statements (for example, an unqualified opinion on the balance sheet but a disclaimer on the other statements) but cannot give an opinion on specific accounts presented within a set of financial statements.

USE OF REPORT OF ANOTHER AUDITOR

A. Most large companies are actually made up of many separate corporations. On occasion, one auditing firm will examine the statements of a portion of these companies while a different firm (**another auditor**) audits the rest. Having two auditors may occur because a part of the company is in a separate geographical area.

1. Management designates a principal auditor to sign the audit report and be the auditor clearly visible to the public. The principal auditor is usually the firm that audits the parent company.

    a. Before accepting the role as principal auditor, firm must have knowledge of entire business and audit a large enough portion of the company to take responsibility as principal auditor.

2. If other auditor did only a small portion of the work, there often will be no division reported; opinion of principal auditor is standard with no mention made of the other auditor.

3. Principal auditor can also decide to indicate the presence of the other auditor (called "dividing the responsibility").

    a. If responsibility is divided, the introductory paragraph provides several pieces of information.

        • Mentions existence of other auditor but rarely identifies other auditor by name. Can only mention name with permission of the other auditor.
        • States the size of the division by giving the total assets and revenue of the part of the company that was examined by the other auditor.
        • States that the opinion being rendered is based on principal's audit and the report of the other auditor.

    b. If responsibility is to be divided, the last sentence of the scope paragraph mentions that the principal's audit "and the report of the other auditor" provided basis for opinion.

c. If responsibility is to be divided, opinion paragraph states that opinion is "based on our audit and the report of the other auditor."

d. A qualification given by the other auditor does not necessarily lead to a qualification of the entire financial statement. Opinion depends on overall materiality of problem.

4. Principal auditor has responsibilities in connection with other auditor.

a. Must always verify the professional reputation of the other auditor.

b. Must always verify the independence of the other auditor.

c. May possibly need to ascertain that other auditor understands applicable GAAP, SEC regulations, tax laws, etc. This step is most likely if other auditor is a very small firm or is located in a foreign country.

d. May also want to review evidence gathered about intercompany balances.

e. If responsibility is not divided, principal auditor should gain assurance of the quality of the work performed by the other auditor. In that case, principal may choose to do some or all of the following:

- Review other auditor's audit program.
- Review the evidence that was gathered and the handling of any problems that were discovered.
- Do some audit testing to confirm work of other auditor.

COMPARATIVE FINANCIAL STATEMENTS

A. A company may change auditors. Subsequently, in connection with comparative statements, the new auditor reports on current year statements, but previous opinion is still applicable for the earlier set of financial statements.

1. Previous opinion can simply be included along with the current audit report. However, previous auditor must agree to inclusion of report. Before giving permission, previous auditor must make certain that original opinion is still appropriate.

a. Previous auditor should review earlier financial statements to make certain that nothing has been changed since original examination.

b. Must also read the current statements and compare to earlier statements to determine that no obvious discrepancies are present.

c. Must obtain a representation letter from current auditors stating that nothing has been found to indicate that the previous statements require adjustment.

d. Must also obtain an updated representation letter from management similar to the one that is required at the end of an audit.

2. The previous report can be omitted, but then current auditor must refer to the earlier report. In that case, the introductory paragraph is changed to include several pieces of information.

   a. The statements being presented that were audited by the previous auditor must be identified, but the name of that firm cannot be given.

   b. Date of the previous report must be included.

   c. Type of opinion given in previous report should be noted along with an explanation if the report varied from a standard unqualified opinion.

B. For nonpublic companies, different levels of assurance may be appropriate for the statements of different years. For example, an audit may be performed in one year but only a review or compilation in another.

   1. The report for the current year should be generated as is appropriate.

   2. A separate paragraph at the end of the current report should be included to indicate the following about the previous statements:

      a. Identification of the previous statements.

      b. Indication of the type of engagement that was performed.

      c. Date and contents of the previous report.

C. Auditor may decide to change an opinion given on an earlier set of financial statements that is being included for comparative purposes.

   1. For example, statements may have been restated to conform with GAAP.

   2. Within current report, an explanatory paragraph is added prior to the opinion paragraph.

      a. Should include date and opinion of previous report.

      b. Should indicate updated opinion on earlier statements and reasons for change.

COMPILATIONS AND REVIEWS

A. Anytime that a CPA is associated with financial statements, a report must be issued to avoid any possible misunderstanding.

   1. This report should indicate level of assurance, if any, that is being given.

2. A CPA is associated with statements when he or she prepares or assists in preparing statements or putting information into the form of financial statements.

B. If CPA is associated with the statements of a publicly held company but has not performed an audit, CPA must state so clearly. ("I have not performed an examination and, therefore, have no opinion.")

   1. No negative assurance should be given. For example, CPA cannot say, "I did not perform an audit but I saw nothing wrong."

   2. Each page should be stamped "unaudited."

   3. If CPA is aware of a problem with the application of GAAP, that information must be included in report.

C. For the interim financial statements of a publicly held company, CPA may perform a limited review.

   1. CPA carries out specified procedures and, if no problems are discovered, states that he or she is not aware of any material modifications that are needed to be in conformity with GAAP.

      a. This wording is known as negative assurance or limited assurance.

      b. Assurance being given is less than that of an audit (reasonable assurance) because no evaluation is made of internal control and insufficient evidence is gathered to form an opinion as to whether material misstatements exist in any of the five assertions made by management about the accounts and the financial statements.

D. If a company is privately-held and an audit is not performed, CPA carries out either a review or a **compilation**. These services can be done on either interim or annual statements. The CPA's work must adhere to the **Statements on Standards for Accounting and Review Services**.

   1. A review is essentially the same as a limited review performed on the interim financial statements of a public company. A review avoids (a) substantive testing of transactions such as through inspection, observation, and confirmation, (b) tests of controls, and (c) tests to corroborate inquiry responses.

   2. There are specific procedures that CPA should do in a review.

      a. The CPA must establish an understanding with the client regarding the work to be done. This understanding includes the objectives of the engagement, the management's responsibilities, the CPA's responsibilities, and an acknowledgement that a review is primarily analytical procedures and inquiries and is substantially less than an audit.

b. Obtain a general knowledge of the company, its systems, its control structure, and the industry in which it operates.

c. Perform analytical procedures. Client balances, percentages, and ratios are compared to auditor's expectations for those same figures. Significant differences indicate areas where risk of misstatement is greatest.

- Auditor expectations are usually stated within a range, and the client figures would be expected to fall within that range.
- Auditor expectations can be based on past years' figures, budgets, financial statements of competitors, industry averages, related nonfinancial information (the local economy has declined so that bad debt expense would be expected to increase), and related financial information (sales have gone up so cost of goods sold should have also gone up).
- For revenues, consider making additional comparisons using disaggregated data, such as comparing revenues by location or by **month**.

d. Make inquiries of the client management looking for potential problems. Areas of inquiry would include the following:

- Whether the interim financial information was prepared according to GAAP.
- The presence of unusual or complex situations that might have an effect on the interim information, such as the following:
    - Business combinations.
    - New or complex revenue recognition methods.
    - Impairment of assets.
    - Disposal of a segment of the business.
    - Adoption of a new stock compensation plan.
    - Restructuring charges.
    - Changes in litigation or contingencies.
    - Application of new accounting principles.
    - Trends and developments affecting accounting estimates.
    - Changes in related parties.
    - Material off-balance sheet transactions.
- The presence of significant transactions at the very end of the interim period.
- The status of previously uncorrected misstatements from earlier reviews and/or audits.
- The status of issues previously questioned.
- The occurrence of any events subsequent to the date of the interim information that could have a material impact on the financial reporting.
- Knowledge of any fraud or suspected fraud
    - which involves management or
    - which could be considered as material.
- Knowledge of any allegations of fraud or suspected fraud.
- Significant journal entries.
- Communications from regulatory agencies.

- Any significant deficiencies in the design or operation of internal control.

   e. Read the financial statements and verify the math on those statements.

   f. Read **minutes of board of directors and stockholders' meetings,** looking for discussion of unusual events or problems.

   g. Get representation letter from the management.

   h. Normally, a lawyer's letter is not sent about contingencies, and no evaluation of the company as a going concern is made. However, if either contingencies or going concern appear to be a concern, the CPA should follow steps similar to an audit.

E. A review report normally has three paragraphs.

   1. First paragraph states that a review was performed and identifies the statements.

      a. Also indicates that the work was in accordance with the Statements on Standards for Accounting and Review Services issued by the American institute of Certified Public Accountants (AICPA).

      b. Specifies that financial statements are the representations of the management.

   2. Second paragraph explains the steps and purpose of a review.

      a. Indicates that a review is mainly inquiries of company personnel and analytical procedures applied to financial data.

      b. Explains that a review is substantially less than an examination made in an audit.

      c. Specifies that no opinion is being expressed.

   3. Third paragraph provides negative (limited) assurance: "Because of my review, I am not aware of any material modifications that should be made ... to be in conformity with GAAP."

   4. Each page of the financial statements must be stamped "see accountant's review report."

   5. During a review, the CPA may become aware of likely misstatements in the financial information. The CPA should make an estimation of the total amount of misstatement that is likely and evaluate, based on the nature, cause, and amount, its materiality.

      a. If the CPA believes that material modifications are needed for the reviewed information to be in conformity with generally accepted accounting principles, the management of the entity should be told.

b. If the management does not do anything in response, the CPA should inform the audit committee.

c. If the audit committee does not do anything in response, the CPA should consider resigning.

d. If modification of the report is required because of a departure from GAAP or inadequate disclosure:

- An explanatory third paragraph is added to describe the situation in question.
- The final (now the fourth) paragraph states, "Based on our review, with the exception of the matter described in the preceding paragraph, we are not aware of..."

F. For a nonpublic company, the CPA can also perform a compilation, which provides no assurance in connection with the statements.

1. A compilation is sometimes referred to as write up work and means that the CPA takes client information and submits it in the form of financial statements.

    a. Footnote disclosure is often omitted in such statements, but, in that case, an extra paragraph should be added to report to indicate that the statements are only intended for people aware of the missing disclosures.

    b. In performing a compilation, CPA should have a general knowledge of the company: its transactions, records, personnel, applicable GAAP, and the industry in which it operates.

    c. CPA must read the final statements and verify the math in order to catch any obvious errors. However, no evidence gathering is performed.

    d. A compilation is one service that can be performed by a CPA who is not independent of the reporting company, although the lack of independence must be disclosed in the report.

2. A compilation report normally has two paragraphs.

    a. The first paragraph identifies the financial statements that were compiled and indicates that the work was done in accordance with the Statements on Standards for Accounting and Review Services issued by the AICPA.

    b. The second paragraph describes the purpose of a compilation as presenting the representations of management in the form of financial statements. An indication is made that no audit or review was made and that no opinion or assurance is being given.

    c. If the CPA is aware of any departure from GAAP, a sentence is added to the second paragraph of the report to note that departure. Then, a third paragraph is added to describe the problem.

d. Each page of the financial statements must be stamped "see accountant's compilation report."

3. If statements will not be seen by any third parties, no compilation report is required with the statements. The CPA can use an engagement letter to indicate that management has agreed that the statements are not to be used by third parties.

   a. A third party is anyone who is not a member of management or does not have an adequate knowledge of the company and the limitations of the financial information (such as the basis of accounting or the assumptions used).

   b. Thus, in this specific situation, a member of management could be viewed as a third party if the person does not have an adequate knowledge of the company or the limitations of the financial information.

   c. Each page of the statements should be stamped "restricted for management's use only."

   d. If it is discovered that third parties are using the statements, the CPA should contact the lawyer and then warn the third parties not to use the statements.

   e. The work to be done by the CPA is not impacted by the restriction of the statements.

AUDIT RISK

A. An independent auditor provides reasonable assurance that the five assertions made by management (and described earlier) are free from material misstatements. Misstatements result from errors, fraud, and direct illegal acts.

   1. Errors are unintentional mistakes that affect the financial statements, such as accidentally capitalizing a repair expense.

   2. Fraud is an intentional act that results in a material misstatement in financial statements. Auditor may encounter two types of fraud.

      a. Fraudulent financial reporting results from manipulation of accounting records, misrepresentation of events in the financial statements, or intentional misapplication of accounting principles.

      b. Misappropriation of assets (also known as defalcation) is the theft of assets, an action that causes the financial statements to be misstated.

   3. A direct illegal act is one that has an immediate impact on the financial statements. Income tax evasion is an example because the reported balances for income tax payable and income tax expense are wrong.

4. Auditor provides only reasonable assurance because (a) not every transaction is examined, (b) human error can occur in the testing, and (c) both fraud and illegal acts are usually hidden.

B. Audit risk is the possibility that a material misstatement will occur and be reported within an entity's financial statements. For each group of accounts, the auditor is not satisfied until audit risk is reduced to an acceptable level. Acceptable audit risk is the amount of risk that the auditor is willing to assume and still provide reasonable assurance of no material misstatements. Audit risk has three components, each of which may be judged quantitatively (for example, a 20% risk of misstatement might be said to exist) or nonquantitatively (one account may be assessed as having maximum risk of misstatement whereas another has minimum risk).

1. The auditor estimates the severity of the first two components of audit risk based on an assessment of the client and the particular group of accounts. Auditor must evaluate the likelihood of a problem.

    a. Inherent risk is the possibility that a material misstatement will occur within the company's accounting system.

    b. Control risk is the possibility that a material misstatement that has occurred will not be detected by the company's control system.

2. The final component of audit risk is based on the quality and quantity of evidence gathered by the auditor.

    a. Detection risk is the possibility that a material misstatement will not be caught by the auditor's testing (often referred to as substantive testing). Auditor continues testing an account group (thereby decreasing detection risk) until the three components taken together indicate that overall audit risk has been reduced to the level judged to be acceptable by the auditor.

    If inherent risk and/or control risk are assessed as high, auditor may have to reduce detection risk further than expected in order for overall audit risk to be acceptable.

    Detection risk decreases whenever auditor gathers more evidence or obtains evidence of a better quality. Evidence is considered to be of a better quality if it is gathered (1) closer to year end, (2) by more experienced auditors, or (3) using more sophisticated techniques (such as statistical sampling rather than judgment sampling).

C. Throughout an audit, the independent CPA must watch for possible problems in the "**fraud triangle**." In other words, whenever concerns appear in one or more of these three, the auditor should be especially careful to look for fraud risk factors.

1. Incentive/pressures—management or other employees have an incentive to commit fraud, or they are under pressures that provide them with a motivation to commit fraud.

2. Opportunity—circumstances exist (the absence of controls, for example) that provide a person with a reasonable chance to commit fraud.

3. Rationalization/attitude—those individuals who could be involved in a fraud are able to rationalize a fraudulent act as being consistent with their personal code of ethics.

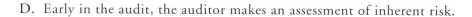

D. Early in the audit, the auditor makes an assessment of inherent risk.

1. Certain factors would increase the possibility that misstatements may have occurred and, therefore, impact the auditor's judgment of inherent risk. These factors would include the following:

   a. It is a first audit.

   b. It is a continuing audit in which misstatements were found in previous years.

   c. Accounts exist with large balances or many transactions.

   d. Significant balances are the result of estimations so that less objective evidence is available.

   e. The accounting system is outdated or understaffed or operated by individuals lacking training or experience.

   f. Discovery is made during the performance of analytical procedures in the initial audit planning stages of client balances that vary significantly from the auditor's expectations.

E. Periodically, during an audit, the audit team (or, at least, the key members of the audit team) should engage in **brainstorming**. This is a discussion of where and how the financial statements might be susceptible to fraud, how management could perpetrate and conceal fraudulent reporting, and how assets could be stolen.

F. The auditor must always be alert for the presence of **fraud risk** factors such as those listed below. The presence of one or more of these factors does not mean that fraud is actually present. However, it does alert the auditor that the risk of fraud is relatively high and should be investigated. The following fraud risk factors are associated specifically with fraudulent financial reporting.

1. Incentive/pressures on employees and/or management to attempt fraudulent financial reporting.

   a. Financial profitability or the company's stability are being threatened.

      - There is a high degree of competition.
      - Company is vulnerable to rapid changes, such as changes in technology and product obsolescence.
      - There has been a decline in customer demand and an increase in business failures in either the industry or the overall economy.

- Operating losses make the threat of bankruptcy or foreclosure imminent.
- Company has recurring negative cash flows from operations while reporting earnings and earnings growth.
- Rapid growth or unusual profitability, especially compared to that of other companies in the same industry.
- Company faces new accounting, statutory, or regulatory requirements.

b. Excessive pressure exists for management to meet the requirements or expectations of third parties due to the following:

- Profitability expectations of investment analysts, investors, or significant creditors.
- Company needs to obtain additional debt or equity financing to stay competitive.
- Company has marginal ability to meet debt repayment or other debt covenant requirements.

c. Information available indicates that management or the board of directors' personal financial situation is threatened by the entity's financial performance arising from the following:

- Significant financial interests in the entity.
- Significant portions of their compensation (for example, bonuses or stock options) are contingent upon achieving aggressive targets, such as stock prices, reported income, or operating cash flows.
- Personal guarantees of the debts of the entity.

2. Opportunities—fraud risk factors dealing with the opportunity of management or employees to carry out fraudulent financial reporting.

a. The nature of the industry or entity's operations to provide opportunities to engage in fraudulent financial reporting can arise from the following:

- Significant related-party transactions not in the ordinary course business.
- A strong financial presence or the ability to dominate a certain industry sector that allows the entity to dictate terms or conditions to suppliers or customers that may result in inappropriate or non-arm's-length transactions.
- The reporting of assets, liabilities, revenues, or expenses is based on significant estimates that involve subjective judgments that are difficult to corroborate.
- Significant, unusual, or highly complex transactions are reported, particularly those close to the end of the period, especially those where the substance may be difficult to ascertain.
- Significant operations are located or conducted across international borders in jurisdictions where differing business environments exist.
- Significant bank accounts or subsidiary operations are in tax-haven jurisdictions for which there appears to be no clear business justification.

b. There is ineffective monitoring of management as a result of the following:

- Domination of management by a single person or small group (in a nonowner-managed business) without compensating controls.
- Ineffective board of directors or audit committee oversight over the financial reporting process and internal control.

c. There is a complex or unstable organizational structure, as evidenced by the following:

- Difficulty in determining the organization or individuals who have controlling interest in the entity.
- Overly complex organizational structure involving unusual legal entities or managerial lines of authority.
- High turnover of senior management, counsel, or board members.

d. Internal control components are deficient as a result of the following:

- Inadequate monitoring of controls.
- High turnover rates for accounting, internal audit, or information technology staff.
- Ineffective accounting and information systems in place.

3. Attitudes/rationalizations—fraud risk factors dealing with the attitudes or possible rationalizations of management or employees who might carry out fraudulent financial reporting.

a. Ineffective communication, implementation, support, or enforcement of the entity's values or ethical standards by management.

b. Nonfinancial management's excessive participation in or preoccupation with the selection of accounting principles or the determination of significant estimates.

c. Known history of violations of securities laws or claims against the entity, its senior management, or board members alleging fraud or violations of laws and regulations.

d. Excessive interest by management in maintaining or increasing the entity's stock price or earnings trend.

e. A practice by management of committing to achieve aggressive or unrealistic forecasts.

f. Management's failure to correct known reportable conditions on a timely basis.

g. Recurring attempts by management to justify marginal or inappropriate accounting on the basis of materiality.

h. The relationship between management and the auditor is strained, as exhibited by the following:

- Frequent disputes with the auditor on accounting, auditing, or reporting matters.
- Unreasonable demands on the auditor, such as unreasonable time constraints regarding the completion of the audit or the issuance of the auditor's report.
- Formal or informal restrictions on the auditor that inappropriately limit access to people or information or the ability to communicate effectively with the board of directors or audit committee.
- Domineering management behavior in dealing with the auditor, especially involving attempts to influence the scope of the auditor's work or the selection or continuance of personnel assigned to the audit engagement.

G. Fraud risk factors can also be associated with misappropriation (although it is not possible to completely separate fraud risk factors between fraudulent financial reporting and misappropriation).

1. Incentives/Pressures—the following are fraud risk factors identified with misappropriation:

    a. Personal debts or other financial obligations may create pressure on management or other employees who have access to cash or other assets susceptible to theft.

    b. Adverse relationships exist between the entity and employees who have access to cash or other assets susceptible to theft that may motivate those employees to misappropriate those assets. For example, adverse relationships may be created by the following:

    - Known or anticipated future employee layoffs.
    - Recent or anticipated changes to employee compensation or benefit plans.
    - Promotions, compensation, or other rewards inconsistent with expectations.

2. Opportunities—the following are fraud risk factors identified with misappropriation:

    a. Certain characteristics or circumstances may increase the susceptibility of assets to misappropriation. For example, opportunities to misappropriate assets increase with the following conditions:

    - Large amounts of cash are on hand or are processed regularly.
    - Inventory items are small in size, of high value, or in high demand.
    - Easily convertible assets are present in the company, such as bearer bonds, diamonds, or computer chips.
    - Fixed assets are present that are small in size, marketable, or lacking observable identification of ownership.

b. Inadequate internal control over assets may increase the susceptibility of misappropriation of those assets. For example, misappropriation of assets may occur because any of the following are present:

- Inadequate segregation of duties or independent checks.
- Inadequate management oversight of employees responsible for assets; for example, inadequate supervision or monitoring of operations at remote locations.
- Inadequate job applicant screening of employees with access to assets.
- Inadequate recordkeeping with respect to assets.
- Inadequate system of authorization and approval of transactions (for example, in purchasing).
- Inadequate physical safeguards over cash, investments, inventory, or fixed assets.
- Lack of complete and timely reconciliations of assets.
- Lack of timely and appropriate documentation of transactions; for example, credits for merchandise returns.
- Lack of mandatory vacations for employees performing key control functions.
- Inadequate management understanding of information technology, which could enable information technology employees to perpetrate a misappropriation.

3. Attitudes/Rationalizations—risk factors reflective of employee attitudes/rationalizations that would allow them to justify misappropriations of assets are generally not susceptible to observation by the auditor. Nevertheless, the auditor who becomes aware of the existence of such information should consider it in identifying the risks of material misstatement arising from misappropriation of assets. For example, auditors may become aware of the following attitudes or behaviors of employees who have access to assets susceptible to misappropriation:

   a. Disregard for the need to monitor or reduce risks related to misappropriations of assets.

   b. Disregard for internal control over misappropriation of assets by overriding existing controls or by failing to correct known internal control deficiencies.

   c. Behavior indicating displeasure or dissatisfaction with the company or its treatment of the employee.

   d. Changes in behavior or lifestyle that may indicate assets have been misappropriated.

H. If actual fraud risk factors are discovered, the auditor should respond in several ways.

1. There should be the assignment of individuals to the audit with specialized skills and experience, a careful consideration of all accounting principles adopted, and an attempt to become more unpredictable in testing (do not always stick with a pattern that the client might come to anticipate).

2. Actual testing procedures (either substantive testing or tests of controls) should be modified.

   a. Additional amounts of testing should be performed.

   b. Tests should be designed to gather more reliable evidence such as (a) relying more on sources from outside of the client, (b) using more physical inspection, and (c) using computer-assisted audit techniques to gather information from within computers.

   c. Do more testing closer to the end of the year instead of at interim times.

   d. Perform analytical procedures at more disaggregated levels of information (by store, for example, rather than for the company as a whole).

I. Auditor's responsibility for detecting illegal acts.

   1. Direct illegal acts—auditor must provide reasonable assurance that no illegal acts have occurred that have a direct and material effect on financial statements. Auditor's responsibility is the same here as it is for errors and fraud.

   2. Other illegal acts such as insider trading and safety hazards only have indirect effects on the financial statements. No account is currently wrong, but a contingency exists; if the act is discovered, company could be punished.

      a. Auditor has no responsibility to look for or find illegal acts that have an indirect impact on financial statements. These actions are outside scope of the audit; in addition, they may well be hidden.

      b. However, auditors must maintain skeptical attitude and, thus, may discover such illegal acts or situations pointing to illegal acts. Questionable events would include unauthorized transactions, improper or slow reporting, and large cash or unspecified payments.

   3. Even for an indirect illegal act, if suspicious situation is encountered, auditor must investigate. If illegal act is discovered, auditor considers potential effect on the fair presentation of financial statements.

      a. Must determine, by talking with management or through investigation, whether a contingency has been incurred that should be disclosed.

      b. If contingency has been incurred, auditor gathers evidence as to amount and proper presentation.

   4. If a material indirect illegal act is found and company will not disclose, auditor renders an opinion qualification. If an act is discovered but its legality cannot be established, the auditor can provide a scope qualification.

J. At any time during an audit, auditor may discover evidence that indicates that a misstatement could possibly exist in the financial records.

1. Auditor must assess whether the possible misstatement could be material. If not, the auditor need only inform members of management at least one level above those involved about the potential problem.

2. If possible misstatement could be material, auditor gathers more evidence to determine if misstatement actually exists.

3. If misstatement does exist, auditor assesses if it is material. If not, auditor tells management and has no other responsibility.

   a. If misstatement is material, auditor talks with management because the statements are the responsibility of management.

   b. Even if material problem is resolved, the audit committee of the board of directors must be informed because the issue had a significant impact on the financial reporting of the company.

   c. If material misstatement is not corrected, auditor gives an opinion qualification or an adverse opinion.

material problem resolved – and must tell aud committee

K. Fraud involving senior management or fraud that causes a material misstatement must be reported to the audit committee. There should be an understanding between the auditor and the audit client as to the reporting of any other fraud that is uncovered.

EVIDENCE GATHERING

A. The audit program is a list of substantive testing procedures to be performed. It is required in an audit; it shows that the work has been adequately planned.

   1. Preliminary draft is often written at the beginning of the audit.

   2. Audit program is finalized after assessment is made of inherent risk and control risk. At that point, auditor knows the level of detection risk that has to be achieved, which affects the nature, extent, and timing of the substantive tests to be carried out.

B. In the year that an auditing firm takes a new engagement, information should be sought from the **predecessor auditor.** Predecessor auditor is one who did previous audit but who has been terminated or resigned or has been told that termination may occur.

   1. Current auditor must always get the client's permission before talking with past auditor (or anyone else). If client refuses to give permission, auditor normally resigns because of fear that management cannot be trusted. However, resignation is not required; auditor should assess reason for refusal.

   2. Successor auditor is required to communicate with predecessor before accepting engagement but should not seek this discussion until after engagement has been

offered. If predecessor's response is limited (if, for example, because of litigation), the limitation should be indicated. Required communications include the following:

   a. Information as to the integrity of management.

   b. Disagreements with management on either accounting or auditing issues.

   c. Communications with audit committee regarding fraud, illegal acts, and internal control-related matters.

   d. The predecessor's understanding of the reason for changing auditors.

3. After accepting an engagement, the successor is urged (but not required) to communicate with predecessor again so as to review prior audit documentation.

   a. This review can help the auditor identify accounting methods that were used in the past so that consistent application can be substantiated.

   b. Successor also needs to substantiate the opening balances of the balance sheet accounts. Successor does not rely on the predecessor's audit documentation; rather, this review is one method of gathering needed evidence.

C. Auditor is required to establish an understanding with the client about each engagement (an audit as well as other attestation services).

1. This understanding must include four areas:

   a. Objective of the work (for an audit, it is the expression of an opinion on the financial statements)

   b. Management's responsibilities—the financial statements, effective internal control, compliance with laws and regulations, making all records available, and a representation letter to the auditor

   c. Auditor's responsibilities—following generally accepted auditing standards and letting the audit committee know of any reportable conditions

   d. Limitations of the engagement—reasonable assurance is given and not absolute assurance, a disclaimer will be rendered if no opinion can be given, and that internal control is only evaluated in order to determine the nature, extent, and timing of audit testing.

2. Other matters can also be included in the understanding: the use of a specialist, the use of internal auditors, discussions with predecessor auditors, etc.

3. Understanding with client must be documented. An engagement letter is recommended for this purpose but not required. A signed memo describing an oral discussion will be adequate, as will a formal contract.

D. Representation letter is obtained by auditor, usually on the last day of fieldwork. Can be dated later than the audit report but no earlier.

1. It is a letter from representatives of the management (signed by both the CEO and CFO and anyone else with sufficient knowledge of financial statements).

2. If representation letter is not received, auditor must give qualified opinion because of the scope limitation. Auditor also has the right to give a disclaimer or withdraw from the engagement.

3. The letter requires management to acknowledge responsibility for financial statements. Management must also state its belief that the financial statements are presented fairly according to generally accepted accounting principles. Management indicates that it is also responsible for correcting any material misstatements and that any uncorrected misstatements are not material. Management indicates that it is responsible for the design and implementation of programs and controls to prevent and detect fraud. In addition, letter confirms and documents the representations made to the auditors during the audit. It also helps to reduce misunderstandings between the parties.

4. Can include a number of representations, such as the following:

    a. Management acknowledges responsibility for financial statements and states belief that they are presented fairly.

    b. States that all records, data, and minutes have been made available.

    c. States that all material transactions have been properly recorded.

    d. States that no fraud has occurred involving management with a significant role in internal control and that no fraud has occurred that has a material effect on the financial statements.

    e. States that the following have been properly disclosed and reported: related party transactions, guarantees, significant estimates, unasserted claims, contingencies and the like.

    f. States that it has no knowledge of any allegations of fraud or suspected fraud. (In other words, members of management do not know of any "whistle-blowers.")

5. Can include information on materiality, in either qualitative or quantitative terms.

E. For publicly held companies, the audit committee of the board of directors must be made up of individuals who are independent from the company's management.

1. The audit committee must be responsible for the appointment and compensation of the external auditors.

2. The external auditors must report to the audit committee rather than to the management. There are several required communications:

   a. All critical accounting policies and practices used by the issuer

   b. All alternative accounting and disclosure treatments of material financial information within generally accepted accounting principles

   c. Other material written communications between the CPA and the management

F. Analytical procedures are used in reviews and they are also required in an audit engagement.

   1. Analytical procedures must be performed in the planning stage of an audit to help auditor assess inherent risk. They also must be carried out in the final review stage of the audit to make certain that no suspicious changes occurred during the audit that were overlooked. Analytical procedures can be used as substantive tests but this use is optional.

   2. Auditor anticipates client figures, ratios, and relationships, such as sales, current ratio, age of inventory, gross profit percentage, etc. These estimations are made within a range. If client figures lie outside of this range, the risk of misstatement increases.

   3. Expected figures come from budgets, figures of previous years, industry averages, reports by competitors, changes in environment or in the company and the like.

   4. The credibility of auditor expectation is improved if information was derived from (1) several sources, (2) outside of the company, (3) an independent party inside of the company, or (4) audited data.

G. In evaluating inherent risk in an audit, the auditor should extend the steps that are traditionally taken to look for anything that indicates the risk that fraud has occurred. To make this assessment, the auditor should do the following. These are steps to be taken, rather than specific fraud risk factors to watch for.

   1. Make inquiries of management, the audit committee, and the internal auditors about the risks of fraud in the company and how they are addressed. The auditors should ask about whether fraud is known or suspected, as well as controls that have been established to reduce the risk of fraud.

   2. Look carefully at unusual or unexpected relationships identified in doing analytical procedures. Several specific comparisons are recommended:

      a. Relationship of net income to cash flows from operating activities

      b. Change from last year to the current year in the figures reported for inventory, accounts payable, sales, and cost of goods sold

c. Company profitability to industry averages

d. Company bad debts to industry averages

e. Sales volume to productivity

3. Look closely at accounts where a high degree of management judgment and subjectivity is present, such as an estimation of restructuring losses.

H. In connection with the recognition of revenue and management's possible override of controls, the auditor should simply presume that there is a risk of material misstatement due to fraud because these have been problem areas for many companies over the past few years.

auto assume risk of material misstmt in rev recog & mgmt override of ctrls

1. In connection with these two areas, the auditor should be especially cautious in connection with (a) the actual recognition of revenues, (b) determining the quantity of inventory on hand, and (c) significant estimations made by management.

2. For example, the auditor should make inquiries of client personnel about sales made near the end of the year, examine the contents of boxed inventory, and review the accuracy of previous management estimations.

3. Because of the possibility of management override, the auditor should also follow a process to examine journal entries and adjusting entries.

   a. Obtain an understanding of the financial reporting process and the controls over journal entries and adjustments.

   b. Select and test actual journal entries and adjustments.

   c. Ask individuals involved in the company about inappropriate or unusual activity in connection with journal entries. The CPA should be particularly interested in entries (1) made to unusual or unrelated accounts, (2) made by individuals who do not normally make entries, and (3) recorded at the end of the period with little or no explanation.

I. Conditions may be identified during audit fieldwork that change (especially increase) the auditor's assessment of the possibility of fraud.

1. Discrepancies may be found in the accounting records.

   a. Transactions are discovered that are not recorded in a timely or complete manner.

   b. Unsupported or unauthorized balances or transactions are discovered.

   c. Last minute adjustments are made that significantly affect the financial results.

d. Evidence of employees' access to systems and records is inconsistent with their duties.

e. Tips or complaints are made to the auditor.

2. Conflicting or missing evidence is found, such as:

    a. Missing documents.

    b. Documents that appear to have been altered.

    c. Original documents are no longer available, only copies.

    d. Significant, unexplained items appear on reconciliations.

    e. Inconsistent or vague responses are given to explain unusual differences found in analytical procedures.

    f. There is missing inventory or other significant assets.

3. Problematic or unusual relationships exist between the auditor and management.

    a. Denial of auditor access to records, facilities, certain employees, customers and the like.

    b. Undue time pressures imposed by management.

    c. Complaints by management about the conduct of the audit.

    d. Unusual delays in providing requested information.

    e. Unwillingness to facilitate the auditor's use of computer-assisted audit techniques.

    f. Unwillingness to add or revise disclosures in the financial statements recommended by the auditor.

J. In every engagement, auditor must maintain an attitude of professional skepticism (a questioning mind that will critically assess the audit evidence uncovered). If auditor has reason to suspect fraud, certain actions may be needed. Additional tests should be designed or additional corroboration should be sought (often from outside third parties). These steps might include the following:

   1. Surprise inspection of assets

   2. Requiring a count of assets closer to year's end

   3. Oral confirmations of balances as well as written ones

   4. Detailed review of large transactions and adjustments

5. Analytical procedures on a more detailed basis (sales by location, for example)

6. Interviews with employees in high risk areas

K. Auditor can make use of an outside specialist in gathering evidence.

1. In some areas, an auditor will not have the expertise necessary for making required judgments. In those cases, auditor may hire and rely on a specialist. For example, this may be done in inventory valuation (diamonds), estimations (percentage of completion), litigation analysis, etc.

2. Before relying on a specialist, auditor must verify the reliability of that party's work.

   a. Auditor checks specialist's professional reputation by examining licenses, certifications, references, client list, etc.

   b. Auditor checks independence. Specialist does not have to be independent but that would weigh on credibility of evidence.

3. Auditor is responsible for making certain that specialist understands what is needed and how the information will be used.

4. If there is a difference between client figures and the results of a specialist, auditor should seek a resolution or get opinion of a second specialist or consider qualifying opinion.

   a. Using the name of specialist in audit opinion is allowed but only if the work of the specialist leads to an opinion that was other than the standard unqualified opinion.

L. Material related party transactions must be disclosed in the footnotes. Auditor must make sure that all have been found and disclosed.

1. Related parties include affiliates of the company, substantial owners, management and their immediate family, and anyone who exerts significant influence over the company.

2. Auditor first gets a list of all related parties by asking client, looking at SEC reports and annual reports, getting a list of management and stockholders, and looking at information found in previous audits.

3. Auditor attempts to find all related party transactions by asking client, giving staff a list of related parties, reading minutes, scanning accounts for unusual amounts or familiar names, and watching for transactions with unusual terms, especially if they occur near the end of the year.

4. If related party transactions have occurred, the nature of the relationship and the terms of the transactions must be disclosed.

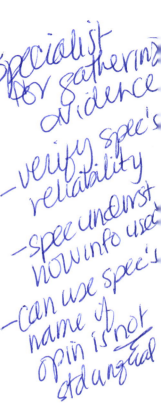

a. Client can also state that transactions were at same terms as transactions with an outside party, but only if that assertion can be substantiated.

M. Auditors are more and more likely to have to audit assets and liabilities reported at **fair value.** Fair value, for example, is significant in the reporting of purchase consolidations and in judging the possible impairment of assets.

1. The auditor must obtain an understanding of the management's process for determining fair value. This understanding should include:

   a. Controls in place to ensure proper reporting

   b. Expertise and experience of those persons involved in the determination

   c. The use of outside specialist by the client

   d. The significant assumptions used in determining fair value

   e. The process used by the management to monitor changes in those assumptions

2. If a fair value account has an observable market price, corroboration should not be especially difficult.

3. Many accounts to be reported at fair value, though, do not have an observable market price. In such cases, management must use other valuation models (such as discounted cash flows).

   a. In such cases, the auditor evaluates the significant assumptions made by management to determine if they are reasonable and consistent with market information, the economic environment, and past experience.

   b. The auditor must also investigate whether the valuation model in use is the most appropriate for this particular account.

   c. The auditor should test the data used by management in determining fair value.

      - The auditor can verify that the information being used came from reliable sources and was complete, consistent with the information that was available, and mathematically correct.
      - As an alternative, the auditor can set up his or her own valuation model to determine fair value to see if there is a material difference with the client figure.
      - The auditor should also review subsequent events for any additional evidence regarding the fair value of the account.

N. Auditor has special problem in corroborating estimations because there is usually a lack of objective evidence.

1. Estimates are found throughout statements: collectibility of receivables, outcome of lawsuits, life of equipment, etc.

2. Auditor evaluates (a) management's system of identifying need for estimates and (b) the method used in making specific estimations.

3. Auditor must also evaluate reasonableness of each significant estimate by (a) looking at past results (for example, how long equipment is normally used); (b) having an independent estimation made, possibly by using an outside specialist; and (c) reviewing subsequent events to determine if they confirm estimations.

O. Auditor must evaluate whether substantial doubt exists that company can remain in business for one year from balance sheet date. Auditor looks for indications of possible evidence that warn of going concern problems.

1. Indicators of possible problems include recurring losses, negative cash flows from operations, a negative working capital position, restructuring of debt, default on loans, lawsuits, unpaid dividends, loss of key customers, etc.

2. If problems are discovered, auditor seeks management's plans as to how problem will be resolved so that the company can continue to operate.

3. If auditor is not satisfied with management's plans, an explanatory paragraph is added after the opinion paragraph to warn readers that substantial doubt exists as to whether company can remain as a going concern. As an alternative, a disclaimer is allowed.

P. All evidence that is gathered to substantiate the CPA's opinion should be accumulated as **audit documentation**. This material should prove that sufficient, competent evidence was obtained to provide reasonable assurance that no material misstatements existed in any of the five assertions made by management. The Sarbanes-Oxley Act requires that registered firms must maintain audit documentation for each audit report for seven years.

1. Current file includes (a) the audit program to indicate adequate planning and show the nature, extent, and timing of the audit procedures that were performed; (b) all evidence gathered to substantiate the opinion along with an indication of which audit team member did the work; (c) indication of proper supervision; and (d) an explanation of all problems encountered and their resolution. Audit documentation must also include an abstract or copy of all significant contracts and agreements examined by the auditor along with an identification of other documents that were examined.

    a. Quality of evidence affects need for quantity. Best quality evidence is any direct personal evidence acquired by auditor (inspection, observation, computation) especially if it is based on information derived from outside of client. Poorest evidence is anything produced by client and given directly to auditor (bill of lading, receiving reports, etc.).

  b. The nature and extent of audit documentation will vary from account to account based on several factors, such as the risk of material misstatement in the account, the extent of judgment required of the auditor, and the nature and extent of any exceptions that were discovered.

 2. Permanent file includes client data that will stay the same for a number of years: account numbers, bond contracts, the company charter, organizational chart, etc.

Q. In an audit, the subsequent period is the time between the end of the client's fiscal year and the last day of the auditor's fieldwork.

 1. Auditor's investigation during this period should provide evidence about the possibility of misstatements in year-end balances. Such testing would include reviewing (a) cash payments as a search for unrecorded liabilities, (b) cash receipts to verify collectibility of receivables, (c) sales to prove reported value of inventory, (d) sales returns to substantiate reported sales figure, etc.

 2. Some subsequent events have no impact on year-end balances but are so significant that they should be disclosed in the footnotes. Examples would include the issuance of capital stock, a large casualty loss, or the incurrence of a large debt.

R. After issuance of an opinion, auditor may discover new information about the financial statements or the audit examination.

 1. After audit is finished, auditor has no further responsibility to do any further investigation. However, information may come to the auditor's attention that indicates a potential problem. In that situation, the auditor's concern is whether the original opinion can still be justified.

 2. Auditor should determine if original opinion continues to be appropriate. If necessary, client should be contacted and asked for help in the investigation.

INTERNAL CONTROL

A. Internal control is a process set up by the board of directors and management to provide reasonable assurance that company goals will be achieved as to (1) the reliability of financial reporting, (2) effectiveness and efficiency of operations, and (3) compliance with laws and regulations.

 1. Control risk is the chance that a material misstatement will not be prevented or detected by the company's internal control.

 2. An inverse relationship exists between assessed level of control risk and the acceptable level of detection risk that has to be achieved through auditor's substantive testing. Thus, assessment of control risk affects nature, extent, and timing of substantive testing.

B. Auditor must always come to an understanding of five components of client's internal control. Knowledge of components must be documented. Documentation can be by questionnaire, flowchart, memorandum, or a combination of these.

1. Control environment—company's commitment to integrity, ethical values, and competence; management's philosophy and style (the amount of risk that the company is willing to take, for example, or conservative nature of reporting); delegation of authority and responsibility; and human resource policies.

2. Risk assessment—company's ability to anticipate potential misstatements and work to prevent them before they occur. Control system should recognize that risk increases because of new people, new operating systems, rapid growth, change in company or environment, new technology, new products, geographical separation and the like.

3. Control activities—policies and procedures installed by company to reduce risk of misstatements to an acceptable level. Can be separated into several classifications.

    a. Performance reviews (such as comparing reported figures to budgets, standards, forecasts, past year figures, etc.) to highlight differences and indicate to officials the possible need for investigation and corrective action.

    b. General controls to help ensure the accuracy of all data processing activities.

    c. Application controls applied to individual transactions to ensure that all transactions are valid, authorized, and properly processed.

    d. Physical controls to safeguard assets.

    e. Segregation of duties within the organization so that different individuals/departments (1) authorize transactions, (2) record transactions, and (3) maintain custody of assets.

4. Information and communication—ability of the accounting system to generate reliable information. System must be able to identify and record all transactions in a timely manner and convey information to those parties who can make use of it.

5. Monitoring—regular assessment of internal control over time so that it does not become outdated or lose its dependability.

C. The client's management has the best chance to perpetuate fraud because its members are in a position that allows them the necessary authority and because they are most likely to benefit from fraud. Thus, the CPA must be careful to watch for any evidence that management is overriding control activities, even though those activities appear to be operating effectively.

D. After coming to an understanding of control components, auditor makes a preliminary assessment of control risk based on the quality of these components, evaluations made in previous audits, discovery of fraud risk factors, competence and objectivity of internal audit department, review of client control documentation, observation of employee performance, and by tracing a sample of transactions through various systems to note proper application of control procedures.

1. Based on this preliminary assessment, significant problems may be apparent and the auditor will assess control risk at a maximum level. Auditor then relies solely on substantive testing to reduce detection risk so that overall audit risk is reduced to acceptable level. Auditor has no reason to perform tests of controls.

2. Based on preliminary assessment, control risk for some assertions may appear to possibly be below maximum. If control risk is eventually assessed as being below the maximum level, auditor will be required to do less substantive testing or can rely on tests of a lower quality.

3. To finalize a preliminary assessment that control risk is below the maximum, the auditor performs tests of specific control activities.

    a. Must determine design of internal control within individual accounting systems. Once again, this understanding can be documented by a questionnaire, flowchart, and/or memorandum.

    b. Control activities are identified within these systems that should help to reduce control risk. Auditor anticipates types of misstatements that could occur and then searches for control activities that would prevent these problems.

    c. The identified control activities are tested to verify that they are actually operating effectively and efficiently as intended. Auditor can take several actions.

        - Talk with personnel about procedures that they follow.
        - Observe employees as they perform critical tasks.
        - Trace the processing of transactions through the system to see if control activities were properly performed. In most cases, control activities are designed to leave some physical proof, such as a check mark.
        - Reperform the activities to ensure that all problems were caught.

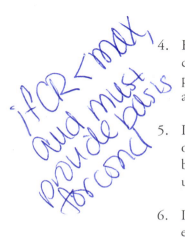
if CR < max, aud must provide basis for concl

4. Even if control risk appears low after preliminary assessment of the five components, further testing of specific controls may take more effort than the potential savings in substantive testing. In those cases, it is more efficient for auditor to assume maximum control risk and move directly to substantive testing.

5. If control risk is assessed at the maximum, auditor must document understanding of the control components and specify the conclusion. If control risk is assessed below the maximum, auditor must also provide basis for this conclusion and understanding of the control activities relied on in the individual systems.

6. In a system where information is transmitted, processed, or maintained electronically, auditor may be unable to carry out enough substantive testing to

reduce detection risk to an acceptable level. Auditor should perform additional tests of controls to gather evidence that might provide adequate assurance.

E. Inherent limitations exist for all systems of internal control. Some amount of risk will always exist; internal control cannot provide perfect assurance.

 1. Collusion by employees can get around most control activities.

 2. Management can override control activities.

 3. Human errors can prevent control activities from working properly.

 4. At some point, the cost of additional control is not worth the additional benefits that accrue.

 5. Internal control as well as the company itself can change quickly over time. Even though control may be excellent at one point in time, that is no assurance it will continue to be sufficient.

F. Internal audit department is responsible for monitoring internal control within a company. It appraises the design and helps assure compliance with all controls (as compared to independent auditor who just assesses financial controls). Fair presentation of financial statements is only an indirect interest of the internal audit department.

 1. Independent auditor determines the actual function of the internal audit department by looking at job descriptions, status in the company, audit plans, etc.

 2. If internal audit department is competent and objective (independent), assessed level of control risk might be reduced so that less substantive testing is needed.

   a. Competence of internal audit department is judged by looking at education, certification, and experience of the individuals. Auditor should also review some of the work of the internal audit department as it relates to financial reporting.

   b. Objectivity of internal audit department is judged by determining whether reporting is done directly to audit committee and/or board of directors. It is also important to make sure that no limitations are placed on work of internal audit department.

 3. If risk of material misstatements is very low for certain assertions (value of prepaid expenses, for example), the work of the internal audit department alone may provide sufficient evidence for the independent auditor.

G. If auditor discovers a reportable condition (a significant deficiency) in a company's internal control, auditor must inform the audit committee.

 1. Communication can be written or oral.

2. If problem has been previously reported and acknowledged by board, but not fixed, auditor has no responsibility to communicate again.

3. If problem constitutes a material weakness in internal control (high level of risk), communication should be made immediately. Otherwise communication can wait until end of the audit.

ACCOUNTS RECEIVABLE AND REVENUES

A. In auditing accounts receivable and related revenue balances, several potential problems exist that could create material misstatements. Some of these would be errors, whereas others would indicate fraud.

1. Reported receivables and sales could be false. Amounts were recorded to manipulate reported amount of income. False sales are especially likely if (a) income to be reported is down for the period, (b) employee compensation or bonuses are based on profits, or (c) company plans to issue capital stock or borrow money in the near future.

2. Incoming cash is stolen and theft is hidden by writing off the receivable as a bad debt.

3. Lapping is being carried out. Cash from one receivable is stolen and covered with cash received from a second customer during the following day or two.

4. The year-end cutoff of transactions is incorrect. Transactions occurring before the end of year could be recorded in the subsequent period (thus, reporting for the initial year is not complete). Transactions after the end of year could be recorded prematurely in the initial year (reported transactions in initial year did not actually exist at the time of the financial statements).

5. Customer is billed incorrectly (because of math errors, wrong quantity, wrong price, wrong items) or customer is just not billed at all for goods that were actually shipped (inventory is gone but no collection is ever made).

6. Transaction is with a related party so that disclosure is needed.

B. Company should have a system in place to record sale, make proper shipment, and control and collect receivable balance.

1. A customer order is received. May be by mail or over telephone or given directly to company employees.

2. On a preprinted, prenumbered sales order form, the sales department lists all relevant information: quantity, description, terms, buyer, address, method of payment, etc.

3. Credit department reviews credit file (which can hold credit report, references, financial statements, payment history of client, etc.). Approval or disapproval of credit is then indicated on the sales order form.

4. If approved, sales order goes to finished goods warehouse where goods are gathered and sent to shipping department. Separate departments are maintained so that goods being removed must be documented. Since asset is being transferred, shipping department should verify description and quantity against sales order form. Condition of goods should also be checked. Shipping then signs and returns a copy of sales order, which is kept by warehouse as a receipt to prove that transfer was made.

5. Shipping department sends goods to customer and prepares a shipping document, often known as a bill of lading. One copy goes with merchandise and a second copy is sent directly to customer.

6. Copy of bill of lading is sent to inventory accounting department which should maintain a perpetual listing of all inventory. An entry is made to remove item from records. Entries are accumulated and forwarded to general accounting department for posting of the overall reduction of inventory account.

7. Copies of all documents go to **billings department.** Comparison is made of quantity and description. If all information agrees, a sales invoice is prepared and sent to client. It is also recorded in sales journal. Summary of sales journal is forwarded to general accounting for recording.

8. Copy of sales invoice is sent to accounts receivable department. Amount is recorded in accounts receivable master file by customer name.

9. Periodically, an aged accounts receivable trial balance is prepared, which lists each account by age. Old accounts are turned over to a collection department.

10. If balance still proves to be uncollectible, both collection and accounts receivable departments file documentation to indicate actions taken. Independent party reviews information before final write-off of balance is approved.

C. A number of substantive testing procedures should be performed to verify the five assertions made by client about accounts receivable and related balances.

1. Perform analytical procedures to identify areas where client figures differ from auditor expectations. Look at overall balance of each account, age of receivables, gross profit percentage, sales returns as a percentage of sales, write off of accounts as compared to previous years, etc.

    a. Analytical procedures are required in planning stage of audit to help assess inherent risk. They are also required in final review stage of audit as a last check. Use as a substantive test of an account balance is optional.

2. Trace one or more transactions through the entire system to see if recording is appropriate at each step. Start with customer order and check all steps until

account and collection are recorded. Auditor is especially interested that all shipments are properly billed.

   a. Whenever auditor starts with transactions at their inception, the completeness assertion is being tested.

3. Vouch one or more entries in the T-account back through system to see if there is adequate support. Whenever auditor starts with a reported balance and seeks corroboration, the existence assertion is being tested.

4. Check math and accuracy of client work where applicable. Re-add accounts receivable master file and compare it to the general ledger account. Verify that aged accounts receivable trial balance is added correctly and individual amounts agree with master file. Re-add sales journal.

5. For three to four days before and three to four days after year end, verify client cutoff procedures to make sure transactions were recorded in correct period. Use the bill of lading and sales invoice to determine when receivable and sale should be recorded. Cash receipts listing provides date for removal of receivable.

6. Auditor reviews any evidence generated in subsequent period (the time from the balance sheet date until the end of fieldwork). For example, cash collections prove the balance and collectibility of a receivable, sales returns should be matched with sales, and bad debts written off may have been uncollectible at year's end.

7. Look for related party transactions that have to be disclosed. For example, the representation letter asks about their existence.

8. Confirm balances directly with customers to prove existence assertion. Usually done early in audit unless inherent and/or control risks are high. In that case, confirmation is carried out closer to year's end.

   a. All confirmations are signed by client but controlled, mailed, and responses received by auditor.

   b. Negative confirmations ask customer for a response only if reported balance is wrong. It is less costly but provides a poorer quality of evidence since nothing tangible is received unless a problem exists. Normally used for small balances, balances that are not old, and where risk appears low.

   c. Positive confirmations ask for response from customer whether balance is correct or incorrect. Because an actual response should be received in all cases, this is viewed as a better technique. Normally used for old balances, large balances, or where risk is high.

   - If no response to positive request is received, a second confirmation can be sent or a direct call made. If auditor still does not get a response, alternative testing must be expanded. All documents should be compared, and cash receipts should be reviewed for subsequent payment.

- In either type of confirmation, reported discrepancies should be investigated to determine whether a problem exists.

d. Accounts which have been written off or which have a zero balance can be confirmed just to make certain that reported facts are accurate.

e. If a confirmation is returned by e-mail or by fax, the auditor may need to call the customer or request that the confirmation be mailed to the auditor in order to get adequate support.

9. Method of estimating bad debt expense should be examined. Auditor wants to make sure that no evidence exists to indicate that client's estimation is not justified. Auditor must be aware of changes that may affect client's previous experience.

10. Auditor must ensure balance sheet presentation and disclosure is appropriate. For example, pledged accounts must be noted.

STATISTICAL SAMPLING

A. Sampling is used in virtually every aspect of auditing. The term refers to making a decision about a whole (a population) by testing only a part of that group (called a sample).

1. Sampling creates a problem; because auditor does not look at every piece of evidence, a chance exists that a material misstatement could be missed. Thus, some risk always remains that the audit opinion will be wrong.

2. There are two reasons why auditor only provides reasonable assurance and not perfect assurance.

   a. Sampling risk is the chance that auditor's conclusion will be wrong because only a portion of the population was examined. A sample may not be representative of the population.

   b. Nonsampling risk is the chance that auditor's conclusion will be wrong for reasons that would happen even if every item had been tested. Includes human errors such as the failure to recognize a misstatement and the misinterpretation of results.

3. Judgment sampling estimates the amount of sampling risk that the auditor faces purely by human guess.

4. Statistical sampling determines sampling risk mathematically.

   a. Auditor sets an acceptable level of sampling risk before beginning a test, and statistical sampling computes the number of items to be tested to reduce risk to that desired level.

b. Auditor can also perform a test and then use statistical sampling to determine the amount of sampling risk that is present. For example, the auditor might use statistical sampling in making the following evaluation: "Based on the results of this test, there is a 10% chance that the client figure is not fairly presented."

B. In general, there are two types of statistical sampling.

1. Attributes sampling estimates a percentage and is often used in the tests of controls because the auditor is interested in the error rate that has occurred in connection with a particular control activity. Auditor is attempting to determine if activity is functioning as intended.

2. Variables sampling estimates a total and is often used in substantive tests where the auditor is attempting to corroborate a reported account balance.

C. Auditor carries out several steps in following an attributes sampling plan.

1. Anticipates the deviation rate for the control activity (or other application) being tested. Expected rate is based on difficulty of activity, experience of person performing the control, results found in previous audits, etc. The more deviations that are anticipated, the larger the sample must be.

2. Sets a tolerable deviation rate. This is the maximum error rate that the auditor could tolerate and still believe the control activity was operating effectively and efficiently. As the rate that the auditor can tolerate gets smaller, sample size must get larger.

3. Sets allowable level of risk that the sample will be misleading. For this particular testing, auditor is especially worried that the sample will look better than the actual population. In that case, auditor may think that the control activity is functioning properly and will set control risk too low and do less substantive testing than is needed. To reduce the level of risk that the sample will be misleading, the size of the sample must be increased.

4. Based on these three figures, a calculation or a chart is used to determine proper sample size. Except with very small populations, the number of items in the population has little or no effect on the sample size.

5. The appropriate number of items is selected from the population. Items must be picked randomly; each item should have an equal chance of selection.

6. Sample items are examined and the number of deviations (usually errors) is determined. That number is restated as a percentage based on sample size.

7. Another chart is used to convert the actual deviation rate of the sample to the potential **upper deviation rate of the population**. Difference between the actual rate and upper deviation rate is called the allowance for sampling risk.

8. Upper deviation rate is compared to maximum tolerable rate. If upper deviation rate is lower, auditor assumes control activity is functioning as intended and will probably set control risk at a low level. If upper deviation rate is more, auditor assumes activity is not functioning as intended; control risk is high.

9. Auditor also examines both the cause and size of the errors that were found. Even if rate is low, the type of deviation may indicate a serious problem.

D. Auditor carries out several steps in a variables sampling plan. There are several variations but following is an example of classical mean-per-unit sampling.

1. Sets the level of a tolerable misstatement. This is the size of the largest misstatement in the account being examined that (when combined with misstatements in all other accounts) would still not cause the financial statements to be materially misstated. If auditor reduces the size of a misstatement that can be tolerated, a bigger sample will be required.

2. Sets allowable risk levels that sample will be misleading. To reduce these risk levels, a larger sample size must be selected.

   a. A misleading sample can cause incorrect acceptance. There is a risk that a sample will substantiate client figure when the population is actually materially misstated. This problem leads to an unqualified opinion being given on statements that are not fairly presented.

   b. A misleading sample can cause incorrect rejection. There is a risk that a sample will not substantiate the client figure even though the population is not materially misstated. This problem leads to additional (unnecessary) testing being performed.

3. Estimates the amount of misstatement in the population. This figure is usually affected by the efficiency of the accounting system and staff. The bigger the expected misstatement, the larger the required sample size.

4. Again, population size has only a little impact on sample size.

5. Auditor takes a preliminary sample to estimate the variability of the items in the population. If the items are all about the same amount, variability is low. Variability is measured by estimating the **standard deviation.** The higher the variability, the more items that have to be selected to get a representative sample.

6. The various factors are entered into mathematical formulas to determine the appropriate sample size.

7. Auditor randomly selects items for the sample and measures the average value of these items. The average of the sample is then extended to the entire population to give a total. Difference between this total and client figure is the **projected misstatement.** If projected misstatement is less than tolerable misstatement, the test has provided evidence that reported balance is fairly presented. If projected

misstatement is more, the test has not provided evidence that balance is fairly presented.

E. In variables sampling, the variability of the items in the population can often be so great that sample size has to be large, causing the auditor to do extensive testing.

1. One alternative is to stratify the population. Items are divided into two or three separate populations based on size. Because they are grouped by size, the variability of each population will be relatively small and the required sample will be reduced.

2. Two other alternatives are ratio and difference estimations. These methods do **not** estimate the average item in the population but rather the average of differences between book values and audited values or the ratio of book values to audited values.

F. Probability proportional to size sampling (PPS sampling) is another way of estimating a total while keeping sample size small. The sampling unit is each dollar in the population and not each document. This approach is also called monetary unit sampling and dollar unit sampling.

1. Instead of selecting every nth item (every 50th invoice, for example), auditor picks every nth dollar (every $5,000th, for example, in a list of invoices). Although the nth dollar is selected, the entire document is tested.

    a. Bigger items have more dollars so they are more likely to get picked. Stratification and the degree of variability are not important.

    b. Sample size is determined mathematically based on tolerable misstatement, expected misstatement in population, allowable risk of incorrect acceptance, and expected number of errors.

    c. Total dollar figure of population is divided by sample size to get sampling interval (such as every $5,000th dollar).

2. If sample has no errors, population total is accepted. If misstatements are found, the size of a projected misstatement must be determined.

    a. For items that are larger than the interval (in this example, an invoice that is over $5,000), the amount of the misstatement is just used in arriving at the projected misstatement.

    b. For items that are smaller than interval, the percentage of the misstatement (called the tainting percentage) is determined and multiplied by the interval. If a $500 item has a 2% error, 2% is multiplied by sampling interval to get figure to include in projected misstatement.

INVENTORY AND ACCOUNTS PAYABLE

A. Auditor should anticipate certain potential problems in auditing **inventory, accounts payable,** and related accounts.

1. Inventory may include damaged or obsolete items so that recorded value must be reduced to net realizable value. This possibility relates to valuation assertion.

2. Inventory might be miscounted, either accidentally or intentionally. Overcounting inflates currently reported earnings; undercounting reduces reported income. If overcounted, problem is with existence assertion. If undercounted, problem is with completeness assertion.

3. End-of-year cutoff could be recorded incorrectly in connection with receipt and shipment of inventory. Again, possible overstatement relates to existence assertion, whereas understatement affects completeness assertion.

4. End of year liabilities may have been omitted because invoice has not been received or because company wants to improve its reported debt position. Problem relates to completeness assertion.

5. Inventory being held by client is on consignment or inventory owned by client is out on consignment.

B. Company should have a system in place to record purchase of inventory (or fixed assets) and the related liability, as well as subsequent payment.

1. For example, assume that a department or individual within the company needs an item. A requisition (sometimes referred to as a material requisition) is completed. A person with appropriate authority reviews and authorizes requisition.

    a. Whenever any document is created, it should be reviewed, authorized, recorded, and a copy kept.

2. Copy of approved requisition goes to warehouse (or store room).

3. If item is available, order is filled. If not, purchase requisition is created and sent to purchasing department.

4. Purchasing department verifies request by checking against budget. Should also check that all documents have been properly authorized. A purchase order should be created after going through a set of prescribed steps, such as getting bids (for expensive items) or checking with a number of vendors (for cheaper items).

    a. Should only buy from vendors listed on a **preapproved vendor list.**

5. Copy of purchase order goes to receiving room to alert that a shipment is to be expected. On this copy, quantity is blanked out to ensure that goods will be counted.

6. Goods are received by receiving room and compared to copy of purchase order to verify make, model, description of item, and condition. If there is a discrepancy or if goods are damaged, they are not accepted. If accepted, a receiving report is prepared, giving all information about goods.

    a. Copy is sent to inventory accounting department to update perpetual inventory records.

    b. Receiving room is separate from warehouse in order to ensure adequate documentation of goods that are received.

7. Goods are transferred to warehouse. Warehouse employees verify quantity, description, and condition and then return a signed copy of the receiving report so that the receiving room has a receipt to verify transfer of goods.

8. Purchase invoice is eventually received from vendor. The price charged, terms of payment, and math need to be verified.

9. Copies of all documents (requisition, purchase requisition, purchase order, receiving report, and purchase invoice) are forwarded to accounts payable department (also referred to as vouchers payable department). Agreement and authorization of all documents is verified.

10. A voucher is prepared by accounts payable to indicate approval to make payment. It is reviewed and authorized. Liability and purchase are recorded in voucher register. Summary of voucher register is forwarded periodically to general accounting to record in general ledger.

11. Voucher and back-up documentation (sometimes referred to as a voucher package) are sent to cash disbursements department and filed by due date.

12. On due date, voucher is reviewed for reasonableness and compared one final time to documentation. Check is written.

13. Second party compares check and voucher and signs check. Amount is recorded in cash disbursements journal as a reduction in cash and liability. Again, a summary will be made and forwarded to general accounting for recording. Voucher is defaced in some manner to avoid repayment. Check is mailed to vendor.

C. A number of substantive testing procedures should be performed to verify the five assertions made by client about inventory, accounts payable, and any related balances.

1. Analytical procedures are performed, both at beginning and end of audit. Auditor expectations are compared to client figures, such as the age of inventory, gross

profit percentage, balance of year-end inventory and liabilities, cost per unit, percentage of inventory that is recorded below cost, etc.

2. Trace one or more transactions through the entire system to see if recording is appropriate at each step. Start with requisition and check all steps until liability is recorded and paid. Whenever auditor starts with initiation of a transaction and follows it through system, the completeness assertion is being tested.

3. Vouch one or more entries in the T-account back through system to see if there is adequate support. Whenever auditor starts with a reported balance and seeks support, the existence assertion is being tested.

4. Check math as well as client work where applicable. Re-add voucher register and cash disbursements journal and compare totals to the general ledger account. Application of LIFO/FIFO should be checked. For manufacturing company, inventory cost figures should be verified.

5. For the three to four days before and three to four days after the end of the year, verify client cutoff procedures to ensure that transactions were recorded in correct period. Use receiving report and purchase invoice to determine when inventory and payable should be recorded. Need to know FOB point and location of inventory on last day of year. Cash disbursements journal provides date for removal of payable.

6. Auditor reviews any evidence generated in subsequent period (the time from the balance sheet date until the end of fieldwork). For example, auditor investigates the following.

    a. Inventory that does not sell in subsequent period should be examined for obsolescence or damage.

    b. Cash payments in subsequent period are reviewed to see if they indicate an unrecorded year-end liability.

    c. Invoices received should be reviewed to see if an unrecorded liability existed at year's end.

    d. Accounts payable can be confirmed but that is not usually done since invoice is received from vendor.

7. Representation letter should ask about presence of obsolete inventory.

8. Auditor looks for evidence that inventory might be out on consignment or that goods are being held on consignment.

    a. Contract file should be examined for evidence of consignment transactions.

    b. Preparation of a bill of lading without a subsequent sales invoice may indicate consignment-out transactions. Receipt of goods without a subsequent purchase invoice may indicate consignment-in transactions.

c. Collections and payments made at irregular intervals may indicate that cash is transferred whenever a sale is made.

d. Confirmations may expose inventory out on consignment that has been recorded by company as a receivable.

e. Auditor should confirm consignment-out balances and may want to make a test count.

9. Auditor should observe client's taking of a **physical inventory**. If company uses a periodic system, count will be at year's end. If it has a perpetual system, count can be any time during year unless risk levels are high. Auditor performs a number of tasks.

    a. Makes sure that counters know what they are doing.

    b. Looks for damaged or obsolete items.

    c. Makes and records a number of test counts.

    d. If tag system is used, records last tag number so no additional inventory can be added at a later time.

10. Client adds cost to ending list of inventory items and arrives at a final total of the inventory cost. Auditor must verify this listing.

    a. Makes sure that quantity listed for the items that were test-counted agrees with recorded amounts.

    b. Verify that last tag number is the same.

    c. Checks a sample of cost figures.

    d. Checks a sample of extensions and footings.

AUDITING AND TECHNOLOGY

A. Control of the Computer Function.

   1. Controls used in connection with computers operating within an accounting system are separated into three broad classifications.

      a. General controls relate to the operation of the entire computer system.

      b. Application controls relate to a specific program or a specified task. Application controls are further divided into (1) programmed application controls and (2) manual follow-up of exception reports.

c. User control procedures are designed to test the completeness and accuracy of computer controls.

2. General controls are divided into four broad categories.

   a. Controls should be in place in connection with the development of new programs.

      - For follow up and testing purposes, new programs should be documented usually by the creation of a detailed run manual.
      - New programs should be properly tested before being approved for actual use in processing data.
         - Test data can be used for this purpose. All conceivable valid and invalid situations are run through the computer to see if program reacts correctly to each.
      - Before a new program is put into use, all parties involved should review and authorize it. Reviewers would include management, user departments, and information system analysts.
      - All computer hardware should be properly programmed to ensure reliability.

   b. A detailed process should be installed to make sure that only authorized changes are made in functioning programs.

      - The details and reasons for all changes should be documented, reviewed, and authorized.
      - Test data can be rerun periodically to ensure that the program still handles all known situations properly.
      - When program is initially developed, a duplicate copy (a **controlled program**) can be safeguarded. Periodically, data is run on current operating program and then on controlled program. Results are matched to see if any discrepancies exist that cannot be explained. This procedure is known as a **parallel simulation**.
         - A code comparison program will automatically compare operating program to controlled program.
      - Programs and hardware can be designed to serve as an **integrated test facility**. Whenever a program is to be run, test data can be included to verify current processing. This approach allows for daily testing. Test data must be coded so that results will not be mixed with live data.

   c. Access to computer, programs, and data should be adequately secured.

      - Computer and all files are locked and access is limited to authorized individuals.
      - Passwords or identification numbers are used to ensure that only authorized individuals have access to the computer. Passwords and numbers are changed regularly.

   d. The computer facility itself should be safeguarded.

- Operators only have access to the portion of run manual dealing with the operating aspects of the program so that they do not have an in-depth understanding of the program.
- Duplicate copies of all programs and backup information are stored at a separate location. Enough data should be kept so that the files can be reconstructed if destroyed.

3. Programmed application controls are specifically designed so that a particular program will function properly.

    a. Self-checking numbers can be used with input information. Computer uses number (employee identification, for example) in a mathematical test to verify that it is proper. One digit (called a check digit) may be placed within the number to create a mathematical verification.

    b. Control totals are predetermined totals that have been computed for data. These totals can be verified at each step in process to make sure that information has not been changed.

    - **Item count** is total of the number of transactions to be processed.
    - **Batch total** is a total derived from some element of the data being processed (total sales for example). Total would have some meaning or importance.
    - **Hash total** is a total derived from some element of the data being processed that would normally not be totaled (total of employee social security numbers, for example). Total is only computed for control purposes.
    - **Limit test** is an upper boundary established for processing purposes. For example, no weekly paycheck might be printed for over $2,000 without some additional testing.
    - **Validity test** is an internal reconciliation of data within computer to make certain that it is legitimate. For example, before printing payroll, computer can check master employee file to make sure that requested checks are only for actual employees.

4. Some application controls are composed of manual follow up steps taken in connection with exception reports.

    a. Whenever computer processes data that may be in error (a check request exceeds the specified limit or a self-checking digit indicates a possible problem), an exception (or error) report is printed and processing is halted.

    b. A control group (an independent team established for review) should resolve exception report problems so that processing can continue.

5. User control procedures are designed to ensure some human testing of computer output.

    a. The control group and/or the department that receives output should test results before authorizing its distribution and use.

b. Verification is made that control totals are in agreement with actual output.

c. On a test basis, individual input items are verified against computer output. For example, payroll checks for a few employees could be computed manually each period to verify balances are correct.

B. **Other Computer Areas**

1. Electronic data interchange (EDI) refers to transmittal of documents directly from a computer in one entity to a computer in another. The Internet is often used for this conveyance. EDI increases the speed of the transmittal and reduces the chance for clerical errors.

    a. Authentication controls are designed to ensure proper submission and delivery of EDI communications.

    b. Encryption makes messages unreadable to unauthorized parties to help ensure that confidential data is not misused.

    c. A value added network (VAN) refers to an organization that gathers and transmits EDI communications. Thus, some part of the communication of information exists outside of the reporting company. An example of a VAN system that enables EDI transactions is a supermarket that allows customers to use a check card to automatically transfer money from their bank accounts to that of the store.

2. On-line, real-time (OLRT) computer systems pose special control problems for a company. On-line means that the computer terminal has direct access to files within main computer. Real-time means that all changes are made immediately to data without any intermediate step.

    a. Typical examples of OLRT systems would include a savings account at a bank and a perpetual inventory system at a furniture store.

    b. Because changes can be made from many locations, company cannot always control who makes changes. Since changes can be made without documentation, auditor has no audit trail to use in verifying that appropriate processing has taken place.

        - OLRT systems rely heavily on **access controls:** input or password numbers must be furnished before access is allowed, access is only allowed from approved terminals and at approved times, large changes require secondary approval.
        - Password numbers should be changed frequently.
        - Computer should be programmed to record unsuccessful attempts to enter system.

    c. Control is improved if documentation is required, which can be reconciled with computer totals periodically. Documentation may not be needed for processing, but only for control purposes.

3. An auditor can make use of a number of computer assisted auditing techniques and other computer audit tools to use the speed and efficiency of the computer in doing certain testing.

   a. Auditing may have or develop a **generalized computer audit software package.**

      - It is designed with considerable flexibility so that it can be adapted to the client's computer.
      - It provides auditor with independent access into computer so that the data can be gathered without having to rely on client personnel and programs.
      - Programs can serve as a **controlled program** so that a **parallel simulation** of data can be carried out and compared to the output of client's programs.
      - Can test data stored within computer. Can do mechanical testing, such as selecting old accounts, internal comparisons, verification of year-end cutoff, and the like.

   b. Spreadsheets can be developed to do many audit tasks. Data can then be entered into the spreadsheet to verify calculations, such as depreciation and interest. Analytical procedures, as well as statistical sampling tests, can be performed using such spreadsheets.

   c. Computer diskettes can be used for audit documentation to allow for easy storage. Items such as flowcharts, questionnaires, representation letters, and engagement letters can be kept on file and printed out when needed.

   d. Testing typically done to control computer, such as the use of test data, code comparison programs, and integrated test facilities, can also be applied by external auditor.

FLOWCHARTING

A. In assessing control risk, the auditor evaluates five **internal control components.** Auditor must also decide whether to perform tests of controls, such as investigating the design of individual accounting systems and the control activities in use. Three approaches can be used in achieving an understanding of controls and systems.

1. Internal control questionnaire is a list of questions about internal control with "yes" answers indicating good control and "no" being a problem.

   a. Auditor anticipates problems that might happen and the control activities that should be in use, both general controls and controls specifically for the system being studied. Each question is designed to ascertain whether a particular control exists and is functioning appropriately.

   b. Thus, a "no" answer would indicate that a control is not functioning properly and, if a misstatement occurs, it may not be caught.

c. The advantages of using a questionnaire are that this is a very thorough technique and problems are noted immediately. The disadvantage is that company personnel often know the appropriate response and may not be completely truthful.

Figure 1: Flowchart Symbols

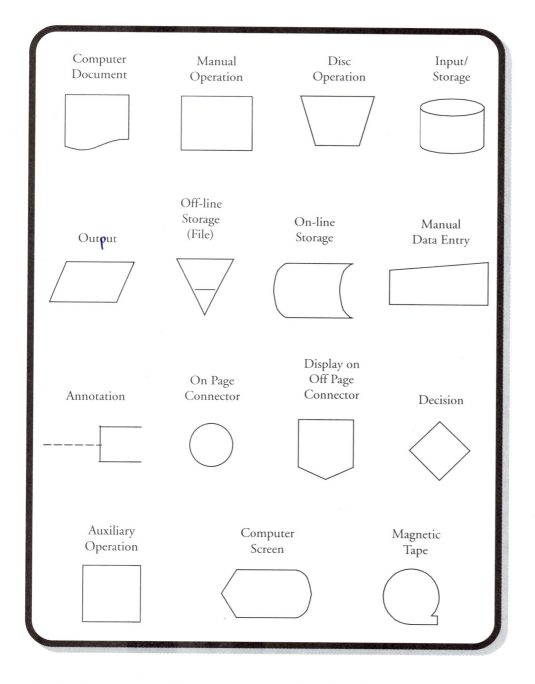

2. Using a memorandum means that auditor physically writes out a description of a system and its control activities.

a. The advantages are that anyone can produce a memo and it requires auditor to gain a good knowledge of a system. The disadvantages are that it takes a long time, problems are not always apparent, and changes are difficult to record.

3. Flowcharting is the symbolic presentation of a system in a sequential order. It is designed to show what each department does, as well as the creation and disposition of all documents.

   a. The advantages are that it provides an excellent depiction of the system and problems may be easier to spot. The disadvantage is that creating and reading a flowchart both take a particular skill.

   b. Numerous flowchart symbols are used. Figure 1.1 shows some of the most common.

CASH RECEIPTS AND CASH BALANCES

A. For auditor, cash receipts and resulting cash balances provide several concerns. Most problems deal with the theft of company's cash and ability of company's internal control to prevent such theft.

B. Company should have a system to record the inflow of cash into company.

   1. As with any transaction, there should be an immediate recording. However, because of the possibility of theft, this step is especially important in connection with cash receipts. The use of a cash register is quite common for this purpose. Cash register tape can be used to make sure money is deposited correctly.

   2. If checks are accepted, they should be required to be in the name of the company and immediately endorsed "For Deposit Only."

   3. Periodically, all cash is delivered to cashier and a signed receipt is used to document conveyance of asset.

   4. Cashier prepares a daily cash summary of all incoming cash with a copy going to general accounting for journal entry purposes.

   5. Money should be deposited in the bank on a daily basis for security purposes and to provide an additional record of the cash amounts.

   6. Cashier prepares bank deposit slip listing individual items. This document is reviewed and approved by second party who makes deposit.

   7. Validated bank deposit slip is mailed by bank directly back to independent party in company who compares total and individual items with daily cash summary to make certain that appropriate cash was deposited each day.

8. Independent party in company performs reconciliation of bank account on a regular basis. Second party reviews reconciliation, especially looking at deposits in transit, outstanding checks, and other items included to get balances to reconcile.

C. If money is mailed into company (for sales or on account), additional control steps should be taken to prevent theft.

1. Ask for payment by check (not cash). Request that checks be made out in the name of the company.

2. Have customer return a remittance slip with the payment which includes information about account. Customer should enter amount of the payment being made.

3. One person opens mail, counts money, and takes custody. A second person records names and amounts, collects remittance slips, and prepares a cash remittance list (which can be used to make certain that money is deposited correctly and that proper reductions are made to accounts receivable).

4. As in any cash system, checks are immediately endorsed "For Deposit Only" and money is conveyed to cashier for inclusion on daily cash summary.

5. Remittance slips go to accounts receivable department to update master file of customer balances.

D. A number of substantive testing procedures should be performed by the auditor to verify the five assertions made by client about cash and cash receipts.

1. Carry out analytical procedures. For example, compare expected cash inflows to actual cash inflows; compare cash inflows by month, looking for any unusual amount; compare items on bank reconciliation to previous reconciliations.

2. Trace a sample of all documents through system to test for completeness: remittance slips, cash remittance list, cash register tape, daily cash summary, bank deposit slip, and journal entries.

3. Vouch entries in Cash account to find support to test for existence. Look for documentation that substantiates entries.

4. Cash remittance list and daily cash summary should be re-added on a test basis.

5. Request a bank cutoff statement for all items clearing account for the first seven to ten days after the end of the year for all checking accounts. As with any confirmation, it is signed by client but controlled by auditor.

6. Year-end bank reconciliation should be reviewed. Math is checked. Items from bank cutoff statement are used to verify outstanding checks and deposits in transit.

7. Test year-end cutoff by looking at receipts and disbursements for a few days before and a few days after the end of the year to make certain transactions are recorded in proper time period.

   a. One of the big concerns at year-end is the chance of **kiting**. In kiting, money is transferred from one account to another with deposit recorded in first period and withdrawal recorded in second period.

   b. Kiting is used to inflate cash in order to (1) allow for recording of false sales or (2) cover stolen funds.

   c. Auditor reviews bank cutoff statement to uncover transfers at year-end, which are then scheduled to ensure that they have been recorded correctly.

8. Cash is only counted if a significant amount is held by client. Should count marketable securities and any other liquid assets at the same time so that funds cannot be moved around to cover a cash shortage.

9. Request a bank confirmation from all banks with which the company has dealt. Confirmations should even be sent to banks where accounts have been closed to make certain that balances have not been hidden. It asks for information about checking accounts, savings accounts, loans and other debts, etc. Confirmation will ask for all balances and terms, including interest rates and security arrangements.

10. Look in subsequent time periods for any unusual cash receipts or cash disbursements. Also watch for any returned checks.

SPECIAL REPORTS AND OTHER REPORTS

A. Several types of special reports exist where auditor can examine information not in the form of financial statements presented according to U.S. generally accepted accounting principles.

   1. One common form of special report is prepared to report on statements produced using a comprehensive basis of accounting other than U.S. generally accepted accounting principles. One example would be reporting on statements prepared on the cash basis.

      a. An additional paragraph is inserted before the opinion paragraph of the report to identify the method of accounting being applied and specify that it is not GAAP.

      b. The opinion paragraph then states whether there is fair presentation based on the specified method in use.

   2. Another type of special report is based on the examination of a single account or schedule—such as sales revenue at a certain location. The CPA can audit the

information and give an opinion based on GAAP (or whatever basis of accounting has been used).

   a. If the basis of accounting is anything other than GAAP, a fourth paragraph is added after opinion paragraph to restrict the distribution of report to those parties who understand what basis was utilized.

B. The attestation function covers any examination and report made by a CPA and can go far beyond the traditional audit of financial statements.

   1. Statements on Standards for Attestation Engagements of the AICPA provide rules for any attestation other than an audit.

   2. One type of attestation is the application of agreed-upon procedures where the CPA is engaged to issue a report of findings based on specific procedures that were performed. In this way, the CPA can report on almost anything—such as the number of votes at the Academy Awards.

      a. CPA may evaluate either a particular subject matter or an assertion.

      b. CPA and the hiring party must agree on work to be carried out and this party must take responsibility for sufficiency of those procedures.

      c. The matter to be examined must be subject to consistent measurement and the criteria must be agreed on by all parties.

      d. The report must be restricted to specified parties who understand what was done.

      e. The report should indicate the subject matter (or assertion), the specified parties to receive the report, the party who was responsible for the subject matter, the procedures performed, and the findings.

C. CPA can be associated with financial forecasts and projections (sometimes known as **prospective financial statements**).

   1. Financial forecast is a general anticipation of a company's future statements. Distribution may be limited or may be given to the general public.

   2. Financial projection indicates effect that a hypothetical event would have on future financial statements. Distribution is restricted to party responsible for projection and to anyone with whom this party is negotiating directly.

   3. CPA may compile statements (no assurance), apply agreed-upon procedures (indicate findings), or exam statements (give positive assurance that assumptions are reasonable). CPA never gives any assurance as to the achievability of the figures.

4. In an examination, CPA also makes certain that all assumptions are disclosed and followed. In report, CPA warns that results will usually be different than projected.

D. Pro forma financial statements are created to indicate effect that a hypothetical event (a merger, for example) would have had on past statements. CPA may either review or exam. Examination and report are similar to that done for a financial projection.

E. Registration statements must be filed by a company with the SEC before new securities can be issued. Normally, these securities are transferred to underwriting companies (stock brokerage houses) which then sell them to the public. Legally, the underwriters must make a reasonable investigation to be certain that information they are using is not false or misleading.

1. To help an underwriter meet these legal requirements, it will seek assurance from auditor who furnishes what is called a comfort letter (or a letter for underwriters). This letter provides assurance beyond that which was given on the financial statements included in the registration statement.

2. Auditor provides positive assurance about independence and that audit followed SEC standards.

3. Auditor provides limited (or negative) assurance for specified information (such as interim data) that is included within the registration statement.

F. An auditor may be engaged to provide an examination and **report on internal control.**

1. In an audit, internal control is studied solely to determine amount of control risk. Any reportable conditions or material weaknesses noted in internal control must be indicated to the board of directors and appropriate members of management.

2. In a separate engagement, examination of internal control is more comprehensive. First, management makes an assertion that internal control is effective. Auditor then makes examination and reports on internal control. As an alternative, auditor can report on management's assertion.

3. Auditor's standard report on internal control has four paragraphs.

   a. First paragraph indicates nature of examination and outlines responsibilities.

   b. Second paragraph indicates that standards established by the AICPA were followed. Also specifies that auditor (1) obtained understanding, (2) tested, and (3) evaluated both design and effectiveness of internal control.

   c. Third paragraph spells out inherent limitations of internal control.

   d. Fourth paragraph indicates whether the company has maintained effective internal control over financial reporting based on criteria established in

"Internal Control-Integrated Framework" issued by the organizations sponsoring the Treadway Commission.

G. If auditor is asked to issue a report on statements that have been condensed, report indicates that the audit was performed on the basic financial statements, gives the date and type of opinion, and indicates whether the condensed statements are fairly stated in all material respects in relation to the basic financial statements.

H. CPA can accept a WebTrust engagement to help give customers assurance about the security of transactions placed through a web site.

1. CPA examines and reports on three principles.

    a. Business Practices Disclosure—all business operating practices used in the web site are disclosed and followed appropriately.

    b. Transaction Integrity—company controls are effective in making certain that customer orders are complete and properly filled.

    c. Information Protection—all information provided by customers is protected.

2. CPA grants company the use of the WebTrust seal. Consumer can then click on this seal to read the CPA's report.

3. The CPA's report will include the following information:

    a. Indication that the web site does conform to the three principles previously listed.

    b. Company is responsible for the assertions made about the web site.

    c. CPA has obtained reasonable assurance that management's assertion about the web site is not materially misstated.

    d. Projections of assurance into future periods are subject to risk.

I. Auditor can perform engagements for governments and agencies receiving government funding. Guidelines may require auditor to follow GAAS, GAS (government audit standards), and/or the Single Audit Act. Governmental auditing standards are set by the Comptroller General of the United States and are accumulated in a volume known as "the Yellow Book."

1. In a financial audit carried out according to GAS, audit may cover an entire set of financial statements or just a segment or schedule.

    a. Reporting is extended. Three different areas must be covered in a combined report or in separate reports.

    - An audit report is provided to indicate whether information is fairly presented according to GAAP.

- An indication is provided as to whether entity has complied with laws and regulations for all material transactions and events. Any material noncompliance must be reported. Positive assurance is given for tested items; negative assurance is given for items not tested.
- A listing is provided of any material weaknesses or reportable conditions found in internal control.

2. Auditor can also carry out performance audits.

   a. In an economy and efficiency audit, auditor indicates whether entity protected and used financial resources efficiently and effectively.

   b. In a program audit, auditor indicates whether desired benefits or results are being achieved.

LONG-TERM LIABILITIES AND CONTINGENCIES

A. In looking at long-term liabilities and **contingencies,** auditor should be aware of certain potential problems.

   1. Auditor is always concerned about the understatement of debt because that would improve the company's reported debt to equity position. Consequently, completeness is a particular worry.

   2. Because of lack of documentation, the mere discovery of contingencies can be difficult. Once discovered, evaluating the likelihood of occurrence and possible amounts poses special problems.

   3. For debts that have been issued, amortization of any discounts and premiums must be verified.

   4. Loan covenants must be properly disclosed. Auditor should also make certain that no covenants have been broken; failure to meet covenants can necessitate debts being reported as current liabilities.

B. Auditor would expect to find certain actions taken by company in connection with long-term liability balances.

   1. Normally, approval for incurring additional debt must be made by board of directors and/or stockholders.

   2. A formal contract (indenture) should be drawn up by lawyers and signed by company officials so that all terms are clearly understood.

   3. The issuance of bonds or other long-term debt may be made through the use of an independent trustee.

   4. Cash received should be recorded in cash summary or cash receipts journal and bank deposit slip to provide documentation.

5. Unpaid interest should be accrued at end of year, along with the recording of any discount or premium amortization.

C. A number of substantive testing procedures should be performed to verify the five assertions made by management about long-term liabilities.

1. Analytical procedures are carried out. For example, cash receipts and interest expense are compared with previous years or with anticipated figures.

2. Debt transactions are traced from initiation through the accounting system to the formal recording in order to substantiate completeness. Because debt must usually be approved by board of directors, minutes should be read to check for approval and for mention of debts that may have gone unrecorded.

3. Entries in ledger are vouched back to source documents to substantiate existence and, possibly, valuation.

4. Amortization of any discount or premium should be recomputed.

5. Interest expense is reconciled to debt balance. If interest is higher than expected, unrecorded liabilities may be present.

6. Verify that any unpaid interest at end of year is accrued.

7. Examine events in subsequent period for evidence of the incurrence of any new debts, a transaction that might require disclosure. Also in subsequent period, look for any payments on debts. May indicate unrecorded liabilities or substantiate balances being reported.

8. On representation letter, ask about any unrecorded debts.

9. Read loan indentures to determine nature of covenants so that verification can be made that they have not been broken.

10. If risk is high, auditor can confirm balances with creditors. Transactions during the year can be confirmed with trustee.

11. Bank confirmations should be reviewed for existence and terms of long-term liabilities.

D. Additional testing should be performed in connection with contingencies.

1. Ask client for (a) a list of contingencies, (b) an evaluation of the possibility of loss for each, and (c) the amounts, if any, expected to be lost.

2. Check files for correspondence with lawyers or insurance companies that might relate to contingencies. Look at invoices from lawyers that might indicate existence of contingencies.

3. Read contracts to see if failure to meet requirements creates a contingency.

4. Lawyers letter should be sent by auditor to company's outside attorneys to substantiate information. Should list all contingencies as well as company's evaluation of each.

   a. Lawyer responds directly to auditor indicating any disagreements. Lawyer should also mention any asserted claims that were not included.

   b. Lawyers do not have to respond about contingencies where they lack adequate knowledge. However, the lawyer must indicate any limitation in the response.

   c. If unasserted claim has been omitted and lawyer believes auditor should be told, lawyer suggests client make disclosure. If not disclosed, lawyer considers resigning.

PAYROLL

A. When auditing payroll balances, auditor should be aware of several potential problems.

   1. Because money is being removed from company, theft is biggest concern. Overpayment can occur for several reasons.

      a. Payment may be for more hours than employee actually worked or for a higher rate than employee earned.

      b. Extra deductions may be taken from one employee in order to increase another employee's paycheck.

      c. Paychecks may be issued in the name of false employees or employees who have quit or been fired. These checks are stolen and cashed.

B. Company should have a well-designed payroll system to ensure that records are correct and payments appropriate.

   1. Personnel department hires employees and sets up a personnel file to accumulate information for computing payroll.

      a. W-4 form lists marital status and number of dependents.

      b. Employee or union contract gives pay rate and terms of fringe benefits.

      c. Deduction authorizations are signed by employee as approval for deducting money for medical insurance, savings bonds, union fees, donations, etc.

      d. Personnel department prepares a payroll input record for each pay period giving list of employees, marital status, pay rate, deductions, etc. Copy is sent to payroll department so that wages can be computed.

2. For employees paid an hourly rate, number of hours worked is maintained by timekeeping **department**. Clock cards or other system is used to determine exact time spent at work.

3. Where applicable, employees keep record of their work on time tickets (or job order cards). This information can be used in determining labor costs charged to each job.

4. Employee's supervisor reviews number of hours being reported and provides authorization. Since overtime hours are usually paid at a higher rate, a special authorization may be necessary.

5. Payroll department computes each employee's gross wages, deductions, and net pay based on hours worked and information from payroll input record.

    a. Salary information is recorded for each employee in payroll register. Totals are forwarded to general accounting for reporting purposes.

    b. Second employee verifies all figures and computations and provides authorization.

6. Payroll register is sent to cash disbursements department in treasurer's office. It is reviewed and approved unless discrepancies are apparent.

7. Paychecks are written on a separate payroll bank account that has no money in it except when payroll is issued. Use of second account reduces the chance and potential amount of theft.

8. Second employee compares checks to register and signs.

9. Paymaster distributes checks to employees, but only after they provide proper identification.

10. Unclaimed paychecks are recorded by paymaster and given to independent party for follow up.

C. A number of substantive testing procedures should be performed to verify the five assertions made by client about payroll.

1. Analytical procedures should be carried out, such as comparing expense to previous years, budgeted figures, and number of employees. May want to compare expense from month to month to note any unusual amounts.

2. Select a sample of employees and trace payroll information from personnel file to payroll input form to clock cards to payroll register to general ledger account to canceled check.

3. Vouch a sample of payroll checks to find supporting documentation.

4. Verify mathematical computation of individual paychecks, including all deductions.

5. Verify extensions and footings in payroll register.

6. Recompute year-end accrual of any unpaid salaries.

7. Observe paymaster's distribution of checks to verify that each employee has proper identification. Investigate the handling of any unclaimed checks.

LAND, BUILDINGS, AND EQUIPMENT

A. In looking at **land, buildings, and equipment**, auditor is aware that several problems could prevent fair presentation.

 1. The cost of new items is not properly capitalized. The cost of additions and other changes in items already in use has not been recorded correctly.

 2. Depreciation is computed incorrectly or is based on estimations that are not reasonable.

 3. Assets are retired or disposed of in some manner without being removed from the accounting records.

B. Auditor performs a number of substantive tests in connection with land, buildings, and equipment.

 1. On a test basis, recompute depreciation amounts.

 2. Physically inspect a sample of assets and compare to records maintained by company.

 3. For assets retired, compare life and residual value to amounts that were anticipated.

 4. Review Repair Expense account and Maintenance Expense accounts to determine if any capitalized amounts have been expensed.

 5. For **constructed assets**, review all cost records for appropriate classification. Make certain that capitalized interest has been appropriately recorded.

 6. For new acquisitions, review vendor invoice and search for any other normal and necessary costs that should be capitalized.

 7. For all additions to land, buildings, and equipment, vouch entries back to source documentation to substantiate balances.

 8. During tours of facilities, look for idle assets that should be reclassified.

9. For capitalized leased assets, review contract and computations.

10. Review cash receipts for an amount that might indicate the sale of a fixed asset. Company may have recorded transaction as miscellaneous income without removing asset.

11. Look over loan agreements to see if any assets have been pledged as security. If so, that information must be disclosed.

INVESTMENTS

A. In looking at investments, auditor is aware that several problems could prevent the fair presentation of reported balances.

1. If control or significant influence exists, the investments must be recorded through consolidation or the equity method. Company may not be aware of this need or may not know how to apply these accounting methods.

2. Interest or dividends can be received by the company and then be stolen.

3. Trading securities and securities available for sale must be reported at market value. Company may not realize this need or may apply the rules incorrectly.

4. A change in market value creates an income effect for a trading security, but only a stockholders' equity effect for a security available for sale. Company may manipulate these classifications in order to impact reported net income.

5. Securities may be sold with the money misappropriated by an employee. At the end of the year, the stock is repurchased and replaced.

6. For **bonds being held to maturity,** any discount or premium must be properly amortized.

B. Auditor should perform a number of substantive tests in connection with investments.

1. Should investigate whether control or significant influence is present. If so, auditor verifies that the proper method of reporting is being utilized and that amounts are being reported properly. Audited financial statements furnished by the investee should be used to verify appropriate financial reporting.

2. For each new purchase, the auditor should review documentation to ensure that capitalized cost figure is correct.

3. For each sale, auditor recomputes gain or loss that is reported.

4. Auditor uses reported amounts of dividend and interest payments to verify amount being reported by company. Dates that individual amounts are recorded should be checked with distribution dates for any unusual delays.

5. If certificates are being held by an independent trustee, auditor should confirm these securities.

6. If certificates are being held within the company, auditor should consider making a surprise inspection to be sure that all documentation is present. Auditor should verify name of company, number of shares or face value, and serial numbers on all stocks and bonds to make sure they have not been switched or replaced.

7. Review company's justification for classifying marketable securities as trading securities, securities available for sale, or bonds to be held until maturity. Look at past history to determine how long investments are usually held.

    a. Auditor may also want to determine company's intentions by examining recorded investment strategy, as well as the minutes of meetings of the board of directors and any investment committees.

    b. Auditor should also consider company's ability to hold securities for an extended period by looking at current financial position, working capital needs, debt agreements and the like.

8. Review company's application of market value to trading securities portfolio and securities available for sale portfolio. Market value can be determined in one of several ways.

    a. Get a quoted market price.

    b. Talk with broker who makes a market in the investment.

    c. If no market price is available, use a valuation pricing model developed by an outsider or by the auditor.

9. Recompute the amortization of any premium or discount on bonds being held to maturity.

10. For investments being held until maturity, a write-down in book value is necessary if a permanent drop in market value has occurred.

    a. A permanent drop in market value should be suspected if one of several events occurs: fair market value is significantly below cost, the entire industry or geographic region is in decline, decline in market value has persisted for an extended period of time, financial condition of issuer has deteriorated, there has been a reduction in dividend distributions, etc.

ESSAY WRITING ON THE CPA EXAM

STUDY MANUAL – AUDITING & ATTESTATION

HOW TO USE THIS COURSE

The Kaplan CPA Review course is designed to get you started on the road to CPA success. Since the essay portion of the exam makes up a significant portion of your score, we created this special essay writing course to help you prepare to write your essays on the exam.

This chapter accompanies a series of videos which are available on our Web site, *www.kaplanCPAreview.com*. The best way to use these materials is to watch the video, then review that section in the chapter before moving on. We'll tackle various steps in the essay-writing process, and we recommend that you review each section carefully. You will review key concepts in grammar, punctuation, and spelling. Finally, you will have the chance to practice what you've learned by writing the practice essays available in the last section of the chapter. You can then review sample answers to the essays.

ESSAYS ON THE CPA EXAM

WHERE THEY APPEAR

As you probably know, the new computer-based CPA exam is divided into multiple-choice questions and case-based simulations. The essay or communication portion of the exam appears as part of the simulations. Three content areas—Financial Accounting and Reporting, Auditing and Attestation, and Regulation—will have two simulations, and each will include one essay. Note that no simulations currently appear on the Business Environment and Concepts section of the exam. You can review the contents of the exam and find sample tutorials by visiting *www.cpa-exam.org*.

HOW THEY APPEAR

Let's take a quick look at a real simulation so you know what the writing component looks like. If you are a student in our full program, you have access to all the FAR online sims. Just select one now, and look at it as you read along. If you purchased only this FAR Study Manual, you have access to four free online sims. You can go to either one of these and read along. Remember, looking at sims on paper is not very useful. The purpose of practice sims is to learn their functionality. Fingers-on-keyboard is the only way to do that!

The first tab will give you the situation, which is the basic knowledge you will need to answer the questions. In order to answer the various questions, you will use the tabs to navigate (click on the Situation Tab to view the information).

The simulation tab that contains the essay will be labeled Communication. On this tab, you will get some information about the question you are expected to answer. In some cases, the essay will be started for you, with a salutation or greeting at the top. You will type your answer into the field at the bottom of the screen. You will also notice that the Communication screen has a toolbar. These are tools that you are probably accustomed to using in word processing programs, including cut, copy, paste, undo/redo, and spell check. Take a look at this by clicking on the Communication Tab now.

HOW MUCH THEY COUNT

The Communication part of your score will be a relatively large portion of your total score. The two essays you will write will count for about 10% of your score. If you are feeling good about the essay portion, this is good news. If you are feeling nervous about the essay portion, you are doing the right thing by committing to a serious schedule of practice for this part of the exam.

WHEN TO DO THEM

Students sometimes ask whether they should do the simulation tabs in the order presented, or whether they should skip around. Usually we tell students that completing the tabs in order is the best way to stay focused. However, if you are particularly anxious about the essay, you may want to try doing it first, so you can be sure that you can give it your best attention. You should make your own decision, based on your experience as you practice.

HOW TO PRACTICE FOR THE ESSAY PORTION

As you work through your Kaplan CPA Review materials, you will be learning lots of ways to cope with the essay portion of the exam. You will want to practice these techniques so that they become second nature. Once you have assimilated our methods, you will find that you can use them on the exam and in all your future business writing.

LEARN FROM THE AICPA

The best way to familiarize yourself with the appearance and behavior of the simulations is to view the official simulation tutorials, which are available at *www.cpa-exam.org*. This will be an essential part of your preparation for the exam. Keep an eye on this Web site, because the AICPA makes frequent updates to the materials available there.

USE YOUR KAPLAN MATERIALS

Make the most of these materials. If you need to watch a video more than once to be sure you are getting the point, go ahead! Write out all the practice essays in the back of this chapter. Take our suggestions, and you are sure to improve your writing, and your score!

STUDY MANUAL – AUDITING & ATTESTATION
ESSAY WRITING ON THE CPA EXAM

PRACTICE WRITING

As you prepare to take the exam, you will run across topics and questions that you know need extra review. Those might be topics studied in your earlier years of college or areas you always struggled with. Try writing short essays on these topics. It will give you excellent practice at writing, and it will also help those tough concepts sink in. Making up your own essay questions will also help you get inside the mind of the test authors, and better understand how CPA essay questions work.

READ CRITICALLY

As you read the newspaper, magazines, or any other non-fiction, take a critical look at the author's writing. Is it solid? Does she make a strong argument? How does he back up his assertions? Think about how you would improve the article, or how you might take the opposite side of an argument. Reading critically will help you to write critically, which is a key component of success on the essay portion.

WHAT GRADERS ARE LOOKING FOR

Kaplan CPA Review has done a careful review of the essay grading system. Unlike the multiple choice part of the exam, your essays will be read by real human graders. They will have very specific criteria to look for, and they will grade you on how closely your response meets those criteria. So what do the essay graders look for?

- **They want your essay to be on topic.** If you stray from the topic at hand or lose focus, you will lose points. In fact, the AICPA says that once the grader starts reading your answer, if your essay is not *on topic,* they will discontinue the grading process and give you no points.
- **Your essay must address the concept of the question.** Your response should answer the question that is being asked! (It is more common than you might imagine for candidates to give a good answer, but to a question other than the one asked on the exam.) When certain accounting concepts come up, the graders want to be sure that you can understand those concepts and write about them.
- **Your essay should have solid structure.** This means that you should be able to construct a strong, well-supported argument, a topic we'll cover later in this chapter.
- **Finally, graders are looking for clear, coherent writing.** This is where concepts like grammar, spelling, sentence structure, and punctuation come in. We will spend time looking at all of these issues later in this chapter.

To write an essay that graders will love, keep these points in mind, and use the Kaplan CPA Review system!

HOW TO ANSWER THE QUESTION

In this section, we will review the same essay that we cover in the video course. That way, you can follow along in your book or you can review what you learned in the video tutorials. If you have already reviewed this essay thoroughly, turn to the last section of this book and practice the essay writing steps with one of the other sample essays that are available for you.

THE IMPORTANCE OF PREWRITING

Prewriting is everything you do before you actually start writing your essay. It includes thinking through the question, planning the structure of your essay, and constructing the basis and support of your argument. Prewriting is an essential part of all writing, but it is particularly important when you have limited time. The prewriting process will help you organize your thoughts and will improve your final product. Prewriting will actually save time in the long run. You will see what we mean as you work through the rest of this chapter.

REPHRASING THE QUESTION

Most essay questions will be very wordy and will include a lot of detail. When you read the question, ask yourself:

- What do the graders want to know?
- How can I cut through the detail and get to the gist?

Following are some examples of rephrasing questions.

1. Easy Question Example

Don Marcus, the partner in charge of the Franken engagement, is considering whether confirmation of accounts receivable is necessary in this engagement. Write a memo to Mr. Marcus describing situations, if any exist, when confirmation of accounts receivable can be omitted.

So what is the question? Translated into plain English, the exam wants to know: Is it always necessary to confirm accounts receivable? If not, describe when it is not necessary.

2. Harder Question Example

Here is another question for you to rephrase.

TFC has hired your firm to audit its financial statements. The president of TFC has heard the term "control risk," but is not sure of its impact on the audit process. Write a memo to the president to explain the nature of control risk. Also describe the work of the external auditor in connection with control risk and the impact of that work on the overall audit.

Translated into English, the exam wants to know: What is control risk? What does the auditor do with control risk? How does control risk relate to the overall audit?

That is a little more complex than the last essay question, but still, you can rely on your knowledge of auditing to come up with the answer.

3. Question Requiring More Information

Take a look at another question.

Garden, Inc. is negotiating the lease of property to FarmCom. Identify the type of lease from the accounting perspective of the lessee, FarmCom, and provide reasons for this classification. Then identify the type of lease from the accounting perspective of the lessor, Garden, Inc., and provide reasons for this classification.

Translated, this question is asking: Based on the information you know about this negotiation, what type of lease is it for the lessee? Why? What type is it for the lessor? Why? (To answer this question, you would obtain facts from the Situation tab of the simulation.)

4. Question Requiring Calculations

Take a look at one more question.

Mr. Roseman is scheduled to receive $200,000 as a result of his wife's life insurance policy. The life insurance company will give him the money immediately or allow him to take ten annual payments of $26,000 each. Write a memo to Mr. Roseman explaining the tax ramifications of this decision.

Translated, the question is: Should the client take the money now, or take annual payments? What are the pros and cons?

To answer this question in detail, you will need background knowledge about the nature of taxation and annual payments. You will also need to apply your knowledge to this specific situation, and perform some basic calculations.

POINTERS ON REPHRASING

If you have trouble translating a question, look for words like "how" and "why." Look for words that point to specific accounting principles. Remember to ask yourself "What do the graders want to know?"

NOTE TAKING

Note taking is a key part of the prewriting process. You will be given scrap paper when you take the exam, and you will want to make good use of it. No one will be grading your notes, so as long as you can read and understand them, they are okay.

Start your notes by writing down your rephrasing of the question. As you progress through the prewriting process, you will want to make notes to track your thoughts. You will use these notes as a basis for writing your essay.

Some things you may want to convey in your notes are lists, like pros and cons. You can write down important numbers and calculations, so you will not have to manipulate numbers when you are trying to write your essay. You can use arrows and symbols to point out specific pieces of information. When your question has multiple parts, you will want to label the questions and notes as A, B, and C. If you do not know every aspect of the answer, write down what you do know.

Essay #1: Note Taking

Here is the first essay we will focus on as we work through the prewriting process.

> Beverage, Inc. (BI) operates beverage machines that do not maintain a record of sales, and accept only cash. BI is a privately held company owned by three investment groups. One of the investor groups serves as the operator. The former auditor for BI went bankrupt due to malpractice claims. The CPA firm Trust LLP is now planning a year-end audit. Provide an overall assessment of BI's risk, and note the impact to the audit process that Trust must execute. In addition, describe specifically how control risk relates to this assessment.

Rephrasing the Questions

Here is how we would translate the questions:

A. How much risk is there and why?
B. What should Trust do about it?
C. What is the control risk implication?

Situation Notes

Now we can start to formulate answers for these questions. Begin by taking notes on the situation.

1. The first sentence tells us: Beverage, Inc. (BI) operates beverage machines that do not maintain a record of sales, and accept only cash. Our notes say: Cash-only bev. corp.

2. The next two sentences say: BI is a privately held corporation owned by three investment groups. One of the investor groups serves as the operator. Our notes say: one op owner.

3. Finally, the last sentences say: The former auditor for BI went bankrupt due to malpractice claims. The CPA firm Trust LLP is now planning a year-end audit. Our notes say: Old auditor no good.

Your notes might look different, but make sure that you have at least covered all the key points of the situation.

Key Concepts Notes

Next, you will want to reread the question and think about the key accounting concepts and principles you will use. Take some notes on these key concepts. Provide an overall assessment of BI's risk, and note the impact to the audit process that Trust must execute. In addition, describe specifically how control risk relates to this assessment.

What key concepts do we need to take into account? Make some notes that make sense to you. Our notes say:

> Internal Controls—Risk Assessment—Substantive Testing—Analytical Procedures—Control risk

QUESTION NOTES

Next you will want to take some notes on the questions so that you have an instant reference when you are ready to write your essay. This is where you will begin to formulate your answers. Our first question, Question A, is: *How much risk is there and why?* Here is our answer: *It is a cash-only industry, there are no good past records, and the past auditor is no help, since he went bankrupt (and is thus unreliable and probably unavailable for comment.)* Make some quick notes about these risk factors under the letter A.

Now let us move on to Question B, which is: *What should Trust do about it?* Here, your notes can come directly from your Key Concepts notes. *The auditing firm needs to think about analytical procedures and substantive tests.* You can abbreviate these however you like.

Question C asks for some detail. *What's the control risk implication?* So what are the specific issues surrounding control risk that we need to cover? *We need to think about material misstatements. We need to consider how trustworthy the operating owner might be. And we need to take into account the issue of opening balances, due to the problem with the previous auditor.* Make some notes on the control risk implications. Make sure they are legible and clear.

HOW TO STRUCTURE YOUR THOUGHTS

STRUCTURE OF AN ARGUMENT

Many of the essay questions on the exam will have relatively simple answers. If they were multiple-choice questions, you would click a choice and that would be all. However, on the essay part of the exam, you cannot just answer the question and move on. If the exam just wanted a quick answer, the test would be all multiple choice. **The graders want to see how well you can construct an argument and back up your theories.** As you well know, accounting is not just playing with a calculator all day. There is a great deal of analytical thought involved in this profession, and the exam wants to be sure that you are ready!

To construct a strong argument, you need to begin with a main point, or thesis. On the CPA exam, your main point is the answer to the question. You also need support for your thesis. This support can consist of facts, key concepts, examples, calculations and other relevant information. As we continue to answer our sample essay question, we will review how you can construct support for your argument.

STUDY MANUAL – AUDITING & ATTESTATION
ESSAY WRITING ON THE CPA EXAM

HOW TO STRUCTURE YOUR ARGUMENT

Here is our question again:

Beverage, Inc. (BI) operates beverage machines that do not maintain a record of sales, and accept only cash. BI is a privately held corporation owned by three investment groups. One of the investor groups serves as the operator. The former auditor for BI went bankrupt due to malpractice claims. The CPA firm Trust LLP is now planning a year-end audit. Provide an overall assessment of BI's risk, and note the impact to the audit process that Trust must execute. In addition, describe specifically how control risk relates to this assessment.

Begin by reviewing your notes:

Situation Notes: Cash-only bev. corp./one op owner/Old auditor no good

Key Concepts Notes: Internal Controls, Risk Assess, Sub testing/An. Proc., Control risk specific

QUESTION A

We will begin our focus with Question A: *How much risk is there and why? Do you think that BI represents a high or low audit risk?* Take a look at all the notes you made about risks, and you can conclude that *BI represents a high audit risk*. That is the main point of your argument.

That is not the end of your answer, though. You also need to explain *why* the risk is high. That is where the rest of your notes will come into play, so let us take a look.

According to the notes for Question A, BI is cash only, there are no good records, and the previous auditor is no help. These details will form the support for your main point. For Question A, you now have the basic underlying structure of your argument.

QUESTION B

Take a look at Question B: *What should Trust do about the high audit risk of BI?* Analytical procedures and substantive testing comprise the basic answer to this question. But again, this is not multiple choice, and we need more information. Where is the support for our main idea? If you get stuck, try asking yourself some questions.

Ask the question: why? Or, in other words: What would be the reason for performing analytical procedures and substantive testing? Well, these are done to gain assurance about the validity of reported revenue.

Now ask the question: How? Or, how could Trust gain the necessary assurance? To answer this question, provide examples. Examples are a great way to provide supporting data for your main point. For example, Trust could look at vendor payments and observe a sales sample to develop estimates. So now Question B has a main idea, and adequate support for that main idea.

QUESTION C

Finally, look at Question C: *What is the control risk implication?* Looking back at our notes, we see that based on the risk of material misstatements, our doubt about the trustworthiness of the operating owner, and our concern about the reliability of the opening balances, we would have to say that internal controls will have a high risk of failure. So that becomes our main point, and the reasons for concern form the support for that main point.

STRUCTURE: QUICK REVIEW

We've organized our notes into an outline, or skeleton, that we can use to write our essay. **Each question has a clear response, with a main point and supporting details. Remember that a well-structured argument is crucial. It is one of the key things that the graders look for.** Be sure that all your main ideas are supported with details, evidence and key concepts.

HOW TO WRITE YOUR ESSAY

ESSAY STRUCTURE

One of the key things that the graders are looking for is an essay with a solid structure. On the CPA exam, structure is your friend. Having a good sense of structure at your fingertips will make it easier to put your answer together quickly and clearly, and that will help you earn points on the exam.

THE THREE OR FIVE PARAGRAPH ESSAY

In high school, you probably learned how to write the five paragraph essay, a classic essay structure. The same type of structure also works well in a three paragraph essay, especially where you have a limited topic and a limited amount of time, as on the CPA exam.

The three or five paragraph essay begins with an *introductory paragraph*. This is where the topic is outlined, and the goal of the essay is stated. If your essay is in response to one question, and has one main idea, this is where you state that main idea. If your essay responds to more than one question, you may or may not want to use this paragraph to express the main ideas, or answers, to all the questions.

The next one or three paragraphs are the *development*. In this section, information is presented, and data and support are supplied. Other opinions and contrary facts can be presented here, if they are relevant.

In the final paragraph, a *conclusion* is drawn, and the author makes a summary of the facts and theories stated in the essay.

Understanding the three or five paragraph essay format will help you structure any essay you write. However, you probably will not need to write a full five paragraphs, and you may not even need to write three paragraphs. There are some essay questions that can be answered without an elaborate introduction or conclusion. There are other questions that may require a different type of structure. With this in mind, let us consider some alternatives.

THE INVERTED PYRAMID STRUCTURE

A structure commonly used in business writing and in journalism is the inverted pyramid structure. In this structure, you begin with the most important point. On the CPA exam, that would be the main point, or the answer to the question. You then follow up with supporting information, like examples, and other supporting details. Finally, you close with any other information, such as less important details.

This structure is called an inverted pyramid because it is large at the top, in terms of importance, and small at the bottom. When no formal introduction or conclusion is called for, the pyramid structure will serve you well.

OTHER STRUCTURES

Now let us talk about a few other types of structure that may come in handy. You may be asked to describe a problem and solution.

> **Example:** *Describe the issues inherent in dischargeability of debts in bankruptcy and propose a solution.* You might need to describe cause and effect.

> **Example:** *What would cause a legal repossession to occur, and what would be the consequences of this result?* You may need to compare and contrast two things.

> **Example:** *What are the similarities and differences between the security interests described here?* You may need to describe a chronology or timeline.

In each of these cases, you want to follow the pattern of the question, answering in the order suggested by the question.

You do not need to memorize all of these structures—what you need to know is that sometimes the structure will be spelled out for you in the question. In these cases, it is better to stick with the structure presented than to try to shoehorn your response into the three or five paragraph structure or the pyramid structure.

STRUCTURING OUR SAMPLE ESSAY

Now that we have described some structures, let us go back to the sample question and decide on a structure for our essay.

> *Question: Provide an overall assessment of BI's risk, and note the impact to the audit process that Trust must execute. In addition, describe specifically how control risk relates to this assessment.*

Here is the translation for the questions that we prepared earlier:

- *How much risk is there and why?*
- *What should Trust do about it?*
- *What is the control risk implication?*

Given these questions, how would you structure this essay? Well, we have three questions, making this one suitable for three paragraphs. The questions go from general to specific, so we can begin with Question A, and move down the line, with one paragraph per question. Let us use the three paragraph essay format.

If we felt a need for an introduction and conclusion, we could expand into the five paragraph format. However, we already have enough to tackle here, and we can omit the added formality of the introduction and conclusion, as long as our argument has a clear structure. We will be sure of that by reinforcing our main points with strong details.

PARAGRAPHS

Paragraphs can have all kinds of structures in articles, essays, stories, and other kinds of writing. The main thing you need to know to do well on the CPA exam is *keep it simple*. There is no need for complex paragraph structure to make your point.

The other thing to keep in mind is that a paragraph is much like a mini-essay. Your main idea is your topic sentence, and your supporting details make up the rest of the paragraph. If your paragraphs have strong structure, your essay will have strong structure.

SENTENCES

Before we begin to write, let us talk very briefly about sentence structure. Once again, keep it simple. You are not going to impress the graders with long, convoluted sentences. You are going to impress them with clear, logical sentences. Keep your sentences logical and well-organized, and you will maximize your points.

TURNING NOTES INTO SENTENCES

The process you will follow here is the same process you will use whenever you translate notes into sentences and paragraphs. Start with your topic sentence, and continue with your support. This is the most basic structure you can use, and it is the best for the CPA exam.

CHOOSING A VOICE

First, we choose a voice. Sometimes you will be asked to write as a certain party, with a certain audience. For example, the question may state that you are an Audit Senior preparing a memo to the Audit Partner. In other cases, you will need to make a decision on your own. In still other cases, a salutation will already be included in the essay writing window, which should make clear which voice you should use.

In this case, we have a choice, since the voice is not specified. Let us write from the perspective of Trust LLP, using the voice "we." This is a pretty safe decision, since there is no specified voice.

Here is one more thing to think about before you begin. You need to keep in mind your *purpose* as you write. Whom are you writing for and why?

- Is the essay intended to be a memo to a client? If so, do not assume that the client will understand abbreviations or accounting jargon. Spell everything out clearly, as you would for an actual client.
- If the essay is intended for a colleague or superior, it is acceptable to assume that she will have knowledge of typical accounting language. However, be careful to answer all parts of the question. You cannot assume that the reader will be able to make inferences from a sketchy essay.

PARAGRAPH 1

Let us take our notes for Question 1, and turn them into the sentences that make up Paragraph 1.

First, there is our main point: *The audit is high risk.* We then need support for the main point. *Our support is that the business is cash only, there are no good records, and the old auditor is no help*

So let us write some sentences! We begin with a topic sentence for Paragraph 1. The topic is that the audit is high risk. Here is a sentence that expresses that:

> *Overall, we have determined that there are several serious issues surrounding the upcoming audit of Beverage, Inc. by Trust LLP.*

Your sentence might be slightly different, but in general, this is a good way to start. Now we need support sentences for Paragraph 1. Try translating your notes into sentences.

> Note: *cash only*
> Sentence: *Beverage, Inc. operates in an industry with no debit or credit card technology, so cash reflects 100% of sales activity.*
>
> Note: *No good records*
> Sentence: *This presents an internal control challenge to BI's management and an audit risk to Trust since there is no written or electronic documentation of each sales transaction.*
>
> Note: *Old auditor no help.*
> Sentence: *Furthermore, the lack of supporting audit documents from previous audits, due to the unreliability of the previous auditor, presents a serious risk of failure.*

Here is our Paragraph 1.

> *Overall, we have determined that there are several serious issues surrounding the upcoming audit of Beverage, Inc. by Trust LLP. Beverage, Inc. operates in an industry with no debit*

or credit card technology, so cash reflects 100% of sales activity. This presents an internal control challenge to BI's management and an audit risk to Trust since there is no written or electronic documentation of each sales transaction. Furthermore, the lack of supporting audit documents from previous audits, due to the unreliability of the previous auditor, presents a serious risk of failure.

Before we move on, let us look at how we used some linking words to contribute to the logic of the paragraph.

- We began with the word "overall," which signals that a general point is about to be made. In this case, it is the main point.
- The last sentence in the paragraph begins with the word "furthermore," which indicates that additional information that is in parallel with the previous information is about to follow.

Using linking words will help to reinforce the logic and structure of your essay.

PARAGRAPH 2

The question we will address in this paragraph is: *What should Trust do about the high audit risk of BI?* Our main idea is that Trust should do analytical procedures and substantive tests. Supporting this main idea is the answer to the question "why?" It is to gain assurance about validity of reported revenue. Let us see if we can turn that into one concise sentence.

Due to the overall risk presented by BI's situation, Trust must execute analytical procedures and related substantive tests to gain assurance regarding the validity of reported revenue.

Now incorporate the examples that will form your support. The examples are: *looking at vendor payments and observing a sales sample to develop estimates.*

Sentences:

Trust could use an analytical procedure where they use vendor payment records. Trust could also observe a sample of vending machine sales to develop an estimate for inventory balances and activity for the fiscal period.

Here is Paragraph 2.

Due to the overall risk presented by BI's situation, Trust must execute analytical procedures and related substantive tests to gain assurance regarding the validity of reported revenue. Trust could use an analytical procedure where they use vendor payment records. Trust could also observe a sample of vending machine sales to develop an estimate for inventory balances and activity for the fiscal period.

PARAGRAPH 3

Paragraph 3 must answer the question: *What is the control risk implication?*

Note: *internal controls have high risk of failure.*
Sentence: *The audit presents certain issues which have specific relevance to high control risk.*

Now let us write the sentences that provide support for the main idea.

Note: *Failure to detect material misstatements*
Sentence: *Without an audit trail of sales transactions, there is a high risk of failure of the internal control system to detect material misstatements in the reporting of revenue for BI for a stated fiscal period.*

Note: *No process to be sure operating owner is accounting for all transactions*
Sentence: *As far as we can determine, there is no internal control process in place to ensure that the operating owner is accounting for all sales transactions during a fiscal period or detecting if any material misstatements have occurred.*

Note: *No way to verify opening balances, due to old auditor*
Sentence: *Since BI's prior auditor is bankrupt, and Trust does not have access to the prior year's auditing audit documents, Trust cannot verify the opening balances for the current fiscal period.*

Here is the third paragraph.

The audit presents certain issues which have specific relevance to high control risk. Without an audit trail of sales transactions, there is a high risk of failure of the internal control system to detect material misstatements in the reporting of revenue for BI for a stated fiscal period. As far as we can determine, there is no internal control process in place to ensure that the operating owner is accounting for all sales transactions during a fiscal period or detecting if any material misstatements have occurred. Since BI's prior auditor is bankrupt, and Trust does not have access to the prior year's audit documents, Trust cannot verify the opening balances for the current fiscal period.

This essay takes on a basic three paragraph essay structure, and there is no need for a formal concluding paragraph.

WRITING THE ESSAY: QUICK REVIEW

When you write your essay, stay focused. Do not go off on tangents or include extra information. Just answer the question as simply as you can. Lay out the simplest possible structure. Use one of the structures we talked about, or follow the structure suggested by the question. Your paragraphs should have one main idea, plus the support for that main idea. Finally, keep your sentences clear and simple. One sentence per idea is usually just right.

EDITING

READING OUT LOUD

One of the most important things you can do when you have finished writing your essay is to read it out loud. During the exam, you will not be able to read it out loud, but you can read silently to yourself. Hearing the voice of your essay in your head will help you to "hear" any mistakes that are there.

DOUBLE-CHECK YOUR PUNCTUATION

- On the CPA exam, you will probably end all of your sentences with *periods. The lessor has met the criteria.* Question marks occasionally come up in business writing when the writer is using a rhetorical style. *Has the lessor met the criteria? Yes, she is qualified.* It is hard to imagine a use for an exclamation point in business communication. (The following is unlikely to gain points on the exam: *The lessor has met the criteria! Hooray!*) Ensure that all your sentences have ending punctuation.
- Use a *comma* to separate parts of dates and places. *January 12, 2007* and *Cleveland, Ohio.* Use a comma to separate items in a series. Examples: *I eat apples, oranges, and bananas. The Sarbanes-Oxley Act of 2002 seeks to institutionalize objectivity, independence, and reliability in corporate governance, audit committee performance, and external auditor activities.*
- *Commas* are used before certain linking words, e.g., *and, but, for, nor,* and *yet.* Examples: *Detection is reduced by carrying out additional substantive testing, or by performing substantive testing that renders a higher quality of audit evidence. The accountant is prepared for a more senior role, yet he lacks experience in certain areas.*
- Use a *comma* to separate an introductory part, or clause, of the sentence from the rest of the sentence. Examples: *If control risk is assessed as high, the auditor will need to gather more evidence. In some cases, the reliability is not strong enough. For example, government confirmations normally require no corroboration.*
- Use a comma to set off descriptive information. Examples: *XMG, a technology firm, has retained our services. Ms. Templeton, an auditor, will be visiting the office today.* Keep in mind that a comma indicates a pause. As you read your essay silently, listen for spots where there should be a pause. Consider adding a comma. If a comma appears where a pause is not called for, consider omitting the comma.
- Use a colon after the salutation in a business letter. Examples: *Dear Investor: Dear Ms. Abernathy:*
- Use a colon to introduce a list of items after a complete sentence. *There are three different classifications of payments by the securitization mechanism: pay-through, pass-through, or revolving-period.* A colon is not required if the list is not preceded by a complete sentence. *The firms retained by the client are Smith, Harvey, and Brustein.* Edit check: Does your salutation end with a colon? Look for lists in your essay. If they are preceded by a complete sentence, there should be a colon before the list.
- Use a semicolon when you are connecting two closely related sentences. *The fair value is known; our information is complete.* Use a semicolon before certain linking words that demonstrate consequence. These are words such as therefore, thus, and consequently. The linking word however also requires a semicolon. *The fair value of the first bond is known; however, the value of the second is unknown.* Edit check: If you

have connected related sentences, consider using a semicolon as the connector. Watch for adverbs such as thus and therefore, and be sure that you have added a semicolon where necessary.

SPELLING: FREQUENTLY CONFUSED WORDS

Spell check on the exam cannot catch everything! Watch out for homonyms, words that sound alike. Learn which ones usually trip you up, and be sure to review and memorize them. Here is a list of words that are commonly confused.

Accept/except
Accept means "to receive." Except means "not including."
We will accept all of the provisions, except the third one.

Access/excess
Access is a noun meaning "the ability to enter." Excess is a noun or adjective meaning "extra."
If you gain access to the storage room, you will find the excess files.

Affect/effect
Affect is a verb that means "to produce an influence or effect on something." Effect is a noun that means "a result" or "a fulfillment." Effect is the word used in the phrase "in effect."
This move will affect our profit margins. The effect will be shrinkage.

Among/between
Use "among" when you are writing about more than two people or things. Use "between" when you are writing about two people.
The client needs to decide among the many accounting firms that are available. The two partners have an agreement between them.

Less/fewer
Less means "not as much," and fewer means "not as many."
Fewer jobs means less income for the city.

Personal/personnel
Personal means "relating to a particular person." Personnel means "staff."
The personal records of our personnel are kept confidential.

Precede/proceed
Precede is a verb meaning "to go before." Proceed is a verb meaning "to go forward, or continue."
The audit will precede the final work paper review. We will proceed with the review after the audit.

Principal/principle
Principal as a noun means the leader of a school. As an adjective, it means "main" or "primary." Principle means a fact or law, like the principles of accounting.
The principal topics on the exam are the principles of accounting.

Edit check: After you have run the spell check, look for frequently confused words. Know which ones give you trouble, and keep a special eye out for those.

APOSTROPHES

Use an apostrophe to substitute for missing letters when you make a contraction. *We will merge = we'll merge. It is prudent = it's prudent. Do not assume = don't assume. The company will not retain = the company won't retain.* Use an apostrophe to indicate possession, the idea that something belongs to someone. *The firm's assets = the assets belonging to the firm. The partner's workload = the workload belonging to the partner. The accountants' case = the case belonging to the accountants.* Note here that there are multiple accountants, so the apostrophe goes after the "s," not before it.

These frequently confused words with apostrophes may come up in your writing: *Its and it's. Your and you're. Whose and who's. Their and they're.*

Its is a possessive word, indicating that something belongs to "it." It's is a contraction meaning "it is." *See the dog? It's wagging its tail. Have you heard about the loss taken by the firm? It's a reflection of its poor management practices.*

Your is a possessive word, indicating that something belongs to "you." You're is a contraction meaning "you are." *You're planning to file your return by April 15, aren't you?*

Whose is a possessive word, indicating that something belongs to "who." Who's is a contraction meaning "who is." *Whose files are these on my desk? Who's going to come to the audit meeting?*

Their is a possessive word, indicating that something belongs to "them." They're is a contraction meaning "they are." *They're on the way to their meeting with the attorneys.*

Edit check: If you are prone to sprinkling extra apostrophes through your writing, do this test as you read through your draft.

- Can the word be expanded? (Does the apostrophe indicate a contraction?)
- Does something belong to someone?

If the answer to both of these questions is no, then the apostrophe is not necessary.

CAPITALIZATION

Each sentence should begin with a capital. Titles such as President or Chairman of the Board begin with capitals. Some abbreviations, such as LLP or FASB, are made up of capitals. Edit check: Do you see capital letters in your draft? Are they necessary according to the conditions above? If not, make them lowercase.

SENTENCE FRAGMENTS

A fragment is an incomplete sentence. Examples: *The goal of this requirement. Providing protection. Consummation of an agreement.* All of these are fragments. A complete sentence requires a subject and a verb. Examples: *The goal of this requirement is to ensure an effective system. Providing protection is the responsibility of the firm. Consummation of an agreement is to be expected within the week.* Edit check: Does your sentence have a subject and a verb?

RUN-ON SENTENCES

A run-on occurs when you have two or more complete sentences without adequate separation. *Management is responsible for maintaining internal controls they must also present an assessment of the effectiveness of the controls.* Fix this run-on this way: *Management is responsible for maintaining internal controls. They must also present an assessment of the effectiveness of the controls.* Or: *Management is responsible for maintaining internal controls, and must also present an assessment of the effectiveness of the controls.* Edit check: If you suspect a run-on, read the sentence again. Does it contain two or more complete sentences, without separation? If so, provide separation, either by breaking it into two sentences, or by adding connecting words and/or punctuation.

SUBJECT-VERB AGREEMENT

In a sentence, your subject and verb must agree. If your subject is singular, your verb must be singular. *John Smith, CPA, undertakes audits.* If your subject is plural, your verb must be plural. *Many CPA firms undertake audits.* The concept of agreement can be tricky with collective nouns like "staff" or "faculty." If a group is working together to perform the same action, you need a singular verb. *The staff prepares for the overhaul. The faculty strives toward excellence.* Be especially careful when the subject and verb are not right next to each other. *The importance of the reports is high.* The importance is high, not the reports. Therefore, we use a singular verb. Edit check: As you read, be sure that each subject and verb agree. Especially watch for collective nouns. If the subject and verb are not next to each other, tune out the words that get in the way, and listen for the right subject-verb agreement.

PARALLEL STRUCTURE

Words that are linked by "and" need to be in the same form, as do words in a list. You can usually diagnose parallelism problems by listening. Listen for the mistake: *The plan will be formulated and I will undertake it in the near future.* Since the verbs are joined by "and," they should be in the same form and tense. Here is the right way to structure this sentence:

The plan will be formulated and undertaken in the near future. Here, formulated and undertaken are in the same, parallel form. Parallel structure is also necessary among ideas in a list. Look for the mistakes in this sentence: *An understanding of internal control is needed to determine the nature, degree to which testing should be performed and when is best to do the substantive testing.* Here is the way to structure this sentence correctly: *An understanding of internal control is needed to determine the nature, extent, and timing of the substantive testing.* Edit check: Listen to your sentence. Any words, phrases, or verbs that are set in parallel structure need to have the same form, tense, and structure.

PRONOUN ANTECEDENTS

A pronoun is a word that substitutes for another word. *John is an accountant. He works very long hours.* "He" stands in for "John." It is clear who we are talking about, so we can say that the pronoun "he" has a clear antecedent. Now read these sentences: *Under some circumstances, the reliability of confirmation of accounts receivable is not strong enough to merit the effort, and the firm may omit the confirmation. They are in a position to gain very little.* To what or to whom does the word "they" refer? The firm? The accounts receivable? Also, what will "they" gain very little of? Reliability? Information? Here is a better follow-up sentence: *In this case, the firm will gain very little information.* Edit check: As you read through your essay, look for pronouns like "he," "she," "it," and "they." Make sure that it will be clear to the reader to whom or to what these pronouns refer.

CLARITY AND CONCISENESS

CPA essay graders will pay special attention to these issues. There are no hard and fast rules here, but here is our key recommendation: think simple. This is not the time to impress anyone with mile-long sentences or ten-dollar vocabulary words. You want to get your answer across as clearly and concisely as possible. The clearest way to say something is usually the simplest way. Minimize the number of phrases and clauses in each sentence, and you are well on your way.

Here is an example of how to avoid wordiness. Instead of: *We intend to take this opportunity to fulfill your request by providing you with the information which it has been our pleasure to enclose.* Try: *Enclosed is the information you requested.* Or: *We are pleased to provide you the enclosed information.* Edit check: Read through your essay. Does any of the language seem excessively wordy? See if you can state your case in a simpler manner.

CHECKLIST FOR EDITING

Use it to check all your practice writing, and the items on the list will become second nature. When you take the exam, you will do this check automatically:

- Is the purpose of the essay clear?
- Is the essay appropriate for the reader?
- Is the answer complete and accurate?
- Is there extra information that should be removed?
- Is any necessary information missing?
- Is the information well-organized?
- Does the flow of the essay make sense?
- Are the paragraphs of reasonable length?
- Does each paragraph have one main idea?
- Should shorter paragraphs be combined, or longer paragraphs be split or trimmed?
- Is the language clear and direct? Is it easy to read?
- Are the grammar, punctuation, and spelling correct?

STUDY MANUAL – AUDITING & ATTESTATION
ESSAY WRITING ON THE CPA EXAM

FINAL REVIEW AND ESSAY #2

So let us take it from the top once again. You are at the exam center, working your way through your exam. You are in one of the simulations, cranking through the drag-and-drop questions, the matching questions, the true/false questions…and then, there is the essay!

The Ulysses Corporation began operations early in Year One and, by the end of that year, the company had generated $400,000 in credit sales. During that year, many of the company's customers made payments on their accounts so that on the last day of Year One, Ulysses was reporting Accounts Receivable of $160,000. Leo Brown is president of the Ulysses Corporation and has hired the CPA firm of Stern and Ross to prepare financial statements for the first year of operations according to United States generally accepted accounting principles. These statements are scheduled to be released on February 16, Year Two. Brown is concerned about the reporting of bad debt expense. Brown believes that approximately 3% of the Year One credit sales will prove to be uncollectible. However, the company will not be able to identify the specific accounts to be written off until June or July of Year Two. Although Brown believes the 3% figure is a reasonable estimation, he realizes that the actual amount of bad accounts could be either higher or lower. Brown has asked the CPA firm as to whether these bad debts should be recognized immediately in Year One or not until Year Two when the actual bad accounts will be determined. You are employed as a staff auditor for Stern and Ross, CPAs. Your supervisor has asked you to write a memo to Leo Brown to explain the proper accounting for bad debts according to United States generally accepted accounting principles.

This essay looks like one that might appear on the Financial Accounting and Reporting section of the exam.

PREWRITING REVIEW: REPHRASING

What do you do first? You read the question and start your prewriting. Remember, prewriting gives you the freedom to construct the best possible sentences without having to think too much about your topic. If it is all there in your notes, you can focus on writing clearly. Begin to prewrite by putting the question into your own words, or rephrasing it. How would you rephrase this question?

Your supervisor has asked you to write a memo to Leo Brown to explain the proper accounting for bad debts according to United States generally accepted accounting principles. It should sound something like … Given the situation provided about the Ulysses Corporation, explain how bad debts are accounted for.

PREWRITING REVIEW: NOTE TAKING

First, take notes on the situation. Your notes might look something like this:

- *400,000 in credit sales*
- *160,000 A/R*
- *About 3% uncollectible*
- *Recognize in Year 1 or Year 2?*

Then, take notes on the key concepts, the principles you will want to take into account. Here is what we wrote as notes.

- *Accrual accounting*
- *The matching principle: recognize expenses in same period as revenues*
- *Reasonable estimation*
- *Report A/R at net realizable value*

PREWRITING REVIEW: STRUCTURING YOUR ARGUMENT

Now find your main point and your support: the structure of your argument. Your main point will be your answer to the question, "How should Ulysses account for bad debt?" and your support will be your review of the key concepts, particularly the matching principle. We are not going to answer the question for you here. Take what we have done so far and work on this one on your own. You will find our sample answer in the last section of this chapter. Keep reading, though, and we'll give you some more pointers.

PREWRITING REVIEW: STRUCTURING YOUR ESSAY

It is time to decide on a structure for your essay. Remember the different types of structure we talked about: the three or five paragraph essay, the pyramid structure, and structure based on the question. What's the best way to structure this essay? *How should Ulysses account for bad debt?* This is a straightforward question. You can begin with your main point—the answer to the question. You can then support that main point with your theoretical key concepts.

Try covering this in three paragraphs, with a basic pyramid structure. Start with the most important information, then fill in the key details you need. Use this structure and attempt to write your own essay. A model solution is provided later in this chapter.

EDITING REVIEW

Before we move on, let us review the key concepts of editing. One of the most important things you can do when you have finished writing your essay is to read it out loud. Hearing the voice of your essay in your head will help you to "hear" any mistakes that are there. Remember that spell check only goes so far. You need to be sure to read and evaluate every word of your writing.

Finally, be sure to use your editing checklist as you practice, and it will become second nature. Know your weaknesses and pay special attention to them as you practice editing.

PREPARING FOR THE EXAM

Let us go over what you can do to prepare for the test. First, remember to *practice writing*. As you prepare to take the exam, write short essays on topics that you need to review. Make up your own essay questions. This will give you great writing practice, and it will also help you with the multiple-choice part of the exam.

The next thing you can do is to *read critically*. Remember to look at the author's argument when you read the newspaper or magazines. Look at the structure of the piece, and search for the support for the main point. Think about how you would improve the article, or how you might take the opposite side of an argument. You will probably find that plenty of professional writers make some of the structure mistakes that we talked about.

Finally, *edit everything* you write, even your e-mails to colleagues or friends. Make every word perfect. If you write a note to your roommate on the fridge, make sure your punctuation and spelling check out. It sounds silly, but proper grammar, punctuation, and spelling are habits. Once you get in the habit, it will help you for the rest of your life. In the next section, you will find several sample essays, complete with notes and sample answers. Use the prewriting and writing process techniques you have learned as you practice writing these essays. The more you practice, the easier it will be to write your essays on the exam. Good luck on exam day!

ESSAY QUESTIONS, OUTLINES, AND ANSWERS

ESSAY #2: SAMPLE QUESTION

The Ulysses Corporation began operations early in Year One and, by the end of that year, the company had generated $400,000 in credit sales. During that year, many of the company's customers made payments on their accounts so that on the last day of Year One, Ulysses was reporting Accounts Receivable of $160,000.

Leo Brown is president of the Ulysses Corporation and has hired the CPA firm of Stern and Ross to prepare financial statements for the first year of operations according to United States generally accepted accounting principles. These statements are scheduled to be released on February 16, Year Two.

Brown is concerned about the reporting of bad debt expense. Brown believes that approximately 3% of the Year One credit sales will prove to be uncollectible. However, the company will not be able to identify the specific accounts to be written off until June or July of Year Two. Although Brown believes the 3% figure is a reasonable estimation, he realizes that the actual amount of bad accounts could be either higher or lower. Brown has asked the CPA firm as to whether these bad debts should be recognized immediately in Year One or not until Year Two when the actual bad accounts will be determined.

You are employed as a staff auditor for Stern and Ross, CPAs. Your supervisor has asked you to write a memo to Leo Brown to explain the proper accounting for bad debts according to United States generally accepted accounting principles.

ESSAY #2: SAMPLE NOTES

Question: Given the situation provided about the Ulysses Corporation, explain how bad debts are accounted for.

Situation: 400,000 in credit sales—160,000 A/R—About 3% uncollectible—Recognize in Year 1 or Year 2?

Key Concepts: Accrual accounting—The matching principle: recognize expenses in same period as revenues—reasonable estimation--report A/R at net realizable value

Structure: Three paragraph pyramid

ESSAY #2: SAMPLE RESPONSE

To: Leo Brown, President of Ulysses Corporation
From: Staff Auditor, Stern and Ross, CPAs
Subject: Recognition of Bad Debt Expense

Bad debt expense of $12,000 (3% of sales) should be recognized in Year One. Under United States generally accepted accounting principles, the timing of revenue and expense recognition is governed by accrual accounting. Here, the issue in question specifically concerns the recording of an expense. According to accrual accounting, the matching principle is used to guide the recognition of an expense. The matching principle states that expenses should be recognized in the same time period as the revenues that they help to generate.

With regard to the Ulysses Corporation, the company incurred uncollectible accounts as a result of the sales process in Year One. These revenues were appropriately recognized in Year One. Thus, the matching principle requires the related bad debt expense to be recognized in the same period. This reporting is used even though the actual amount and identity of the uncollectible accounts will not be known until Year Two. The company, though, must be able to make a reasonable estimation of the amount of expense to be reported.

Recognition of the uncollectible accounts in Year One also reduces the reported year-end balance of Accounts Receivable to its net realizable value, the amount that the company expects to collect. Reporting this asset at the lower net realizable value figure is conservative, and this approach is favored by United States generally accepted accounting principles.

ESSAY #3: SAMPLE QUESTION

To: Information Technology Partner
From: Engagement Partner
Re: ConnMart's supply-chain management process
Date: May 17, Year 6

ConnMart, a publicly held entity, operates in a paperless environment. The complete supply-chain management process, including the purchase order, delivery, and vendor payment, is electronic.

The recent issuance of the Public Company Accounting Oversight Board Auditing Standard No. 2 requires our firm to issue a separate report regarding the system of internal controls developed, documented, maintained, and evaluated by management. We want to verify the reliability and effectiveness of ConnMart's system of internal controls over their supply-chain management process.

STUDY MANUAL – AUDITING & ATTESTATION
ESSAY WRITING ON THE CPA EXAM

Please direct your information systems audit team to assist in the development of substantive testing procedures to verify the accuracy, reliability, and completeness of the financial information reported by the supply-chain management system.

ESSAY #3: SAMPLE NOTES

Question: Describe the necessary substantive testing procedures.

Situation: Supply-chain management system: paperless,

Legal entity: publicly held, subject to Sarbanes-Oxley Act of 2002

Auditor: must be registered with PCAOB

Key Concepts: Internal controls, substantive testing to confirm inventory balances, expenses and related liabilities along with revenue, analytical procedures, expenses, liabilities

Computer-based auditing procedures—Revenue

- Program analysis
- Program testing
- Continuous auditing

Structure: Two paragraphs, each describing a key aspect of the question to be answered

ESSAY #3: SAMPLE RESPONSE

To: Engagement Partner, Little Rock, Arkansas
From: Information Technology Partner, Little Rock, Arkansas
Reference: ConnMart's supply-chain management process
Date: May 17, Year 6

The information audit team has considered the outcome of the risk assessment process, and the team will develop the following substantive testing procedures. The audit team can use analytical procedures to gain insight into the reliability and reasonableness of the financial information reported by ConnMart's supply-chain management system. For example, the team can develop contribution margin ratios for each inventory category and compare these to sales activity, vendor payment activity, and inventory activity to determine reasonableness. The auditors can project the level of sales, costs, and remaining inventory using this technique. In addition, the team can review management's forecast, annual budget, and monthly operational reports to detect trends, and can compare these to the current results. This should identify any major variances and areas where additional investigation is required.

As for computer-based auditing procedures, the audit team can use program software to analyze various aspects of the supply-chain system, and can implement controls to ensure the accuracy of data output. They can review the existing system to ensure there are no coding problems that would lead to errors. The team can also run audit software to trace actual transactions from purchase order to vendor payment to the reorder process when a sale occurs. The team can input dummy transactions to ensure accurate processing throughout the system, and they can install a continuous auditing feature to monitor transactions as they occur. Finally, the team can run audit software that will allow for parallel simulation of actual data to be compared to output from the supply-chain management system.

ESSAY #4: SAMPLE QUESTION

Netco, Inc. filed for an Initial Public Offering in Year 6. Also in Year 6, Netco experienced significant sales growth and generated a profit of approximately $85 million on sales of almost $1 billion.

Netco launched the IPO to generate additional capital to finance growth and expansion as well as provide additional incentives for employees. Specifically, Netco used the funds to acquire new buildings and equipment to expand their technology infrastructure, and to establish a stock option plan. When the CFO directs the generation of the statement of cash flows for the year ending December 31, Year 6, describe the impact of the following in terms of the three sections of the statement of cash flows:

- Generation of equity and related proceeds from the sale of stock via the IPO.
- Treatment of costs for going public.
- Acquisition of buildings.
- Purchase of equipment.
- Creation of stock option plan.
- Generation of net income.

ESSAY #4: SAMPLE NOTES

Question: Describe the impact of the listed items on the statement of cash flows.

Situation: Company industry: Internet; Legal entity: issued an IPO; Acquisitions: purchased new buildings and equipment; Revenue: generated $1 billion with net income of $85 million

Key Concepts: Statement of Cash Flows, Investing activities, Financing activities, Operating activities, Accruals, Direct and indirect approach

Structure: Introduction, plus three paragraphs, each focused on an aspect of the statement of cash flows.

ESSAY #4: SAMPLE RESPONSE

The CFO of Netco, Inc. will translate the key events for the current fiscal period into the three areas of the statement of cash flows as follows:

With regard to operating activities, the revenue generated from routine sales activities, adjusted for accruals and other non-cash transactions such as depreciation, will result in cash flow from operations. Specifically, the $85 million in net income will be adjusted for the net impact of current accounts and non-cash activities, such as amortization, to establish the cash flow from operations.

As for financing activities, the proceeds from the IPO represent an equity-based transaction that generated cash flow. The use of the funds is not relevant, but the net effect from the equity-based activity represents cash flows from financing. The costs for an IPO are expensed as part of the issuance and are included in the net proceeds amount and, accordingly, there is no amortization. The creation of a stock option plan does not constitute an investing or financing activity until the stock is exercised.

As for investing activities, the acquisition of a long-term asset, such as a building or equipment, represents an investing activity. In this case, cash flows were used to invest in the expansion of assets.

ESSAY #5: SAMPLE QUESTION

To: General Counsel, Construction Firm Inc.
From: CFO, Construction Firm Inc.
Reference: Plaintiffs and Municipal Airport Project Subcontractors
Date: May 11, Year 6

Construction Firm, Inc. (CFI) has received a letter of intent to litigate from counsel representing a contractor who responded to our Request for Quotation to provide electrical and mechanical services for the Municipal Airport Project. The letter claims that counsel's client has incurred proposal costs, as well as injury to his business, because CFI elected to perform the work internally instead of using an external contractor. CFI's Request for Quotation is the industry standard solicitation that requests that potential and eligible suppliers provide their estimated price schedule for a specified set of goods and services. We clearly indicate that this RFQ is not a binding agreement that constitutes a contract between CFI and the offeror. Furthermore, we indicate that CFI reserves the right to secure the specified goods and services. Finally, the RFQ also states that all information submitted by the offeror becomes the property of CFI.

The overall claim of the plaintiff is that CFI improperly used the RFQ process to obtain prices and to use that information as a resource base to direct internal resources to secure the goods and services to support the Municipal Airport Project.

As the CFI general counsel, we need your opinion on this potential lawsuit. Specifically, does the RFQ process commit CFI to an obligation to select a potential supplier and execute a procurement contract?

ESSAY #5: SAMPLE NOTES

Question: Is CFI committed to this selection and contract execution?

Situation: Company industry: construction; contract issue: municipal airport project; legal entity: corporation; sourcing: decision to in-source or out-source a project

Key Concepts: Outline the appropriate key contract law terms related to the memorandum:

Contract law, Existence of an offer, Evidence of consideration, Acceptance of an offer, Invitation to make an offer versus an offer, Definiteness of terms, Type of agreement (written, oral, unilateral or bilateral), Uniform Commercial Code

Structure: Introduction stating the answer, plus two paragraphs of support describing reasons for the answer

ESSAY #5: SAMPLE RESPONSE

The plaintiff does not have legal recourse against CFI for our decision to use internal resources to provide electrical and mechanical services for the Municipal Airport Project for the following reasons.

An offer is a definite proposal or undertaking made by one party to another that, by its terms, is conditional upon an act or return promise given in exchange. An RFQ is not an offer, but an invitation to bid in the same manner as an advertisement. As such, an RFQ does not constitute an offer or any legally binding event.

The RFQ does possess the three essential components of an offer: intent, communication, and definite and certain. However, the CFI RFQ clearly indicates the intent to solicit non-binding prices, and not bids. Further, there was no commitment to select a respondent for procurement. Consequently, the criteria for an offer were not met, and there is no binding element.

ESSAY #6: SAMPLE QUESTION

The passage of Sarbanes-Oxley Act of 2002 represents the most significant changes to the regulation of capital markets, corporate governance, and the auditing profession since the Securities Acts of 1933 and 1934. Congress passed the Act in response to an unprecedented wave of fraudulent financial reporting that ultimately led to the erosion of investor confidence in capital markets.

The Act targets management, auditors, and audit committees, among other stakeholders, and charges them with responsibilities. Outline the major requirements of the Act as it relates to one of the three stakeholders. Also discuss the purpose and implications of the Act for restoring investor confidence in each of the three respective responses for the stakeholders.

ESSAY #6: SAMPLE NOTES

Question: Identify the major points of Sarbanes-Oxley for one of the three stakeholders. Note that you only need to choose one stakeholder to write about. Discuss purpose of the act as it relates to investor confidence.

Situation: Outline the appropriate key aspects of Sarbanes-Oxley related to the essay; Major rules as they relate to management, audit committee, or external auditor, PCAOB.

Key Concepts: Fraudulent financial reporting, Corporate governance, Investor confidence, Role of audit committee, Role of external auditor.

Structure: Two paragraphs, each addressing one of the two aspects of the question.

ESSAY #6: SAMPLE RESPONSE—THREE OPTIONS FOR YOUR RESPONSE

1. Management

The Sarbanes-Oxley Act mandates that management is responsible for creating and maintaining adequate internal controls, and presenting its assessment of the effectiveness of those controls. The goal of this requirement is to ensure that there is an effective system to prevent material misstatements in the financial statements generated by management.

The wave of fraudulent financial reporting cases caused significant erosion to investor confidence in the reliability, accuracy, objectivity, and validity of financial information disclosed by corporate America. The Act requires that the CEO and CFO must sign a separate statement to accompany the financial statements certifying the propriety, reliability, fairness, and completeness of the financial reports. It also requires that the financial reports and disclosures fairly present the company's operations and the financial condition. This sends a signal to investors that management is ultimately responsible for the financial information released and will be held accountable, including being held liable and subject to criminal prosecution for any known false statements.

2. Audit Committee

The Sarbanes-Oxley Act outlines a comprehensive role for the audit committee that did not exist in the past. The audit committee is responsible for ensuring that management adheres to the rules of the Act, including the establishment of a system of internal controls. The act requires that the audit committee oversee the relationship with the registered external audit firm, including hiring, compensation, and verification of their continued independence. The Act also specifies that the audit committee should consist of independent directors and a financial expert.

The increased role of the audit committee ensures that there is an independent and strong monitoring function on the Board of Directors that will review both management and external auditor activities. This will help to ensure that external auditor performance is optimal. The Act further requires that audit committees have procedures in place to receive and address complaints regarding accounting, internal control, or auditing issues. Further, it provides protection for corporate whistle blowers by specifying that audit committees establish procedures for handling employees' anonymous submission of concerns regarding accounting or auditing matters.

3. External Auditor

The Sarbanes-Oxley Act prescribes the nature of the relationship of the external auditor with the company, and identifies the services that an auditor can provide to a company for which it performs an audit. The Act also details services that are prohibited, such as executing accounting services or performing the functions of management. The audit committee must approve all services that are allowed per the Act, such as tax services, prior to consummating an agreement.

In addition, the Act created the Public Company Accounting Oversight Board. The PCAOB is granted the authority by the Act to publicize auditing rules, regulate registered accounting firms, and invoke sanctions for any violations. Accounting firms must register with the PCAOB, and must adhere to its standards for independence and its auditing standards. The creation of the PCAOB seeks to enhance the regulation and performance monitoring of the external auditor, who plays a key role in ensuring the reliability of financial reports.

EXAM STRATEGIES

STUDY MANUAL – AUDITING & ATTESTATION

OVERVIEW

Kaplan CPA Review applauds your desire to earn the CPA designation, one of the most prestigious and respected professional credentials in the world. Employing Kaplan's proven system for CPA examination preparation, you will be giving yourself a tremendous advantage in your efforts to join the more than 340,000 fellow CPAs and members of the American Institute of Certified Public Accountants (AICPA).

We have assembled some of the best minds in academia, along with a highly skilled professional staff, to develop a comprehensive review course for enhancing your chances of passing the CPA exam. We recommend that you follow the guidelines in this book and use the supporting course materials to ensure your success.

You should also be commended for working hard to complete your accounting degree. It is one of the most rigorous programs in business. With Kaplan's proven tools and CPA exam preparation formula, we can assist you with taking the knowledge you have acquired through the years and applying it to the CPA exam. Rigorous study alone will not ensure success. Your approach must focus your energy in a logical and organized manner, combining hard work with more effective and successful techniques. **Once you see that the "how" of studying is as crucial as the "what" to study, the effort and results will become readily apparent.**

This Tips and Techniques chapter will serve as a valuable tool to help you navigate the Kaplan course material, organize your study approach, and gain an understanding of the big picture regarding the CPA exam. We know that your chances for success will increase if you begin with this chapter and follow its recommendations, instructions, and advice.

The chapter is divided into six sections, which cover the following:

- Exam preparation.
- Strategy development.
- Multiple choice and simulation study strategies.
- Recommendations for exam day.
- Post-exam activities.

STUDY MANUAL – AUDITING & ATTESTATION
EXAM STRATEGIES

PLANNING TO TAKE THE EXAM

AICPA TESTING GOALS

You are taking the exam in a new era, one that will recognize the context of your current educational environment and work experience. The old, paper-based exam sought to test problem-solving skills and knowledge of financial literature. It required more memorization than demonstration of critical thinking and analytical and communication skills. Today's computerized exam focus requires more than a general familiarity with the material. It requires a complete grasp of the concepts and the ability to clearly communicate your knowledge to the graders. This reflects today's business environment, which requires more advanced skills in researching technical information; applying informed, sound judgment in decision making; and communicating more effectively with many different stakeholder groups.

What is the driving force behind all this change? Corporations and other organizations are demanding accounting professionals who possess skills in communication, critical thinking, and problem and opportunity definition and analysis to guide their institutions in the 21st century's global economy. Accountants have become business partners and not just "bean counters." In response to the growing need for CPAs to possess broader skills, curricula are changing at colleges and universities to promote more experiential and cooperative learning (e.g., group projects and class presentations). Likewise, the AICPA has incorporated the demands of the marketplace into the new CPA exam by transforming it from a paper-based to computer-based test and leveraging the benefits of a technology-based environment. Specifically, the computerized exam expands the learning goals and expectations beyond simply content and problem-solving skills. On the CBT exam, the candidate is expected to demonstrate mastery of the competencies listed below.

- *Research relevant financial literature.* The candidate should possess the ability to review current rules, regulations, and interpretations in a particular context, such as revenue recognition or impairment of goodwill. The CBT exam requires the candidate to demonstrate the ability to research an issue, identify the appropriate authoritative literature, understand its application to the issue, and offer an opinion or structure a transaction in compliance with the proper rules. This is now tested under the simulation dimension of the exam. The questions will require you to access, during the exam, an online database of literature from which you will retrieve your answer.
- *Communicate business information.* Through analysis, evaluation, and conclusion, a candidate should demonstrate the ability to conduct the appropriate research of financial literature. Findings must then be communicated in an effective, clear, and relevant manner. This part of the exam, requiring written communications, will be graded manually by the AICPA. Scoring will focus on your ability to write well—including developing, organizing, and expressing your ideas—as well as the technical content of your answer.
- *Analyze and interpret business information.* The candidate will review and evaluate information in context (e.g., business combinations), in order to offer opinions, conclusions, further discussions, or actions related to the analysis.

- *Render judgment based on available business information.* Traditional quantitative problems focus on generating an exact answer [e.g., net present value (NPV) of a proposed capital investment]. The computerized exam will test the candidate's ability to review the business context and relevant information, and offer an opinion beyond the formula. For example, while the NPV of a project may be positive, other risk factors, such as declining revenue and increasing expenses, may render the validity of the underlying assumptions (e.g., cash flow predictions) less reliable. Perhaps management should consider these issues prior to authorizing the investment.
- *Gain an understanding of key business terms, facts, and processes.* One major complaint by accounting firms and corporations has been that accounting graduates are not familiar with business in general, but know only how to record accounting entries. The pencil and paper CPA exam did not historically test for a breadth of understanding behind these entries. The paper-based exam assessed the candidate's proficiency in answering quantitative problems and memorizing rules. The essence of accounting is the interpretation of economic events and the translation of events into financial information. Therefore, it is critical for the candidate to understand the business environment and operations to ensure the proper evaluation of economic events along with their related recording and disclosure.

We feel confident that the knowledge gained from your college curriculum and current professional work experience, along with our guidance, will help you successfully demonstrate your mastery of these competencies.

So, yes, the CPA exam has entered the 21st century. It is more relevant than before. It is testing different skills, and testing the same skills in different ways. Does this make it more difficult to pass? Not really. Read on. There are actually some new features that will make you happy. This is not your grandfather's CPA exam!

ADVANTAGES OF THE COMPUTERIZED CPA EXAM

Probably the biggest advantage of the computerized exam is that you no longer have to prepare for all four parts of the exam at once. This is the best thing that has ever happened to a CPA exam candidate!

The CPA exam was changed from a paper-based test to a computer-based test (CBT) in April 2004. The CBT exam allows candidates to plan and schedule the time that they wish to take the exam, based on the following requirements:

- The exam is offered in more than 300 Prometric centers across the United States and its jurisdictions.
- Candidates can take the exam two months out of each quarter each year (January–February, April–May, July–August, and October–November).
- Candidates can take only one or as many as all four sections at a time and in any order desired.
- Each section is graded independently, and the outcome does not impact the other section results or qualification.
- Once you pass a section and earn credit, you have 18 months to pass the other three sections of the exam.
- There is no minimum score requirement for failed sections.

The new exam mirrors the flexibility that technology has brought to the workplace, most notably through telecommuting and flexible work arrangements. Candidates can now schedule sections within a testing window (i.e., 2-month period) and take the sections of the exam at a pace that meets their work schedule, study/readiness plan, and general preference.

Candidates should be careful to understand the rules imposed by the CBT exam. Under the paper-based method, there was a lack of uniformity among the jurisdictions in qualifying for sections as they were passed. For example, in some jurisdictions, you had to have a minimum score on all parts taken, or your passing grade on another part was not accepted. All jurisdictions now follow the same guidelines for granting credit. Each section is graded independently, without regard to your score on another section of the exam.

However, once you pass any section, your time clock begins, and you have 18 months from that passing notification to complete the remaining sections. It is imperative that you fully understand the time constraint that is imposed once a section is passed. Your professional career or personal demands could easily consume months, and before you know it, time has expired and you could be working under pressure to pass or face forfeiture of the sections for which you previously earned credit.

We will assist you in passing the exam as soon as possible to avoid this potential planning and scheduling challenge. We want you to be aware of the potential risk and avoid it with effective planning.

Do not procrastinate. Once you pass the first part of the exam, maintain your study schedule, with appropriate rest breaks, and keep going. Prepare for and pass sections on a time schedule that works for you, but just ensure that you pass all four sections before that 18-month period slips by!

CBT VS. PAPER-BASED EXAM

A CBT exam presents some unique advantages, which were noted above, along with some limitations listed below:

- The examination is linear; you must take each portion of an exam section (called a "testlet") in a series. You cannot start in the middle of the exam as you could do in the paper-based mode.
- Once you complete a portion (testlet) and exit from it, you cannot go back to review and/or change answers.
- The time limits are even more critical as the system will close the testlet once the time expires. There is no flexibility in allocating your time to portions or questions, which existed in the paper-based mode.

The candidate should visit the AICPA's Web site, *www.cpa-exam.org,* to become familiar with the CBT exam. The AICPA has developed and made available a free comprehensive tutorial, use of which is highly recommended. The tutorial provides examples of test questions and, more importantly, the technical mode of presentation and delivery. Utilizing these resources will ensure that you will be confident, prepared, and efficient when the time comes. **We cannot overemphasize the importance of this step in your preparation.** The actual exam administration location (i.e., the Prometric Center) is not the place to learn what the new exam looks like!

Remember the last time you drove a car that you had never seen before? You had to get in, locate all the buttons and dials, adjust the seat, set the air conditioner and radio, etc. This is similar to how you will become familiar with the new exam experience. Do this on your own time with the tutorial, and our online materials, not at the exam, where your time is precious!

We recognize that you began your career in the information age, and you are probably quite adept at using technology. However, one aspect of technology is navigation, and it is essential that you gain an understanding of the software and mode of operation used for the CPA exam prior to exam day. Coaches and their players often visit a football field in advance of the game to ensure they know the stadium and the unique dimensions of the field, and to remove the fear of the unknown. Likewise, we want you to invest the necessary effort with the AICPA's tutorial and the Kaplan online materials. Take the opportunity to practice in a CBT environment similar to that where the test will be given. We want you to be free of exam-day jitters and be ready to pass.

EXAMINATION OVERVIEW

The CPA exam is prepared and administered by the AICPA for the 55 jurisdictions, including the District of Columbia, Virgin Islands, Puerto Rico, Guam, and the Commonwealth of the Northern Mariana Islands (CNMI). The AICPA is responsible for exam development, administration, and scoring. The AICPA has partnered with Prometrics Testing Services to administer the computerized examination at Prometric centers within the 55 jurisdictions.

Each state and jurisdiction has its own board of accountancy that administers the licensing function. For example, if you live, sit for, and pass the exam in Houston, Texas, the Texas State Board of Accountancy will issue your license to practice and your CPA certificate. The requirements for licensure vary from state to state. Be sure to check with your own state's board of accountancy for the requirements, both to sit for the exam and to become licensed after you pass.

The CPA exam is given in four sections as follows:

Section	Test Format	Allowed Time
Auditing and Attestation	• Multiple choice given in three separate testlets of 24 to 30 questions each • 2 Simulation questions	4.5 hours
Financial Accounting and Reporting	• Multiple choice given in three separate testlets of 24 to 30 questions each • 2 Simulation questions	4.0 hours
Regulation	• Multiple choice given in three separate testlets of 24 to 30 questions each • 2 Simulation questions	3.0 hours
Business Environment and Concepts	• Multiple choice given in three separate testlets of 24 to 30 questions each (no sims)	2.5 hours
Total		14 hours

Topic coverage of CPA exam:

Section	Content Coverage Percent	Relevant Supporting Literature
Auditing and Attestation	• 100%	• Generally Accepted Auditing Standards • Standards for Attestation Engagements • Accounting and Review Services • Government Auditing Standards • Audit Risk Alerts • PCAOB Standards • For sims, a research database such as the AICPA Standards database

Financial Accounting and Reporting	• Business Enterprises—80%
	• Government Entities—10%
	• Not-for-Profits—10%
		• Generally Accepted Accounting Principles for:
		  - Business enterprises
		  - Not-for-profit organizations
		  - Government entities
		• For sims, a research database such as FARS

Regulation	• Federal Taxation—60% • Law and Professional Responsibilities—40%	• Internal Revenue Code • Ethics pronouncements of AICPA • Sarbanes-Oxley Act of 2002
		• PCAOB Pronouncements • Business Law textbook • For sims, a tax research database tool
Business Environment and Concepts	• Business Structures—20% • Economics—15% • Finance—20% • I.T.—25% • Planning & Measurement—25%	• Current textbooks and business periodicals provide good coverage for BEC • There are currently no plans to include sims on BEC

Note: Because the ability to research technical questions is tested in the simulations, the AICPA makes a sample research database available to candidates for a period of time while they are preparing for the CPA exam. See *www.cpa-exam.org* for more details. Kaplan's simulations also provide a sample research tool for your use in practicing with simulations.

Your initial response could be "Wow! That is a lot of material to cover in such a short period of time," or "I have never had an exam that lasted more than three hours, even when I had back-to-back exams in college." Please relax. We will teach you how to navigate through the material, develop an effective study plan, and efficiently use your time to focus on the relevant topics required to successfully pass the exam.

Remember: You are *not* learning all these topics for the first time; you are learning how to pass the exam. There's a big difference. You are not trying to become an expert in all of these topical areas. What you need is a structured and focused review and a proper strategic approach. We will provide that, along with flexibility and content to support any areas where you have had little or no prior exposure.

Hopefully, after looking at this schedule, you can begin to see how this guide, along with other Kaplan materials, will assist you in using your time wisely. For example, you may not have taken a course in college; not everyone does. Since this is an important topic for the exam, you may want to spend a little more time to cover this topic well. Perhaps you took Individual Taxation in college, and you will be able to adequately cover this topic in less time than needed for the Corporation tax rules. This allows you to more effectively plan your time to properly manage the volume of material and breadth of topic coverage. With Kaplan materials, your focus can easily be tailored to reflect your particular background and you can efficiently and effectively prepare for the CPA exam.

BENEFITS OF THE KAPLAN CPA REVIEW MATERIALS

Kaplan has developed a comprehensive set of materials that will greatly assist candidates in their preparation to pass the CPA exam. The following is a guideline for each study aid and its recommended use and value:

Study Tool	Recommended Use	Benefit
Lesson Video	• Background material for a topic (e.g., basic auditing standards).	• Provides audio/visual lecture in a dynamic, interesting, and comprehensive manner.
Problems Video	• Demonstration of how to effectively solve problems in a specific content area (e.g., lease accounting).	• Provides a dynamic illustration of how to solve a problem.
Problems PDF	• Practice responding to problem-oriented questions within a topic area.	• Provides an opportunity for candidates to test their understanding and ability to complete CPA exam–like questions within a topic area.
Study Manuals	• Reference guides to support the review and study process for each topic.	• Provides a comprehensive resource for each topic area for ongoing reference and review.

	• Also includes essential outlines, exam strategy and technique, and a writing styles guide.	• Provides summary outlines for quick review. • Helps you understand the exam and the entire exam process. • Helps you structure your writing assignment in the sims to gain maximum points.
Kaplan Activity Planners	• Schedule the practice and review time in order to prepare for the CPA exam. • Impose discipline on your study schedule.	• Provides a terrific planning tool that integrates all of the Kaplan CPA Review materials by topic with a suggested study approach.
Kaplan Audio CDs	• A question/answer format to reinforce the content.	• Allows you to listen while you commute, go for a run or walk, or any other time it is appropriate for you to multi-task!
Kaplan Flashcards	• More than 2,000 cards organized by exam topic, in question-and-answer format.	• Provides additional reinforcement of the topics, in a format that is convenient to use and carry with you.
Kaplan Online Exam Testlets	• Evaluation mechanism to determine progress and areas where more work is required.	• Provides an opportunity for candidates to evaluate progress in an environment that simulates the actual CPA exam CBT format. This is an invaluable opportunity for candidates, not only to demonstrate their readiness in terms of the topic coverage, but also to increase their level of comfort with navigating the computerized exam environment.
Kaplan Online Exam Simulations	• Sims provide the opportunity to practice with exam-like case problems and with an online research database tool. • While simulations definitely give you the opportunity to reinforce content, the major benefit of using sims is to practice with the functionality of the software and the use of the research tool.	• Provides an opportunity for candidates to evaluate progress in an environment that simulates the actual CPA exam CBT format. Since the simulations are the newest component of the CPA exam, it is critical that the candidate understand the process and functionality of the software in this testing context. The simulations consist of multiple points and clicks, screen accesses, and other navigational requirements (e.g., professional literature review prior to responding to the specific questions). You should feel very comfortable with this process prior to exam day to ensure that you can maximize your available time to answer the questions, as opposed to being confused by the functions of the software. We want to minimize your stress on exam day by preparing you to anticipate every dimension of the exam, including content and operation.
Kaplan Online Question Bank	• True/False questions sequenced to develop your learning of the topics; multiple-choice questions that are similar to exam questions.	• Provides candidates with additional testing opportunities to identify strengths and weaknesses.

E-mail a Kaplan Professor	• Resource for timely response to your questions.	• Provides candidates with a feedback mechanism to address issues and concerns as they arise. This is where our course becomes a personal tool, as this will complement any of our materials with the ability for you to ask specific questions. We also use this as a course material based on responses from candidates such as you. We want you to view this function as having access to a personal coach who will ensure that, as you practice, any issues or concerns you have will be addressed in a timely manner. We will be there for you and with you throughout this whole preparation period. You are not alone!

KEY STEPS FOR PASSING THE EXAM

We recommend that you follow these guidelines to ensure that you maximize your time and appropriately utilize the resources made available through the Kaplan course.

1. **Visit the AICPA dedicated Web site for the CPA exam to gain a thorough understanding of the exam.** Take the tutorial, which gives you a sample of the test questions and mode of examination: *www.cpa-exam.org*. The AICPA has created for eligible candidates a wealth of free instructional information, such as tutorials, guides, and resources. This will allow you to be clear on the nature of the exam in terms of content and operation. It will also give you guidance on preparation and other critical information, such as scheduling the exam. **Be sure to obtain and read the Candidate Bulletin from that Web site.**

2. **Enroll in the following:** The AICPA is offering eligible candidates (refer to above Web site for more information) a 6-month free subscription to the AICPA Professional Standards, FASB Current Text, and FASB Original Pronouncements, which will provide students with a rich resource base to prepare for the research element of the simulation questions. Since the simulation questions will require research of the professional literature, the AICPA is offering a free subscription so you can practice conducting research prior to the exam. This will allow you to become familiar with both the content and the operation. This will greatly benefit you on exam day because you would have already mastered the research and the navigation effort. And it's free. What a great bargain!

3. **Determine when you plan to take the exam and contact your state board of accountancy and Prometric Center to apply and schedule a time.** As working professionals or students nearing graduation, your time is both limited and precious. Make sure you fully understand the "testing windows" concept and your availability prior to scheduling the exam. Keep in mind that you have new flexibility that was not previously available. But also note that you have an 18-month limitation once you pass a section to complete the rest of the exam. We want you to avoid the last-minute or "cram" approach to the exam. Your success depends on having sufficient time to study for and pass the exam.

4. **Use the Kaplan materials in conjunction with your study plan to ensure your readiness on exam day.** The Kaplan materials have been developed to support each section of the exam. The Kaplan materials also help prepare the candidate to perform effectively within the new computerized exam environment by providing CBT examples relevant to each topic and testing format (i.e., multiple choice or simulations). We strongly urge you to use these materials to prepare for the exam.

5. **Follow the suggestions in the Kaplan CPA Survival Guide (see *www.kaplanCPAreview.com*, under CPA Info and Resources).** This guide is a personal reminder to make sure you plan, prepare, relax, and succeed. Kaplan understands that you will work very hard to prepare for the exam. We will assist you in planning your time effectively so your preparation activities are efficient and effective. This should ensure that you can physically and mentally relax, both during your preparation and on exam day. We do encourage dedicated days off to refresh and rejuvenate during the practice period. Finally, we feel that if you are properly prepared, you can relax and minimize or even eliminate stress before and on exam day. We want you to just go out and do your very best. Remember: you practiced, practiced, and practiced; all you have to do now is demonstrate what you know. And, while there is no such thing as being overly prepared, you do want to reach your exam day in an optimistic frame of mind.

DEVELOPING A STUDY PLAN

Once you have determined that you are fully committed to taking the exam, we recommend you develop a careful, sensible, and comprehensive study plan. This will ensure that you use your time and Kaplan materials effectively and efficiently. This will help you manage the process of preparation and control the degree of stress that is often related to such endeavors. As you progress with your studies, you will also begin to see that, while this is a big effort, it is absolutely not an impossible effort. You will begin to develop the confidence needed to believe in yourself and to keep heading toward your goal.

The CBT exam is more focused on assessing the competencies previously noted in Chapter 1 than on the memorization of certain rules and techniques. A quote from a recent presentation by an AICPA representative, "More thought than rote," indicates a focus toward more critical thinking. It is essential that you invest the proper time to plan, because the process of demonstrating mastery of the five competencies is different from a cursory memorization process.

The paper-based exam emphasized the ability to recall facts and rules. Several review course providers recommended that candidates spend effort learning how to memorize certain facts (e.g., the four criteria for determining a lease) by using such aids as developing mnemonics. Preparing for the new exam requires effective application of the accounting foundation you acquired in college and/or work to the various contextual situations found throughout the exam.

Our review process focuses on providing you with adequate time to practice applying your knowledge, enhancing your knowledge in areas where you need support, and learning the testing environment. Therefore, you can relax and not be overwhelmed with the amount of material covered, or be concerned about your ability to memorize the complete set of GAAP and GAAS. We will help you prepare for this exam with proven methods that are relevant to the current expectations. We cannot emphasize enough that *how* you study is as important as *what* you study.

PREPARATION FRAMEWORK

When coaches prepare their teams for the forthcoming season, they develop a comprehensive plan that seeks to address every dimension of the competitive environment: game plan, winning strategy, physical component, and their team's mental readiness. Likewise, serving as your coach, Kaplan fully recognizes your world-class talent and capabilities and seeks to ensure that you walk away from the exam having given a winning effort.

We also want to address every key aspect of the CPA exam, relative to your strengths, talents, and professional, personal, and physical dimensions, so you are adequately prepared. Specifically, we will focus on strengthening and conditioning the following dimensions of your life related to preparing for the exam:

- Knowing the rules.
- Knowing how to implement the rules.
- Managing your emotional and mental energy while preparing.
- Maintaining your health and energy during the preparation period.

This chapter and our free weekly "CPA Exam Lesson" e-mails will provide you with a comprehensive and current review of the rules of the CPA exam (sign up for these lessons on our Web site under CPA Info and Resources). These Kaplan references provide a complete description of the exam and its objectives, explanation of its administration, registration information, and recommendations on how to leverage knowledge of the rules to your advantage. It is critical that you understand how the exam works. We go beyond the basics, giving you a background of the exam so you can fully appreciate why the current exam has been transformed from a paper-based, memorization-oriented test into a computerized exam that emphasizes critical thinking and analytical skills. We also feel it is important for you to know the registration process so you can make sure you are enrolled and eligible to sit for the exam when the time comes.

Kaplan will provide you with a rich set of tools that will assist in your preparation for the CPA exam. These tools include: lesson videos, problem videos, problems PDF, study manuals, Kaplan Activity Planner, Kaplan Online Test Bank and Testlets, research library, and simulation questions. Kaplan's tools are your manual for success, ensuring that your talents and mental attitude are ready to be put to the test.

We make an all-out effort to support your mental attitude by acting as your coach and cheerleader. This is especially true of our "E-mail Lessons" (mentioned above) and our interaction with you via our Web site announcements and our "e-mail the professor" feature. We know you have already worked hard to become eligible for the exam. We feel that our proven techniques will not only provide adequate preparation, but will instill the confidence needed to face the challenges of the CPA exam. In addition, if you ever feel an anxiety attack approaching, you can e-mail us via "E-mail a Kaplan Professor" and we will provide helpful feedback to resolve whatever issues are causing you stress. We will be there for you throughout the preparation period. Your coach will be on the sideline cheering, encouraging, and providing guidance right up to exam day.

The Kaplan Activity Planner, the "CPA Exam Lesson" e-mails, and the Kaplan CPA Survival Guide all encourage you to rest, relax, and refresh your energy throughout the preparation period. We recognize the fatigue that will arise from executing the recommended preparation schedule. We strongly encourage you to take periodic breaks at least once a week and also right before the exam. We want you to have the energy to rally all of your talents and knowledge to achieve peak performance. We want you to be as stress-free as possible during the preparation period. In fact, we want you to enjoy this process and anticipate and visualize your success. Most of all, we want you to enjoy the relief, satisfaction, and professional recognition that will come your way when you pass. So keeping healthy, alert, and confident is a very important part of this process.

DEVELOPING A STUDY PLAN AND SCHEDULE

Now that you fully understand the rules of the game, we need to focus on learning to play the game by practice, practice, and more practice. However, we want you to practice in an efficient, effective, and organized manner, and not just plunge into a set of materials. Besides not being very efficient, a haphazard approach may even lead to burnout.

We have developed a 4-step process for you to design a comprehensive study plan. This will prepare you for the planned "testing window" when you seek to take the exam. You must consider your level of knowledge section by section, your schedule, and the rules of your jurisdiction to outline a plan that will lead to successfully passing the exam.

Please review the following steps and begin to design your study plan.

Determine when you are going to take the exam and calculate how many weeks of study you have available. We recommend a minimum of 40 available days to study prior to taking the examination. Your schedule should also include planned days of NO study to provide balance and an opportunity to refresh and relax; this will help you avoid burnout and a negative attitude. We want you to be extremely realistic when considering your current responsibilities, and professional and personal commitments, and then, with our Kaplan Activity Planner, outline a study plan that you can fulfill. It is essential that you commit to the study days as well as to the days off. We want you to develop a balanced preparation approach that considers your intellectual efforts, as well as the need to maintain your mental and physical health. Another reason to be realistic in planning your study schedule is to ensure that you do not "over-schedule" yourself and then feel negative about yourself when you cannot meet that schedule. Set yourself up for success by being realistic from the beginning. Remember: this is really not a difficult exam, but it is a very long exam! Have someone who knows you well review your planned schedule and offer their opinion on whether you have a great chance of sticking with it.

Access the Kaplan CPA Review Kaplan Activity Planner that is available for each topic. Your Planner is a booklet that arrives in the box with all your other study materials. A video describing the Planner and the Kaplan approach to CPA Review can be viewed at *www.kaplanCPAreview* under Online Lessons. We urge you to view this video as a part of your planning process.

- The planner provides a recommended schedule that offers a 40- or 70-day option for REG, AUD, and BEC, and a 50- or 80-day option for FAR.
- The appropriate Kaplan review course material is outlined within the topical study plan and schedule. For example, day one of the AUD requires the following action steps:
    - Read the introduction to the planner.
    - Watch an instructional video.
    - Activate your Kaplan e-mail accounts.
    - Read sections of the Study Manual.
    - Watch lesson videos.
    - Answer questions in software.

The nature of the planner makes it easy for the candidate to identify the course material required and the recommended use of that material for each topical area. The candidate needs to execute the first step, which is to identify an appropriate schedule and implement the planner accordingly. Once you determine the number of days to study, you can select the appropriate Kaplan Activity Planner. We have identified the specific course materials discussed earlier in this chapter and made recommendations for how to use them during the selected preparation period (e.g., 40 or 70 days for AUD). However, you can adjust this plan as you deem appropriate based on your unique schedule.

For example, alternative job schedules allow some people to be off every other Friday or Monday or to select a day off every week. Individuals who telecommute have the option of selecting schedules they prefer. This may impact your study schedule, however, and the Kaplan Activity Planner can be adjusted accordingly. This is your personal plan, and it should reflect your time availability and individual preparation needs. We have done the detailed work for you; all you need to do is adjust it to meet your personal circumstances.

UNDERSTAND THE "TESTING WINDOWS" FOR TAKING THE CPA EXAM AT THE PROMETRIC CENTERS

Testing Windows*	Closed Periods per Quarter
January and February	March
April and May	June
July and August	September
October and November	December

*A window is a consecutive 2-month period within a quarter that the exam is available via Prometric. Candidates can take one or all four parts or a combination thereof during a "window." Candidates cannot repeat a part during a window.

As noted earlier in this chapter, the CBT exam gives the candidate considerable flexibility. For example, during the January and February window, a candidate could elect to take Auditing and Attestation during the first week of January. This could be followed by

Regulation during the third week of January. They could then take Financial Accounting and Reporting during the second week of February and complete the exam with the Business Environment and Concepts section during the last week of February.

Another candidate might elect to take two of the sections during this period and defer the other two to the April and May window. Or another candidate might elect to take one section per window to complete the whole exam in a year. The number of sections you elect to take during a window is your choice. Just remember, you cannot repeat a section within a window. In other words, you cannot take Regulation twice in the January and February window.

The improved flexibility in the exam scheduling is a great benefit to candidates. Not only does it allow you to create your own schedule, but it also enables you to prepare for and take only one section at a time. Compared to the old exam requirement of sitting for all four sections at once, this is a huge stress reliever for you. If you have not experienced preparing for and sitting for all four sections over two days, just ask some of your colleagues at work how much fun that was!

Along with this great benefit from flexibility comes a huge responsibility. (There is no free lunch, right?) You have the responsibility to discipline yourself to begin the process. It is far too easy for some people to say, "Oh, well, I'll just take it next month." While it is much better for you to have this flexible scheduling, it is also easier for you to let yourself procrastinate. Think about this. Do not put it off. Get the process out of the way, and move on to other learning opportunities in your life and career. The hardest part of a difficult undertaking is just taking the first step.

Another scheduling consideration is when to schedule a re-take in the event something unexpected arises that prevents you from preparing sufficiently. You always want to get your scores on a section of the exam before you schedule a re-take. Realistically, you will probably not receive your grades in time to retake a section within the same window. Thus, the AICPA has a rule allowing you to take a section only once per window. In addition, we would want you to spend sufficient time addressing the weaknesses noted on any failed section so that we can assist you in avoiding the same mistakes. With adequate preparation, you can expect to pass. If something prevents you from preparing completely, we will help you assess what your next steps should be.

Here's another point to consider. Experience shows that few people leave the exam site saying, "Oh, great, I passed that with no problem." It just doesn't happen. Most candidates leave the exam with at least some doubt as to whether they passed. This is perfectly normal. Many of them find out their immediate assessment was wrong, and they did pass. So *always* know your score before scheduling another sitting of any part of the exam. In fact, the best thing to do after a part is over is to make note of any areas you felt very weak in while taking the exam, and then put away that note until you get your score. Next, go have some fun! You earned it. After a few days off, you can start preparing for the next section of the exam you plan to take.

Before going any further, take the time to review your plan. Consider whether the schedule you selected is realistic. For example, if you have just been promoted and your new position will require extensive travel, will you have online access to the Kaplan materials while you are on the road? Will you have the time to study adequately? We do

©2007 Kaplan CPA Review

not want you to design a plan that is not attainable. It is essential that you develop a program that makes sense for your professional and personal schedule, commitments, and responsibilities.

We want you to be committed to your schedule. Our tools, such as the Kaplan Activity Planner by section, are very useful. But these tools are only as good as how you use them to support your practice and preparation period. We recommend you document this plan in your PDA, online, or in the tool that best keeps you organized. This will provide an additional mechanism and the ability to track your progress, modify plans as your schedule changes, and ensure that you have considered all aspects of your professional and personal activities.

REGISTER TO TAKE THE EXAM

We want you to be mentally, physically, and emotionally ready for the exam. However, it will all be moot if you do not follow the process of enrollment and eligibility. We urge you to take sufficient time to understand the specific rules for registering to take the exam in your jurisdiction.

We have provided a list of steps for you to follow, which are relevant in each of the 55 jurisdictions.

Please note, these steps are general and you need to augment them after researching your respective jurisdiction.

Apply to your state board of accountancy. Your jurisdiction should have a Web site containing the registration information online. We recommend you pay particular attention to the eligibility rules (e.g., number of college credits and the lead time for filing). For example, if you seek to sit for the exam in the April through May "testing window," identify the deadline for registering for that time. This is critical, since missing the deadline to register for a desired testing window will impact your study plan.

Be sure to notice your jurisdictions's requirements for number of credits in accounting courses, number of credits in other business courses, rules for accepting online courses, and any requirement for courses specifically dedicated to Accounting Ethics (not general ethics). Some states are adopting new rules in these areas. Be sure you know exactly what is required to be eligible to sit for the exam. Don't make the assumption that because you hold an accounting degree, you have met all requirements. Do your research to be sure. We will assist you in this area if you have questions.

Obtain your Notice to Schedule (NTS). This is your confirmation of eligibility to sit for the exam. You will need to keep this in a safe place since it will be required for admission [along with the approved form(s) of identification] to the Prometric Center where you take the exam. The NTS also qualifies you for enrollment in the AICPA Professional Literature subscription, as noted previously.

DETERMINE YOUR TESTING WINDOW SCHEDULE BASED ON THE STUDY PLAN YOU HAVE DEVELOPED

Again, you need to consider your professional and personal commitments. The rules for changing your testing window and any related refund for registration will vary by jurisdiction. We feel it is better to be certain and retain your scheduled testing window unless there is an emergency.

Schedule your examination appointment with Prometric. You can use the online or telephone contact information below. We recommend that you make your appointment as soon as you receive your NTS from your jurisdiction. This will ensure that your planned time and location are available.

- *www.prometric.com/cpa* (there is some very useful information on this site; visit it early in your planning).
- 800-580-9648.

We recommend you take the time to visit the Web site for the state board of accountancy in your jurisdiction to learn the process. Some states process applications directly, and some have delegated this function to the National Association of State Boards of Accountancy (NASBA). NASBA is the central organization that the AICPA works with to facilitate the grade distribution process. Some states have authorized NASBA to serve as the registration unit for their candidates. It is imperative that you know what organization is responsible for registration. This will allow you to determine their procedures, gather the appropriate information, and complete the application in a timely manner. Completion will include verification of your eligibility (i.e., sufficient hours in accounting and undergraduate coursework in compliance with your jurisdiction's requirements, which may be 150 hours).

AICPA GRADING PROCESS

We have given you information regarding the rules of the exam, which have included a comprehensive description of the how, what, when, and why of the exam's administration and delivery processes. It is important that you also know how your performance will be evaluated by the AICPA. Remember, we are concerned about you in every aspect and want to eliminate any ambiguity regarding the grading process. This will help eliminate any stress you may have over this particular issue.

The following table provides an outline of the process that occurs once you complete the exam, whether you take one section or all four sections. The table makes a distinction between the multiple-choice testlets and the simulation testlets, since the latter possess a written portion, which is manually, rather than electronically, graded.

Function	Performer	Action
CPA exam	Candidate	Complete scheduled section(s) of exam. Once you finish a section, it is independently graded and processed. Each section is graded separately, based on its own merit. Multiple-choice testlets are graded electronically; simulations are graded both electronically (the objective questions) and manually (the writing assignment).
Exam distribution	Prometric Testing Services	Distributes candidate's electronic files to AICPA. The AICPA has the sole responsibility for grading, assembling the grades, and distributing the grades to NASBA and/or the candidate's jurisdiction.
Grading—multiple-choice testlets and objective portions of simulation testlets	AICPA	Conduct a sampling of answers to determine grading scales and any adjustments for defective questions with multiple answers. This allows the AICPA to calibrate the grading scales to reflect desired passing ranges and to consider overall candidate responses for each question. For example, if there is a noted trend on a multiple-choice question, it may indicate that the question is defective or that the intended clarity was not achieved, and consideration for an alternative answer may be valid. Review answers electronically and assign scores to candidates. Once the grading scales have been calibrated, the scoring process is electronically completed, summarized, and prepared for distribution.

Grading—written communications portion of simulation testlets	AICPA	Conduct a sampling of written questions to develop a grading guide for point assignment. This process mirrors the paper-based examination in regard to its manual nature in that it is still graded by humans rather than a computer. Fortunately, the graders do not have to navigate the various challenges of legibility issues that handwritten responses presented. However, they must read your response for both content and writing proficiency. The clarity, organization, accuracy, relevance, and content of your responses are critical because these characteristics will impact the graders' ability to determine your grade. If your response is not clear, then just as in the paper-based exam, the grader will make a quick determination that you are not worthy of passing the written portion of this simulation question. While the CBT exam spreads out the thousands of candidate responses throughout the year and within the window period, graders still have a large workload and have less than three minutes to look at your particular response. If in the first minute they feel you do not communicate effectively, they will suspend their effort and make a general assessment of failure.
		Execute manual review, evaluation, and grading of written communications. The written communication portion of the simulation questions is one of the reasons the exam is not like those of other professional certifications (e.g., Certified Management Accountant) that are also CBT and give immediate scoring. The written portion is still manually graded. In addition, the other professional accounting exams do not possess the public responsibility of a CPA. As a result, the AICPA and NASBA seek to control the grade distribution process, and, consequently, there will not be an immediate feedback mechanism used.
Grade distribution	NASBA/State Board of Accountancy	Distribute grades to candidate. You will receive a notice of your performance via the United States Post Office. You will not receive an e-mail or voice mail. You will receive the same paper-based notification that was used under the old exam. This is done for security and control purposes.

Now you have a customized study plan that reflects your practice and preparation needs and considers your professional and personal commitments. This plan will be your critical guide over the coming weeks to help you navigate the process of being prepared for exam day. You should congratulate yourself for reaching this stage, because it reflects your commitment to investing the appropriate resources to pass the CPA exam.

TYPES OF QUESTIONS ON THE CPA EXAM

In order to prepare efficiently, you need to understand how the CPA exam questions are designed, the types of answers that are expected, and the recommended solution approach that will best help you achieve your goal of passing the CPA exam.

This chapter provides a guide based on the current approach the AICPA has developed for the CBT exam. We will discuss the multiple-choice question testlets for each section and address the different types of multiple-choice questions and recommended approaches to providing an answer. We will also do the same for the simulation questions that will be used on all of the sections except the Business Environment and Concepts.

PRESENTATION OF MULTIPLE-CHOICE QUESTIONS (MCQs)

In the rest of this chapter, you will see representative samples of every type of multiple-choice question from each of the four sections of the exam. It is key to your success that you become familiar with all the various types of questions, and that you practice with them in our materials and on the *www.cpa-exam.org* Web site. Strategy is undeniably important to your success on the exam. Take a look at the kinds of questions, and you will feel less like you are going into a mysterious event called the CPA exam. You will know what to expect, and that in itself is worth some points in your score!

We have selected multiple-choice questions (MCQs) and simulation questions from our online materials to help reinforce your study approach. This will allow you to refer to the actual section online for further review or to go back later to ensure that you understand both the question and the way it was presented.

SCREEN OUTLINE FOR MULTIPLE-CHOICE QUESTIONS

The screen for MCQs is outlined as follows for the CBT CPA exam. We feel it is important that through the AICPA tutorial and our online testlets and question bank, you become familiar and proficient with using this format and the related available tools, such as a calculator or review selection feature.

Top of Screen from Left to Right

- *AICPA logo.*
- *Testlet number* (e.g., Testlet 1 of 5).
- *Question number* (e.g., 1 of 25).
- *Time clock.* Shows remaining time for the total section, so it is counting down to zero.
- *Calculator.* You should use this online calculator for various exercises to ensure that you are comfortable with its operations. Yes, it looks and operates like the handheld calculators, as well as the one on your PC or laptop. However, we want you to feel confident with its operation so that on exam day you will not waste any unnecessary energy learning to use it.

- *Help.* Provides guidance on the CBT technical dimension, the MCQ aspect of the exam, and what to do if you need to ask a Prometric representative a question (does not provide help with correct answers! Sorry!).
- *Done.* Indicates that you have completed the section. Just as with most Windows-based operations, it will ask you to confirm (yes or no) your decision to leave the section through the appearance of a dialogue box.

Bottom of the Screen from Left to Right

- *Answer status.*
  - A check in one box indicates that you answered the question and are finished with that one.
  - A check in the other box indicates that you marked the question for another review. This is an important feature, whereby the question will be highlighted in a sequential list, allowing you to quickly determine which questions you need to complete prior to clicking the *Done* button.
- *Mark for review.* Allows you to mark an individual question for review, enabling a check mark to appear in the Status box.
- *Previous.* Allows you to return to the previous question when clicked.
- *Question sequence.* Indicates the answer status as follows:
  - Answered questions appear in a white box.
  - The current question appears in a black box.
  - Questions marked for review have a check that appears below the number. This allows you to identify the unanswered questions quickly so that they may be completed. We will discuss this in more detail at the end of this chapter.
- *Next.* Allows you to move to the next question.

The actual question appears in the middle of the screen in a format that you will see illustrated in the following sections. The MCQs operate in the manner of a traditional MCQ as you select your answer by clicking on a button next to one of the four answer choices. The answer status boxes will indicate your completion and election to mark for review.

It is critically important to become familiar with the screen design and the online practice tests so that you can position yourself to be successful on exam day and not be overwhelmed by the exam's method of delivery. We cannot overemphasize how important it is to be prepared for the "look and feel" of the screens.

TYPES OF MULTIPLE-CHOICE QUESTIONS

Let's first discuss the types of MCQs that exist. The two primary categories are *qualitative* and *quantitative*. *Qualitative* MCQs seek to determine your understanding of a principle and/or rule or its application, in view of a set of presented facts or procedures. In addition, some qualitative questions ask you to evaluate the four answer choices by selecting the "best," "least," or "most likely" answer. *Quantitative* questions require that you make a calculation based on a set of facts.

We have provided examples of both qualitative and quantitative MCQs with solutions from the online materials to get you familiar with both types. In addition, we have provided commentary regarding the type of information that was required to answer the question correctly, such as knowledge of a specific rule.

You have probably heard this advice before, but it bears repeating: Most MCQs will have a best answer, an almost correct answer, and two other answers that are much less correct! Be sure to read all the answers before making your choice. At least two of the distractors (wrong answers) are usually close to being correct. And, if you read the question too fast, or do not give adequate consideration to each answer, it will be easy for you to select the "almost" right answer. And never leave an answer blank. If you should run out of time, or have no idea, try to make an educated guess and record something. Even if you do not know the answer, you have a 25% chance of getting it correct by guessing!

AUDITING & ATTESTATION

The examination of Auditing and Attestation focuses on your ability to interpret a set of facts and select the answer based on the generally accepted auditing standards (GAAS). The nature of this topic lends itself to qualitative versus quantitative MCQs since GAAS and the related pronouncements are policies-, principles-and procedures-based.

This also makes the choices tougher to select unless you are properly prepared. As you will see during our discussion, various types of qualitative MCQs can be used. By using our online material and this information, you should feel comfortable and confident when seeing questions similar to these on exam day!

MCQ TESTING A SPECIFIC RULE OR PRINCIPLE

When a company issues an income statement but no statement of cash flows, what is the only opinion that can be rendered?
A. Adverse.
B. Qualified.
C. Unqualified with an explanatory paragraph.
D. Unqualified.

The correct answer is B. The auditor must issue a *qualified* report. This question is designed to test a specific auditing rule, which states that when an income statement is provided, but no statement of cash flows is included, the CPA must give a qualified opinion. Neither an adverse opinion nor an unqualified opinion can be given in this particular case. In this example you needed to know the specific rule regarding issuing an audit report.

MCQ TESTING AN APPLICATION BASED ON A SET OF FACTS

A client has $1 million in assets and $600,000 in income. Which of the following is *most likely* to be material?
A. Accidentally expensing a $20,000 asset.
B. An extraordinary item of $30,000 was reported.
C. The treasurer making an illegal bribe in a foreign country of $15,000.
D. Accidentally capitalizing an expense of $12,000.

The correct answer is C. An illegal act is always material due to the fact that a violation of a law exists. In deciding about materiality, the CPA faces both a quantitative issue as well as a qualitative issue. The *quantitative* issue is purely a question of size and all of the misstatements here are relatively the same size. The *qualitative* issue rests on the seriousness and/or the nature of the problem. In other words, the cause would concern the auditor even if the discovered result were comparatively small. Here, the bribe will cause the most worry because it is both an intentional and illegal act. Moreover, it can be representative of a wider problem that needs to be further examined.

This question required you to identify which item was material. You had to compare the amount noted in each choice to the asset and income size of the company to determine if it was material. Initially, you may have thought "none of these are material." So, your next step would be to determine "what is there about these answers that makes one of them stand out from the others?" Choice "C" involved an illegal act, whereas "A" and "D" are both accidents, and "B" is a legitimate transaction. The existence of fraud or illegal activity renders any transaction as material because of its nature. Thus, you could have selected "C" without any further analysis. **Tip:** Finding the correct answer efficiently and effectively allows you to save time for a subsequent review prior to exiting and closing the testlet.

MCQ Requiring the Evaluation the Four Answer Choices

The following question is one where you need to know the rule and apply it by evaluating the four choices to select "the least." In this question, you should know the reasons why auditors must hire a specialist and then select which reason is the *least likely*.

> The CPA firm of Acme and Ball has hired an outside specialist to help with the audit of Keystone Corporation. Which of the following is the *least likely* reason for hiring the specialist?
> A. Keystone is an art gallery and the firm wants to determine the value of the inventory of paintings.
> B. Keystone is a jewelry store and the firm wants to determine the value of the diamonds held in inventory.
> C. Keystone is a construction company and the firm wants to determine the degree of completion of several big projects.
> D. Keystone owns an office supply company and the firm wants to determine the assessed value of its warehouse.

First, in reading this question, note the italicized words; these are the keys to getting this question correct.

The correct answer is D. The nature of office supply inventory does not merit the hiring of a specialist. A specialist is most often hired when the CPA needs certain information that is not readily available in any other way, or the nature of the information needed is highly technical and outside the breadth of the CPA's knowledge. For example, the **value of assets** in A and B and the **status of completion** for construction projects would be essential information in an audit and very few auditors possess the expertise to make that determination without the use of a specialist. However, an **assessed value** is done for tax purposes and really provides little value to the auditor. In addition, the client should have physical proof from the government of the assessment so the auditor would not need a specialist. In this case, the question asked for the "least likely." Therefore, answer choice D is the least likely in view of the other three answer choices.

It is essential that you become familiar with these very common forms of questions. Often, all of the answers will be correct to some degree, but only one is the right selection—or more correct than the others—in the context of the question.

QUANTITATIVE MULTIPLE CHOICE QUESTIONS

Quantitative MCQs require you to review a set of data and then perform a calculation. The CBT exam has a built-in calculator, which appears as an icon on the top right of the screen. You can use this calculator at any time. Quantitative questions require you to know the underlying accounting or regulatory principle, as well as the procedure for executing the calculation. Therefore, we recommend plenty of practice so you can become very familiar with how concepts can be presented and tested. This will allow you to effectively and efficiently respond to each quantitative MCQ.

QUANTITATIVE AUDITING AND ATTESTATION QUESTION

The next question requires you to understand the concept of audit sampling and related procedures for establishing an error rate or tolerance level. You must then apply the formulas for calculating a sample size.

> A client has processed 200,000 sales invoices, and the CPA must consider the error rate associated with these invoices. The auditor expects 2% to have mistakes but could tolerate having mistakes up to 6%. A sample of 200 invoices was selected and three were found to have errors. Using a statistical sampling chart, an upper deviation rate of 5% was determined. What was the allowance for sampling risk?
> A. 1.5%.
> B. 2.0%.
> C. 3.5%.
> D. 4.0%.

The correct answer is C, which is the difference between the upper deviation rate of 5%, less the actual upper level rate of occurrence, which is 1.5%. In a sampling for attributes plan such as this, the difference between the sample rate (1.5% or 3 out of 200) and the upper deviation rate determined statistically (5%) is known as the allowance for sampling risk.

This question required you to understand sampling procedures, the auditor's role in establishing a tolerance rate, and how to apply the two concepts to select the best answer. The goal is to have practiced enough of these questions from our question material that you can effectively identify the appropriate approach and calculate the answer efficiently.

STUDY MANUAL – AUDITING & ATTESTATION
EXAM STRATEGIES

COMBINATION MULTIPLE CHOICE QUESTIONS

We have illustrated both quantitative and qualitative questions in terms of the types and approach within Auditing and Attestation. There is also a presentation approach for the *answer choices*, which applies to both qualitative and quantitative MCQs. Both types of MCQs can use the following types of answer choices:

- *Combination Choices.* You are given a set of facts about a situation, where a *selection* of the facts make up the answer. For example, you are given a list of various cash flows, and asked which one(s) are Investing Cash Flows. Or, you must choose answers with multiple variable choices for each lettered answer (e.g., balances for both current assets and retained earnings). These are like two questions in one!

COMBINATION AUDITING AND ATTESTATION QUESTION—EXAMPLES

Here, you are presented with two situations and you must determine if the correct answer is one of them, both of them, or none of them.

> In reviewing the financial statements of a nonpublic entity, an accountant is required to modify the standard review report for which of the following reasons?
> 1. Inability to assess the risk of material misstatement due to fraud.
> 2. Discovery of significant deficiencies in the design of the entity's internal control.
> A. Both require modification.
> B. Neither requires modification.
> C. Only 1. requires modification.
> D. Only 2. requires modification.

The correct answer is B. According to GAAS, a review does not mandate procedures that would affect the report. In a review, the CPA uses analytical procedures and inquiry to ascertain the possibility that a material misstatement exists. Other than asking about changes in the company's internal control, the CPA does not study internal control or the possibility of fraud in these types of engagements. You had to select a combination of facts and then respond with answer choices that considered the combination of facts.

In the following question, you must answer two questions, "yes" or "no" for each column heading:

> An auditor would express an unqualified opinion with an explanatory paragraph added to the auditor's report for:
>
> | | An unjustified accounting change | A material weakness in the internal control structure |
> |---|---|---|
> | A. | Yes | Yes |
> | B. | Yes | No |
> | C. | No | Yes |
> | D. | No | No |

©2007 Kaplan CPA Review

The correct answer is D. Both of these conditions mandate a qualified opinion. If the auditors are not satisfied that management's justification for a change in accounting principle is appropriate, their opinion should be qualified for a departure from GAAP. Material weaknesses in internal control must be reported to the audit committee. Such weaknesses affect the design of substantive tests, but are not noted in the auditor's opinion. Answers A, B, and C are incorrect because an unqualified opinion would not be issued when there is a departure from GAAP, and an explanatory paragraph would not be added for internal control weaknesses.

There are numerous examples of all these question types in our Kaplan materials, whether you are using the online multiple choice questions or the books. Practice, practice, practice is the key to getting used to these styles of questions. And, if in doubt, you can usually eliminate 2 of the answers with your base of knowledge. (That's just how multiple choice questions are designed!) So, even if there is a question where you are unsure, you will usually have a 50/50 chance of getting it right on that basis alone.

FINAL COMMENTS ABOUT MCQs

The CBT CPA exam offers a valuable tool to assist you with executing your review process—*mark for review*. As described previously, this feature allows you to visually see all of the questions you have not completed. Once you have sequentially gone through a testlet and answered as many questions as possible, you should go back through and complete those that remain unanswered.

We want you to use your time wisely. When you approach a question, review the context of the question or its actual "question" prior to looking at the answer choices. Then apply the recommended approach to selecting an answer. If a question appears to be too difficult to resolve, continue on to the next question. Do not let a question frustrate you or cause any stress. Do not waste a lot of time on a question you do not know the answer to. The key is to remain positive and confident, so do what is necessary to maintain your composure and progress through the exam, knowing that you are managing your time toward a successful completion.

Once you have answered all of the questions you feel comfortable with, return to those you skipped. Perhaps by answering the other questions, your memory was jolted and/or your confidence has been boosted so that you can tackle these remaining questions effectively. Amazingly, sometimes you may "learn" an idea in a subsequent question that reminds you of the answer to a previous one.

It is critical that you complete every question. The CPA exam does not penalize guessing like some other exams you may have taken. While we want you to be prepared and minimize guessing—please do not leave any question blank. Your attempt will at least increase the possibility of receiving some points—and we hope we have prepared you to take an educated guess on those questions where you are unclear of the approach. Never, never, never leave blanks.

Finally, time management is a required skill of CPAs; it was expected on the paper-based exam, and it is just as essential on the CBT exam. Always be aware of your time and keep an eye on the "remaining time" feature on your screens. You will actually have plenty of time, and many candidates will leave early. You will probably be surprised to learn that you do have sufficient time. But use that time wisely and maximize the amount of benefit in terms of points scored! Practice working with time constraints when you are preparing for the exam.

SIMULATION QUESTIONS

Now that you understand MCQs, we will continue with the other type of question on the CPA exam—the simulations.

The simulation questions are structured to reflect real-world scenarios by going beyond the static nature of a long problem or essay that offers only historical information. Simulation questions require the candidate to respond to a multiple set of objective questions, which could include true/false, multiple choice, matching, or journal entries. In addition, simulation questions include a subjective component. This component will require a written response based on the candidate's interpretation of a given situation and research of the appropriate auditing, tax, or financial accounting literature.

The simulation format attempts to place the candidate in a "real world" environment. In the real world, you will be faced with a situation, such as a potential merger or acquisition, or the spin-off of a line of business, that demands an informal decision be made concerning accounting or auditing issues. To effectively develop a response, you would consult the current financial accounting literature (GAAP) or generally accepted auditing standards (GAAS) for guidance.

The REG, FAR, and AUD sections of the exam contain three testlets of MCQs and two testlets of simulation questions. There are no plans at the current time to include sims on BEC. In this section, we will discuss both the nature and operation of the simulation questions to assist you in becoming proficient at solving them on the exam. It is particularly important that you become familiar and comfortable with how simulation questions operate, since you must be able to navigate the software and access multiple tabs in order to answer the question. For example, you will be required to access related authoritative literature on some questions, requiring use of the appropriate tab to execute your research effort.

Tip: We highly recommend that you take the time to practice using both the AICPA tutorial and our replication of the CPA exam simulations. Both will provide valuable experience with respect to content and functional format. However, the most beneficial aspect of the practice simulations is your practice with the functionality of the software. The content is presented elsewhere in the program. Your major goal in working sims should be to learn the software and practice timing yourself.

DIAGRAM OF A SIMULATION QUESTION

You should understand why the CBT exam contains simulation questions. Let's go back to our earlier discussion where we noted that the profession was asked by key stakeholders, such as employers, to test the following competencies:

- Research, interpretation, and application of current financial literature.

- Communication of business information.
- Analysis and interpretation of business information.
- Render judgment based on available business information.
- Gain an understanding of key business terms, facts, and processes.

Simulations create the opportunity to meet these testing goals in a way that multiple-choice questions cannot.

SCREEN OUTLINE FOR SIMULATION QUESTIONS

You are able to access simulations on our Web site, *www.kaplanCPAreview.com*. If you purchased our entire program, you have access to all our online sims. If you purchased only the Study Manual for AUD, you can access a limited number of sims under Free Resources. As you read the following paragraphs about sims, it will be helpful to have the online sims available to you for examination of their features.

The screen for simulation questions is outlined as follows for the CBT CPA exam. We strongly believe it is important that, through the AICPA tutorial and our online testlets and question bank, you become familiar and proficient with using this format and related available tools (e.g., calculator or professional literature feature).

Top of Screen

Top Bar

The top of the screen on the top bar contains a series of buttons and windows, providing an array of tools and resources to assist you in completing the simulation questions. The tools include such things as calculators and access tabs to the authoritative literature. As you read through the descriptions below, try clicking on the various buttons to experience the functionality.

Top of Screen from Left to Right

- *AICPA CBT CPA exam logo.*
- *Testlet window.* Provides an indication of testlet number (e.g., 3 of 5).
- *Time clock.* Shows remaining time for the total section (e.g., 3 hours and 5 minutes). This is a critical and valuable tool that will assist with time management as you complete the exam. Please use the clock as a tool and do not let it alarm you as you proceed. With practice, you will learn how to use your time wisely during the exam, and we will provide you with the necessary guidance to do so.
- *Copy.* Provides the same copy function as the copy button provides in Microsoft Word.
- *Paste.* Used in concert with the copy button to move text within or between documents.
- *Calculator.* You should use this online calculator for various exercises to ensure that you are comfortable with its operations.
- *Spreadsheet.* A worksheet similar to Excel, used to facilitate calculations or arrange data.

- *Standards.* This button is used to conduct research online within the set of prescribed authoritative literature. You have an opportunity to become familiar with online research for free if you take advantage of the AICPA's offer of a free subscription to their Research Database. (See *www.cpa-exam.org*.)
- *Help.* Provides you with guidance on the CBT technical dimension, on the simulation questions part of the exam, and what to do if you need to ask a Prometric representative a question. (Does not "help" you with answers to the exam!)
- *Split.* This feature allows you to split the screen in the same manner as the Windows Excel program. Specifically, this function splits the screen between the situation tab and the current tab you have selected (e.g., communication). It also allows you to split the screen between the Research Standards tab and the Research Answer tab. You must be in split screen mode (either vertical or horizontal) to answer the Research question. Please see below for further discussion regarding "tabs."
- *Done.* Indicates that you have completed the section. Just as with most Windows-based operations, it will ask you to confirm (yes or no) your decision to leave the section through the appearance of a dialogue box.

We have just outlined how the simulation questions look in terms of their online design, features, and functionality. Next we will discuss the contents of the questions in a manner similar to our earlier coverage of the MCQs. This is where you can begin to experience these questions in their actual environment.

Tip: We highly recommend that after reviewing this section, you maintain your schedule according to the *Kaplan Activity Planner* and practice using the online version of the simulation questions. Remember, practice will help your confidence and your knowledge, both of which will lead to success on exam day.

Lower Top Bar

This bar consists of "tabs" that you can click as buttons to obtain information, resources, or an objective or subjective question. The tabs, which contain objective or subjective questions, are noted as "work" tabs by the AICPA.

Tabs

- *Directions.* Provides a source of instruction regarding the overall simulation question (e.g., how to approach the simulation question), such as selecting the simulation question tab to begin.
- *Situation.* Provides the essence of the question and set of conditions and facts (e.g., an accounting firm has been requested to consider a new engagement and they need to determine if it will be a compilation, review, or audit client).
- *Series of multipart objective and subjective questions.* Each of these work tabs will ask a series of objective questions, including formats such as true/false or MCQ. In addition, they could also be "check the box" type questions where you indicate whether this condition or fact is applicable to the given set of circumstances.
- *Written Communication.* Used when you need to write a memorandum to someone regarding an issue. Depending on the particular simulation, you may be addressing the accountant, the CFO, or the partner of the CPA firm. In any case, pay attention to the addressee of your communication and consider that when developing your answer. You may write differently to the CFO versus the entry-level staff accountant because

of their differing levels of experience with the topic. *Note*: The simulation questions allow you to click on the tab labeled "standards" to conduct your literature review.

- *Research.* Allows you to review relevant literature prior to answering specific research-oriented questions.
- *Resources.* Provides tools that can be used with the spreadsheet function (e.g., a present value table or formula specific to the simulation question). Resources will vary from question to question depending on the tools required for answering that question.

Note: The objective question work tabs will be graded electronically by the AICPA. The written communication and research components will be graded manually.

TYPES OF SIMULATION QUESTIONS

Simulation questions represent a combination of objective and subjective questions. Objective questions can include multiple choice, completion, matching, and true/false formats. They can also include questions that require completion of a spreadsheet, calculation of amounts, and preparation of journal entries.

As we noted in the MCQ section, there are various types of MCQs, and the same applies to the broader category of objective questions. The two primary categories are qualitative- and quantitative-based objective questions. Qualitative objective questions are based on a specific rule or set of facts, where there is only one answer based on that set of facts. Objective questions can also be quantitative, requiring a calculation based on a specific rule or set of facts (e.g., what is the book value for the building after the first year?). The answer options for both qualitative and quantitative can include MCQ, where there is more than one choice and you have to select one, or you must fill in a box to indicate if a set of facts is true or false.

Each simulation question consists of two subjective questions, written communications, and research. Like objective questions, subjective questions are also based on facts, conditions, circumstances, and other criteria. However, unlike objective questions, subjective questions do not list a set of answer choices for you to select as correct or true/false. Rather, you must provide a written response. Written responses can vary in terms of the specific words used, but must meet the key criteria for the question. Your response must reflect an authoritative literature-based answer. The AICPA expects that you will be specific, clear, and concise, using language that indicates your understanding of the situation. The graders will be looking for sentences and paragraphs that are well written, and you should avoid simply making lists with bullet points.

TIME OUT! LET'S SEE WHERE WE ARE

Let's take a break to review what we have covered. By summarizing the following seven key points, it will be easier for you to practice and apply what you've learned.

1. Simulation questions are divided into objective and subjective parts, which appear in separate work tabs.

2. The objective and subjective questions are based on a situation that presents a set of facts.

3. Each of the objective work tabs will contain a series of questions, which could be in MCQ, completion, true/false, matching, or some combination.

4. The work tabs and the series of questions contained therein are independent, but they share the common situation.

5. You should answer the work tabs in order. Select the questions within each work tab that you understand and can definitively answer. This will allow you to reduce the number of questions on which you have to guess.

6. Answering the questions in order will help you on each subsequent question, since all the questions are based on the same situation and require an understanding of the same set of authoritative literature.

7. If you practice using our online material, the objective questions should not be difficult for you to answer and should help prepare you to respond to the subjective questions.

Hopefully you feel more comfortable regarding the objective questions and understand how they are presented so that you can effectively practice and prepare for the exam.

PREPARATION FOR THE EXAM

Now it's time to practice, and, as they say, practice makes perfect. You are now aware of how the exam is scheduled throughout the year, as well as what is required in terms of your eligibility to sit for the exam. Let's now concentrate on how to practice, so you will be prepared on exam day.

APPROACH

All work and no play will burn you out and result in fatigue, impairing your ability to be successful on exam day. To avoid this problem, we have developed a holistic approach to studying for the exam. Our Kaplan Activity Planner balances your preparation period by considering what it will take to pass the exam, while also recognizing that you have a full personal and professional life. We do not recommend that you put your personal life, including social and health management–related activities, completely on hold until you take the exam. In fact, we strongly encourage you to take time out, enjoy yourself, and relax periodically. This will allow you to return to your preparation activities with energy, enthusiasm, and clarity.

Now that you have elected to take the exam, you must look ahead at your schedule and consider your forthcoming personal and professional commitments. You may then make a realistic decision on how many sections of the exam you will take and when. You have 18 months to complete the entire exam successfully once you have passed any one of the four sections. For example, if you pass Auditing and Attestation in the January/February testing window, you have 18 months from that time forward to pass the other three sections. We feel confident that our process for exam preparation will enable you to complete the exam successfully within this time period.

PROGRESS EVALUATION

Kaplan has assembled an array of online materials to assist you with monitoring your preparation, as well as its quality and effectiveness. By using Kaplan's tools, you will always know how your study is progressing. The tools will indicate whether or not you have mastered a given subject matter and focus your attention on areas where you are not performing as well.

So how can you measure your progress? Each time you take a test in a specific subject area, you receive a comprehensive view of where you stand. Testing also gives you the chance to see the actual testing condition. Once you complete the testlet, you can review your scores as well as an explanation for each answer to determine why you missed any particular question. This will provide you with a progress evaluation that should agree with what you have documented on your planner.

As you proceed through the practice season, the Planner will identify specific testlets for you to complete, which, as noted earlier, will serve as an ongoing evaluation of your performance. You will also receive daily progress reports as you complete each set of assigned problems. Our online material will allow you to score your performance immediately, with detailed results and answer solutions. In essence, our comprehensive program provides a continuous evaluation mechanism in the form of the assigned questions and problems, testlets, and simulation questions. In addition, you have the opportunity to go beyond the recommended questions for more practice in a particular subject area. Each of these additional tests operates in the same manner as the assigned problems, allowing you to obtain immediate feedback.

We hope this method of evaluation will serve as a source of encouragement. As you progress, we expect that your scores will improve. Use your improvement to boost your self esteem and confidence, and know that your hard work will pay off on exam day. Are you still visualizing that CPA certificate on your wall?

FINAL STRETCH

It's the fourth quarter and you have a comfortable lead. You have scheduled to take the exam on July 10, and it is now July 1. You may have told all of your friends and relatives that you cannot attend any of the Fourth of July festivities. Wrong! Now is just the time to take a break, and we will show you how to take a break and still be prepared. Having some fun in the final stretch is okay. After working so hard, you deserve a break!

We have outlined some key steps to follow during that final stretch period. Following, you will find a reference tool that you can use during the final few days before the exam to guide your activities effectively. Keep in mind, if you have consistently tested at a level of 80% or more, you are already testing at a level above the minimum passing rate of 75%. This fact should help keep your anxiety level down and enhance your confidence.

Also, understand there are certain things you should not do during the following few days. Do not try to learn new material. Doing so will cause unnecessary stress. Do not focus on areas of material that you don't know well or have consistently failed during the review period. Instead, focus on those areas where you have performed well and feel confident. Remember, you do not need to score 100%. Relax and look back at how well you have done during the practice period. You should review with a smile on your face, knowing that your hard work will allow you to take the exam with confidence.

FINAL STRETCH REFERENCE GUIDE

Use the following guide on July 1 to review your work during the practice season. The guide serves as a checklist and, hopefully, confirmation of your efforts to pass the CPA exam. We have listed seven questions, which we want you to answer.

Tip: Print this guide and place it on top of each of the planners that you have in use (e.g., Financial Accounting and Reporting).

Once you have completed your comments next to each question, step back and see where you stand. Answering yes to questions 1, 2, and 3 indicates that you have followed our recommendations for executing a structured process of exam preparation. It also shows that your hard work has consistently scored at 75% or better, which is what you need to pass the exam. Answering "no" to any of the seven questions is your indication of where to review during the coming days.

The remaining four questions will determine how you feel about navigating the exam (e.g., MCQ or simulation questions, or the specific CBT technology). If you have issues or concerns in this area, please feel free to e-mail us, or review the AICPA tutorial again to make sure you are comfortable with the technology. In terms of format issues, you can also go back to Chapter 3 in this chapter for additional review.

Assuming you launch the Final Stretch period on July 1, you have nine days to answer questions 1 through 7 in the Final Stretch Reference Guide. This will allow you time to review what you have covered, evaluate how well you performed, review the technology, and determine your proficiency in answering questions in a variety of formats. Hopefully, you will complete the guide and get the big picture! That is: you have read, reviewed, and completed a vast amount of material over the past 40 days; you were committed, faithful, and diligent; and you are ready to give your best on exam day.

It is critical that you do not allow the rigors of the preparation process to overwhelm, discourage, or distract you from the overall goal of becoming a CPA. Yes, it is a lot of work, but the rewards are outstanding, and you deserve to experience all of them. Therefore, we have developed a "CPA Survival Guide," which is a digital pocket guide of recommendations that we hope you will use to succeed in your goal of becoming a CPA.

Action Steps	Candidates Review Comments
1. Have you completed all key steps outlined in the Kaplan Activity Planner?	

2. Did you score at least 75% on all of the key topic areas?	
3. Did you review any area where you did not score 75%? If so, how did you do on the next test?	
4. Are there any areas where you still have trouble? What are they? What is the expected coverage on the exam?	
5. Overall, how do you feel about the qualitative multiple-choice questions?	
6. Overall, how do you feel about the qualitative/subjective simulation questions?	
7. Do you feel comfortable with the exam technology? Did you use the tutorial on the AICPA Web site? Have you used our testlets, which look just like the new CBT CPA exam technology? Did you have any trouble navigating through the technology?	

In the next section, we will continue with our review of preparation for the exam, but our focus will be on exam day. We will use the same example (i.e., sitting for the exam on July 10) to help illustrate our key points.

REST, REST, AND REST

It is the night before the exam, and all through the house not a soul is stirring, not even your computer mouse. That is exactly the atmosphere we want for you: peaceful and quiet the evening before the exam. The Final Stretch Reference Tool provided above will direct you to conduct a high-level review, but we don't want you to do anything on the day before the exam other than the following:

1. **Take the day of July 9 off from work; schedule a vacation or personal day, whatever is available.** If your family environment mandates, check into a hotel the night before the exam. Yes, that means in addition to the day(s) required to sit for two sections, you will also need a day of rest prior to the exam. Therefore, assuming you take one section per day, you will need a minimum of three days.

2. **Locate your Notice to Schedule (NTS).** Make sure you place the NTS next to your two forms of identification to ensure you will have it with you when you proceed to the exam on July 10.

3. **Go to the Internet and print out the directions to the testing site.** We actually recommend you do this when you first receive your NTS. Hopefully, you have physically visited the location and know all of the alternative routes in case of heavy traffic.

4. **Review the rules for Prometric Testing Centers.** The AICPA and NASBA, along with Prometric's standard policies, prohibit candidates from wearing certain articles of clothing without significant security reviews. This is intended to prevent the use of electronic devices such as hidden cameras or unauthorized transmitters.
   We recommend that you go to *www.prometric.com/Sites/TestCenterTour.htm* and take the Test Center Tour. The tour will give you a feel for the site, your expected arrival time, a description of the process, and a list of "do's and don'ts."

5. **Look in your closet and locate comfortable clothes.** Remember to follow the instructions from the Prometric Web site, and adhere to the limitations of what you can wear and take to the exam.

6. **Go to your kitchen and identify what you will eat for breakfast.** Make sure the breakfast you select is something that will promote energy, rather than upset your stomach or cause any other unwanted side effects.

7. **Get a good night's sleep.** Now it is time to go to bed. If you have cable or satellite service, find a comedian, listen to a joke, and go to bed prepared to sleep and dream about the sweet success to come.

GUIDANCE ON EXAM DAY

Finally, it's July 10 and it's a beautiful morning. It is time to go outside and conquer the world of passing the CPA exam. This is the day we have been waiting for. Just like the Olympians who practice very hard in hopes of earning a gold medal, you have also worked very hard. Just remember, a bronze is good enough to pass the exam, but keep your eye on the gold medal.

So here we are. We have done what we promised. If you followed our steps, you should be prepared and ready to demonstrate just how well you know the underlying material. Before you leave for the Prometric Testing Center, please remember the following:

1. Be confident—you worked really hard to be prepared.

2. Do not forget your NTS and two forms of identification (e.g., driver's license and passport).

3. You will be provided with calculators, scratch paper, and pencils, along with lockers for small bags or wallets. Based on our discussions in Chapter 3, these are the only items you should bring to the exam. The only other thing to bring is the knowledge that you have acquired over the past few weeks and the confidence that you are prepared!

4. Remember to view the Prometric site at *www.prometric.com/cpa* or take the tour of the testing center at *www.prometric.com/Sites/TestCenterTour.htm* and make sure you follow their specific instructions.

5. Do not bring large bags, briefcases, or laptops, because they will not be allowed and they do not fit in the lockers. If you bring such items, you will have to go back to your car or even back home (if you did not drive), which could adversely impact your time.

One last thing before you leave home: look in the mirror and what do you see? We see a CPA in the making, and the next step is successfully passing the sections you are taking today.

POST-EXAM ANALYSIS

You have just completed one of the most significant testing marathons of your life. How do you feel? You may be exhausted, but, hopefully, you feel relieved and confident. If you followed our program, you should have had some time to relax as you studied for the exam. Now you have to wait for the results. Even though the exam is computer-based, there are still portions that are manually graded the old-fashioned way. What should you do in the mean time? Do you wonder what you missed and think back about each question to see if you made a mistake? Certainly not! We want you to enjoy the break and think ahead to the remaining sections with optimism. Do not spend time reliving the exam you just completed. Most people who spend time trying to analyze their own results will underestimate how well they did. Move on. Have some fun. Don't try to mentally grade your own exam. Wait for the results before you even think about that section again.

The CBT is still too new to assess pass rates and trends. However, the AICPA has noted that the first CBT exam takers passed at a rate of around 45%. This rate is higher than the pass rate of the paper-based test. We sincerely hope that you are in that 45% group, and feel that we can make the difference when it comes to your success. We now recommend that you resume your regular schedule and not dwell on or worry about the results.

IT'S IN THE MAIL

The scores have finally arrived. Let's have a drum roll as you open the envelope. You open the envelope and find that you passed Financial Accounting and Reporting with a score of 76%, but failed to pass Auditing and Attestation at 65%. Congratulations, you deserve to celebrate! You have just passed part of the CPA exam, and you are on your way to earning one of the toughest professional certifications in the world.

What we need to do now is find out what happened with Auditing and Attestation. You did so well on the practice questions, testlets, and simulations that we were sure you would pass. Let's go back to the score reporting envelope and look at the diagnostic analysis of your score by each testlet, along with the additional analysis of your score by the AICPA Content Specification Outline (see the Appendix for further details). This analysis should tell you how you performed on the MCQs, and two simulation testlets by topic area. For example, you will know if you did well on the MCQs but performed poorly on the simulation tests. Use this information to direct your review for the next exam.

You should also review your score for the section that you passed to identify any trends (e.g., you performed marginally on the simulation questions in that section as well). Any such trends would suggest the need to work harder at becoming more proficient and comfortable with the simulation format questions.

So now you know your score. You passed one of the two sections and came very close to passing the other section. We still want you to celebrate and have some fun. When you return, we have more work to do; you now have 18 months remaining to become a CPA.

We hope you have found this chapter to be a beneficial preparation tool. As you continue preparing for the remainder of the CPA exam, be sure to use this chapter as one of your central resources for navigation and support.

INDEX

A

acceptable audit risk 117
accepting the audit 22
accepting the engagement 19
access control and security software 314
accounting estimates 422
accounting principles 18
accounts payable 204
accounts payable and accrued liabilities 293
accounts payable confirmations 293
accounts receivable 201, 203
accounts receivable and revenue 492
adverse opinion 57, 67
agreed-upon procedure 10
AICPA 14, 558, 566, 567
AICPA testing goals 551
analytical procedures 30, 146, 147, 151
apostrophes 537
applicability and importance of specific controls 189
application controls 187, 309, 310
application of agreed-upon procedures 348, 355
assertions 12
associated with the financial statements 62
assurance 13
attestation engagements 366
attribute sampling 265, 267
audit committee 19, 197
audit conference 21
audit documents 153
audit function 455
audit objectives 144
audit of a client using IT 303
audit opinions 461
audit planning 26
audit planning procedures 28
audit procedures 145, 146, 255
audit procedures performed for accounts receivable 257
audit program 32, 141
audit report 56
audit risk 140, 265, 471
audit risk model 116, 140
audit strategy 26

auditing and technology 502
auditing around the computer 312
auditing cash 331
auditing inventories 291
auditing investments 409
auditing long-term liabilities 382
auditing property, plant, and equipment 399
auditing receivables 256
auditing stockholders' equity 416
auditing through the computer 312
auditor's consideration of internal control 191
auditor's judgment of inherent risk 117
auditor's standard report on internal controls 74
authoritative GAAP 19
authorization of transactions 202, 206, 209, 212, 215
automated audit document software 315

B

batch processing 305
block sampling 274
brainstorm 118

C

capitalization 537
cash disbursements cycle 204
cash receipts 201, 203
cash receipts and cash balances 508
cash receipts cycle 203
Category I: Other information in documents containing audited financial statements 338
Category II: Required supplementary information 338
Category III: Other information in auditor submitted documents 338
checklist for editing 539
clarity and conciseness 539
client representation letters 420
client's industry 28
communicating with the audit committee 197
communications with the predecessor auditor 30
comparability 60
comparative financial statements 69, 465
comparison programs 312

comparisons 203, 207, 210, 213
competence of internal auditors 190
competent audit evidence 18, 138
compilation engagement 96
compilation of prospective financial statements 352
compilation report 96, 101
compilations and reviews 466
completeness 12, 143
compliance auditing 364
compliance with a contractual agreement 349
comprehensive basis of accounting other than GAAP 346
computer operations 308
computer operator 308
computer-assisted audit techniques (CAAT) 304
computerized audit tools 314
confirmations 146, 148
consistency 18, 60
contingent liabilities 64
continuity of controls 311
continuous or concurrent testing 313
control 196, 502
control activities 186, 192
control environment 185, 191
control procedures 328
control procedures and related management assertions 219
control risk 17, 116, 140, 193, 199
control risk at the maximum 194
control risk below the maximum level 195
control totals 310
controlled reprocessing 313
controls over changes to existing programs and systems 307
controls over the development of new programs and systems 307
corroborating evidence 141
CPA exam 552
current audit file 154
custody of assets 203, 206, 210, 213, 215

D

data entry operator 308
date of the report 58
decision tables 193
deficiencies in the internal control 218
departure from GAAP 67
dependence of other controls on controls over computer processing 306
detection risk 116, 140, 196
disclaimer 66, 67
disclaimer of opinion 57, 62, 68

disclosures 61
discovery sampling 269
distributed processing 305
division of responsibility for the opinion 62
document the understanding of internal control 193
downgrading an engagement 338
dual read check 308

E

elements of internal control 185
embedded audit modules and audit hooks 313
emphasis of a matter 65
engagement letters 19, 23
error 12
errors and fraud 118
essay grading system 523
essay writing 521
essays on the CPA exam 521
evidence 138, 141
evidence collection procedures 146
evidence gathering 479
exam day 583
exam strategies 550
examination 10
examination of prospective financial statements 353
examination reports on prospective financial statements 354
existence or occurrence 12, 143
explanatory language 56
express an opinion 18
extended records 313

F

fair value 425
fieldwork standards for financial audits 361
fieldwork standards for performance audits 368
files control 311
filing under federal securities statutes 357
financial audits 360
financial statement audits 360
financial-related audits 360
financing cycle 216
First Standard of Reporting 59
fixed versus sequential sample size 269
flowchart symbols 220, 329
flowcharting 193, 326, 506
flowcharting software 312
Foreign Corrupt Practices Act 188

Fourth Standard of Reporting 62
fraud 12, 118
fraud risk factors 118
fraud triangle 118
fraudulent financial reporting 118
functions within the IT department 308

G

general controls 187, 307
general standards 15
general standards for financial audits 360
general standards for performance audits 368
generalized audit software (GAS) 314
generally accepted accounting principles 59
generally accepted auditing standards (GAAS) 14
generally accepted government auditing standards (GAGAS) 360
going concern considerations 430
going concern issues 64
government audits 360
governmental auditing 359
governmental auditing standards 363
grade distribution 567
grading 566, 567
grading process 565

H

haphazard sampling 274
how to write your essay 529

I

illegal act 12
illegal acts 13
independence 16
Independent Auditor's Report 58
information and communication 187, 192
information processing 186
information technology (IT) 303, 305
inherent risk 116
input controls 309
inquiries 147
inquiry of a client's lawyer 424
inspection 147
integrated test facility (ITF) 313
internal auditors 190
internal control 17, 31, 185, 488
internal control in operating cycles 199

internal control questionnaire 193
internal inquiries and comparisons 146
inventories 150
inventories and production cycle 207
inventory and accounts payable 499
investing cycle 217
investments 408, 519
IT controls 304
IT department 308
IT hardware controls 308
IT risks to internal control 307
IT skills 304

J

job accounting data/operating systems logs 314
judgmental sampling 264

K

Kaplan Activity Planner 560, 561

L

lack of independence 67
land, buildings, and equipment 398, 518
lapping 257
letters for underwriters 356
librarian 308
library management software 314
limitations 188
limited reporting engagement 66
long-term liabilities and contingencies 381, 514

M

management responsibility 188
management's assertion regarding internal control 74
management's assertions 27, 142, 217, 290, 328
management's representations 422
master files 311
material weakness 198
materiality 12, 27
methods of processing data 306
misappropriation of assets 118
misstatements 12
monitoring 188, 192
multiple-choice questions 568

N

narrative 193
National Association of State Boards of Accountancy (NASBA) 565, 567
negative confirmations 149
new risk assessment standards 123
nonpublic companies 77
nonsampling risk 266
nonstatistical sampling 264
note taking 525
Notice to Schedule (NTS) 564

O

objectivity of the internal audit staff 190
observation 150
observation and physical examination 147
observation of inventories 150
obtain an understanding of internal control 191
omitted disclosures 18
omitted procedures detected after the report date 434
online processing 305
operating cycles 199
operational audits 337
opinion directly on the effectiveness of internal control 74
opinion on management's assessment process 74
opinion paragraph 58
opinions 56
other reports 337, 510
output controls 311

P

parallel simulation 313
parallel structure 538
parity check 308
partial presentations 351
payroll 389, 516
performance audits 367
permanent file 154
personnel and payroll cycle 211
physical controls 187, 309
piecemeal opinion 57
planning an audit 11
planning and supervision 17
positive confirmations 149
potential for errors and fraud 306
PPS samples 275
precision 267

predecessor auditors 21
preliminary assessment of control risk 194
preparation for the exam 579
presentation and disclosure 12, 142
probability-proportional-to-size sampling (PPS) 272
processing controls 310
processing of transactions by service organizations 315
professional care 16
program analysis 312
program and data controls 309
program code checking 312
program tracing and mapping 312
programmer 308
Prometric centers 562
Prometric Testing Services 565, 566
pronoun antecedents 539
property, plant, and equipment cycle 214
prospective financial statements 350
public companies 74
Public Company Accounting Oversight Board (PCAOB) 14, 46, 543, 549
purchases 204
purpose of auditing 10

Q

qualified opinion 56, 65, 67

R

random-number sampling 273
read after write 308
real-time processing 305
reasonable assurance 13, 188
recalculation 147
recording of transactions 203, 206, 209, 212, 215
related-party transactions 426
relevance of audit evidence 138
reliability 267
reportable condition 197, 198
reporting on condensed financial statements and selected financial data 358
reporting on financial statements prepared for use in other countries 359
reporting on information accompanying audited financial statements 338
reporting on transactions 349
reporting requirements 18
reporting standards for financial audits 362
reporting standards for performance audits 368

STUDY MANUAL – AUDITING & ATTESTATION
INDEX

reports 56
reports on a printed form 349
reports on internal control 74
responsibilities of management 23
responsibilities of the auditor 24
review 10
review engagement 98
review of interim (quarterly) financial statements 342
review of operating systems 314
review report 99, 101
rights and obligations 12, 143
risk 116
risk assessment 186, 192, 196
risk assessment procedures 125
risk assessment process 124
risk assessment standards 125
risk of incorrect acceptance 267
risk of incorrect rejection 267
risk of overreliance 266
risk of underreliance 266
roles of management, board of directors, and audit committee 11
run-on sentences 538

S

sales 201, 202
sample audit engagement letter 25
sample deviation rate 270
sample size 268
sampling risk 266
sampling risk in attribute sampling 266
Sarbanes-Oxley Act 46, 74, 153, 189, 458
scope limitations 65
scope paragraph 58
search and verification 146
Second Standard of Reporting 60
section 302 189
section 404 74, 189
section 906 189
segment information 341
segregation of duties 187
segregation of functions 204, 207, 211, 213, 216, 306
sentence fragments 537
sequential sampling 269
simulation questions 575
single audit act 364
snapshot 312
special reports 337, 345, 510
specialists 423

specified elements, accounts, or items of a financial statement 347
spelling: frequently confused words 536
standard interim review report 344
standard report 57
standards of fieldwork 15
standards of reporting 15
state board of accountancy 564, 567
Statements on Auditing Standards (SAS) 14
statistical sampling 264, 495
stratification 274
structure of an argument 527
study plan 559
subject-verb agreement 538
subsequent discovery of facts existing at the date of the auditor's report 433
subsequent events 59, 431
substantive audit procedures performed for expenses 420
substantive audit procedures performed for revenue 419
substantive testing 18, 116, 140, 191
substantive testing procedures 145
successor auditor 22
sufficiency (quantity) of audit evidence 139
supervision requirements 32
systematic sampling 274
systems analyst 308
systems control audit review files (SCARF) 313

T

test control procedures 199
test data 312
testing windows 562
tests of balances 146, 255, 290, 330
tests of controls 191, 193, 196
tests of controls procedures 145
tests of details 255, 290, 330
tests of details of transactions 146
Third Standard of Reporting 61
timing of audit procedures 33
trace 147
training and proficiency 15
transaction files 311
transaction or audit trails 306
transaction tagging 313

U

uncertainties 64
uniform processing of transactions 306
unqualified opinion 56
use of report of another auditor 464

V

validity of evidence 139
valuation or allocation 12, 143
variables sampling 265, 271
vouch 147

W

work of other auditors 63

Notes